COMPUTER DESIGN

Glen G. Langdon, Jr.

In some endeavors there is no substitute for experience. *Those without it worry about the wrong problems and ask the wrong questions.*

COMPUTER DESIGN

Glen G. Langdon, Jr.

IBM CORPORATION
SAN JOSE, CALIFORNIA

1982

COMPUTEACH PRESS INC.

San Jose

Library of Congress Cataloging in Publication Data

Langdon, Glen G.
    Computer design.

    Bibliography: p.
    Includes index.
    1. Electronic digital computers--Design and construc-
tion. 2. Computer architecture. I. Title.
TK7888.3.L29   621.3819'582   81-71785
ISBN 0-9607864-0-6   AACR2

Copyright 1982 by Computeach Press Inc.
P.O. Box 20851, San Jose CA 95160

Figure 0.2 is a likeness, reprinted by permission of Sterling Publishing
Company, Incorporated, from the book, *The Complete Book of Puppets and
Puppeteering,* by Robert Ten Eyck Hanford. Copyright 1976 by Robert
Ten Eyck Hanford.
    Figure 1.4 was digitally half-toned from gray scale by computer algor-
ithms developed by the IBM Research Division, and printed on an Autolog-
ic APS-5.

ISBN 0-9607864-0-6

10 9 8 7 6 5 4 3 2

To Marian

CONTENTS

Chapter 6. Microprogrammed and Bit-Slice Computer Design   362

Appendix A.   A Course Outline with a Design Project   424

Appendix B.   Electronic Devices and Useful Interface Circuits   434

* PREFACE *

SCOPE

This book is about real-world engineering design as applied to computers. A two-pronged approach integrates computer *organization* concepts
(data flow, instruction interpretation, memory systems, interfacing, microprogramming) with practical and systematic digital *design* methods
(behavioral versus structural descriptions, divide-and-conquer, hierarchical
conceptual levels, trade-offs, iteration, and postponement of detail). The
approach teaches the *relative importance* and *applicability* of the concepts
and methods. The book also serves two purposes: (1) as a *reference* for
computer professionals interested in broadening their background in digital
system design methodology and computer organization, and (2) as a *text* for
a second course in computer engineering. The book is based on experience,
both as a practitioner in the field and as a lecturer in the classroom. Material in this book has both teaching and practical value. To enhance its use as
a reference, I have tried to include a wide variety of common terms and
their synonyms in the subject index.

An indirect result of this book should be a heightened appreciation for
the pragmatic aspect of design. A cost-effective design speaks for itself.
Ultimately, the goal of most digital designs is a physical object offered for
sale. We do not support teaching a design method which is not competitive.

OBJECTIVE: THE DESIGN PROCESS

To make the approach realistic, we design a computer: a problem
which possesses *complexity*. Problems at the homework level deal in only a

few building blocks. It is deceptively easy to coerce a homework design problem to work, but this unsystematic application of "intuition" is too time-consuming for real problems.

It is easy to make a problem overly complex. Computers are often *represented* in a complex manner: detailed logic schematics of integrated circuit chips which also show the physical location of the components, sockets, wires, pins, cables, etc. Most designers have learned computer design by first studying a particular design at this low level. However, designs ought not be *created* at such a low level (through bad habits they often are). The learning process is much more efficient at *higher* conceptual levels where the design process *really* takes place. The detailed logic circuit diagrams are the ending point of a nontrivial design, and should not be confused with the starting point.

The design methodology is based on a data flow design, a data flow cycle, and a control flow comprised of major control states and microoperations (data flow dependent register transfers). The method encompasses microprogrammed control flow: the microprogram address is the control state and the action fields of the microinstruction are the microoperations. Methods such as the Algorithmic State Machine (ASM), while useful for controllers and giving valuable design experience, are too weak for attacking more complex system problems. The ASM represents only one way to handle control state sequencing, and typically deals directly in lower-level control point activations instead of microoperations. In contrast, our method scales down for use on simple problems.

The design methodology presented here will not surprise experienced designers. The notions of conceptual levels, microoperations, data flow components, and timing charts appear in the literature of the first generation computers. The engineering *trade-off* aspect of design has been with us for many centuries, where conflicting design goals are resolved by compromises. The *iterative* aspect of design is visible in slow motion to the archeologist who studies the evolution of tools. The fist hatchet was used before a handle was affixed, and the spear preceded the bow and arrow.

A DESIGN PROJECT

Where does the book lead? Our *goal* is to teach the reader how to design a nontrivial digital system. Thus we assume the student has enough motivation to learn a realistic digital design procedure. A design project described in Appendix A provides the focus.

Can digital design *really* be taught? The answer is "yes". Design strategies *can* be taught in a classroom. But the student must play an *active* role in the teaching process. Many of our students felt that through the design project they were teaching themselves. Students at the University of

São Paulo designed and built a small computer called the *Patinho Feio*. At the University of Santa Clara, we have graded many respectable design projects submitted by our students.

Here is an interesting challenge. Is it possible to concentrate on the useful and practical aspects of design, while remaining relatively independent of a particular technology? Can we teach a design methodology which will not become obsolete with technological advances? We can, thanks to an increased awareness of how to treat complexity, how to deal with different conceptual levels, and due to technological advances. Moreover, our confidence in the method is reinforced by a historical perspective of computer design experience: approaches which were good for the technologies of thirty years ago and are still good today will continue to be good tomorrow.

Technology yields increasingly convenient building blocks. The semiconductor industry has provided ever decreasing circuit sizes, such that global interconnections and their associated cost tend to dominate the cost of the physical result. However, short local interconnections which connect components to neighbors remain relatively inexpensive. This is as true for a VLSI chip as it is for a pc board. What has emerged are *higher-level digital building blocks:* adders, shifters, registers, multiplexers, PLAs, etc. These functional *data flow components,* based on *inexpensive local connections,* are convenient to implement in any digital technology we choose.

We develop our design to the level of the higher-level building blocks which in turn are implemented in a straightforward fashion in the technology at hand. The same MSI-level blocks are readily available in the TTL, ECL, and CMOS technologies. For custom or semi-custom VLSI chips, these *same* building blocks are available as "macro cells" in a computer-aided design library. The message is clear: we teach how to think and design at the level of technology-independent *functional units* above the level of gates and flip-flops.

We heavily employ the notion of *microoperation* to describe a small information processing action or event. Microoperations were first used to describe control unit behavior over thirty years ago. The *control flow* concerns the sequencing of microoperations performed by the data flow. Many *register transfer* design languages have evolved from the well-known and widely accepted microoperation. Having spanned many technologies, the microoperation concept has clearly demonstrated its technological independence. Once the microoperations to control the digital structure have been determined, one of several alternative control unit structures may be obtained by "turning the crank".

Thus, our defense against technological obsolescence is now supported by universal data flow components and microoperations. We need a third support: sequencing and synchronization (timing). Current circuit technology and performance-oriented data flows which provide for concurrency favor the use of clocked timing schemes. *The employment of a fixed clock cycle is perhaps the simplest and most powerful technique known to coordinate and synchronize concurrent microoperations.* We treat both a single-phase and two-phase clock cycle. All other clocked schemes are combinations or variations of these two schemes. All submit to the general notions of setup times, propagation delays, and clock skew.

The foundations of this book are: (1) data flow components as higher-level structural parts, (2) microoperations for describing the behavior or control flow, and (3) clocked synchronization concepts. We may well ask where the technology enters the picture: no designer attacks a nontrivial problem without some technology in mind! Yet, a new or different technology does not imply that a new design approach must be learned. For example, the IBM S/370 Model 168 employed essentially the same design approach as the earlier IBM S/360 Model 85.

An implementation in a new technology amounts to going through the same design process while making new trade-offs to new parameters. Digital technology is characterized by parameters: cost, propagation delays, interconnection delays, power consumption, package size, circuit density (area), pins, etc. Before a technology is developed, these parameters are determined as part of the proposal. The designer studies the parameters and makes design *trade-offs:* for instance, the choice of cycle time, or less expensive narrow data paths versus wider paths.

Within a given technology, the designer employs *implementation techniques* dealing with fan-in, fan-out capabilities, type of flip-flop available, etc. Many low-level techniques are self-evident. The reader who has mastered the higher-level design process easily reinvents the lower-level tricks which relate to a particular technology.

The approach based on data flow components, microoperations, and timing techniques is general enough for designing *any* digital system, not just computers. We employ the *same* design approach to design memory controls, an IO controller interface, and a cache controller. The approach is particularly crucial to VLSI design. Relatively high development costs require a hierarchical or structural design method. We carry the design to higher-level building blocks, the control flow, and system timing. This level represents the most important part of the design, and cannot be easily automated. The higher-level description is the natural entry point to a computer-aided design system, whose purpose is to replace that description with a maze of interconnected transistors on a chip.

A REVIEW OF THE CHAPTERS

The book bridges from the data flow component level (registers, adders) to the instruction set processor level. We assume the reader is familiar with material covered in introductory or "first course" texts (boolean logic, multiplexers, adders, and registers). It is unrealistic to provide a nontrivial treatment of computer design in the same course as the prerequisite material.

The Prologue should be skimmed first, to appreciate the point that design in a complex environment cannot be reduced to a simple step-by-step procedure. The Prologue will make interesting reading following the design example in Chapter 5.

In Chapter 1 we present some basic material on computers in the tone and philosophy of the book. Following Chapter 1, the reader should skim the appendices. The goal of the book is embodied in the design project of Appendix A. The remaining appendices present prerequisites: technological details in Appendix B, and the well-known data flow components or data handling functional units in Appendices C and D. To introduce microoperations in a familiar setting, the appendices describe behavior in a register transfer notation (RTN).

Students like to know where they are being led. We avoid toiling up hill in the dark, and then presenting a beautiful view from a mountain top in the morning. Students want to know why the mountain should be climbed before they learn to climb. In Chapter 2 we present a general view of instruction sets, since the primary function of a computer is to execute instructions. To readers with a background in assembler languages, Chapter 2 is a refresher.

People learn by example. We begin the teaching of design in Chapter 3, with a simple example computer called TM-16. The TM-16 provides an easy environment for acquiring a "taste" of computer design. We use RTN to describe the actions which take place to fetch and execute an instruction. Chapter 3 also shows the importance of the main memory and its interface. Following a relatively naive design of the TM-16 data flow, the RTN statements are down-converted to boolean statements, representing a gate-level realization of the TM-16 control unit.

With motivation from the TM-16 example, Chapter 4 covers the main memory system. Most of this chapter constitutes reference material. Relative to the book's primary design goal, we need stress only the basic concepts of the memory bus (MBUS), its cycle, and the interconnection concepts of modular memory units. Chapter 4 offers ample opportunity to acquire an appreciation for the descriptive power of a timing diagram.

Once a simple example is established, more complex cases are explained with reference to the example. In Chapter 5, the simple TM-16 instruction set is expanded to the more sophisticated SC-16 architecture.

The nontrivial SC-16 is a realistic vehicle for displaying complexity and design detail. Data flow trade-offs are covered, and a systematic design approach is used. As is often the case in real designs, *auxiliary circuits* are incorporated to solve particular problems at the interface between data flow and control flow. The system clock cycle is two-phased, but some of the registers operate in single-phase mode. The control unit design follows the "hardwired" approach, which is later seen to yield fewer cycles per instruction execution than the microprogrammed approach.

Chapter 6 broadens the reader's knowledge of design alternatives by covering microprogrammed and *bit-sliced* design. First, we control the same SC-16 data flow of Chapter 5 by a microprogrammed control unit. Second, a bit-slice data flow chip is used as a data flow component in a new system data flow, and controlled by its own microprogram. The performance of the hardwired and microprogrammed versions are compared.

The computer architectures we implement in Chapters 3, 5, and 6 are hypothetical. The important point is not *what* we design, but *how* we design it: the main objective is to *teach design*. A design method is necessarily independent of the particular (nontrivial) instruction set being implemented as an example. Each step in the design process is described, and the reasons for the design decisions are explained by the actual designer. The designs are our own, so we can safely say some bugs are included for the reader to find. (The probable cause is an incomplete follow-up to a change made after the initial iteration.)

TEACHING ASPECTS

A great song writer might make a poor accountant. Good managers who understand how to motivate people need not be great designers or vice-versa. Not all students think about problems in the most efficient way. Poets excel in verbal thought, but engineers need a *spatial visualization* ability which we seek to reinforce in this book. Different aspects of design evoke different mental images. Acquiring the proper viewpoint can greatly simplify a problem. We use the pictorial form which we find simplest for each aspect of the problem. Several sections of the book are "picture-driven": the design was done in the form of drawings and followed up with explanatory text. In these places, the reader should concentrate on absorbing the "picture" being presented.

We also lead the reader over a longer, simpler route than the one an experienced designer would take. For example, in preparing the original lectures on the subject, the designer of the SC-16H control unit (yours truly) jumped directly to the *table of microoperations* once the data flow was done. However, the table of microoperations turned out to be a "short cut" not well appreciated by the students in the lecture. We have learned to take the longer route of creating *event schematics* for each instruction. The descriptive flow diagrams can then be merged by noting common or similar activities in each instruction.

When one becomes familiar with the design process, short cuts suggest themselves. Many designers have the digital part numbers and pinouts memorized. On small projects they can form a mental image of the data flow, and directly implement the design result onto paper.

CONTRIBUTIONS OF THIS BOOK

Experienced designers will find the individual concepts familiar, so what is new about this design approach? We have integrated the concepts, and made them come alive through design examples suitable for teaching. In an analogy to languages, we not only give examples of how to construct sentences, but more importantly we explain the underlying grammatical structure.

We provide motivation by being introspective about how we solve a design problem. Control unit design is given two treatments, hardwired and microprogrammed, both in the context of the same architecture.

We give unique exposure to timing diagrams, and data flow design. We introduce control flow design, especially with concepts below RTN: conditional execution, p-term implicants, control point activations, and control signal gathering. We introduce conceptual levels and other notions for attacking complexity, and reinforce them throughout the book.

Descriptive techniques are given the importance they deserve. We resolve the dispute between the program-like language approach of VLSI silicon compilers versus the use of two-dimensional drawings on a graphics terminal as follows. Each approach is useful in its own place: a *language* for control logic and *drawings* for the data flow.

GLEN LANGDON
San Jose, California
July 1982

Note on Second Printing

Uncommon design detail is a two-edged sword; it makes the design clear, but may also introduce "bugs". The second printing has corrected all known problems, and incorporates many clarifying comments. I thank the many students and their instructors who have brought the errata items and problems requiring rewording to my attention.

GGL, *June 1984*

ACKNOWLEDGMENTS

To my students of EECS307 at the University of Santa Clara, particularly those who used my cryptic lecture notes in 1978, I owe the largest debt. Andres Goforth, one of those students, was a *major* assistance in reviewing the manuscript. Dan Lewis of SCU permitted the use of the lecture notes, and contributed to the notions of the logic-to-physical mapping.

I am indebted to students and faculty at the University of São Paulo, where I taught in the early 1970s. This book had its genesis in Brazil. Prof. Helio Vieira provided a stimulating teaching environment, and I share many teaching ideas and design notions with Profs. Edson Fregni and Wilson Ruggiero.

I owe a large debt to IBM's long-standing commitment to education. I took graduate courses at an IBM development laboratory, and received my doctorate as an employee under an IBM fellowship. I taught at the University of São Paulo as a work assignment. IBM provided support through Pat Mantey, Kwan Wong, and Ron Arps. The book has been done with the aid of IBM computer systems and IBM word processing software. I appreciate the help and cooperation of the machine room operators.

Helping with portions of the manuscript were Ray Voith, Keith Duke, Carl Hamacher, and Dan Helman. Calvin Tang reviewed Chapter 4. Prof. Tom Brubaker used parts of Chapter 6 for a microprogramming course at CSU.

Lance Levanthal provided many helpful general and organizational comments. Harold Stone helped alter the orientation of the book. Adam Osborne helped with the decision to consider self-publishing, and Nils Nilsson of Tioga Publishing Company extended valuable advice based on his own experience. Jim Rudolph, Martin Freeman, Ron Hoelzeman, Tom Cain, Bill Fletcher, Frank Moore, Bruce Brodie, Bob Stewart, Lee Hollaar, and John Wakerly provided interest and encouragement. Ted Friedman and Roger Haskin helped with some terminology.

Lori Vissiere conscientiously typed the earliest version of this book. Most of the art work was ably done by Francisco Moreira, at the suggestion of Jorge Teixeira, who also provided information on art work. Lois Romano and John Stotts provided additional information. Jim King helped with technical information on computer typesetting and photocomposition. Jack DeLany, Jean Chen, and Karen Bryan provided advice on line art and photoreduction. Ralph Linnell of IBM Endicott helped with a photograph. Sig Nin and Mitch Zolliker helped to half-tone it.

My father-in-law Eric Jacobsen kindly provided some sketches. My brother-in-law John Jacobsen of White Oak Design Inc. designed the cover. My daughter Karen shared time with the book project and did some figure paste-up. I owe a great debt to my wife Marian, who did the final manuscript typing and commands for the computer typesetting program.

COMPUTER DESIGN

✳ PROLOGUE ✳

A HIERARCHICAL VIEW
OF COMPLEX SYSTEMS

0.1. INTRODUCTION

The prologue discusses the practice of engineering design in the realm of information processing. Before plunging into the details of computer design, we consider some important global aspects to the problem which often go unstated. The ideas discussed here have a wider applicability than just to the profession of computer design.

Computer design has an aspect of *complexity*. The building blocks are weak and the computer itself is powerful. Design choices are many. Engineers have successfully encountered complex systems in other fields. They have built complex aircraft and have placed men on the moon. In dealing with complexity, we have invariably adopted a hierarchical view of the problem, which breaks the large problem into smaller problems at lower levels of detail. We provide some general concepts which exist in some form at any level of detail in an information system hierarchy. The concepts are useful whether we design a complex computer program, a distributed microprocessor system, or a digital computer.

We have found that graduate students with at least a year of engineering or programming experience perform noticeably better. At first it appeared that the inexperienced students lacked the fundamental prerequisites. However, students with programming work experience have the same

1

hardware prerequisite courses as the full-time students. It seems that work experience provides a global perspective via a design environment complex enough for "ad hoc" or heuristic design approaches. Complexity forces the designer to use experience and reasoning to break up the problem into pieces small enough that the implementation is straightforward.

In the first part of the prologue, we explain "the way things are". We define an information processing system and relate its organization and design to engineering. Engineering is compared with athletics and contrasted to the study of science and mathematics.

In the second part of the prologue, we explain ways to adapt our thought processes to the way things are. We give a *model* for design based on data processing functions and functional units and explain their behavioral and structural aspects. Design strategies are given.

0.2. THE NATURE OF INFORMATION PROCESSING

0.2.1. An Information Processing System

What are the key aspects of information processing? **Figure 0.1** depicts a generalized information processing system diagram which is valid for a powerful data processor as well as for a tiny microprocessor controlling a traffic signal. Before information or data can be processed, the system must first acquire the information. It should be stressed that digital information is a *representation* of some state of the real world. Transducers convert real world values into digital form, suitable for processing. An *information processing function* or digital function accepts items of information as inputs, and delivers information as outputs. An analogy can be made with a mathematical function f, which for each *argument* value x determines a corresponding value $f(x)$. That value $f(x)$ may be assigned to a variable which becomes an argument of another function g, for example composite function $g(f(x),y)$. As in mathematics, digital functions are combined. The output of one function serves as an input to another function, or even to itself.

The term *digital function* is used here with an abstract meaning to indicate *behavior,* i.e. *what* the function does and not *how* the data is manipulated. Digital functions are defined broadly. They can store information for later retrieval, convert data for printed page or plotter for "hard copy" output, or display data on a TV (or CRT) for "soft copy" output. Digital functions can provide outputs which close switches or relays, turn lights on or off, open or close valves, ring an alarm, provide an electrical signal to control motor speeds, light intensities, focal length of a lens, etc.

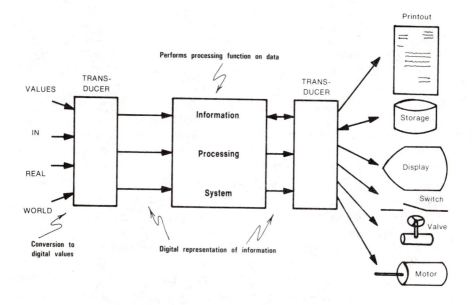

Figure 0.1. *Information processing.*

0.2.2. Engineering deals with Results

Engineers are problem solvers. What they design and build has a *cost* and delivers a *performance*. The engineer begins with a *problem statement*. This could be vague: "Let's build a bridge across the Golden Gate." The engineer then assesses the building blocks at hand (steel, concrete, suspension cables, etc.) and the environment.

Design is the organization of the basic components (building blocks) such that the result solves the problem and meets the design goal. Once designed on paper, the design is *implemented* using the parts which reflect the structure of the solution. In real life, *choices* contribute to the complexity of the design problem. Consider the *space-time trade-off* of digital processing. A design can employ more equipment (which takes space) and reduce the time to perform a task, or the designer can allow for more time and reduce the size of the equipment.

Engineers are pragmatic; *the design result must work*. If a better way to design or build something is found, engineers adopt the better way. There are no theorems defining the best product; there is this element of imprecision to engineering. Certain approaches are better in some applications but not in others. We use the computer design approach explained in this book, because from our experience it is the best available.

The field of athletics has this similarity with engineering: performance is the key to developing approaches to things like swinging a golf club or high jumping. The engineer is like a coach who adopts the strategy which has the best chance of winning. Athletes and engineers both generally discover the successful approaches by experience.

Consider the golf swing as being subdivided into a coordinated sequence of body actions, many happening concurrently. The golf swing is complex enough to cause the beginner to wonder if it will ever be remembered. The swing is also intricate enough to cause an advanced player to omit occasionally one of the coordinated movements. Is ensuring the employment of golf instructors the only justification for the current golf swing? The correct golf swing exists for a stronger reason: it produces superior results. The swing evolved over a period of time as the early golfers acquired experience.

Cost effective performance as determined by experience justifies current practice in computer design. Ferguson [1] concludes that this is the *nature* of design. The early motorcycle designers had no guidelines from science as to where the engine, battery, fuel tank, etc. should go. Bad decisions were ultimately discovered, but by an *experimental process* rather than a scientific analysis. Experienced designers can develop an intuition which spares them a few bad decisions, but not all.

Design techniques change slowly, and the changes are generally motivated by technological or political changes that alter relative costs. Also, as in athletics, two distinct approaches may yield very competitive results, as in the two high jumping styles (the "roll" versus the "flop"). Nevertheless, *cost effectiveness* and *performance* are very powerful filters which trap and destroy otherwise fine ideas and approaches.

0.2.3. Engineering is neither Science nor Mathematics

Simon [2] has reflected upon artificial phenomena versus natural phenomena in his monograph. Among natural phenomena such as plants, animals, and stars, things are the way they are. Scientists attempt to discover fundamental natural laws. In information systems and other fields, engineers deal in man-made things which *originate in the mind,* and not in nature. An engineer must conceive the idea of a bridge before setting about to construct it.

Zemanek [3] comments that computer scientists are also engineers: *engineers of abstract objects.* In data processing, the computer instruction performs a relatively modest digital function, but the design result, a computer program, performs a more powerful task, and meets the requirements of the application.

On the other hand, mathematics is based on assumptions, and deals with what may be possible or not possible according to the assumptions.

Mathematics provides the engineer with valuable analytical tools when the problem meets the assumptions.

0.2.4. Complexity: "Forewarned is Forearmed"

Complexity is a problem shared by many fields. In data processing, the problem of complexity arises during the development of large computer programs. Dijkstra [4] feels that underestimation of the difficulties of size is a major cause of data processing problems.

A problem is complex if its solution requires the use of a large number of interacting primitive building blocks. Complexity is the consequence of a large *conceptual gap* [4; p. 208] between the functional capability of the system and the primitive building blocks. A computer with powerful arithmetic instructions, and many addressing modes, but built from only 4-input NAND gates, presents a conceptual gap.

Simon [2] develops a central theme that complexity frequently takes the form of a *hierarchy*. Matter can be viewed in a hierarchical fashion, being composed of molecules, in turn composed of atoms, and in turn composed of yet more elementary particles like the electron, proton and neutron. Simon notes that a complex system is analyzed by successive sets of subsystems. Such systems appear in books, for example (chapters, sections, subsections, paragraphs, sentences). In information systems, the hierarchy takes the form of *conceptual levels,* which decompose powerful digital functions into interacting less powerful digital functions.

The notion of *our inability to do much* [4; p. 1] reinforces the connection between complex systems and hierarchical structure. Our brains are not capable of precise thinking about more than about seven items at a time [5]. This suggests that we bridge a large conceptual gap in small steps.

Another attribute of the way we think favors a hierarchical approach. We focus on the usual or normal situations, preferring to suppress exceptional details, which reduces complexity. See Winograd [6]. In a design situation, we can think of a building block at a higher level in the hierarchy in an imprecise way. Later we fill in the exceptions at a lower level.

In teaching a new concept, we can teach the normal case as if there are no exceptions. The student becomes familiar with the simple basic concept and assimilates the concept where it belongs. Later the student may learn the exceptions. Knuth [7] uses the technique in a manual, and admits to not always telling the whole truth the first time.

There is another source of complexity. When building blocks are very small, there is great freedom to select the intermediate levels of abstraction. Brooks [8] speaks of *arbitrary* complexity. There are many alternative choices where the cost effectiveness is not affected by the decision. How often have we wasted time choosing between arbitrary alternatives?

The variety of *combinations* grows rapidly with alternatives. If the problem (at some conceptual level) is decomposed into five subproblems, with three alternative solutions or approaches available for each subproblem, then we have three raised to the fifth power (3^5), or 243 possible problem solutions. The wide variety of choice is evident in the broad cost versus performance spectrum which may be achieved simply through the way a computer is organized. The models of the IBM System/360 series spanned a performance range of 100 to 1 with a technology family whose circuit delays would account for only a 4 to 1 performance range.

Individual design choices are interrelated. A solution to one subproblem may have an impact on feasible solutions to other subproblems. The combination of approaches yielding the best overall system will not be immediately obvious.

Many students have not encountered complexity in prior course work, and may be unaware of and unprepared for design problems with two or more conceptual levels. The next section describes the tools available for solving complex multilevel problems.

0.2.5. "Any General Law is bound to have two Exceptions."

The large conceptual gap allows sufficient organizational freedom to defeat "absolute laws" or theorems. The choices available to the systems designer are often too broad to be constrained by any narrow assumptions. As assumptions are broadened, then theorems become less sharp. Weinberg [9] comments that general theorems or laws are proposed which hold "most of the time". Slight inaccuracies are employed in order to teach a general point. The "Law of Unhappy Peculiarities" states that "any general law is bound to have at least two exceptions".

"Rules of thumb" may not always hold, but they always make a point. As a concept is developed in greater detail, annoying exceptions may surface. However, the student who can discover exceptions to a rule has also progressed to the stage where the general rule can be appreciated for what it is: a guidepost.

In the field of computer systems, there are no "absolutes". Knowledgeable people disagree on topics such as the impact of newer technologies, or what should be emphasized in design, and so on. We do not wish to hide this aspect of the field: "the first step to knowledge is the confession of ignorance" [9].

0.2.6. The Active–Passive Duality: a Curious Parallelism

The active-passive duality occurs at all conceptual levels in computer systems. Most design subproblems and subtasks have an active part and a passive part. The duality leads to a convenient way to decompose prob-

Table 0.1. Active-Passive Duality

Democritus	*Heraclitus*	*Reference*
things	process	Waddington [10]
mechanism	vitalism	,,
things	happenings	Ross and Schoman [13]
data	activities	,,
nouns	verbs	,,
substances	events	,,
passive	active	,,
objects	operations	,, and Babbage [14]
structure	function	Pattee [15]
structure hierarchy	control hierarchy	,,
object	action	Wirth [11]
data structure	algorithm	Wirth [12], Hoare [4]
white box	black box	Weinberg [9]
state description	process description	Simon [2]
data flow	control unit	
structural description	behavioral description	

lems. We summarize the terms used by several authors to describe the active-passive duality in **Table 0.1**.

C. H. Waddington [10] has noted that the duality of views can be traced back to the ancient Greeks. A *passive* view was proposed by Democritus, who asserted that the world was composed of matter called atoms. Democritus' view places *things* at the center of focus. On the other hand, the classical spokesman for the *active* view is Heraclitus, who emphasized the notion of *process*. Both views occur in language. In a sentence, the subjects and objects are nouns (things) connected by a verb (action or process). In the computer programming field, followers of Democritus would emphasize the data structure aspect of the problem, whereas the followers of Heraclitus would emphasize the algorithmic or procedural part. Dahl et. al. [4] emphasize *both aspects;* they show the close connections between the design of the data structure and the design of the procedural part. Wirth [11] defines an *action* as a fundamental notion, and requires an *object* to change state to note the effect of the action. He emphasizes the duality in the title of the book, *Algorithms + Data Structures = Programs* [12].

The active-passive duality arises in digital systems design. In a data processor, the local registers and arithmetic unit are the objects; the control unit provides the action. We do not emphasize one aspect over the other.

Some digital system problems are *data-intensive* whereas others are *algorithm-intensive*. Some problems can be attacked either way. In hand-held calculators, the trigonometric functions are calculated by an algorithm, whereas in some vector graphics processors it may be more convenient to look up the values in a large data structure (table).

In software design, Ross and Schoman [13] see the duality as *things* and *happenings* and note that they only exist together. Their object is to specify software, recognizing both aspects of the duality. The sentiment is reflected by Hoare [4]: "decisions about structuring data cannot be made without knowledge of the algorithms applied to the data and that vice-

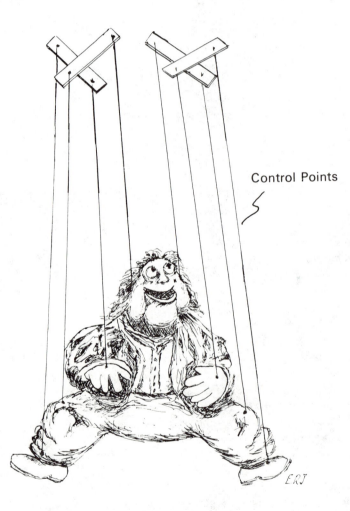

Control Points

Figure 0.2. *A puppet with its control points.*

versa, the structure and choice of algorithms often strongly depend on the structure of the underlying data''.

As an analogy, we view a bicycle as a passive element, capable of certain actions such as forward motion, turning right or left, or braking. Its control points are the handle bars, brakes, and pedals. The active part is provided by the human who rides the bicycle. Another analogy with a human as the active part is the puppet of **Figure 0.2.** The control points are the strings tied to the joints and extremities of the puppet. The actions and the passive parts are at the same conceptual level, and provide a useful way to divide the level into two parts. The puppet is analogous to the data flow of a data processor (CPU), as seen in **Figure 0.3.**

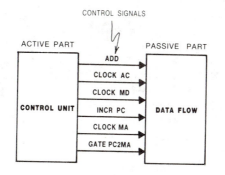

Figure 0.3. *Control points activated by control signals in a CPU.*

We note that the data flow of a digital system is capable of manipulating data. The *control flow* represents the sequencing or control of the actions which the data flow is capable of performing. *The designer can unravel and simplify many complex problems by the simple expedient of separating the control flow from the data flow.*

This separation is not always easy: some logic circuits (which we call *auxiliary circuits)* are difficult to assign a strict data handling or control role. However there is another impediment to the separation of data from control: old habits. There is a mathematical elegance which favors generality and unifying concepts. The Turing machine is an early example. Control information may be stored on the tape and operated on as data. Computer architects also store both instructions and data in a common main memory, where instructions may be operated on as data. In logic design, the logic circuits used to build the data flow are also used to build the control unit.

Chemical engineers are more fortunate. The apparatus for holding and treating the materials of a chemical process does not also control the sequencing of operations involving these same components. Nor are design automation tools for laying out the chemical process components used to lay out the process control algorithm.

0.2.7. Behavior versus Structure

In digital systems, there are two ways to describe a data processing function. A behavioral description deals with what outputs to expect for what input values. A structural description deals with how the building blocks are put together.

Simon [2] notes that, in the context of a system description, the active aspect of a system is manifested in a description of its *behavior*. The passive aspect is the description of its *structure*. In Simon's terms, these are *process descriptions* and *state descriptions,* respectively. Simon's *state* description of a circle is "the locus of all points in a plane equidistant from the center", whereas the *process* description is a recipe for constructing a circle with a compass. In circuit theory, *analysis* begins with the structural description of a circuit and derives the corresponding behavioral description. The problem of circuit *synthesis* (which corresponds to design) begins with a behavioral description and derives the corresponding structural description.

Electrical engineers are quite familiar with the notion of a *black box*. See **Figure 0.4.** A black box hides the structure of what is inside, but permits the observer to note the behavior of the input and output. Weinberg [9] describes a *white box* as the opposite: the structure is exposed but the behavior (what it does) must be determined. Weinberg links the white box with system simulation. In computer design, the (synthesis) problem to be solved is very complex. The behavioral description may be implemented in many different ways, subject not only to environmental constraints but also to cost and performance objectives. As a design progresses, it is tempting to change the behavioral description in the light of new insight.

Simon [2] views problem solving as beginning with a given state of affairs and ending with a desired state of affairs: "find the difference between these two states and then find the correlating process which will erase the difference". He observes, "problem solving requires continual translation between the state and process descriptions of the same complex reality." Weinberg says the designer bounces back and forth from white box to black box viewpoints. This suggests the *cut-and-try* technique: propose a solution structure (a first cut), and compare its behavior against the desired behavior. If the structure does not behave as desired, modify it. Hopefully, the desired behavior is more closely met by each new modification (cut). Iterations continue until the structure behaves satisfactorily.

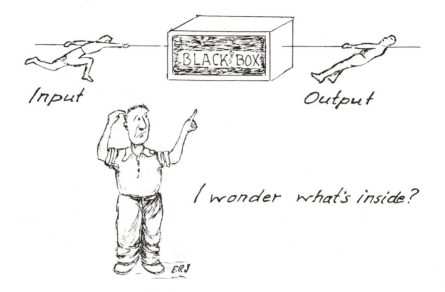

Figure 0.4. *A black box.*

0.3. A DESIGNER'S MODEL FOR STRUCTURE

In the previous section we saw how hierarchical approaches and the notion of conceptual level arise naturally from complex problem environments where the building blocks are weak. In this section, we are interested in abstract concepts relating to digital function structures (building blocks) which are suitable over a hierarchy of conceptual levels. We introduce **Figure 0.5** as an abstract model for these concepts. This model includes the structural primitives of the SARA [16] approach. Three concepts relating to structure are used:

- functional unit,
- connection point (data and control, input and output), and
- interconnection.

The *functional unit* is the embodiment of the digital function itself, and is the most important part of this model. The term *unit* stresses its role as a structural component. The concepts of connection point and interconnection support the functional unit with means to handle inputs and outputs. Corresponding to these structural entities is a counterpart dealing with behavior. The functional unit implements the behavior of the digital function. Corresponding to the *connection point* is what the point *does* (how it influences behavior). The connection point is also an *interface point* to other functional units at the same conceptual level. Corresponding to an *interconnection* is a *protocol* governing the use of the interconnection. Thus, the digital function has data inputs, and in accordance with the control information inputs (describing what to do with the data values), operates on the input data and delivers output data.

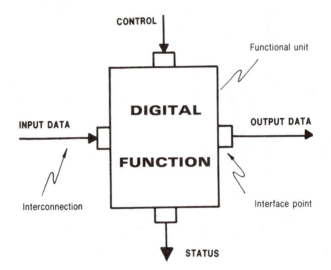

Figure 0.5. *A digital function.*

We can ask, *why bother about this model?* In many courses, only one conceptual level is bridged. In homework problems of introductory courses, we often treat small building blocks as functional units and interconnect them to form a more powerful building block. In computer engineering, sooner or later we must learn to think in terms of a hierarchy of levels. The easiest time to learn a hierarchical approach is the first time we encounter a multilevel problem. At a higher conceptual level, a newly constructed building block is again a functional unit. As we move up or down the hierarchy, the notions of functional unit, connection point, and interconnection remain with us.

A powerful motivation for isolating digital functions is the technological "wave of the future": the technology provides for more function on ever smaller integrated circuit chips. One must learn to conceptualize these circuits as providing a digital function. To take advantage of these circuits on a chip, we must learn what the function is, how to control the function through its connection point values, and how to interconnect the chip into the system. These three important concepts are covered by the model.

At the application programming level, programming costs make the *reusable code* approach economical. This approach is the computer software "wave of the future" according to Belady [17], because it avoids reprogramming digital functions with minor differences. A subfunction is programmed and debugged once and for all in a general-purpose way, and is reused as a component in new applications. To reuse the subfunction, we must know three things: its *function* (behavior), its *connection points* (the location and meaning of values), and how to interconnect it (transfer values between it and the system).

The model we describe also satisfies the important properties of a distributed system, which is the system organization "wave of the future" for many applications. A distributed system is a collection of subsystems, and each subsystem has some autonomy. The individual subsystems perform a nontrivial digital function, and are interconnected to the other subsystems. For example, microprocessors as functional units provide a digital function at low cost; they can be used with one or more specialized digital functions implemented in hardware (including additional microprocessors) for cost-effective solutions to many data processing problems.

As will be seen, the model also illustrates the distinction between structure and behavior at many levels, and further explains the notion of *design* in an information processing environment. The model is also useful in defining a task. A digital function such as a handheld calculator cannot perform *work* unless it is fed input values and told what to do. A processing *task* is a digital function together with input data and control parameters defining what to do. A function corresponds to a mapping from *each* argument value to a resulting value in the function's *range,* whereas a task corresponds to a *particular argument and particular result.* A task is a *single evaluation* of the function: given an argument the evaluation provides the corresponding value in the range. A function is like a vending machine waiting to be used. The machine performs a task when coins are deposited and a pushbutton activation tells it what to do.

0.3.1. The Digital Function or Functional Unit

The functional unit is called a "module" in SARA [16]. We call it a digital function when emphasizing its behavioral properties: a digital function *does* something. It transforms data. It processes information. It implements a control algorithm. By drawing a box around a digital function and assigning connection points, it is viewed as a structural component: a *functional unit* or *building block,* or simply block. In some large programs, a subprogram is called a module. In *structured analysis* [18], a program or subprogram is called a process. We suppress the details of precisely *how* the function is accomplished when treating the unit as a building block.

As designers, we also may apply *requirements* or constraints to the function. For example, we may not be able to tolerate too long a wait for the outputs. Or we may require the digital function to follow a certain sequence or procedure (protocol) in interacting with the environment. (Once a digital function is implemented, of course, the shoe is on the other foot; it is the environment which must follow the rules in interacting with the functional unit.)

In a formal sense, we identify a digital function with a *sequential machine* or *finite state machine* (FSM). An FSM has an internal state, and provides a status output (as well as a data output value) describing something about the internal state [19]. (See Appendix D.) The finite state machine is useful in viewing the algorithmic part of a digital system [20]. The FSM has also been used to design programs [21] and to specify complex software systems precisely [22]. The definition of complex interfacing protocols is also described in terms of the state transition diagram of a finite state machine [23].

The digital function itself can be very simple or very complex. The model trivially applies to the elementary 2-input AND circuit, which is a "1-state" finite state machine, i.e. a combinational circuit. There are two data input bits, one output bit, and no control parameter inputs or status outputs. At this low a level, the model offers no conceptual advantage to the designer.

The notion of digital function is broad, and no distinction is explicitly made between active or algorithmic digital functions, and the more passive data storage. We give some examples.

An arithmetic unit receives the value of two operands as input data, a control parameter, and delivers the value of the result. In many cases, the control parameter defines the function to be either the sum or the difference of the two input operands.

A computer memory consists of locations numbered 0,1,...,n. The memory delivers the data value at a given location if presented with the location number and the "read operation" control parameter. The memory stores a data value in a location if presented the location number, the data value, and the "write operation" control parameter.

At a more abstract conceptual level, computer instructions are digital functions, although the notion of a functional unit as a physical circuit is lost. Computer instructions operate primarily on values in memory. The "add" instruction will add the value in a second operand location to the value in a first operand location.

At a yet higher conceptual level is the handheld calculator. The information is keyed in, operations are performed, and output information is displayed. Keys are of two types. Numeric *data* can be entered. But there are *control parameter* keys such as the "+" key which describe what to do with the data. The output display also has two purposes. Normally, it displays numeric *data*. But it provides *status* information as well. For example, if the batteries are low, the display may appear as all decimal points. If 30 seconds have expired since the last key stroke, the display may be blank.

For purposes of economy, the handheld calculator provides common support components such as power supply, display, and keyboard. Also, some means to do arithmetic are included. Instead of supplying a separate calculator for each computation type (square roots, trigonometric functions, etc.), the support components are provided in common and the control parameter describes the particular computation.

The use of control parameters is a widely used technique. The control parameters go by several names: selection, modifier, tag, mode, control. The technique is found in products as diverse as washing machines and automobile transmissions. A functional unit does a class of operations which have something in common. For each task (each evaluation and/or state change made by the processing function), a control parameter specifies the variation.

The *data items* are quite general. A data item can be a value representing temperature, or an integer corresponding to the index of an item in a sequence, or a character string corresponding to a street address. Data can also mean a data structure: a vector or matrix of data values. Some computer instructions can operate on data structures composed of an arrangement of data items.

0.3.2. Connection Points, Interconnections, and Protocols

The functional unit is capable of processing data, but cannot do so without an external environment which feeds data and control information, and accepts the response (output data and/or status). The functional unit needs connection points or "doorways" through which information passes. These points are *interfaces* between what is internal to the processing function and what is external. For computer hardware, the doorways are *pins* (or pin-outs) at the chip level, and connectors or sockets at a higher level. For memory systems, the connection points are often called ports. In computer programs, the connection points may be global variables, or external symbols or identifiers. In the SARA system [16], the connection point is called a socket. The terms "input" and "output" are too broad: they fail to distinguish the *doorway itself* (a connection point) from the *information values which pass through the doorway.* (The distinction is the same as between a variable, and the value taken on by the variable.)

An *interconnection* transports or transfers *values* from output connection points to input connection points. In the case of a computer program, this operation may be one which moves a data value from one location in memory to another. The output variable of one program is the input variable for another. In hardware, the interconnection may be a flat cable between two sockets, or a wire between two pins.

Many transactions in our everyday lives are analogous to this model. Consider the bank transaction where we deposit our pay check but keep some of it in cash. We transmit the check and a deposit slip through the connection point, the *teller window,* which is capable of transferring information in two directions. The teller is the functional unit and accepts the documents and acts upon them. The deposit slip is a control parameter, explaining what to do with the check. The teller output is the cash, and the stamped deposit slip, informing us of the status of the transaction. (The cash of course is to be spent as input to another functional unit, the sooner the better.)

The model of a digital function is extremely general if we accept the existence of space-time trade-offs. Connection points can be time-shared. Sometimes the teller accepts data and control information as inputs through the window, and at other times delivers status and data as outputs, as is governed by prior agreement or the protocol between the two units. In hardware, the two-way teller window has its counterpart in bidirectional bus interfaces. In software, the two-way connection point might be a memory location which provides the input data to a square root subroutine, and the subroutine uses the same memory location to return the result.

Implicit in the use of interconnections between connection points of subsystems is a *protocol.* The protocol is the method by which the output value from one connection point becomes the input value of another connection point, with the intended meaning attached to the value. The protocol may also be involved in the procedure for selecting a digital function to be performed.

Many functional units at higher conceptual levels undergo three phases in the performance of a task: (1) setup phase (receive control parameters and data), (2) operational phase (operate on the data and get the result), and (3) clean-up phase (deliver or check results or error status).

0.3.3. Decomposing a Function

In the handheld calculator, the connection points interact directly with a person. Within a functional unit, however, the function may be *decomposed* into interconnected subfunctions. When a function is decomposed, our interest turns to how the higher-level function is implemented. *When a large function is decomposed into an interconnected set of smaller subfunctions, a span in the conceptual hierarchy is being bridged.* The interconnection of subfunctions represents the *structure* at that conceptual level. In information processing, then, a design result is the interconnection or composition of the primitive functions such that the interconnected structure performs the overall function desired. An analogy is a stereo sound system which provides music from a selection of several sources (tape, phono, radio), when the components are properly interconnected. Note that some connection points are interfaces in the hierarchical decomposition process. An internal connection within the higher-level functional unit may be a connection point at a lower level.

0.3.4. Functional Units in the Hierarchy

It is naive to assume that functional units at a high level in the conceptual hierarchy have a great deal in common with functional units at a low level. The designer should anticipate this, and be prepared to employ concepts and techniques which pertain only to a given conceptual level. In particular, interconnections and connection points take on different forms depending on whether they are above or below the hardware/software interface. In structured analysis [18], the data file is given special attention by its classification as a primitive. For data file transactions and processing, the storage, retrieval and restructuring of data is important enough to treat the data file as a primitive distinct from a digital function implemented as a computer program. In structured analysis, it is beneficial to make the designer aware of the algorithm and data structure duality.

At the lower conceptual levels, the task concepts of setup, operate, and clean-up do not exist when referring to the humble NAND gate. Gates also do not have "status" output values as opposed to "data" output values.

0.4. DESIGN STRATEGIES

A *strategy* implies a design concept or approach which has broad applicability within the engineering field. A *technique* is more specialized. Often, a design technique represents an alternative approach in an implementation trade-off situation.

Many information processing problems have no recipe or algorithm for deriving the solution. Simon [2] characterizes problem solving as a form of means–ends analysis. The ends are the desired results, and the means are the ways of achieving the results. Designs iterate; they proceed by trial and error. The designer "knows" when the desired result is achieved and stops iterating. We summarize the characteristics as follows:

- no recipes,
- a conceptual gap,
- many design alternatives available,
- space-time trade-offs, and
- iteration.

0.4.1. Divide and Conquer

Most design strategies serve to *divide and conquer:* to partition the problem into smaller pieces. A problem may be decomposed in several ways.

1. Partition into active and passive subsystems at same level (horizontal partition).
2. Partition the algorithmic part into sequential steps (dynamic refinement).
3. Partition elements of the objects or data structure (static refinement).
4. Repeat at lower level of the hierarchy (vertical partition).

The first item recognizes the active-passive duality, and suggests a block be decomposed (horizontally) into an active part and a passive part. Items 2 and 3 note that the respective active and passive parts may be further decomposed. Item 4 notes that each resulting part may itself be viewed as a composition of active and passive parts at a lower conceptual level.

0.4.2. Top-Down versus Bottom-Up

Two design philosophies are prevalent, the *top-down* and the *bottom-up*. The top-down approach is the successive decomposition of a large problem into smaller subproblems, until suitable primitive building blocks are reached. This is a popular approach for computer programming, where the primitives are computer instructions. Dijkstra [4] describes this strategy as *stepwise refinement*. Each refinement defines a new conceptual level (level of detail).

In the *bottom-up* approach, the basic primitives are used to build useful and more powerful problem-oriented building blocks. These "super instructions" are used to build still more powerful application-oriented constructs. Dahl and Hoare [4; Chap. 3] give examples of program constructions illustrating both bottom-up and top-down approaches.

0.4.3. A Mixed Approach

In digital systems, we favor a mixed strategy. A pure top-down approach lacks safeguards against devising a subsystem which is too expensive or too slow in the implementation technology. On the other hand, a pure bottom-up approach may lose sight of the overall system objectives. We prefer to begin with a top-down approach, first decomposing the original problem into smaller subproblems. Then, we consider feasibility by composing some critical (high relative importance) components at the lowest level of detail. This step could conceivably check that the protocol requirements can be met. For decomposing or refining at the major sub-function level, if each functional unit is decomposed into five to ten sub-functions, the conceptual gap is somewhat less than for the original problem. As the conceptual gap closes toward the primitive building blocks, the designer's knowledge of what useful "superblocks" can be built from the primitives provides a strong "bottom-up" influence.

The conceptual gap is bounded above by the functional specification of the problem, and below by the primitive building blocks. *Any technique which serves to close the gap is beneficial.* Close to the top boundary, decomposition or refinement appears most effective. Close to the primitive level, more powerful blocks built from the primitives are effective. The bottom-up approach is most successful when performed by an experienced designer, who has already dealt with the conceptual level above the primitives, and has some notion of what blocks are general and useful. Computer designers think in terms of higher-level functional units such as adders, buses, shifters, and counters which are built from more primitive circuits. Although a completed design may have come about from a mixed approach, from our teaching experience, students prefer to be motivated and learn about the design from the top down. The student is unmotivated if taught the bottom-up parts with no apparent goal.

0.4.4. Iteration

A characteristic of computer design is the iterative way a design result is achieved. Dahl and Hoare [4] note that insights obtained at later stages of the design cause revisions and reconstruction at earlier stages. Also, there is interplay between the passive or data structure part and the control or actions which create the state changes. The iterative aspect comes about for several reasons, including the presence of the conceptual gap. Due to the cost versus performance constraint present in a real design environment, the design is usually targeted to fill a particular market requirement. Naturally, marketing people want the resulting cost to be as small as is feasible for a given performance level. Therefore, some iterations are to be expected when trying ideas to improve performance and decrease cost. Further, as the design progresses, certain aspects will emerge as being more important than others. Understanding the *relative importance* of things seems to be primarily acquired by experience. As the important aspects emerge, design modifications result.

In some fields, such as the architecture or form of a man-machine interface, a direct design procedure appears not to exist. Alexander [24] shows that discovering and removing "misfits" is the way to fit a design to its requirements: "A good fit is the absence of misfits". Brooks [8; p. 634] concludes that "the only effective design methodologies will be those built around the iterative approach".

0.5. THE LANGUAGE OF DESIGN

In our experience, the descriptive techniques used in design are very important, and worthy of special emphasis. Concise and informative descriptive techniques greatly aid the computer designer. In a sense, the descriptive language and the way we think about the design are correlated. Wirth [12] states, "My strong desire to teach using a notation in which structures of processes and data emerge clearly and systematically rests on the observation that most people stick forever to that language". Ford [25] expresses it another way, "The language in which the student is taught to express his ideas profoundly influences his habits of thought and invention." In this book we stress the use of *block diagrams* for the data flow, a notation to describe actions or *microoperations,* and *timing charts* to describe interconnection and sequencing protocols.

0.6. SUMMARY OF DESIGN PHILOSOPHY

Computer design is a discipline in which designs originate in the mind, and bridge a conceptual gap. Designs must be cost-effective, and many choices are available to the designer. The conceptual gap plus a wide range of design possibilities render the problem complex. The complexity coupled with our mind's inability to interrelate more than about seven items point to a hierarchical structure of conceptual levels.

In the information processing field, a concept which appears to be independent of conceptual level is the functional unit, its connection points, and the interconnections themselves.

In attacking a design problem, one of the first aspects to be studied is how to separate the data handling and manipulation from the control and sequencing part.

Design alternatives are different ways of structuring the solution. Alternatives are considered in the order of their importance. As the design progresses, items of high relative importance will surface, as well as design decisions which result in a misfit. These create normal design iterations, which give a trial-and-error aspect to design.

Design strategies incorporate ways to *divide and conquer,* including refinement or decomposition (top-down design) and building application-oriented super primitives (bottom-up design). The language of design is important, and it is necessary to use concise, informative descriptive techniques for each aspect of the design.

REFERENCES

1. E. S. Ferguson, "The Mind's Eye: Nonverbal Thought in Technology", *Science,* v. 197, n. 4306, August 26, 1977, 827-836.

2. H. A. Simon, *The Sciences of the Artificial,* MIT Press, Cambridge, MA, 1969.
3. H. Zemanek, "Was ist Informatik?", *Elektronishe Rechenanlagen,* v. 13, n. 4, August 1971, 14.
4. O.-J. Dahl, E. W. Dijkstra and C. A. R. Hoare, *Structured Programming,* Academic Press, New York, 1972.
5. G. A. Miller, "The Magical Number Seven, Plus or Minus Two", *Psychological Review,* v. 63, 1956, 81-97.
6. Terry Winograd, "Beyond Programming Languages", *Comm. ACM,* v. 22, n. 7, July 1979, 391-401.
7. Donald E. Knuth, *TAU EPSILON CHI, A System for Technical Text,* American Mathematical Society, Providence, RI, 1979.
8. F. P. Brooks, Jr., "The Computer Scientist as a Toolsmith - Studies in Interactive Computer Graphics", *Information Processing 77,* Proc. IFIP 1977, North-Holland Publishing Co., Amsterdam, 1977, 625-634.
9. G. M. Weinberg, *An Introduction to General Systems Thinking,* Wiley, New York, 1975.
10. C. H. Waddington, *Tools for Thought,* Basic Books, New York, 1977.
11. N. Wirth, *Systematic Programming: An Introduction,* Prentice-Hall, Englewood Cliffs, NJ, 1973.
12. N. Wirth, *Algorithms + Data Structures = Programs,* Prentice-Hall, Englewood Cliffs, NJ, 1976.
13. D. T. Ross and K. E. Schoman, Jr. "Structured Analysis for Requirements Definition", *IEEE Transactions on Software Engineering,* v. SE-3, n. 3, January 1977, 6-15.
14. P. Morrison and E. Morrison (Eds.), *Charles Babbage and his Calculating Engines,* Dover Publications, New York, 1961.
15. H. A. Pattee, Ed. *Hierarchy Theory,* George Braziller, New York, 1973.
16. Gerald Estrin, "A Methodology for Design of Digital Systems - Supported by SARA at the Age of One", *AFIPS Conference Proceedings,* vol. 47, National Computer Conference, 1978.
17. L. A. Belady, "Evolved Software for the 80's", *Computer,* February 1979, 79-82.
18. Tom DeMarco, *Structured Analysis and System Specification,* Prentice-Hall, Englewood Cliffs, NJ, 1979.
19. M. Minsky, *Computation: Finite and Infinite Machines,* Prentice-Hall, Englewood Cliffs, NJ, 1967.
20. C. R. Clare, *Designing Logic Systems using State Machines,* McGraw-Hill, New York, 1973.
21. R. E. Heistand, "An Executive System Implemented as a Finite State Machine", *Comm. ACM,* v. 7, 1964, 669-677.
22. A. B. Ferrentino and H. D. Mills, "State Machines and their Semantics in Software Engineering", *COMPSAC '77,* IEEE Publication 77CH1291-4C, 1977, 242-251.
23. D. E. Knoblock, D. C. Loughry, and C.A. Vissers, "Insight into Interfacing", *IEEE Spectrum,* May 1975, 50-57.
24. C. Alexander, *Notes on the Synthesis of Form,* Harvard University Press, Cambridge, MA, 1964, Chapter 2.
25. G. A. Ford, "Comments on PASCAL, Learning how to Program, and Small Systems", *Byte Magazine,* v. 4, May 1978, 136-142.

* CHAPTER 1 *

INTRODUCTION AND BACKGROUND

1.1. COMPUTER SYSTEM ORGANIZATION

In 1834 the English mathematician and designer Charles Babbage designed an Analytic Engine, with a 1000-number 50-digit memory, an arithmetic unit, and instructions. The instructions were based on the Jacquard loom, a machine to control the weaving of colored threads. The Analytic Engine was never built because it was too ambitious for 19th Century technology. A "paper design" was completed in enough detail to demonstrate that Babbage had grasped ideas and principles about programming and operations on data. These principles were only rediscovered after the relay and vacuum tube technology made computing machines feasible. Babbage was not only the first computer designer, but also the first to underestimate the importance of designing the machine to the existing technology. Claws, ratchets, cams, links, gear wheels, etc. were required to be built by gauged standards. As described in Morrison [1], Babbage's less ambitious but still unrealized Difference Engine design would have weighed about two tons. This is not to say the Difference Engine was unbuildable. A Stockholm printer, George Scheutz, built a simple version of the Difference Engine after many years of work.

22

1.1.1. The Components of a Computer

The block diagram of a simple computer system is shown in **Figure 1.1.**
The major components are the central processing unit (CPU), primary
memory (main memory), and input and output (IO) devices. The system is
controlled by a program in main memory which is executed by the CPU.
The IO devices or peripherals either store programs and data records
(secondary storage), or, as in the case of keyboards and printers, convert
information between a form suitable for a computer and a form suitable for
people.

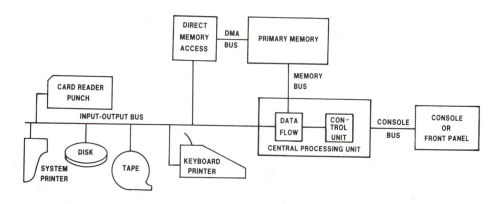

Figure 1.1. *Block diagram of a computer system.*

In quite small systems, the CPU controls a single repetitive function (a
traffic light, for example), and is the most important component. However,
in many larger data processing applications where the computer is shared
among several applications and users, greater insight is gained if the
primary memory and secondary storage are treated as the most important
components. Data processing equipment originated as mechanical and
electromechanical machinery (e.g. the Hollerith punched card machines
used by the U.S. Census Bureau in the early 1900s). Computer engineers
continue to apply the term "machine" to electronic digital systems which
perform the data processing function.

Throughout this book, we shall be interested in the parts which constitute a function, or conversely the building blocks out of which a larger
entity is built. ("Part", "component", and "building block" are used
interchangeably.) Not all parts need to be circuits. For example, a computer program is built from computer instructions and data words. A
macroinstruction is a sequence of instructions more powerful than a single
instruction, but less powerful than a program.

The CPU is the "engine" of the machine which fetches instructions and executes them. The CPU has two major parts, the data flow and the control unit. The *data flow* (also called data path) is capable of accepting, holding, processing and delivering data items. The building blocks comprising the data flow include the set of CPU registers (accumulator, index registers, instruction register, etc.), the arithmetic unit, and the buses which interconnect these components. These blocks are *data flow components*. The *control unit* governs or controls the data flow, providing the control and coordination (timing) signals which interface to other units in the system. The data flow alone is capable of processing data but does not know what to do. The control unit knows what to do, i.e. provides the *control flow*, but does not have any processing capability. The data flow components and control unit themselves are physically built from digital logic blocks, elements or *gates*. Digital logic *gate-level* blocks are the primitive or basic logic decision elements such as AND and OR gates, and primitive 1-bit (0 or 1) memory elements called *flip-flops*. Gate-level blocks or logic elements are built from components (transistors, diodes, etc.) provided by the technology.

This book addresses computer design in general, but most examples use small computers. Small computers convey the same design concepts which apply to larger systems. The boundary lines between small, medium, and large computers are blurred. Small computers generally have from 800 to 8000 gates, whereas large computers may have several hundred thousand gates. Small computers tend to use 8-bit or 16-bit data word sizes whereas large computers use 32-bit to 64-bit data word sizes. Typical minicomputer systems have buses as shown in Fig. 1.1, whereas microcomputers coalesce the individual buses into a single "system bus".

1.1.2. Some Historical Considerations

Tremendous technological advances have been made since the early computer days of the 1940s. Many of the plateaus have been assigned generation numbers. Some early computers were implemented in the relay technology developed by the telephone industry. Others were developed in the vacuum tube circuitry used in World War II radar equipment. Today, the term *first generation* computer is applied to the machines of the 1946-1956 time period. First generation processors used vacuum tube technology for the primitive gate-level logic elements.

In the first generation, when data processors were gaining a foothold in the business world, the most popular justification to acquire the new "status symbol" was the payroll application. A payroll program reads a record which has th employee's salary, and another record with the hours worked. The program makes the appropriate deductions and calculates the amounts to be paid and to be withheld. Punched cards served as the storage media for payroll data records (one card per record) in many early systems. Later, magnetic tape served as storage for records for payroll and similar data processing programming applications. The collection of programs which cause the computer system to process data is called *software.*

Input-output (IO) operations occur when records are transferred between main memory and external media or IO devices. Computer instructions cause data records to be read into main memory for updating. The updated records, under computer control, are put out to another tape, the output tape. Output in user-readable form, alphabetic or numeric (alphanumeric) characters, is assembled in memory and then sent to the printer for hardcopy output. This documents the transactions.

In the first generation, these programs were generally written in *symbolic* instructions using symbolic addresses, in a language called *assembler* (or assembly) *language.* The language was machine-dependent, and only served the particular computer for which the *assembler program* was written. An assembler program accepts the symbolic instructions as alphanumeric characters, and delivers "binary" *machine language* instructions as output. The binary 0's and 1's are understood and interpreted by the machine's central processing unit. As computer designers, we are very interested in these 0's and 1's. This is the machine language level of the system, the *hardware-software interface* between the computer *architecture* (at which the computer programmer works) and the computer *implementation* (performed by computer and logic designers).

The *second generation* (1956-1964) was keyed to the discrete transistor, fabricated in the semiconductor technology and mounted on a *printed circuit* (pc) board or card. The ubiquitous two-sided pc board is a sheet of fiberglass to which a sheet of copper is laminated to the top and the bottom sides. The circuit connections are made by printing a wiring pattern on the copper and etching away the unwanted copper. Connections are made from one side to the other by drilling holes in the board which are then filled with a conductor.

In the second generation, higher-level languages independent of the particular machine architecture became widespread, and small supervisor or monitor programs handled one program at a time in a "batch processing" environment.

Higher-level languages are converted to machine language by a *compiler* program. The existence of higher-level (machine-independent) languages does not eliminate assembler language programming. Although the present trend is otherwise, many compilers have been written in assembler language. Where execution times are to be minimized, programmers generally use assembler language. A characteristic of many compilers is the relatively inefficient use of machine language in the compiled program.

The *third generation* (1965 - ?) introduced the semiconductor *integrated circuit* (IC) technology, at a level of integration now called *small scale integration* (SSI). Gate-level circuits or logic blocks are equivalent to SSI. As the level of integration increased (circuit size decreased), useful building blocks at the data flow component level were built in *medium scale integration* (MSI) circuits. Since 1972, *large scale integration* (LSI) building blocks of microprocessors and memories and other powerful functional units have become available. The third generation introduced sophisticated operating system programs to control *multiprogrammed systems* where main memory typically held more than one program in some state of execution. *System software* consists of the *operating system,* the set of programs supplied to control the flow of jobs through the system, and other programs such as language processors to handle the assembly or compilation of other programs. *Application software* is the set of programs which performs the data processing applications work of the system.

The current semiconductor technology of *very large scale integration* (VLSI) encourages the distribution of even greater computing power to smaller functional units. The direct execution or interpretation of higher-level languages is now feasible.

1.1.3. The Family Concept

The onset of the third generation is also distinguished for the compatible family concept which sharpened the notion of computer architecture. Prior to this time it was customary for the manufacturers to accompany technological advances and new computer announcements with a new machine language. This practice consumed considerable resources for rewriting compilers and converting application software in the field to the new language. The advantage to the user of a higher-performance computer was accompanied by a "conversion headache". (Some employers found they had programmers who would rather switch jobs than convert.) In the family concept the manufacturers offered a single line of compatible models. When each model has the same *architecture,* or hardware-software interface, a user can upgrade to a more powerful *model* without converting the application programs. The *architecture* of one notable family is the IBM System/360 (S/360); the Model 25 through the Model 195 (S360/M25 – S360/M195) spanned a performance range of over one to one hundred. The family concept is an illustration of a *cost-performance* trade-off; the user can increase the cost to achieve a higher performance. "Grosch's Law" of the late 1940s stated that doubling the cost gives four times the performance (i.e. the performance is proportional to the square of the cost) [2].

In this book, computer architecture is based on the instruction set design and system organization of which the CPU is a component. *Computer design* is defined to be the activity performed by a design group which results in an implementation of a computer architecture. Since a computer is an instance of a digital system, computer design is the application of digital system design techniques with a computer as the end result. Many techniques employed in the design of a computer are in fact applicable to most digital systems.

1.2. ASPECTS OF SEMICONDUCTOR TECHNOLOGY

The important concepts of computer and logic design can be expressed in terms of the logic element abstractions, independent of any particular logic or memory technology. In this section, we briefly discuss the underlying semiconductor technology, or microelectronics. See Appendix B for a tutorial on simple electronic devices intended for the reader with little technical background.

To the package designer, the semiconductor chip is a "black box" which requires power and interconnections to its pins, and which generates heat which must be carried off. Our present interest pertains to what is inside the chip package. The logic of most digital systems today is implemented in semiconductor integrated circuits. The term "integrated circuit" (IC) comes from the fact that the fabrication steps which create the circuits on the chip are also used to create the chip interconnections. Many IC technologies exist; the most popular today is probably transistor transistor logic (TTL). Others include emitter coupled logic (ECL), complementary metal oxide semiconductor (CMOS) logic, and integrated injection logic (IIL). These technologies are described in Taub and Schilling [3], and there is no need to describe them here. Once the function of the IC is understood, the computer designer treats it as a building block.

1.2.1. The Manufacturing or Fabrication Process

The IC manufacturing operation is a process and the basic ingredient is the semiconductor silicon. See **Figure 1.2**. A slice from a specially prepared or grown cylinder of silicon is called a wafer. Many chips of the same type are processed on the same wafer. The process steps of importance include diffusion, oxidation, masking, etching, and metalization. The wafer is then diced into chips. Chips which pass their tests at this stage are bonded or mounted on a ceramic substrate and the chip signal pads are connected to pins, as shown in the blow-up to the right. The package is capped and tested again. The two parallel rows of pins on the long periphery of the substrate give rise to the name *dual in-line package* (DIP). The terms "IC" and "chip" are often used when DIP or IC module would be more specific. For a survey article on the fabrication process, see Oldham [4] or Allen [5].

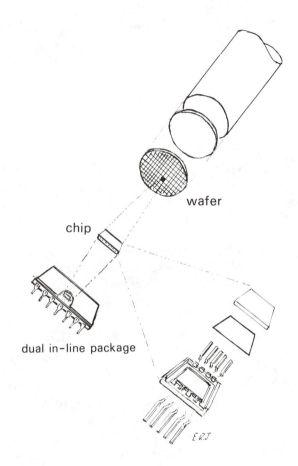

chip

wafer

dual in-line package

Figure 1.2. *Integrated circuit manufacture.*

1.2.2. LSI and VLSI

Computer technology has reached a certain level of maturity, due to advances in integrated circuits. Successive reductions in circuit density have allowed more and more gates per chip. The size of the pins of the DIP or any other package predominate over the size of the logic circuits. The earlier ICs used 14 pins, two for power and ground and the remaining 12 pins for logic signals. The SSI DIPs contain gates of a varying number of inputs (fan-in), or flip-flops or latches. Many of the MSI packages have 16 pins and comprise common functional circuits such as counters, registers, multiplexers (data selectors), decoders, and shift registers. LSI packages include 4-bit arithmetic units, microprocessor CPU chips, peripheral adapter chips, memory chips and programmed logic arrays. Once the SSI scale of integration was reached, lesser scales, such as discrete devices, tended toward obsolescence. However, the arrival of MSI and (V)LSI has not made SSI obsolete. The SSI circuits are employed on cards and boards for controlling and interconnecting large chips.

Semiconductor circuits have been getting smaller but pins haven't. In placing logic functions onto chips under pin and area constraints, the designer is more likely to exhaust the available pins before exhausting the area for circuits. In order to get more logic function into (V)LSI packages with a given number of pins, that function must be specialized somewhat, and have a low *pin-to-circuit ratio,* because connections today are more expensive than gates and flip-flops. General SSI packages are still required to connect together the higher function packages.

The utility of a given functional unit is independent of the technology. The same MSI package types appear in TTL, ECL, or CMOS, as well as in VLSI macro or standard cell libraries. Two directions seem clear. First, a knowledge of the SSI building block types continues to be useful. Second, *the designer must learn to assimilate and think in terms of larger functional units* in order to exploit them properly. It therefore makes sense to present digital systems design in terms of building blocks above the gate and flip-flop level, as future technologies will continue to implement them.

1.2.3. Environments

There are generally two environments in which a computer designer may find himself. In the pc board environment, SSI, MSI and LSI packages are mounted on a pc board or card. This is the environment from which most of the examples in this book are drawn. In the VLSI chip design environment, the common SSI building blocks are in a macro circuit or cell library of a *computer-aided design* (design automation) system for the chip technology. Unless the convenient MSI building blocks have been added to the library, the designer does not have them available.

In the VLSI and LSI chip design arena, the designer has a physical limitation on the "active area" of the chip available. Most of the active area is dedicated to logic circuits, but some portion (perhaps 1/3 to 1/5) must be devoted to interconnections. In this environment, design and implementation decisions are subject to different trade-offs. In the MSI and pc board environment, a designer may choose to implement a register using IC "A" instead of IC "B", because IC "A" has the same number of flip-flops and pins as IC "B", but is edge-triggered. On the other hand, an LSI chip designer may choose the less powerful latch function of IC "B" because it takes up less active area and draws less power, than IC "A". In SSI and MSI packages, the functions are generally pin-limited rather than area-limited. Perhaps the most tedious design environment is LSI microprocessors. Without higher-level macros, functional units such as the ALU are laid out gate by gate. If a cell takes too much width, it is squeezed narrower or reoriented. In the VLSI design environment, design automation tools facilitate the design process.

1.2.4. The IC "Part Number" Problem

The part number problem concerns the undesirable amount of effort to design, produce, document, test, and inventory a large number of distinct parts. Development and bookkeeping efforts are better employed on a small number of parts, where the volume of each part is high. This promotes the design of general-purpose ICs. Chips which are not general-purpose and are intended for a unique function in a unique machine, are said to be *custom-designed*. As a rule, the total number of ICs goes down, and the performance goes up, if the machine is implemented with custom-designed chips. The designers must assess the cost of generating the new part numbers, and the volume of parts to be produced, against the overall cost and performance benefits.

In general, volumes somewhere between 10,000 and 100,000 parts can justify a custom design and the generation of a new part number. Intermediate approaches, which have some merit, use design automation systems on a standardized chip, a library of cells, and constraints to provide wiring area. The cell is a functional unit such as a NAND or flip-flop, which can be placed in a rectangular area of the chip. The *master-slice* approach provides a predetermined selection of functional units already placed into rectangular areas of the chip, with interconnection areas or channels left "open". The user interconnects the functional units as desired, using the open areas for the interconnections. The *semi-custom* approach leaves the interconnections to the user as in the master-slice approach, but also gives the user a selection of the function in each rectangular area.

In VLSI, the master-slice approach has evolved to *gate arrays,* and the use of computer programs to aid in assigning and interconnecting the gates. In the gate array, identical cells are placed on the chip and the metalization layers are personalized to construct gates from cells, and interconnect the gates. Areas occupied by unused cells can be used for wiring.

1.2.5. Forecast

The growth of the computer field has seen a rapid change in the technology. There has been a feeling at universities about "hardware" oriented subjects such as switching theory, that it is important to teach the subject independent of the technology. In this way, the student does not learn subject matter which will soon become obsolete.

We feel the set of building blocks implemented in computer technology has reached a certain level of maturity. This began with the introduction of the IC circuit and its subsequent dominance. Eventually, the size of the pins to interconnect the circuits came to exceed the size of the IC chips themselves. The early ICs provided approximately 14 pins, with "unit logic" (NAND, NOR) gates on the chip. As densities improved, useful interconnected functional units or building blocks appeared. As a result, many skills such as the minimization of switching functions are less important to the designer.

The pin size and pin-to-circuit ratio problems are solved by the definition of useful MSI- and LSI-level functional building blocks. These new digital system components are defined independent of the logic technology. It therefore makes sense to present digital systems design techniques in terms of these building blocks. Furthermore, in applications such as custom VLSI chip design, the design can be built up from a library of MSI-level building blocks, which is conceptually above the gate (SSI) level. The availability of higher-level building blocks should not be construed as making "gate-level" design obsolete. First, the building blocks themselves are designed at the gate level. Second, the building blocks or LSI circuits are the "bricks", in a system where SSI circuits are the "mortar".

1.3. PHYSICAL ASPECTS OF A COMPUTER SYSTEM

1.3.1. Subdividing the Physical System

To motivate the discussion on the physical (and geometric) aspect of a computer system, the reader is invited to consider how to actually *build* the computer for which a "paper design" has been done. The detailed paper design consists of logic diagrams of AND, OR, NAND or NOR gates, and flip-flops, and shows how they are interconnected. The first job is to convert the logic diagram blocks to physical parts. Many designers actually skip this step by not using abstract blocks and designing directly to a set of available physical parts or components [6]. For *packaging,* the parts must be assigned to packaging units (cards, boards, cages) and then interconnected, provided with power and a cooling system to carry off the heat generated by the circuits.

Packaging is an important part of computer engineering. More than the discipline of logic design is involved, as powering, cooling, noise radiation, and mechanical and thermal robustness are also considerations. An overview of the problem with examples from some actual computer systems appears in Bell et. al. [7]. Thirty years ago, computers of modest performance took up an entire room.

Today, the semiconductor technology has achieved a small CPU plus read/write memory and read-only control memory on a single chip. The physical size of keyboards, printers, and magnetic tapes have not been reduced much over the years, but the CPU and its main memory have undergone dramatic reductions in size. As may be anticipated, the traditional data processors are housed in a "main frame" containing power supplies, power distribution cables, cooling equipment (fans in the case of forced air cooling), and a gate (which swings out for maintenance) for the logic circuits. The gate subdivides into pc boards or a frame which supports an array of sockets. The pc cards plug into the socket from one side, and backplane wiring appears on the other side. Integrated circuit packages are mounted on the cards.

Some smaller computer systems are rack mounted. Electronic equipment and instruments have been rack mounted for years, predating the computer industry. The standard width for rack mounting is 19 inches, and the height is a multiple of 1 3/4 inches. A card cage or enclosure for such a package might be 19 inches wide and of a suitable height and depth. Edge board connector sockets are mounted vertically to the rear of the cage, and vertically positioned cards are slid in from the front. (There is no standard for computer packages, however, as the Data General NOVA cards are oriented horizontally.) Micro and minicomputer manufacturers tend to choose their own edge board connector type and printed circuit card form factor (size). Many microcomputers use the pc board to package functional units. A system may consist of a CPU card, several memory cards, and some peripheral or device control cards.

Knowledge of the card and card cage or motherboard size, in terms of the number of gates and cable or edge signals accommodated, affects the realization of the system. For example, the logic designers of the S370/M145 computer thought in terms of useful functions which could be accommodated on a pc card. Cards were assigned to backplane boards later. On the other hand, the logic designers of the larger more powerful S370/M158 computer thought in terms of backplane boards. Later, the board logic was partitioned into cards.

We classify the important elements of the physical system:

1. electronic or electromechanical components,
2. printed circuit cards or boards,
3. interconnections (sockets, wires, cables),
4. power and power distribution subsystem,
5. cooling subsystem, and
6. frame, enclosure and covers.

Current components use the integrated circuit technology. Most commercially available chips are mounted in the dual in-line package (DIP). For larger and denser chips, another package is the quad in-line package (QUIP), which has four rows of pins, and can save 40% of the space over an equivalent DIP.

Phister [8] views the interconnection system as including the printed circuit card or board. This is true historically, but due to the pc card's important role as a functionally testable and field replaceable unit, we

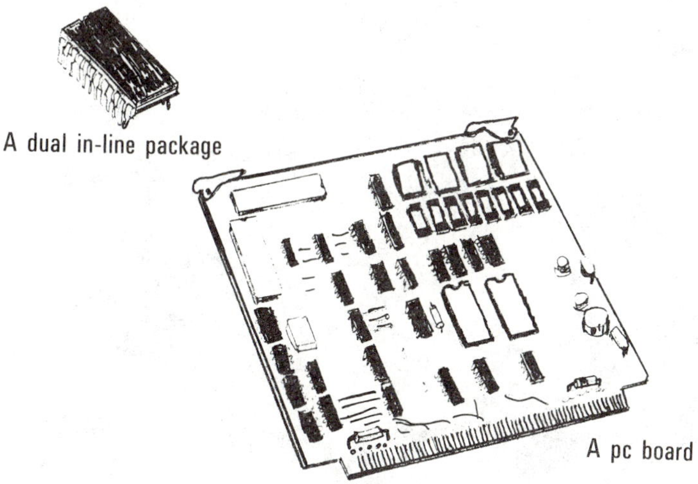

A dual in-line package

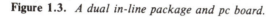

A pc board

Figure 1.3. *A dual in-line package and pc board.*

prefer to consider it an important category in its own right. See **Figure 1.3** for an example of a pc card. Other parts of the connection system include socket and edge board connectors, backplane wiring, and cables between boards or racks. Pc cards can be slid into a cage, with the fingers of the edge connector sliding into a backplane socket.

The system must have power supplies and a power distribution system. In small systems, the power supply may occupy a corner of the chassis and the distribution may be done by ordinary backplane wiring. In large systems, heavy copper conductors and buss bars are used. Logic circuits generate heat. In smaller systems, circuits are properly spaced to avoid a concentration of hot spots, and boards are mounted vertically to allow natural convection to cool the system. Other systems may have a fan to draw air over the circuits. Large high-performance systems may use liquid cooling, with chilled water cooling pipes passing close to the circuits. The IBM S360/M91, for example, had an impressive amount of "plumbing".

The frame or cabinet must house all of the subsystems. It should also provide for ease of maintenance by providing access to the cards and backplane. The location of covers and air vents is important for convection or forced air cooled systems. Mudge [9] includes a description of a 1976 packaging scheme for the PDP-11/60, a mid-range minicomputer.

Perhaps the most awesome aspect of the physical system is the space taken up by interconnections at each packaging level. If we take into account that a 5 mm × 5 mm chip has a nontrivial share of its area already

Figure 1.4. *An IBM 4341 board with 18 logic cards, showing one card with 28-millimeter metallized ceramic modules with 116 pins.* (Courtesy of IBM).

taken up by the "integrated" wiring, and the "space expansion" at the pc card level for pins, cables and connectors, then over 99.5% of the volume occupied by a digital system is required as interconnection space. (In actual fact, the need to cool the circuits is another reason for increasing the volume of the package.) Nevertheless, the semiconductor circuits themselves only occupy from 0.1% to 1% of the space. There is thus a trend to reduce the size of the package. A densely packaged system designed at the IBM Endicott Development Laboratory, the IBM 4341, is shown in **Figure 1.4.** The package uses multilayered, multichip, array modules with up to 361 pins per substrate and nine chips per module.

1.3.2. Breadboarding and Prototyping

Breadboarding is a term which predates the computer industry. It means constructing a circuit in an experimental fashion in order to check out the design. For circuits which can fit on one pc card, it is convenient to use components which easily plug in or out of a socket, and for which the wiring can be easily changed. Breadboarding logic is useful for educational purposes in computer laboratory courses.

Prototyping is the building of a system which behaves quite closely to the system intended to be manufactured. Often the cards may be wire-wrapped [10] for the prototype machine, and interconnected by printed circuits in the final product. For its first product, the Amdahl Corporation custom-designed a set of functional IC chips. These were each prototyped with a pc card. The prototype machine had a pc card for each IC chip in the final product. Many breadboarding and prototyping schemes are commercially available. Trade journals periodically review the kinds of equipment on the market [11].

1.3.3. An Apportionment of Costs

It is also instructive to know the portion of the system cost attributable to the cost of the circuit. Powering, packaging, and cooling constitute the remainder of the system hardware cost. Blakeslee [12] has studied system cost for a 50-IC board, wire-wrapped backplane, apportioning frame, power, assembler and test, and front panel. Sutherland and Mead [13] also apportion power and packaging costs on a per IC basis. This information is shown in **Table 1.1.**

<table>
<tr><td colspan="3">**Table 1.1.**
Package and Power Cost Apportioned on IC</td></tr>
<tr><td>*Item*</td><td>*Blakeslee*</td><td>*Sutherland and Mead*</td></tr>
<tr><td>Pc board and connector</td><td>$0.50</td><td>$1.00</td></tr>
<tr><td>Card cage (rack) and power</td><td>0.35</td><td>0.20</td></tr>
<tr><td>Backplane</td><td>0.10</td><td>0.15</td></tr>
<tr><td>System, board, IC test</td><td>0.38</td><td></td></tr>
</table>

Phister [8] has studied extensively the costs of a typical computer system of 1974. **Table 1.2** defines Phister's percentages.

The cost of the pc board "space" is seen to be a major item. This cost is not independent of the IC type, as 24-pin and 40-pin ICs take up much more space than a 14-pin or 16-pin SSI or MSI part.

The cost of the IC itself can vary widely also. Some 14-pin SSI parts cost $0.25 whereas some (V)LSI parts cost a few hundred dollars when first available. The industry is volume-sensitive, and experiences a "learning curve" phenomenon: traditionally, the price halves with each doubling of the volume produced. With sufficient volume, any current LSI

Table 1.2.
Apportionment of Computer Manufacturing Costs

Item	*Manufacturing Cost (%)*
Components	45%
Printed circuit cards	24%
Other interconnections	14%
Cooling and frame	8%
Powering	7%
Assembly and test	2%

part should have an "ultimate" cost of less than $10.00 (1981 dollars). The 8080 microprocessor chip, once priced over $100, sells for less than $4.00. Most MSI parts cost less than $2.00. VLSI parts, with larger chip sizes, and lower yields, can command higher prices.

1.3.4. Assigning Components to Packaging Levels

Packaging levels for the physical system are listed below:

- Cabinet
- Rack, card cage, or enclosure
- Pc card
- IC part

The assignment of IC parts to pc cards to racks is called *partitioning*. The goal of partitioning is to reduce the interconnections going in and out of the partition. Thus, circuits which are interconnected among themselves should be assigned to the same partition. Once the ICs have been assigned to pc cards, the next step is *placement* of the ICs to DIP or module locations on the card. The goal of placement is to reduce the mean length of each interconnection. The strategy is to place ICs close to each other if they are directly connected. This facilitates the wiring *layout* for the card. (The term layout refers to the geometric positioning of circuits and wires, and applies equally well to an IC chip.) If packaging is dense and only two wiring planes are available on the pc card, one can conceive of many placements which are not wirable.

Partitioning, placement, and wiring problems are amenable to design automation [14], or computer-aided design (CAD). Since packaging constraints and geometries vary from project to project, the algorithms are heuristic in nature. The wiring programs, in particular, generally fail to perform as well as a human. However computer programs can test a lot of possibilities quickly, suggesting an interactive approach. Computer programs have been used for some time to aid in the more routine documentation, simulation, drafting, and layout phases of design [15].

1.3.5. Rent's Rule

Computer engineers tend to search for common denominators and useful "rules of thumb" which may help estimate costs or package sizes for future designs. In this section, we describe an item of popular lore, dealing with the pin/circuit ratio at various packaging levels.

In 1960, E. Rent of the IBM Endicott Development Laboratory studied partitions of random logic in the IBM 1401 computer. From this study, he devised the formula $P = A \times C^p$, where P is the number of pins (external connections) to a logic partition containing C logic gates. For Rent's study, the constant of proportionality A was 4.8 and the exponent p was 2/3. The formula has been studied extensively and generalized [16]. For most logic, the constant A is 2 to 4, and at the chip package level, represents the average number of pins for a logic gate. (A 4-input NAND has 5 pins, and a 2-input NAND has 3 pins.) The exponent p varies from 0.47 to 0.75, and is related to the overall number of blocks and the overall number of input and output pins needed by the circuit under study.

Rent's rule deals with "random" logic, which is presently defined. In the first and second generations, microprogramming was not prevalent. The CPU control units were primarily *hardwired* control logic. Microprogramming (see Chapter 6) implies a microprogram memory, and hence the term *stored control logic*. Memory arrays are implemented as *regular* structures on IC chips. Similarly, registers and data paths show a degree of regularity, if only because a single data-bit path is replicated a certain number of times. The term *random logic* is applied to a collection of logic gates (AND, OR, etc.) which appear to be interconnected in a random fashion. In a CPU with a hardwired control unit, perhaps half the logic gates can be in this category.

Rent's rule is a reminder that the LSI technology, which is pin-limited, is not generous to random logic. With the value of A at 2.3, and an exponent p of 0.6, Rent's Rule shows that a 100-gate partition of random logic would need about 35 pins for the IC chip. The only solution to the problem is to design with functions whose overall pin count is small. In keeping with "first things first", single chip microprocessor designs are usually begun by deciding how many pins are available in the package, and how these pins are to be assigned. Techniques such as bidirectional buses and time-shared bus usage are employed to conserve pins.

1.4. THE COMPUTER DESIGN PROFESSION

Babbage stated, "It is not a bad definition of *man* to describe him as a 'tool-making animal'." Computers are tools, and like anything else designed by engineers, are built out of parts in order to perform a function in a cost effective manner. *A design result is not unique.* It is the result of compromises and is influenced by the interplay of various factors. A (V)LSI chip designer, for example, is constrained by circuit speed, power, chip area, and pins (pin-outs, pads). Often there is no a priori reason for choosing one compromise over another, but having done a preliminary design the engineer can always see how to improve the design. *Design is iterative in nature.* Some aspects of design are routine and straightforward, but it would be sad for us indeed if all aspects of computer design could be reduced to a computer program. Where then would the interest and challenge be?

The semiconductor industry has brought about a rapid change in the packaging boundaries of computer systems. Formerly a small CPU comprised a rack of printed circuit cards. Today, large scale integration has produced a CPU, some program control memory, and some addressable data memory on a single chip. *The packaging boundaries have changed,* changing some constraints and modifying some of the trade-offs available to the computer designer. *The basic design principles have not changed.* The problems and approaches described in the design of the Intel 8086 processor chip [17] are very familiar to experienced computer designers.

Computer design expertise is acquired by experience, not by reading books. As a consequence, individual approaches to the problem tend to develop. In 1958 at the Western Joint Computer Conference, proponents of the "Eastern" school debated proponents of the "Western" school on the best way to design the logic of a computer [18, 19]. Individual approaches give rise to the rediscovery and renaming of old ideas. This has been particularly true in recent years with the microprocessor designers [20]. As a result, the same item goes by many names. The MSI multiplexer (MUX) part is also called assembler, funnel, data selector, and in-gate. On the other hand, some techniques (e.g. residual control) go unnamed for years until someone gives them a name in a book or paper. Worse is the misapplication of a term which has had a well-defined meaning for decades. For example, microprogramming is a control unit implementation technique, and *not* the act of writing an application program for a microprocessor. In this work we try to mention parenthetically synonyms for the same concept in case the reader has encountered the concept under another name. The reader is kept alert by our use of synonyms, e.g., MUX and data selector. We use our judgment in assigning names to concepts which have been known for years, but for which no accepted term seems to have emerged.

The terms "conditional information", "conditional execution", "anticipation" and "race-through problem" are possibly in this category.

1.4.1. The Computer Designer

Ideally, the computer designer has an electrical engineering background. We say this, partly out of our own experience, but also because most of the supportive or foundation disciplines are electrical. **Figure 1.5** shows a hierarchy of disciplines which influence or support computer design. If an individual is interested in learning "about" computers, starting with a course in computer design is inefficient. Knowledge "about" computers is a course prerequisite. In order to appreciate how to *design* a computer, the reader should know something about assembler language programming, and be familiar with switching theory and logic design. Do not naively jump into computer design without these valuable tools. The assembler language level defines the computer designer's implementation goal. For example, instructions such as an indirect subroutine jump or a two's complement binary subtraction must be implemented. These concepts are covered in assembler language programming courses. Books by Osborne [21], Sloan [22], and Tanenbaum [23] are suggested. Moreover, Chapter 2 reviews instruction set level concepts.

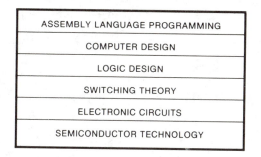

| ASSEMBLY LANGUAGE PROGRAMMING |
| COMPUTER DESIGN |
| LOGIC DESIGN |
| SWITCHING THEORY |
| ELECTRONIC CIRCUITS |
| SEMICONDUCTOR TECHNOLOGY |

Figure 1.5. *Coursework foundations for computer design.*

For supportive detailed levels, the student needs a switching theory and logic design course covering some electronics, boolean algebra, logic gates and flip-flops, and techniques for building logic circuits from these SSI parts. Such a course provides the student with the basic building blocks and concepts for designing a wide variety of simple digital systems. The digital building block bridges the large gap between the weak gate level and the powerful CPU level. The prerequisite materials for computer design form courses in their own right. There is enough complexity and uniqueness to computer design to justify excluding lower-level material from the main topic. For fundamentals in combinational and sequential circuits, books by Fletcher [24], Peatman [25], Blakeslee [12] and Greenfield [10] are useful. A review of building blocks and their timing appears in Appendices C and D.

Finally, we view computer design primarily as an engineering profession, and secondarily as an academic discipline. The design result is intended to compete in the market place where clever but impractical ideas don't stand a chance. Cost and performance issues are of more than academic interest: they serve the interests of the profession. Although we admit to the normal number of oversights, in this book we do not promote techniques which currently lack cost effectiveness. Nor do we teach an approach which works on simple problems but fails on problems as complex as CPU design.

1.4.2. Hierarchical Computer Organization: an Example

We list here a way to structure a computer system as a hierarchy of levels, the "higher level" first, the more detailed level last.

- Problem-oriented (higher-level application) languages
- Assembler language and machine language
- CPU data flow (register transfer or microprogram) level

At the problem-oriented language level, we find statements such as

"C = A + B".

This language is reminiscent of algebra which has equations of the type:

$$F(x) = x^2 + 2x - 6.$$

When given a value for variable "x", the equation *evaluates* to a number in the range of $F(x)$. This value is *assigned* to variable F. (In computer languages F is also a variable.) So "C = A + B" means to add the values of A and B, and assign the result to variable C. Variables A and B provide the source values, and variable C is the destination of the result. In higher-level languages, the "=" (or "←" or ":=", etc.) means to evaluate the expression on the right and assign that value to the variable on the left. The statement C = A + B may be broken down (decomposed) by a compiler into a program segment (block) of assembler level instructions such as:

LOAD   A
ADD   B
STORE C

These assembler level instructions correspond directly to machine language instructions. The machine language resides in main memory (a passive functional unit), and is executed by the central processor (an active functional unit).

To us, *conceptual level* corresponds to *level of abstraction* in the software field. Below the machine language level, the levels are not "abstract", hence our preference for the term "conceptual level". The CPU data flow level is the next refinement below machine language. Not all CPUs are microprogrammed, but all have a data flow. The data flow performs actions described by register transfers or by a microprogram.

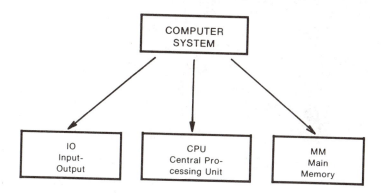

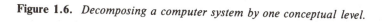

Figure 1.6. *Decomposing a computer system by one conceptual level.*

A partition for a computer system is shown in **Figure 1.6.** It consists of the input-output unit, central processing unit, and the main memory. A more detailed decomposition of the CPU is shown in **Figure 1.7.** The decomposition is both a static and a dynamic refinement because one subsystem, the data flow, is considered to be the static or passive part. The other subsystems, the system timing and the control unit, are active parts. The system timing unit, or central clock, provides signals which are used in sequencing the control unit microoperations. In effect they are used to provide the protocol by which data is transferred. An example of static refinement is the arithmetic unit. The circuits which perform the sum, carry lookahead, and (boolean) logic operations may be grouped separately.

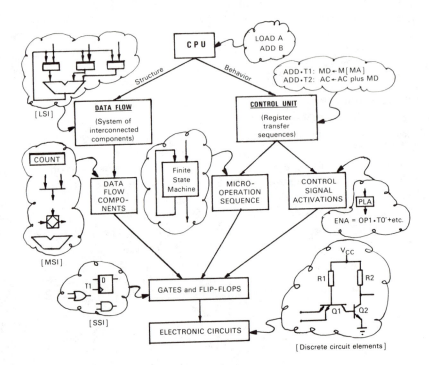

Figure 1.7. *Conceptual levels for computer designers.*

Figure 1.8. *A dynamic refinement model for many data processing applications.*

An example of dynamic refinement is shown in **Figure 1.8.** This decomposition reflects a time succession of activities. Many structured programming methodologies are based upon this model, and its utility should not be overlooked by the digital systems designer.

We now consider the data flow level. Assume a CPU has five registers:

1. PC - program counter; holds the pointer to next instruction.
2. MA - memory address register; holds the main memory address.
3. MD - memory data register; holds data for transfer to or from memory.
4. IR - instruction register; holds the instruction to be executed.
5. AC - accumulator; holds a data operand.

The instruction "ADD B" may result in the register transfer level sequence of microoperations shown. The sequence begins with the reading of the instruction from memory.

Notation	*Meaning*
1. MA←PC; READ	Place contents of PC in MA, do memory read. (Use next instruction address.)
2. MD←M[MA]	Transfer contents of memory location MA to MD. (MD now contains the next instruction.)
3. IR←MD	Place the instruction in the IR.
4. MA←IR(address)	Place address portion of IR (address of "B" for "ADD B") in MA.
5. MD←M[MA]	Place the operand B value into MD, from its location in memory.
6. AC←AC plus MD	Add MD value (operand B) to AC value, with result in AC register.
7. PC←PC plus 1	Increment value in PC to point to the next instruction.

With notations 1 through 7, we are defining the register transfer concept by example. The left arrow (←) corresponds to the *assignment* of the value determined by the right hand side to the register on the left hand side. A more detailed definition of statements in register transfer notation appears in §1.6. To implement (at the gate level) a register transfer operation or a *microoperation,* more detail is required than we are prepared to discuss at the present time. The refinement of microoperations into "control signal activations" is covered in Chapter 3.

In digital hardware, the active-passive duality is manifested as the data part and the control part. The data part is called the *data flow,* which consists of data registers, data buses, and functional units (such as an adder) which transform the data. The registers and adders may be decomposed or down-converted to flip-flops and gates. The data flow, in addition to the data inputs and outputs, has input signals called *control points.* In digital hardware, the *control unit* is the active or control part, and dictates the control flow. The control points are connection points for control parameters, and are connected to *control signals* which are activated and deactivated by the control unit. Microoperations such as MA←PC are decomposed or down-converted into *control signal activations,* or control signal activation logic, which may be implemented in array logic or programmed logic arrays (PLAs). In the case of microoperation MA←PC, one control point selects PC as the input for MA, and another control point activation clocks the data into MA. At a lower level, resistors, transistors and capacitors are the primitives for the electronic circuit designer.

1.4.3. Primitive Elements for Computer Design

The book by Bell, Grason, and Newell [26] is perhaps the first on digital system design to start at the register transfer conceptual level. Before that, it was customary to start at the lower gate level. Bell et al. [26] mention the lack of agreed upon register transfer level primitives. Without "lots of designs" being created in terms of those primitives, such a design level cannot become accepted. We observe the active-passive duality (see Prologue) and support a *dual view* of the decomposition at the register transfer level, where data organization items such as the *data flow components* (registers, shifters, adders, buses, etc.) define the *passive* part. *Register transfer notation* (RTN) describes algorithmic *behavior:* actions, or microoperations. Together with a set of major control states as conditional information, RTN may describe the sequencing of data flow operations. Thus RTN defines the *active* part. In our view, the fundamental conceptual level for computer design rests upon the functional power of the data flow components. This level of digital function should be the agreed upon primitives which define the data flow level. Our criticism with using RTN to "define" any conceptual level is that RTN spans too many levels. RTN can describe behavior at the levels of gate, data flow component, or instruction set. In IBM, the data flow block diagram (known as a "second level logic drawing") is used as an intermediate conceptual level. Once a data flow has been designed, RTN which *depends on* that data flow (dependent RTN) can describe the desired behavior of the control unit. We therefore assume data flow components as the starting point for the book, and presume this level of knowledge on the part of the reader.

In treating data flow components as building blocks, we feel a different type of thought process or emphasis is required than is normally taught in the traditional switching theory course. Combinational and sequential circuits are presented in building block and RTN terms in the appendices, in case the reader needs to be reeducated. Like Bell, Grason, and Newell [26], we consider gates and flip-flops to be too low a level to be the primitives for a course in computer design. Although the gate-level design of an adder, look-ahead unit, or multiplier presents an interesting intellectual puzzle, we feel that rearranging gates *is not the major theme* of computer design. Therefore, this low-level material does not appear in the body of the book.

1.4.4. The Design Phases and Conceptual Levels

The overall design process for a computer can be viewed in four phases, corresponding to design activities. These phases often overlap and it is difficult to assign well-defined boundaries. The phases are listed in **Table 1.3.**

Table 1.3. Design Phases	
Phase	**_Activity_**
1. Architectural	Define behavior as programmer sees CPU.
2. Implementation	Design data flow and control microoperations.
3. Realization	Map the design to physical components, assign packaging levels and wiring.
4. Check-out	Build prototype and debug system.

The first is the *architectural phase,* where the behavior of the computer, as the user sees it, is specified. The second phase is the *implementation* phase, where the major components (registers, adders) and their interconnections (buses and control points) and the system timing and control is defined. The result of this phase is a "paper design". The third phase is the *physical realization* phase. Gate, flip-flop, and building block pin-outs are of interest. The components are assigned locations on the pc boards, wiring lists are made, and cables and edge board pin connector assignments are made. The fourth phase is the *check-out and documentation* phase. The design is not complete until it works and is documented. The first phase is the province of computer architects, and the last three phases are performed by computer and logic designers. In some small systems and microprocessor organizations, computer designers also do the architecture.

In this book, the primary concern is the implementation phase, which to us is the most interesting. The realization phase is a relatively straight-forward "turn the crank" process if the design at the implementation level has been properly done. The instruction set architecture phase is more an art, and is covered for motivational and background purposes in Chapter 2. In most cases, the designer is asked to implement an existing architecture or a variation of one. There is much overlap between the implementation and the realization phases. The implementation is influenced by the gate or combinational circuit delays, the flip-flop clocking, and flip-flop setup and propagation delays. Knowledge of these delays is needed in order to devise the system timing cycle.

The realization phase can be viewed as having two parts. First, the larger functional blocks are down-converted (decomposed) into their physical parts. Then, these parts are assigned locations, wiring and cabling lists are compiled, power supplies, the power distribution subsystem, and the cooling subsystem are specified, and the system is assembled.

1.4.5. Managing Computer and Logic Design Projects

In the early days of computer engineering, the different logic design activities were not well recognized. Typically, the engineers built the machine and the machine itself defined the architecture. That was the opposite of what is done today, although some early microprocessor architectures have some aberrations which are clearly a result of space limitations on a semiconductor chip. Some of the first generation machines were built by the engineers, who then hoped the programmers could do something with them. Today, the engineers who design the machines can no longer afford to be ignorant of the machine's intended application.

In discussing the design of a computer system, there is one item of folklore worth remembering. Most digital systems projects, hardware or software, take longer to complete than anticipated. This has been true since Babbage. The engineers of the IAS project (begun in 1946) coined the phrase "von Neumann constant": no matter how close to completion the project, there were always a few more things to do. Much of the delay resulted from failing to "freeze" the design at some less than "perfect" state. (The design job is "open-ended", and one can always improve it.)

A problem in digital systems design has traditionally been the orders of magnitude disparity between the computing power of the design result (a computer) versus the computing power of the NAND gate. We compare the situation to building a house out of matchsticks. The design problem is now being alleviated by the availability of data flow components as building blocks. The designer must learn to think in terms of more powerful functional units.

An underrated aspect of design is the *documentation*. Lack of adequate descriptive techniques is an impediment to effective design, debug and maintenance. Descriptive techniques involve all aspects of design. In one aspect, a block diagram showing the functional units and their interconnections is called for. The designer must know how the functional unit behaves: what is fed in, and what comes out in turn. An awareness of the timing relationships and propagation delays through the unit is also necessary. Timing relationships are another aspect of a design description: the relation along the time axis of the control and data signals in the system. Some descriptive techniques are covered in §1.6.

The designer should *think* in terms of higher-level building blocks, their control points and microoperations. For the data flow, we favor a *structural* description based on two-dimensional block diagrams to aid spatial visualization. For the control unit, a *behavioral* description based on RTN is more appropriate. The merits of design approaches based on block diagrams versus those based on symbolic (register transfer) statements were debated at a session at the 1958 Western Joint Computer Conference. As is often the case, each approach is useful in its own way. A third dimension is time. The relative timing of control point activations and deactivations is are often depicted with *timing charts* of the control and timing signals. For instruction executions, actions and timing can be combined together on instruction event schematics; see Chapter 3.

1.4.6. Good Design Habits

Our design approach handles problems where a large conceptual gap is to be bridged. The desired behavior, including any requirements or protocol, must be stated explicitly before the design is begun. Also, the components available as building blocks should be known. The strategies to be covered in this section are summarized in **Table 1.4.**

Table 1.4. Design Strategies
1. Top-down: Refine a large problem into smaller ones.
2. Work on the most important items, or more frequent cases, first. (First things first.)
3. At a given level, postpone lower-level details.
4. Handle exceptions or less frequent cases after the major case is done.
5. Bottom-up: Build more powerful tools from the basic tools, thus raising the level of thought about the problem.
6. The design *iterates*, but toward the final phases, "freeze" the decisions at the higher conceptual levels and work down.
7. Maintain updated documents of the design result.

In computers, the designer builds powerful functions from simple parts. Design techniques must take into account the existence of the large number of alternative or functionally equivalent ways of arranging the logic blocks. This problem was observed by Babbage [1]. When asked what he considered his greatest difficulty in designing his machine, Babbage replied it was not that of "contriving a mechanism to execute each movement ... but it really arose from the almost innumerable *combinations* amongst all these contrivances." He compared the problem to that of a general commanding a vast army in battle. We attempt to present decisions in the proper order and systematically reduce the number of alternatives.

For complex problems, we fill a large conceptual gap with one or more intermediate levels. In the top-down approach, the large problem is divided into subproblems: "divide-and-conquer". (No problem is so complex it cannot be broken into two parts!) It is beneficial to work initially on the most important subproblem: the most critical to cost and performance.

If decisions on the *most important item* on a level are made first, then items on the same level may be less subject to change later. At whatever level, we recommend: "first things first". This forces the designer to consider the *priorities* of the problem. In dealing with the most important item(s), lesser items or details at a lower conceptual level can be deferred. Considering important items first reduces complexity as well: if we select only items with at least a 15% influence on the problem, then no more than six items need be considered.

A solution which works *most of the time* can be called a *first cut* or "bare bones" solution. This permits other work to proceed at that conceptual level. Once a solution for "most of the time" is found, it can be tested against less frequent cases by thinking of *"what if?"* situations.

The benefits of the *bottom-up* approach should not be overlooked, in spite of current interest in top-down "structured" approaches. The bottom-up approach has been employed successfully by IC manufacturers in the design of MSI circuits such as the ALU, counter, data selector, decoder, etc. Further, even more powerful bottom-up parts have been developed, such as programmable peripheral controller chips. For the proper application of the bottom-up approach, general-purpose "superparts" are designed from more basic parts. Although more complex than basic parts, the designer must know what the superpart can do, how to control it, and what the timing relationships are. In this way, by thinking in terms of more powerful building blocks, the conceptual level is raised, and the designer is closer to the solution. Just as ingenuity is required in subdividing a larger problem into smaller problems, perhaps even more ingenuity is required in discovering useful "superparts" out of which solutions to some interesting class of problems can be configured. The development of the FORTRAN language, which relieved scientific programmers of writing in assembler language, is a bottom-up solution for a large class of problems.

The design process is *iterative* in nature; we deal with a *design loop*. To initiate the iteration, a system or solution should be proposed to fill the gap to be bridged by the design, even if it is not the best. A performance analysis may illuminate weak points of the design not otherwise apparent. By experimenting with ideas, the cost-effectiveness of the system can be improved. At some point the highest conceptual level should be "frozen" and not subjected to further iteration activity. Lower levels should be frozen in turn. Otherwise the "von Neumann constant" will dominate and the design will never be finished.

Documentation is an activity which takes on greater importance with the size of a project. For small "hobby" projects the designer can scribble on paper. In larger projects the design decisions must be properly written down: "If it isn't written down, it doesn't exist." For the build and debug of a prototype, it is recommended the project have a log book for dating and recording when things happened, the nature of "bugs", changes, etc. Brooks [27] and Levanthal [28] make some excellent points on this subject.

Once a design has been realized in the technology (chips or pc boards usually), logic drawings or schematics are the rule. These schematics reflect how the system is *built,* not how it was designed. Schematics show where chips are located and how pins are interconnected. Unfortunately, the physical design is usually the only up-to-date document at the end of the design. Although the top-down approach is the proper way to learn about a particular design, often the new engineers on the project are forced to learn it from the bottom, through the detailed logic diagrams. The schematics are not bad for the data flow, which is primarily a structure, but are horrible for learning the control flow, which concerns the sequencing of events.

Since the nature of design is continual change, particularly in the debugging phase, any documentation scheme must accommodate change. Logic corrections are usually made to the module, chip or gate level. This is usually the level where the bugs are found; hence it is inconvenient to update higher-level block diagrams or timing charts used in earlier design phases. We feel, however, that reflecting the changes upward and updating the higher-level documents is valuable for teaching purposes.

1.4.7. A Summary of the Computer Design Problem

We recall the characterization of a computer as a digital system or machine which executes computer programs. The program is expressed in a language defined by the machine architecture, and is located in the machine's main memory. The program consists of a sequence of machine language instructions which operate on data or operands also stored in the main memory. Some operands may be stored in machine registers. The central processor or CPU consists of the machine registers, the necessary functional units to perform the instruction operations, interconnection paths or buses, and the control unit.

It is the designer's task to define and interconnect registers and other functional units, and to arrange the necessary control signal activations. The changing values on the control signals cause the machine to fetch each instruction in turn from memory, to decode it (discover what to do), locate the operands, and perform or execute the required operation.

The designer's task is not easy. The designer must have have knowledge of many topics:

- the building blocks provided by the technology,
- binary number systems and arithmetic algorithms,
- busing and worst-case delay analysis,
- the setup of a system clock cycle,
- the organization of the control unit, and
- the breakdown of each instruction into a sequence of actions.

The designer should also employ design approaches which reduce the complexity of the problem, viewing the design in a top-down as well as bottom-up fashion, and should be aware of the conceptual levels encountered. The logic designer should understand the importance of good design documentation, and be familiar with the descriptive tools available for expressing designs at different levels of abstraction.

We summarize the general assumptions on which our approach is based. The reader should be aware of these points while learning the design process.

1. Computer systems are complex, and possess a hierarchy of conceptual levels.
2. One level is the instruction set, the interpretation of which is the design goal.
3. The designer's foundation must be the building blocks the technology provides. Their functions must be assimilated.
4. Design is an iterative process, guided by "first things first" and postponement of details.
5. There is an active-passive duality. The units with which the designer works, at each level, have both structural and behavioral aspects.
6. The designer's descriptive techniques should match the conceptual level and the aspect (structure or behavior).

For an exposition of the levels of abstraction of a computer system, centered at the instruction set level, the reader is referred to Bell and Newell [29].

1.5. BINARY NUMBERS AND ARITHMETIC

In this section some of the numbering conventions used in this book are explained. Common sense is combined with a desire to minimize the "unlearning" required of the novice or "lay person". (A lay person is either someone in awe of computers, or a high school sophomore.) As a reminder of what the novice is accustomed to, we use the term *pencil and paper rule:* how would the lay person, with no particular computer bias, write something down on paper? The pencil and paper rule follows the *natural order* we learn in childhood. In reading and writing, we start in the upper left part of the page, and proceed to the right. At the end of the line, a "carriage return" operation brings us to the left position of the next line down. If asked to write something vertically, we write from top to bottom. In reciting numbers, we start at the lower numbers and proceed to the higher. In reciting the alphabet we start with "A" and end with "Z". To illustrate, consider the construction of a three-variable truth table, with input variables named A, B, and C. We find the column headings in the order "C B A" to be surprising, and might attach something mysterious to this unexpected event. After all, the "expert" who wrote it this way must really have some inside knowledge, to *reverse the natural order* on purpose! In this case, the curious novice who is eager to resolve the mystery will be disappointed. Columns labeled C B A serve only to confuse. The pencil and paper rule is a simple reminder to label columns "A B C", and reserve the surprises for situations where the lay person should *really* be in awe. (This illustration of the rule may seem trivial, but the nonmysterious use of "C B A" can actually be found in the product literature.) Whenever possible, *sequences should have the natural order:* horizontally from left to right, and vertically from top down. By the same common sense reasoning, the lay person expects to see digit-by-digit additions and subtractions starting from the right (low-order end) and working to the left (high-order end).

One area where experience is offended is in the numbering of things where the first item in the list is labeled "0" instead of "1". For example, the lay person is accustomed to counting 1, 2, ..., 8 for a list of eight items. Instead, logic designers make the itemization 0, 1, ..., 7. In this case, there actually *is* a "mystery" to spark the curiosity of the novice. When three binary digits are used to distinguish eight items, in the binary number system, the eight combinations of numbers become 0 (000), 1 (001), ..., 7 (111). Computer memory address locations are typically itemized in this fashion. A higher-level language, APL, addresses this problem by giving the user a choice. In the *zero-origin* convention, the index origin for numbering elements is "0". In the *one-origin* convention, the origin is "1". The zero-origin numbering convention has found its way into computer engineering jargon. The engineers who are with a project from the very beginning are said to be with the project "since day zero". Zero-origin numbering also appears in the numbering of decades and centuries. For example, "the 1900s" correspond to the 20th century, just as address 19 corresponds to the 20th location in a memory.

1.5.1. Bit Numbering Schemes

In most computing systems, the addressing of main memory is done in the binary number system. For this reason, computer people soon learn about numbers which are powers of 2. With eight bits, there are 2^8 or 256 combinations. In addressing, a 10-bit address is capable of addressing 2^{10}, or 1024, or 1K locations. The *memory address space* is 1024 locations. These 1024 addresses range from 00 0000 0000, 00 0000 0001, through 11 1111 1111. In decimal, the address or location numbers are 0, 1, etc., through 1023. Since the addresses form a sequence, the memory space is said to be linear. At each location, a computer word of n bits is stored. In this book, the bits within the word are designated, from the left, bit 0 through bit n−1, *consistent* with the zero-origin convention and with the way location numbers are assigned to words within memory. See **Figure 1.9.** The left-to-right bit numbering convention is also consistent with the usage of the first quarter century of electronic computers. Many current computer systems ranging from the PDP-8 to the IBM S/360 and S/370, employ this bit numbering scheme. The most significant bit (MSB) of a word is designated bit 0. For this reason it is called the *MSB 0* scheme. Although this scheme is a result of the application of the pencil and paper rule to a zero-origin system, there is not universal agreement about numbering the bits in a word.

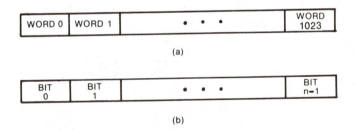

(a)

(b)

Figure 1.9. *Assigning numbers to word and bit locations consistent with pencil and paper rule.* (a) Word addresses within a 1024-word memory. (b) Bit position numbering within an n-bit word.

Another bit numbering scheme popular in microcomputers is called *LSB 0*, because the least significant bit is designated 0. This scheme numbers the bit positions backwards, from right to left, instead of from left to right. The LSB 0 scheme is motivated by the following convenience: if the data word being considered is a fixed point integer, we can calculate the value of a 1 located in position "i" as 2^i. The LSB 0 has the characteristic that the more significant the bit the larger the bit position number.

Since the computer can function without knowing how the designers named the bit positions, the bit designation scheme is *arbitrary*. However, the consistency of the MSB 0 scheme with the method of numbering word locations in main memory offers a singular advantage (in addition to following the pencil and paper rule). In grouping together adjacent memory words to increase the precision of arithmetic operations, as in double precision arithmetic, the word with the leftmost (lower) address (Fig. 1.9) is the most significant word as would be written on paper.

In the IBM S/370 architecture, the word size is 32 bits, composed of four 8-bit bytes. An 8-bit byte can be further subdivided into two 4-bit digits. It is convenient for the bit numbering scheme to extend naturally to these other subdivisions of words. The subdivision of a 16-bit word appears in **Figure 1.10,** where the natural extension of the MSB 0 scheme is shown.

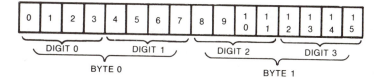

Figure 1.10. *Consistent left-to-right naming of digits and bytes within a 16-bit word.*

Unfortunately, if we are to retain the left-to-right numbering of memory positions, systems which use the LSB 0 bit numbering scheme *inconsistently* treat the problem of multibyte words. Consider the situation where the LSB 0 scheme is used on 16-bit numbers, but the system employs addressing to the 8-bit byte. It is convenient to name the high-order and low-order bytes within the 16-bit word. Two choices are possible:

1. the high-order (left hand) byte can be byte 0, consistent with the addressing, or
2. the high-order byte can be byte 1, consistent with the LSB 0 numbering scheme.

Consider word address 0, comprising the first two bytes of memory, as shown in **Figure 1.11.** The two choices considered are shown as (a) and (b) respectively, and not all users of LSB 0 schemes are in agreement. For *either* choice, *unlearning* is required. Since reading from left to right is deeply ingrained in the western world, the situation in Fig. 1.11(b) requires the most unlearning, and is less desirable.

The choice of a bit numbering scheme is not usually ours to make; it has been chosen for us by our employer or by the manufacturer of the

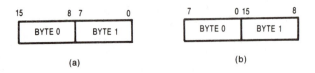

Figure 1.11. *LSB 0 scheme consistency problems when applied to 16-bit words, using byte addressing.* (a) Inconsistent with LSB 0 right-to-left naming. (b) Byte naming right-to-left, with byte 0 least significant, leaves bit 0 adjacent to bit 15, inconsistent with writing digits of a number from left to right in memory.

computer system available to us. Many mainframe systems use MSB 0 and many microcomputer systems use LSB 0. Therefore the computer engineer should be familiar with *both* the MSB 0 and LSB 0 numbering schemes.

When alphabetic or text information is accepted or delivered by a computer, an interchange code is used. An American standard code is called ASCII. The S/370 system uses the Extended Binary Coded Decimal Interchange (EBCDIC) code. Such codes generally use one byte to represent each character. Such data is called *alphanumeric* (alphabetic and numeric). Alphanumeric information is often stored in the computer memory in the form of a character (or text) string. When character string information is read to memory, the characters are normally stored from lower-valued addresses to higher-valued locations. This is consistent with the pencil and paper rule of reading or writing from left to right (or top to bottom); see **Figure 1.12.** Addressing is to the byte. Byte 49 contains "cr", the code for "carriage return", a delimiter to mark the end of a line of text.

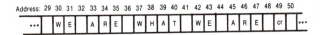

Figure 1.12. *Alphanumeric data stored in a byte-addressed memory.*

Another type of data encountered in a computer memory is called *packed decimal.* Two digits occupy (are packed into) one byte. (In ASCII a decimal digit would occupy one byte.) The number "2001" would appear as shown in **Figure 1.13.** Fig. 1.13(a) shows the unpacked version in the EBCDIC code.

Due to the inconvenience of using bits, binary numbers often are converted to base 16 or hexadecimal (hex) numbers. In hex, the EBCDIC

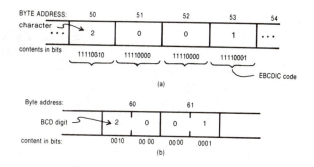

Figure 1.13. *A decimal number stored in memory.* (a) Unpacked. (b) Packed.

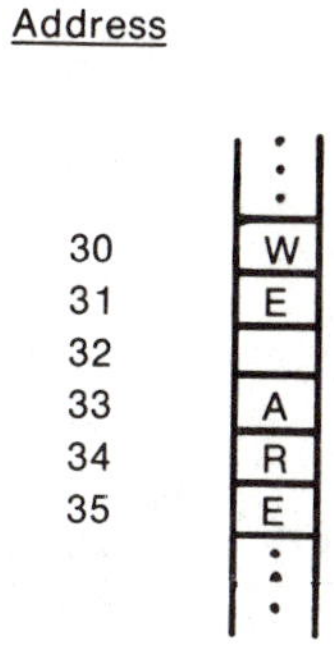

Address

```
30   W
31   E
32
33   A
34   R
35   E
```

Figure 1.14. *Depicting a linear memory vertically.*

code for "2001" is "F2F0F0F1". As with alphanumeric data, digits are placed in memory horizontally from left to right (vertically from top to bottom) as would a lay person. In performing packed decimal addition, the computer designer would cause the CPU to begin with digits at the low-order end (which is to the right) and work toward the high-order end digits to the left. This is consistent with how a lay person would work from right to left in solving problems of addition digit-by-digit with a pencil and paper, and requires no unlearning.

A linearly addressed memory is most often depicted vertically. When this is done, consistency with the pencil and paper rule would place the lowest address on top and the highest address on the bottom. See **Figure 1.14** for a vertically depicted memory which requires no unlearning.

1.5.2. Binary Number Representations for Integers

People are familiar with the decimal number scheme. The *radix* or number base is ten, and digits in the number represent powers of this base. In the binary system, digits are 0 and 1, and the radix is two. Using the MSB 0 numbering scheme, the MSB or bit 0 is usually the sign bit of the integer. For 16-bit numbers, this leaves 15 magnitude bits, so that the integers from −32,767 to +32,767 can be represented. This range and precision is sufficient for many applications, a fact favoring the popularity of machines using a 16-bit word. The sign bit values are 0 for positive and 1 for negative numbers. The most familiar representation is the sign followed by the magnitude. Thus, for 4-bit sign and magnitude numbers, 0111 is +7 decimal, and 1111 is −7 decimal. For binary numbers, three representations have been used, as shown in **Table 1.5.**

Table 1.5. 4–Bit Signed Integers			
N *Sign Magnitude*		*One's Complement*	*Two's Complement*
+7	0111	0111	0111
+6	0110	0110	0110
+5	0101	0101	0101
+4	0100	0100	0100
+3	0011	0011	0011
+2	0010	0010	0010
+1	0001	0001	0001
+0	0000	0000	0000
−0	1000	1111	doesn't exist
−1	1001	1110	1111
−2	1010	1101	1110
−3	1011	1100	1101
−4	1100	1011	1100
−5	1101	1010	1011
−6	1110	1001	1010
−7	1111	1000	1001
−8	*	*	1000
* No 4-bit representation			

The signed magnitude (sign and magnitude) number system is shown in the first column of Table 1.5. It is not popular with computer designers for the following reason. In the *addition* of a positive number and a negative number, the actual arithmetic operation to be performed is the *difference* operation: a "subtraction" and not an "addition". In the *subtraction* of the same two positive and negative numbers, the actual operation on the magnitudes is a *sum*.

Consider an arithmetic unit as a building block capable of calculating the sum or the difference of two numbers. Of course the unit must be told which. To handle addition and subtraction in the sign and magnitude representation, two decisions need to be made: should the sum or difference operation be performed, and what is the sign of the result?

Because of the technical problems inherent in the signed magnitude number representation, two other negative number representations have been devised by computer designers, *radix complement* and the *radix-minus-one complement*. These number representations do not require decisions about the sum versus difference operation, or about the sign of the result. In binary number systems, the radix is two, and these negative number representations are called the two's complement and the one's complement representations. For binary *one's complement* numbers, the negative number is the bit-for-bit complement of the positive number. A significant property of one's complement numbers is the existence of the number *minus zero* (−0), which is 1111 in the 4-bit system. The *two's complement* number system is most easily explained in terms of one's complement numbers. The two's complement of a number is the one's complement plus one. To find the two's complement of a number, complement the number bit for bit, then add one, ignoring any carry-out of the highest (sign) position. Thus, adding one to the one's complement for −7 (1000) gives the two's complement of −7: 1001. Taking the two's complement of 1001 gives 0110 from complementation and 0111 from adding one. The result, 0111, is +7 as expected.

1.5.3. Binary Addition

The truth table for the binary sum of two binary bits A and B with carry-in CIN, and resulting sum SUM and carry-out COUT is shown in **Table 1.6.**

Table 1.6 is the behavioral description for a single bit position of an adder. A realization of this truth table with gates is shown in **Figure 1.15.** Fig. 1.15 is thus the structural description of a 1-bit adder. An intermediate signal, "A xor B" is called the *half-sum*. The half-sum is exclusive-OR gated with the carry-in CIN to form the resulting sum bit. To implement a parallel adder, the circuit of Fig. 1.15 is copied for each bit position. In a *ripple-carry adder,* the 1-bit adder circuits are cascaded together by feeding the COUT signal of the lesser significant bit position to the CIN input of the adjacent more significant bit position.

The adder circuit is independent of the number representation: it simply adds the binary magnitudes presented to it. The designer's task is to

Table 1.6. **Truth Table for a 1–Bit Binary Adder**				
_A_	_B_	_CIN_	_COUT_	_SUM_
0	0	0	0	0
0	0	1	0	1
0	1	0	0	1
0	1	1	1	0
1	0	0	0	1
1	0	1	1	0
1	1	0	1	0
1	1	1	1	1

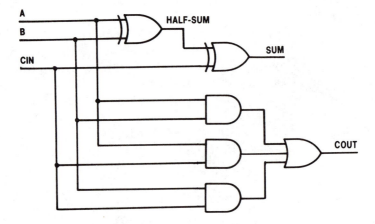

Figure 1.15. *A 1-bit binary adder.*

control the data fed to the adder, and to handle properly the least signifi-cant carry-in signal and the carry-out of the most significant bit position.

The advantage of the one's and two's complement representation is that with the adder as described, positive and negative numbers alike may be correctly added with very little additional logic. For the sign and magni-tude representation, special decision logic must be provided to examine the sign information and the "add" or "subtract" control signal to determine whether a sum or difference operation is called for.

In one's complement addition, the adder must be modified to handle the "end-around-carry". The end-around-carry (EAC) is the detection of a carry-out from the MSB (sign) position, as a condition to add one into the lowest bit position. The "add one" operation is necessary because both operands include the "minus zero" combination. As an example, let −3 be added to −4, in both one's complement and two's complement numbers.

	One's Complement		Two's Complement	
	1100	(−3)	1101	
	1011	(−4)	1100	
carry: 1	0111		1001	(−7)
	1	← EAC		
	1000	← Correct sum, −7		

The requirement to handle the EAC is the primary reason that the one's complement representation is not popular. For n-bit numbers, a situation may exist where the n-bit adder outputs may not stabilize in the desired amount of time [30]. A second disadvantage of the EAC occurs for multiple precision arithmetic, because an EAC at the high-order word must be propagated to the low-order word. This problem does not exist for two's complement numbers, a fact which contributes to its popularity. ·

1.5.4. Binary Subtraction

For subtracting binary numbers, the truth table for a 1-bit subtracter can be generated and then implemented. However, with a few extra circuits, a binary adder can be persuaded to perform subtraction through the technique of *subtrahend complementation*. To subtract the number B (subtrahend) from number A (minuend), one can add the negative of B (−B) to A:

$$A - B = A + (-B).$$

When negative numbers are represented in complement form, it is a simple matter to invert each bit to form the one's complement of a number. In fact, the exclusive-OR gate can be used selectively to invert a bit. See **Figure 1.16.** Data bit B passes to the output uncomplemented if control input ONESCOMP is inactive. If ONESCOMP is active, then the OPERAND output is the complement of B. The second operand can be selectively complemented before feeding the adder input by such a circuit. The designer provides for the EAC in a one's complement adder.

With two's complement numbers, simply inverting each subtrahend bit is not enough, as a 1 must also be added to the LSB. Adding 1 is conveniently accomplished by the *forced carry* technique: activating the carry-in input for the LSB position of the adder. There is no lower-order bit position below the LSB, so the carry-in input (LSB) signal is available for control purposes. For binary addition, the LSB carry-in (CIN) input is

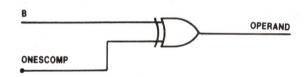

Figure 1.16. *Use of exclusive-OR as selective inverter of data bit.*

inactive for two's complement numbers, whereas it is used for the EAC in one's complement representation schemes.

Consider the example of 7 − 3, converted to 7 + (−3):

One's Complement		*Two's Complement*	
0111	(+7)	0111	
1100	(−3)	1100	
		1	← forced carry
carry: 1 0011	(+3)	0100	(+4)
1	← EAC		
0100	← Correct sum, +4		

1.5.5. Overflow

Using signed binary integers of n bits, an *overflow* occurs if the result of an arithmetic operation exceeds the representable range: for 16-bit fixed point numbers, the range is any result greater than +32,767 or less than −32,767. There is danger of overflow when numbers of like sign are added, or when numbers of unlike sign are subtracted. The occurrence of arithmetic overflow must be detected because it means the result is incorrect. The sign bit for the complement number representations is the most significant bit (MSB) position. When this is the case, for the two's complement representation, there is a convenient rule for overflow detection (OVF): when the carry-in of the sign bit position differs from the carry-out of the sign bit position. The overflow condition is expressed by Eq. 1.1:

$$OVF = CIN(MSB) \text{ xor } COUT(MSB) \qquad (1.1)$$

Eq. 1.1 is valid for one's and two's complement binary adders for addition, and for subtraction by subtrahend complementation. However, for double-precision one's complement numbers, consider the case when one summand is minus zero (11...1) and the other is the smallest representable negative number (10...0). Here, when the most significant portions are added, the rule at first indicates an overflow because COUT(MSB) (EAC) is active with CIN(MSB) inactive. However, after the EAC is propagated, CIN(MSB) becomes active.

1.5.6. Sophisticated Arithmetic Operations

Many small CPUs provide no more than addition and subtraction instructions. The problems of doing multiplication, division, double precision arithmetic, and floating point arithmetic are left to program subroutines. As a result, perhaps the majority of computer designers are relieved of the task of dealing with arithmetic units more sophisticated than an adder. Adders are commercially available as ICs. One should not be intimidated by them; an adder is a simple combinational circuit, and no great conceptual gap need be bridged. Arithmetic unit design does not capture enough of the spirit of computer design to merit much attention in this book. For our purposes, the following mental picture of a 4-bit binary adder as a functional unit is sufficient. Independent of the number representation, if one adder input is 1011, and the other is 0101, and the carry-in signal is active, then the 4-bit sum is 0001 and the carry-out signal is active. If the structure of a 4-bit adder is required, see [6].

For additional information on computer arithmetic, see Hwang [31]. Computer arithmetic is a problem concerning a single conceptual level. In our experience, one's recollection of the principles is refreshed by doing a few examples. We do not attach great importance to computer arithmetic, because we do not find it mysterious. We prefer to view the passive arithmetic unit as a component to be interfaced by the designer. Only larger more powerful CPUs, or special-purpose processors have sophisticated arithmetic units. When the designer is faced with a problem dealing with arithmetic, many solutions to these well-known problems are available in the literature.

1.6. DESCRIPTION AND DOCUMENTATION

1.6.1. Descriptive Languages

Language is important. Once people learn one language, they have difficulty acquiring another unless there is motivation to do so. Ideally, a language should mirror our thoughts. In the field of engineering design, we are in the realm of nonverbal thought.

The skill of spatial and temporal visualization needs to be developed. Spatial visualization is aided by block diagrams, and temporal visualization is aided by timing diagrams. *Block diagrams* are two-dimensional representations of functional units and their interconnections. *Timing charts* are waveforms where the horizontal axis is time and the cause-and-effect relationship of different events is displayed along the time axis. For describing behavior in terms of a sequence of events, we prefer *register transfer notation* (RTN). RTN is a way to describe microoperations capable of being performed by the data flow. These techniques are useful in the intermediate conceptual level of computer design.

In mathematics, generalization can be beautiful. In engineering, generalization can be a disaster. A mathematician seeks to generalize and unify fields of mathematical knowledge. For example, ordinary arithmetic (add, subtract, multiply and divide) can be explained in terms of the more general (and less structured) set theory. However the cost of generalization and unification is an increased distance between the concepts and their practical application. The "set theory" approach can lead to a generation of schoolchildren who know all "about" arithmetic except how to do it.

In computer design, we think about different things in special ways. Timing charts are used in describing the signal coordination or *transactions* between two semi-autonomous functional units, such as the interface protocol between the CPU and main memory. The timing chart is a special-purpose descriptive technique, whereas the other two techniques (block diagrams and RTN) are more general-purpose. The fact remains we would like to use a hammer on nails and a screw driver on screws. RTN is general enough to replace block diagrams, and block diagrams can replace RTN. However, we recommend using each in its intended purpose.

When dealing with the *structural* aspects of a digital system, the two-dimensional property of the block diagram is indispensable. The block diagram can be broken down nicely into a gate-level description used in building the system. RTN comes naturally when thinking about the *behavioral* or action-like aspect of functional units (or a system of functional units). It is futile to debate the merits of each technique as if we should choose one to the exclusion of the other. Each mirrors different types of thought processes.

How do RTN and block diagrams affect the computer designer? For complex structures such as the cascaded carry-save adder arrays which do multiplication, the data part dominates and block diagrams are most useful. For communications controllers, the algorithmic part dealing with protocols dominates and RTN is useful. The data part and control part of CPUs are equally important. Block diagrams, timing charts, and RTN evolved naturally. Block diagrams have been used since the beginning of electronics. Timing charts are found in all early IBM maintenance manuals, and are used in an early book on switching circuits [32]. RTN was used in a June 1946 memo by Burks, Goldstine and von Neumann, on ideas leading to the IAS computer [33]. Reed [34] recalls his early experiences with a register transfer notation which was used in the design of the CG24 computer [35]. Since that time, the implementation of a register transfer language was always a good PhD dissertation topic for electrical engineers. The utility of an RTN "shorthand" hardly needs to be taught, and once one notation is mastered the others seem to be variations.

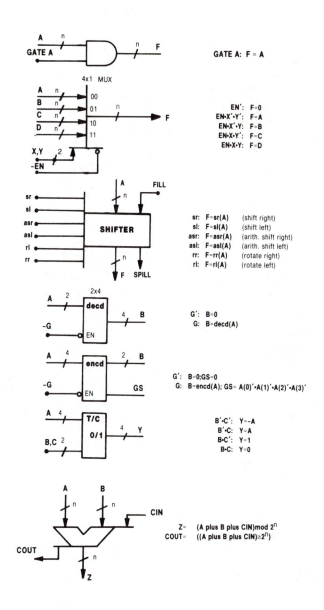

GATE A: F = A

EN': F=0
EN·X'·Y': F=A
EN·X'·Y: F=B
EN·X·Y': F=C
EN·X·Y: F=D

sr: F=sr(A)   (shift right)
sl: F=sl(A)   (shift left)
asr: F=asr(A)   (arith. shift right)
asl: F=asl(A)   (arith. shift left)
rr: F=rr(A)   (rotate right)
rl: F=rl(A)   (rotate left)

G': B=0
G: B=decd(A)

G': B=0;GS=0
G: B=encd(A); GS= A(0)'·A(1)'·A(2)'·A(3)'

B'·C': Y=-A
B'·C: Y=A
B·C': Y=1
B·C: Y=0

Z= (A plus B plus CIN)mod 2^n
COUT= ((A plus B plus CIN)≥2^n)

Figure 1.17. *Summary of combinational circuit blocks with RTN descriptions.*

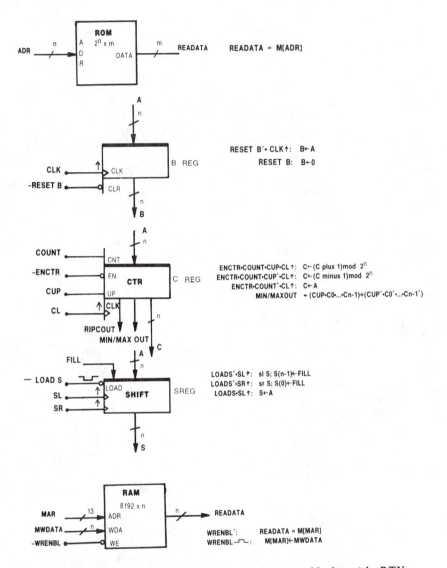

Figure 1.18. *Summary of sequential circuit blocks with RTN descriptions.*

Appendices C and D review many convenient data flow level building blocks. The descriptive techniques are applied to these components. A brief summary for the combinational building blocks of Appendix C appears in **Figure 1.17,** and the sequential building blocks of Appendix D are summarized in **Figure 1.18.** The general form is *condition: action.* A left arrow ($\leftarrow$) implies that the value to the right is stored in the item to the left. An equal sign ($=$) indicates a combinational circuit function. A semicolon (;) separates concurrent actions implied by the same conditional information.

Higher-level block diagrams and RTN serve two useful functions. First, the techniques are a means for the designer to document decisions on the intermediate conceptual levels of the design. We assume the mental picture comes first. Then the designer transfers the idea to paper. Second, once documented, others can *efficiently* learn the design at the higher level. The reader should be able to look at the diagram and recreate the designer's mental picture. Lamentably, the lowest level logic schematics of the physical structure are often the only up-to-date documents to survive the rigors of the hectic debugging phase. Trying to reconstruct the designer's mental picture from gate-level schematics is an extremely inefficient use of an engineer's time. In the remainder of this section, an overview of these descriptive techniques is provided.

1.6.2. Block Diagrams

Block diagrams aid spatial visualization; they are popular for conceptualizing certain relationships such as which functional unit's outputs feed which functional unit's inputs. Ferguson [36] has studied the role of nonverbal thought in technological developments by engineers, designers and craftsmen. He concludes that "thinking with pictures" is essential. A picture in the designer's mind is drawn on paper in order to stimulate a similar picture in another mind. In this sense, the engineer who deals in nonverbal thought shares this aspect of his profession with the artist, who also thinks in pictures.

Consider the following verbal statement made by a male speaker, "John's son is my daughter's father." The relationship described gives one pause. If the statement is diagrammed with an arrow denoting the parent-child relationship, as in **Figure 1.19,** it is evident immediately that John is the speaker's father. Grammarians know the pedagogical value of the two-dimensional sentence diagram to teach the roles of subject, object, adjectives and adverbs.

Block diagrams offer more economy of space when dealing with conceptually simple, yet structurally complex, higher-level functions such as an adder. As an example, we represent the 1-bit adder circuit of Fig. 1.15 by the symbol of **Figure 1.20.** Using Fig. 1.20, we now draw a 4-bit adder as shown in **Figure 1.21.** Fig. 1.21 represents considerable economy over the more complex gate-level diagram which would result from replicating Fig. 1.15 four times and making the appropriate parallel and cascade interconnections.

In block diagrams, the "pencil and paper" rule implies signals should flow from left to right or from top to bottom. The carry chain of Fig. 1.21 appears to violate this. However, when addition is done with pencil and

Figure 1.19. *The solution to a riddle is its formation as a diagram.*

paper, the carries also propagate from right to left. Further, the most significant bit appears on the left as it should. Thus this manner of representation does not force the reader to unlearn anything.

The economical Fig. 1.21 still has unneeded interconnection "clutter". The function performed is that of a 4-bit adder, which can be represented with a single symbol as shown in **Figure 1.22.** Data lines A and B have a slash and the nearby numeral "4" denotes a path width of four bits.

The width of the input and output lines imply the width of the adder is also four bits. Lines with no slash are presumed to be a single wire, as for

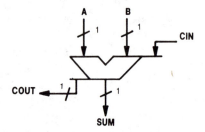

Figure 1.20. *A single-bit adder symbol.*

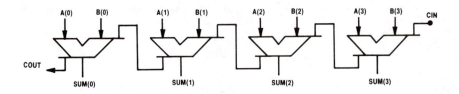

Figure 1.21. *A 4-bit adder built from 1-bit adders.*

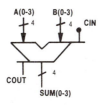

Figure 1.22. *A single-symbol 4-bit adder.*

the carry-in (CIN) and carry-out (COUT) signals. The adder is a functional unit, and its function can and should be assimilated in the designer's mind. Since the adder is a combinational circuit, it is *always* presenting the sum of a value A and B on its output (following a propagation delay). This "always performing its functions" concept is sometimes difficult for a student with a programming background to grasp. Programmers are accustomed to a digital system which does nothing unless it is told. In contrast, a combinational adder circuit needs no instruction to cause it to add; it continually adds its inputs and delivers the output. The programmer's "ADD" makes use of the output by causing it to be fed to a result location at the end of the instruction execution.

With the technological advances of LSI, sophisticated functions are placed on a chip. To exploit the technology properly the designer must "think" of the higher-level functional unit as a building block. Unless the block has a distinctive shape like an adder, the function is represented as a rectangle on block diagrams. The data inputs should all be presented to one of the sides, and the data outputs should come from the opposite side. Control signals should feed either the data input side, or feed one of the other sides, but not the output side. If these rules are not followed, and input and output lines are drawn to whichever of the four sides is closest, that unit's role in the system is difficult to grasp.

If the functional unit contains a data register, we prefer (following IBM) to use a heavy line on the input side of the rectangle to indicate the storage function. The absence of such a heavy line indicates a combinational circuit. It is also desirable to distinguish data lines from control lines. A black dot on a line indicates a control line; if control lines are bused, a black dot is placed where the slash denoting bus width intersects the bus.

Figure 1.23 summarizes some interconnection notation for block diagrams. Note that Fig. 1.23(f) shows the use of an arrow where a driver connects to a bidirectional bus. We use higher-level block diagrams for data flows in the book. However it should be understood that if the generation of a gate-level data flow diagram is necessary, it is easily done. The

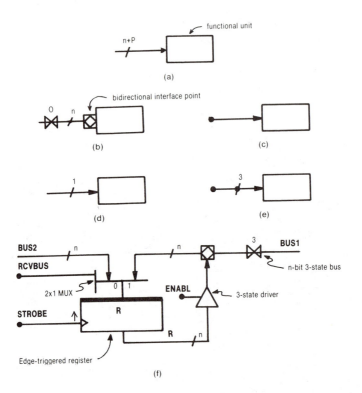

Figure 1.23. *Some notations for block diagram interconnections.*
(a) Unidirectional n-bit data bus with parity. (b) Bidirectional n-bit
data bus, open collector. (c) Single control line. (d) Single data line.
(e) Three bused control lines. (f) Register connected to an n-bit bidirectional tri-state (3-state) data bus (BUS1) and a second source (BUS2).

composition process which took us from Fig. 1.15 to Fig. 1.21 is reversed,
and becomes a decomposition or down-conversion process.

To illustrate the information-conveying properties of block diagrams,
Figure 1.24 is the block diagram of address selection for a video look-up
table for the refreshing of a raster-scan CRT color display. The 8-bit
picture element (pixel) for both the odd and even scan rows are multiplexed to the address register per the condition of the odd field being
refreshed (or the complement case where the even field is being refreshed).
Also sharing the diagram (although not directly related) is a 4-clock time
delay applied to the composite blanking signal CBLKG.

Contrast the block diagram of Fig. 1.24 to the corresponding gate-
level diagram of **Figure 1.25.** Although already cluttered, not all gates are
actually shown. Rather, the blocks represent TTL DIPs, assigned to socket

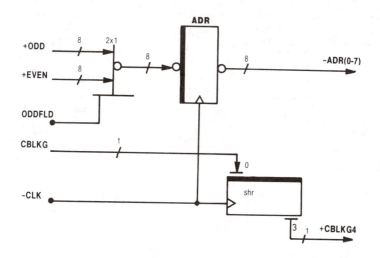

Figure 1.24. *A block diagram example.*

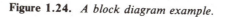

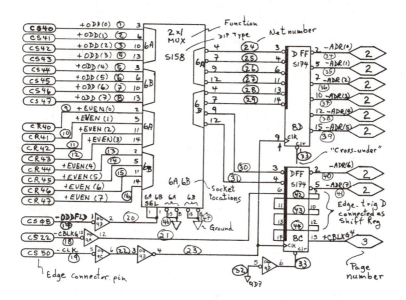

Figure 1.25. *Detailed logic schematic of example.*

locations 6A, 6B, 8C, and 8D. Inverters are used from DIPs in sockets 9A, 9C, and 9D. Note that not all signal lines deserve names, although all have net numbers. The *net* (IBM term) is the set of interconnected pins. The circled net numbers are used to make up a wire list. The uncircled numbers above where the signal wire enters or leaves the block is the pin number of the socket. For convenience, since sockets 6A and 6B together compose the 2×1 MUX which happens to be eight bits wide, the MUX is shown as one block. This enhances the readability of the diagram. Nevertheless, it can be appreciated that the less detailed diagram of Fig. 1.24 captures the essential design concept of the function, and more nearly reflects the designer's thoughts. The block diagram helps the reader assimilate efficiently what the circuit does. In contrast, prototyping and maintenance documents describe exactly the details of the physical system.

1.6.3. Register Transfer Notation

Designers of computers have devised many languages and notations to describe the register transfer (RT) level of design. Many text books introduce some sort of language for this conceptual level. The languages are made general by providing for a way to declare the existence of memories, registers and other functional units, and the paths between them. These declarations parallel the role of two-dimensional data flow diagrams. The incorporation of the two-dimensional data flow structure into the language, plus the capability to define clock pulses, and to manipulate gate-level signals, makes it possible to simulate the behavior of the resulting system by a computer program. However, without block diagrams and timing charts, such languages are unsuitable for teaching purposes.

On the other hand, RTN is an excellent vehicle for describing events, microoperations, actions, or register transfers which can take place, together with the *conditional information* in the system which caused the action to come about. Since our purpose is to teach computer design, rather than the (typically bad) user interface features of a simulation program, we do not attempt to push RTN statements into an area where there exists a better descriptive method. Data flow design is best learned from block diagrams. Once one has acquired skill in this level of spatial visualization, one is free to use register transfer languages. Our "shorthand" for microoperations is called a *notation* rather than a language, to emphasize its limited scope in the teaching aspect of computer design.

Babbage [1] was the first computer designer to recognize the need for a notation which worked together with diagrams. In Babbage's technology, the parts were readily seen but the mechanical motions and timing of interactions were not. This caused him to "contrive a notation which ought, if possible, to be at once simple and expressive, easily understood at the commencement, and capable of being retained in memory". The notation was called Mechanical Notation and enabled Babbage to scrutinize all contemporaneous actions.

The computer's instruction set is interpreted by actions which control the data flow. The actions are described in RTN. There are two kinds of RTN. When RTN is used after the data flow is assumed to be "frozen", a route we recommend, we call it *dependent RTN.* If dependent, then no register transfer can take place over a path that does not exist, and no statement implies a function the data flow is incapable of performing. The second kind of RTN is called *independent RTN.* In a more general setting, RTN can be used to describe behavior. For example, independent RTN can describe actions on the registers known to the programmer without regard to the existence or nonexistence of direct paths or intermediate registers. In independent RTN no data flow is predefined. Independent RTN is used in Chapter 2 to describe addressing modes.

Bell and Newell [29] have defined a descriptive technique called the instruction set processor or ISP descriptive system. ISP was used to describe over forty instruction sets in a uniform manner, independent of timings or of a particular data flow. As such, its original usage was as independent RTN. Later, DEC expanded ISP and employed it in the description, simulation, and microprogramming of machines. Thus, the terms "dependent RTN" and "independent RTN" apply to the *usage* of the RT level description rather than the notation or language itself. The reader is alerted that although independent RTN may imply an underlying data flow structure, we stress that data flow design is a separate activity. Independent RTN is for defining behavior and not machine structure. Dependent RTN and the underlying data flow are mutually supportive, such that the design of the action part does not compromise the design of the controlled part and vice versa. The RTN used in this book is typical of that found in other books and papers.

The statement

$$A \leftarrow B \qquad\qquad (1.2)$$

means that a copy of the data in entity B (typically a register) is placed in Register A. Use of the left arrow means A possesses the property of storage. Statements of the form "destination ← source" mean the source is supplying a *copy* of its value (or contents), and the destination (dest) entity is changing the value it *stores* to conform to the source's value. Eq. 1.2 states to *evaluate* the right-hand side and *assign* the resulting value to the variable on the left-hand side. If the destination register has fewer bits than the source, the destination accepts only the lowest-order bits. If the destination has more bits than the source, the value of the source is sign extended to the left.

The left assignment arrow conforms to the evaluation aspect of mathematical notation ($f(x) = 5x + 2$) and to the less dynamic expression ("the destination receives the source value"). Many prefer the more active expression ("the source value goes to the destination") and use a right arrow: source → destination. We use the left arrow only because it appears to be the more prevalent.

Use of an equal sign (=) instead of an assignment arrow, as in

$$\text{CTL} \cdot \text{T0}: \quad A = B \tag{1.3}$$

means the contents of B are presented to the input of combinational circuit A. Where storage takes place, the assignment arrow is used.

A boolean statement to the left of a colon (:) represents *conditional information* in the system. In Eq. 1.3, when control signal (or condition) CTL is active and signal T0 is active, then the *action* on the right of the colon takes place. If more than one independent action shares the same conditional information, the individual actions are separated by semi-colons. For example, the general format of an RTN statement with two actions is:

Conditional information: Action1; Action2

The conditional information most often is an AND of literals (status and control signals) in the system, which represents a *p-term*. The p-term is said to *imply* the action.

If a storage function is involved, we assume the action takes place on the trailing edge of the condition. (See Appendix D.) For each project, a "global groundrule" on system timing should cover this point. RTN statements rest upon a foundation where time has been quantized. If level-sensitive and edge-sensitive memory elements are both in the system, it may be advantageous to add a special graphic to the signal which provides the edge: e.g. an up arrow or down arrow after the name.

Memory locations are indicated by square brackets following the symbol for the memory, such as M[adr]. Here "adr" indicates the address itself, or something to be evaluated, such as a register which contains the address. Thus M[PC] is the memory location with the next instruction, because the address is indicated by the Program Counter PC, whose value points to the next instruction. The statement:

MD ← M[MA]

means that the Memory Data (MD) register receives the contents of the main memory (M) as addressed from the Memory Address (MA) register.

Register fields are indicated by parentheses. Bit AC(0) is bit 0 of the accumulator AC. The operation of concatenation is denoted by a comma (,). Thus "AC(0),AC(1),AC(2),AC(3)" denotes AC bits 0, 1, 2, and 3. However, this is somewhat awkward, and the common "shorthand" form is AC(0-3). The comma is also useful in "merging" data from two source buses into a single bus: "PC(0-3),MD(4-15)". This represents a 16-bit value whose four high-order bits come from the PC register, and whose 12 low-order bits come from the corresponding bits of the MD register.

Sometimes it is desirable to indicate the activation of a control signal or data flow control point at a particular time. In this case, the action simply consists of the name of the control signal which is to be activated. For example:

E•T3: CLRWRITE

The control signal CLRWRITE is activated when the condition E•T3 is active.

1.6.4. Register Transfers versus Block Diagrams: an Example

We find that describing things as actions at the register level, versus describing things as structures at the block diagram level may produce different solutions to the same problem. Consider the problem:

"If condition 'COMPLEMENT' is valid, place the complement of each bit of XREG onto DBUS; otherwise pass the value of XREG to DBUS unchanged."

A flowchart, and RTN statements for this problem appear in **Figure 1.26.** A solution based on Fig. 1.26 is shown in **Figure 1.27.** The contents of the XREG are complemented, and a MUX element selects the desired data. However, a conceptually simpler solution is shown in **Figure 1.28.** The latter solution is obtained from a knowledge of the available building blocks and *how to use them,* rather than from implementing the problem statement by rote. (Of course, once the solution of Fig. 1.28 is found, the problem statement can be rewritten to conform to it.)

It is worth mentioning that after people gain experience doing tasks in an area, be it carpentry or driving a car, the brain seems to sort out the important points and allows one to get things done more efficiently. This phenomenon is often called the *learning curve.* The same is true of logic design; experienced logic designers use two-dimensional drawings and knowledge of the building blocks in order to solve problems.

1.7. THE IMPORTANCE OF COMPUTER DESIGN

It can be stated safely that the majority of computer engineers or logic designers is not engaged in computer design. For every computer designed, many more engineers are involved in its application and interfacing. Why then teach a course for which there appears to be a very limited need? (The same question could be asked of a computer architecture course since there are probably even fewer computer architects than designers.)

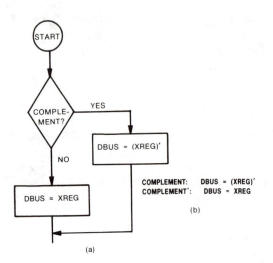

(a)

(b)

Figure 1.26. *A problem statement.* (a) Flow chart. (b) RTN statements.

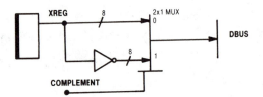

Figure 1.27. *A first solution to the problem.*

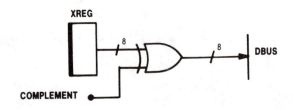

Figure 1.28. *A second solution to the problem.*

In this section, we offer several reasons supporting the importance of a course in computer design. We feel that the primary reason is that computer design is an important *example* of digital system design. Digital logic terminology and techniques are learned in the more interesting (at least to us) context of CPU design. We believe that any computer engineer capable of designing a CPU is capable of designing *any* digital system. We have used the same digital system design techniques described here in a variety of digital system design projects. The use of more buses for increased concurrency, the separation of data from controls, the need for waveform charts and the study of timing problems, the behavior of different flip-flop types, etc. are all pertinent to the general field of digital systems design. Moreover, the functional unit with its connection points and interconnection protocol represents an important basis for the design of distributed systems.

Second, in a changing technological climate, there is continual competitive pressure to reimplement existing architectures (for which software already exists) in more cost-effective technologies. Many instances also exist where performance requirements make a special-purpose CPU a solution to a functional requirement. Technological advances create a continual need for computer designers.

Third, logic designers engaged in interfacing peripheral devices to computers should be aware of how and why computer design decisions were made. To do interfacing, basic timing cycles and the memory-CPU interface should be understood. These topics are a proper part of computer design.

Fourth, there are subfields of computer engineering for which the participants should know something of computer design. The field of design automation (DA) furnishes the computer designer with design aids. (DA of digital systems is typically one aspect of computer aided design (CAD), which includes architecture of buildings, aircraft design, or ship design, etc. Some members in this field would like to automate the designer as well!) Traditionally the programmers working on design aids know little of design, and are fully capable of naively asking the designer not to use the wire-OR or tri-state driver because the DA program cannot handle them. A second subfield is fault-tolerant and fail-safe system design. The incorporation of redundancy into a computer system to reduce the chance of failure, and/or to detect and diagnose failures, is an important and nontrivial engineering task. We feel the engineers who attack this problem should have an appreciation for the computer design activity.

Last, we note that computer design has many characteristics of any engineering design problem. A designer is given an objective for the final design result, and must solve the problem with the technological tools at hand. A systematic attack, methods to subdivide the problem into smaller subproblems, and the lack of a "recipe" to be blindly followed, are characteristic of engineering practice. The "open-endedness" of the design problem, the existence of alternative approaches, the ability to redefine the problem, and the different trade-offs to be made, are all part of the real world. The algorithm versus data organization duality, and the hierarchy of conceptual levels are properties of the information processing field, and not just computer design. Software algorithms can also be subdivided into a sequence control part and a part which performs operations or actions on the data. Knowledge of how to solve a computer design problem provides the engineer with increased confidence in his own general problem solving abilities.

1.8.   THE FUTURE OF COMPUTER DESIGN

What is in store for the computer designer and digital system designer? We see increasing designer interaction with CAD systems. In this section we touch on CAD tools and their desirable features.

The computer design role is being influenced by the changing packaging boundaries. The building blocks are more complex and powerful. For some designers, the job will be to interconnect these higher-level parts at the card or board level. These designers will think in terms of higher-level units, learning their behavior, and how to apply them. For other designers, the job is to implement these higher-level parts on chips. For this second task, the designer is not able to probe or replace individual gates. In either case we support the conclusion that the designers will become increasingly dependent on CAD systems.

CAD systems are surveyed by vanCleemput [37]. The coming VLSI revolution is previewed by Rice [38]. T. C. Raymond [39] provides a brief tutorial on design automation for (V)LSI.

Packaging boundaries have moved such that the digital function which was once placed on a card can now be placed on a chip. The design of a card or board using SSI or MSI circuits can proceed by ordering the low-level parts, and prototyping the system. Debugging is done by adding or replacing components and rewiring interconnections. Higher-level VLSI chip designs isolate the designer from dealing with gate-level parts in a "hands on" fashion. The "hands on" aspect will be relative to "paper design" documents, or to interaction with a "soft copy" document at a computer terminal. The design of the interface of a CAD system to the user is important.

1.8.1.   Data Flow and Control Unit Level

For the data flow and control unit conceptual level, very few CAD tools exist. Such tools are in an experimental phase. In this book, we teach how to design the data flow and implement the behavior (control unit) by motivated examples.   Tseng and Siewiorek [40] have studied algorithms for designing the data flow once the required data transfers and concurrency constraints are specified.   In [40], the term *bus style primitive* is equivalent to our term data flow component.   Another approach to data flow design is proposed in [41].

Once the data flow and a specification of behavior is given, Evangelisti et al. [42] propose a method to generate the control unit for a clocked digital machine.

1.8.2. Data Flow Component Level

At the next lower (data flow component) conceptual level, CAD systems exist which are capable of handling the hierarchical levels downward to gates and cells.   These systems can perform expansion or "downconversion" of data flow components such as decomposing 16-bit wide MUXes or registers into a collection of individual gates.   Programs such as SCALD [43] and ALEX [44] replicate, cascade, or parallel gates, and "do the right thing" with interconnections.   The result is a realization of n-bit wide data flow components from 1-bit wide primitive cells or gates.   If a change is made at the gate-level description level of a data flow, this change can be reflected up in a straightforward manner to a higher description level (block diagram).

A similar hierarchy for control logic is less straightforward.   In Chapters 3 and 5 we treat the decomposition of RTN statements into *control signal activation logic* (CSAL).   (See Fig. 1.7, where the CSAL is shown as a PLA.)   Often during the debugging phase, changes are made to the CSAL.   These changes are rather difficult to reflect up to the RTN description.   We find it desirable, for the purpose of describing and teaching the behavior of a functional unit, that such behavior changes at the CSAL level be reflected up to the RTN level.

1.8.3. Gate Arrays

We see an increasing use of master-slice and gate array chips.   In the LSI era of microprocessors, designers such as Shima [45] developed hand-crafted custom-designed chips.   VLSI technology is capable of providing more gates on a chip than is feasible to lay out and wire manually.   The design time of VLSI logic chips can be shortened by employing gate arrays.   Larger chips implement increasingly complex digital functions, which increase the need for CAD.

The IBM 43xx series of computers employs gate arrays.   (See Fig. 1.4.)   According to Cave of DEC, gate arrays were employed in the VAX-11/750 due to a lack of enough layout designers to do 40 designs in 18 months [46].   In gate arrays, efficient use of silicon area is sacrificed in order to use standard cells.   A beneficial effect is that the logic designer requires less knowledge about the particular silicon technology. A well-structured hierarchical CAD system can further raise the conceptual level at which the logic designer deals with a particular technology.

1.8.4. Technology Dependence

Since CAD systems provide the same functions for different technologies, CAD systems should be organized in a modular fashion. The modules which handle the technology-independent aspects, such as are dealt with in this book, can be reused. At some point, however, the designer must face up to reality, and address technology-dependent parameters characterizing the building blocks. See Tobias [47].

Technology parameters of interest include the gates and pins per chip (or card), wirability and testability constraints, preference for register clocking schemes, and gate and interconnection (line) delays. For example, the need for activating control signals on time may eliminate the use of a PLA output for certain control signals whose activation is needed early in the cycle.

With increased circuit speeds, interconnection delays become an important part of worst-case cycle time calculations [39] [48]. Line delays are primarily due to charging and discharging line capacitance, and are a function of line length. Line length depends on circuit placement and wiring, which is typically done late in the design cycle; thus the design iteration loop is lengthened [39].

1.8.5. Testing

There are some activities in the design loop which proceed concurrently with the logic implementation and physical design. These include the incorporation of a strategy for testing the chip or card, and the design verification of the logic by computer simulation.

There are two times when testing is required. First a component is tested in isolation of its role in a system. The component is tested following manufacturing and before sale to a customer. Second, the component is tested as a part of a system. If the system once worked and subsequently fails, then a *fault location test* is required to determine the faulty replaceable component or subsystem.

The chip test problem is one which the designer cannot ignore. The chip implements a complex sequence-dependent mapping from a sequence of input values to a sequence of output values, and this behavior must be verified. The chip should be testable, which usually entails rearranging circuits and/or including extra circuits. Moreover, test patterns for the chip must be generated.

One approach to chip testing is called *functional testing:* does the chip perform all functions for which it was designed? For a microprocessor chip, a functional test ensures that all instructions execute properly on various data values.   Memory chips generally undergo a functional test: patterns of bits known to catch most problems are stored and retrieved.

A lower-level testing approach is based on the fact that combinational circuits are not sequence-dependent; hence testing is relatively simple. We describe the *scan-in scan-out* used on the IBM S360/50. The system clock was two-phased. To test the combinational circuit between phase 1 and phase 2, the phase 1 latches were loaded (scanned in). Then the phase 2 latches were clocked, receiving the result of the digital function performed by the intervening combinational circuit. The phase 2 latches were then scanned out and compared against the correct result. The combinational circuit between the phase 2 and phase 1 latches was tested similarly.

A derivative of scan-in scan-out, proposed in 1971 [49] and since improved, is called LSSD (level-sensitive design) [50]. The basic storage element is called a shift register latch (SRL). During ordinary operation, the SRLs behave as normal data latches performing their required functions. In shift register mode, the SRLs are interconnected as shift registers. The scan-in operation is performed in shift register mode. Next, the system clock is applied with the SRLs behaving normally. The result of the combinational circuit function is captured in the latches of the following phase. The latch interconnections are returned to shift register mode and the test result is scanned out. Finally, the test result is compared against a known value.

The LSSD approach may be used for either component test or system test. System test can be simplified for many systems which possess an instruction set processor. The processor executes diagnostic routines (or microinstruction routines) as a self-test when power is first applied to the system. Diagnostics, or even an internal sequential machine, may also be available to the user in a push-to-test strategy. The user may have a self-test manual which provides a procedure and values against which a test value displayed by the system is compared; see Peatman [51].

1.8.6. Simulation

When the system design is complete, with additional circuitry for test purposes, the design result must be verified. In reality, *design verification* can be performed earlier on subsections of the design concurrently with the design of other subsections. Design verification is performed by computer simulation of the logic, and can be performed at various levels; see [52]. The designer creates input patterns, and studies output patterns to ensure that the logic behaves as desired. (It has been suggested that these same tests be captured by the CAD system for subsequent use in testing.) Simulation is relatively tedious, and a poor user interface for this task can greatly aggravate the designer. In chasing some bugs, having an interactive simulator provides a tremendous gain in productivity.

Another use of simulation is to simulate the effect of faults. For these simulators, a logic interconnection of the "good" machine may be stuck high or stuck low, and the input patterns are those generated for the fault location tests.

1.9. SUMMARY

This chapter provides a backdrop for the chapters to come. It has reviewed some material with which the reader should already be acquainted, and introduces some commentary on design and documentation techniques. Computer design seeks to interpret instruction sets using digital logic. The designer needs a basis in combinational and sequential circuits, and must be aware of the hierarchy of conceptual levels involved. The creative part of the design is at the data flow component and register transfer conceptual level. Once the data flow and interpretive microoperations are properly defined, it is a relatively straightforward procedure to generate the gate-level or part-level drawings needed to build a prototype. The designer must "think big" about block diagram function units and design the actions and system behavior at that level. The designer must "absorb" the building block functional capability and the means to control it. The structural and behavioral aspects of the design are distinct, but they interact. Each favors its own descriptive technique, and we discourage "unifying" the descriptive techniques. Each type of visualization or mental image justifies its own representation on paper.

We mention the importance of documentation, and recommend that higher-level documents be used and kept. On naming conventions, we do not favor "mystery". The "pencil and paper" rule is a reminder to keep drawings and names as simple as possible, and minimize the unlearning required to understand the conventions.

Babbage was the first to appreciate the complexities involved in the design of a data processing system. He filled the intermediate conceptual gap with mechanical functional units, and then controlled those units to perform arithmetic and control operations. His knowledge was acquired by the experience of doing a paper design, since he never succeeded in building the Analytical Engine. Today, we benefit from the thirty-year history of computer design by the definition and availability of data flow component parts. Like Babbage, the reader can acquire some experience and knowledge of computer design by working out solutions on paper. But we are more fortunate than Babbage, for today's technology has progressed to where the step from the paper design to the realization is, barring unusual constraints, no special problem.

REFERENCES

1. P. Morrison and E. Morrison (Eds.), *Charles Babbage and his Calculating Engines,* Dover Publications, New York, 1961.
2. K. E. Knight, "Changes in Computer Performance", *Datamation,* v. 12, n. 9, 1966.
3. H. Taub and D. Schilling, *Digital Integrated Electronics,* McGraw-Hill, New York, 1977.
4. W. G. Oldham, "The Fabrication of Microelectronic Circuits", *Scientific American,* v. 237, n. 3, September 1977, 110-128.
5. Roger Allen, "Semiconductors: Toeing the (microfine) Line", *IEEE Spectrum,* v. 14, n. 12, December 1977, 34-40.
6. Anon., *TTL Data Book,* Second Edition, Texas Instruments, Dallas, TX, 1976.
7. C. G. Bell, J. C. Mudge, and J. E. McNamara, *Computer Engineering: A DEC View of Hardware System Design,* Digital Press, Bedford, MA, 1978.
8. M. Phister, *Data Processing Technologies and Economics,* Santa Monica Publishing Co., Santa Monica, CA, 1976.
9. J. Craig Mudge, "Design Decisions Achieve Price/Performance in Mid-Range Minicomputers", *Computer Design,* v. 16, n. 8, August 1977, 87-96.
10. J. D. Greenfield, *Practical Digital Design Using ICs,* Wiley, New York, 1977.
11. J. F. Masor, "Reports on Breadboards", *Electronic Design,* v. 22, n. 8, April 12, 1974, 30-40.
12. T. R. Blakeslee, *Digital Design with Standard MSI and LSI,* Wiley, New York, 1975.
13. I. E. Sutherland and C. A. Mead, "Microelectronics and Computer Science", *Scientific American,* v. 237, n. 3, September 1977, 210-228.
14. M. Breuer, Editor, *Design Automation of Digital Systems,* v. 1, Prentice-Hall, Englewood Cliffs, NJ, 1971.
15. P. W. Case et. al., "Solid Logic Design Automation for IBM System/360", *IBM Jl. Res. Develop.,* v. 8, 1964, 127-140.
16. B. S. Landman and R. L. Russo, "On a Pin-vs-Block Relationship to Partitions of Logic Graphs", *IEEE Trans. Computers,* v. C-20, December 1971, 1469.
17. J. McKevitt and J. Bayless, "New Options from Big Chips", *IEEE Spectrum,* v. 16, n. 3, March 1979, 28-34.
18. L. S. Bensky, "Block Diagrams in Logic Design", *Proc. AFIPS,* (Western Joint Computer Conference), v. 13, 1958, 177-178.
19. H. L. Engel, "Machine Language in Computer Design", *Proc. AFIPS* (Western Joint Computer Conference), v. 13, 1958, 182-186.
20. Bill Bottari, "The Jungle of Computer Jargon", *Appliance Engineer,* v. 13, n. 4, August 1979, 45.
21. Adam Osborne, *An Introduction to Microprocessors,* v. 1, Osborne and Associates, Berkeley, CA, 1976.
22. M. E. Sloan, *Computer Hardware and Organization,* SRA, Palo Alto, CA, 1976.
23. A. Tanenbaum, *Structured Computer Organization,* Prentice-Hall, Englewood Cliffs, NJ, 1976.
24. William I. Fletcher, *An Engineering Approach to Digital Design,* Prentice-Hall, Englewood Cliffs, NJ, 1980.
25. J. B. Peatman, *The Design of Digital Systems,* McGraw-Hill, New York, 1972.
26. C. G. Bell, J. Grason, and A. Newell, *Designing Computers and Digital Systems,* Digital Press, Maynard, MA, 1972.
27. F. P. Brooks, Jr. *The Mythical Man Month,* Addison-Wesley, Reading, MA, 1975.
28. Lance A. Levanthal, *8080A/8085 Assembly Language Programming,* A. Osborne and Associates, Berkeley, CA, 1978.
29. C. G. Bell and A. Newell, *Computer Structures: Readings and Examples,* McGraw-Hill, New York, 1971.
30. J. J. Shedletsky, "Comment on the Sequential and Indeterminate Behavior of an End-around-carry Adder", *IEEE Trans. Computers,* v. C-26, March 1977, 271-272.

31. K. Hwang, *Computer Arithmetic,* Wiley, New York, 1979.
32. W. Keister, A. E. Ritchie, and S. H. Washburn, *The Design of Switching Circuits,* Van Nostrand-Reinhold, Princeton, NJ, 1951.
33. A. Burks, H. Goldstine, and J. von Neumann, "Preliminary Discussion of the Logical Design of an Electronic Computing Instrument", in John von Neumann, *Collected Works,* vol. 5, Macmillan, New York, 1963, 34-79. (See also *Datamation,* September 1962, 24-31 and October 1962, 36-41).
34. I. S. Reed, "Symbolic Design Techniques Applied to a Generalized Computer", *Computer,* v. 5, May/June 1972, 47-52.
35. G. P. Dinneen, I. L. Lebow, and I. S. Reed, "The Logical Design of CG24", *Proc. AFIPS,* v. 14 (EJCC), December 1958, 91-94.
36. E. S. Ferguson, "The Mind's Eye: Nonverbal Thought in Technology", *Science,* v. 197, n. 4306, August 26, 1977, 827-836.
37. W. M. vanCleemput, Editor, *Tutorial on Computer-Aided Design: Tools for Digital Systems,* Second Edition, IEEE Computer Society, EHO 132-1, Los Alamitos, CA, 1979.
38. Rex Rice, *Tutorial on VLSI: The Coming Revolution in Applications and Design,* IEEE Computer Society EHO 158-6, Los Alamitos, CA, 1980.
39. T. C. Raymond, "LSI/VLSI Design Automation", *Computer,* vol. 14, n. 7, July 1981, 89-101.
40. Chia-Jeng Tseng and Daniel P. Siewiorek, "The Modeling and Synthesis of Bus Systems", *Proc. 18th Design Automation Conference,* IEEE, 1981, 471-478.
41. Louis Hafer and Alice C. Parker, "A Formal Method for the Specification, Analysis, and Design of Register-Transfer Level Digital Logic", *Proc. 18th Design Automation Conference,* IEEE, 1981, 846-853.
42. C. J. Evangelisti, G. Goertzel, and H. Ofek, "Using the Dataflow Analyzer on LCD Descriptions of Machines to Generate Control", *Proc. 4th International Symposium on Computer Hardware Description Languages,* IEEE Computer Society 79CH1436-5C, 1979, 109-115.
43. T. M. McWilliams and L. Curt Widdoes, Jr., "SCALD: Structured Computer-Aided Logic Design", *Proc. 15th Design Automation Conference,* IEEE, 1978. Reprinted in [37].
44. Keith A. Duke and Klim Maling, "ALEX: A Conversational Hierarchical Logic Design System", *Proc. 17th Annual Design Automation Conference,* ACM, 1980, 318-327.
45. Masatoshi Shima, "Demystifying Microprocessor Design", *IEEE Spectrum,* vol. 16, n. 7, July 1979, 22-30.
46. Anon., "Semi-Custom Logic: Computerized Design Tools", *EET,* June 22, 1981, 31.
47. J. R. Tobias, "LSI/VLSI Building Blocks", *Computer,* vol. 14, no. 8, August 1981, 83-101.
48. T. M. McWilliams, "Verification of Timing Constraints on Large Digital Systems", *Proc. 17th Annual Design Automation Conference,* ACM, 1980, 139-147.
49. Edward B. Eichelberger, private communication, January 1971.
50. E. B. Eichelberger and T. W. Williams, "A Logic Design Structure for Testability", *Proc. 14th Design Automation Conference,* IEEE, 1977. Reprinted in [38].
51. John B. Peatman, *Digital Hardware Design,* McGraw-Hill, New York, 1980. See Chapter 3.
52. C. Hemming and J. Hemphill, "Digital Logic Simulation: Models and Evolving Technology", *Proc. 12th Design Automation Conference,* IEEE, 1975. Reprinted in [38].

✻ CHAPTER 2 ✻

INSTRUCTION SET ARCHITECTURE
AND DESIGN

2.1. INTRODUCTION

The purpose of this book is to teach the design of a computer which interprets an *instruction set*. The instruction set is that selection of operations the hardware will be capable of performing. In Chapter 1, the starting points were covered: the technology, the building blocks, and the language of descriptive techniques. The subject of the present chapter is computer architecture. The *architecture* defines the behavioral specification of the central processor unit (CPU). The behavior and any additional requirements (cost, speed, etc.) must be incorporated into the design result by digital system engineers (computer designers). The computer designer should understand architecture and appreciate the characteristics of instruction sets. (In many small computer architectures, the architect was also the computer designer.) The computer engineer should know how to *use* a computer from the programmer's viewpoint.

A data processor is fed data and programs through *input units,* and delivers results through *output units*. Data transferred to and from the user is generally in some alphanumeric code, such as EBCDIC (an 8-bit code defined by IBM) or ASCII (an American National Standards Institute standard 7-bit code). Input-output data in human-readable alphanumeric characters is called *primary input-output*. Often the system contains disk or drum devices for the storage of business files, system or compiler programs, or an application program library. This storage, if available *on-line* (under system control) is called *secondary storage*. *Off-line storage* can be made available by mounting removable media onto a device (tape reels on tape drives, disk packs on disk drives, etc.).

Writing and debugging computer programs is desirable experience for a computer designer. Familiarity with instruction types and their uses, addressing modes, assemblers, binary arithmetic, IO routines and interrupt structure, and the console or front panel functions provides the designer with insight. This chapter reviews the key elements found at the instruction set (architecture) level.

The computer system does its work through computer programs, which are written by programmers. In general, a *task* is a computer program and its input data, in a state of execution. Work is done by changing the state of things. The result of the task may be updated or new data files, the performance of actions at a peripheral device, or the control of valves, switches or motors in a process control environment. The task consists of two parts. The active part is the program (analogous to an algorithm), and the passive part is the data acted upon by the program. Information processing *work* is accomplished by changing the *state* of memory, in particular by changing the value of data items stored in main memory. Later the new values can be printed on a page, or transferred to a communications line, or translated to voltages for electromechanical control purposes.

System programs are variously called the operating system, monitor, supervisor, or executive. These programs control the resources of the system, or benefit the user, or facilitate the running of application programs. Resources include peripheral devices, main memory, and the CPU. Supervisors allocate the main memory resource, interpret higher-level input-output operation requests, and queue hard copy (paper) output tasks to the system printer. Supervisors also handle interruptions (interrupts) from all causes, including such program bugs as generating an out-of-range address or encountering an illegal instruction. Supervisors also may have high-level routines to provide access to storage devices in a uniform manner.

Language processors or translators are used to generate machine instructions from the program written by the programmer. The programmer uses symbolic names for data variables, and *mnemonics* for actions on those variables. MOVE, ADD, LOAD, PRINT, DO, etc. are typical symbolic mnemonics for actions. The program is typed into the computer as a text or character string. The text consists of a sequence of statements, and each statement is written on one line. The statement ends with the alphanumeric code for a "Carriage Return" character as a delimiter. In punched card systems, prevalent in the second generation, there was one statement per card. The program, as a text string in the alphanumeric code of the machine (e.g. EBCDIC or ASCII), is called the *source code.* The size of the program is generally measured in *lines of code* or in number of locations used. For variables, the assembler or compiler makes a symbol table and assigns binary addresses, and for actions generates the proper codes in bits. The result of a program assembly is called the *object code,* and is an instruction word consisting of 0's and 1's.

The assembler language is not considered a higher-level language. Its conceptual level is close to the computer's machine language. Higher-level languages are usually compiled into machine language instructions which are then run on the machine. (An alternative is for the CPU to *interpret* directly the higher-level language or some equivalent intermediate form of the same conceptual level.)

The *instruction set* is an important conceptual level. In most systems, the instructions define the interface between the programmer and the computer, and between computer architecture and computer design. In a system with a new architecture, the software designers and hardware designers can work concurrently and more or less independently. The software engineers build more complex functions using the instructions as the basic building blocks. The hardware engineers bridge the gap from the instruction set to the technology.

Historically, instruction set design has been closely linked to computer design. In the first and second generation computers, each "instruction set design" had one computer design to implement it. This has also been true of the first two waves of microprocessors. In fact, instruction set architecture was a responsibility of the computer designers. When a new computer reached the market, it was difficult for a user to upgrade or convert his computer system without extensive reprogramming of application programs. Moreover, the early instruction sets left much to be desired, and were considerably improved from one machine to the next. Further, due to the high cost of hardware, machine "architecture" (then called "organization" or "planning") was very dependent on technology and implementation techniques. In fact, the early machine implementers tended to dictate the architecture, just as microprocessor architectures are often dictated by technological constraints and design trade-offs.

Today, it is recognized that decisions made to convenience the relatively small group of implementers or logic designers during the one-to-three year development cycle, may inconvenience the larger group of programmers and users over the one or more decades of lifetime of the instruction set. Computer architecture is viewed as a specification based on concepts and principles, such specification to be, of course, feasible and practical. Architecture enjoys an independence from particular implementation constraints. The third generation of computers witnessed the separation of instruction set design from computer design.

Instruction set design requires some experience. F. P. Brooks [1] characterizes the senior architects of the IBM S/360 family as having gained experience and judgment through development of several prior computer specifications. Instruction set design is something like designing a crossword puzzle. All the pieces must fit together properly. Instruction set design is also something like the coding of information. Each instruction is divided into fields, and within each field, mutually exclusive information can be specified. The fields should be chosen to "pack" the most information in the smallest size. A successful design results in smaller machine language program sizes, consuming less storage space.

Good instruction sets should be powerful enough that no frequently needed data processing operation requires an inordinate number of instructions. Some common omissions are instructions which shift data across word boundaries conveniently, or which increment or decrement words or registers used as address pointers. Other omissions include instructions which search character strings for a given character or word.

Good designs are "consistent" or uniform. The programmer should not have to remember minor details on top of minor details. No one wants to remember something like "the indirect indexed mode can only be used with the XYZ, ZYX, and XZY opcodes, and only with the XZY opcode if the preceding instruction was YZX and the branch was not taken." It is much simpler for address modes to work uniformly for *all* opcodes, and for operations to work uniformly for *all* data types.

In this chapter we cover some basic properties of instruction sets, primarily based on the *single-address* class of instruction. In single-address architectures, the instruction has an address part which specifies how to obtain one operand. In single-address machines, the second operand is an accumulator register. In a 4-accumulator machine, a 2-bit field in the instruction specifies which accumulator.

Other instruction set architecture classes exist. The *memory-to-memory* architecture operates with both operands in main memory and leaves the result in main memory. *Stack* architectures use a stack to store the operands in the order required. Cragon [2] has studied several architectural approaches to see if any offers significant savings in the amount of code (machine language instruction) space or memory cycles to perform a data processing function of a certain power. Cragon discovered there were no significant differences, and concluded that a given number of instruction bits can be used effectively by any well-designed architecture. From our experience, we would have been surprised had this conclusion not been reached. The result explains why "experts" can honestly disagree on the architectural worth of ideas. Many such debates are expensive to resolve (few "experts" want to build a machine to prove a point).

With the knowledge that any well-designed approach performs about as well in code space and memory cycles as another, we suggest the term

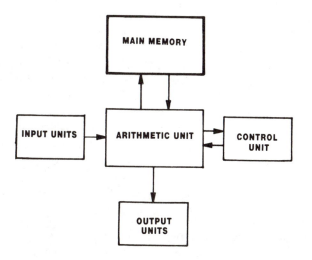

Figure 2.1. *"Classical" machine organization.*

"powerful" for instruction sets which raise the conceptual level used by the programmer. The benefit is less program development time.

The ideas behind the stored program concept as known to Babbage were rediscovered in discussions by the ENIAC design group. These ideas appeared in a 1946 report by Burks, Goldstine and von Neumann [3]. A stored program consists of instructions which are fetched, then executed (interpreted). Instructions and data are stored in the same main memory and this has come to be called a "von Neumann" machine. The ideas were incorporated in a computer built in Princeton, NJ, at the Institute for Advanced Study, called the IAS computer. **Figure 2.1** shows the general machine organization of this computer. The "arithmetic unit" part has been called the *data flow* for some time by IBM and other designers. The *control unit* is responsible for controlling the fetch of the next instruction from main memory (called the "instruction fetch", I-state, or I-fetch phase) and controlling its execution (called the "execution" or E-state). In this task, the control unit activates and deactivates control signals, causing register transfers in the data flow. The data flow is passive and the control unit is active. The control unit and data flow together comprise the central processor unit, or CPU. The CPU performs as a slave to the stored program instructions. System control clearly resides in the active program, written by a programmer. (Of course, if the programmer fails to handle a situation in the program, the "computer" is often blamed for the resulting "goof" resulting from the "bug".)

2.2. MAIN MEMORY

The first generation memory technology presented cost and reliability problems to the computer designers. The ENIAC used vacuum tube flip-flop registers, which cost over $10 per bit. Some early computers used magnetic drums. Others used mercury or sonic delay lines for main memory. Still others used a CRT storage tube. In the second and third generation computers, the technology of ferrite magnetic cores was so widespread that "core" became a synonym for main memory. Today one can purchase a memory chip with tens of thousands of bytes of storage for $5 to $10, an indication of the tremendous advance in memory technology.

2.2.1. Main Memory Organization

Main memory stores n-bit words. The *capacity* is the number of words stored. Common capacities are found in powers of 2 because of the prevalence of binary addresses. A 10-bit address field can address 1024 distinct words. Word sizes vary from system to system. **Table 2.1** gives some indication of the variety.

Table 2.1. Word Sizes	
System	*Size (Bits)*
Intel 4004	4
IBM 1401, Intel 8080, MC6800	8
CDC-160, PDP-8	12
Whirlwind I, HP2116B, PDP-11, MC68000	16
Univac 1218, PDP-1	18
SDS 910, CDC 924	24
IBM S/360, S/370	32
IBM 7070, ERA 1101	36
IAS	40
Burroughs B5000, CDC 1604	48
CDC 6600	60
IBM 7030 (STRETCH)	64

Traditionally, small computers have used 8-bit or 16-bit words as the addressable quantity. The word location is taken to be the value of its binary address. Thus, with a 10-bit address, the first word's address is 00 0000 0000 and is called word 0. The last address is binary 11 1111 1111 and is word "1023". Memory is viewed as a linear sequence of words, as in **Figure 2.2**. Fig. 2.2(a) (horizontal representation) is

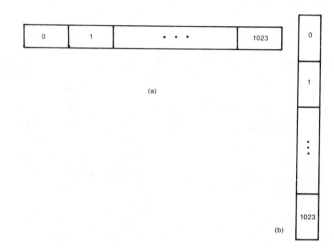

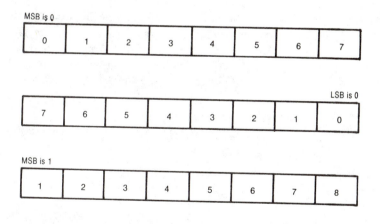

Figure 2.2. *Memory maps of 1K-word memory as a linear structure.*
(a) Horizontal depiction. (b) Vertical depiction.

Figure 2.3. *Alternate bit-numbering schemes for bits in a word.*

useful where storage is used for alphanumeric quantities such as names.
The vertical representation of Fig. 2.2(b) is useful to depict tables and
programs. Refer to Chapter 1 for the numbering of bits within the words.
This book uses the MSB 0 scheme described in §1.5. See **Figure 2.3.**

2.2.2. Memory Boundaries

A character size which has prevailed is the 8-bit *byte*. (A 4-bit quantity is known as a "nibble".) The magical quantity of eight bits has the advantage of being a power of 2, but this in itself does not account for its popularity. Many first generation machines used a character size of six bits, whose 64 combinations provided upper and lowercase alphanumeric characters and many of the special graphics and punctuation symbols. However, with the advent of communications, when combinations intended for line handling purposes were added to the character set, the character acquired seven bits. The current ASCII standard is an example of such a character set. To transmit or receive an ASCII character, a parity bit may also be specified, creating a need to handle 8-bit characters.

Some small computers use a memory word of 16 bits, but provide addressing to the byte. This gives rise to a situation called *alignment*. When addressing a 2-byte word, the even-numbered address is used. For example, bytes 0 and 1 are brought out when reading memory location 0. The "even" byte address is the most significant byte and the "odd" byte address is the least significant byte. When 2-byte words are stored in memory with the most significant byte in the "even" byte address, the 2-byte word is *aligned* to the memory word boundary.

The word boundary problem in a byte addressing architecture is a performance issue. Higher-performing processors will read many bytes out of memory at a time, aligned on word boundaries. If a data item is "split" across a word boundary, then the CPU would be required to access memory twice to fetch each half of the data item. The IBM S/360 and DEC PDP-11 architectures use byte addressing with a larger word size, and maintain the notion of word boundary alignment. In the IBM S/370, the word boundary problem is handled by the computer designer, not by the programmer or compiler writer.

2.3. IAS COMPUTER ARCHITECTURE

The IAS computer was developed at the Institute for Advanced Study under John von Neumann between 1946 and 1950 [4]. There are reasons why we study an obsolete machine architecture. The IAS has historical significance because many binary single-address instruction sets trace their ancestry to it. In addition, the IAS architecture is relatively simple, and is a convenient starting point for a field which is quite complex. While it is important to know the definition of concepts when asked, it is essential also to know their *relative importance*. What problems are solved by each technique? Which concepts represent alternative approaches, which are independent, and which are refinements of more basic ideas? A sense of relative importance results from learning the IAS architecture and then seeing how the field progressed historically.

The IAS was intended for scientific calculations. It used a 40-bit data word to produce results of good precision. The number system chosen was binary. Binary systems have greater bit efficiency than decimal systems, and their arithmetic algorithms are simpler. The sign bit is the leftmost bit in the word.

The CPU had three 40-bit data registers, an *accumulator* (called AC here), an *arithmetic register* (MQ) for holding the multiplier during the multiplication operation and quotient during the division operation, and a *memory data register* (MD) for buffering data transfers to and from main memory. A *program counter* (PC) stored the location of the next instruction to be executed. The term "counter" is used because after fetching the current instruction, the PC register is "counted up" (incremented) by one to point to the next instruction. Unless a jump or branch occurs, instructions are executed sequentially. The CPU also possessed an *instruction register* (IR) to hold the instruction being executed. These registers have been fundamental to many subsequent architectures.

2.3.1. The IAS Instruction

The IAS "packed" two 20-bit instructions into one 40-bit memory word. An odd/even flip-flop was provided to remember whether the next instruction was the odd (low-order) or even (high-order) half of the 40-bit word.

The original design called for 4K words of memory, requiring a 12-bit address. Therefore, the instruction *format* (see **Figure 2.4**) had a 12-bit (full direct) *address field* and an 8-bit *operation code* (opcode) field. The final design provided only 1K words of main memory, permitting a 10-bit address field and a 10-bit opcode field.

Figure 2.4. *Original IAS computer instruction format.*

The address to be used in the execution of the instruction was that found in the address field. This is known as the *direct addressing mode*. The address was either a 40-bit data operand or, in the case of a branch or jump instruction, a 40-bit word containing an instruction to be executed next. Direct addressing is a basic concept which now has many variations.

2.3.2. Branching or Jump Instructions

Program control by branching is fundamental, and today many variations exist. For an *unconditional branch*, the next instruction is never indicated by the PC value, and always by the address field. In the IAS computer, the *target* of the branch instruction (pointed to by the address field) could be the odd or even instruction of a word. Two opcodes for the branch instruction were used, one for the odd instruction and the other for the even instruction. The only *conditional branch* instruction in the IAS computer was a branch if the accumulator was positive. For the conditional branch, if the AC was negative the next instruction was the one following the current instruction, and if the AC was positive the next instruction was taken from the location indicated by the instruction address field and opcode.

The designers of the IAS computer contemplated program loops, but in a rudimentary fashion. Indexing had not been invented. Instructions in the loops were loaded into the AC and incremented or decremented to change the address field. Architectures which require instructions to be modified are often difficult to debug.

2.3.3. Memory-Reference Instructions

Memory-reference instructions can be data movement or arithmetic. The IAS memory-reference instructions which move data included loading and storing the MQ and the AC. In two-operand operations, one of the operands was assumed to be the accumulator AC. (This specification of the AC was "implied".) The "add" instruction had eight variations, as denoted by the value of three additional bits. The variations included add or subtract, load versus add, or use of absolute values instead of signed values. Two other arithmetic instructions were multiply and divide. For multiplication, the referenced operand was the multiplier (brought to the MQ) and the AC was the multiplicand. For division, the memory operand was the divisor, and the AC was the dividend. The location of the binary point was on the left of the MSB such that all numbers were fractions. The multiplication of two 39-bit operands results in a 78-bit product. The high-order 39 bits were retained in AC and the low-order bits were left in the MQ register.

2.3.4. Register-Reference Instructions

The IAS register-reference instruction type did not involve an operand in main memory. There were ten such instructions. Eight of these corresponded to the memory-reference arithmetic instructions, except that the second operand was the contents of the MQ register. The remaining two instructions were shifts, involving both the AC and MQ registers as one register. Recall that in performing a shift, one bit *spills* off one end, and another bit must *fill* in at the other end. In a rotation, the spill bit feeds the fill bit position.

In the IAS left shift, the AC spill bit fed the MQ fill bit which effectively placed the MQ to the left of AC. The AC fill bit was 0 (zero-fill). For a right shift the AC was to the left of MQ, and the AC sign bit was retained. A shift which retains the sign bit value is called an arithmetic shift.

Memory-reference and register-reference instructions cause data values to change, which is how a computer performs work.

2.3.5. Input–Output (IO) Instructions

Input and output on the IAS computer was typical of first generation systems. There was no common IO interface, nor was any concurrency possible. The interfaces were custom-designed to each IO device. The instruction following the IO operation waited until the IO operation was completed.

The three IO media were the punched card, paper teletype tape, and a magnetic drum. Information was transferred in fixed blocks of "n" words each. The instruction address field pointed to the first word of the block in memory. For the card the block size was 12; for the drum the block size was 32.

2.3.6. Descendents of the IAS Architecture

MIT's Whirlwind I computer [5] was a derivative of the IAS architecture. Speed was more important than mathematical precision because of its use as a real-time aircraft simulator. The data word and instruction were 16 bits. Data used the binary one's complement scheme. The instruction used a 5-bit opcode field and an 11-bit direct address field. The Whirlwind is the forerunner of many 16-bit minicomputer architectures.

Another derivative of the IAS machine was the IBM 701 computer. The 701 was tailored to scientific calculation, and used a 36-bit word. The 36-bit word was amenable to packing six 6-bit alphanumeric characters, or two 18-bit instructions. The IBM 701 was the forerunner of the IBM 704, 709, 7090, and 7094 series of large binary scientific computers. However, the later machines had 36-bit instructions.

2.3.7. IAS Architectural Summary and Shortcomings

The IAS computer stored the program and data in the same memory. This feature has been called a "von Neumann" or "Princeton" class architecture. The IAS computer used an instruction format with an opcode field and an address field. Memory-reference, arithmetic, branching, and IO instructions were provided.

Modern instruction architecture has progressed considerably since the IAS computer. Providing only direct addressing was a shortcoming. Many instruction loops require the modification of address pointers. Today, an index register relieves the programmer of modifying operand addresses within a loop. The index is added to a base address to form an *effective address*. Prior to a subsequent pass in the loop, the programmer increments or decrements the index register. On the next trip through the loop, all indexed operand addresses point to the next data word as operand. Another improvement is *indirect addressing*. The instruction address field indicates a data word in memory which itself is a pointer or indirect address. This pointer is the operand address.

The branching capabilities of the IAS computer were very weak. Many types of conditional branches are commonplace today. Improved program techniques include the concept of a *subroutine,* called from several points in the program. The subroutine is useful for implementing "super instructions" in the bottom-up approach. Early scientific computers used subroutine packages. The subroutine is passed one or more operands called *parameters,* and delivers the results to known locations. The companion notion of *procedure,* found in higher-level languages, is a useful top-down tool.

The IAS provided no facilities for handling data structures. It is convenient to have *block move* instructions to move contiguous blocks of data words in memory. A powerful data structure is the *stack*. In a stack, the last item stored is the first item retrieved, which gives rise to the acronym LIFO (Last In First Out). Instructions and addressing techniques exist to facilitate the implementation of LIFO structures in memory.

Devices were attached to the IAS computer in an "ad hoc" fashion. *Input-output architecture* has been improved by the definition and use of general-purpose standard interfaces. Interrupt structures now permit input-output operations to overlap with CPU processing. These and other advances are covered in greater detail in the following sections.

2.4. DATA TYPES IN MAIN MEMORY

This section covers the basic data items operated on by the instruction set of the computer. In the IAS architecture, the single data type was a 40-bit word. The data registers in the CPU and the locations in main memory accommodated the 40-bit word. Today's architectures admit a wide variety of data types.

2.4.1. Word Size

The choice of word size involves a trade-off. The 8-bit byte is a convenient quantity for character string manipulation, data communications systems, and text editing. For process control applications, 16-bit data words provide sufficient precision most of the time. The sensor inputs are rarely capable of refining more than four or five decimal digits of precision, which is also true of set-point outputs. *Double precision* (or even multiple precision) techniques are used in applications such as numerical analysis where a single precision word size proves inadequate. A 16-bit word is capable of little more than four decimal digits of precision. Two adjacent 16-bit words treated as a single 32-bit value result in approximately nine digits of precision.

Double precision arithmetic instructions and data registers can be provided in the architecture, such as in the IBM S/360. Alternatively, interword shift and carry propagation capability can be provided in the instruction set, leaving to software subroutines the implementation of the remaining double precision requirements and capabilities. 32-bit word sizes are convenient for powerful processors where a large addressable main memory is needed. Indirect address pointers of 32 bits provide a *memory address space* of over 4 billion words. In his study of microprocessor architectures, Brooks [6] notes that historically, the most common and damaging mistake made by architects is the failure to provide a large enough memory address space.

Instruction size is another consideration. In the IAS computer, instructions were half the data word size. In some machines the data word is the byte. The Intel 8080 and many other 8-bit microprocessors have instruction lengths of one, two, or three bytes. The length is defined by the opcode in the first byte. Instruction length is a trade-off involving the size of the eventual program versus the processing power of an individual instruction. The value of "powerful" instructions is difficult to quantify. Power comes in two varieties. The designer can increase the size of the address field to provide more powerful addressing capability, or the size of the opcode field to provide a richer set of data processing and program control operations. A human factors consideration is that richer opcodes are next to useless if they are too complicated for the programmer to assimilate. Richer addressing modes follow suit if they are inconsistently related to the opcodes.

The notions of "complexity" and "inconsistency" are intuitive and difficult to quantify. One instruction set may be more complex than another if more statements are required to describe the first instruction set. Inconsistency involves the existence of exceptions to an otherwise general rule or statement. The more the exceptional cases, the longer the description of the instruction set.

2.4.2. Data Types

Many computers have only one data type, the fixed point binary number. Any other type must be implemented by software. Additional data types include floating point numbers and decimal numbers. Typically, decimal digits are coded in a 4-bit "nibble" in binary coded decimal (BCD). Some early decimal machines used a decimal address (e.g. the IBM 1401); others used a binary address for greater efficiency. In the second generation, the preference for binary over decimal number schemes for business applications was the subject of a debate among computer users. Many microprocessors have a "six-correct" capability which permits software subroutines to handle decimal arithmetic conveniently. Some microcomputer architectures have a decimal add and subtract instruction, which is implemented in the hardware.

In the foregoing cases, the digital logic which interprets the instruction set assumes the data type implied by the instruction. Thus, the data operand found at the effective address of a decimal add instruction is presumed to be in BCD form. (If not, a "data exception" interruption may be generated, as in the S/370 architecture.) Another approach is to provide a single "add" instruction, and a "tag" field with the data which describes its type. The digital logic which interprets the add instruction must examine the tagged data and "do the right thing". For example, if a fixed point number is added to a floating point number, some sophisticated architectures convert the fixed data type to floating data type, and generate a floating point result. The extra operation involved is called *data conversion,* and is a well-known problem to compiler writers.

In the "von Neumann" or "Princeton" class architectures, the instructions and the data words share the same addressable memory. In many architectures, there is nothing to prevent a branch target address from being data. A programmer can place "garbage" into the computer, get it out of the computer, and even execute it! "Wild branches" can execute data for some time with very unpredictable and often unreproducible results. To avoid such pitfalls, the tag field can also identify a data type as being an "instruction". The programmer may have less hilarious bugs, but they'll be far easier to detect. The *separation of programs from data* produces programs that are easier to understand and to debug. In some organizations a programmer is subject to a reprimand if he generates a "self-modifying" program (the program treats its own instructions as data).

2.4.3. Multiple Accumulators and General Registers

In programs written for the "classical" single-address instruction architecture, the accumulator is continually being used as a "switch". Data is loaded, tested, stored, reloaded, retested, etc. Having more than one accumulator reduces some of this traffic and improves programmer efficiency. Some of the accumulators not assigned a specific function may be called general-purpose registers (GPRs). The Data General NOVA computer architecture has four accumulators, the DEC PDP-11 and IBM Series/1 have eight accumulators, and the IBM S/370 and Zilog Z8000 have sixteen. The term "register file" also applies to the multiple accumulator concept.

Figure 2.5. *Instruction format with multiple accumulators.*

For two-operand instructions, an additional field in the instruction specifies which accumulator is to take part. In **Figure 2.5,** the "R" (register) field specifies the accumulator register. In a multiple register machine, the operations can take place between the registers, and the address field is not needed. One popular design technique for these register-to-register (register-reference) instructions is to assign a specific opcode combination for general "register-reference" operations. The otherwise unused bits in the address field, now called *modifier* bits, determine the register-reference operation. Redefining the address field to be the modifier field is an instance of *field redefinition.*

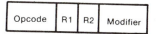

Figure 2.6. *Instruction format for register-to-register operations.*

The instruction format of the two-operand instruction appears in **Figure 2.6.** This represents a departure from having a single instruction format; now the format depends on the instruction's opcode. Instruction formats can be made quite flexible. Some designs, in fact, have a variable length opcode field at the left hand side of the instruction format.

2.5. ADDRESSING MODES

In the IAS, Whirlwind I, and IBM 701 computers, the address field of the instruction was sufficiently wide (in bits) to address the available memory space directly. The address field was the *full direct address,* and the architecture only provided direct addressing. First generation computer designers were happily unaware of the "address space" problem. Von Neumann stated that 2000 words of memory was more than any program should need. Two decades later, Brooks [7] said "more main memory is the universal elixir of computer systems". System programmers, when asked by computer designers what "features" they would like in an instruction set, will respond, "Save money on fancy and powerful instructions. Just give us more main memory!"

This section discusses methods to obtain the operand or operand address. The *effective address* (ea) is the address of the branch target or of the operand (if it is in main memory). A direct address field is included with the memory-reference instruction format. This field may have too few bits to be a full memory address, in which case we call it the *partial direct address* (pda) field. Different architectures employ the pda in different ways, so it may have different names. In S/370 architecture the pda is called the displacement; some architectures call the pda field the offset. The *full direct address* (fda) is an address which has the full number of address bits. The fda is obtainable from the pda field and another instruction field called the *address mode* (am) field. The address mode field has an important function: it indicates *how* the effective address is to be obtained from the full direct address. For indexing, the effective address is the sum of the full direct address and an index. For indirect addressing, the effective address is the value in the memory location specified by the direct address.

2.5.1. The Full Direct Address Problem

In typical 16-bit minicomputers, the registers (including the PC) and memory word are 16 bits. Using a data word or PC register as an address provides a capability to address a 64K-word address space. This is the largest address space which is convenient and efficient for 16-bit architectures. If the instruction is a 16-bit word, and the opcode and address mode fields take up some bits, then the instruction address field may have only 8 to 12 bits. The partial direct address (pda) field must somehow be augmented to become a full direct address of 16 bits. The problem of augmenting the partial address is called the *full direct address problem*. Several solutions to this problem are considered in the following subsections.

2.5.2. Fixed Pages

The Hewlett-Packard HP2100 computer has a 10-bit partial direct address field, permitting 1024 directly addressable words. In one approach to the problem, the pda field is the ten low-order address bits or offset. This approach divides memory into fixed "blocks" of 1024 words. Now the six high-order bits must be obtained somehow. Normally, the high-order six bits of the PC define which of the 64 blocks in the address space is being addressed. In many 16-bit architectures, this block is called a *page*. (The term "page" has another meaning in the context of a virtual memory; see Chapter 4.)

In the HP2100, the high-order six bits which help form the full direct address are defined according to the value of a 1-bit field of the instruction called the *page bit*. If the page bit is 0, then the six high-order bits are all 0, and *page 0* is referenced. If the page bit is 1, then the six high-order bits are obtained from the corresponding bits in the PC, and the *current page* is referenced.

In independent RTN statements, the formation of the full direct address on the HP2100 is described as follows:

Page 0: fda = 000000,pda
Current Page: fda = PC(0-5),pda

If indirect addressing is used, the indirect pointer must reside in the referenced page. However, the indirect address can point anywhere in the address space. The pages are "fixed"; when the PC is incremented, it crosses a page boundary, and words in the previous page are no longer directly accessible.

2.5.3. Relative Pages

An alternative to fixed page boundaries is the concept of the *relative page*. In the case of the 10-bit pda, 1024 addresses can be specified. In a relative or "floating" page, the leftmost bit is treated as a sign bit and this field is algebraically added to the PC. This is done in digital logic by *sign extending* (SE) the 10-bit pda, making it a "relative offset". (The 10-bit SE of binary 0110 is 00 0000 0110, and the 10-bit SE of 1010 is 11 1111 1010.) The 10-bit sign extension technique with the two's complement negative number representation defines a "floating page" of plus 511 or minus 512 words of the current instruction. The following RTN statement describes the procedure:

PC-relative: fda = PC plus SE(pda)

The problem of organizing programs into fixed page boundaries disappears with PC-relative addressing, but it is still necessary to arrange data words to be close at hand.

2.5.4. Base Registers

In the IBM S/370 architecture, a 4-bit *base field* (bf) in the instruction specifies one of the 16 general-purpose registers to be the *base register* BR. The full direct address is the sum of BR and the 12-bit pda (displacement) treated as a positive number. If register 0 (R0) is selected as the base, page 0 is addressed regardless of R0's contents. In a simple variation, the pda could be treated as a signed integer by doing sign extension. The base register technique is described by the following RTN statements:

$$bf = 0: \qquad fda = SE(0,pda)$$
$$bf \neq 0: \qquad fda = BR \text{ plus } SE(0,pda)$$

2.5.5. Register Addressing

Register addressing is another form of addressing which uses base registers with 0 displacements. Instruction bits are freed for other uses. Register addressing is used in several microprocessors (such as the Fairchild F8) and in the PDP-11 minicomputer for obtaining the full direct address. (Osborne [8] uses the term "data counter" to describe such a register.) In register addressing, the fda is the value in the register. The RTN statement for register addressing using Register "n" (Rn) is:

$$\text{Register Rn addressing:} \qquad fda = Rn$$

2.5.6. Indirect Addressing

In *single-level indirect addressing*, the instruction's address field is used to access a memory word (pointer) which itself is the operand address. The instruction provides the "address of the address" of the operand, hence the origin of the term *indirect address*. A bit in the address mode field of the instruction format is provided which specifies direct or indirect addressing. The concept is shown in **Figure 2.7(a)**. The following RTN statement describes the mode:

$$\text{Indirect mode:} \quad ea = M[fda]$$

Some architectures have *multiple-level indirect addressing,* e.g. HP2100. In these architectures, one of the bits in the pointer may be an "indirect" bit, or *flag*. In logic design and programming alike, a flag is a useful device. A flag is a 1-bit value which has an assigned meaning. Flags are generally spoken of as being "on" (in the active state) or "off" (in the inactive state). If the indirect flag bit is "on" (1), it invokes another level of indirection. This form of indirect addressing is illustrated in Fig. 2.7(b). The possibility of multilevel indirect addressing invites a special form of "endless loop" or "hang-up" where none of the address pointers in the pointer chain have the "indirect" flag bit off. Multilevel indirect addressing can be used to implement a storage structure of a "last-in, first-out" nature. From our experience, one level of indirection is quite sufficient. Single-level indirect addressing allows all bits of the data word to be arbitrary, which permits twice the address space to be reached indirectly.

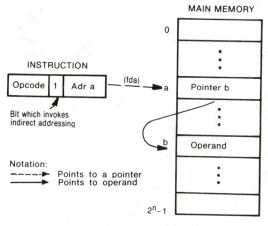

(a)

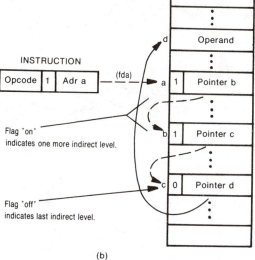

(b)

Figure 2.7. *Indirect addressing.* (a) Single level. (b) Multiple levels.

2.5.7. Indexing

Systems with an index register XR, but with no indirect addressing, can use the same instruction format as Fig. 2.7. The address mode field distinguishes between direct addressing mode and *index mode*. In architectures with indirect addressing, the programmer can manipulate the pointer by bringing it into the accumulator and treating it as data. In some architectures with indexing, a particular register is distinguished as the index register (XR) with special instructions to increment, decrement, load or store it. In architectures using the multiple "general-purpose register" (GPR) philosophy, any register (except possibly register 0) can be an index register. Any register contents, including those of the index registers, can be manipulated as data. In some early designs, the index register was located in word 0 of main memory, and was accessed and treated as a memory data word. Effective address calculation by use of an index register is described by the following RTN statement:

Index mode: ea = XR plus fda

Some architectures provide for both index and indirect addressing. An example is the SC-16 computer architecture of Chapter 5. See **Figure 2.8** for the format. The index and indirect modes can be employed either together or separately. When used together, two possibilities exist, according to when the index value is added. In the first case, the indirect pointer is found at the full direct address. Adding the indirect pointer to the index value forms the effective address. This approach is called *post-indexing,* and the RTN statement is:

Post-indexing: ea = XR plus M[fda]

Post-indexing is useful in accessing information stored in blocks of a fixed known format, such as system control blocks. The index register contains the offset within the block; the direct address is a location which always points to the current control block.

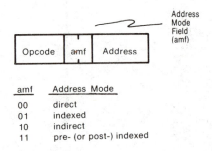

amf	Address Mode
00	direct
01	indexed
10	indirect
11	pre- (or post-) indexed

Figure 2.8. *Instruction format for mixed indirect and indexed modes.*

Second, the index can be added to the full direct address to form the pointer address. This is called *pre-indexing:*

Pre-indexing: ea = M[XR plus fda]

Pre-indexing is useful for the construction of a multiway branch table. The direct address of the instruction points to the base of a branch table. The index register now contains a value controlling the program's future action. In all likelihood the branch table contains pointers to a set of routines which define mutually exclusive actions the program is capable of doing at that point in the program.

Most systems employ either pre-indexing or post-indexing, but not both. Perhaps the opcode could distinguish the alternative as follows. Pre-indexing is indicated with branch opcodes; otherwise post-indexing is used. Of course, the effect of pre-indexing and post-indexing can be achieved by manipulating the pointer before using it. Therefore the existence of pre- or post-indexing is justified only in architectures with powerful, convenient index register manipulation facilities such as automatic incrementing or decrementing.

2.5.8. Immediate Addressing

Immediate addressing is a technique which uses what "normally" is the partial address field to specify the *value* of the operand itself. The address field thus supplies a constant value to the program. The high-order bit of the field is a sign bit, which is sign extended to the full data word size in bits. The *immediate* value is sometimes called a *literal*. For example, consider a single-address architecture which has the *immediate mode*. An "ADD" instruction with the address mode field indicating "immediate" and an offset or pda field of "127" would add "127" to the accumulator.

Immediate addressing is an example of field redefinition. In this case, the field which is redefined is the partial direct address field. Depending on a bit combination elsewhere in the instruction, the pda is redefined to be the operand itself, with sign extension (SE).

Nonimmediate: Operand = M[ea]
Immediate: Operand = SE(pda)

2.5.9. Stack Addressing

The stack is a useful data structure. Stacks appeared in the second generation, and have achieved some popularity with microprocessors. Stacks can be used conveniently for operands, as in the Burroughs 5000 architecture and its derivatives. In the B5000, instructions are provided to place items from main memory on the stack (PUSH operation), and move operands from the stack to main memory (POP operation). The B5000 "add" instruction consists only of the opcode, because the two operands are *implied* to be the top two data items on the stack. The sum replaces these operands on the stack. The instruction type which uses a stack in this manner is called a *zero address* instruction. A stack operation example is shown in **Figure 2.9**. The stack is initially as shown in Fig. 2.9(a). The result of the "Add" operation replaces the two top values (A and B) with their sum, as shown in Fig. 2.9(b). Compiler programs tend to parse the compiler language arithmetic expressions such that executions can be handled by an operand stack in this fashion. Many hand-held calculators utilize a stack for operand storage. There is general disagreement as to whether shorter program size results from the use of operand stacks in conjunction with the instruction set. (See [9] and its references).

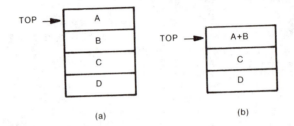

Figure 2.9. *Contents of the stack.* (a) Before an ADD operation. (b) After an ADD operation.

Figure 2.10 gives an example of implementing a stack in main memory using a *stack pointer* (SP). Initially, the pointer indicates the first location reserved for the stack, as shown in Fig. 2.10(a). Item A is *pushed* (placed) on the stack in a two-step process. The pointer is used to write the item to the stack in step 1, and then the pointer is incremented in step 2. Fig. 2.10(b) shows the result of the two-step process, which is described here in RTN statements.

PUSH•STEP1:	$M[SP] \leftarrow A$
PUSH•STEP2:	$SP \leftarrow SP$ plus 1

Item A is *popped* (removed) from the stack in a two-step process. First, the stack pointer is decremented, and second the pointer is used the memory READ operation. Thus, for the PUSH operation for initialization as in Fig. 2.10(a), the pointer must be incremented *after* the memory operation, whereas in the the POP operation, the stack pointer is decremented *before* the memory operation.

A convenient instruction for data stacks is the COPY operation, where the top data item is copied to a register, and not popped. The scheme of Fig. 2.10 shows that to implement the COPY, the pointer needs to be decremented, the item read, and finally the pointer incremented. The pointer manipulation is undesirable, and can be avoided as follows.

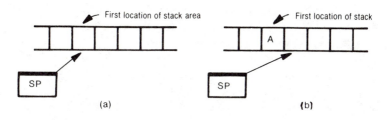

Figure 2.10. *Stack pointer is initialized to point to first location.*
(a) Empty stack. (b) Item "A" PUSHed onto stack.

In **Figure 2.11,** the stack pointer is initialized to one location *less* than the first item on the stack. To push an item A, the stack pointer is first incremented, followed by the memory write operation. To pop an item, the item is first read, then the pointer is decremented. To copy the top item of the stack, the pointer value is not changed. The simple copy operation is provided in Knuth's [10] description of this stack algorithm. The RTN statements are:

PUSH•STEP1:	SP ← SP plus 1
PUSH•STEP2:	M[SP] ← A
POP•STEP1:	A ← M[SP]
POP•STEP2:	SP ← SP minus 1
COPY:	A ← M[SP]
	(SP unchanged)

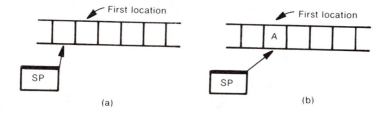

Figure 2.11. *Stack pointer initialized to one location less than first stack location facilitates COPY.* (a) Empty stack. (b) Item "A" PUSHed onto stack.

2.5.10. Pointer Adjusting

Pointers (either index registers or indirect addresses) are useful in processing character strings, in searching tables, and in loading and storing blocks of memory words. When used in loops, pointers are adjusted up (incremented) or down (decremented) on each trip through the loop. The most convenient method (to the assembler language programmer) is for the instruction set to provide for *automatic adjustment* (bumping) during the execution of memory-reference instructions. In automatic adjustment, a field within the same memory-reference instruction using the pointer has an *adjust amount* field to control whether the pointer is left alone, is incremented, or decremented. In some systems, the amount incremented or decremented can be controlled by the programmer. Another point to be resolved is *when* to adjust the pointer. From the preceding discussion on implementing stacks, the reader can see the importance of whether the pointer is adjusted before or after its use.

The ability to increment *or* decrement pointers is useful. Pointer decrementing is needed to handle multiple precision arithmetic numbers in the right-to-left fashion as done with pencil and paper. On the other hand, pointer incrementing is needed to operate on a character string in the normal left-to-right fashion. Character string operations are commonly performed by assemblers, compilers, interpreters, and text editor or word processing programs.

2.6. SOME EXAMPLES OF OPERAND ADDRESSING

2.6.1. The PDP-8 Minicomputer

The DEC PDP-8 employs direct addressing to page 0 or to the current page, and provides indirect addressing. See **Figure 2.12.** A pointer bumping capability called "autoindexing" is provided for memory locations 8 through 15. Autoindexing is described in terms of the following global "convention", or "constraint", or "groundrule":

> "Whenever one of locations 8 through 15 is used as an indirect address (instead of as an operand), the content of the location is incremented (by one) prior to its use in fetching the operand."

The incrementation function is invoked by convention. In programming, something like a pointer being incremented without an explicit instruction is often called a *side-effect*. The values in the designated addresses cannot be used as indirect pointers *without* being incremented. On the other hand, no valuable bits in the instruction format are spent to achieve the function of autoindexing. The definition of functions by

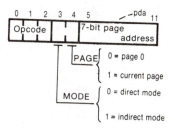

Figure 2.12. *PDP-8 instruction format.*

convention, and the use of global groundrules are important and powerful design tools.

Another point illustrated by autoindexing is that in most first generation computers, all addresses were treated the same. Autoindexing is an example of an "address-dependent" action on the part of the architecture. Such techniques have become common practice. In the PDP-8 case, the power of the architecture increased at no expense in instruction format bits. However, the technique can be overdone. Programmers ought not to be forced to learn a complex jumble of side-effects before they are able to write programs.

2.6.2. The PDP-11

The DEC PDP-11 has a flexible addressing scheme. It has single-address and double-address instruction formats. See **Figure 2.13.** In each case, there are two 3-bit address fields per operand: MODE and REG. The MODE field specifies one of eight modes; mode 0 through mode 7. The REG field specifies one of eight 16-bit general registers or accumulators, R0 through R7. We shall use the notation "Rn" to denote a selectable accumulator, where "n" can be 0 through 7. Register R6 is a stack pointer (SP) and R7 is the program counter (PC). Thus, six bits denote the effective address of an operand: three bits for selecting an address mode, and three bits for selecting register Rn. In describing the addressing modes, we reflect common practice and use the term "indirect" where the PDP-11 manuals use "deferred".

The first mode (mode 0) is called the *register* mode. The assembler language notation for this mode is Rn. The operand value is contained in register Rn itself:

Rn: operand = Rn

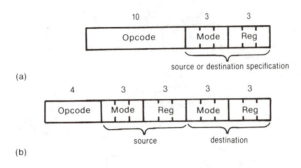

Figure 2.13. *PDP-11 memory-reference instruction formats.*
(a) Single-address instructions. (b) Double-address instructions.

In all other modes, the operand value resides in main memory, so an effective address must be determined:

Other modes: operand = M[ea].

The second address mode (mode 1) is very simple: the selected register Rn contains the effective address, which means Rn points to the operand. This mode is *register indirect,* and denoted (Rn):

(Rn): ea = Rn.

These first two modes are summarized here.

Mode	*Name*	*Notation*	*RTN*
0	Register	Rn	operand = Rn
1	Register Indirect	(Rn)	ea = Rn

We call address modes 2 through 5 the "autobump" modes. Mode 2 is obtained by combining automatic incrementing with mode 1, and is called *autoincrement* mode, denoted (Rn)+. Following the use of Rn as a pointer in step 1, Rn is incremented in step 2. The "+" is placed after Rn to reflect this sequence. Mode 3 is obtained from mode 2 by applying an additional level of indirection. The "at" symbol (@) is employed to indicate indirection, so mode 3 is called *autoincrement indirect* and is denoted @(Rn)+. Address modes 4 and 5 decrement register Rn, and are similar to modes 2 and 3. The difference is that in modes 4 and 5 the value in register Rn is *decremented before* its use as a pointer, instead of being *incremented after*. The "before" versus "after" aspect facilitates the programming of stack addressing. Modes 4 and 5 are respectively denoted "–(Rn)" and "@–(Rn)". The name and notation of the autobump modes are summarized as follows.

Mode	*Name*	*Notation*
2	Autoincrement	(Rn)+
3	Autoincrement Indirect	@(Rn)+
4	Autodecrement	–(Rn)
5	Autodecrement Indirect	@–(Rn)

The behavior of the autobump modes is described as follows, where the bump amount is assumed to be 1.

(Rn)+:   Step 1: ea = Rn;   Step 2: Rn ← Rn plus 1

@(Rn)+:   Step 1: ea = M[Rn];   Step 2: Rn ← Rn plus 1

–(Rn):   Step 1: Rn ← Rn minus 1; Step 2: ea = Rn

@–(Rn):   Step 1: Rn ← Rn minus 1; Step 2: ea = M[Rn]

The address mode field, if 2 through 5, tells us whether to increment or decrement, but does not specify the *bump amount*. How can we determine how much the pointer is bumped? The architecture defines the bump amount based on a "do the right thing" philosophy which we now describe.

The PDP-11 is a 16-bit machine with addressing to the byte. The opcode determines whether the memory operand is a byte or a 16-bit word. For the autoincrement (autodecrement) address modes, the amount of the increment or decrement is 1 or 2 according to whether the operand is a byte or a word respectively. The exception is when stack pointer R6 or program counter R7 are used. The stack and PC use 16-bit words, so the amount of the bump for R6 and R7 is always 2.

Note that in the autobump modes, the value of Rn is incremented *after* its use. In autodecrement, Rn is decremented *before* its use. This is *opposite* to the convention used by Knuth [10]. As a result, when stacks are implemented to facilitate the copy capability, the memory diagram of a PDP-11 stack does not follow the "pencil and paper" rule. (The top of the stack is on the bottom of the diagram.)

The remaining modes (6 and 7) are *indexed* and *indexed indirect*, denoted X(Rn) and @X(Rn) respectively. The two indexed modes use two 16-bit words per instruction, because the 16-bit word following the first instruction word is the full direct address. The index is the value of Rn, which is added to the fda to form the indexed address. The indexed indirect mode adds one level of indirection to the indexed address. The notation "CI" denotes the location of the current instruction. Thus, the fda following the instruction is at location "CI plus 2". (Since the PC is incremented following instruction fetch, the PC actually points to "CI plus

2" at execution time.) We now summarize the indexed modes 6 and 7.

Mode	RTN	
6	X(Rn):	ea = M[CI plus 2] plus Rn
7	@X(Rn):	ea = M[M[CI plus 2] plus Rn]

Use of program counter R7 in the address modes is possible. By PDP-11 convention, whenever R7 is used to acquire a word from memory, R7 is automatically incremented by 2 after a memory read operation. For the instruction fetch phase, this convention ensures that R7 points to the next sequential instruction. However, the convention also holds for operand fetches. The combination of this convention with the selection of R7 as the REG field of the address format gives rise to four useful R7 addressing modes: modes 1, 3, 6 and 7.

Mode 1, Register Indirect, when combined with R7, is renamed *immediate,* and denoted "#n". In immediate mode, the operand value itself follows the instruction.

Mode 3, Autoincrement Indirect, when combined with R7, is renamed *absolute,* and denoted "@#A". In absolute mode, the word following the instruction contains the absolute address of the operand.

The indexed modes 6 and 7 become *relative* and *relative indirect* modes when combined with R7, denoted "A" and "@A" respectively. Recall the indexed modes use location "CI plus 2" as the fda, where CI is the location of the current instruction. Further, R7 is automatically incremented by 2 following the read operation which fetches the fda. Therefore the value in R7 when the relative effective address is computed is "CI plus 4", where CI is the address of the first word of the current instruction.

We now summarize the R7 modes. "CI" denotes the byte address of the current instruction as before. Note that value "CI plus 4" is in R7 at the start of the determination of the effective address (after the fda has been read).

Mode	RTN	
1	#n:	ea = CI plus 2;
3	@#A:	ea = M[CI plus 2]
6	A:	ea = M[CI plus 2] plus CI plus 4.
7	@A:	ea = M[M[CI plus 2] plus CI plus 4].

The PDP-11 also has a number of double-address instructions. These instructions require two 6-bit operand fields. Double-address instructions make it unnecessary for the programmer to bring operands from main memory to the accumulators, operate on their values, and return them to main memory. Rather, the program conceptually processes data directly in main memory with "storage-to-storage" operations. (Of course, the control unit brings the data to the CPU for processing, but this occurs at a conceptual level beneath that of the programmer.) For double-address instructions, the accumulators behave as address pointers.

2.6.3. PACE

The 16-bit PACE architecture of National Semiconductor is an outgrowth of the earlier IMP-16 microcomputer. It has four 16-bit CPU registers or accumulators called AC0, AC1, AC2, and AC3. In some instructions with no register field, AC0 is the implied operand, an example of definition by constraint. The CPU has a 16-bit status register called "Flags".

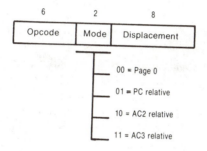

Figure 2.14. *PACE memory-reference instruction format.*

The basic instruction format is shown in **Figure 2.14.** Four address modes are shown; page 0, PC relative, AC2 relative, and AC3 relative. For page 0 addressing, the displacement is generally treated as an 8-bit unsigned positive number between 0 and 255. On the chip, a pin can be wired to change this to words 0 through 127 and words (hexadecimal) X'FF80' through X'FFFF'. The PC-relative mode provides a "floating" relative page which avoids concern about fixed page boundary problems. The AC2 and AC3 relative modes have been called *accumulator relative*, and are similar to PC-relative addressing. In combination with these modes, some opcodes permit one level of indirection. These include Load and Store AC0, Jump, and Subroutine Jump. No automatic bumping capability exists. The architecture permits three "immediate" instructions; Add and Skip on Zero, Load, and Complement and Add. The format for the immediate instructions is shown in **Figure 2.15.**

PACE also has a 10-word stack in the CPU. Generally the stack is not used for operands, but to save return addresses from subroutines or a program interruption. The stack may also store the contents of the Flag register via Push and Pop (Pull) instructions. There is no Copy instruction, but an "Exchange Register and Stack" instruction exists.

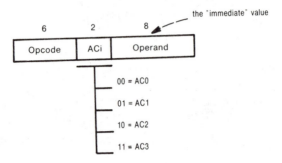

Figure 2.15. *PACE immediate instruction format.*

2.7. PROGRAM SEQUENCING INSTRUCTIONS

The *program sequencing* instructions are used for decision-making operations. Normally, instructions execute sequentially, one after the other. The PC points to the *next sequential instruction,* and is incremented after each instruction. Sometimes the next instruction to be executed is not the next sequential instruction. If this is the case, another address must be specified as the location of the next instruction. This occurs with a *BRANCH* or *JUMP*.

At the computer design level, program sequence control is no more than answering the question "What next?" The answer is the address used in fetching the next instruction. In microprogramming, the next instruction address calculation can be quite complex. In some early computers such as the IBM 650, the current instruction brought along the address of the next instruction.

2.7.1. Target Address for Branching

The effective address of a branch instruction is the *target* of the branch. In general, branch instruction target addresses can be formed in the same manner as operand addresses. In practice, the branch address is generated in less sophisticated ways than the operand address. With a partial address field, the PC-relative technique for the full direct address is popular, and PC-relative with indirection is very popular. Stacks and index registers may also be employed for branch target addresses. These last two techniques are covered in the section on subroutines.

2.7.2. Conditional and Unconditional Branching

The IAS computer had only two program control instructions: the unconditional branch and the branch on accumulator positive. Both used a direct address for the target. The branching capability of today's computers is far more flexible.

A programmer can test many status bits or conditions within the system with a conditional branch instruction. For example, two operands may be compared and generate five branch conditions: (1) equal, (2) greater than, (3) less than, (4) equal to or greater than and (5) equal to or less than. A single operand may be tested for zero, positive, or negative magnitude. Other conditions test status bits on 0 or on 1, or equal (or not equal) to a supplied value. CPU status bits include the carry flip-flop, overflow flip-flop, "ALU zero", "negative result", etc. Like the indirect bit referred to in §§2.5.6, status bits belong to the general class of *flags*. The *state* of the status bit is changed by the operations of "set" (turn on), "clear" (turn off), or "complement". (In contrast, *data* bit *values* are 0 or 1, and are changed by "loading" a new value.)

2.7.3. Condition Codes

In the IBM S/370 architecture, many branch conditions are coalesced and given a unified treatment through the definition of a *condition code* register. Following the execution of data operation instructions such as Add, Subtract, Load Register, Compare, etc., the instruction execution leaves the condition code register in a data-dependent state indicative of the result of the operation. For example, following a Load Register instruction, the condition code indicates whether the value loaded was zero, or negative. A subsequent Branch on Condition instruction can test for a desired condition code bit or bits.

The DEC PDP-11 also uses a condition code register. Basically, four conditions are saved in four status bits: N (negative), C (carry), Z (zero), and V (overflow). Many instructions affect these status bits for subsequent conditional branching purposes.

The PACE architecture incorporates a 4-bit condition field to select one of 16 mutually exclusive conditions for conditional branching. These include: stack full, AC0 is zero, positive, negative, odd, or even, link bit "on", carry, overflow, and interrupt enabled.

2.7.4. Skip Instructions

SKIP is a convenient program control instruction from the architect's viewpoint. (The programmer might prefer a conditional branch.) If a given condition is met, the SKIP causes the PC to be incremented one more time before fetching the next instruction. Thus, the instruction *immediately* following the SKIP is skipped and the *next* one is executed. *No address field is needed.* The redefinition of the address field provides many bits with which to indicate a large number of skip conditions. Skip condition specification is a simple application of the field redefinition technique.

Conditional branching can be done in two instructions with a skip instruction followed by an unconditional branch instruction. This two-instruction technique means that an instruction which contains a branch target address need not have a conditional branch specification (condition) field, thus conserving bits in the instruction format. To raise the conceptual level of the programmer, the assembler could have a conditional branch macroinstruction which generates the proper two machine language instruction sequence. The skip followed by an unconditional branch is useful in implementing program loops. The branch target is the first address of the loop. In some applications of the skip, the skipped instruction is not a branch. For example, the absolute value of a number in the AC can be obtained using a skip instruction as follows. If the AC is positive it is already the absolute value. We let the skip occur if the AC is positive. The skipped instruction complements the accumulator.

Many architectures provide the *indexed skip*. The indexed skip instruction has no condition field, but contains an address field to specify the operand. The address field is usually the same address mode and displacement as for data manipulation instructions. The operand is typically a "loop" index or counter, and is either incremented or decremented. In some architectures, the direction of the bump is fixed (no choice). In the PDP-8, the counter is always incremented. Other architectures provide the indexed skip instruction with a field which defines the direction or amount of the bump. Following the bumping of the counter, if the result is zero, the skip is taken. Otherwise the next instruction is executed. In the loop counter application, the next instruction is a branch back to the beginning of the loop.

The indexed skip can also be used in situations where the next instruction is always executed (never skipped). Consider the application of bumping an indirect pointer. The pointer, being an address, should not go through 0. This example is a secondary and perhaps "tricky" use of the indexed skip instruction. The beginning programmer may be slightly confused when first encountering this application in a program listing, and wonder why the program is mysteriously testing an address for a zero value. The mystery is solved when it becomes clear the program is doing no more than bumping an indirect address. In architectures where the index register is an assigned memory address, the indexed skip instruction can also be used to bump the index value.

2.7.5. Repeat Instructions

Another program control function which appears in some architectures is the *REPEAT*. The instruction specifies that the next, or next two, instructions are to be repeated "n" times, where "n" is the loop count.

Count "n" may be a field in the instruction or in a predefined location. The REPEAT is most useful in architectures whose addressing techniques provide for the concurrent or repeated bumping of pointers or indices. The designer takes advantage of the repeat instruction by saving the memory instruction fetch time on each execution.

2.8. SUBROUTINE CONTROL

The subroutine technique was originally employed to conserve program memory, but experienced programmers use subroutines (or procedures) to structure and organize programs in a top-down fashion. Subroutines are also used for common subprogram segments which are to be performed in various places of the program, and thus serve as bottom-up "super instructions". The subroutine instructions could, of course, be replicated "in line" in the program wherever needed. This, however, is time consuming for the programmer and costly in terms of memory use.

The transfer of program sequence control to the subroutine is known as a subroutine *call* operation. When the subroutine has performed its task, sequence control returns to the calling program by means of a subroutine *return* operation. A subroutine is *called* by an instruction in the *main line* of the program. The *linkage* concerns how to return to the main line program, and is an important part of the execution of the subroutine jump instruction. Once completed, the subroutine must transfer program control back to the main line program *return address* so that the main line program may be resumed. This operation is called the subroutine return.

The call or subroutine jump instruction must provide a *branch* to the subroutine, and must also set up the return linkage. The return linkage function requires that the return address (address of the next main line instruction, usually PC plus 1) be saved, where the call instruction is in location PC. The return address is subsequently used in the subroutine return operation.

Many subroutines operate on data operands, often called *parameters*. For example, a subroutine which calculates the sine of an angle must know the value of the angle whose sine is desired. Parameters are also used to select a subroutine option. Instead of separate routines to calculate sine, cosine and tangent, perhaps the program provides a trigonometric subroutine. The subroutine user can select the calculation desired with a second parameter value. Parameters are *passed* from the main line program to the subroutine by various methods. To complete its job, the subroutine must return a result to the main line program. The method of treating the "parameter passing" and "result returning" is a part of the *linkage convention*. The CPU registers are convenient locations for passing parameters and returning results. An operand stack can also be used: operands are placed on the stack and the result is returned on the stack.

Three techniques for implementing the subroutine linkage are described in the following sections. These techniques differ primarily in where the return address is stored.

2.8.1. The LGP-30 Subroutine Jump (SRJ)

The Librascope LGP-30 was a first generation computer which implemented the return linkage by storing the return address in the branch (target) address. See **Figure 2.16**. The location following the branch address contains the first instruction of the subroutine. The address used by the CPU for storing the return address is incremented and loaded into the PC, which now points to this first instruction. Upon completion of the subroutine, a jump instruction (JMP) with indirect addressing mode returns control to the main line program using the previously stored return address as the indirect pointer. Upon return and resumption of the main line, a subsequent call to the same subroutine will store a different return address in the branch target address, and the indirect jump at the end of the subroutine returns control to the new calling location.

Now consider the passing of parameters to the subroutine. In a technique suited to the LGP-30 subroutine jump, the operands may be stored in main line locations, as shown in **Figure 2.17**. At (1), main line instructions store the operands in consecutive locations following the subroutine jump (SRJ) instruction. At (2), the execution of the SRJ instruction stores the address of the first parameter in the target address. At (3), the subroutine

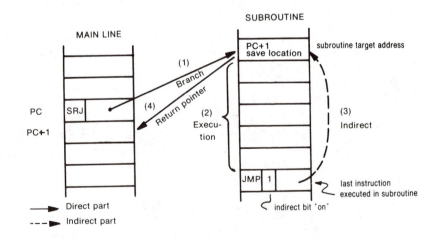

Figure 2.16. *Mechanics of LGP-30 subroutine jump instruction.*

is executed. The subroutine fetches the parameters indirectly through the return address (now used as a pointer) located in the subroutine target address. Following each parameter fetch, the subroutine increments the return address. After fetching the last parameter, the return address refers to the next executable instruction in the main line program, which is where control should be returned. At (4), the subroutine has completed execution and performs the return indirectly through the subroutine target address.

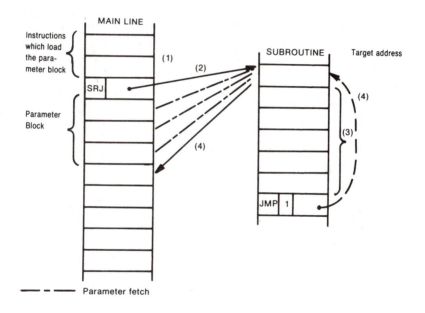

Figure 2.17. *Passing a block of parameters to a subroutine.*

The LGP-30 type of subroutine jump has not been popular in microprocessor architectures. Many microprocessors have subroutines which reside in read-only memory. The target address cannot be written into, but the problem can be circumvented with local memory techniques. Another problem is that the LGP-30 subroutine jump is not good for reentrant subroutines. However, two other means exist for jumping to subroutines.

2.8.2. Branch and Link (BAL)

The IBM 704 computer was a follow-on machine to the IBM 701. Unlike the 701, the IBM 704 provided the programmer with an index register. For the Branch and Link (BAL) instruction, the return address

PC plus 1 is stored in the index register. The branch instruction effective address can be determined in the indexed mode. To return to the main line program, the subroutine branches to full direct address 0, indexed by the return address. The effective address is the return address, and control is returned to the main line. Unless the main program resides in read-only memory, parameters can be passed as in Fig. 2.17, and the index register may be used to advantage in retrieving the parameters. In cases where the subroutine uses indexing, the return address may be saved somewhere else such as in a local variable (a variable whose location is known only to the subroutine.) The BAL instruction type is used in the S/370 architecture, where most of the 16 general-purpose registers may be used to receive the return address. The register so specified is called the *link register.*

In more complex systems, it is not uncommon to have a subroutine call instruction within a subroutine. We refer to subroutines calling other subroutines as *nesting.* Each new call increases the *level* or depth of the nest. Each return decreases the level. For the BAL type of subroutine call, different levels must agree to use distinct link registers, or else each subroutine must save the return address in a local variable.

2.8.3. Subroutine Stack (CALL)

For a call in a subroutine stack architecture, the value PC plus 1 of the main line program is PUSHed on the stack. For a return, the top stack item is POPped and placed in the PC. This scheme favors the nesting of subroutines, because the order of returning from nested subroutines is the inverse of the order in which the subroutines are called. The scheme also works well for reentrant subroutines. A CALL is analogous to "push", and the return is analogous to "pop". If subroutine A calls subroutine B, which calls subroutine C, the calling order is A, B, and C. Upon completion, C returns to B, which returns to A, which returns control to the main line. The order of subroutine return is C, B, and A. The function of a LIFO stack is evident: A, B, and C is the order of pushing items on the stack, and C, B, and A is the order for popping items off the stack.

If instructions are available for manipulating values on the subroutine return stack, the stack data structure can also be used for passing parameters. Such is the case in the PACE architecture. However, because the return address is on the top of the stack on subroutine entry, it is a slight nuisance for the programmer to access the operands. A more powerful approach separates the operand stack from the subroutine return stack.

2.9. INSTRUCTIONS FOR DATA MANIPULATION

The computer performs work for the user by doing functional transformations on data. The ENIAC computer performed ballistics calculations resulting in tables useful in artillery. The payroll calculation function is a typical example of a commercial data processing application. The outcome of the task is an amount for the employee and an amount for the tax collectors. The actual work is accomplished by data manipulation instructions. Program sequence control instructions such as branch and skip do not actually process the data, but provide algorithmic control.

2.9.1. Fixed Point Arithmetic

Small computers tend to have modest arithmetic capabilities. In the PDP-8, the two's complement add (TAD) instruction performs two's complement addition of the AC and the operand. For two's complement addition, the resulting bits are the same as for unsigned (ordinary) binary addition. (The reader is invited to verify this by working a few examples.) Thus the ordinary binary sum of a positive and negative two's complement binary number gives a correct result in the two's complement number system (provided overflow does not occur). The ability to add, to shift, and to complement the AC are the only arithmetic instructions in the PDP-8 (if we do not consider the indexed skip an arithmetic instruction). Subtraction is performed by complementing and incrementing the AC and adding the result to the operand.

Multiplication and division routines may be programmed in any architecture with the capability of adding, subtracting, shifting or rotating right, and testing the value of bits and the carry flip-flop. Some architectures provide multiply and divide instructions. Others follow an intermediate approach with "multiply step" and "divide step" instructions to perform a 1-bit multiply or divide respectively. These instructions are used in a program loop for multiplication and division. The multiply step and divide step instructions imply that the architecture should have a double-length register capable of being shifted and another shiftable register to hold an operand (multiplier or quotient). The AMD Am2903 is a popular "bit-slice" chip, intended for the data flow part of a CPU. This chip was obviously designed with the multiply step and divide step in mind. A control sequencer chip is provided with a "repeat" function to take advantage of the Am2903's multiply and divide steps.

Another arithmetic requirement is the capability to do double or multiple precision arithmetic. 16-bit machines must be able to add and subtract 32-bit signed operands. This requirement is met by propagating any carry or borrow up to the high-order words of the double or multiple precision operands. In the PDP-8, this capability is provided by the Link flip-flop, which may be viewed as being the leftmost bit of the AC. During the TAD instruction, the carry-out is exclusive-ORed with the old Link value to generate the new Link value. To propagate the carry, the Link bit must be tested. If it is "on", a 1 is added to one of the next higher operand words.

Alternatively, a Carry flip-flop can save the carry-out bit, which is added to the next higher-order words. We mention two ways to add the double precision interword carry. (1) The PDP-11 minicomputer has the "Add Carry" reference instruction which adds the value of the carry flip-flop to the designated register. (2) The Intel 8080 architecture provides two separate instructions of the memory-reference class for addition. In the "Add" instruction, the addition is performed normally, which is equivalent to the low-order carry-in being 0. For the "Add with Carry" instruction, the execution is like the Add instruction, except that the Carry flip-flop value is added as well. The IBM 1130, a 16-bit architecture, had an additional (upper accumulator) register and a double precision addition instruction. Programmers find it most convenient when the double precision arithmetic problem is handled by hardware implementation. Double precision arithmetic raises the conceptual level at which the programmer thinks about the program to be written.

2.9.2. Decimal Arithmetic

For some time, the minicomputer field tended to ignore the existence of BCD arithmetic (see Chapter 1) and the convenience of doing some calculations in decimal. Perhaps the use of BCD in hand-held calculators reawakened interest in BCD numbers. Today, some microcomputer architectures are providing a BCD capability. Of course, one approach provides opcodes for the direct addition and subtraction of numbers in BCD form: a "decimal add" instruction. (Some ingenuity may be required to do subtraction.) A more economical approach is to provide an instruction which can *decimal adjust* (or "six-correct") a result. The numbers can be added by performing a binary addition first and the decimal adjust operation next.

In reality, the digital logic to convert a binary adder to a selectable BCD/binary adder is relatively modest. The binary number system is quite capable of effectively handling the decimal integers, but has some limitations in dealing with decimal fractions. It is well known that one can convert fractions to binary, operate on them in binary, reconvert to decimal, and get the wrong answer! The problem lies in the *round-off errors* made during the conversions of fractions. (To avoid problems with fractions when dealing with dollars and cents in a binary machine, the programmer should by all means use common cents!)

The Electronic Arrays EA9002 microprocessor chip had good decimal capabilities without the use of special opcodes. The EA9002 used the technique of *residual control*. (Residual control has been used extensively in microprogrammed CPUs, in particular in the S/360 family.) In the

EA9002, if a decimal status flag is "on", it causes the arithmetic unit to "think" decimal, and all 8-bit Add, Increment, Decrement and Complement instructions, are performed in BCD. Further, if the number 0 (or any other operand) is added to an 8-bit binary integer when decimal mode is "on", the result is correct in BCD provided the result does not exceed 199. (The 100's position is represented by the value of the carry-out.) Clearing the decimal status flip-flop returns the machine to binary mode.

2.9.3. Floating Point Arithmetic

Floating point arithmetic is available in many large machines. A floating point number consists of an exponent and a mantissa. Floating point arithmetic is the normal case in the Burroughs B5000 architecture and its derivatives. A fixed point (integer) number occurs as the special case of a "floating point" number whose exponent is 0.

Many floating point schemes use either a binary or hexadecimal designation for the exponent, and represent the mantissa respectively as a binary or hexadecimal fraction. We feel that since input to, and output from, the computer system is decimal, the use of a decimal system for representing floating point numbers is superior in view of the binary fraction round-off problem. Floating decimal numbers are readily rejected in cost-sensitive systems as a matter of course. However, on a system basis which includes the programming costs over the life of the architecture, implementing floating decimal arithmetic should compensate the slight extra hardware cost.

2.9.4. Data Movement

An important class of data manipulation functions are those which move blocks of storage. The IBM S/370 architecture has a variety of data movement instructions. Data can be moved from left to right, or right to left. In some cases, the source block can overlap the destination block. Block data movement instructions are useful when main memory areas are used for input and output buffers. Output data is moved to an output buffer area, and the output operation can proceed asynchronously with the processing of more data.

2.9.5. Logical Operations

Logical operations are also data manipulation functions. (The term "logical" is derived from the phrase "boolean logic" and does not mean the operations have been particularly well thought out.) Logical operations apply on a bit-by-bit (bit-wise) basis. For the AND operation between two 16-bit operands, the nth bit of the result is the AND of the nth bit of each operand. Boolean functions are useful in at least two instances. The first is to implement programs which simulate digital logic, or which implement algorithms for minimizing boolean functions. In this first use, the data manipulation directly involves two operands. The second use is *bit manipulation,* also known as bit "fiddling" or "twiddling". Individual bits of a status word (flags) are set, cleared or complemented by the respective boolean functions of OR with 1, AND with 0, and exclusive-OR with 1. In each of these cases, one of the operands is a constant. Bit fiddling can also be accomplished by instructions which "set under mask" (or "clear under mask"). The *mask* operand is a string of 0's and 1's. In dealing with individual (flag) bits, the bit value is *on* if it is a 1, and *off* if it is a 0. Only data operand bits whose positions correspond to an "on" mask bit are set (or cleared).

Bit testing is commonly done with a skip instruction requiring no address field. The address field can be redefined to indicate which bit (or bits) are to be tested, and for which state the skip is to take place. Alternatively, the following approach can be used. The word is placed in the AC and ANDed with a constant which has a single 1 in the bit position to be tested. The result in the AC can be tested for the "AC is zero" case. Bit testing may also be done with the shift instructions. The bit to be tested can be shifted to the sign position of the AC (or carry bit) and the AC can be tested for negative status (or for carry set).

Shift instructions are also useful for data "packing" and "unpacking". Often, 4-bit or 6-bit fields are given special meanings in data records. In manipulating fields within a word, the programmer becomes frustrated if there is no place to save the "spill" bits from the shifting operations. (The spill bits are the positions which are shifted out; see Appendix C.) In these instances, a double-word shift is very useful.

2.9.6. Text String Operations

Human-readable input and output consists of character strings or text strings. A character or text symbol is usually represented by an 8-bit byte. A computer program is generated as a text string. Program translation, where *source* code is translated to *object* (machine) code, is an instance of operations on text or character strings. The word processing application of editing reports and documents also utilizes instructions to move character strings and search tables.

In studying architectural advances as incorporated in microprocessor architectures, one of the "surprises" to Brooks [6] was the absence of text string handling instructions.

Another useful instruction, found in the S/370 architecture, is the "Translate and Test" instruction. This instruction searches a character string and delivers the index of the first instance of a given character. If the character is not found, the condition code so indicates. The instruction is useful in searching an input stream to locate delimiters.

Another text string instruction is Translate, which performs a table look-up function on each character of the source string. The first operand address points to the source string and the second address points to a look-up table. Each 8-bit source string symbol is treated as a look-up table offset, and is replaced by its corresponding value in the look-up table.

2.10. REGISTER-REFERENCE INSTRUCTIONS

One class of instructions, called register-reference, involves only a single operand, usually the accumulator (AC). Since a memory reference is not required, the operand specification field is redefined to indicate the desired operation on the AC (or other CPU register).

Operations on an accumulator (or a general-purpose register) include taking the radix or radix-minus-one complement, clearing to zero, incrementing or decrementing, setting all bits to 1 or 0, decimal adjusting, shifting (with many options), exchanging values with an index register, and adding the Carry flip-flop value.

The redefined instruction field used for specifying the desired register-reference operation may itself be subdivided into mutually exclusive fields. Each field can define independent *microorders*. The PDP-8 architecture followed this approach and made many operations available to the programmer. For example, the AC is set to all 1's by first clearing the AC with an order in one instruction field, and then complementing the AC with an order in a second field. The action in the second field is performed later in the cycle of the same instruction.

2.11. THE INTERRUPTION OF PROGRAMS

First generation machine architectures did not provide the capability to *interrupt* a running program. Today the interrupt concept has been highly developed and is a convenient method to coordinate or synchronize external events or IO devices. Interrupts also measure the passage of time (timer interrupt) and notify the system program of a failure or error condition (machine check interrupt). A program interruption is defined as the *execution of a set of instructions not in the normal sequence.* (The answer to the "What next?" question is an unexpected intruder.) In the absence of an interrupt, the PC defines the normal sequence. If an interrupt occurs, the address of the interrupt sequence needs to be put into the PC by some means.

2.11.1. Interrupt Acceptance and Clearance

The computer *accepts* an interrupt when the CPU control unit saves the "old" ("What next?") PC value as a return address, and uses the out-of-sequence (interrupt) address to fetch the next instruction. In other words, a branch is "forced" with the *interrupt address* as the target. This is done by special hardware and is not of direct concern to the programmer. The hardware must be made to provide the address at which the programmer inserted the interrupt routine. The interrupt address contains the first instruction of an *interrupt handler* program or *interrupt service routine*. An interrupt handler is that portion of the system software which accepts the interrupt and determines the cause of the interrupt. Once the cause is determined, control passes to the interrupt service routine belonging to the cause. After the service routine treats the cause, the interrupt is *cleared*.

Upon termination of the interrupt service routine, the saved value of the PC is restored, and the interrupted program continues where it left off. An interrupt is very similar to a subroutine jump. In fact, in many architectures, saving the old PC is done expediently; the first instruction in the interrupt handler is a subroutine jump instruction which automatically saves the contents of the PC register (old PC).

The transfer of control by an interrupt is more complicated than a subroutine jump because more than the PC must be saved. Consider a program which has performed an addition and is about to test the value of the Carry latch when interrupted. The interrupt handler must save the Carry latch value. Otherwise, when the interrupted program is resumed, it may take the wrong branch because of the change in the environment. The next subsection treats this problem.

2.11.2. The Processor State and Context Switching

The program executes in an *environment* which includes the state of all the registers (AC, accumulators, index register, PC, etc.) and status (Carry bit, overflow bit, and any other bits such as flags, condition code, etc.). This information is called the *processor state*.

At the end of the execution of one instruction, the processor state provides the *context* for the execution of the next instruction. An interrupt changes the execution environment and constitutes a *context switch,* whereby the old processor state must be saved. Prior to resuming the interrupted program, the processor state must be restored. One common solution to this problem is to provide instructions to store all processor state data. A software convention may require the interrupt handler to save the processor state before doing anything else. The interrupt handler must not use any unsaved register, or modify any status of the interrupted program's processor state. In the IBM S/370 architecture, the Program Status Word (PSW) consists of the PC, condition code, and other status items. The processor state consists of the PSW, 16 general registers, and 4 floating point registers. The S/370 architecture automatically saves (restores) the PSW upon acceptance (clearance) of an interrupt. Thus the interrupt handler is only concerned with saving and restoring the registers.

2.11.3. The Trap

Once the interrupt concept became well known, architects discovered that interrupts could be employed to solve a class of vexing problems. When two numbers are added, the result may be too large to be represented in the number of bits available. *Overflow* results. (Overflow can also happen in floating point operations if the exponent becomes too large to be represented. *Underflow* occurs when floating point operations generate a result whose exponent is too negative to be represented.) Overflow can be handled by defining an overflow flip-flop and setting it when overflow occurs. The programmer must test the overflow latch. Similarly, one can require the programmer to test a divisor for the "0" value before attempting to divide. An alternative solution to problems such as these, which are data-dependent, is to provide for a synchronous interrupt, called a *trap*. In contrast to interrupts from external events, which can occur asynchronously with the running program, traps are repeatable and occur synchronously with the program. The same program running on the same data will trap on the same exceptional condition at the same place and time in the program.

The architecture of larger systems provides for a supervisor, monitor, or executive program to control certain system resources such as the peripheral devices. In this case, the trap concept can be employed to call the supervisor program, and the supervisor program in effect becomes the interrupt handler. Some second generation architectures (Westinghouse Prodac 580, SDS 941, Ferranti ATLAS) caused the unimplemented opcodes to trap to a handling routine. These "illegal" opcodes (called "psuedo ops" or "extracodes") were actually subroutine calls to the supervisor. In ATLAS, extracodes corresponded to fixed subroutines in a read-only memory, and performed functions such as the calculation of sine or cosine. In other systems, the pseudo ops were precursors to the supervisor call instructions which handle privileged operations such as input and output functions.

2.12. IO INSTRUCTIONS

Input and output (IO) operations transfer data between peripheral devices and main memory. In a typical application, the programmer will cause data to be brought into main memory. When in memory, the data can be manipulated. Subsequently, the program will have data to transfer from main memory to a peripheral device such as a printer. In order to coordinate the proper transfer of data, the programmer must be aware of how the device is to be controlled. For example, following the reading of data from a reel of magnetic tape, the programmer may wish to cause the tape to be rewound. Communicating this desire to the tape control unit involves *control* or *command* information (as opposed to data). When a device control unit receives an information word from the CPU, it is essential that the IO architecture provide some means to distinguish ordinary data words from control or command words.

It may also be necessary to acquire status information from the device. For example, before reading the first punched card from a card reader, the program should check the "ready" status to make sure the operator has placed the card deck in the read hopper. This is an instance where *status* rather than input data is transferred from the device to the program. Four kinds of transfers are indicated: data in, data out, status in and control out. The architect should provide ways to treat these different transfers conveniently. When the same data bus is used to convey four kinds of information, then an *information discrimination* problem exists. This problem is easily solved if the bus has a *tag* field which accompanies the information.

Another technique for data discrimination at the device is to assign more than one address to each device. This technique is available to designs which fail to provide control tags. Data received by the device through one of its addresses can be interpreted differently from data received through another address. Typically, one address is used to transmit control information, and another for the data bytes of a block transfer.

2.12.1. Special–Purpose Programmed Transfers

Because of their inherent simplicity, the IO instructions of an early (second generation) computer, the IBM 1401, are briefly described. The 1401 was character-oriented and dealt primarily with commercial operations called "unit record" processing. The "unit record" is the 80 column punched card (one card = one record).

The IO technique of the IBM 1401 was *special-purpose*. For example, the 1401 opcode "1" caused the card in the card reader to be read, and the input data placed in locations 1 through 80 of the 1401 main memory. The programmer was given no choice of the input buffer location, as locations 1-80 of main memory were *dedicated* to the card reader input. The next instruction in the program was not executed until the card had been read. No overlapping of IO operations with computing was envisioned. Actually, the card had already been read and the data was waiting in a buffer in the card reader control unit. The "read card" command not only transferred the data, but also initiated the reading of the next card contents to the card reader's buffer. The first card was buffered when the operator depressed the "Ready" button.

The dedicated buffer concept also applied to the card punch and the printer of the 1401 system. Magnetic tape and disk used a programmer-defined buffer. In all cases, each IO instruction transferred a full record or a block of characters. The next instruction was not executed until the entire transfer had taken place. This method is quite simple to understand.

2.12.2. General-Purpose Programmed Transfers

Requiring a special-purpose interface to the device is an expensive disadvantage of special-purpose IO instructions. It is also difficult to add new devices to the system without changing the instruction set. Thus, flexibility is lost. Today, most small computers use generalized IO instructions and a general-purpose IO interface bus. The IO instructions have an address field which indicates the particular device for which the instruction is intended. The *device address* is sometimes called a *select code*. The address field of the IO instruction determines the device address space. Systems with an 8-bit device address permit 256 device addresses.

In the simplest case, the programmed IO transfers take place through the CPU registers (e.g. the AC), one data word at a time. This approach is more difficult for the programmer, but the computer designer's task is easier and the logic circuit cost is low. The programmer must control the device itself as well as control the data transfers. Thus the programmer needs a way to read device status and to pass control information (a control word) to the device. The bits of a control word may take on an individual significance (as 1-bit fields), depending on the device. The same applies to the device status word: the meanings of status bits are device-dependent.

When transferring a block of data between devices and main memory, the program must determine when the device is available to accept the next data transfer. Typically, there is a one-word register at the device (or at its interface logic) which serves as a data buffer. On input operations, the program reads the data buffer contents and clears a "Busy" flag. On output operations, when the data buffer is empty, the device is "Not Busy". The program loads the data buffer register with the next word, and the flag shows "Busy" until the device disposes of the buffer register contents. (Sometimes the flag may be called "Ready", with "Busy" corresponding to "Not Ready".)

The HP2100 computer provides an example of a simple programmed IO scheme. IO instructions use a CPU register (A or B register) as the source or destination register for the CPU side of the transfer. The device address is specified by a 6-bit Select Code in the instruction. As the data bus is common to all devices, the value of the Select Code on the device address bus distinguishes the using device. Each device decodes its own Select Code. The HP2100 has two IO input instructions, LIA and LIB (one for each of the A and B registers), which cause the addressed device to place a data word on the IO data bus (IODATABUS). The data word is loaded to the A or B register at the CPU. SC denotes the value of the Select Code, and DATA[SC] denotes the value in the data register of the selected device.

$$\text{LIA: } A \leftarrow \text{IODATABUS} = \text{DATA[SC]}$$
$$\text{LIB: } B \leftarrow \text{IODATABUS} = \text{DATA[SC]}$$

Two output instructions OTA and OTB cause the data word in A or B to be placed on the IO data bus. The value on the IO data bus is received by the data buffer register of the addressed device. The RTN statements are:

$$\text{OTA: } \text{DATA[SC]} \leftarrow \text{IODATABUS} = A$$
$$\text{OTB: } \text{DATA[SC]} \leftarrow \text{IODATABUS} = B$$

The IO architecture must also provide for the synchronization (coordination or control) of the data transfer. For example, the programmer may wish to have a program loop which reads a new data word from the device for each trip through the loop. It is undesirable to read the old data word under the belief that it is a new word; the data transfers must be coordinated. In the HP2100, synchronization is done through *Flag* and *Control* flip-flops at each device. The programmer can set and clear the Flag and Control flip-flops with Instructions STC, CLC, STF, and CLF. When set, the Control flip-flop is a "start" signal to the device. When cleared, the Control flip-flop is a "halt" signal. The Flag flip-flop is used for coordinating data transfers, and behaves as a "ready" signal. The device can only set Flag when some condition is met signalling the end of a device-dependent operation. The programmer can test the status of the device with two Skip on Flag instructions: SFS (if Flag is set) and SFC (if Flag is clear). A typical data word input operation to register A is as follows:

1. Set Control (STC) and clear Flag (CLF). This initiates an input operation for the device.
2. Skip on Flag (SFS) and loop back until Flag is set, signifying input data is ready.
3. Flag is set. Read in data word with LIA instruction and clear Flag with CLF.

An output operation is similar, except the CPU first transfers output data to the device (with OTA or OTB) before starting the device with STC.

These instructions lack the ability to transfer device-dependent control (or status) information. However, the IO data bus is 16 bits wide. If the device operates on a character basis, the unused bits can become a "tag" field to convey control or command information. Alternately, control information can be time-dependent, such as the first data output or input following a "start" (STC) instruction.

If the IO architecture only provides a means to identify the direction of data transfer, then ingenuity is required when sending command words and receiving status words. The information discrimination problem can be solved by using unique addresses for control words. In this approach, a single device is assigned more than one device address or select code. Only one of the addresses is used for data. The Intel 8080 microprocessor has two programmed IO instructions, appropriately called "IN" and "OUT". The device address of eight bits provides for 256 devices, sufficient to permit each device to have multiple addresses. On input, the Intel 8080 places the device address on the address bus, and activates the IN strobe. The device, upon recognizing its address, places data on the data bus.

The Data General NOVA computer incorporates an information discrimination technique based on tag signals. The architecture defines three registers A, B, and C at each device. The programmer has instructions for outputting and inputting to or from each of the A, B, or C registers in the device. At the interface bus level, the device receives information as to what to do on six mutually exclusive tag lines (to or from A, B, or C). The assignment of these registers to data, status, and control is a device-dependent function defined by the host software as distinguished from the host architecture.

In programmed IO, it is customary for the CPU to wait on the IO device, so the system progresses at the slower IO speed. The CPU processes data, then waits for an IO transfer. It is interesting to contrast the general-purpose programmed transfers to the method used by the IBM 1401. The 1401 IO data transfers were between buffer areas of the IO devices and buffer areas of main memory, conceptually bypassing the CPU registers. The 1401 waited until the transfer was done before continuing the CPU program. Following a block transfer from the card reader, the reader's device buffer was automatically being refilled with the contents of the next card. Thus the 1401 achieved the overlap of CPU processing of the last card (in the memory input buffer) with the reading of the next card (to the device buffer).

Most general-purpose programmed transfers use CPU registers. Programmed IO requires the programmer to use memory-reference instructions to move data from or to main memory. The programmer is further burdened by the need to handle each data word in a block. Also, the programmer must use "skip on flag" instructions to coordinate the transfer between successive data words. Such a technique is called the *busy wait,* because the CPU is not idle or halted, but no data is processed until the flag being tested changes state.

In *overlapped IO,* the system attempts to overlap waiting on an IO transfer with further CPU processing. Of course, if the program has data to process during an IO wait, the general-purpose programmed IO technique is still flexible enough to permit the overlap of processing with the IO wait.

While transferring a record of information between a device such as a magnetic tape drive, and the CPU, the transfer is time-critical, and the CPU must handle its part of the data transfer within a time constraint. The time constraint is due to the speed of the physical motion of the tape across the read-write head, and the inability to interrupt this motion in the middle of a record without loss of data. If data is not picked up (delivered) at the tape drive when needed, the resulting loss of data is called *overrun.* If the CPU program is otherwise busy when the read-write head is in the middle of an active tape record (being read or written), the device must be serviced when it is ready for the next data word transfer. In the next section, it is seen that the interrupt technique permits CPU-IO overlap by relieving the CPU from the wasteful "busy-wait" loop. A rapid response to an IO device in need of service is handled by interrupting the data processing program.

2.13. SYNCHRONIZATION BY INTERRUPTS

2.13.1. The Interrupt Enable Bit

To control the interrupt system, some architectures make use of a set of CPU control flip-flops called the "interrupt enable" word (or mask). Each bit of the interrupt enable word corresponds to a device. An external event at the device generates an *interrupt request* signal. With the interrupt bit enabled (on, or unmasked) for a given device, the CPU receives the interrupt request. An interrupt request is typically the indication of readiness for the next data transfer. In the HP2100, setting the device Flag flip-flop corresponds to an interrupt request. If a device's interrupt enable bit is off, the CPU does not receive the interrupt request. The request must wait until the enable bit is turned on.

2.13.2. Single-Level Interrupt Systems

If the main CPU program is running when an interrupt request is received, the interrupt is accepted and the running program is interrupted immediately. If another device has already interrupted the main program, what happens next depends upon the architecture. In a multilevel system, the higher-priority device gains the CPU. Thus a slow paper tape reader can interrupt a low-level program, and then the high-speed disk can interrupt the paper tape reader.

If the system has a *single-priority level,* also called a single level of interrupt, then only one interrupt is allowed at a time. Thus if one device's interrupt service routine is running, the interrupt enable bit is off, and an interrupt from a second device must wait (the interrupt is deferred). Single-priority level schemes are in one of two mutually exclusive states: not interrupted (level 0) or interrupted (level 1). In level 1, all interrupt requests are deferred until the priority system returns to level 0. Single-level systems are inherently simple, and only one processor state needs to be saved at a time. Simple machines usually save only the value of the PC at the time the interrupt is accepted. Control returns to level 0, and any interrupts generated while in level 1 are said to be *pending* or outstanding. Only one of the pending interrupts can be selected first for servicing. The policy for choosing the first pending interrupt is resolved by a "static" priority mechanism. The PDP-8 CPU handles the static priority by a software *polling* routine. The PDP-8 interrupt handler executes a "Skip on Flag" instruction in search of a device whose Flag flip-flop is set. (The interrupt is caused by the OR of individual device Flag flip-flops.) The program segment which successively examines flags is called a *skip chain.* When the interrupting device is found, the interrupt handler branches to the device's service routine. The order of static priority is the order in which the device addresses are polled in the skip chain.

A more expensive technique uses a digital logic priority network. The programmer is provided with an IO instruction which requests the interrupting device to place its device address on the IO data bus. The priority network ensures that only the highest priority requesting device answers this request.

In some architectures, the highest-priority interrupting device presents the CPU with the address of its interrupt service routine. Such an architecture has a *vectored interrupt* system, where the vector is the address of the interrupt service routine. Vectored systems can also be implemented by a vectoring table. In such systems, CPU control logic uses the device address as a table offset to access an instruction from main memory. This is a subroutine jump instruction which saves the value of the PC. If a vectoring table is used, the device need not remember the address of its interrupt service routine.

2.13.3. Multilevel Priority Schemes

Multilevel schemes are similar, except that an interrupt request at a higher level can interrupt a handler running at a lower level. The multilevel schemes tend to be more complicated, particularly if several devices are placed on one level. A popular scheme, generally called *vectored priority interrupt,* combines the multilevel priority scheme with the vectored interrupt technique.

The interrupt capability allows the computer to respond to requests in real time. An interrupt scheme facilitates the overlap of CPU processing with device data transfers: the CPU program is freed from periodically testing device Flag flip-flops. Multilevel priority schemes quickly divert the CPU program to the most time-critical task to be handled. Typically the device most likely to overrun is given the highest priority.

2.13.4. Applications other than Device Servicing

Once implemented, the interrupt scheme can be employed for other ends. One common application is the "power fail" interrupt. The CPU plugs in to a power outlet in the building. The incoming power alternates at 50 or 60 Hz (cycles per second). A power failure can be detected within a half cycle. The CPU's own power supply usually has enough energy stored to sustain operation for a few tens of milliseconds. Since the memory cycle is on the order of microseconds, an interrupt service routine can save the "state" of the computation in nonvolatile storage, or switch to battery backup power. Upon restoration of power, the system can recover where it was interrupted.

Another application is the "machine check" or "processor check" interrupt. These interrupts are caused by the detection of bad parity or an error in the arithmetic unit. The service routine may determine the running program and leave an indication of the problem on the console.

Note that the interrupt concept *supplements* but does not replace programmed IO transfers. Once an interrupt is accepted, programmed IO instructions are used to transfer data words, control words and status words across the IO bus. In particular, the programmer is not relieved of using memory-reference instructions to transfer data words in and out of main memory. The next section offers a solution to this problem.

2.14. DIRECT MEMORY ACCESS (DMA)

The DMA concept, or *cycle-stealing,* relieves the programmer of handling each word in a data *block transfer.* Here, a block is a sequence of data words in memory. The DMA technique requires programmed control word transfers to *set up* the DMA unit or channel for the transfer of the block of words. The DMA unit uses the program interrupt to indicate the termination of the block transfer.

Before describing the DMA technique, we introduce some terminology. The transfer does not disturb the CPU registers; conceptually there is a path from the IO device to the main memory. The path is often called a *DMA port,* a data channel, or a DMA bus. A portion of main memory is designated as the *IO buffer* for the data block involved in the transfer. The DMA unit must know the main memory IO buffer's *starting address* and its size. The size is called the *count* and indicates the number of data words in the block.

When a block transfer between a device and main memory is taking place, both the CPU and the DMA unit can request a main memory cycle at the same time. If the main memory can only service one request, it resolves the conflict by granting the cycle to the DMA unit. The CPU is caused to wait. Thus the DMA unit "steals" one or more cycles from the CPU. In a DMA operation, programmed IO instructions set up (initialize) the DMA unit with the direction of the transfer, the starting address pointer, and the count. The DMA unit transfers the block one data word at a time by cycle-stealing. For each data word transferred, the address pointer and count are bumped appropriately until the count reaches zero. Upon completion, the DMA unit generates an interrupt request to the CPU.

DMA operations are *more efficient* than programmed IO transfers. It is faster to "steal" one memory cycle per data word than to interrupt the CPU program, save the PC, run the interrupt handler, and resume the interrupted program. The HP2100 provides two DMA channels, which are software assignable (via control bits) to peripheral devices. Each channel has its own address pointer and count register and the means to request a memory cycle. When the cycle has been granted, the DMA channel presents memory with the address, transfers the data word to or from the IO bus, and updates the count.

In contrast to the HP2100, for Data General NOVA computers any device may perform DMA (Data Channel) operations. However, to do DMA operations on the NOVA bus, the device must have the appropriate control logic for manipulating the address pointer and the count register. The programmer loads these registers with the programmed IO instructions, using the A, B, or C registers at the device. The device activates the Data Channel Request (DCRQ) signal when it wants a transfer. The memory unit responds with an acknowledgement. The device next places the memory address pointer on the 16-bit bidirectional IO data bus, which the memory unit copies. The device removes the address, freeing the same IO data bus for the data part of the transfer. The CPU waits when it wants to use memory and a data channel transfer is underway. One data transfer is made for each Data General DMA transfer, and the device updates the count. This procedure, beginning with a new data channel request, is followed for each data word. When the last data word has been transferred, the device activates the program interrupt to the CPU.

2.15. MEMORY-MAPPED IO

Memory-mapped IO employs addresses in the memory address space for device addresses. The device address space coincides with a portion of the memory address space. The technique has many names, including phantom IO, or implicit IO. Memory-mapped IO occurs primarily in single bus architectures. With memory addresses recognized as device addresses, ordinary memory-reference instructions can be used to transfer data between devices and the CPU. When the architecture provides explicit opcodes for the programmed IO instructions, the term *explicit IO* is sometimes used.

Many microcomputers use memory-mapped IO. In *single bus* systems, the same data bus transfers data words between the CPU and main memory and also between main memory and IO devices. See **Figure 2.18**. Using a single data bus for memory and IO does not of itself imply memory-mapped IO. The Intel 8080 is one microprocessor which does not use memory-mapped IO, but can still use a single data and address bus. In the Intel 8080, a device address is distinguishable from a program memory address by the use of distinct control tags for each. In memory-mapped systems, only the address itself distinguishes memory addresses from device addresses. A designer can choose to do memory-mapped IO with the 8080, but is not obligated to. The 8080 has mutually exclusive tag signals to distinguish an IO data transfer from a memory transfer so the device address space can be made distinct from the memory address space. Memory-mapped IO has the limitation that only memory address space exists, with certain addresses assigned to devices. All data transfers on the bus follow the memory operation protocol. Since the memory-mapped technique was first employed in the PDP-11 system, we now describe the PDP-11 scheme as an example.

The PDP-11 architecture uses a common system bus called the *Unibus*. The system provides 18 bits of memory address. Memory is addressed to the byte, allowing for a maximum memory capacity of 256K bytes or 128K 16-bit words. (Chapter 4 treats the use of a 16-bit pointer where an 18-bit address is required.) The high-order 4K words are reserved for device addresses. Each real device possesses more than one address and each address assigned has a special meaning. Bus transfers are initiated by a

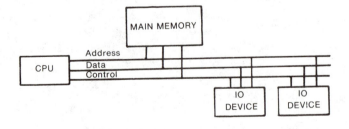

Figure 2.18. *A single bus system.*

unit requesting a bus cycle from the bus *arbiter*. The requesting unit becomes the bus master when granted the bus. The bus master places an address on the address bus, and indicates the direction of transfer (to or from the master). The addressed unit is the slave, and either delivers data to, or removes data from, the data bus. The master is usually the CPU, and the slave is usually main memory. However, the scheme readily permits DMA because a DMA unit can request a bus cycle and transfer data to or from main memory. Program instructions can load specific addresses in the designated high-order 4K-word area of the memory space in order to initialize a DMA unit.

The memory-mapped IO concept is relatively independent of the program interrupt concept, so it may coexist with the common interrupt architectures. One potential disadvantage of memory-mapped IO is that an undebugged program may write into the designated 4K-byte IO area and produce some surprising results.

2.16. THE CONSOLE OR FRONT PANEL

2.16.1. Physical and Human Factor Considerations

The console or front panel may be viewed as an input-output device. The computer operator communicates with the computer through the console. The console functions are used to operate and maintain the computer. These functions typically use switches, pushbuttons or keyboards for input, and lights, display panels, or cathode ray tubes (CRTs) for output. Although comprising relatively few logic circuits, these functions are quite important. The console is a part of the man-machine interface; its design must take into account the fact that inexperienced people will be using it. Pushbuttons can be pushed in unexpected ways.

It is important to be able to read and write main memory from the console, particularly during maintenance and debugging operations. To load memory, the operator must specify an address and data. The first data word read from the switches or keyboard is a value for the address register. The keyboard can be used to specify the data value to be loaded to memory. Since the user may wish to load a block of sequential data this way, the address register should be bumped automatically after each usage. The address bumping principle also holds for displaying memory, where the data word is displayed in lights. It is also desirable to be able to load and display the CPU registers from the console.

2.16.2. The Initial Program Load (IPL)

Another required function is called "initial program load" (IPL). In the IPL function, a loader program is brought to memory. This function is often called *bootstrapping,* and the initial loader program is called a *bootstrap.* Of course, manual entry is the most tedious way to enter the loader. Some systems have a read-only memory which contains the bootstrap. The bootstrap can be selected by a switch, or can be a permanent part of the memory space (as are some monitor and debugger programs for microprocessors). A more sophisticated solution selects an "IPL device" and causes the control unit to load a record from that device. The IBM 1130 used the punched card reader to load memory from the device. The floppy disk had its origins as an IPL device for some IBM S/370 CPUs.

2.16.3. The HALT State and Address Stopping

For small computers, programs must be halted and then restarted. Two methods are generally available: (1) a halt (wait) instruction in the program, and (2) a halt button on the console. In the halted state, the program context or processor state retains its value, unless changed by console functions. A function called *single-step* is available. Here, the CPU executes one instruction and halts. The operator can examine the registers to determine what happened. An extremely useful function for debugging programs is the *address stop.* A *stop address* is set into the console switches. In address stop mode, the control unit enters the halt state when the machine attempts to execute the instruction at the stop address. Normally, the undebugged program is loaded, and the address stop is used to run the program quickly through the debugged initial portion, to arrive at the place in the program suspected of the bug. The machine is then single-stepped through the suspicious portion of the program.

Some computers provide a "wait" as well as a "halt". In the wait state, the interrupt handlers and DMA channels are allowed to run, permitting pending interrupts to be serviced, and IO operations to run to completion. This is distinguished from a "hard stop" halt, where the CPU central clock is, for all practical purposes, stopped.

2.17. MULTIPROGRAMMING CONSIDERATIONS

The concept of *multiprogramming* was explored in the late second generation systems [11, 12]. In multiprogramming, more than one program or task is in a state of execution at one time. When the running program must wait for an external operation such as an input-output operation, the operating system can suspend it and activate another program. The operation is called a *task switch.* The operating system saves the processor state of one task and activates another program by restoring its processor state.

In multiprogrammed systems, either the application programs must be very well-behaved, or the operating system must be able to protect the system from being "clobbered" by an undebugged program. Protective mechanisms are a part of the architectural definition of systems intended for multiprogramming. (Obviously, an application program executing the HALT instruction should not stop the entire system.) One of the early multiprogrammed systems was STRETCH, where four architectural entities facilitated multiprogramming [11]:

1. flexible interrupt system,
2. timer and timer interrupts,
3. memory protection, and
4. interpretive console.

The flexible interrupt system provided the operating system with the ability to determine the completion of all IO tasks. The interrupt system made it possible to operate input-output channels concurrently with the CPU. The "trap" technique detected such program data errors as dividing by zero.

The operating system could impose time limits with the timer interrupt. The system could ensure that the application program was not in an "endless" loop. The operating system also used the timer to allocate the CPU resource to a particular program no more than one "time slice" at a time.

The memory protection system ensured that no program could store data outside of its assigned locations. The *base and bound* technique was employed. Each program was assigned a lower and an upper bound on the memory addresses available to it.

The interpretive console was treated as an IO device, and did not have a fixed assignment to the bits and switches. The console was programmable. A console-defining routine of the operating system assigned the meanings.

A subsequent notion, not present in the STRETCH instruction set, but which has become very important for multiprogrammed systems, is that of *privileged* instructions. An operating system must control all the system resources properly; it must not permit user programs to execute IO instructions. The memory protection system should not be subject to change by a user program. Privileged instructions can only be executed for a program which is in *supervisor mode*. They include the IO instructions, and all instructions which can alter the state of the memory protection or interrupt system.

The operating system treats the CPU, memory, and IO devices as *resources* which it *allocates* to users as needed. To accomplish this, two instruction types are included in the IBM S/370 instruction set. The first is the "Supervisor Call" (SVC) instruction, made by a user program to request anything requiring a privileged instruction. Thus, if a user program needs to write a data record to a storage device, the program makes that fact known by executing an SVC instruction. Of course, the operating system must provide a linkage convention similar to subroutine calls to pass the parameters and return the results.

The second instruction in S/370 is the "Test and Set" (TS) instruction. This instruction implements a "semaphore" between cooperating tasks, or can be used to share a resource that is available to only one task at a time. The TS instruction "queues" users to such a resource. The instruction operand is called a "lock byte". When the TS instruction is executed, the lock byte is retrieved from memory and restored as a "1111 1111" in one *uninterruptible* memory operation. The TS instruction sets information into the condition code to inform the program of the value of the sign bit. If the sign bit is "off", then the resource is free and the condition code is "00". If the sign bit is "on", then the resource is busy and the condition code is "01".

2.18. SUMMARY

Instruction set design can be somewhat "fun", in the sense that designing or solving a crossword puzzle can be fun. The problem offers ample opportunity to be creative or original. However, the task is not without its pitfalls. Most successful designs are carried out by two or three people. A "committee" approach may run into the danger of incorporating too many "pet" ideas. Designers are sometimes *unaware* of what the programmer requires, or of techniques used by competitors for providing more powerful features at little extra expense. For example, when autoincrement and autodecrement are provided, it is advantageous as well as trivial to do the pointer manipulation in such a way that the programmer can implement a stack data structure conveniently. Machines doing character manipulation, or handling floating point numbers, or converting character information to or from 4-bit decimal digits, should possess a double word shift capability (or other facilities for packing and unpacking data).

Unfortunately, designers sometimes create an "overly rich" instruction set. Good assembler language programmers write straightforward, easily understood programs which make very little use of exotic instructions. Compiler-generated code uses perhaps less than half of the available instructions in a sophisticated architecture. Small computers with a large number of opcodes must not be presumed to be superior by that fact alone. A danger exists if instruction sets are inflated inconsistently, unnecessarily increasing complexity and decreasing understandability. Inconsistency encourages programmer errors. Many programmers would prefer a flexible and consistent memory addressing capability to the use of more powerful opcodes.

PROBLEMS

2.1. In architectures whose address modes include both register addressing and a partial direct address, we note that the pda field is unused in register addressing mode. In such architectures can the pda be used to bump Rn? How?

2.2. Some higher-level languages have a "DO CASE" instruction. Relate "DO CASE" to preindexed address formation.

2.3. Not all stack algorithms need follow the "pencil and paper" rule. Discuss the case when the stack grows toward the lower addresses.

2.4. Suppose a printer is provided with a new capability (perhaps to print lines of eight characters per inch in addition to an existing capability to print six characters per inch). Discuss the IO commands needed to invoke the new feature. Suppose such commands have been defined. What else must be done before the user can print documents at eight characters per inch?

REFERENCES

1. F. P. Brooks, Jr., "The Future of Computer Architecture", *Proc. IFIP Congress,* New York, 1964, 87-91.
2. H. G. Cragon, "An Evaluation of Code Space Requirements and Performance of Various Architectures", *Computer Architecture News,* v. 7, n. 5, February 1979, 5-21.
3. A. Burks, H. Goldstine, and J. von Neumann, "Preliminary Discussion of the Logical Design of an Electronic Computing Instrument", in John von Neumann, *Collected Works,* vol. 5, Macmillan, New York, 1963, 34-79. (See also *Datamation,* September 1962, 24-31 and October 1962, 36-41).
4. G. Estrin, "The Electronic Computer at the Institute for Advanced Study", *Math. Tables and Other Aids to Computation,* v. 7, 1953, 108-114.
5. R. R. Everett, "The Whirlwind I Computer", *Rev. Electron. Digital Computers,* Joint AIEE-IRE Computer Conference, Philadelphia, PA, December 10-12, 1951, 70-74. Published as AIEE Special Publication S-44, 1952.
6. F. P. Brooks, Jr., "An Overview of Microcomputer Architecture and Software", *Proceedings of Second Euromicro Symposium on Microprocessing and Microprogramming,* North-Holland Publishing, Amsterdam, 1976, 1-3a, (Invited Keynote Address).
7. F. P. Brooks, Jr., "Mass Memory in Computer Systems", *IEEE Trans. on Magnetics,* Vol. MAG-5, No. 3, September 1969, 635-639.
8. A. Osborne, *An Introduction to Microprocessors,* v. 1, Osborne and Associates, Berkeley, CA, 1976.
9. J. L. Keedy, "More on the Use of Stacks in the Evaluation of Expressions", *Computer Architecture News,* v. 7, n. 8, June 1979, 18-22.
10. D. Knuth, *Fundamental Algorithms,* Second Edition, Addison-Wesley, Reading, MA, 1973.
11. W. Buchholz (Ed.), *Planning a Computer System,* McGraw-Hill, New York, 1962.
12. N. Lourie et. al., "Arithmetic and Control Techniques in a Multiprogram Computer", *Proc. AFIPS,* vol. 16, EJCC 1959, 75-81.

ADDITIONAL REFERENCES

Harry Katzan, Jr., *Computer Organization and the S/370,* Van Nostrand Reinhold, 1971.
Peter Freeman (Ed.), *Software Systems Principles: A Survey,* Science Research Associates,

Palo Alto, CA, 1975 (Chapter 2).

C. G. Bell and W. D. Strecker, "Computer Structures: What have We Learned from the PDP-11?", *Proc. 4th Symposium on Computer Architecture,* IEEE Press, 1975.

P. F. Conklin and D. P. Rodgers, "Advanced Minicomputer Designed by Team Evaluation of Hardware/Software Tradeoffs", *Computer Design,* v. 17, n. 4, April 1978, 129-137.

G. M. Amdahl, G. A. Blaauw, F. P. Brooks, Jr., "Architecture of the IBM System/360", *IBM J. of Res. and Develop.,* vol. 8, 1964, 87-101.

✻ CHAPTER 3 ✻

THE DESIGN OF THE TM-16

3.1. INTRODUCTION

This chapter begins to address design problems. We use the combinational and sequential building blocks and timing of Appendices C and D. Background in instruction sets, addressing, input-output instructions, and a simple interrupt system is provided in Chapter 2.

We design a very simple machine. The design implementation is simplified, but not to the point of poor cost-effectiveness. The machine is called the TM-16, with TM for "Teacher's Machine", and "16" to reflect the 16-bit word size. The student is given a quick overview of the design process, with introspective digressions. Inefficiencies are incorporated, and later criticized as a way *not* to implement a machine.

Major goals are learning the concepts of major control state, and the "actions" or microoperations in interpreting an instruction set. The composition of the central processor as a data flow (controlled part) and a control unit (controlling part) is demonstrated. The control unit and data flow are defined at a higher level by a list of RTN statements. Next, at a lower level, the actual control signal implementations controlling the data flow are obtained from the microoperations. A *control signal* gathering or tabulation process employs the *conditional information* of the RTN statements. Intermediate design steps are covered:

- data flow design,
- machine cycle timing,
- major control states,
- register transfer notation for the behavior of the control unit,
- a rudimentary input-output scheme, and
- control unit implementation.

3.2. INSTRUCTION INTERPRETATION

The function of a computer or CPU is as a slave to the program in main memory. Each instruction is fetched and executed. The CPU follows a "What next?" rule to determine the location of the next instruction, and then *interprets* (fetches and executes) that instruction. The CPU is in an endless loop, with an insatiable appetite for interpreting instructions. The interpretation process stops only when power is removed from the system, or a "Halt" instruction is executed, or by a console command from the computer operator.

Since our primary job is to cause the CPU to interpret instructions, let us imagine we are the CPU. Assume the instruction to be interpreted is an ADD instruction. We must form the sum of the accumulator contents and a second operand, and leave the result in the accumulator. A flowchart of the major steps in the interpretation procedure is shown in **Figure 3.1.** We must begin somewhere, so assume we are in possession of the address of the instruction to be interpreted. Using the address, step 1 brings the present instruction from main memory. (Until the instruction is retrieved, we don't know what to do.) Knowing the instruction type and address mode, at step 2 we calculate the effective operand address. This process may involve indexing or indirect addressing, etc. When the operand has been fetched at step 3, the addition can take place in step 4. When the accumulator is updated with the result, the next instruction interpretation is almost ready to begin. The address of the next instruction must be determined in step 5 according to the "What next?" rule. In most computers, this is the next sequential instruction address, obtained from the present instruction address by incrementation. In practice, this incrementation often takes place in step 1 while the CPU is waiting for the instruction from memory. The designer has some freedom in arranging the step-by-step interpretation procedure, and Fig. 3.1 is only one such procedure.

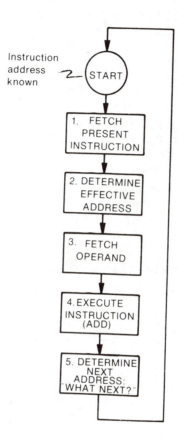

Figure 3.1. *Interpretation procedure for ADD instruction.*

Unconditional branch instructions do not have an execution step as such. Once the effective address is calculated, that result already is the answer to the "What next?" question. For conditional branch instructions, the branch condition must be resolved before the "What next?" question can be answered.

3.3. COMPONENTS

3.3.1. Data Flow Registers

The TM-16, like many simple computer architectures, follows the single-address instruction architecture. This implies the existence of *five standard CPU registers*. These registers are the *program counter* (PC), the *memory data* register (MD), the *memory address* register (MA), the *instruction register* (IR), and the *accumulator* (AC). The first four registers are present in one form or another in almost all computers. The fifth (accumulator) is a property of single-address architectures. The program counter PC holds the main memory address of, or pointer to, the next instruction to be executed. The memory data register MD holds data read from or being written into main memory. The memory address register MA holds the address while main memory is being accessed or written into. The instruction register IR holds the instruction which the CPU is currently executing. The accumulator AC is the register which holds the implied operand for two-operand instructions. Most of the task of instruction execution involves manipulating the contents of these registers, and/or commanding the main memory to read or to write. The CPU registers usually provide the source, destination or address for the memory operations.

3.3.2. Memory Interface Terminology

Some explanation is helpful regarding the terminology of the memory data interface. To the CPU designer, "memory data-in" means data read from memory. To the memory designer, "memory data-in" means data which is to be written into memory. To avoid the ambiguity of the terms "data in" and "data out" as regards main memory, we shall only use these terms where the meaning is clear. The term "read data" unambiguously means data which is read out of memory, and the term "write data" means data which is written to memory. In the TM-16, data which is read from memory comes on the MREAD bus. Data written to memory goes out on the MWRITE bus.

3.3.3. Data Flow

The computer designer places paths as needed between the CPU registers and the arithmetic unit. The generalized block diagram of a single-address class computer appears in **Figure 3.2**. The major components are the CPU and main memory, interconnected by the Memory Read, Memory Write, and Address buses. Most computers can be understood as a variation of this structure. Sometimes MA and/or MD are considered to belong to the main memory system. The memory bus interface may be a single, shared, bidirectional bus. The AC can be implemented as a local memory or a register file of 4, 8, or 16 general registers. In a register file, the PC can be a dedicated memory location or a general register.

The two parts of the CPU are the *data flow* and the *control unit*. Both parts are constructed of the same primitive building blocks: logic gates. As a result, the interface between the data (passive) and control (active) parts may be blurred. In a chemical plant, the distinction is more obvious. The

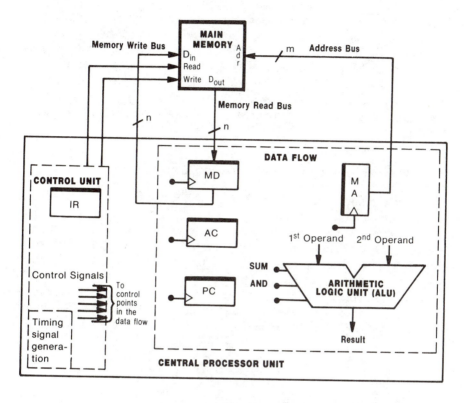

Figure 3.2. *Generalized block diagram of a small computer.*

"data flow", so to speak, consists of pipe and vats for transferring and processing fluid. The controls are electrical signals driving pumps, valves, or motors.

3.3.4. Data Flow Control Points

The data flow has all of the CPU registers except the IR which belongs to the control unit. The data flow has the data paths and data processing functional units such as the ALU. The data flow and control unit interface at connection points called *control points*.

Control points are activated or deactivated by values on *control signal* lines emanating from the control unit. The control signal activations govern the flow of information through the data flow, as traffic lights direct the flow of traffic. Most signals within the CPU can be classified as having either a data or a control purpose.

Of interest for data signals is when the data is *valid* or stable within the timing cycle. For control signals the important aspect is whether the signal is *active* or *inactive.* Control points govern the *source* register of a data transfer via MUX (data selector) elements, select options for functional units such as the ALU or shifters, and govern the *destination* registers. ALU options include whether to complement the second operand on input, to add with carry-in of 0 or 1, or to select the value of a carry flip-flop. Shifter options might include shift right, no shift, or shift left. The control unit also provides control signals which cause the memory system to read or write. Control points may also exist to set and clear flag bits or status flip-flops.

3.4. TM-16 INSTRUCTION SET ARCHITECTURE

The instruction format of the TM-16 is shown in **Figure 3.3.** Words are 16 bits, and a 16-bit memory word can be a two's complement data word, or an instruction. The operation code portion of the instruction is the high-order 3-bit field, which provides for eight opcodes. The direct address field comprises the remaining 13 bits of the instruction word, which provides for addressing up to 8K (8192) 16-bit words. Because the only addressing mode provided in the TM-16 is direct addressing, the maximum main memory capacity for this architecture is 8K words. The instruction opcodes, mnemonic (name), and meaning are shown in **Table 3.1.**

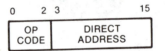

Figure 3.3. *TM-16 instruction format.*

Table 3.1. TM-16 Instruction Set		
Op	*Name*	*Meaning*
0	JMP	Unconditional jump to address
1	SRJ	Subroutine jump to address
2	IRJ	Indirect return jump (from subroutine)
3	JAN	Conditional jump on accumulator negative
4	LAC	Load accumulator from address
5	SAC	Store accumulator at address
6	ADD	Add contents of address to accumulator
7	DIO	Do IO using control field as command

Some of these instructions are self-explanatory. The subroutine jump instruction SRJ uses the LGP-30 technique of storing the PC in the first location of the subroutine. For example, if SQRT is the label (address) of the square root subroutine, the instruction "SRJ SQRT" would store the current 13-bit PC in the low-order 13 bits of the word in main memory whose label is SQRT. Word SQRT now contains the subroutine's return address. The next instruction executed is the SRJ located at SQRT plus 1, which is the first instruction of the square root subroutine. The called subroutine, when it has finished executing, ends with the instruction IRJ SQRT. This is an indirect return jump through the return address in location SQRT. Instruction IRJ is executed by reading the contents in location SQRT and loading the low-order 13 bits of that value in the PC.

The JAN instruction tests the accumulator sign bit AC(0), and if AC(0) is 1, causes the PC to be loaded with the instruction's address field, IR(3-15). Since the PC is used to fetch the next instruction, this is suffi-cient to cause the jump. If AC(0) is 0, the PC is incremented and the next sequential instruction is executed.

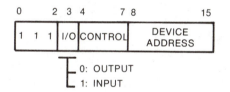

Figure 3.4. *Instruction format of the DIO instruction.*

The DIO instruction is the only instruction which does not need a memory address. See **Figure 3.4**. Input data uses the AC as the destina-tion, and on output the AC is the source. Thus the 13-bit address field of the DIO instruction is available for specifying to the input or output device exactly what is expected of it. In the TM-16, bit 3 will determine if the operation is an input or an output operation: 0 is for output and 1 is for input. Instruction bits 4-7 form a 4-bit field CONTROL which is transmit-ted to the device and determines what the device is to do. This field is device-dependent; the CPU merely passes it onto the IO bus. The remain-ing 8-bit instruction field is the device address. This address is also driven onto the IO bus, and each device must recognize its own address. Device address 0 is reserved for the CPU itself, the console switches and lights. §3.8 examines the DIO instruction in detail.

3.5. DECOMPOSING THE CPU

In a structural decomposition of the CPU, the major subcomponents are the data flow and the control unit. The control unit provides the system timing cycle, and implements the microoperations which cause the data flow events (register transfers) to occur. These three parts, data flow, microoperations, and system timing cycle, are not independent. This presents something of a dilemma: which should be designed first? The answer may depend on the instruction set, technological trade-off considerations, and some trial-and-error design to fill a conceptual gap. The *data flow cycle* is a fundamental timing concept. Typically, in this cycle, two source registers are added and the result is stored in a destination register. The process of addition is the most time consuming, due to adder propagation delays. It is important to have a good estimate of the time expended in a data flow cycle. During a data flow cycle, other data flow events may occur concurrently with the use of the arithmetic unit. If data paths are available, register transfers and memory operations may take place. However, provision for parallel data paths comes at the cost of additional data selector (MUX) elements.

3.5.1. Placing Data Flow Paths: Test some Ideas

A cost-oriented design decision, usually made early in the design cycle, is how to organize the basic CPU registers. Traditionally, these registers have been implemented as flip-flop registers. However, another approach locates the major CPU registers in a local read-write memory array (local RAM). The CPU control unit can address, read, or write the local RAM as required. The RAM approach provides a cost savings over the flip-flop register approach, but results in some loss of concurrency. In a mixed approach, some of the registers can be implemented as flip-flop registers, and others in local RAM. The mixed approach is treated in Chapter 6. We cover the flip-flop register approach here.

The present approach permits parallel data transfers and thus potentially a higher performance. A single-phase data flow cycle is also permitted where the flip-flop registers are edge-sensitive. To illustrate the point, the TM-16 data flow is implemented with the edge-triggered D type flip-flop. Another early decision concerns determination of the data paths. To "fill the gap" and obtain some notion of the data path requirements, it is instructive to lay out sequences of microoperations for some of the more important instructions. We show a possible microoperation sequence for the load accumulator instruction LAC in **Table 3.2**.

The Table 3.2 sequences have implications for the data flow paths. For example, step 1 implies a path from the PC to MA; step 6 implies a path from MD to AC. The data flow paths required for the machine are

Table 3.2. LAC Microoperation Sequence

Microoperation	_Remarks_
1. MA ← PC	Program counter value to address reg MA.
2. incr PC (PC ← PC plus 1)	Increment PC to point to next instruction.
3. MD ← M[MA]	Read instruction M[MA] location to MD.
4. IR ← MD(0-2); MA ← MD(3-15)	Opcode to IR, Address field to MA.
5. MD ← M[MA]	Read operand at address MA to MD, allowing for access time.
6. AC ← MD	Place operand into AC.

the totality of the paths implied by all microoperations for all instructions. For the ADD instruction, the following microoperation implies additional paths:

$$AC ← AC \text{ plus } MD. \qquad \text{(Replacing step 6 of Table 3.2 for LAC instruction.)}$$

The foregoing microoperation *implies* paths from AC and MD feeding their respective adder inputs, and a path from the adder output to the AC. Thus, a considerable number of paths may be *implied* by "blindly" handling the control sequences of microoperations first, before giving thought to the structure of the data flow. Alternatively, with the data flow organization defined first, the designer is obliged to generate only *dependent* register transfers for which paths are available. Many microprocessors use a single bus data flow to conserve chip area. A single bus reduces the possibility of concurrency and results in lower performance. In the earliest microprocessor days, the small chip sizes dictated the trade-off "low performance or nothing". In the TM-16, we shall design the data flow based on considering some microoperations first.

3.5.2. System Timing: Synchronous Data Flow Cycle

We consider next the third powerful influence at this stage of the computer design: *system timing*. We only consider synchronous systems for the CPU, due to performance considerations. The *CPU performance* in executing each instruction is strongly influenced by how many memory cycles are needed to execute the instruction, and how long each memory cycle takes. CPU performance suffers if the memory is idle while the CPU is determining what to do next. Since main memory is cyclic, the CPU uses a system timing cycle which "fits" the main memory cycle. The duration of the CPU clock period is generally determined as the time chosen for the *data flow cycle time.* In a data flow cycle, each functional unit can be used once; each data flow register can acquire one new value. The synchronous assumption leads to use of an integral number of data flow cycles per memory cycle.

The problem in timing organization now becomes one of determining what *events* happen on a data flow cycle, and how much time is allowed for the cycle. The duration of the data flow cycle is dependent on the flip-flop setup and propagation delay times, and combinational circuit propagation delays. The problem can be appreciated by using the following microoperations as examples.

Microoperation

1. MA ← PC
2. incr PC
3. MD ← M[MA]
4. AC ← AC plus MD

Microoperation 1 is a simple register transfer which should not take long if a direct path is available. Microoperation 2 implies the PC is a counting register, and should not take long either. In fact, since data paths are not required if the PC is implemented as a counter element, the incrementation can take place concurrently with register transfers. Microoperation 3 must not occur too soon after MA becomes valid, because the access delay to main memory must be paid. In some systems, the CPU must idle (do nothing) while waiting for data from a slow main memory. Microoperation 4 must allow for the adder delay from when the operands are valid at the adder input, to when the valid result appears at the AC inputs. These varying demands must be worked into a system timing cycle.

In practice, microoperation 4 represents the longest delay within a cycle. This is an "important" microoperation because it may limit the speed of the data flow cycle; it is usually handled first. Microoperations such as "MA ← PC" and "incr PC" are allowed to take a full data flow cycle, even though less time is required. Alternately, a simple register transfer could be the dominant operation in a data flow cycle, and two data flow cycle times could be allotted for an adder operation. A similar strategy is used for memory cycle times. Operations such as "MD ← M[MA]" are allowed from one to three (or sometimes more) data flow cycle times. If the memory cycle time is the same as the data flow cycle time, then one is coupling too expensive a memory to the CPU, or the CPU designers have paid the price in circuits to give the data flow sufficient concurrency to keep the memory busy. Some microprocessors are designed to receive valid memory data one data flow cycle time following the address loading in MA. The interconnection to slower memories is permitted by providing a CPU input controlled by the memory which forces the CPU to "idle" while waiting for the read data. Our experience with small CPU design has been that events can be controlled which allow efficient use of a memory whose cycle time is twice that of the data flow cycle time.

3.5.3. First Data Flow and Timing Iteration

Determination of the data flow organization helps fill the conceptual gap between implementation and behavior. One approach to data flow design, often used in medium- to high-performance CPUs, is outlined here.

1. Propose microoperation sequences (independent RTN) for some typical instructions (load, store, add, subroutine jump) and some addressing modes, and determine the implied data paths.
2. Design a tentative data flow subject to any constraints.
3. Determine the typical data flow cycle, and system cycle.
4. Lay out the microoperation sequence for each instruction.

In low-cost designs, an economical data flow is a dominant concern, and step 2 is usually done first.

The design can proceed by iterating on the first three items. Once the data flow and data flow cycle timing have been determined, item 4 can be attacked. Each instruction in turn may be "laid out" into its sequence of microoperations. The design can iterate still more, adjusting the data flow paths and microoperations accordingly.

For the typical TM-16 instructions (LAC, SAC, ADD, SRJ) the implied data paths yield the data flow of **Figure 3.5.** The Program Counter PC is implemented as a counter. Labels X and Y have been given to the left and right adder input points. In the design which follows, we presume only the existence of these paths when laying out the other microoperation sequences. If it turns out that another path is required, then that path is added. Such is the iterative nature of design.

Figure 3.6 shows the time delay chain of what is typically the most time-consuming operation of the data flow cycle:

$$AC \leftarrow MD \text{ plus } AC.$$

Note: *Worst-case delays are stacked serially end-to-end in order of their occurrence.* If some delays occur in parallel, they should not be added serially. The designer seeks to have more delays occurring in parallel, and fewer occurring serially. *A lowercase* t *followed by a digit is used to reference a timing event in the text.*

At t0 we assume AC is valid and the loading of MD is initiated. The *minimum* time in which the data flow can be cycled, called *Tmin*, is a function of the *maximum* (worst-case) delays expected in the cycle. The delays occur as data flows through the functional units (adder, multiplexer) and registers. At t1, the worst-case propagation delay through MD is

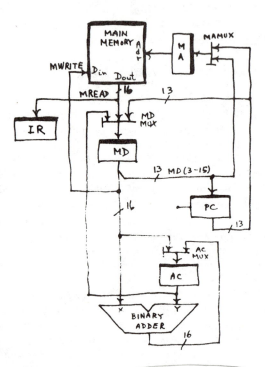

Figure 3.5. *TM-16 data flow (tentative).*

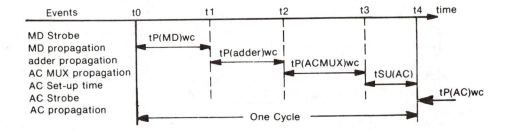

Figure 3.6. *A time delay chain for estimating minimum data flow cycle time.*

accounted for, and at t2 the adder output is stable. At t3, the ACMUX delay has been paid, and at t4 the AC setup time tSU(AC) is paid. At time t4, the AC strobe can occur, and AC input data is guaranteed to be stable. (Note that the AC propagation delay tP(AC) occurs at the start of the *next* cycle.) The data flow cycle time should not be less than time t0-to-t4, or

Tmin. The cycle time can, of course, take more time than Tmin. The designer controls the cycle time by controlling the rate at which the periodic timing signals repeat.

3.6. DATA FLOW CYCLE

The data flow cycle is typically the major subdivision of an instruction interpretation. Instruction interpretations occur in an integral number of data flow cycles. A data flow cycle can be refined into *timing points* or clock times. In a single-phase clocking scheme, the data flow cycle is defined by a single clock signal. One or more data flow cycles can correspond to a *major control state,* which is often called a machine cycle or major cycle. A major control state corresponds to the internal state of a sequential (finite state) machine. In some simple processors, the major control state might be simply a counter which steps through a fixed count sequence. However for many complex processors, the finite state machine may have a "normal" sequence, with deviations or exceptions to skip some states or pass through others. Notice in Table 3.2 that the first four steps are always done, independent of the instruction. This sequence is called *instruction fetch,* I-fetch, or I-cycles. In the TM-16, this sequence of four microoperations is made a major control state, called I. The control state is subdivided into four data flow cycles, each clocked by one of the timing signals T0, T1, T2, and T3. These timing signals can be generated from a basic oscillator signal OSC as shown in **Figure 3.7**. The trailing edge of T3 can be used to change the major control state. Four data flow cycles comprise a major state cycle.

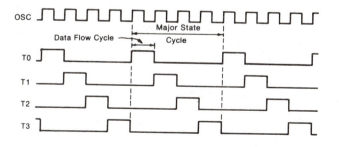

Figure 3.7. *TM-16 major state cycle.*

The execution phase of instruction execution is assigned major state E. Now state E follows state I. The system timing is described in **Figure 3.8**. Fig. 3.8(a) shows how the repetitive waveforms appear in a timing chart. A compact representation is shown in Fig. 3.8(b). Control state E is also subdivided into four data flow cycles. No computational work is done on a cycle without some value being clocked into a register, or written into main memory. As another *groundrule*, the trailing edge of the clock signals T0 through T3 is used to strobe data into the edge-triggered data flow registers.

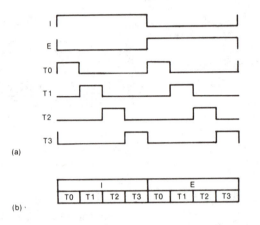

(a)

(b) ·

Figure 3.8. *System timing cycle for TM-16.* (a) Waveform method. (b) Compact representation.

One more groundrule is useful before proceeding. There are several control flip-flops in the implementation. Consider a flip-flop called WRITE which is active when the memory is performing a write operation. To activate the WRITE flip-flop, an action called SETWRITE will appear to the right of the conditional information of an RTN statement. To clear the WRITE flip-flop, an action called CLRWRITE will appear in the action part of an RTN statement. As with the data flip-flops, the convention specifies that the change take place on the *trailing edge* of the timing point of the conditional information.

3.7. INSTRUCTION INTERPRETATION

The primary purpose of the CPU is to execute instructions. To execute an instruction it must be fetched. Then the operands must be fetched or calculated, and the operation performed. This process is called *instruction interpretation*, whether done by hardware, microprogram, or program. Instruction addressing is handled by proper control of the contents of the PC. In the TM-16, operand addressing could not be simpler since the architecture only provides direct addressing. Execution is also simple, with a small number of weak instruction types.

For most instruction interpretations, the memory is accessed twice, once for the instruction and once for an operand. We assume as a ground-rule that memory is always reading the location defined by the MA register, and that the access time is less than two data flow cycles. In practical terms, if the MA is loaded on the trailing edge to T0, the MD register can be strobed on the trailing edge of T2.

Two data flow cycles are similarly allowed for the memory write cycle. Let MA and MD be valid following the trailing edge of T0, and at the same edge let the write command be given. MA and MD cannot be changed until the trailing edge of T2. We make another timing assumption: the adder can form a valid result and present that result to the destination register in one data flow cycle. Thus, at the beginning of T3, for example, the AC and MD can be gated to their respective adder inputs and the result is ready for strobing into AC at the trailing edge of T3.

We assume the PC register has parallel load capability, and is also an up counter. The MD, AC, and IR registers are 16 bits wide and the PC and MA are 13 bits wide.

At the behavioral level, the interpretation of each instruction is divided into a two-part sequence: (1) in *control state I* (I cycles), the instruction is fetched and the memory read operation for the operand is initiated; (2) in *control state E* (E cycles), the instruction is executed.

3.7.1. Control State I

A program instruction is interpreted by a *macrosequence* of microoperations. During each new data flow cycle, the functional units and buses can be reused. In the system timing, data flow cycles are identified by ANDing the control state signal I with the individual signals T0, T1, T2, and T3. Consider the RTN statements for the data flow cycles in state I (I cycles). We assume that at the start of state I the MA does not contain the address of the next instruction. Therefore the first microoperation must load the MA with the contents of the PC. While waiting for the instruction to be delivered from memory, the PC may be incremented. Following the access time, the memory read data is loaded into MD from the MREAD bus. We know MD has an instruction (it was fetched using PC), so the IR is loaded from MD. Also, since all instructions except DIO use the address field to indicate the operand, the MA can be loaded from MD(3-15). In fact, it would be more costly, in time and circuits, *not* to transfer MD(3-15) to MA at this time. (As will be seen, the execution of the DIO instruction makes use of the fact that the address field is in MA.) The microoperations for state I are summarized in **Table 3.3**.

Transfers take place at the *end* of the indicated clock time. The first clock time of state E follows the last clock time of state I. This is indicated for I•T3 by activation of control signal ECYNEXT. Similarly, at the end

Table 3.3. TM-16 State I Macrosequence *Fetch*	
I•T0:	MA←PC
I•T1:	incr PC
I•T2:	MD←M[MA]
I•T3:	IR←MD(0-3); MA←MD(3-15); ECYNEXT

of state E, the major control state is changed to I by the activation of a control signal called ICYNEXT. We assume a lower-level digital logic circuit which receives these control signals as inputs and handles the major control state changes properly. Later, when our attention is drawn deeper into the implementation details, we design a circuit to govern the major control state aspect of the control unit.

3.7.2. Control State E

When state E is entered, the direct address is in MA, and the instruction opcode is in IR.

To execute an instruction, the opcode must be known. In the control unit, the four high-order bits of the instruction (bits 0-3) are in IR, and are decoded as shown in **Figure 3.9.**

Note that for DIO, IR(3) distinguishes an IO input operation from an IO output operation. The opcode control signals are intended for use as

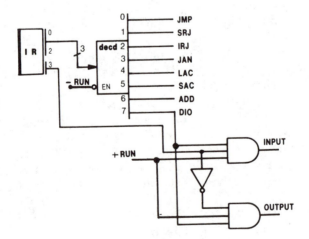

Figure 3.9. *Instruction opcode decoder.*

conditional information on microoperations. If the machine is *not* in the RUN state, the decoder is disabled. (The RUN state is explained later.)

Execution of the JMP Instruction

The jump instruction (JMP) is executed by the following RTN statement:

E•JMP•T0:   PC←MD(3-15); ICYNEXT

Since the next instruction is to be from the target address stored in MD(3-15), the target address value is loaded into the PC. The PC is loaded during the first timing point (T0) of state E. Waiting for the clock to go through T1, T2, and T3 times before activating state I would be a waste of time. Therefore control signal ICYNEXT is activated. This causes major control state I and timing point T0 to become active following the next OSC edge. We shall also assume that if state E and T3 time is reached, an AND gate causes signal ICYNEXT to become active. In the execution statements for instructions whose execution takes the full four timing points of state E, we do not explicitly indicate ICYNEXT. ICYNEXT causes the cycle controls to activate state I, T0 time.

Execution of the SRJ Instruction

The RTN statements for the execution of the subroutine jump (SRJ) are:

E•SRJ•T0:   MD(0-2)←0; MD(3-15)←PC; PC←MD(3-15);
             SETWRITE
E•SRJ•T1:   incr PC
E•SRJ•T2:   ICYNEXT; CLRWRITE

For the SRJ instruction, the value of the PC must be transferred to the MD, with the high-order bits set to zeros. The PC is to be written into memory at the first subroutine location. Also, before returning to state I, the memory address must be incremented and placed in the PC. In this way execution can start at the second subroutine location. It is seen from Fig. 3.5 that a path from MD to PC exists. Since the registers are edge-triggered, the contents of PC and MD may be swapped in data flow cycle T0. In T0, a "SETWRITE" signal is activated, which sets the WRITE flip-flop at end of T0 time. We use the convention that flip-flops change state on the trailing edge of the conditional information stating the change. Thus the WRITE flip-flop is set at the beginning of T1 time. Once WRITE is set, the memory is given the write command during T1, because MA was already set up at the end of state I. The PC must be incremented, which is done in T1. The two data flow cycles which comprise the memory write operation are T1 and T2. At the trailing edge of T2, signal CLRWRITE being active causes the WRITE flip-flop to be cleared. At the end of T2, control returns to state I. During T2, signal ICYNEXT is activated.

Execution of the IRJ Instruction

E•IRJ•T1:   MD←M [MA]
E•IRJ•T2:   PC←MD(3-15); ICYNEXT

The indirect return jump (IRJ) accesses memory to obtain the value to be loaded into PC. Since MA was set up with the valid address at the end of T3 in state I, the first half of the memory read operation takes place in T0 time. The desired value can be loaded to MD at the end of T1 (of state E). Note that T0 is used to allow time to access memory. From there it is routed to the PC during T2 time. This new PC value should not be incremented, since the incrementation took place in state I of the SRJ instruction which stored it in memory.

Execution of the JAN Instruction

E•JAN•AC(0)•T0:   PC←MD(3-15)
E•JAN•T0:   ICYNEXT

The purpose of the jump on accumulator negative (JAN) instruction is to determine the proper value to be in the PC. If the accumulator is positive, the PC is left alone (it was incremented in state I). If AC is negative, AC(0) is 1, and in T0, the target address in MD(3-15) is loaded to PC.

Execution of the LAC Instruction

E•LAC•T1:   MD←M[MA]
E•LAC•T2:   AC←MD; ICYNEXT

The load accumulator (LAC) instruction waits for the memory access time (T0) then loads MD in T1. In T2 the data value in MD is transferred to the AC.

Execution of the SAC Instruction

E•SAC•T0:   MD←AC; SETWRITE
E•SAC•T1:   (First part of memory write operation)
E•SAC•T2:   ICYNEXT; CLRWRITE

The store accumulator (SAC) instruction transfers the contents of the AC to MD for writing to memory. Register MD always feeds the MWRITE bus (Fig. 3.5.). MA already has the proper address, so SET-WRITE is activated causing the write operation to take place in times T1-T2. The control of the memory write operation is the same as for SRJ. At the end of T0, the WRITE flip-flop is activated, T1 is used to allow for memory access delay, and at the end of T2 the WRITE flip-flop is deactivated.

Execution of the ADD Instruction

E•ADD•T1: MD←M[MA]
E•ADD•T2: AC←AC plus MD; ICYNEXT

The add to accumulator (ADD) instruction is executed by fetching the second operand from main memory to the MD, then routing it from there to the second adder input. The first operand is the AC which feeds the first operand adder input. The result is placed in the AC.

3.8. INPUT–OUTPUT OPERATIONS

Before interpreting the DIO instruction, the IO architecture of the TM-16 must first be defined. The input-output data transfer capability of the TM-16 is a simple "programmed IO" instruction with the AC acting as a buffer register between the device and main memory. See **Figure 3.10** for the data structure of the IO bus. As shown in Fig. 3.10(a), the data bus is DOT-OR bidirectional, driven from the AC on output and by the addressed device on input. In Fig. 3.10(b), the device address (DEVADR) portion is driven to the IO devices from the MA, since the device address resides in MA at this time anyway. The devices are connected (tied) to the IO interface bus. The bus has five signal types: data, device address, device control, timing and control strobes, and interrupt. The last three types are collectively called the control portion of the IO bus; see Fig. 3.10(c). The device address and device control signals are unidirectional.

At the end of state I, MD(3-15) is transferred to MA, where the bits are renamed MA(0-12). Since the DIO instruction's device address and device control specification fields are already loaded into MA, we can share these lines for the IO bus DEVADR and DEVCTL fields. This explains why Fig. 3.10(b) shows DEVADR and DEVCTL driven from MA. Each device, however, must ignore its address in the absence of a control strobe. Device address 0 is used within the CPU, and is shown decoded as DEVADR0.

Fig. 3.10(c) shows the control strobe and interrupt line timing. Control strobe –INP is active-low for three clock times, from the trailing edge of T0 to the trailing edge of T3 in state E of DIO input instructions. Strobe –OUTP is active-low for the same three clock times of DIO output instructions. Timing signal T2 is inverted and driven out as an active-low timing pulse for use by the device interface designer.

The interrupt signal is a single unidirectional DOT-OR signal from the devices to the CPU control unit. The control unit looks at this interrupt request line INT at the last part of the execution cycle for which

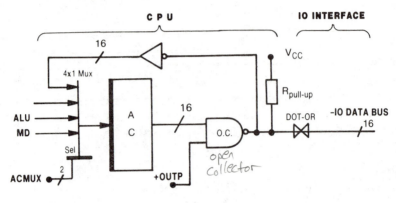

(a)

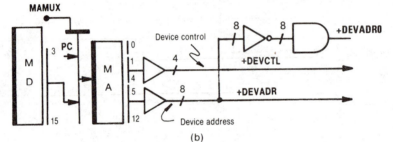

(b)

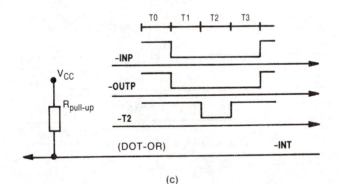

(c)

Figure 3.10. *TM-16 IO interface signals.* (a) IO data bus.
(b) Address and control. (c) IO control signals with timing
superimposed.

ICYNEXT is active. Therefore, the devices must use the trailing edge of
T2 to set or clear their interrupt flip-flops, to meet the CPU setup time for
the trailing edge of T3.

The control unit executes the DIO instruction in the following fashion. If MA(0) is 0, an output instruction is specified and signal OUTP is activated for clock times T1-T3. The active value of OUTP gates the AC value onto the IO Data Bus. The addressed device must use time T2 (from timing signal −T2) to load its input buffer register. If the device has more than one buffer register, the device control field may determine which buffer register should be loaded by the device from the IO Data Bus. The meaning of the four device control bits is determined by the device interface designer and/or the programmer for the device handling routines. In many small computer applications, these decisions may be made by the same person.

If MA(0) is 1, a DIO input instruction is being executed. SETINP at the end of T0 means control signal INP is made active at time T1. This alerts the addressed device to gate one of its buffer registers onto the IO Data Bus for the duration of INP. The device control bits may perform register selection if the device interface has more than one buffer register. At the end of T3, CLRINP deactivates signal INP.

The device interface designers know that unless control strobes INP or OUTP are activated, DEVCTL and DEVADR are to be ignored. The bus sharing of the memory address lines with IO address lines is commonly done in microprocessor designs.

Table 3.4. Execution of DIO Instruction

E•DIO•IR(3)′•T0:	SETOUTP (OUTP: IODATA BUS = AC)
E•DIO•IR(3)•T0:	SETINP
E•DIO•IR(3)•T2:	AC←IODATA BUS
E•DIO•T3:	CLROUTP; CLRINP

The microoperations for the execution of the DIO instruction are in **Table 3.4.** The control of the two IO bus strobes INP and OUTP is assumed to be via edge-triggered flip-flops. The JK type flip-flop is best suited to this purpose. Signals SETOUTP and SETINP activate OUTP and INP respectively at the trailing edge of the clock time. Similarly, the activation of signals CLROUTP and CLRINP respectively clear the flip-flops which generate IO bus strobes OUTP and INP. Thus if a strobe is active, it is active from T1 through T3.

Table 3.4 accounts for the purpose and use of all the IO interface signals except one: the −INT signal. The interrupt scheme is treated in the next section.

3.9. INTERRUPT ARCHITECTURE

An *interrupt request* is a signal (INT in the TM-16 case) indicating the need for a sequence of instructions to be executed. The consequence of the *interrupt* is the execution of one or more instructions not in the normal (or "main" program) sequence. The normal instruction sequence is suspended to accommodate the interrupting (out-of-normal-sequence) instruction.

Once the interrupt has been handled, the normal sequence is restarted (begun again) at the point where it was suspended. The analogy to a subroutine jump is immediate, because the PC must be saved, and later restored in order to resume the suspended program.

3.9.1. A Single-Level Scheme

The TM-16 permits only one level of interrupt, hence is a *single-level* scheme. An interrupt is accepted when ICYNEXT is active, that is, when leaving state E, if the interrupt enable (IEN) flip-flop is active. When an interrupt is accepted, flip-flop IEN is deactivated. The IEN flip-flop may be set and cleared by DIO instructions to device address 0 (the CPU). Upon acceptance of an interrupt, a control flip-flop RUPT is set and is active during control states I and E. When state I and RUPT are active, the current program is suspended, and the PC is loaded with the address of the interrupt routine. The suspension of the current program must be done so that a subsequent return to where it left off is possible.

3.9.2. Interrupt Acceptance and Saving the Old PC

In the TM-16 computer, memory locations 0 and 1 are reserved for the interrupt system. Memory location 0 is reserved as the save location for the PC when an interrupt is accepted. Location 1 should contain an unconditional jump instruction to the interrupt handler or service routine (or the handler itself may start at location 1).

To modify state I when RUPT is active, we perform the necessary "housekeeping" to ensure that when we enter the following state E, the control unit "thinks" it is executing a subroutine jump instruction to location 0. What we are actually doing is breaking the "unwritten groundrule" that the next instruction come from main memory. We are also practicing the art of "fooling" the machine to do what we, in our "superior wisdom", want it to do. Computer programmers are equally adept at fooling the machine.

Observe that all instructions are "executed" in one major control cycle. This major execution cycle is preceded by the "instruction fetch" major cycle. When changing from control state E to state I, the following statement handles the acceptance of an interrupt during the transition:

ICYNEXT•IEN•INT: SETRUPT; CLRIEN

In the foregoing RTN statement, if the interrupt system is enabled, the RUPT flip-flop will be set in state I. Also, the IEN flip-flop is cleared, ensuring that no other interrupt will succeed while the interrupt handler program is running. In this way, only a single level of interrupt is implemented.

If RUPT is active, then state I must be modified. This is shown in **Table 3.5.**

Table 3.5. New I State, which Treats Interrupts	
I•T0:	MA←PC
I•RUPT'•T2:	MD←M[MA]; incr PC
I•RUPT•T2:	MD(0-2)←001; MD(3-15)←0
I•T3:	IR←MD(0-3); MA←MD(3-15)

Note that since conditions IEN and INT activate signal RUPT, we can more economically use control signal RUPT for distinguishing the state I actions based on whether or not an interrupt is to be accepted.

By inhibiting the incrementing of the PC in state I if an interrupt is being accepted, we preserve the value of PC. Saving the old PC is done with the "forced" SRJ instruction; opcode 001 is placed in MD(0-2) before passing it to IR(0-2). The destination of the forced SRJ instruction is 0, which is placed in MD(3-15), from where it goes to MA. In T2 time, control signal RUPT is needed to select what goes into the MD register. Since the RUPT signal has to be generated at T2 time, the incrementing of the PC is moved to T2 time. This takes advantage of an existing control condition: the *condition* for "incr PC" (p-term I•RUPT'•T2) is shared with the action of loading MD from memory.

For state I following the forced SRJ, flip-flop RUPT is always cleared, because IEN is inactive.

3.9.3. Interrupt Servicing and Return

In Table 3.5, the microoperations to effect a transfer of control to the interrupt handler have been done. Once in the interrupt handler, the programmer must discover which device generated the interrupt by the "skip chain" or polling technique (see Chapter 2). After the device service routine performs its job, it resets the interrupt. To return to the normal program, an indirect return jump (IRJ) to location 0 restores the old PC. However, we must first enable interrupts again. It appears there are no opcodes for this, so we have to display some creativity. Note that the DIO instruction with device address 0, decoded as "DEVADR0" in the control unit, is reserved for the CPU. See Fig. 3.10(b). *We use two control field combinations, 0 and 1, respectively, to clear and set the IEN flip-flop.* **Figure 3.11** shows the circuits and a timing diagram for the implementation of the interrupt sequence. AND gates 1 and 2 respectively set (control combination 1) and clear (control combination 0) the IEN flip-flop via CPU instructions. One input to the AND clocking the JK flip-flop is ICYNEXT, so IEN is only changed on the transition *to* state I. The programmer uses DIO output instructions to set or clear IEN.

The timing of the enabling of interrupts by setting IEN is somewhat tricky. We must retain the ability to return from an interrupt. This implies we cannot overwrite a valid return address in location 0. The problem is solved as follows. We allow the instruction following the "Set IEN" to be executed because this instruction is the IRJ returning control to the interrupted routine. This "following IRJ" instruction is indeed executed even if signal INT is active, because IEN is set only by the trailing edge of T3. In this and many computer designs, the enabling of the interrupt system (setting IEN) has been timed so that one more instruction is allowed to execute before being susceptible to an interrupt. In such cases the following instruction is the IRJ which clears the RUPT flip-flop and restores the old PC of the interrupted program. This is illustrated in the waveform of Fig. 3.11(b), where the IRJ '0' instruction of Note 2 executes before a second interrupt is serviced.

The approach employed here of designing state I without worrying about the interrupt, then coming back to modify it to handle the interrupt, is called *postponement of detail*. This is an example of the "iterative" design technique. For complex design problems, *planned iteration* appears to be the most successful approach. One handles the *major* considerations on a "first pass", then returns to handle the exceptions or minor considerations. (Unplanned iterations may result from worrying about too many unimportant or minor considerations on the "first pass".)

3.9.4. Using the DIO Instruction for the System

The system architects can allow system programs for the TM-16 to use the DIO instruction to accomplish system functions. Device address 0 has been assigned to the CPU itself, and control functions can be assigned as desired. Only device control field (DEVCTL) combinations "0000" (DEVCTL0) and "0001" (DEVCTL1) have been used so far; see Fig. 3.11(a), gates 1 and 2. Other combinations may be employed for functions such as "supervisor call".

We shall implement the HALT instruction as a DIO instruction to device 0, with DEVCTL field assignment "0010" (DEVCTL2). This instruction activates the HALT control signal, which clears the RUN

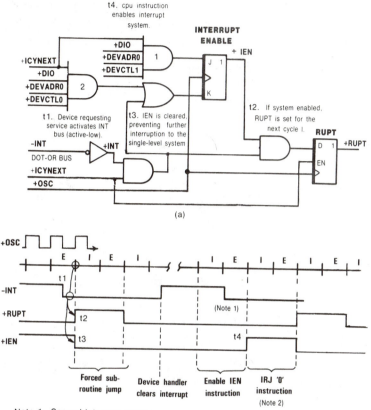

(a)

(b)

Note 1: Second Interrupt occurs.

Note 2: Uses loc 0 to return from first interrupt before second interrupt is serviced.

Figure 3.11. *An implementation of interruption circuits for the TM-16, and waveform of an interrupt sequence.* (a) An implementation of the controls for the RUPT flip-flop. (b) Waveforms of interruption sequence.

flip-flop at the proper time. The design of the RUN flip-flop controls is postponed until the console operations are discussed.

Fig. 3.11 illustrates the implementation for the single-level interrupt architecture (no new interrupts accepted while the current one is being handled) of TM-16. Fig. 3.11(a) shows the circuit implementation with signals and gates keyed to the important activities. Fig. 3.11(b) shows a timing chart keyed to these same activities.

3.9.5. TM-16 Summary

We summarize the RTN statements for the opcodes designed so far.

I State

I•T0:	MA←PC
I•RUPT'•T2:	MD←M[MA]; incr PC
I•RUPT•T2:	MD(0-2)←001; MD(3-15)←0
I•T3:	IR←MD(0-3); MA←MD(3-15)

E State

ICYNEXT•IEN•INT•OSC: SETRUPT; CLRIEN

JMP

E•JMP•T0:	PC←MD(3-15); ICYNEXT

SRJ

E•SRJ•T0:	MD(0-2)←0; MD(3-15)←PC; PC←MD(3-15); SETWRITE
E•SRJ•T1:	incr PC
E•SRJ•T2:	ICYNEXT; CLRWRITE

IRJ

E•IRJ•T1:	MD←M [MA]
E•IRJ•T2:	PC←MD(3-15); ICYNEXT

JAN

E•JAN•AC(0)•T0:	PC←MD(3-15)
E•JAN•T0:	ICYNEXT

LAC

E•LAC•T1:	MD←M[MA]
E•LAC•T2:	AC←MD; ICYNEXT

SAC

E•SAC•T0:	MD←AC; SETWRITE
E•SAC•T2:	ICYNEXT; CLRWRITE

ADD

E•ADD•T1:	MD←M[MA]
E•ADD•T2:	AC←AC plus MD; ICYNEXT

DIO (See also Fig. 3.11)

$E \cdot DIO \cdot IR(3)' \cdot T0$:   SETOUTP; (OUTP: IODATA BUS = AC)

$E \cdot DIO \cdot IR(3) \cdot T0$:   SETINP

$E \cdot DIO \cdot IR(3) \cdot T2$: $AC \leftarrow IODATA\ BUS$

$E \cdot DIO \cdot T3$:   CLROUTP; CLRINP

$DEVADR0 = MA(5)' \cdot \ldots \cdot MA(12)'$

$DEVCTL0 = MA(1)' \cdot MA(2)' \cdot MA(3)' \cdot MA(4)'$

$DEVCTL1 = MA(1)' \cdot MA(2)' \cdot MA(3)' \cdot MA(4)$

3.10. THE DATA FLOW AND REGISTER CLOCKING

We can now examine the microoperations of the RTN statements in §§3.9.5 for data paths. We lay out the final data flow as shown in **Figure 3.12**. The edge-triggered registers employed are those with clock enabling, so signal +OSC is sent to all registers. The control points are shown as lines terminating with a solid bubble. The control points are primarily the MUX select signals and the register clock enable signals.

The generation of the basic timing signals is shown in **Figure 3.13**. The clock times T0, T1, T2, and T3 are generated by a ring counter. Since the rise of OSC is the active transition, this *always* precedes a change in Ti. The system timing generator is basically a 4-bit shift register in which a 1-bit (bit whose value is 1) is circulated, with the provision that activating ICYNEXT moves the counter to T0. The counter as shown is "self-starting" in that if it ever gets two or more 1-bits, or no 1-bits in the ring, it will eventually return to the state of circulating a single 1-bit. The power-on reset (POR) condition also initializes the clock time to T0.

Fig. 3.13(b) shows how the major (control) state machine might be implemented in a "first pass". The POR condition leaves the machine in state I. The major control state system behaves as a ring counter, circulating a 1-bit between the two I and E flip-flops. The flip-flops are enabled by signal NEWCY, which is the OR of ECYNEXT and ICYNEXT. The major state changes at ECYNEXT or ICYNEXT, whichever comes first. NEWCY is active, the flip-flops advance at the next active transition of OSC.

By using signal +OSC as the clock, with clock times Ti as enabling signals, a register enabled by time +T3, for example, will actually change state at the *trailing edge* of +T3. At the leading edge of T3, the positive OSC transition has "gone away", because that transition caused the change to T3. In the RTN statements we imply that changes take place at the trailing edge of Ti.

With the data flow cycle and the system cycle worked out, it is possible to describe the macrosequence for the execution of each instruction by an *event schematic*. The event schematic has clock times blocked out on the

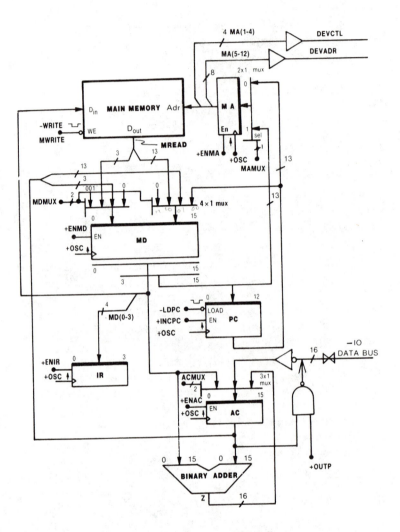

Figure 3.12. *TM-16 data flow.*

horizontal scale, and within each block is placed the RTN statements of the microoperations (if any) which take place at that time. This descriptive form is found in some microprocessor manuals. If the instructions have a manageable amount of conditional execution microoperations, the event schematic is a convenient descriptive form. The event schematic for the load accumulator instruction (LAC) is shown in **Figure 3.14.** An instruction event schematic can be represented by a table of RTN statements. The inclusion of conditional information is a difficulty with event schematics. We suggest event schematics as a convenient starting point for "laying

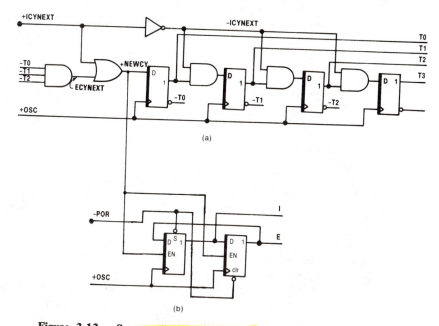

(a)

(b)

Figure 3.13. *System timing and control.* (a) Ring counter clock. (b) First try at machine cycle (major state) machine.

RUPT':

	I				E		
MA←PC	1st memory half-cycle	MD←M[MA] incr PC	IR←MD(0-3) MA←MD(3-15)	1st memory half-cycle	MD←M[MA]	ICYNEXT AC←MD	skipped
T0	T1	T2	T3	T0	T1	T2	T3

Figure 3.14. *Event schematic for load accumulator instruction.*

out" each instruction, i.e. determining how each instruction is to be executed. The student must first learn to handle "one thing at a time". Chapter 5 makes use of this approach. Since the event schematic lacks conditional information, we recommend the use of a table of RTN statements as in §§3.9.5 to describe the control flow. A straightforward implementation procedure from such a table, called control point gathering, is described in §§3.12.1.

3.11. THE TM-16 CONTROL PANEL

In this section we address the control panel or console. It is through the console that the user communicates with the computer at a very basic level. The control panel is used during both hardware and software debug, and to get a program initially loaded into memory. Only the Run/Halt operation is worked out in detail here; the other operations are deferred.

3.11.1. Control Panel Architecture

We design a control panel for the TM-16; see **Figure 3.15.** The panel has 16 lights, 16 switches (SW(0-15)), a 4-position control knob with settings "RUN", "READ", "WRITE", and "LOAD", and a debounced pushbutton PB to initiate one of these four control knob actions. When the control knob is removed from the RUN setting, the machine halts. When in READ mode, with the pushbutton PB depressed, the address in PC is presented to main memory, the PC is incremented, and the memory contents are placed in the AC for display. When PB is activated in WRITE mode, the address in PC is presented to memory, and the value in the switches SW(0-15) is placed in the AC and written to main memory. The PC is then incremented. When in the LOAD setting with the pushbutton PB depressed, the contents of the switches SW(0-15) are loaded into the AC. At the same time, SW(3-15) is loaded to the PC and MA. The AC is continually being displayed on the lights, providing feedback to the user. For loading and storing data, or reading it from main memory, the address is in the PC.

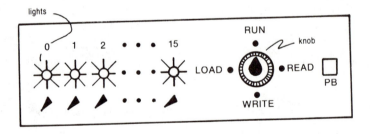

Figure 3.15. *A control panel for TM-16.*

The purpose of incrementing the PC afterward is to facilitate reading or writing blocks of data from the console. When the machine is initially "brought up", instructions can be "manually bootstrapped" to successive main memory read/write locations via the console switch operations. With the initial program loaded, the starting instruction address is loaded to the

PC, the control knob placed in RUN mode, and the pushbutton activated. The CPU executes the loaded program, which usually is capable of reading a larger program into main memory from an IO device. The act of getting the initial program into the machine is called "initial program load" or IPL. An approach which avoids manually entering the bootstrap program to certain memory locations is to place it in a ROM addressed by those locations.

3.11.2. Run/Halt Controls

In implementing the Run/Halt console operations, the designer must first determine how to stop the "fetch-execute" syndrome, and cause the machine to rest (do nothing). In general there are two approaches to this challenge. In the first approach, the basic clock, in this case +OSC, is stopped. Without +OSC, the timing ring is not advanced and the machine does not progress to the next clock time. In general, this approach has the problem of generating "runt" +OSC pulses when entering or leaving the "halt" state. We recommend a second approach: inhibit all major control state signals. The clock times T0, ..., T3 still appear, so the "runt" pulse problem is avoided. For the recommended scheme to work, all data flow control signals should have one of the major control states as a condition. For example, performing a microoperation on the condition E′ would also cause that microoperation to occur in the halt state. For this reason, we avoid implementing the control state machine as a single flip-flop where state E′ would be I. We would avoid encoding four major control states into two flip-flops for the same reason. Due to its simplicity and under-standability, we prefer one flip-flop per major control state.

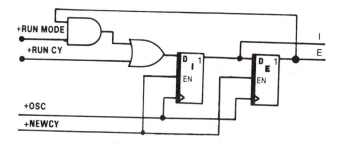

Figure 3.16. *Design of major state machine.*

The problem now is to deactivate simultaneously both major control states. It would suffice to prevent state I from reactivating. In this way, were it decided to halt the machine during state I, the following state E would still be allowed to occur, which has the beneficial effect of not leaving an instruction half executed. Now we must generate conditions which cause the machine to execute instructions normally, or which cause it to halt. Assume the existence of a flip-flop called "RUN MODE" to distinguish these two conditions.

In **Figure 3.16** the final major state machine is designed. An AND gate senses the deactivation of RUN MODE and prevents state I from activation. This circuit effects the transition from "running" to "halted" very nicely by requiring the machine to be in RUN MODE before following state E with state I. However, once the TM-16 is halted, both I and E are deactivated. Signal RUN MODE being reactivated will not remove the major control state machine from this halted state. We need something to give it an "initial push". For this we design a signal controlling the transition from the halted to the running condition called RUN CY. In order to start state I with clock time T0, RUN CY should be activated during clock time T3. Signal RUN CY is ORed through to place a 1 on the I flip-flop D input causing the next machine control state to be state I. **Figure 3.17** shows the timing cycle for the control state machine. Cycle 1 is state I, and cycle 2 is state E. In cycle 2, the RUN MODE is deactivated; in cycle 3 the halt state is entered. The machine remains in this state until cycle 4, when RUN CY becomes active. On cycle 5, state I begins again, as does RUN MODE.

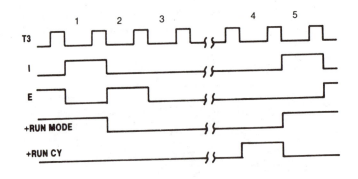

Figure 3.17. *The sequencing of the major state machine.*

The particular design presented here is by no means the only way to accomplish the simultaneous deactivation of the control state signals I and E. The flip-flop outputs I and E could each be passed through their own AND gate, with the other input being the RUN MODE signal.

3.11.3. Design of Timing Signals

What remains is to interface the console knob and pushbutton PB to generate the signals RUN MODE and RUN CY. Timing signals are required for all console functions, so we design a timing signal generator useful to all console operations.

The RUN and HALT controls must ensure that states I and E are not cut short, or begin at the wrong time. We summarize some requirements.

1. The switch and pushbutton must be synchronized with the CPU clock.
2. Major state cycle controls for the console functions are needed.
3. The timing of state I for RUN must begin with clock time T0.

Since the console operations are initiated with the pushbutton, the pushbutton is synchronized with the system clock and used to generate major state control signals CONCY1 and CONCY2. As with control state I, the console states are valid from the start of one T0 time to the end of the succeeding T3 time.

In synchronizing a pushbutton with a clock, we generally have the choice of using the depression or the release of the pushbutton to activate the operation. For summoning an elevator, for example, one may wish to activate the summons on the button depression, in order that the elevator come faster.

The choice is arbitrary, but we prefer to use the release of the button. Buttons are traditionally noisy, and by performing on the depression, there is a chance the subsequent release may cause an intermittent problem. By performing on the release, there is always the chance any intermittent problems from the depression are neutralized by the operation called for. Also, debugging a system may entail use of an oscilloscope in an awkward position. It is easier to depress the button, position oneself to observe the scope, and then release it, rather than positioning oneself first, then fumbling for the pushbutton.

The common timing signals for the execution of the console operations are shown in **Figure 3.18,** with the timing chain of Fig. 3.18(b) initiated by the release of the pushbutton. The trailing edge of PB triggers FF1, whose data input is tied to $+V_{CC}$ through a resistor, yielding value "1". The other three flip-flops are strobed by +OSC gated by +T3. (This is an alternate way to clock an edge-triggered flip-flop register with a common clock enable, but it introduces clock skew.) In the timing diagram, the arrow labeled "1" indicates that the positive edge of −PB causes the change in FF1. Arrow 2 shows that with FF1 active, at the clock edge, FF2 changes. FF1 output may or may not get to FF2 with adequate setup time, so the danger of an ambiguous output on FF2 exists. This danger is waited out one full clock cycle before clocking either a 0 or 1 into FF3, as indicated by arrow 3. With FF3 (CONCY1) active, in a similar fashion, the next

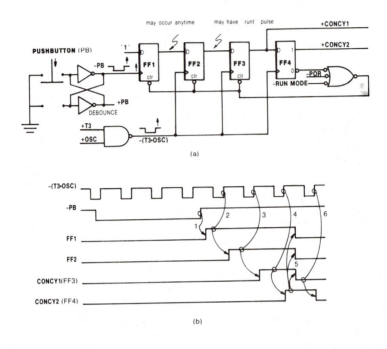

Figure 3.18. *Generation of timing signals for console operations.*

(a) Circuit for console operations timing generator. (b) Timing diagram.

clock pulse −(T3•OSC) activates CONCY2. This activation causes the level-sensitive clear of the first three flip-flops, as seen by arrow 4. At the next clock active transition, indicated by arrow 6, the low level on FF3 causes FF4 to go low. The "clean" timing signals CONCY1 and CONCY2 may now be used to implement the console operations.

Figure 3.19 illustrates control of the RUN MODE flip-flop. Assume the RUN flip-flop is initially set. To halt the computer, the control knob need only be moved off the RUN position to one of the other positions. This gives a level-sensitive clear to the RUN flip-flop. With this flip-flop clear, the level-sensitive clear via signal −RUN MODE is removed from the first three console timing generator circuit flip-flops, and the machine will respond when the pushbutton is depressed and released. Signal +CONCY1 and T3 activates signal +RUN CY. The trailing edge of this signal turns RUN MODE on. We note here that power-on reset (POR) will clear the RUN flip-flop, as will signal +HALT. We can allow the programmer to activate the +HALT signal by a DIO instruction, to device address 0, with a special control subop signifying HALT.

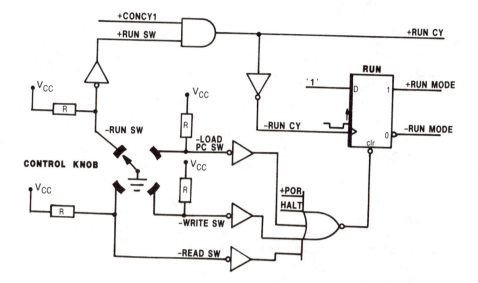

Figure 3.19. *Control knob and RUN operation.*

3.11.4. Console Operation Implementation

The LOAD, READ, and WRITE console operations can now be implemented, with RTN statements, during CONCY1 of the console operation timing generator. At some point in the data flow, the switches SW(0-15) must be brought in to a register. Our choice is to use the AC register for this purpose, by expanding its 3×1 MUX to a 4×1 MUX. Bringing SW through MD would be preferable, but MDMUX already is a 4×1 MUX; the resulting 5×1 MUX would be cumbersome.

3.12. TM-16 CONTROL UNIT IMPLEMENTATION

We have implemented the system clock, the Run/Halt controls, and the console operation cycle timing signals. The data flow is as shown in Fig. 3.12, and is implemented in straightforward fashion with MSI building blocks. The control unit governs the behavior of the data flow to interpret the instructions of a computer program. A sequence of microoperations defines the control unit behavior. Each microoperation takes place when the conditional information is satisfied. The control unit is defined by the RTN statements of §§3.9.5. What remains is to further decompose the RTN statements into *control signal activations.*

3.12.1. Control Point Gathering

Each RTN statement describes *behavior*. For example, the statement

E•LAC•T2:   AC←MD

means that whenever *condition* "E•LAC•T2" exists, then MD is routed to and strobed into the AC. We must convert this statement of behavior into control unit *structure*. The data routing is accomplished by selecting the proper combination for the ACMUX control points; the strobing into AC is done by activating the AC enable control point ENAC. The condition which causes this, E•LAC•T2, is a *p-term* in the terminology of boolean algebra. For our purposes, a p-term converts to the structural part known as an AND gate. The p-term E•LAC•T2 *implies* control signal ENAC because that p-term *activates* the "Enable AC" control point of the data flow. In what follows, we let ENAC denote both the control point "Enable AC" as well as the control signal feeding that point. In other words, corresponding to the data flow *connection point* labeled "Enable AC", there is an *interconnection* of the same meaning. The interconnection feeds the data flow control point from the control unit.

E•LAC•T2 is not the only p-term which activates ENAC. The design of control signal ENAC is the result of the boolean OR (or gathering) of all its p-terms. The problem at hand uses boolean algebra, but we do not start with a truth table in our design of control signal ENAC. Our starting point is the set of RTN statements of §§3.9.5, and we must discover for ourselves the p-terms which imply each of the date flow control signals. We *gather* the p-terms for each control point. The operation is performed by searching the list of RTN statements for all instances in which the AC should be enabled. The result of this operation is the control signal activation logic.

3.12.2. Identification of Control Points

To fix our direction, we list the data flow control points, and the setting and clearing of miscellaneous control flip-flops (such as interrupt enable IEN), in **Table 3.6**. The control points are broken down into one of three categories according to the three columns. The signals in each category receive similar treatment.

3.12.3. Microoperations Imply Control Point Activations

On the left-hand side of the RTN statements (before the colon) are the conditions or p-terms. Table 3.6 lists the control points which the p-terms may imply. The question to be answered next is, "Which p-terms imply which control signals?" The answer is found in the microoperation: each microoperation implies that certain control signals should be activated.

Table 3.6. TM-16 Control Points

Register Clocking	Multiplexer Controls	Control Flip-flops
ENAC	ACMUX(0,1)*	IEN
ENIR	MAMUX	INP
ENMA	MDMUX(0,1)*	OUPT
ENMD		RUPT
LDPC (Load PC)		WRITE
INCPC (Incr PC)		

* Note: A 4×1 MUX has two encoded control points.

Table 3.7. From Microoperations to Control Points

Destination	Microoperation	Activated Control Points
AC	AC←MD	ENAC ACMUX
	AC←MD plus AC	ENAC ACMUX
	AC←IO Data Bus	ENAC ACMUX
	AC←SW (console, not implemented)	ENAC ACMUX
IR	IR←MD(0-3)	ENIR
MA	MA←PC	ENMA MAMUX
	MA←MD(3-15)	ENMA MAMUX
MD	MD←M[MA]	ENMD MDMUX
	MD←0,PC	ENMD MDMUX
	MD←AC	ENMD MDMUX
	MD←0010 0000 0000 0000	ENMD MDMUX
PC	INCR PC	INCPC
	PC←MD(3-15)	LDPC

Table 3.7 lists the microoperations generated by the interpretation of the instructions, and the relevant control points which they activate. Table 3.7 brings out a characteristic of the busing system being used in the TM-16. The bus control signals are concerned with the destination register of the data transfer. In bidirectional bus systems, control signals also deal with the source register. Were the TM-16 to use a single bidirectional bus,

then the microoperation AC←MD would imply control signal ENAC as usual, but it would also imply a control signal to place the contents of the MD register on the bidirectional bus.

3.12.4. Detailed Gathering of Control Point Implicants

We now proceed with the more detailed implementation. Basically the control points are of two kinds, register clock enabling signals, and MUX control signals. First we handle the clock enabling signals, by searching Table 3.6 for each instance a register receives data:

$$ENAC = E{\cdot}LAC{\cdot}T2 + E{\cdot}ADD{\cdot}T2 + E{\cdot}DIO{\cdot}IR(3){\cdot}T2 \tag{3.1}$$

$$
\begin{aligned}
LDPC = {} & E{\cdot}JMP{\cdot}T0 + E{\cdot}SRJ{\cdot}T0 + E{\cdot}IRJ{\cdot}T2 \\
& + E{\cdot}JAN{\cdot}AC(0){\cdot}T0
\end{aligned} \tag{3.2}
$$

$$
\begin{aligned}
ENMD = {} & I{\cdot}T2 + E{\cdot}SRJ{\cdot}T0 + E{\cdot}IRJ{\cdot}T1 \\
& + E{\cdot}LAC{\cdot}T1 + E{\cdot}SAC{\cdot}T0 + E{\cdot}ADD{\cdot}T1
\end{aligned} \tag{3.3}
$$

$$ENMA = I{\cdot}T0 + I{\cdot}T3 \tag{3.4}$$

$$ENIR = I{\cdot}T3 \tag{3.5}$$

3.12.5. Special Treatment for MUX Select Controls

The multiplexer select signals are an encoding of individual gating signals. For example, the select for MAMUX which feeds MA must be in one state when the PC is to pass, and in another when MD(3-15) is to pass. The PC source is assigned state 0 and the MD source is assigned state 1 of control signal MAMUX. The actual problem of the synthesis of the control signal contains many "don't care" conditions, because MAMUX need only be in the 0 state for "I·T0" and in the 1 state for "I·T3". The simplest solution is:

$$MAMUX = T3 \tag{3.6}$$

This assignment assumes nothing bad will happen in E·T3, which the reader can verify: looking at Eq. (3.4), the MA is never clocked in state E. Proceeding to the synthesis of ACMUX feeding AC, the combinational problem is one where, in effect, the designer has partial control over the truth table specification of the circuit. **Table 3.8** tabulates the p-terms to pass each of the four sources for AC.

Let the two bits of ACMUX be ACMUX(0) and ACMUX(1). Suppose the source selection is made according to **Table 3.9.**

The assignment shown in Table 3.9 is arbitrary, and we know of no algorithm for achieving a minimal implementation in the general case. For the assignment made for Table 3.9, the following solution is obtained:

$$ACMUX(0) = ADD \tag{3.7}$$
$$ACMUX(1) = DIO \tag{3.8}$$

The solution is obtained from Tables 3.8 and 3.9. Ignoring the switches as the source, from Table 3.9, ACMUX(0) must be 1 when Z is passed. From Table 3.8, this occurs when "E•ADD•T2" is active. Similarly, from Table 3.9, ACMUX(1) must be 1 when IODATA BUS is to be passed, which from Table 3.8 is when "E•DIO•IR(3)•T2" is active.

Table 3.8. Four Sources for the AC, and their p-terms

_MD_	_IODATA BUS_	_Z_	_SW_
E•LAC•T2	E•DIO•IR(3)•T2	E•ADD•T2	(not implemented)

Table 3.9. ACMUX Selection Assignment for Sources

ACMUX(0)	_ACMUX(1)_	_Source_
0	0	Pass MD
0	1	Pass IODATA BUS
1	0	Pass Z
1	1	Pass Switches (SW)

Due to the ability to manipulate the "truth" table of Table 3.9, and the large number of "don't cares", a simple solution resulted from what appeared to be a difficult problem. When the machine is halted, the IR register might contain the opcodes for ADD or DIO, which might be bad for the console operations. However, note from Fig. 3.9 that the decoder for the opcodes is disabled when not in the RUN state. When not in RUN mode, the IR could contain anything, which could disrupt the console operations unless inhibited.

Table 3.10. P-terms for Sources on MDMUX to MD

MREAD BUS	_SRJ Forced_	_PC_	_AC_
I•RUPT'•T2	I•RUPT•T2	E•SRJ•T0	E•SAC•T0
E•IRJ•T1			
E•LAC•T1			
E•ADD•T1			

For MDMUX, the p-term table appears as **Table 3.10.** Note that one of the MDMUX select signal combinations has four p-terms; the others have one.

Table 3.11. MDMUX Assignment of Sources		
MDMUX(0)	**_MDMUX(1)_**	**Sources**
0	0	AC
0	1	MREAD BUS
1	0	PC
1	1	SRJ
		(forced SRJ to address 0)

wrong

With the source combinations assigned as shown in **Table 3.11,** the equations for the MDMUX selection inputs are:

$$\text{MDMUX}(0) = \text{SRJ} + \text{RUPT} \qquad (3.9)$$
$$\text{MDMUX}(1) = \text{T1} + \text{T2} \qquad (3.10)$$

The reader may verify from Table 3.11 that whenever the MD is clocked, the correct source is selected. Again, the large number of "don't care" conditions has permitted a relatively simple encoding of the select bits for a 4×1 MUX.

3.12.6. Miscellaneous Control Signals

The design includes control flip-flops RUPT, INP, OUTP, WRITE, and IEN, and incrementing the PC. Control flip-flops RUPT and IEN have been implemented as auxiliary circuits in Fig. 3.11. The remaining control flip-flops are implemented in the following fashion. In the action part of an RTN statement, the requirement that the flip-flop be set is expressed by an action of the form SETFF. For example:

E·SRJ·T0: SETWRITE

For that statement, the conditional information (to the right of the colon) represents a setting p-term which should feed input JFF of a JK flip-flop. We similarly handle *conditional information* implying control signals of the type SETFF (or CLRFF). The conditional information of RTN statements which activate (or deactivate) flip-flops represent p-terms which cause the flip-flop to be set (or cleared). These p-terms are implicants of the relevant JK flip-flop input J (or K).

The equations are tabulated here. The common JK flip-flop clock signal is OSC. Changes take place on the leading edge of OSC which is at the beginning of a clock time period.

$$JINP = \qquad E \cdot DIO \cdot IR(3) \cdot T0 \tag{3.11}$$

$$KINP = \qquad E \cdot T3 \tag{3.12}$$

$$JOUTP = \qquad E \cdot DIO \cdot IR(3)' \cdot T0 \tag{3.13}$$

$$KOUTP = \qquad E \cdot T3 \tag{3.14}$$

$$JWRITE = \qquad E \cdot SRJ \cdot T0 + E \cdot SAC \cdot T0 \tag{3.15}$$

$$KWRITE = \qquad E \cdot T2 \tag{3.16}$$

The following equation implements the HALT control signal, employed in Fig. 3.19.

$$HALT = \qquad E \cdot DIO \cdot DEVADR0 \cdot DEVCTL2 \tag{3.17}$$

The following equation describes when the PC is to be incremented:

$$INCPC = \qquad I \cdot RUPT' \cdot T2 + E \cdot SRJ \cdot T1 \tag{3.18}$$

INCPC may be gated against OSC through a NAND (as in Fig. 3.18(a)) for $(T3 \cdot OSC)'$ to provide a positive edge only when desired. Alternatively, if the PC counter has an enable input, signal INCPC could feed the enable input and the clocking edge could be provided by OSC.

Equations (3.1) through (3.18) represent the control signal activation logic. Each equation results from the "gathering" of the implicants for that control point signal. The equations can be converted directly into AND and OR gates. For the purpose of implementation, these equations describe the lower-level structure (circuit level) of a portion of the control unit. We have thus converted the portion of the RTN statements describing flip-flop behavior at the data flow component level, into boolean statements related to circuit structure.

3.12.7. Control Signal Timing Charts

We can now construct timing charts for control states I and E for each instruction type and address mode, as well as for the interrupt sequence. Figure 3.20 shows the timing chart of the control signals for state I assuming no interrupt (RUPT is inactive).

The portions of the control unit not described by the RTN statements are *auxiliary circuits*. Auxiliary circuits implement groundrules or conventions, or are concerned with lower-level details, or are some of the basic timing and control circuits such as the RUN flip-flop.

3.13. SUMMARIZING COMMENTS

The general topics of relevance to the computer design problem are:

1. definition of data flow or internal organization, and control points,
2. timing cycles: definition of data flow cycle, control state cycle, memory cycle,
3. instruction set interpretation via RTN statements, and
4. implementation of data flow, and generation of control signals.

We view the TM-16 as an introduction to design. Even though the TM-16 design problem is simple, we introduce and employ the most important concepts required for more complex designs. We address the data flow

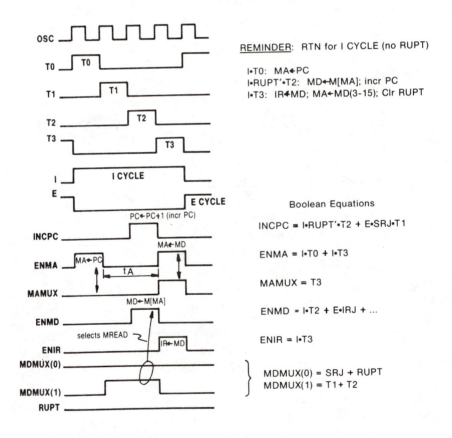

Figure 3.20. *Timing chart for relevant control points of I cycle, no interrupt.*

component and RTN level of the problem without the detail of a complicated instruction set. The instruction set is quite weak, and the system timing cycle is simplistic. The data flow is strongly influenced by the RTN approach, and as a consequence has some unnecessary data paths.

However, many important teaching objectives are met. The interpretation of instructions as a sequence of microoperations or actions is illustrated. Register transfers dominate the actions. RTN statements are convenient to express data flow events which are to take place. A single RTN statement may result in the activation of many control points.

We show that the data flow is like a marionette, with the marionette strings corresponding to control points. RTN statements correspond to coordinated actions or movements for which the puppeteer may manipulate several strings.

The block diagram for the data flow and RTN statements for the control part illustrate the "data organization/procedure" duality present in most information systems. The action part subdivides into two parts; one part deals with the data flow events whereas the other part deals with the control state of the system. The major state control, the interrupt enable flip-flop IEN, RUN flip-flop, and timing point generation, relate to the state of the system.

The straightforward design of the instruction interpreter is contrasted with the design of the interface to the front panel or console. The front panel design is characteristic of *random control logic* and appears to be "ad hoc". Systematic procedures exist in the form of tabular or flow table approaches, but such approaches treat all inputs equally. Unfortunately in the real world some inputs are more important than others, and in a hierarchical or iterative approach the most important signals must be handled first. Later the design is refined to include the effects of the less important signals. In handling any kind of complex problem, the "divide and conquer" approach is used. For the console operations, the method of starting and stopping the RUNMODE major states of I and E is first designed. Then we designed the circuit for the console operations timing generator (Fig. 3.18(a)). This functional unit recurs often in digital systems design, and it soon becomes a part of the logic designer's stock-in-trade. Note that we needed the signal +RUNMODE, which starts and stops the cycling of the I and E states (Fig. 3.16). With the console timing generator implemented, the RUN mode circuit design of Fig. 3.19 is relatively easy. Fig. 3.19 *generates* the needed RUNMODE signal. Once the timing environment is known, other console operations which operate on the data flow can be designed at the higher conceptual level of RTN statements.

Where RTN statements are applicable, the designer has a powerful higher-level tool. However we have seen that not all problems seem to be amenable to the RTN approach. This is most true in dealing with detailed timing circuits, which we implemented by planned iteration.

Once a circuit has been built, such as the realization of Equations 3.1 through 3.18, the designer tends to think at the gate level. It is at that level that bugs are discovered and fixed. The physical circuit is changed in order to get on with debugging, and thoughts are directed to the shapes and blocks of the diagram representing that circuit. There is no RTN intermediary. When bugs are fixed by modifying the physical circuit, the RTN statements may soon become outdated as a description of the implementation. This is unfortunate. We recommend that the RTN level document, which is so useful in teaching the system to others, be kept up to date.

Timing charts are an important tool. The timing figures have been included as a reflection of our own experience in visualizing what is happening on the screen of an oscilloscope or logic analyzer. Computer engineers soon learn to think in terms of timing charts.

The design procedure is neither characterized as strictly top-down nor as bottom-up. For the console operations, we began at the top with the decision as to the functional units or component "pieces" of the system. Then we dealt with the bottom level in constructing some functional units. Finally, we reached a point where RTN statements could be written to handle switches to memory, or memory to display operations. A theory which has gained credence in the field of natural languages is: the language *in which* a person thinks will influence the *way* he thinks. We feel the theory is applicable to descriptive techniques as well. For this reason, we have sought to present this material using the descriptive tool appropriate to the particular thought process involved.

One interesting point for the reader to ponder is the question of analogies between computer programming and digital systems design. We feel there are sufficient differences in the way of thinking about digital design to discourage an approach that characterizes digital design as "like programming". Our basis for this feeling centers on the use of conditional information to decide what should be done in any given timing period. The point is more obvious for the more complex SC-16 of Chapter 5.

Digital design and program design have surprisingly many similarities, and appreciating them is helpful for the additional insights provided. Both involve solving complex problems and both must divide and conquer. Both often have bugs at interfaces between components and the outside world. In programming, the specification of something which does not need to be done costs time. In hardware, control signals can be activated when not needed, provided no harm is done. The concept of a combinational circuit always doing its job sometimes takes a programmer a while to grasp. The programmer is accustomed to generating an "ADD" instruction to obtain a sum, and does not immediately appreciate the fact that an adder circuit is *always* generating a sum.

PROBLEMS

3.1.   Treat the following flip-flops as components of the global major state of the TM-16: CONCY1, CONCY2, FF1 (from Fig. 3.18(a)), I, and E (Fig. 3.16), and RUNMODE flip-flop (Fig. 3.19). Let PB denote the pushbutton input which generates CONCY1 on the trailing edge. Draw a state transition diagram for the TM-16 with primary inputs PB, RUN, LOAD, WRITE, READ, and the HALT instruction being executed.

3.2.   Suppose the JAN instruction were replaced by an ISZ (Increment and Skip if Zero) instruction, described as follows:

$$MD \leftarrow M[MA]$$
$$MD \leftarrow MD \text{ plus } 1$$
$$(MD = ZERO): \quad PC \leftarrow PC \text{ plus } 1$$
$$M[MA] \leftarrow MD$$

To implement the instruction, what changes would you make to the data flow? Why? Describe the new state I and state E RTN statements for the execution of this instruction. Use time T4 with partial loss of credit if you find no other way to avoid another execution cycle.

3.3.   Make a timing chart of the following signals during the execution cycles of the SRJ instruction:

T0, T1, T2, T3, E, MDMUX(0), MDMUX(1),
ENMD, LDPC, INCPC.

3.4.   Redraw the timing chart of the relevant signals in Fig. 3.20 (timing chart for state I) which would be different with the RUPT flip-flop in the active state.

3.5.   "What if" the TM-16 is in RUN mode, and someone accidentally depresses key PB? What would you expect *should* happen?

3.6.   (a) Can the RUPT flip-flop be cleared at the start of state E? (b) Redesign the circuit of Fig. 3.11 using a JK flip-flop for RUPT.

3.7.   Do the RTN implementation for the TM-16 using the data flow shown below. Compare cost and performance with the data flow of Fig. 3.12. The MW (Memory Write) register replaces the MD register for writing. Instead of direct register-to-register paths, the adder is used as a switch by disabling the second operand. The PC is incremented by adding CIN through the adder.

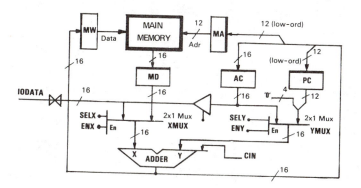

* CHAPTER 4 *

MEMORY SYSTEM DESIGN

4.1. INTRODUCTION

4.1.1. Primary versus Secondary Storage

Memory systems, like anything else, have a price and deliver a function. Primary and secondary storage represent a *physical* hierarchy involving cost and access time. *Main memory* (or primary storage) stores computer programs and data, and IO buffers. Main memory is *program addressable*, a significant property. The program counter points to a location or address in main memory. The result of the effective address calculation performed during instruction execution is a primary memory location. The program and its variables refer to primary storage; IO operations handle transfers between primary and secondary storage. The *work* of a computer system is accomplished by bringing data into main memory, modifying it, and returning the new values to secondary storage and/or to the user.

Main memory is usually in scarce supply for two reasons. First, the system performance or amount of work done per unit of time is very dependent on how fast main memory can be cycled. However, the faster the memory cycle, the more expensive the memory. Second, the instructions themselves must address operands in main memory. Many address bits are required if main memory is large. A 32-bit address pointer takes up twice as much space as a 16-bit address pointer. To reduce address pointer size, many small systems do not permit a large amount of main memory. Some systems such as the IBM System/38 business computer have devised a way to allow all of secondary storage to be addressed from the programming language, with very large address pointers. Such techniques are discussed later in conjunction with architectural considerations.

Secondary storage typically stores data records or files and copies of programs. Programs are treated as files when in secondary storage, but the system monitor can *load* a program into primary storage preparatory to running it. Secondary storage is distinguished in that it is accessed through the input-output class of instructions, and data transfers take place over the IO bus or channel. One of the active areas of computer architecture involves changing the traditional or "classical" separation of primary and secondary storage.

Media for secondary storage include direct access devices such as drums and disks, and sequential access devices such as magnetic tape. Secondary storage is slower and costs less per bit than main memory. Architectural aspects of IO are covered in Chapter 2. Direct memory access (DMA), IO channel, and memory-mapped IO techniques concern the memory system designer because of their effect on the memory interface.

4.1.2. Memory Technologies

The system performance is highly dependent upon main memory. The first generation computers employed several main memory technologies: latching relays, mercury or sonic delay lines, magnetic drums, and cathode ray storage tubes. Except for the storage tube, these technologies were relatively slow, and the storage tube was not without its reliability problems. In most early systems, the memory technology was chosen first and the CPU was designed around it.

The invention of the magnetic core memory system provided the second and third generation computers with a reliable random access (RAM) technology for main memories. The anachronistic term "random access" has come to mean that any location is equally accessible in time, as distinguished from the "sequential access" property of drums or delay lines. Magnetic core main memories so predominated the second generation computers that the term "core" became synonymous with memory; "low core" meant the lower addresses of main memory reserved for the monitor, "core dump" a printout of memory location values, and "more core" expressed the programmer's most fervent wish. Main memory was expensive enough to cause computer installation managers to have their programmers try to squeeze as much program function as possible into a small space. Today, VLSI semiconductor memories and virtual memory techniques are answering the programmer's wish for "more core".

In this chapter, we concentrate on monolithic (semiconductor) main memories. Semiconductors dominate main memory technology today, and have the advantage of great simplicity. For many years, magnetic cores were dominant, and are still in use where *nonvolatility* is important: core memories retain their contents after power is turned off.

4.1.3. Architectural and Organizational Aspects

The main memory system, in its most basic or fundamental implementation, is *single-level* (nonhierarchical). All memory locations are implemented in the same technology, and are equally accessible. The addresses generated by the programs are the actual physical (real) memory locations. The *cache technique* is a method for using a high-speed memory to retain recently used addresses. The cache memory is "backed up" by a slow main memory whose contents represent the physical capacity of main memory.

At program generation time the program has symbolic or named variables which the assembler or compiler program translates into a program *address space* or *name space*. An address in name space is sometimes called a *logical* or *absolute* address. On the other hand, the computer system possesses a physical or real main memory which defines a set of memory locations called the *memory space*. Addresses in the memory space are sometimes called *physical* or *real* locations or addresses. The mapping between the address space and memory space in small unsophisticated systems is trivial: the address space *is* the memory space and vice-versa. The simplest virtual-to-real address translation mapping occurs when the addresses generated by the programs are the actual physical (real) memory locations. See **Figure 4.1.**

In a *virtual memory,* an *address translation* function **F** maps addresses in the address space to locations in the virtual memory space. In virtual memory, we have a bottom-up construct which raises the programmer's conceptual level of memory. At a lower level of detail, the computer hardware and software handle the address translation, and bridge the

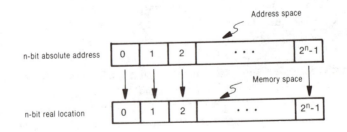

Figure 4.1. *The identity mapping from the address space to the memory space.*

conceptual gap. A virtual memory is little more than an address translation mechanism followed by a real memory. For convenience in implementing the mapping function, the mapping is performed on blocks of contiguous virtual addresses, as determined by high-order address bits. See **Figure 4.2.** In Fig. 4.2(a) the arrows show a mapping from virtual addresses to physical locations. Blocks 0 and 2 are mapped to blocks in real memory. If real memory is smaller than virtual memory, some virtual blocks (blocks 1 and K) must be mapped to secondary storage. Fig. 4.2(b) shows the address translation performed by mapping function **F,** where secondary storage is represented by a drum.

Address values in *linear* memory represent an unbroken sequence of address locations: the "next" contiguous address location in the sequence is one greater than the previous address location. Another term for linear is "one dimensional." The (real) memory space goes from location 0 to the highest location value.

In a *segmented* memory the address space is broken into distinct segments. The highest location value in one segment is not logically "next"

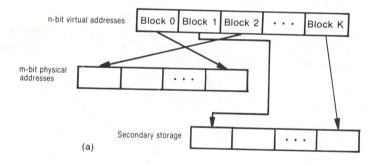

(a)

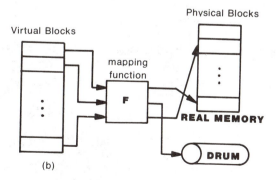

(b)

Figure 4.2. *Address translation.* (a) Mapping of blocks of addresses. (b) View showing physical locations of blocks.

or contiguous to the lowest address in the segment with the next higher segment number. Segments are independent memory spaces which themselves are linear and possibly subject to some address translation.

We define a *real memory* to be an unmapped linear memory system, with location numbers ranging from 0 to the highest physical location number. We first treat the memory system in terms of the more easily understood real memory model. Unmapped real memories are quite adequate for most low-cost microcomputer systems. Hierarchical memories (of two or more levels) and virtual memories are more complex; they require greater programming system awareness, and are more expensive to implement.

4.1.4. Memory Interface

A higher-level language programmer may generate the program statement "C = A + B". This is broken down into several memory-reference instruction (e.g. load accumulator and store accumulator) at the object code (machine language) level. Of course, *how* the instructions and data are transferred between main memory and the CPU is of no concern to the programmer, who is confident that the CPU designer has taken care of that matter. One of the objectives of this chapter is to show how the CPU designers and memory system designers follow the correct protocol in getting words into and out of main memory.

4.2. SYSTEM BALANCE CONSIDERATIONS

In this section, we first introduce some performance notions of the major elements of a computer system and the relationships among them. These relationships are derived empirically from systems which satisfy our intuition about being "in balance". They can help estimate the main memory *speed* and *capacity* required in a particular system, or the amount of *IO traffic* the main memory system is expected to sustain. The designer needs these estimates when considering the primary memory system design.

Figure 4.3 shows a block diagram with the main memory system as a component interfaced to the CPU and to secondary storage.

4.2.1. Some Characteristics and Performance Parameters

System organization is influenced by questions of cost-effectiveness. Main memory is an expensive system component, and its cost and performance should be in "balance" with the other system components. An important memory system specification is the *cycle time:* how frequently can one get a new word from memory? A related performance parameter is the memory *data rate* or *bandwidth,* which is the maximum number of bytes per

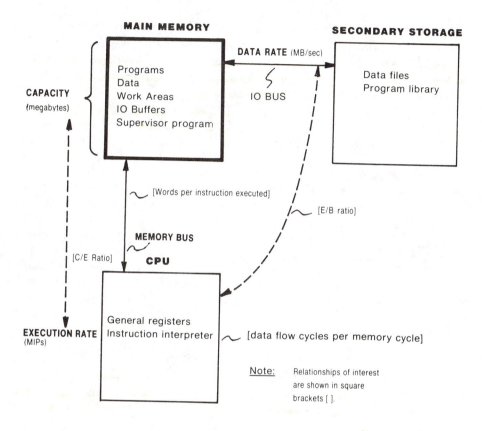

Figure 4.3. *Activity and relationships in a computer system.*

second that the system can accept or deliver. Present day memories measure bandwidth in megabytes per second (MB/sec). For main memories, bandwidth is the product of the number of bytes per access and the maximum number of memory cycles per second. Given a memory cycle time, the bandwidth can always be doubled by doubling the width of the word accessed. However, other system components may not make efficient use of the double-length data word.

In the case of secondary storage, the bandwidth does not completely describe device performance. Data rate generally refers to the *transfer time* once the first data byte has been accessed. Transfer times are on the order of hundreds of thousands or millions of bytes per second. However, secondary storage devices have delays: interrecord gaps, rotational delays (latency) of drum and disk storage, and seek time delay (the time to position the arm of a movable read/write head of a disk). The *access time* to the first byte may be several milliseconds. The secondary storage access situation somewhat resembles using tomato catsup from a half empty bottle. It takes some time for the first amount of catsup to be transferred to the plate, but then the rest of the bottle's contents follow rapidly!

Main memory cycle times are on the order of hundreds of nanoseconds, and access times to secondary storage are on the order of milliseconds; this difference is called the *access gap.*

The CPU performance is the instruction *execution rate,* traditionally measured in millions of instructions per second (MIPs). Of course, some instructions take less time to execute than others; the performance (average execution rate) will depend on the particular instruction sequence in the program. Each instruction's execution time is weighted by frequency of occurrence, to derive an average execution rate. An assignment of a frequency to each instruction is called an *instruction mix,* and is determined experimentally. The "MIP" rate, as it is also called, is a useful comparison factor between members of the same computer family architecture. However, the MIP rate can be misleading when referring to different architectures. A 1-MIP 8-bit wide microprocessor is not as powerful as a 1-MIP main frame data processor which handles 32-bit words and possesses a powerful set of machine language instructions and built-in operating system capabilities.

4.2.2.   CPU and Main Memory Bandwidth Relationships

For single-address machine language architectures, most instructions require two memory cycles: one cycle for the instruction fetch and a second cycle for the operand. Generally, the *memory cycle* is an integral number of data flow cycles. In the second generation, many systems used four data flow cycles per memory cycle. In the second and early third generation, the transistor logic circuit technology was much faster than the slower magnetic core memory technology. This mismatch gave rise to memory *interleaving* techniques to increase memory bandwidth in higher-performance machines. In interleaved memory systems, independent memory modules were defined on the basis of the low-order address bits.

Interleaving real memory directly to the CPU for performance purposes has been succeeded by the cache technique, discussed in §4.15. With a cache, interleaving plays a supporting role, and is almost always used to transfer multiword blocks of data between main memory and cache. This purpose of interleaving is to reduce peak power demand and bus width. The advent of semiconductor memory has provided performance comparable to the logic technology, so designers of modern systems have a wider choice of trade-offs.

Another useful parameter is the average number of memory cycles required per instruction execution. We can obtain this parameter from the same instruction mix used to calculate the average instruction execution rate. The number of memory cycles each instruction demands is weighted by its frequency of occurrence. Typically, between two and three memory references occur for each instruction executed.

4.2.3. Some Empirical Relationships

Our attention has been focused on the primary memory system. Let us now delve into some "computer lore" relating CPU MIP rates, main memory capacity, and IO bus data rate. In particular, studies have been made relating memory capacity to CPU execution rates (the C/E ratio), and the number of instructions executed for each byte transferred across the IO bus (the E/B ratio or Amdahl constant). Before explaining these relationships, and drawing conclusions, it is helpful to have a sample system in mind to serve as a crude "activity model".

We visualize the CPU running a transaction-oriented application program. The program receives input on a magnetic tape, updates files on a disk, and generates a report on a printer. Control of the system lies in the computer program which is running. The CPU slavishly fetches and executes instructions at its MIP rate. Input-output routines get input tape records and disk file records to main memory, and put updated records and lines of print to the disk and printer respectively. Main memory is employed for the storage of the application program and its "work" areas, and buffers for the input and output routines. Most systems have an operating system or monitor program to manage the IO and work flow.

4.2.4. The E/B Ratio: Executions per IO Bytes Transferred

A result of a study of IBM 7090 scientific programs showed that on average, one bit of IO data was transferred for each instruction executed. The term *E/B ratio* is used: E denotes instruction executions and B denotes 8-bit bytes transferred over the IO bus or channel. This phenomenon is also called the Amdahl constant (although it is not constant). For the IBM 7090 scientific programs, the ratio is about 8 (8 executions per 8-bit byte). One would expect a lower ratio for a simple interactive inquiry application such as playing "Adventure" on a time-shared system. Matick [1] gives some approximate E/B values of 8, 4, and 1+ for scientific, commercial or business processing (e.g. COBOL), and interactive terminal systems, respectively.

4.2.5. The Capacity per Execution Ratio (C/E)

An interesting empirical relationship exists between main memory capacity and CPU power. The amount of memory required by a computer system seems to grow. It is easy to underestimate memory requirements.

John von Neumann felt that 2,000 words was more than enough for a first generation computer. 18 to 20 years later, Brooks [2] was to characterize the addition of more main memory as the "universal elixir" for curing problems in the system.

Since the first generation, both CPU power and main memory capacity have increased. Amdahl [3] noted that memory capacity is historically directly proportional to CPU power. Recently, Matick [1] studied this relationship: a CPU with a given performance of m MIPs has a main memory capacity averaging between one-half to one times m megabytes. Thus, if the CPU power of a traditional system doubles, so should the main memory capacity, to keep "in balance".

Why should the memory capacity increase in proportion to the CPU speed? We can do no better, at this point, than offer an intuitive explanation. The C/E ratio tends to remain constant as CPU performance increases due to the existence of the access gap. If CPU power increases with no commensurate increase in secondary storage access time, the system becomes more "IO bound": the CPU waits a larger portion of time on secondary storage accesses. The E/B ratio indicates that higher-performance systems must handle a higher data rate. To reduce CPU idle time caused by IO waits, and to increase system throughput, the technique of *multiprogramming* was devised [4]. In principle, while one program enters the wait state due to an IO operation, the CPU resource is given to another program which is ready to continue because its IO operation has completed. Of course, multiprogramming requires a complicated supervisor or monitor program. As the number of programs in main memory increases, each requires some memory space, and a larger main memory is needed. To further minimize the effect of large access times, many systems transfer bigger blocks between main memory and secondary storage. As a result, more bytes are transferred, but the larger buffers consume more main memory capacity.

The *space-time* trade-off is also worth mentioning. Programmers can generally use more memory (a larger space requirement) to reduce the time it takes to execute a program. Similarly, computer designers often employ more memory to improve performance, or trade memory for logic circuits. Thus, the C/E ratio is not independent of the relative costs of CPU logic and main memory bits.

4.2.6. A Synopsis of System Balance Considerations

We can now devise a simplified, high-level picture of the computer system. The running program is in the driver's seat, but the execution speed is a function of the CPU power. A problem occurs if the CPU fails to transfer IO data due to slow primary or secondary storage devices. To achieve its potential, a system needs a main memory whose capacity is predictably related to the CPU execution rate. Moreover, to sustain the CPU execution rate, the secondary storage system must accept and deliver data at predictable rates. Higher-performance CPUs must possess a secondary storage system capable of meeting that data rate requirement [5].

Also of interest is the portion of the main memory bandwidth used by the IO system. An example is a 1-MIP CPU with a 16-bit instruction and data word. At two memory references per instruction, the execution rate places a bandwidth demand on main memory of four MB/second. Now consider the IO and an E/B of four. At a 1-MIP instruction execution rate and four executions/byte, the bandwidth requirement for IO is 250 KB/second, or 1/8 that of the instruction execution stream. We conclude that *the dominant user of main memory bandwidth is the CPU.* From the standpoint of computer system design, this discourages any trade-off which reduces memory bus performance as a concession to the IO traffic.

4.3. THE MAIN MEMORY BUS

Several approaches exist for interfacing the primary memory into the computing system. A simple but nontrivial approach is shown in **Figure 4.4.** A *system bus* serves main memory, the CPU, and IO devices, an approach most often found in low-cost and low-performance microcomputer systems. The single bus prevents data transfer concurrency at this level, but does not require the expense of a second bus. The CPU communicates with and controls IO devices over the same bus as it accesses main memory.

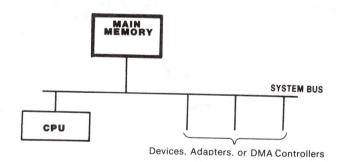

Figure 4.4. *A simple single-bus scheme.*

Figure 4.5 shows a more sophisticated *two-bus scheme:* the CPU communicates with IO devices over the IO Bus while accessing main memory over a memory bus. Employing two buses improves the performance of IO instructions and permits a higher-speed memory bus with a shorter inter-

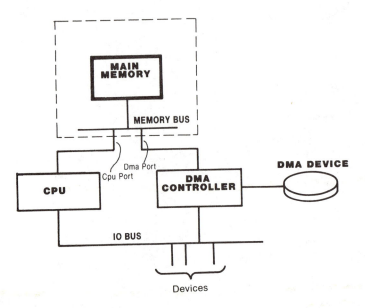

Figure 4.5. *Two-bus scheme for small systems.*

connection (wire) length. The IO data and IO address bus widths can now be smaller. Also shown in the figure is a DMA (direct memory access) controller. Many variations in DMA exist. Basically the DMA operation needs a data register, a count register, and a memory address register for each *port* (interconnection plus buffers). For the configuration of Fig. 4.5, these values are held in the DMA controller. Sometimes the main memory system is provided with an address and data register for each port. The system has an internal scheme which handles and coordinates each port. The arrangement is called a multiport memory system and is illustrated in Fig. 4.5 in dotted lines. Some late third generation systems used multiprocessed CPUs which shared the same modular main memory system, and the CPUs interfaced to individual ports of the main memory modules.

Figure 4.6 shows a configuration common to the IBM S/360 and S/370 architecture. The CPU and the IO channels communicate with memory over the memory bus. Each channel has its own control lines and IO Bus. The channels execute a "channel program" in main memory. The memory data bus may be 32 bits wide, whereas the IO bus usually has an 8-bit sub-bus. Several channels can be active at a time, increasing the possibility for concurrency in the system.

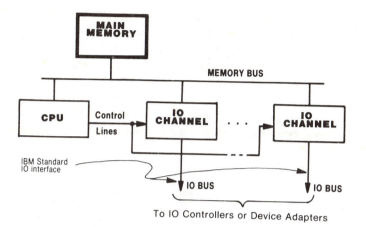

Figure 4.6. *Single memory bus and multiple IO buses.*

4.4. THE COMPOSITION OF THE INTERFACE BUSES

The memory bus, IO bus and system bus interconnections (Figs. 4.4 and 4.5) are themselves composed of three fields or sub-buses: (1) the *data bus* (if bidirectional) or data buses (read-data and write-data if unidirectional), (2) an *address* bus, and (3) a *control* bus. (In some systems such as the IBM Standard IO interface, the data and address buses are time-shared.) The control bus is loosely defined as signal lines that cannot be identified as data or address. The address bus identifies a memory location or IO device (or subdevice).

If a system uses a single system bus, it takes the place of both the IO bus and memory bus. Some simple system buses use the value on the address bus to determine whether or not an IO device is addressed. In a more flexible and powerful approach, distinct control bus states (or IO strobe signals distinct from memory strobe signals) determine whether the system bus is being used as a memory bus or an IO bus. In one state, main memory delivers or accepts data bus information, and in the other state an IO device performs this function.

4.4.1. A Single-User Memory Example (One-Way Control)

Before discussing the general requirements of the memory bus, we first consider the important data transfer concepts for a simple single-user case. In some single-purpose microcomputer applications with programmed IO (such as control of a traffic signal light), the exclusive use of the memory is to fetch instructions and transfer operands to the CPU. The memory is a complete slave to the CPU and does only what it is *told,* namely either to read or to write. When the memory has no chance to respond, the interface is under *one-way control;* i.e. control signalling is only one-way.

A block diagram of this simple system is shown in **Figure 4.7.** Fig. 4.7 illustrates the point of the memory system as a *functional unit.* The memory interface bus provides the *connection points.* There is one *control point,* WRITE. Data input connections are the address and write-data buses. The data output connection is the read-data bus. The behavior of the memory system is simply described: to receive or deliver data to or from the addressed location.

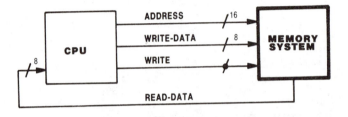

Figure 4.7. *A simple memory bus interface, using one-way control.*

Note that from the viewpoint of the memory system designer, read-data is "data out". To the CPU designer, read-data is "data in": the "data out" of the memory is "data in" to the CPU. "Read-data" is a term both would find unambiguous. The second type of data on the memory interface bus is write-data, data to be written to memory. Since read-data and write-data are mutually exclusive, many memory interfaces have a bidirectional data bus.

The second type of information on the memory bus is the address (or location) of each data word in memory. What remains is the control portion. Technically, the only control line needed in a memory environment with one-way control is a signal signifying a write operation. The remainder of the interface specification can be handled by timing agreements: when the WRITE control signal is inactive and the address lines have been stable for time tA(ad) nanoseconds, the memory system designer ensures that the read-data lines are valid with M[Address]. The data flow cycle and memory cycle are synchronized to meet the timing requirements. This simple memory system was present in the TM-16 machine of the previous chapter.

At the microoperations level, the designer thinks in terms of a *read operation* ("get me the word at address *m*"), or a *write operation* ("take this word and store it at address *m*"). At a greater level of detail the designer must be concerned with the timing, to insure that data has time to become valid following a change of address or control signals, before being accepted by the recipient.

The simplest CPU memory interface occurs when only the CPU uses the memory. The CPU always addresses memory at the same time in the system timing cycle, and the memory always delivers the read-data after the same access delay. In this approach, the CPU cycle and memory cycle are driven by the same system clock. When the "CPU Wait" technique is added to this approach, the resulting memory system can accommodate other users.

4.4.2. The Need for Autonomy (Interlocking)

Many single-user "local" or buffer monolithic memories are designed for one-way control, i.e., without need of a response from the memory. In most applications, although a servant, the memory system has some autonomy. The memory bus handles transactions in a cooperative spirit. Instead of *telling* the memory to read or write, the memory is politely *requested* to read or write. If the memory cannot satisfy the request in time, it so informs the requester. This capability gives the interface an interlocking mechanism; the CPU designer is forced to solve the problem of a memory cycle not being available when requested.

The desire for memory autonomy results from two considerations: *organizational* and *technological*. Organizationally, the memory may serve more than one requester. When an IO channel and the CPU both request the same memory cycle, one of them (usually the CPU) must be prepared to wait. A status or feedback signal from memory indicating temporary denial of a request is needed. The feedback signal provides means for a response, allowing for *two-way control*. The memory is regarded as a shared resource, requiring some means of apportioning or prioritizing its use.

The second consideration, technological, results because the memory cannot always respond within a predetermined time. Some memory technologies, such as dynamic semiconductor RAM, require a memory cycle periodically to *refresh* the memory contents. (Dynamic RAM is like an automobile battery, which loses its charge after a period of time. Dynamic RAM memory cells must be "recharged" thousands of times per second.) Another memory technique stores more recently used memory data in *cache* memory buffer locations whose access is faster [6, 7]. The requester will have to wait if data is not in the cache. A further example is a system which uses a high-speed memory for some locations and a low-speed memory for other locations in the same memory space. In such a system, the memory response is a function of whether the data is in the high-speed memory or not. In summary, two-way control coordinates the temporary denial of a request at the requesting functional unit. This coordination may be handled in many ways.

4.5. MEMORY INTERFACE CONSIDERATIONS

4.5.1. Custom versus Standard Interfaces

Historically, the CPU-to-main-memory interface has been custom-designed for each system. When the memory and CPU design are done by the same manufacturer, cost effectiveness is achieved through a custom-designed bus, tailored to the chosen memory and packaging technology. When the CPU is denied a memory access request, the memory system can simply turn off (idle) the CPU timing signal or clock. In the IBM S/360 Model 65, sometimes the data flow needed data by the third data flow cycle from the request, and at other times after the fourth data flow cycle. The memory supplied a special signal along with the CPU read request to indicate which of these needs existed. As a result, a data flow cycle was "saved" whenever a 4-cycle request could not have been satisfied in three cycles. The bus was custom-designed, and here was an opportunity to spend a few gate level circuits and some wiring to buy increased system performance. Such "tricks" are not as easily implemented with standard-ized buses.

Some lower-performance microprocessor systems benefit from the greater flexibility of a standardized bus. Altair developed one of the earliest such buses, now called the S-100, for use in a computer hobbyist system. The bus definition has two parts of interest to the logic designer: (1) an identification of the function assigned to edge connector fingers of a pc card, and (2) a set of timing dependencies or constraints. The back-plane of a card cage which uses the bus can have pins of the same function wired together, such as the bidirectional data or address portions of the bus.

4.5.2. Centralized versus Decentralized Control

Packaging considerations and the desire to define a "memory card" which can be replicated for increased memory capacity influence the memo-ry bus. Two possibilities exist. One uses a *centralized* controller (see Frankenberg and Cross [8]). Another uses *distributed control;* each memory card is provided with its own address, and read and write control logic. See **Figure 4.8**. With a memory controller, the address and data registers and the high-order address decoder are centralized as in Fig. 4.8(a). Distribut-ed control, shown in Fig. 4.8(b), prevails in memory cards which are pluggable into standard buses such as for the Intel Multibus and its Single Board Computer (SBC) product line.

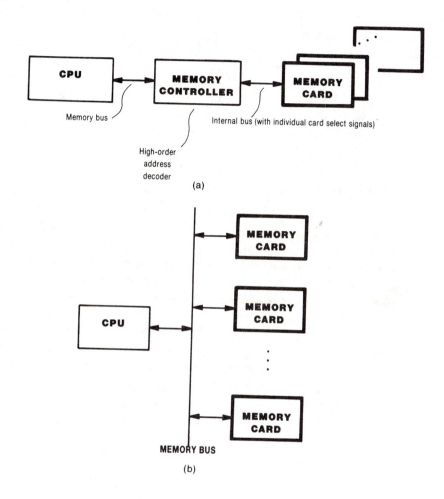

Figure 4.8. *Centralized vs. distributed controls.* (a) Centralized controller. (b) Distributed controller.

4.5.3. Synchronous versus Asynchronous Interface

The interface scheme can be designed especially for a particular CPU, and receive its clock timing from the system clock. Alternatively, the interface can have its own internal clock and be applicable to many different CPUs. In the latter case, a "handshaking" protocol is convenient; the memory receives an asynchronous "start" command, to which the memory responds with a "busy" signal. When "busy" goes inactive, the read-data bus is valid for a specified interval surrounding the trailing edge of the busy signal.

Synchronous memory interfacing needs two-way control, as the system is not immune from some kind of feedback signalling. The CPU is rarely the exclusive user of the memory. The input-output system may have its own requirement for an interface to the memory. In this case, when the IO is "stealing" a memory cycle, the memory system can "turn off" the CPU clock. Some microprocessor CPUs have a "wait" or "hold" input which places the CPU in an idle state. Such a state is also useful in "mixed" memory systems which incorporate some memory chips with slower access time than the CPU normally expects.

4.5.4. Who has the Data and Address Registers?

In a more autonomous and sophisticated memory system, the memory controller logic provides registers for the address and data. The CPU need only meet the setup time specifications when requesting a memory cycle. In a more economical approach, the memory system may employ the memory address and data registers in the CPU to hold the information valid for the specified durations of the memory cycle. This approach shares the use of these registers between the CPU and memory.

A related question concerns the multiplexing or directionality of the address and data buses. In a simple system, in which all IO goes through the CPU, the address lines are exclusively from the CPU to the memory. In more complicated systems, the address bus connective may use the wire-OR or tri-state technique, with a bus arbiter or controller to ensure only one user acquires the bus at any time. There may be two unidirectional data buses, one for read-data and another for write-data. Alternatively, there may be a single bidirectional data bus whose direction is defined by the current memory cycle being a read or a write operation.

4.6. MBUS: A CPU-CONTROLLED MEMORY BUS

In this section, we specify a synchronous memory bus interface called MBUS. In the following section, we design a memory system to interface with MBUS. MBUS is not a standard; it is customized. The CPU is the single user and provides the address and control fields of the interface. The MBUS interface signal lines are identified and named as shown in **Figure 4.9.** The CPU supplies the memory write-data over the MWRI-DATA bus for a write operation. The memory provides the read-data over the MREADATA bus on a read operation. A two-way control response is provided through a signal called MWAIT whose source is the memory system.

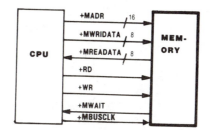

Figure 4.9. *A CPU-controlled memory bus, MBUS.*

4.6.1. Synchronization to the CPU Data Flow Cycle

The MBUS is *synchronous* because the CPU furnishes a periodic signal, MBUSCLK, to synchronize bus data transfers and the CPU "wait" function. Like many custom buses, this particular bus is defined for the convenience of the CPU designer. The read and write cycles of the TM-16 are assumed to be two data flow cycles each. Clearly, if the memory cannot meet that specification, the CPU must "wait". It is also most convenient from a design standpoint that the CPU wait in increments of a data flow cycle. When the "wait" time is an integral but variable (not predetermined) number of cycles of the bus clock, the system is *semisynchronous*. Timing synchronizer "glitches" should be avoided, and the memory should be synchronized to the same central clock as the CPU data flow cycle.

4.6.2. A Memory Cycle is two Data Flow Cycles

In normal operations, the CPU must inform the memory of the nature of the operation (read or write) and when the CPU expects data (for a read) or can change the address and data (for a write). The CPU has two control lines for this purpose: RD and WR. Signal RD is activated shortly after the start of the first MBUSCLK cycle of the read operation, and WR is similarly activated for a write operation.

The read and write operations each require two data flow cycles. If the memory cannot comply with the 2-MBUSCLK cycle requirement, there must be some agreement (protocol or specification) on when and how the memory is to ask the CPU to idle or "wait". In our case, memory activates the MWAIT signal before the end of the second cycle. When the request is satisfied by the memory system, feedback signal MWAIT is deactivated, allowing the CPU to continue.

Figure 4.10 shows the timing for the normal and delayed read operations, and the CPU data flow cycle defined by MBUSCLK. The data flow cycles are numbered 1 through 8. Shortly into cycle 1, RD is activated. It

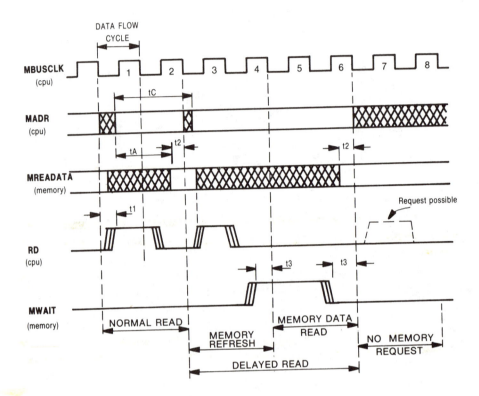

Figure 4.10. *Normal and delayed read cycles.*

must activate within timing specification t1 nanoseconds after the fall of MBUSCLK. Time t1 allows for propagation delays in the generation of the control signal RD. Also, the address bus MADR must be made valid by time t1. When RD activates, the read-data bus MREADATA is assumed to be invalid. Within timing specification t2 prior to the fall of MBUSCLK in the second cycle, the MREADATA bus must be valid. This allows for the register setup time within the CPU, preparatory to strobing in the MREA-DATA bus with the fall of MBUSCLK at the end of cycle 2. The time elapsed between the validity of the address and the validity of the data is the access time, denoted tA. Feedback signal MWAIT remains inactive throughout data flow cycles 1 and 2, so the cycle is normal. The cycle time tC is the time elapsed between successive presentations of a valid address to the memory.

Next, consider a delayed read cycle. In data flow cycle 3, RD is activated again for another read cycle. Assume that the memory system is refreshing dynamic memory in data flow cycles 3 and 4. During refresh,

CPU read-data will not be valid at the end of cycle 4 when normally expected, so signal MWAIT is activated. There must be time for propagation delays for the CPU to enter an idle state or to inhibit the CPU internal clock. Timing specification t3 requires that the activation of MWAIT precede the fall of MBUSCLK by t3 ns. On the data flow cycle that data becomes valid, MWAIT must be deactivated t3 ns before the fall of MBUSCLK as shown in cycle 6. In cycle 7, the CPU is making no memory request. If the memory initiates a refresh cycle, and if no memory request is made for cycle 8, then there is no need to activate MWAIT. Since the CPU does not expect data, there is no point in causing it to idle. Note that it does no harm if the old data remains valid on the MREADATA bus in cycles 7 and 8.

A timing diagram for the write operation is shown in **Figure 4.11**. Cycles 1 and 2 are normal; the CPU places valid write-data and the address on respective buses MWRIDATA and MADR within time t1 of the fall of MBUSCLK. In reality, the address and write-data are not necessarily clocked at the same time as might be assumed from Fig. 4.11. However, both buses must be valid by time tP following the trailing edge of

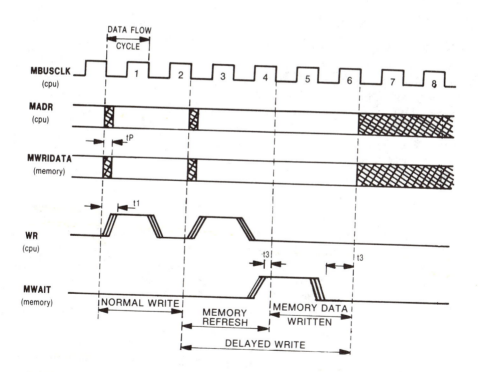

Figure 4.11. *Normal and delayed write cycles.*

MBUSCLK. At the end of the second cycle, with feedback signal MWAIT inactive, the CPU can remove the data and the address from the bus. In the third cycle, a write operation is initiated which must be delayed. Signal MWAIT is activated in cycle 4, so the CPU must maintain bus MWRIDATA stable through cycle 6. In cycle 6, MWAIT is deactivated.

The MREADATA and MWRIDATA buses have been made unidirectional here for the purpose of explanation. These data buses can be coalesced into a single bidirectional bus by the use of the wire-OR or tri-state bus connectives. A bidirectional bus requires the data source to let the bus "float" following the last data flow cycle of the memory access operation.

4.7. A SIMPLE MEMORY SYSTEM DESIGN

This section describes in block diagram form a 16KB memory card design using the memory bus interface of the previous section. The CPU-memory organization uses decentralized controls as in Fig. 4.8(b). The high-order address bits select the proper memory card. The design remains at the block diagram level at this point. We postpone the detailed discussion of the memory chips and their timing specifications. Once memory chips have been covered, we will return to complete the design.

The behavioral description of the memory is relatively simple. We implement the design with a data flow and control flow. The data flow of the card design is shown in **Figure 4.12**. This diagram also shows some auxiliary circuits. Following an explanation of the data flow, we describe a simple state machine for control state sequencing. Then we generate the control signal activation logic. The external interconnections are shown in Fig. 4.9. The control logic of Fig. 4.12 interfaces the memory array subunit to MBUS.

4.7.1. The Memory Array Subunit

The memory array subunit is a *functional unit* composed of four columns of eight rows of memory chips. For the basic memory component, we assume a simple low-capacity 4K words by 1 bit dynamic MOS memory chip, the Intel 2107C. This chip requires refreshing but does not have address multiplexing. (Larger capacity memory chips have a more complicated time-multiplexed address input bus, where the address is strobed onto the chip seven or eight bits at a time.) Having an input pin for each address bit simplifies timing constraints. A complication does exist in that the chip must be refreshed; however this makes the design problem more interesting. The data connection points include the address, input data, and output data. The control points are *chip select* (CSi), *chip enable,* and *write enable.* We describe the memory chip timing parameters later.

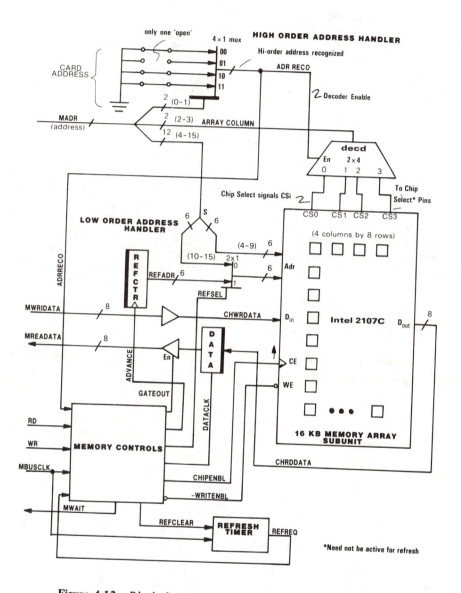

Figure 4.12. *Block diagram of a 16KB dynamic memory card.*

Each column contains 4K bytes, each of the eight chips stores $4K \times 1$ bits, hence requires a 12-bit address. A column is activated for reading or writing by a common chip select signal, CS0, CS1, CS2, or CS3. Each of the eight rows provides one of the eight bits of the data byte. The 12 address bits are fed to all chips. The tri-state data-out bit lines in the same row are wired together to form a tri-state bus. Only the chip data-out (read-data) line in the addressed column is active (not high impedance). The eight chip write-data lines CHWRDATA are fanned out one line to each row of the memory array.

Consider the control of the chips. The active-low write enable interconnection signal line (WRITENBL) controls the operation (read or write). If WRITENBL is active, a write operation is performed; otherwise a read operation is performed. Two control signals, chip enable (CHIPENBL) and the chip select, control whether or not the chip participates in the operation. The operation is initiated by an active transition on the chip enable input line. This is accomplished by the leading edge of the CHIP-ENBL signal, which is fed to all chips in the array. The four chip select signals CS0, CS1, CS2, and CS3 are mutually exclusive; at most one is active at a time. Only the column of selected chips (whose chip select input pin is active) perform the read or write operation. However, all chips receiving the active transition on the chip enable input are refreshed. The refresh address requires only six bits because all 64 memory cells sharing the same six low-order address bit values are simultaneously refreshed. We cover the timing of data and control relationships at the chip level later.

4.7.2. Address Handling

Consider the incoming address. The high-order 2-bit field MADR(0-1) determines the 16KB card selected. The internal decoder function of a 4×1 MUX (top of Fig. 4.12) activates signal ADRRECO when the card address is recognized. ADRRECO is activated when ADR(0-1) assumes the value "01". The next two high-order bits ADR(2-3) are decoded (assuming the card is selected and the 2×4 decoder DECD is enabled) to provide the CSi signals which select one of the four array columns to take part in the memory operation.

In summary, the 4×1 MUX and the 2×4 Decoder handle the high-order address bits: they generate the status signal ADRRECO that the card has been selected (an input to the Memory Control block of Fig. 4.12) and they activate the proper chip select signal. The 12 low address bit signal values are bused to the chip address pins after signal amplification. The six low-order bits (ADR(10-15)) are first gated through the 2×1 MUX. The second source for the 2×1 MUX is the refresh address REFCTR.

4.7.3. Refresh Logic

Each cell must be *refreshed* every two ms, which means that a 6-bit address should be refreshed approximately every 31 microseconds (μs). If the period of MBUSCLK is 200 ns, then following each 155 clock times the Refresh Timer block (bottom of Fig. 4.12) activates signal REFREQ which calls for a refresh cycle. The next refresh address REFADR is stored in a refresh counter (REFCTR). REFCTR is incremented at the end of each refresh cycle, by activation of signal ADVANCE. Except during the refresh cycle, REFCTR always contains the next address to be refreshed. The ADVANCE control signal, among others, is generated in the block labeled Memory Controls.

Refresh controller chips are commercially available. These chips have a refresh counter whose output is multiplexed with the low-order address bits from the MBUS address field. Provision exists for an asynchronous timer delay, and the basic operation mode is asynchronous.

4.7.4. Memory Control Logic

The memory card performs three operations; *refresh, read,* and *write*. The refresh request is internally generated by the timer, and the read and write requests are externally generated. These operations can be informally described with independent RTN statements as follows.

Refresh: ARRAYADR(11-15) = REFCTR; REFCTR←REFCTR plus 1
Read: ARRAYADR = MADR(2-15); MREADATA = M[ARRAYADR]
Write: ARRAYADR = MADR(2-15); M[ARRAYADR]←MWRIDATA

We implement the refresh, read, and write RTN statements, with a macrosequence of two MBUSCLK cycles for each operation. The timing charts of Figs. 4.10 and 4.11 point to the requirements of the RD and WR memory control inputs. Observe that the RD and WR signals are active (within a propagation delay) after the start of a data flow cycle, and go inactive within the next data flow cycle. This is true even when the memory is busy during refresh. The first conclusion is that the RD and WR control signals must be latched up in the Memory Controls block, in flip-flops RDREQ and WRREQ respectively. A second conclusion is that generally the Memory Controls must often wait for the data flow cycle to begin before deciding what is to be done during that cycle. An exception occurs when RD is activated in a data flow cycle where the memory is not busy: the next data flow cycle is known to be the second half of the memory read operation.

In order to sequence the memory control signals properly, we define a three-state sequential machine. The state transition diagram which describes the control state sequencing is shown in **Figure 4.13**. The "normal" control state is "FIRSTCY". In FIRSTCY the memory is ready to accept a refresh, read or write request. If no valid request is made, the next control state is again FIRSTCY. The control state "self-loops" in FIRSTCY until the arrival of a request. Due to the volatility of the dynamic memory, a refresh request takes priority over the read or write requests. When REF-REQ is active in state FIRSTCY, a refresh operation is performed, and the control state following FIRSTCY is called REFCY2 (refresh cycle 2).

Following state REFCY2, the memory is ready to accept another request, so control returns to state FIRSTCY.

In state FIRSTCY, if REFREQ is inactive, the memory accepts read or write requests. The memory card accepts a read operation (write operation) if the proper high-order bits are recognized (ADRRECO is active; see Fig. 4.12) and if input signal RD (WR) occurs or has occurred during a refresh operation. These signals are generated by RD and WR respectively in conjunction with ADRRECO as shown in **Figure 4.14.** Thus we use RDREQ (WRREQ), which is latched only if the proper high-order address has selected this memory card. The flip-flops are normally clear. If ADRRECO is active (high-order address bits are recognized) when RD (or WR) is active, the respective flip-flop set input (S) is activated, setting

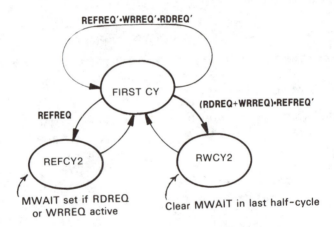

Figure 4.13. *State transition diagram for memory control state sequencer.*

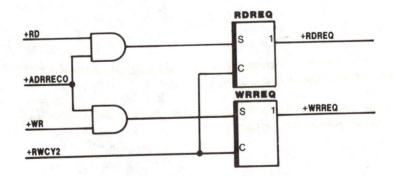

Figure 4.14. *Latching of RD and WR request pulses.*

flip-flop RDREQ (or WRREQ). The flip-flop remains set until cleared by the active transition which ends the read (or write) operation, ensuring that RDREQ (or WRREQ) remains valid throughout the operation. If a read or write operation is accepted in state FIRSTCY, the next control state is called RWCY2 (read/write cycle 2). As with the second refresh cycle control state, RWCY2 is always followed by state FIRSTCY.

Each control state FIRSTCY, REFCY, and RWCY is implemented with a single edge-triggered flip-flop whose active transition is the fall of signal MBUSCLK. The flip-flop next-state inputs are called FIRSTCYN, REFCY2N, and RWCY2N respectively; they represent *control points* for which control signals must be generated. The result is shown in **Figure 4.15**. With the present complement of control states and control point names, it is now possible to describe the desired behavior of the Memory Controls block of the memory card using dependent RTN statements. Actually, the RTN statements simply describe the cycle in which the control signals are activated or deactivated. We will cover the exact timing of these signals when the memory chips are described.

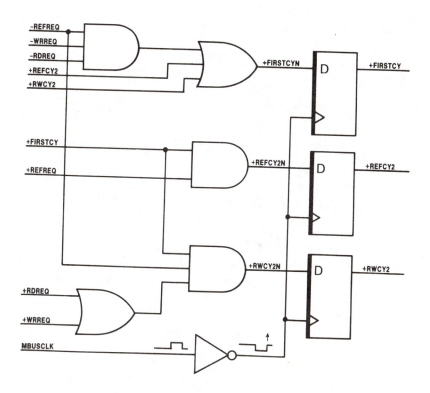

Figure 4.15. *Logic design of control state sequencer.*

	Stmt Nr	Control Signal Activation Statement
Refresh Operation	1	FIRSTCY•REFREQ: REFSEL; CHIPENBL[1]
	2	REFCY2: REFSEL; CHIPENBL[2]; REFCLR
	3	REFCY2•MBUSCLK↓: ADVANCE↑
Read Operation	4	FIRSTCY•REFREQ'•RDREQ: CHIPENBL[1]
	5	RWCY2•RDREQ: GATEOUT; DATACLK[1][2]; CHIPENBL[2]
Write Operation	6	FIRSTCY•REFREQ'•WRREQ: CHIPENBL[1]; WRITENBL[2]
	7	RWCY2•WRREQ: CHIPENBL[2]; WRITENBL[2]

NOTES:

(1) The timing of this signal has not yet been covered. It is activated some time early or midway in this cycle.

(2) This control signal is deactivated sometime toward the end of this cycle.

Figure 4.16. *RTN statements for memory controls.*

Figure 4.16 lists the control signal activation statements directly. This represents one level of detail greater than register transfers. The next-state function does not appear in these statements, having been described by Fig. 4.13. Statements 1 and 2 cover the first and second refresh operation cycles. The chips are enabled and the refresh address is gated to the chip through the 2×1 MUX. In REFCY2, the refresh timer is reset. Statement 3 means that at the end of REFCY2, the refresh counter is advanced by the activation of control signal ADVANCE. This can be accomplished by a NAND gate fed by REFCY2 and MBUSCLK. At the fall of MBUSCLK, the NAND output (ADVANCE) experiences the active transition. Statement 4 covers the first cycle of the read operation. The chips are enabled by activating control signal CHIPENBL. The 2×1 MUX normally selects the read address. Statement 5 describes the second bus cycle. Memory array read-data (the CHRDDATA bus) in Fig. 4.12 is latched by the leading edge of DATACLK, and the register DATA is driven to read-data bus MREADATA by a tri-state driver activated by control signal GATE-OUT. Later in the cycle, CHIPENBL, DATACLK and GATEOUT are deactivated. Statement 6 describes the first cycle of the write operation. The chips are enabled as for the read operation and sometime in this cycle the write enable input to the chips, WRITENBL, is activated. Statement 7 is the second write operation cycle, when CHIPENBL and WRITENBL chip input signals are deactivated.

4.8. A CENTRALIZED MEMORY CONTROLLER

We now illustrate the wide variation in approaches available in memory system design. In the previous section, each memory card had its own control logic. This section discusses the problem of a centralized memory controller. See **Figure 4.17.** The discussion is based on a simplification of a design by Frankenberg and Cross [8]. The controller is fully buffered, which means that address, read-data, and write-data registers are provided. The memory cards of today have a greater storage capacity, but the design techniques remain the same.

The memory cards connect to a common bidirectional data bus INTMDATA. A 4-bit module address MODULEAD is decoded on each card. Buses CHIPADR and MODCOL are fed to each card, as are the two control signals chip enable (CE) and write enable (WE).

The controller is asynchronous; there is no central clock. Read and write operations are initiated by active transitions. Although Frankenberg and Cross use dynamic memories, the block diagram of the controller presented in **Figure 4.18** assumes the more easily interfaced static memory chips. Another simplification is one-way control signalling; the data transfer memory is non-interlocked.

The controller can handle up to 16 memory modules. Each module stores 16K words, and consists of one pc card. The system comprises a maximum capacity of 256K words, necessitating 18 bits of address. The four high-order address bits are the module address, and each 16K-word memory module has jumpers available to recognize its own unique module number. (Jumper usage is covered in Appendix B.) The chip employed is $4K \times 1$, using a 12-bit chip address as in the previous section. Each module decodes address bits (4-5) to form chip enable signals for the module columns.

The CPU interface is asynchronous. For a read operation, the CPU activates signal READ, initiating a timing chain of events which first loads the address register. Subsequently, the chip enable CE which feeds the memory modules is made active. Following the read access time, the internal data bus is strobed into the READDATA register, and CE is

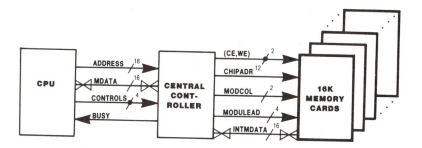

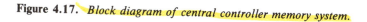

Figure 4.17. *Block diagram of central controller memory system.*

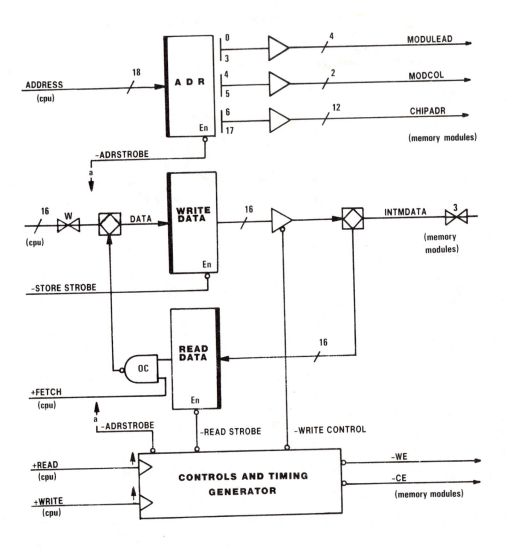

Figure 4.18. *Block diagram of controller data flow.*

deactivated. The directionality of the external data bus is under control of the CPU. When the CPU wants the data, it activates the FETCH control signal. For a write operation, the CPU must load the WRITEDATA register by the time the leading edge of the WRITE signal occurs. The active transition on WRITE loads the ADR register, activates write enable WE, and subsequently activates the module's chip enable. At a time following the minimum specification for the chip enable pulse width, CE is deactivated causing memory to be written. WE is subsequently deactivated.

The memory system designer is concerned with power supply requirements, heat dissipation, the package, cabling and cross-talk problems, chip type and density, cost, parts quality and availability, signal drive or fan-out capability, access and cycle times, testability, etc. The excellent series of articles by Frankenberg [9] covers these and other aspects of semiconductor memories. Many of the memory testing and servicing aspects mentioned are common to all digital systems products, and not just to memory cards.

4.9. A REVIEW OF THE MEMORY SYSTEM LEVEL

The real memory system has thus far been described as a system component. In a given computer system design, the "rules of thumb" of past experience can be used to estimate the capacity and performance requirements, and the amount of IO traffic expected of the memory system. *The buses should be designed to handle the peak traffic and not the average traffic.*

Next in line with the "first things first" philosophy is to define or specify the number and type of memory, IO, or system buses in the system. The actual desired behavior of the memory system depends heavily on the memory bus interface specification (synchronous, asynchronous, provision for DMA, IO, two-way Wait/Ready signalling, etc.). The designer may consider a decentralized control where each "like" functional memory unit is "wired" to recognize its own address. Alternatively, the designer may consider a centralized memory controller with an "internal" bus connecting "like" memory array cards. In the treatment at this level, one of the "black boxes" is the memory array itself. The initial top-down approach embraces the problem, and then leads to the bottom (detailed) conceptual level comprising the basic building block: the semiconductor memory chip. We study the memory chip as a basic part, and then build a more powerful higher-level block: the memory array of chips encountered in Fig. 4.12. We used a mixed top-down/bottom-up design approach.

4.10. MONOLITHIC MEMORIES

Core memories read words by a *destructive read* process where all bits in the word are sensed by clearing them to zero. The destructive read process implies we must rewrite the contents of the word. The monolithic memory technology performs *nondestructive read,* relieving the memory system designer of rewriting the accessed word. Monolithic memories have independent read and write cycles; any number of consecutive read cycle requests can be issued. Further, monolithic memories share the same package as the logic (e.g. dual in-line package), and are relatively inexpensive. Their good speed (access time) eases the requirement that the CPU data flow cycle be synchronized (or "in step") with the main memory cycle. When monolithic memory was first introduced it saw limited application due to its high cost. An early user was the IBM S/360 Model 25 (1968); a monolithic memory replaced the data flow registers which otherwise would have been implemented in more expensive SSI flip-flops. The S/370 Model 145, announced in 1971, also employed a monolithic main memory; it was the first commercial system which was entirely semiconductor. Prior to that, the S/360 Model 85 used a monolithic cache or look-aside buffer memory for storing the contents of the more recently used main memory locations. This hierarchical technique enabled the S/360 Model 85 system designers to match the data flow cycle to the high-speed cache, while employing a less expensive, slower magnetic core memory for the full memory capacity. Since the cache capacity was only 16K bytes (optionally 32K bytes), and typical systems used 1M to 4M bytes of real main memory, the trade-off worked well. In general the cache had the desired data over 90% of the time and the system generally performed at 80% or better of the maximum achievable (*all* main memory references satisfied at cache speeds).

4.10.1. Monolithic Memory Chips

Monolithic memory systems consist of memory chips (or memory array chips) coupled with *support* chips on a printed circuit card or other suitable packaging scheme. Support chips provide conversions from one voltage level to another, do multiplexing on read-data, fan-out powering (buffering) on write-data and address lines, and perform high-order address bit decoding.

Monolithic memories are of two basic types, *static* and *dynamic*. In static designs, the memory bit storage element consists of at least two transistors, cross-coupled in a flip-flop arrangement. For the storage of a 0, one transistor is on, the other off. To store a 1 the first transistor is off and the second is on. In the dynamic designs, a one-transistor cell is the storage element, and the bit is stored as the presence or absence of an electrical charge, generally in the capacitor defined by the gate electrode of an MOS transistor. This charge is slowly lost, so the dynamic memory contents must be periodically *refreshed*. As a result, the static RAM is the simplest read-write memory chip to incorporate into a design. **Figure 4.19** shows the general lay-out for a memory chip. Chips are generally organized to deliver or accept one bit, to or from any of the locations defined by the *n* address bits. In Fig. 4.19, there are 10 address lines, hence 1024 (1K) memory locations. The memory is organized as 1K (words) by 1 (bits per word). Some chips of 1024 bits capacity are organized as 256 words by 4 bits per word, specified as "256×4".

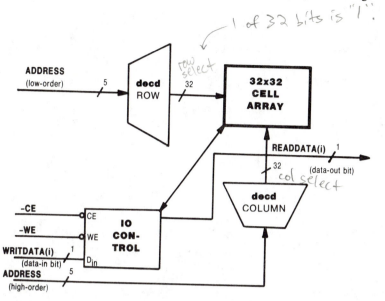

Figure 4.19. *Block diagram of 1K-bit memory chip.*

4.10.2. Chip Connection Points

The chip connection points or pins are the address and data lines, and the two control points are chip enable (CE) and write enable (WE). If the CE signal is inactive, there is no valid data on the chip output pins. To read information, CE must be active. To write information into a cell, both CE and WE must be active. The output driver may be one of two types: an open-collector for wire-ORing together the data outputs of many chips, or a tri-state output driver. The open-collector output requires a pull-up resistor external to the chip; with the tri-state output, care must be taken to ensure that only one source of the data bus is enabled at one time.

The chip enable input CE is useful in building larger capacity memories from the basic building block, by accepting externally decoded high-order address signals as shown in **Figure 4.20**. Also shown is the busing of the open-collector output READDATA. The data-out signals in each column are wire-ORed to a common pull-up resistor. In this figure, 16 interconnected chips form a 4K by 4 bit memory unit. The ten low-order address bits drive all memory chips; the two high-order bits decoded provide the chip enable function. At any one time, only four of the memory chips (those along the same row) receive a valid enabling signal. The decoder is provided with a strobe input "–STROBE DECODE", which can be made inactive if all the memory chips are to be disabled.

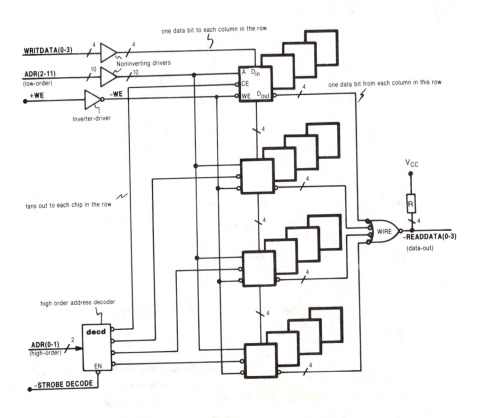

Figure 4.20. *A memory array of memory chips and support chips.*

The signal polarities shown for the memory chips conform with many actual parts. Decoders which deliver their outputs in complement form can connect directly to the chip enable input which expects this complement polarity. The memory designer should be aware that, in the case of the data signals, some memory chips provide the complement polarity of what was input. In Fig. 4.20, the memory data input (write-data) is in true form. The chip data output (read-data), in complement form, is wire-ORed and provides a complement form input to a READDATA register.

4.10.3. RAM Timing Relationships

Fig. 4.20 fails to bring out one area of memory system design: the timing requirements. The time relationships between control signal activation and data validity is important. A memory cycle is generally dominated by the propagation delays within the memory chip itself. In addition, of course, are the support circuitry delays. These memory chip timing specifications (relationships, switching characteristics, or parameters) have some common ground with flip-flop timing.

We review some terminology. The specifications deal with the stability of input or output *values* relative to some *event.* An event is the activation or deactivation of an indicated signal. One or both value and event names may appear within the parentheses following the notation of the timing relationship. A *setup* time tSU is the required time an earlier input signal value must be held stable *prior* to some event. It is important to note that a "0" setup time does not imply there is no setup time. *A tSU of "0" means that the input signal value cannot stabilize later than the occurrence of the event.* A *hold time* tH is the required time an input value must be stable *following* some indicated event. If the hold time is negative, the input signal value may change before the indicated event. A negative hold time is often called a *release* time. Another type of hold time is the *output hold* tOH. It guarantees how long an *output* value remains stable following some event. The *manufacturer* of the part guarantees the tOH specification; it should not be confused with the (input) hold time tH which the *designer* must guarantee for an input. The propagation time is called *access time* tA. The value tA includes the propagation delay of the on-chip address decoder, the multiplexing delay for the selected bit value to reach the sensor, and the propagation delay of the sensor output buffer. The *cycle time* tC is the time interval before reinitiating a memory operation or cycle. Implicit in the cycle time may be a *recovery* time. In dynamic memories the recovery time is called the precharge time.

Following the delay specification type is an indication in parentheses of the relative signals involved. For example tA(CE) is the access time relative to the event defined by the activation of the chip enable signal. In many cases, the specification of interest is a minimum or a maximum value; in most cases whether it is a min or max is obvious. In static memories, the access time tA and *minimum* cycle time tCmin are usually specified by the manufacturer to be the same. In this case, tCmin may be deceptive because no time is allowed for delays external to the chip for changing the value of the address or having a setup time to clock read-data into a register. Dynamic memories usually will have a nonzero recovery time: tC exceeds tA. Also note that the *system's* access time may be greater than the *chip* access time, due to delays in the support circuits.

In memory chip timing specifications, two timing events of interest are: (1) the acquisition or change of an input or output value, and (2) a signal transition. If both events are on the inputs, then the memory designer (as chip user) must ensure the timing specification. Setup and hold times usually fall into this category. Access time tA(ad), between an input event and output event, is a specification which the memory chip manufacturer guarantees, and upon which the memory system designer depends. Output hold and propagation delays or access times fall into this category. In addition, a timing specification may involve the same signal for both edges; here, the system designer must guarantee a maximum or minimum pulse width (tW) specification, or minimum cycle time tC. Thus, tW(WE) is the time during which write enable is active, and tW(WE′) is the time write enable is inactive.

The interface timing concepts and specifications just explained in connection with memory chips are useful concepts for interfacing and properly using a "building block" (MSI- or LSI-level digital part) or functional unit. Many specifications are based on worst-case and best-case delays within the building block. The notation for these concepts generally varies from manufacturer to manufacturer.

4.11. STATIC MONOLITHIC MEMORY CHIPS

4.11.1. The Read Cycle

The operation of the static monolithic memory for a read cycle is very simple. When not writing, the write enable signal is false; the memory is always outputting the read-data value of the addressed memory word. Of course, when the address changes, there is a delay tA analogous to a propagation delay before READDATA (data-out) bus becomes valid again. See **Figure 4.21.** An address change causes a chain of two events: (1) after a best-case delay analogous to an output hold time tOH(ad), the READ-DATA bus becomes ambiguous, and (2) after a worst-case access delay tA analogous to a propagation delay, the READDATA bus becomes valid with the new data. Recall that for *output hold* time tOH(ad), the old address may be changed tOH(ad) nanoseconds *before* data goes invalid. This chain of events can be initiated by a change in value on either the chip enable line or an address line. The access and output hold times are defined by Fig. 4.21 where events (1) and (2) are depicted on the timing diagram.

The respective access and output hold times for the two control inputs are shown in **Figure 4.22** for a full read cycle from when the address is valid to when the chip enable deactivates. Following a valid address, the chip enable signal CE may become active. Following a delay, the chip read-data becomes valid. It is not guaranteed valid prior to tA(CE) from the activation of CE or prior to tA(ad) from address validity. Typically, tA(ad) is the larger delay; therefore signal CE is designed to be activated within time duration tA(ad)–tA(CE) following the validity of the address. This allows time for the high-order address decoder propagation delay (Fig. 4.20). The output hold time specification tOH(CE′)min states how long after the deactivation of CE that chip read-data becomes invalid. Specification tOH(ad) has a similar meaning, but usually has a nonzero value corresponding to a minimum (best-case) delay through the on-chip address decoders.

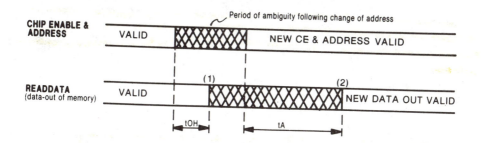

Figure 4.21. *Timing of a static monolithic memory chip in read mode.*

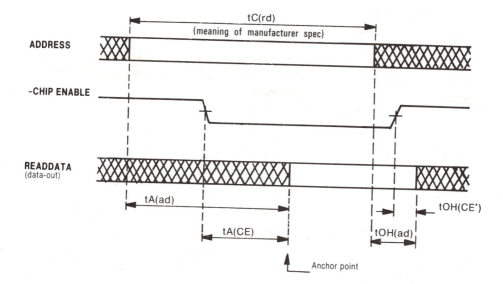

Figure 4.22. *Timing specifications for the basic read cycle of a simply addressed static memory chip.*

In designing with monolithic memory chips, the designer's useful "anchor point" of the read cycle timing is the point at which the read-data becomes valid. In integrating the chip into a memory array subunit, the designer determines the time chip read-data should become valid, and then works backwards to ensure that the address and chip enable CE are valid within the required time. Usually, the address validity is the most critical input event.

In the subsystem for which the memory chip is a component (memory array subunit), the system designer must ensure that the chip read-data bus is strobed into a memory system output buffer register for subsequent use. Read-data cannot be stored before the chip read-data becomes valid. Moreover, read-data should not be stored following loss of either the CE signal or address validity plus output hold time tOH, as it may have gone invalid. Some memory chips provide an on-chip data latch, which stores and buffers the last data bit read out until replaced by new data.

4.11.2. The Write Cycle

The write cycle for a static memory chip is slightly more complicated than the read cycle. The additional complications come from the transitions of the *write enable* control signal WE (sometimes called R/W). A basic write cycle is shown in **Figure 4.23.** Basically, to write into the memory, the address bus, chip write-data bus (WRITDATA), and signal CE must remain valid for a specified period of time called the address setup tSU(ad), write-data setup tSU(da), and CE setup tSU(CE), respectively. Signal WE is activated for a specified minimum period of time, tW(WE), and is then deactivated. The *trailing edge* of write enable, denoted in the timing notation as WE′, is an active transition which latches the value on the chip write-data pin into the memory cell. The data must be valid for time tSU(da-WE′). In some cases, depending on the memory chip design, it may be necessary to maintain one or more of these chip input values stable for a short hold time tH(da).

In Fig. 4.23, the address becomes valid and the chip is enabled as in read mode. The write enable signal is activated, following a suitable setup time tSU(ad-WE) from the address validity. Write enable must be active a specified minimum length of time tW(WE). Write-data (WRITDATA) setup time tSU(da) and chip enable setup time tSU(CE) are referenced to the cycle "anchor point", which is the trailing edge of write enable, denoted WE′. The trailing edge of write enable causes the actual storage of the data. This is shown in Fig. 4.23 as tSU(da-WE′) and tSU(CE-WE′). These are the setup times from data valid to WE′ and the chip enable activation to anchor point WE′. In some cases, it may be required that the address, the chip enable, and WRITDATA each maintain or hold their values for a hold time tH(ad), tH(CE) and tH(da) respectively. The specification from one address valid time to the next address valid time is the minimum write cycle time tC(wr). Since the address must be invalid for a time while it is changing, as with the minimum read cycle time, the actual write cycle time must exceed the the manufacturer's "minimum" tC(wr).

The designer working out the memory system timing specifications uses the trailing edge of write enable as an anchor point for the write cycle; see Fig. 4.23. The designer then works backward to determine when the data, address, CE and leading edge of WE should occur. For some chips,

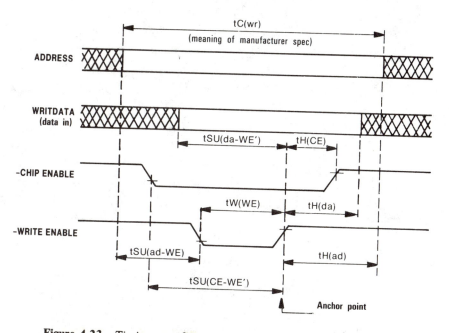

Figure 4.23. *Timing specification for write cycle of a static memory chip.*

the leading edge of WE is also a reference edge and anchor point for satisfying other setup times.

4.11.3. The Read–Modify–Write Cycle

Suppose you read a value, increment that value, and write it to the same address. The read cycle can be immediately followed by a write cycle to the same address so that the address to write enable setup time $tSU(ad-WE)$ need not be paid. The write cycle generally has a longer time specification from the address validity to the trailing edge of WE, than the corresponding read cycle specification. The shorter specification $tSU(da-WE')$ from write-data allows some time to "modify" the read-data without paying the full price in time of an independent read cycle followed by an independent write cycle.

For many static memories, read access time tA and write cycle $tC(wr)$ take the same amount of time. Thus, in a synchronous system, it is not uncommon for the system cycle repetition rate to equal the memory system cycle time. The timing chart for a basic read-modify-write cycle is shown in **Figure 4.24.** It is seen that this cycle has a minimum specification of $tC(rd)+tW(WE)+tH(ad)$.

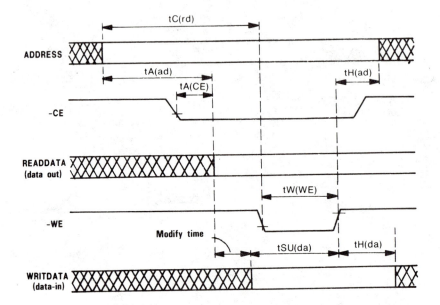

Figure 4.24. *Timing chart for read-modify-write cycle.*

	Table 4.1.	
Timing Specifications for Static Intel 2102 Static Chip		
	Time in Nanoseconds	
Read Cycle	*2102A*	*2102-2*
tA(ad)max	350	650
tA(CE)max	180	400
tOH(ad)min	40	50
tOH(CE')min	0	0
tC(rd)min	350	650
Write Cycle		
tSU(ad-WE)min	100	200
tSU(CE)min	250	550
tSU(da)min	250	450
tH(ad)min	0	50
tH(CE)min	0	50
tH(da)min	0	100
tW(WE)min	250	400
tC(wr)min	350	650

4.11.4. The Intel 2102 Static Chip

Table 4.1 describes two memory chips from the same family, the Intel 2102A and 2102-2. Generally the semiconductor masks and processing are the same for each, but one chip time tests out faster than the other. Note that the minimum cycle time tC is the same as the access time of the read cycle. This cycle time will generally not be met at the actual system cycle level due to address line skews and the setup time required to clock the read-data into a register.

4.12. DYNAMIC RAM MEMORY CHIPS

4.12.1. The Refresh Requirement

In dynamic memories, the bits are stored as electrical charges. Because leakage current will ultimately bleed off the charge, the contents of dynamic memories must be periodically recharged or refreshed. Consider a typical case: a 4K-bit dynamic memory chip organized as 64 rows by 64 columns. For the read-out of a particular bit in a selected row and column, the charge in all cells of the selected row is transferred to special cells, one for each column. From these special cells, the memory cells of the selected row are recharged. Also, the content of the special cell corresponding to the selected column is sensed and placed on the read-data (data out) pin. The cells of an entire row are refreshed simply by reading a cell position of that row. The entire 4K-bit memory chip can be refreshed in 64 refresh cycles. Typically, each cell must be refreshed every 2 ms. Apportioning the time evenly between rows means that at least one row should be refreshed every 32 μs. Three methods are currently in use: the "transparent" method, "cycle-steal" (as for Fig. 4.12), or "burst". The "transparent" method is used in some microprocessor systems where only half of the available dynamic memory cycles are required by the CPU. Cycles not required by the CPU are assigned for refresh. In the "cycle-steal" method a time-out signal generates a cycle-steal request at periods of 32 μs, to refresh a single row. The "burst" mode is similar to the cycle-steal, but a request is generated every 2 ms and all 64 rows are refreshed in succession. For all three cases, a modulo 64 counter is used to generate the refresh address. In an application where the memory is continually cycled through all rows, a special refresh circuit is not required. For example, in refresh buffer memories for CRT displays, refresh of the dynamic memory comes "free" with the application.

4.12.2. Comparison with Static Memories

The absence of a refresh requirement makes static memories the easiest to interface. More recent dynamic memory designs incorporate refresh logic on the chip itself, relieving the system designer of this task. Also, some CPU chips have built-in refresh controls. The provision for two-way control must still be inherent in the support circuits. A simpler cell design makes dynamic memories more dense, hence less expensive on a per-bit basis. Dynamic memories also tend to consume less power. Some dynamic memories can be placed in "standby" mode where the per-bit power dissipation is very low. Some of this cost saving is lost because a more expensive power supply is needed. In static memories the demand for current is relatively steady; dynamic memories place a heavy peak load on the power supply for very short periods of time. Dynamic memories require a larger number of high-frequency ceramic bypass capacitors on the pc board. Further, static memories tend to use fewer power supply voltages. In small quantities, static RAMs are favored; in large quantities the costlier support circuits for dynamic memories are apportioned over a larger number of bits. (Some dynamic memories with built-in refresh circuits may be competitive even in smaller capacities.)

For static RAMs, the access time and cycle time are generally the same. For dynamic RAMs, following the access time, some additional "precharge" time or recovery time may be required before the initiation of the next cycle.

4.12.3. The Intel 2107C Chip

As an example of some of the important specifications in dynamic memory chips, we consider the Intel 2107C family which can be used with the Intel 8080 microprocessor. The chip has three control points: pins chip select, chip enable, and write enable. The chip enable function in static RAMs is apportioned to two control signals in this dynamic RAM. The chip select pins receive the decoder outputs of the high-order address bits, used when the chips are organized into a memory system whose capacity exceeds 4K words. The active chip select signal causes the writing of data when write enable is active, and also places the chip read-data bit value onto the tri-state chip output bus. The chip enable pin accepts a timing signal whose leading edge initiates a timing sequence within the chip. First, CE causes the address and chip select state to be stored on the chip (on-chip flip-flops). On-chip address storage gives the designer the option of changing the contents of the off-chip address register earlier in the cycle than the access time. Dynamic RAMs do not conform to the useful "model" of the static memory chip always reading out the addressed word unless told otherwise. For dynamic RAMs, the leading edge of the chip enable pin together with the state of the write enable signal (0 or 1) define a read operation or a write operation. As with the static RAM, the read operation is nondestructive.

4.12.4. Dynamic Read Cycle

The read cycle of the Intel 2107C is shown in **Figure 4.25.** The CE input is active-high, rather than the more popular active-low. The address lines, and the chip select and WE control signals must be stable prior to the leading edge of CE, tSU(ad)min. Once the address and chip select signals have met their minimum hold time specification tH(ad)min from CE, they may be changed. WE, however, must remain inactive until after CE goes inactive, denoted CE' in the specification tH(WE-CE')min.

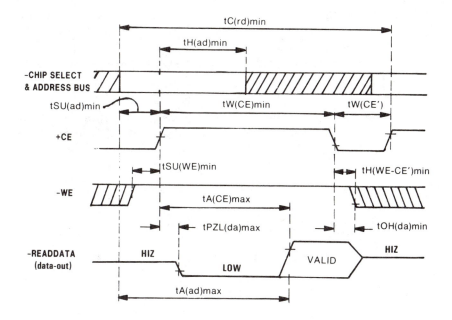

Figure 4.25. *Dynamic memory read cycle timing.*

In Fig. 4.25, delay tPZL(da) denotes the propagation delay from the activation of CE to when the tri-state read-data signal value READDATA goes from the high-impedance state (Z) to the low voltage state (L). Chip enable must remain active for at least pulse width tW(CE)min. The chip read-data signal is guaranteed to be valid following tA(CE)max or tA(ad)max, whichever occurs later in the cycle. When CE goes inactive, chip read-data is guaranteed stable no longer than tOH(da)min from CE'. Chip enable must remain inactive at least tW(CE')min before another cycle can be initiated. This is the precharge time.

4.12.5. Dynamic Write Cycle

A write cycle timing diagram is shown in **Figure 4.26**. Again, the cycle is initiated by the leading edge of CE, and the address and chip select signals behave as for a read cycle. Signal WE must be active for at least tSU(WE)min prior to the trailing edge CE' of chip enable, and WE must be active for at least tW(WE)min. The chip write-data value must be stable tSU(WE)min before the trailing edge of write enable (WE'). To guarantee that the write-data bit WRITDATA is written correctly, the chip write-data bit value must remain stable for tH(da-WE')min after the same WE' edge, and for tH(da-CE')min after the trailing edge of CE. The chip enable pulse widths have specified minimums for both active and inactive states, called tW(CE)min and tW(CE')min respectively. See **Table 4.2** for the switching or timing characteristics of two members of the Intel 2107C family. As with Table 4.1, the specifications are in nanoseconds.

4.12.6. Read–Modify–Write Cycle

A read-modify-write cycle may be achieved by paying a hold time tH(CE-WE)min from the leading edge of chip enable CE to the leading edge of write enable WE. Such a hold time is long enough to endure through the read cycle; it is 230 ns for the 2107C-4 and 180 ns for the 2107C-2.

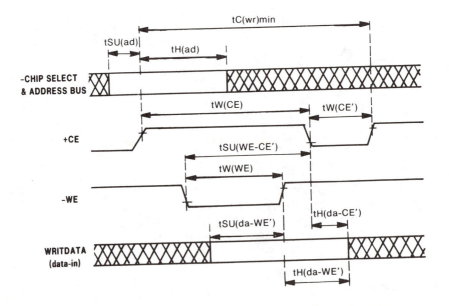

Figure 4.26. *Dynamic memory write cycle timing.*

Table 4.2.
Timing Specifications for the Intel 2107C Dynamic RAM Chip

Read Cycle	2107C-4		2107C-2	
	Min	**Max**	**Min**	**Max**
tC(rd)	470		400	
tSU(ad)	0		0	
tSU(WE)	0		0	
tH(ad)	125		100	
tPLZ(da)		175		125
tW(CE)	300	4000	230	4000
tW(CE')	130		130	
tA(CE)		280		180
tA(ad)		300		200
Write Cycle				
tC(wr)	470		400	
tSU(ad)	0		0	
tH(ad)	120		100	
tSU(WE-CE')	240		210	
tW(CE)	300	4000	230	4000
tW(CE')	130		130	
tW(WE)	200		180	
tSU(da-WE')	180		160	
tH(da-WE')	30		10	
tH(da-CE')	0		0	

The advantage of having both chip select and chip enable control points is apparent from refresh considerations. The chip select controls the read-data and write enable circuits such that a chip need not be selected in order to be refreshed. A given row of each chip in the entire memory system is refreshed at one time. Alternative dynamic chip designs which use only one chip enable signal place the memory in a low power standby mode unless the chip enable signal is active. To refresh such a system at once, all chip enables must be active, necessitating a more complicated refresh circuit.

4.13. ADDITIONAL CHIP CONSIDERATIONS

4.13.1. On–Chip Address Register

Static RAMs can also be provided with an address register on the chip. There must be some means to inform the chip as to when the address should be strobed. The leading edge of the chip enable signal is used for this purpose. The on-chip address buffer relieves the memory system designer of the requirement to maintain a stable address bus throughout the entire read or write cycle. However, this simplification implies some additional timing requirements, specifically an address setup time tSU(ad-CE) for the leading edge of chip enable. Further, before initiating another cycle, the chip enable must be deactivated for a minimum period of time tW(CE'). This would imply use of a strobe on the decoder which provides the individual chip enable signals; see Fig. 4.20. In order for the access time to be less dependent on the leading edge of chip enable, the address lines can be decoded while the chip enable signal is deactivated. Alternatively, some designs use the leading edge of chip enable to initiate an internal timing chain for the read cycle, and the access time is referenced only to this active transition.

4.13.2. On–Chip Read–Data Buffer

Some memory chips store the read-data bit. This capability is most often found on dynamic memory chips. Other memory chips provide the additional ability to remove the data-out bit from the output bus. This is normally done by an inactive chip select signal. However, in the system bus approach (Fig. 4.4), the data bus has sources other than the memory chips. An independent *output enable* (OE) or *output disable* (OD) control signal can be provided to remove memory data from the bus when the bus is preempted by another system component. This capability to "get off" the bus is essential if the memory chip uses the same pin for data-in and data-out, and is very convenient for the bidirectional data busing encountered outside the chip.

Memory chips using the leading edge of chip enable to initiate a read cycle can provide an on-chip read-data latch which is latched on the trailing edge of chip enable or some other suitable timing signal. In this way, another system component can overlap the access time using a shared data bus. When the bus is free, the output enable control point can be activated, to gate data out onto the shared data bus. The output data latch is cleared by the next leading edge of the chip enable signal.

4.13.3. Multiplexing Addresses

The increasing densities of monolithic memories and the desire to keep the pin count low gave rise to the multiplexed address technique. In multiplexing, address fields are successively strobed to their on-chip register positions. For example, a 16K×1 memory chip can have a 7-bit address bus. First, the seven "row" address bits are strobed into the row address register by the leading edge of the *row address strobe* (RAS) control signal. Next, the 7-bit column address field is strobed into the column address register by the leading edge of the *column address strobe* (CAS) control signal. The CAS strobe also acts as the chip enable signal to initiate the memory operation cycle. The RAS and CAS together are analogous to the chip enable signal of a nonmultiplexed dynamic chip (e.g. the Intel 2107C) which loads the nonmultiplexed address into the address register on the chip. By specifying that the row address must be loaded prior to the column address, the leading edge of CAS starts the internal timing chain for the read cycle, such that following delay tA(CAS)max, the read-data lines are guaranteed to be valid. The technique generalizes so that in very dense memories, a third address strobe could provide means to multiplex the address using three fields. For example, a 7-bit address bus can be multiplexed three times to provide a 21-bit address suitable for addressing 2M words. Since the address is stored on the chip, the write enable pin may be subsequently activated to initiate the write subcycle of a read-modify-write operation cycle, as shown in **Figure 4.27**. Fig. 4.27 also demonstrates the benefit of providing an on-chip flip-flop to store the data-out bit, as READDATA is valid through the write operation.

In dynamic memory chips with address multiplexing, a single RAS strobe signal is generally distributed to all chips for refresh. High-order address decoding provides the individual CAS signals which are distributed only to those chips actually accessed each cycle.

4.13.4. Bipolar and MOS Memories

Static memories are implemented in either the *bipolar* or the *MOS* technologies. Bipolar memories are faster, less dense, and consume more power. Bipolar chips are used for high-speed cache memories. Medium performance static memories are generally made in the MOS technology. The dynamic memories are MOS, and are used in low-cost applications where a high-speed cycle is not required.

4.13.5. Chip Summary

The cycle types which have been covered are quite basic. The read-modify-write cycle is useful in computer systems which have a *semaphore* for coordinating concurrent programs (e.g. the IBM S/370 architecture's

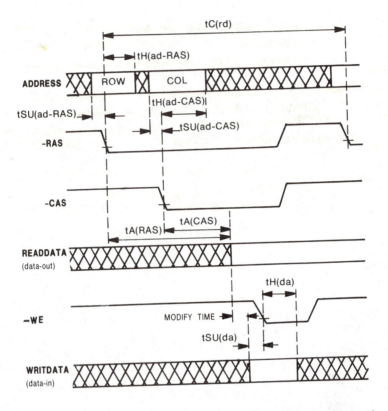

Figure 4.27. *A read-modify-write cycle for a memory chip with multiplexed addressing.*

use of the Test and Set instruction). What is required is the ability to read a memory word and rewrite that word as an *uninterruptible* primitive operation. This property is not satisfied by a memory which services independent read and write operations. For a semaphore operation, another user should not be able to access the memory between the semaphore read operation and the rewrite operation.

Other cycle types are possible: write-verify-read, and read-while-write. Additional features create other dependencies and/or active transitions. For example, if the storage of the address on the chip occurs on the active transition of CE, then the read access time is specified with respect to the leading edge of CE.

The timing specifications at the chip level, as seen in Table 4.1, dominate the timing of a memory system such as Fig. 4.20. However, propagation delays through flip-flops, buffer inverters, and the decoder, must be appropriately accounted for. The access and cycles times at the system level are calculated taking into account delays in the support circuits.

Properties such as a semaphore or Test-and-Set operation, or write-verify-read, or read-while-write, etc., are easily within the capability of the memory chips. However, control circuits in the memory control unit are required to pass these capabilities on to the user. Moreover, the memory interface must possess commands to utilize these capabilities. The simple MBUS interface of §4.6 (Fig. 4.9) is incapable of providing additional function; there is no control or tag field or the like for specifying the function desired.

4.14. DESIGN CONTINUATION: MEMORY ARRAY

We now complete the design begun in §4.7. The synchronous memory bus MBUS defined in §4.6 is assumed; see Fig. 4.8(b). The reader should reflect at this point on the design approach. In a top-down operation, we described a data flow block diagram for a 16KB memory card with decentralized control with Fig. 4.12. We postponed our discussion on the monolithic chip memory array until now. We worked out the read and write operation timing, with respect to the MBUS clock. Next, we dropped to the chip level, and studied chip timing and behavior. Now we need to integrate the *chip* timing with the *system* timing. The material is relatively straightforward, but requires some effort to understand.

We now treat a type of logic design activity characteristic of *interfacing*. We must ensure that certain signals are active (or valid) or inactive at certain times within a cycle. This type of activity is not generally treated in books, perhaps because it cannot be described as a step-by-step procedure valid for all situations. Nevertheless, this is a common design activity which should be understood by anyone involved with interfaces.

4.14.1. The Array Read Operation

Monolithic memory chips are organized into memory array subunits such as in Fig. 4.12. The chip enable input signal CHIPENBL, chip select signals CSi, chip write-data bus CHWRDATA, and the write enable input signal WRITENBL may be powered by buffer inverters. Powering is needed because each line may drive (fan out to) many chips. The interconnection of these signals is quite simple and straightforward. Less obvious is the integration of the chip timing parameters with the overall system timing cycle. Generally, for static memory chips, the system level cycle time is slower than the tC(rd)min or tC(wr)min specified at the chip level. Address line skew, chip enable skew, data setup and clock skew at the destination register for bus MREADATA, can cause the time duration of a memory operation to exceed the chip minimum cycle tCmin. Designers, of course, prefer that the cycle time be as small as possible. For dynamic memory chips, these delays can overlap the precharge time, and the system cycle need not exceed the minimum chip cycle by more than the skew of a control signal.

A timing "worksheet" for the design of the timing of the control signals for the read operation is shown in **Figure 4.28.** The critical events in the timing are shown with an integer enclosed in parentheses, in order of occurrence. We solve the problem by an *iterative* procedure, in which some assumptions are made, and then adjusted. At best we can guide the reader

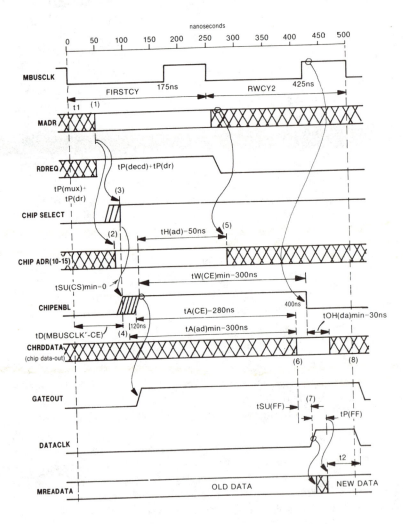

Figure 4.28. *Timing worksheet for read cycle timing integrated with chip.*

through the analysis. The reader must make the effort to "absorb" the essence of an activity which could be likened to solving an elastic jig-saw puzzle.

Referring to Fig. 4.28, at time (1), the MBUS signals are assumed to be valid. For the purpose of this exercise, memory bus timing specifications t1 and t2 of Fig. 4.10 are assumed to be 50 ns each. Specification t1 means that RDREQ and MADR become valid within 50 ns of the fall of MBUSCLK. Specification t2 means that MREADATA is to become valid 50 ns prior to the end of the following MBUSCLK cycle. At t1, propagation delay chains beginning with the validity of the address and RDREQ signals are initiated. These delay chains are deduced from the sequence of propagation delays of Fig. 4.12. At time (2), the chip address lines should be valid, following the delay of a 2×1 MUX and driver. A greater delay is assumed for arriving at the valid chip select line at time (3); there is an additional delay in recognizing the high-order address bits to enable the decoder with signal ADRRECO. The decoder delay is followed by the driver delay. *The setup time tSU for chip select to chip enable is 0 ns, which means that the chip input CE cannot be activated before the chip address or chip select are stable.*

At time (4), the chip enable signal CHIPENBL is activated following a delay tD(MBUSCLK'-CE) from the fall of the bus clock. The delay tD ending at time (4) guarantees that the chip address and select lines are stable. With specification t1 at 50 ns, and assuming the decoder and driver delay at 50 ns, the delay tD must be at least 100 ns, the worst-case delay time for CHIP SELECT to become active (see time (3)). The access time tA(ad) from the stable address is 300 ns, whereas the access time from an active chip enable is 20 ns less (280 ns). Therefore, CHIPENBL can be activated as late as 120-ns time without impacting the overall chip access time. Thus delay tD(MBUSCLK'-CE) can be 110 ns ± 10 ns.

Time (5) occurs nominally at about 250-ns time plus a small delay. (We say "nominally" at this preliminary stage of the design iteration; later a more detailed analysis can bound the time more precisely.) The MADR input lines may change at time (5). We easily meet the 50-ns hold time specification tH(ad) from the activation of CE.

At time (6), nominally 400-ns time (time (3) plus tA(ad)), chip read-data (CHRDDATA) is valid. Also at time (6), since tA(CE) is 280 ns, we can work backward in time and confirm that CHIPENBL can be activated as late as 120-ns time. The only critical reference at time (6) is that chip read-data CHRDDATA must be valid early enough in the cycle to pay the setup time tSU(FF) of the register DATA. The system MREADATA bus must be valid t2 ns before the fall of MBUSCLK, as specified by the MBUS protocol.

The time tSU(FF) is thus keyed to the active transition on the DATA register at time (7). If time (6) is at 400-ns time, and if tSU(FF) is 10 ns and tP(FF) is 10 ns, then the chip read-data output should be valid by 420-ns time. Working backward, with a value t2 of 50 ns, the MREADA-TA bus must be stable by 450-ns time. So far, this specification is met with 30 ns to spare. We will see, however, that "spare" time is required later in the design to account for clock skew. At time (7), keyed to 425-ns time by the leading edge of signal MBUSCLK, signal CHIPENBL is deactivated and signal DATACLK undergoes an active transition.

4.14.2. Control Signal Generation for the Read Operation

Although the trailing edge of MBUSCLK defines the data flow cycle, the time of its leading edge is a "free" specification. This specification is a function of the pulse width tW(MBUSCLK). A judiciously chosen tW(MBUSCLK) will help in the design of properly timed control signals. Let tW(MBUSCLK) be 75 ns. Let CHIPENBL be generated by a set-clear flip-flop. At time (7), let the condition RWCY2 and MBUSCLK clear the flip-flop to deactivate CHIPENBL at 425-ns time, and also activate DA-TACLK, which loads edge-triggered register DATA.

Another control signal to be activated during the read operation is GATEOUT which gates DATA onto the MREADATA bus. To avoid delaying the validity of MREADATA, the GATEOUT signal should be activated before DATA is stable. We set a flip-flop for GATEOUT at 175-ns time with CHIPENBL and RDREQ active. Since the MREADATA bus is unidirectional, the GATEOUT flip-flop can be cleared before another activation of signal RD. GATEOUT should be deactivated at the end of the RWCY2 cycle because the data bus may soon have a new "owner".

GATEOUT is implemented as shown in **Figure 4.29**. The delay tD is obtained from a delay element. (See Appendix D.) Since the chip enable inputs to the memory chip are also activated for write operations, the CHIPENBL flip-flop is set in either case. The CHIPENBL flip-flop is cleared at 425-ns time by the signal DATACLK. The flip-flop for GATE-OUT is set at 175-ns time in the FIRSTCY control state, and cleared at 0-ns time in the next FIRSTCY control state.

4.14.3. The Write Operation

The worksheet for the write operation is shown in **Figure 4.30**, and events in the cycle are numbered and enclosed in parentheses. The chip enable input to the array subunit has been generated as in Fig. 4.29. Signals DATACLK and GATEOUT are inactive, and only the proper activation and deactivation of the write enable control point WE is needed to complete the design of the control of the array subunit. The chip timing specifications place few constraints on the signal WE.

With the aid of the worksheet, we analyze the chip timing specifications of the chip input connection point WE. At time (1), the data to be

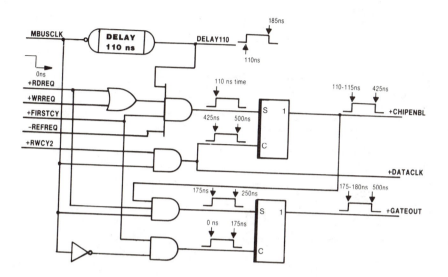

Figure 4.29. *Control signal generation for read operation.*

written is valid, which is much earlier than required. At time (2) the signal driving control point WE becomes valid. A critical specification here is that activation of chip input WE must precede the deactivation of chip input CE (which in our design occurs at 425-ns time) by at least tSU(WE-CE')min = 240 ns. Thus WE must be activated before 185-ns time. If WE is activated at 185-ns time, then tW(WE)min is 200 ns, and WE must be active at least until time (3) at 385-ns time. (If WE activates sooner, it can deactivate sooner). At 500-ns time, the write cycle is over, and following a short delay, chip input CHWRDATA will no longer be valid. Bus MWRIDATA may change any time after 500-ns time. With hold time tH(WE'-da) of 30 ns, WE must be deactivated before time (5) at 470 ns. The constraints at WE allow for many alternative solutions to the implementation of the control signal (WRITENBL) which drives the chip control points labeled WE. Perhaps the simplest solution is that the activation and deactivation times for CHIPENBL also suffice for signal WRITENBL, as shown in **Figure 4.31.**

4.14.4. Clock Skew

The memory card we have designed is synchronized by the MBUSCLK signal, and we must consider the effect of clock skew. Regarding specification t1 (the time by which the address MADR is stable or valid), the

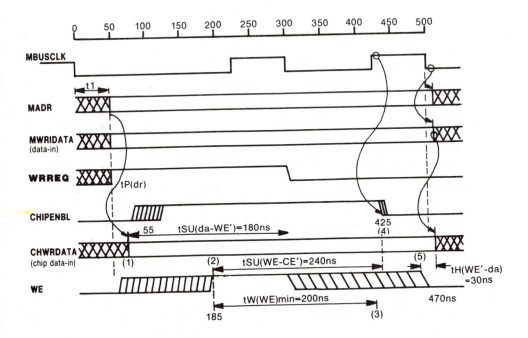

Figure 4.30. *Worksheet for integration of system write operation timing with chip level timing.*

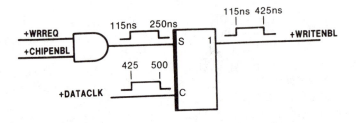

Figure 4.31. *Generation of write enable signal.*

functional unit which presents MADR must ensure that the address is stable within t1 ns of the fall of MBUSCLK, taking into account the presence of skew. With this in mind, the activation of CHIPENBL at "nominal" 110-ns time is subject to skew. The time delay element tD of Fig. 4.29 provides a 110-ns delay. This delay begins with the deactivation of MBUSCLK. At the end of the delay, plus or minus the delay time tolerance, CHIPENBL occurs, however early or late the deactivation of

MBUSCLK. Thus, the activation of CHIPENBL is not adversely affected by skew in MBUSCLK.

Next consider the read operation and the activation of DATACLK of Figs. 4.12 and 4.28 at 425-ns time. Let $t_{SU}(FF)$ be 10 ns, meaning that CHRDDATA must be valid at 400-ns time. With this assumption, and assuming CHIPENBL is activated exactly 110 ns after MBUSCLK falls, a relative skew of 15 ns is the maximum tolerable for the leading edge of MBUSCLK, else valid data CHRDDATA (Fig. 4.12) may not arrive at the DATA register in time. Any skew in the delay element value t_D decreases the tolerable skew in MBUSCLK by the same amount.

Consider now the effect of skew on the minimum width specification $t_W(CE)$ for the chip enable input to the chips. With CHIPENBL activated at 110-ns time, and deactivated at 425-ns time, it is clear that the width of CHIPENBL can tolerate 15 ns of skew in MBUSCLK.

In dealing with a value of skew t_{SK} for MBUSCLK, we assume the source of MBUSCLK is crystal-controlled, hence not subject to variation of more than 0.1% in frequency. On an absolute time scale, the leading and trailing edges of MBUSCLK can be assumed to occur within plus or minus one half t_{SK} on the absolute time scale. If t_{SK} is 10 ns, then FIRSTCY could end at 255-ns time instead of 250-ns time on a "worst case" distribution of delay, or it could end at 245-ns time with a "best case" distribution of delays. However, it is not true that the following cycle, RWCY2, can end at $500+5+5 = 510$-ns time. If a worst-case distribution of delays again occurs, then RWCY2 will again end at 505-ns (absolute) time.

4.15. CACHE MEMORY ARCHITECTURE

This section describes the concept of cache memory. As CPU speeds increase, "balance" considerations necessitate a memory with both large capacity (following the C/E ratio) and high speed (to match the CPU cycle). *These properties conflict.* The problem is nicely resolved by a memory hierarchy: meeting the CPU cycle requirement with a low-capacity high-speed memory buffer called a *cache,* and implementing the large-capacity main memory (also called a backing store) in a slower less expensive technology. The cache memory holds the most recently used information and in principle satisfies most CPU memory requests. The cache memory is transparent to the computer user, who visualizes only a single main memory.

Gibson [10] has written an excellent tutorial on cache memories, which traces the historical developments from the roots of the concept through the use of a cache on a system with virtual memory.

4.15.1.   Some Background and Definitions of Cache Memory

The CPU presents real addresses as usual; the memory cycle time depends on whether the address has been allocated a slot in the cache. If the cache contains a copy of the data stored at the address presented by the CPU, a *hit* occurs; otherwise the presented address is a *miss*. The *hit ratio HR* is the percentage of addresses which are hits, and the *miss ratio MR* is the percentage of misses. These ratios are program-dependent. Some of the concepts discussed here were developed at the University of Manchester, and incorporated in the Ferranti Atlas computer [11]. The IBM S/360 Model 85 (S360/M85) computer demonstrated the commercial viability of the cache concept [7]. Today the majority of high-performance systems use a cache.

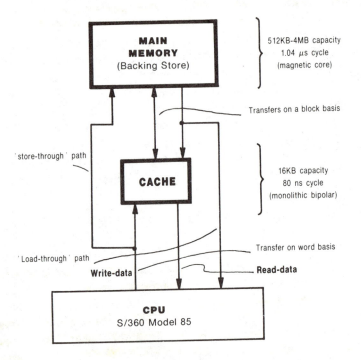

Figure 4.32. *Block diagram of IBM S/360 Model 85 cache.*

A block diagram of the system is shown in **Figure 4.32.** Data transfers to the CPU are on a word basis. To increase memory bandwidth, main memory transfers take place in units of a *block* of words. In the S360/M85, a block consisted of two words of four bytes each. Main memory was from 512K to 4M bytes with a 1.04 μs memory cycle time.

The cache was 16K bytes with an 80-ns cycle time. The CPU cycle was also 80 ns. The cache system organization resulted from many program trace simulations to determine hit ratios and CPU performance for various configurations [12]. The cache scheme is cost-effective because computer programs exhibit a *locality of reference:* address references tend to "cluster" rather than occur randomly. Locality of reference is responsible for the high hit ratios which favor use of the cache technique. For the *ideal* CPU performance, all main memory has an 80-ns cycle time. The S360/M85 performed at about 80% to 85% of the ideal with hit ratios from 92% to 99%. In typical systems, cache cycle times are one to two CPU (data flow) cycles; the main memory cycle time is about 8 to 12 times the cache cycle. If the main memory cycle is much slower than 20 times that of the cache, the mean access time tends to be dominated by the slow main memory cycle. In the case of the Ferranti Atlas machine, the main memory was a drum whose access was on the order of milliseconds.

If write operations are ignored, the mean access time TAM for the "read" case is given by the following formula, where TAC is the access time of the cache, TAMM is the access time of the main (backing) memory, and MR is the miss ratio.

$$TAM = TAC + (MR) \times (TAMM) \qquad (4.1)$$

Assuming TAC is one cycle, TAMM is 20 cycles, and the miss ratio is 5%, then the mean access is $1 + (.05) \times (20) = 2$ cycles. In real applications, the backing memory must be written, and the actual mean cycle time is somewhat larger than the mean read access time.

4.15.2. Cache Management and Bookkeeping Problems

We ignore for the moment the problems associated with write operations. **Figure 4.33** describes the read operation in which real address RA is presented to the memory system. The flowchart raises three questions. First, does the presented address RA give a hit? Second, *if* a copy of the data is in the cache, *where* is it? Third, *if* a copy of the data is not in the cache, then *where* should the data go when it is brought in? Matick [1] calls these problems the IF and WHERE problems. In the event of a miss, the incoming data block overwrites or *replaces* the block of data previously residing in the slot. Which block should be replaced? This decision is performed by the *replacement algorithm*.

We now consider alternatives for the write operation. Where should we store the write-data presented by the CPU? We discuss three mutually exclusive approaches. (1) The *store-through* approach always stores the write-data back to main memory. If a copy is also residing in the cache, that copy is updated. (2) In the *store-wherever* approach, if the copy resides in cache, then only that copy is updated. If no copy resides in the cache,

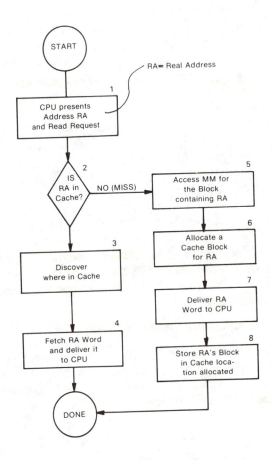

Figure 4.33. *Flow chart of read operation.*

then only main memory is updated. When only the cache copy is updated, the main memory copy is *out of date* (outdated). Cache control must remember this fact; when the updated word in cache (corresponding to an outdated word in main memory) is replaced, that block must be written back to main memory. This is called a *write-back* operation. (3) In the *store-to-cache* approach, write data is always written to the cache. If the block in which the word resides does not occupy a slot in cache, then a slot must be allocated by the replacement algorithm and a copy of the block brought in from main memory. Of course, the write-data is written to the appropriate word in the cache slot. As with the store-wherever approach, the store-to-cache approach requires a write-back operation when a block is replaced for which the block in main memory is outdated.

4.15.3. The Set Associative Method of Cache Management

The *set associative* technique [13] is a solution to the IF and WHERE questions. The real address is subdivided into fields as shown in **Figure 4.34.** The fields are "TAG", "SET" and "WORD". The WORD field is an offset into a block. With cache allocation done on a block basis, the problem of locating the word is narrowed down to locating the block. The desired word within the block is indicated by the WORD field of the address. The TAG and SET fields are used to locate the block. The field called SET divides main memory into nonoverlapping sets, or congruence classes, of blocks. Each congruence class shares the same bit combination in the SET field of the address. A 7-bit SET field defines 2^7, or 128,

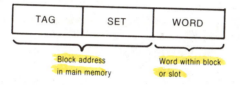

Figure 4.34. *Address fields used for cache control.*

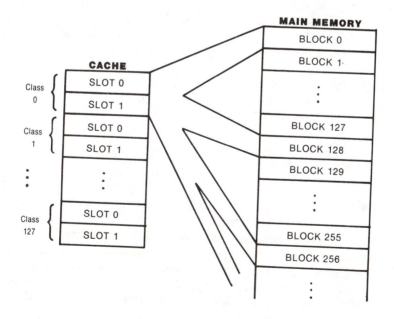

Figure 4.35. *A 7-bit SET mapping in a cache with two slots per class.*

congruence classes. The cache is similarly partitioned into these congruence classes. Only data copies of blocks belonging to congruence class "0" in main memory can reside in partition 0 of cache. This "restriction" is more than compensated for by the ease of implementation: the problem of determining where a block is located in the cache is reduced to the smaller problem of locating a block within its partition. The cache partitions are subdivided into slots, and each cache slot holds a copy of a main memory block. The key to simplifying the WHERE problem lies in having only a small number of slots per cache partition. The "temporary occupant" of a cache slot (a block of address space) is identified by the TAG field. Assigning from two to eight slots per congruence class partition is common practice. **Figure 4.35** shows a mapping of a 128-congruence class main memory to a 128-partition cache, with two slots per partition.

A small control memory called the *cache directory* retains information on blocks currently in each slot of each cache partition. The directory address is formed from the low-order bits of the memory address which indicate the block. The directory stores the tag of every block allocated to the partition [6]. The directory tag consists of the high-order TAG bits of the real address. IF and WHERE an addressed block resides in cache is determined by an *associative* search of that partition's directory contents.

Figure 4.36 shows graphically an associative search for two-slot partitions. The 7-bit SET field of the address ADR(SET) reads the tags of the blocks allocated to the two slots in the congruence class. These tags are compared against the tag ADR(TAG) of the addressed block. This is the "associative search" phase. If the address is a hit, the slot location is known from which TAG comparison results in the hit. If the address is a miss, then a main memory cycle is required.

The directory can also have a control field for storing *flags* useful for write-back or block replacement. The use of flags in the directory is illustrated in the next section.

4.16. A CACHE DESIGN EXAMPLE

We outline the design of a small 1024-word cache scheme, using the set associative technique. The CPU data interface is 16 bits wide; the word size is 16 bits. The 16-bit address field is subdivided into fields as shown in **Figure 4.37**. The cache is organized as two words per slot; a block consists of an odd word and an even word. The addressed word within the block is determined by bit LSBA, the least significant bit of the address. The 32-bit block is also the unit of transfer between main memory and the cache. The cache has 512 slots, and can store 1024 words. If two slots are assigned to each congruence class, then 256 classes result, meaning the SET field of the address is eight bits wide. Since one bit is the odd/even word

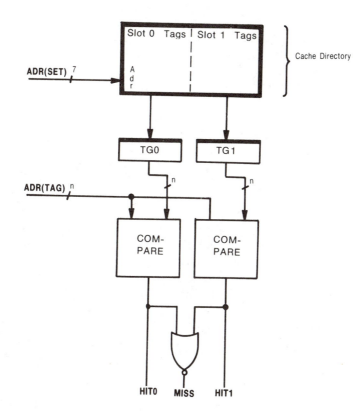

Figure 4.36. *Use of cache directory to solve IF and WHERE problem.*

bit of the slot, the TAG field is seven bits wide. (For a cache of double the size, the designer would probably double the number of congruence classes to 512.) The SET field is named CONGR and the word field is only a single bit.

4.16.1. The CPU to Memory Interface

We define a simple protocol (or groundrules) for controlling the CPU to cache/main memory interface. We shall use the MBUS interface, which is the synchronous custom bus of §4.6. The data portion of the bus is 16 bits wide instead of eight bits as used before. The bus is synchronized by signal MBUSCLK which defines the CPU cycle. If the addressed word is in cache, the memory system responds as expected and interface signal MWAIT remains inactive. If the address presented is not in cache, then signal MWAIT is activated in the second cycle and does not deactivate until

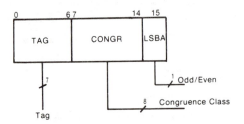

Figure 4.37. *Fields of 16-bit address MADR.*

the last cycle in which the operation requested is satisfied. On the cycle following the deactivation of MWAIT, the CPU may make another memory request. In this example, one cache cycle is two data flow cycles. In high-performance systems, one data flow cycle is usually one cache cycle.

A timing chart illustrating the cache-main memory protocol is shown in **Figure 4.38.** In bus cycle 1, the CPU initiates a read or write operation. In cycle 2, prior to the activation of MBUSCLK, signal MWAIT is activated at time t1 to cause the CPU to wait. Bus cycle "n" is the last cycle of the requested operation. MWAIT is deactivated at t2. In cycle "n+1", the bus is free, and at t3 the CPU can request another operation.

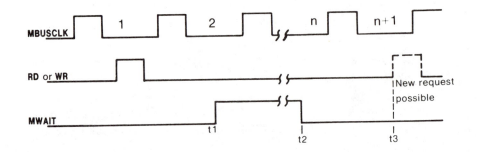

Figure 4.38. *CPU-to-memory communication using MWAIT signal.*

4.16.2. Data Transfers

The simplest data bus scheme uses a single internal bidirectional bus of 16 bits width, called MDATA. See the data paths of **Figure 4.39.** In this design, we initially propose a simple data bus solution. We may find out as the design progresses that the "first cut" should be changed to accommodate some problem not presently considered. Registers MDWR and MDRD buffer the data interface to the CPU. These registers "uncouple" the CPU from the internal bus MDATA. A cache miss results in one or more data transfers between the cache and main memory, so write-data from the CPU should not tie up or occupy the MDATA bus. We shall assume the bus connective is the tri-state driver technology. Since the bus is 16 bits wide, and the block of data transferred to or from main memory is 32 bits (a 16-bit even word and 16-bit odd word), the bus must be time-shared for the transfer. *This generally does not decrease performance because the bus data transfer times are fast relative to the cache access time.* However, it suggests that main memory be split into two modules, one for the odd words and the other for the even words. Further, each module is supplied with its own write-data buffer register. These registers free the MDATA bus for use by the cache when data is being written to main memory.

4.16.3. The Strategy for the Write Operation

In managing the cache, we must make several decisions. In particular, there are many ways to handle the write operation. The present design

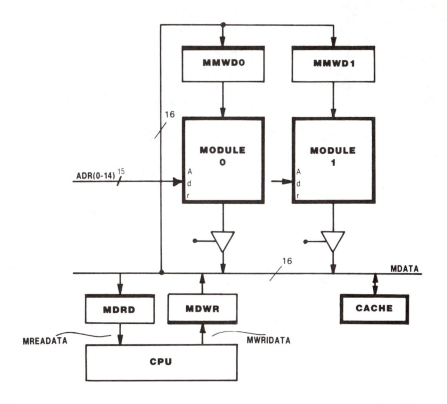

Figure 4.39. *Block diagram of cache design with single bus MDATA.*

uses the store-to-cache strategy. When a cache miss occurs, replacement is made on a slot basis; a cache block which has been updated with write-data must be written back to main memory. A "modified" bit in a control field of the tag memory data word is set whenever a slot is written into, and cleared whenever the slot is reallocated. Bit "M0" is used for slot 0 and "M1" for slot 1. When a slot is replaced whose "modified" bit is set, the block in main memory is outdated and a write-back operation is required. If the "modified" bit is still clear when a slot is replaced, the slot can be overwritten as the main memory block has a valid data copy.

4.16.4. Block Replacement Strategy

We now decide on the block to be replaced for a miss in a given congruence class. Experiments have shown that a random choice strategy does not perform too poorly. An alternative strategy is called "least recently used"; in the two-block case it keeps the last slot referenced and replaces the other. We choose to record the complement of the slot last hit or used for each congruence class as the "RS" bit in tag memory. In the event of a miss, this bit indicates the replacement slot.

We have made enough decisions now to describe the tag memory (cache directory) used by the memory controller. Tag memory helps implement the "bookkeeping" required for cache management. The tag memory is composed of three independently controlled modules. However, all receive the same address which corresponds to the congruence class (SET) address field CONGR. See **Figure 4.40**. Modules MTG0 and MTG1 respectively hold the tags for slot 0 (TG0) and slot 1 (TG1). Module MTCTL holds the three control bits (flags) M0, M1, and RS. Flag "RS" remembers which block is to be replaced when a miss occurs.

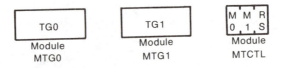

Figure 4.40. *Cache directory memory word, with three independently controlled modules.*

4.16.5. Write-Back Strategy

When a read miss occurs and the slot to be replaced was written into, the slot contents must be written back to the main memory block as indicated by the TAG and CONGR fields of Fig. 4.37. A read miss results in two main memory cycles, one to read the requested data and another for the write-back operation. If the read operation is done first, the data can be passed to the CPU sooner, and the CPU can continue its instruction interpretation task sooner. On the other hand, if the write-back operation is performed first, the CPU is forced to wait longer for its data. The present design therefore performs the write-back operation last. This can be done because registers MMWD0 and MMWD1 buffer (temporarily store) the write-back data block. Similarly we shall define register WBADR to buffer the write-back address.

A cache slot must be allocated in the case of a write miss. Since the CPU furnishes only one of the two words for the block, the other word must come from main memory. A write miss thus requires a main memory read operation.

4.16.6. The Cache Directory

We can now draw data paths involving the directory and address paths; see **Figure 4.41.** Incoming bus MADR from the CPU presents the data address. The low-order address bit is called LSBA and goes to the cache controller where it is used for control purposes. The 8-bit congruence class field CONGR, selected as bits MADR(7-14), is fed to the directory and the cache. The cache is subdivided into four modules, one for each of the four 16-bit words belonging to the addressed congruence class.

The directory is a very high speed memory. It can be read in one MBUSCLK clock cycle. The address field TAG (MADR(0-6)) is compared against tags TG0 and TG1, and HIT0 or HIT1 is activated in the event of a hit. Otherwise the cache controller must handle the miss situation. Tag control bits M0, M1, and RS are inputs to the cache controller. The cache is *simultaneously* read, taking two clock cycles.

With a read hit, the directory determines the desired 16-bit word. This word is to be routed to MDATA and strobed into the MDRD register (shown in Fig. 4.39). With a miss, the two data words to be replaced are available for transfer to registers MMWD0 and MMWD1 (shown in Fig. 4.39) for buffering in case a write-back operation is required. With a write-back cycle, the high-order address bits TG of the write-back address WBADR are selected by data selector TMUX (Fig. 4.41) whose select input is the RS bit. The other write-back address bits of the replaced block are its class CONGR. Words are stored on even byte boundaries.

The main memory block at location MADR(0-14) must be accessed for a read miss. This is a 15-bit block address; bit LSBA is not needed by main memory, as both words are always transferred. In Fig. 4.41, the data selector AMUX selects the main memory address. Signal SELWB generated in the memory controller controls AMUX.

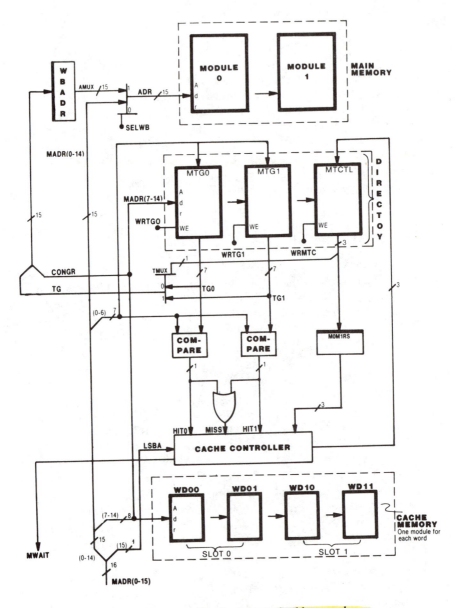

Figure 4.41. *Cache directory and address paths.*

4.16.7. Cache Macrosequences

There are six possible cache macrosequences (or "tasks"): three for a read operation and three for a write operation. These are summarized in Table 4.3.

Table 4.3. Cache Task Sequence Names	
Read	***Write***
Read hit	Write hit
Read miss, no write-back	Write miss, no write-back
Read miss, write-back	Write miss, write-back

Each of the six tasks is subdivided into a time sequence of data transfer operations or microoperations. We need some notation to describe these microoperations. Binary variable HSL (a 0 or 1) denotes the slot for which the hit occurred. An independent memory module is indicated by a name in parentheses following name MM for main memory or CM for cache. Thus CM(HSL,LSBA) denotes the cache memory module whose slot was hit, and hence contains the addressed word. CM(HSL,LSBA') denotes the same cache slot but the module containing the other word of the block. (LSBA' denotes the complement of bit LSBA.) MM(LSBA) denotes the main memory module containing the addressed word, and MM(LSBA') denotes the other main memory module. CM(RS,0) denotes the cache module containing word 0 of the slot to be replaced.

4.16.8. Data Transfer Strategy

The simplest treatment follows from a hit. For a *read hit* cache operation, the addressed word from the cache is transferred to the MDRD register:

Read hit: MDRD ← CM(HSL,LSBA)[CONGR].

On a *write hit*, the MDWR register contains the write-data:

Write hit: CM(HSL,LSBA)[CONGR] ← MDWR.

On a *read miss with no write-back*, main memory is read. The output of the MM module containing the addressed word is transferred first, the value going to register MDRD as well as to CM(RS,LSBA) [CONGR]. Next the other MM module word is transferred to CM(RS,LSBA') [CONGR]. Since a cache cycle is about two MBUSCLK cycles, two buffer registers are used to hold cache write data, CWD0 and CWD1. This frees the MDATA bus for other transfers when the cache is being written.

The bus cycle is subdivided as shown in **Figure 4.42**. Two words can be transferred to or from MM across the MDATA bus in one MBUSCLK cycle by defining two subcycles, A (SCYA) and B (SCYB). This can be accomplished by generating a timing pulse which activates in the middle of an MBUSCLK cycle. A delay element assists in providing such a signal.

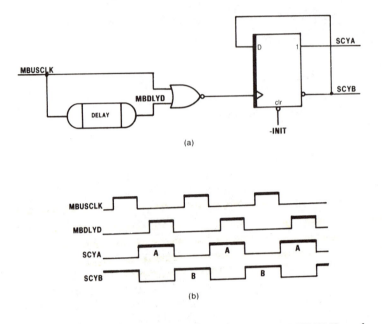

(a)

(b)

Figure 4.42. *Timing for two bus cycles per MBUSCLK cycle.*
(a) Circuit. (b) Timing charts.

The circuit of Fig. 4.42(a) generates the subcycle signals SCYA and SCYB. The circuit must be initialized to ensure SCYA is active for the first half cycle. The timing chart is shown in Fig. 4.42(b).

The two main memory modules can be cycled together or separately. Cycling them together is simpler, but no performance is lost by delaying by one-half MBUSCLK cycle the initiation of the module whose data is to be transferred during subcycle B. Such a delay, for instance, might ease the power supply peak current requirement. For the present design, we shall adopt the simpler approach of cycling the modules together.

We have defined the two-cycle cache write data registers CWD0 and CWD1, as shown in **Figure 4.43**. The designer converts the controller description in microoperation (RTN) form to control signal activations by a straightforward procedure called control signal gathering. The data registers are edge-triggered D flip-flops with an enable input (EN). For the read miss with write-back macrosequence, the contents of the replaced block are transferred to registers MMWD0 and MMWD1. The write-back address is stored in register WBADR (shown in Fig. 4.41). Meanwhile, address MADR(0-15) (originating in the CPU; see Fig. 4.41) is valid at the main memory and a read operation is initiated. Referring to Fig. 4.43, when the MM read-data is valid, in the next SCYA cycle, the requested word is transferred first to register MDRD and to the CWD register indicated by signal LSBA. In cycle SCYB, the remaining word of

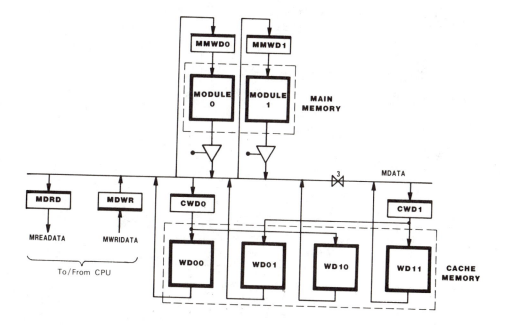

Figure 4.43. *More detailed diagram of cache system data paths.*

the block is transferred to the other CWD register. At this point, the MDATA bus is free and the MWAIT signal to the CPU can be deactivated. However two things remain to be done. First, the new block is written to the cache block from registers CWD0 and CWD1. Second, the main memory undergoes a write-back cycle. To coordinate the next memory request properly, we define two control signals, cache busy (CMBUSY) and main memory busy (MMBUSY). The tag memory cycle which initiates the response to a CPU request is delayed if signal CMBUSY is active. When CMBUSY deactivates, the cache is available and any CPU requests which result in a hit can be satisfied. If a miss occurs and MMBUSY is active, then the system waits until MMBUSY deactivates. The alternative to these "interlocking" signals CMBUSY and MMBUSY would be to delay the deactivation of MWAIT to the CPU until the memory cache and main memory were free. This delay would unnecessarily reduce performance.

The data transfer microoperations for the three read macrosequences are listed in **Table 4.4,** without control or timing information. Similarly, the three write macrosequences are listed in **Table 4.5.**

Table 4.4. Data Transfer Microoperations for Read Macrosequences

Read Hit

    MDRD ← CM(HSL,LSBA)[CONGR]

Read Miss, No Write-back (RDNOWB)

    CM(RS,LSBA)[CONGR] /MDRD ← MM(LSBA)[MADR]
    CM(RS,LSBA')[CONGR] ← MM(LSBA')

Read Miss, Write-back (RDWB)

    WBADR ← TMUX,CONGR
    MMWD0 ← CM(RS,0)[CONGR]
    MMWD1 ← CM(RS,1)[CONGR]
    CM(RS,LSBA)[CONGR] /MDRD ← MM(LSBA)[MADR]
    CM(RS,LSBA')[CONGR] ← MM(LSBA')[MADR]
    MM[WBADR] ← MMWD0,MMWD1

Table 4.5. Data Transfer Microoperations for Write Macrosequences

Write Hit

    CM(HSL,LSBA)[CONGR] ← MDWR

Write Miss, No Write-back (WRNOWB)

    CM(HSL,LSBA)[CONGR] ← MDWR
    CM(HSL,LSBA')[CONGR] ← MM(LSBA')[ADR]

Write Miss, Write-back (WRWB)

    WBADR ← TMUX,CONGR
    MMWD0 ← CM(RS,0)[CONGR]
    MMWD1 ← CM(RS,1)[CONGR]
    CM(RS,LSBA)[CONGR]/MDRD ← MDWR
    CM(RS,LSBA')[CONGR] ← MM(LSBA')[MADR]
    MM[WBADR] ← MMWD0,MMWD1

4.16.9. Additional Design Considerations

We have designed a cache data flow, and described the macrosequences in terms of RTN statements. We have not implemented the control unit beyond this point, nor have we designed the writing of data into the cache directory. We summarize the overall strategy. The first cycle of a macrosequence is initiated with both status signals MWAIT and CMBUSY inactive. At the end of the first cycle, the directory entry has been read and enough information is available to determine which of the six macrosequences is required. Only one more cycle is needed in the event of a hit, as the cache access is already underway. If a miss occurs, one of four macrosequences is to be performed. The control state flip-flops for each are: RDNOWB, RDWB, WRNOWB, and WRWB. The flip-flop outputs can serve as "opcodes" to control the microoperations for each macrosequence. With MMBUSY inactive, we advance a cycle counter CYCOUNT, to distinguish and control the microoperations for each cycle. Corresponding to each macrosequence flip-flop and cycle count, we can activate the appropriate control signals implied by the microoperation.

The cache control unit is not implemented in detail here. We have demonstrated the decisions and strategies employed in cache designs, and indicated the complexity of the design problem. The example given here is relatively simple; the CPU is the only user of main memory, and there is no virtual memory address translation.

4.17. VIRTUAL MEMORY SYSTEM ARCHITECTURES

The real memory provides physical locations to store data words in the memory space. The program generates instruction and operand references to its program name space. At some time the program name space or address space must be mapped to locations in real memory. See **Figure 4.44.** This mapping is called *static binding* if it is performed before the program is to run (program generation, assembly or loading time). Binding resolves the symbolic addresses to *absolute* addresses. Another technique is *dynamic relocation;* a dynamic address translation (DAT) unit accepts an address in name space and converts it to a real memory address every time the name is used. When the DAT technique is used, the absolute address is called a *virtual address.* Binding and dynamic relocation are not mutually exclusive. Binding techniques deliver the absolute or virtual address, which can then be dynamically relocated to real memory. Virtual-to-real address translation is not without cost, because a DAT unit is built from logic circuits. A DAT unit also consumes time, which reduces performance. Each address must undergo the DAT process, which increases memory access time. The IBM S360/M67 had an access time of 600 ns without translation; at best, it was 750 ns with translation. With no translation, static binding techniques are performed "once and for all" for the running of the program, and the generated addresses are already the addresses which go to real memory. Dynamic address translation adds another step to the process of accessing memory. The question must be asked, why pay extra circuits and reduce performance in order to do dynamic mapping? We examine some reasons in the next subsection.

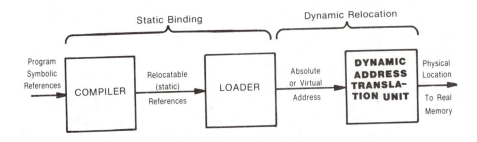

Figure 4.44. *Relationship of static binding to dynamic relocation.*

4.17.1. Architecture of the Program Address Space

Computer system users generally encounter the problem of too little memory capacity. We define the *overlay problem* as running a program in a smaller amount of memory space than the size of the full program in its address space. To solve the overlay problem, not all parts of the program can be in the memory space at the same time. Some of the memory space must hold one part of the program at one time and be overlaid by another part of the program at another time. Second generation computers employed the technique of *manual memory overlays;* see Pankhurst [14]. A portion of the memory space available to the programmer is assigned the role of *overlay area*. See **Figure 4.45.** The principal or root program always occupies a portion of the remaining space, together with data areas. The overlay area is used for successively transferring program overlays and/or data overlays between secondary storage and the main memory space. In this way, a large program can be written for a small memory space. However, the manual overlay technique increases programming and debugging time, due to the additional complexity of scheduling the use of the overlay area. Programmers prefer to write programs as if the memory space constraint did not exist, and concentrate instead on solving problems dealing with their application.

Third generation computer system architects of multiprogrammed systems faced another problem dealing with memory: program *relocatability*. In second generation programming systems, the programmer uses an "ORG" statement to define the location (higher than the monitor program) at which the first word of the object program is to be loaded. This location is called the *origin*. The act of specifying the origin is an instance of static binding. In a wider sense, binding is the assignment of an actual or absolute address to a symbolic or logical address. When the assembler or compiler generates the object program, the target addresses of branch instructions and the operand address fields are calculated relative to this origin. The situation where programs are "bound" at program generation time   is called early binding. Many factors, including greater flexibility, make it desirable to postpone the binding time. We now describe some reasons favoring a late binding time.

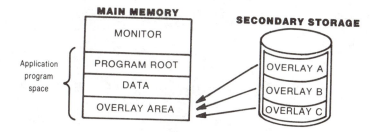

MAIN MEMORY

MONITOR

PROGRAM ROOT

DATA

OVERLAY AREA

Application program space

SECONDARY STORAGE

OVERLAY A

OVERLAY B

OVERLAY C

Figure 4.45. *Memory overlay concept.*

System monitors tend to grow in size and encroach upon the memory origin of the application programs. This forces the application programs to be reassembled. When an object program is generated for the same source program with a new origin, only the values in the address fields are changed. To avoid the time-consuming reassembly process, the concept of a *relocating loader* program was introduced. A relocating loader is told the origin, and modifies the instruction address fields accordingly as the object program is loaded into memory. Of course, not all words of the object code undergo this process, so when the object code is first generated, a list of the offsets of the modifiable words must be generated by the assembler program and placed at the beginning of the object code. At load time, the relocating loader is supplied with the program origin. From this origin the loader calculates the relocation constant to be added to the address fields in the instructions. As a result, the binding time has been postponed to program load time. Binding the program origin at load time is essential to multiprogrammed systems; several programs occupy memory space at the same time. The location of where the next program is to be loaded is a function of which active program is the next to finish.

Third generation instruction set architectures facilitate program relocatability by minimizing the number of words in the object program which require modification by the relocation constant. For example, where PC relative addressing (see Chapter 2) is used, no relocation constant is involved. The IBM S/370 architecture uses base register addressing. The loader needs only to store the correct values in the locations from which the base registers are loaded.

The development of time-sharing systems [15] created a need for postponing the binding time still further. For time-sharing, many users at terminals are being served, and human response times are such that not all user programs and data need be in main memory at the same time. According to a scheduling algorithm, user programs (and their data) are swapped between main memory and secondary storage. Thus, programs are continually being swapped in and out of main memory. A program which is swapped out may be "suspended" somewhere in mid-execution. System programmers may find it more convenient to swap the program back to a different main memory location, which creates a need for dynamic relocation.

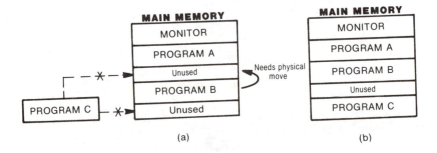

Figure 4.46. *Illustration of how relocation benefits fragmentation problems.* (a) Fragmentation, C won't fit. (b) B relocated, C fits.

Multiprogrammed systems may also employ dynamic relocation to advantage. When a large program is waiting to be run in main memory, and several small programs have finished, the case of *external fragmentation* occurs. See **Figure 4.46.** Here, the amount of memory required by a large program may be available, but only in small pieces, as shown in Fig. 4.46(a). By dynamically relocating a smaller program as shown in Fig. 4.46(b), the required contiguous memory space for the large program is now available.

4.17.2. Dynamic Address Translation Techniques

What is known to the programmer as dynamic relocation, the designer implements with a dynamic address translation unit. The DAT unit receives a program address as input and delivers a location number in the real memory as output. Conceptually the idea appears in **Figure 4.47,** where N virtual addresses are mapped by function F to M real addresses. The map to address "NULL" indicates addresses not currently assigned a real address. It becomes expensive to have each individual virtual word mapped arbitrarily to an individual physical location. Each group of contiguous addresses in the virtual address space is mapped to a block of contiguous addresses in real space. A design parameter is the size of the group which takes part in the mapping function. In practical terms, only the high-order address bits take part in the mapping.

Translating every address emitted by the CPU calls for a mapping function which can be implemented rapidly, preferably in a single operation, so as not to add excessive delay to the access time. The architecture of a system using dynamic relocation cannot really ignore the implementation aspects of the mapping mechanism. *Successful address mapping architectures use both software and digital logic in the implementation.* Software routines allocate real memory, load registers and tables, control data movement in real memory, and between real memory and secondary storage. Digital logic assists in the actual translation of each address for the memory operations.

An early technique for dynamic relocation employed the use of a *relocation register,* where the entire program and data is the translated group. The contents of the relocation register were added to the program address to form the real address. Before running the program, the operating system could load the relocation register. This solved the problem of being able to swap out a program and swap it back into main memory

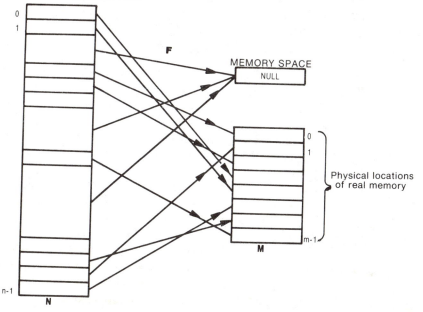

VIRTUAL MEMORY NAME SPACE

Figure 4.47. *Mapping function F.*

somewhere else. Relocation can also be used to eliminate external fragmentation by physically moving programs. However, the relocation register technique does not solve the overlay problem because the output of the mapping unit is simply the input address plus some number. Modern DAT units are based upon the more flexible table look-up form of mapping. We discuss two techniques: *paging* and *segmentation.*

4.17.3. Paging

To reduce the table space required by DAT units, the look-up for relocation is only done on the high-order address bits, partitioning a linear memory space into blocks which are usually small relative to the program size. The low-order address bits represent an offset within the block or *page* defined by the high-order address bits. The use of fixed-sized pages and table look-up which permits a noncontiguous mapping is called *paging.*

Unfortunately the word "page" has two connotations in regard to memory addressing, and both imply a fixed-size block of contiguous linear addresses or locations. In the context of dynamic relocation, the page is the smallest unit or "granule" of addresses mapped by the DAT unit. The second connotation for page occurs in the context of instruction set architecture. The "offset" within the "page" comes from the partial direct address field of the instruction. The page address is determined according to the instruction set architecture dealing with the full direct address. This use of the term page was most probably popularized by the "page 0/current page" bit of the PDP-8 instruction set.

For dynamic relocation purposes, typical page sizes range from 512 bytes to 4K bytes. A page size of memory space is called a *page slot* (or page frame in IBM manuals), because it holds one page of the program address space. Thus, the DAT maps a page in the address space to a page slot in the memory space.

The technique of table look-up on pages permits a response to the CPU of the form, "This page is not present in real memory." An advantage in permitting such a response is that it solves the overlay problem: not all of a program's pages need be assigned memory space in order for the program to run. A *page fault* occurs when the page table indicates the absence of the referenced page in the memory space. The computer operating system is notified of the fault so that the missing page can be brought into the real memory. See **Figure 4.48.** One of the program pages in real memory must be *replaced* in order to provide the slot for the new page. The technique of waiting for a page fault before transferring the page into real memory is called *demand paging* (or page-on-demand). The question arises: where are the unused pages? Copies of all pages customarily reside on a *paging device,* a direct access unit (usually a drum-like device having relatively high-speed access times). The need for a paging device is evident from the following situation. Suppose a local variable (e.g. a "loop" variable) is modified on a program page which was brought in from the program copy permanently residing in secondary storage. If the page is selected for replacement, that page cannot be written back on top of the original program copy. Having a separate paging device provides a place to hold the replaced page temporarily. The paging device is formatted to a record size equal to the page size. Programs and data not in page-formatted records can be read from the library, converted to page format, and written to the paging device before execution of the program.

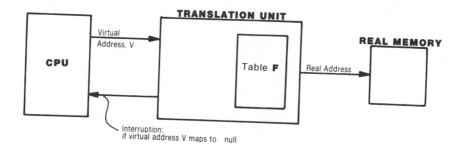

Figure 4.48. *The translation unit.*

Pages not assigned a page slot are called external pages. Their location is determined from an *external page table.* Upon receipt of a page fault, the operating system searches the external page table to find the location of the missing page. This is a requirement absent in cache memory systems. (In cache systems, when the IF question is answered as a miss, then the WHERE is in main memory at the given address.) When the page is in real memory, the page translation table is updated to reflect its slot allocation.

Perhaps one of the most important features of the table look-up technique on pages is that, by incorporating information into the tables on which program is requesting the page, each program is able to use the entire address space defined by the instruction set architecture. Of course, this means that quite large programs can be supported by these architectures. Without identifying the program address with the individual program, address m of program 1 and address m of program 2 would map to the same real address. This problem is solved by providing each program with its own user identification number (user ID) and its own paging tables. Paging allows addresses which are contiguous in the user address space to be non-contiguous in the real memory. In effect, a program's pages can be scattered throughout the real memory. This capability effectively solves the external fragmentation problem without the need to physically move contiguous programs in real memory. However, with fixed-size pages, a condition known as *internal fragmentation* occurs. Suppose a system has a page size of 4K bytes, and a program has a size of 13K bytes. The program must be assigned four pages totalling 16K bytes. In this example, internal fragmentation in the fourth page has caused a loss of real memory of 3K bytes.

The success of the paging approach in making efficient use of real memory depends on the same program locality of reference property exploited by the cache technique. However the locality property cannot be abused by allocating too few slots to a program, else a phenomenon known as *thrashing* occurs. Thrashing is caused by the replacement of pages which are still being actively referenced, creating excessive traffic between main memory and the paging device.

4.17.4. Segmentation in the Virtual Address Space

The term *segmentation* has traditionally been applied to the virtual address space. Consider the context of virtual memories. Segmentation as employed by the Burroughs 5500 had two distinguishing properties: (1) a segment is *an independent linear address space* defined by the user; (2) the segment is *a variable-size unit of transfer between secondary storage and real memory*, as opposed to a page of fixed size. The second property of segmentation is an implementation consideration; more recent systems have retained the notion of independent address space without requiring that the entire segment be used as a unit of transfer. Motivation for variable-size segments appears in Barton [16]. Dennis [17] provides reasons for using a collection of independent linear address spaces.

In a pure paging system, the user's virtual memory is one-dimensional. In a segmented address space, *each segment is itself an independent linear address space*. Segmentation thus adds another dimension to the user's address space, and provides a convenient tool for handling data structures which expand and contract in size. Compiler symbol tables tend to grow, and stack structures tend to expand and contract with time. In general, segments can be procedures, subroutines, utility programs, as well as data structures such as stacks, symbol tables and matrices.

Multiprogrammed systems favor the existence of logically independent address spaces; segments can be individually shared and protected. In particular, programs can be kept distinct from data by assignment to different segments.

Segments are of variable size up to some maximum. When the segment is used as a unit of transfer between real memory and secondary storage, there is no internal fragmentation. But in compensation, the external fragmentation problem is not solved by segmentation without physically moving blocks of contiguous data in real memory. If a segment grows beyond the allocated size (but is still below the maximum provided in the address space), then additional room must be found by moving data. The overlay problem is not solved because the programmer is still free to define one large program in the address space of a single segment which could exceed the amount of real memory available.

In segmented virtual memories, a segment table stores the base address of the page table. The low-order bits of the address indicate the offset within the segment. When a segment not in real memory is referenced, the operating system must perform the necessary IO operations to secondary storage to transfer the entire segment to real memory. The operating system may first need to replace one or more segments to provide memory space for the new segment.

4.17.5. Segmentation with Paging

Paging allows the use of a smaller real memory with a large linear address space. External fragmentation does not occur because contiguous pages in the address space need not occupy contiguous slots in real memory. Thus paging makes efficient use of real memory and takes advantage of the locality of reference inherent in programs.

Segmentation permits the programmer to partition programs in the program address space (in virtual memory) more logically for protection and sharing purposes. Segmentation also accommodates data structures whose size fluctuates, but does not suppress external fragmentation. The variable-size segments do not have internal fragmentation.

The advantages of both segmentation and paging accrue to the system if each segment defines a linear memory space which itself is paged. Segmentation is applied to the user's virtual space, and paging is applied to the real memory. The Multics system pioneered at M.I.T. employed this approach, as did the IBM S360/M67. Segmentation and paging are implemented as a double look-up on two tables, a segment table and a page table. **Figure 4.49** illustrates the two-table mapping.

The segment and page tables have an "available" flag bit. The segment table points to the origin of the relevant page table. If the page available flag is on, the page has been allocated a slot of real memory. This satisfies the IF question. The table entry itself answers the WHERE question if the page is a hit. For a miss, the external page table indicates the page location, either on the paging device or in the user program library.

In the S360/M67, the 24-bit virtual address is partitioned into three fields, a 4-bit segment field, an 8-bit page field, and a 12-bit displacement or word field. This provides 16 segments of 256 pages per segment. These tables are normally stored in main memory. To avoid an associative table

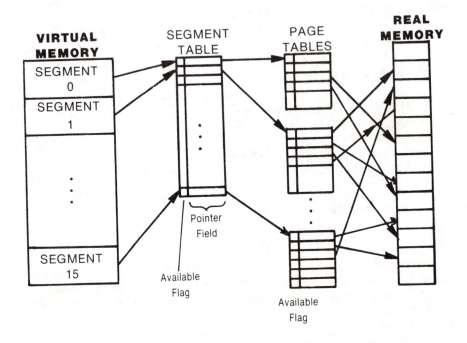

Figure 4.49. *Architecture of the double look-up technique.*

search to find the page slot, the 4-bit segment field is an offset to the segment table; the pointer to the page table is obtained by one memory reference. The page table is similarly constructed, with the page number acting as an offset to permit immediate access to the page slot. The address calculation process is depicted graphically in **Figure 4.50.**

The page tables, if full-sized, would require considerable space in memory: 4096 words. However, many segments use less than 256 pages. Therefore, within each segment, the page numbers actually used range sequentially from page 0 to however large the segment is. Page tables are made short so that unused pages in virtual memory address space do not take up more table space than needed.

In the IBM S360/M67, the double look-up takes 2.1 μs; this is prohibitive relative to a CPU designed to a 600-ns access time. To increase the mean access time, the designers employed a *directory lookaside table* (DLAT), also called a translation table lookaside array. See **Figure 4.51.** The page slots of the eight most recently used pages are stored in a register array. Another array of virtual page registers stores the 12-bit "virtual page", or the segment and page numbers, in an arrangement of associative lookaside registers. When an address is presented, the addressed virtual page is simultaneously compared against the eight most recently used virtual pages as shown in Fig. 4.51. This process takes 150 ns. With a hit,

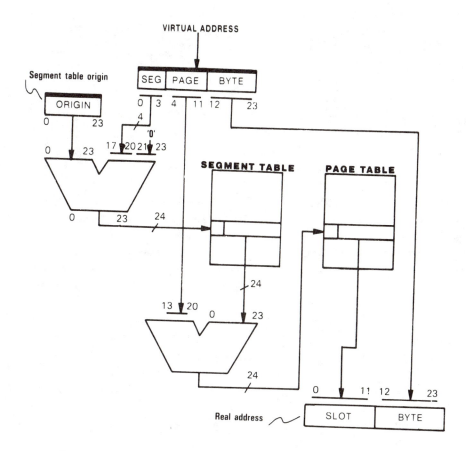

Figure 4.50. *IBM S/360 Model 67 architectural definition of the real address.*

the corresponding 12-bit page slot is the high-order 12 bits of the memory address, and the displacement field is the low-order 12 bits of the byte address. With a DLAT hit, the access time is 750 ns. With a miss, a special control register previously loaded by software is used to obtain the origin of the user program segment table in real memory. Using this value as a pointer, the DAT unit performs a 2.1 μs double look-up and replaces the contents of the least recently used associative lookaside register with the segment, page and slot just used. Fortunately, when only a few pages are involved, a simple digital circuit exists to identify the least recently used page. (See Problem 4.15.)

If the DAT unit discovers either the segment or page "available-bit" off during the double look-up, a *page fault interrupt* to the supervisor is generated. The supervisor puts the application program in the wait queue,

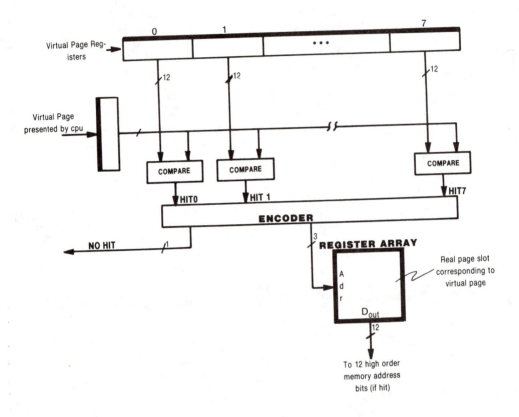

Figure 4.51. *Data flow for directory lookaside table (DLAT).*

allocates a slot, and effects the page transfers to and from secondary storage or the paging device. This operation is analogous to the cache miss operation, and uses the "modified bit" technique to save a write-back operation. Upon loading the addressed page to its slot, the supervisor turns on the available-bit and returns the suspended program to the active queue.

To handle its paging responsibilities, the supervisor program must have privileged instructions to control the system. The supervisor must run some operations in real memory rather than virtual memory. Since the supervisor must access at least part of real memory directly, the DAT must be capable of being told to treat the virtual address as a real address. Also, the supervisor will wish to determine the real address of IO buffers and of the segment and page tables for user programs, so it has a "Load Real Address" instruction. The IO channels use real addresses; they are not expected to do address translation and thereby risk overrun situations. Further, when a new application program with its own virtual memory is started, the special control register contains a new value for the segment table origin, and the eight associative lookaside register contents of the DLAT in the DAT unit are outdated. The supervisor needs an instruction which reinitializes the DLAT associative lookaside registers in the DAT.

4.17.6. Virtual Memory Summary

Successful virtual memory system architectures employ both digital logic (or hardware) and software in a cost-effective manner. A flexible address translation function results from the use of a look-up into an address translation table on the high-order address bits. Even more flexible is the double table look-up which provides the system with both segmentation and paging. The time-consuming look-up is avoided most of the time by a hit in the DLAT. This technique remembers the set of eight (or however many the designer chooses) most recently referenced pages. If the current virtual page belongs to this set of eight pages, then a very small overhead in time is added to the memory access time.

4.18. CACHE STRATEGIES FOR VIRTUAL ADDRESSES

In the cache design example of §4.16, the address presented by the CPU to the memory system was already a real address. We briefly consider strategies for implementing a cache in a system which uses virtual addressing. Early examples include the IBM S370/M158 and S370/M168. A descriptive example of the S370/M168 cache appears in Matick [1]. The main memory system, or program addressable storage, is a three-level hierarchy composed of (1) cache, (2) the main (real) memory, and (3) the paging device. In this section we examine two alternatives for combining a cache with DAT.

For the first alternative, suppose we proceed from the fact that most address references are to data residing in the cache, and that the address presented is a virtual address. This immediately suggests that the tag portion of the cache directory contain the high-order virtual address bits (rather than a real address). In this way the requested memory operation is quickly and conveniently satisfied with a cache read or write cycle. With a hit, the information of which unit gave the successful set associative compare is all that is needed to locate the cache slot. With a cache miss, the next likely possibility is that the referenced page is in main memory and belongs to the set of most recently used pages. Therefore a set of associative lookaside registers or DLAT can determine the page slot. In the event of a miss to the DLAT lookaside registers, the double look-up must be performed and the eventuality of a page fault handled. As before, software can handle the page fault situation. However, functions such as this become candidates for firmware or hardware implementation.

In a second alternative, employed by the S370/M68, the cache directory uses a *real* address for the tag. The reasoning is as follows. The low-order address bits are independent of the virtual or real part, and can be used to address the cache directory. If the addressed block has a slot in cache, then the page to which that block belongs must also have a page slot in real memory. While the cache directory is being accessed for the main memory tag, the virtual part of the address is *simultaneously* used to access the associative lookaside registers (DLAT) for the real main memory page slot. This is another application of the technique of *anticipation,* needed anyway in the event of a cache miss. The real address part from the associative registers is compared with the tag. This second approach provides a bookkeeping advantage. By referencing the associative lookaside registers, the least recently used page can be kept up to date. Also, by referencing the lookaside array, *a hit cannot occur on a cache block whose page in main memory has been replaced.* Lastly, there may be a small cost advantage to performing the set associative comparison for the cache on the high-order real address bits instead of the virtual address: there are fewer real address bits.

In this discussion we have not touched on all the complexities of the management of a three-level memory hierarchy. In the IBM S/370 architecture, many operating systems have implemented the software aspects of the dynamic address translation architecture (e.g. page replacement strategies) in different ways. In the various S/370 models, the computer designers have also made different trade-offs in the digital logic portion of the implementation. Tang [18] confronts the problem of cache design in a shared main memory multiprocessor environment. Tang also discusses sharing this cache design with dynamic address translation, storage protection, and system clocks.

The implementation trade-off opportunities we have encountered in cache memories, main memory data path widths, cache directories, and translation table lookaside arrays are typical of many computer design problems. See Clark et. al. [19] for a description of a memory system design. The designer must consider digital logic costs and the resulting performance. Techniques which can save time or cost are developed and applied. A cost is associated with a capability; any increase in function that may not be utilized should be carefully studied and possibly eliminated. Further, the designer should assure the design provides for all eventualities by asking questions of the type "What if ... ?"

4.19. EXTENDING A SMALL ADDRESS SPACE

For some time, the notion of minicomputer was closely identified with a 16-bit memory word and the 16-bit registers and indirect address so implied. A 16-bit address limits the programmer's address space to 64K words. Minicomputer users have uncovered many applications for which a 64K-word capacity is insufficient. This section studies ways to extend addressability of a small program address space. For a survey, see Poppendieck and Desautels [20].

An early architecture which encountered the limitations of a small address space was the DEC PDP-8 and its predecessor, the PDP-5. The architecture provides a 12-bit word and indirect address, hence an address space of 4K words. A physical memory space of 32K words is achieved by the technique of *bank switching*. Eight banks of 4K words each are defined. The basic PDP-8 instruction set has the ability to load two 3-bit bank registers, one for an instruction bank and another for a data operand bank. At any one time, the programmer can address at most one 4K-word program bank and one 4K-word data bank. To achieve more memory, the programmer must employ thought processes similar to those required for program overlaying. Portions of programs and data are assigned banks. The programmer loads the appropriate 3-bit value in the register as needed by accesses or branches to code outside the current operand or instruction bank. After loading the instruction bank, one more instruction is executed in the previous instruction bank. That last instruction is a branch to the appropriate location in the new instruction bank.

Raphael [21] describes some additional methods for use with a microprocessor with a 16-bit byte address. A one-megabyte memory is proposed, requiring a 20-bit address. The memory is divided into 32K-byte blocks, and the byte within the block is determined by the 15 low-order bits ADR(1-15) of the 16-bit address ADR. A 5-bit register BLK is used to indicate the high-order five bits of the 20-bit address. This register is loaded over the IO bus by the use of IO instructions. The most significant address bit ADR(0) behaves as a "block select" line. If ADR(0) is 0, then the 5-bit register BLK is not used and the five high-order bits of the 20-bit address are forced to 0. The other 15 bits are ADR(1-15), and block 0 is referenced. On the other hand, if ADR(0) is 1, then the contents of the 5-bit register BLK are concatenated with the field ADR(1-15) to form the 20-bit address. The block whose 5-bit number was last loaded into register BLK is referenced.

Another way to use a megabyte memory with a 16-bit address architecture is to define a 20-bit register called BASE which is loaded by means of IO instructions. The memory system forms the real address dynamically by adding the contents of BASE to the 16-bit address generated by the program. *In either case, at any one time, the programmer is limited to only 64K bytes of address space.*

By manipulating register BLK in one case or BASE in the other, the programmer can make overlays available. Alternatively, a program can be written without regard to the small address space, and an assembler or compiler program can insert the IO instructions for controlling the bank, block or base registers as needed. However, this approach can be quite inefficient if symbols are not assigned to banks with care.

Some systems such as the IBM Series/1 perform dynamic address translation on 2K-byte blocks or pages. (They are also called segments; see Schoeffler [22].) This technique can provide the *system* with a large address space, but not the individual program which uses machine language instructions limited to 16 bits of address. In a multiprogrammed system, several tasks can exist in, say, 256K bytes of real memory, where each task uses no more than 64K bytes. If a single application requires more than 64K bytes of memory, then the designer of the application should consider splitting the application into cooperating tasks. (In fact, such an exercise might illuminate a simpler way to approach the application.) Data and utility routines shared between tasks can be shared in a paged system by the supervisor loading pointers to the common areas in the task page tables.

4.20. SUMMARY

We have introduced some important aspects of the main memory system. These include the concepts of address space (of programs) and memory space (physical locations). Also considered are system balance, performance parameters, and memory interfacing. We used a simple memory interface bus (MBUS) to illustrate system memory design. We employed the design methodology on an example using commercially available chips to interface with MBUS. We discussed static and dynamic memory chips and their timing specifications. We completed the design example by adjusting the memory array control signal activation and deactivation times to conform to the chip specifications. This last design problem lies at a lower conceptual level than microoperations, and illustrates how many interface design problems are treated.

A simple cache memory system illustrated the design of cache memory controllers. The scheme interfaces to the same memory bus defined earlier (MBUS). Cache control is aided by the use of a cache directory for tags. We defined the control of the system at the macrosequence level, and suggested a timing arrangement to support the more detailed microoperations. However, the design was not carried to this level of detail.

The memory and cache controller examples follow the same design methodology as for CPU design. We first attended to the *data path* design, and organized a *basic timing cycle*. For each timing cycle, data is moved and operated upon by functional units, at the end of which new values are stored. The control unit provides *major control states* which control each cycle's *microoperations* or actions. A macrosequence is a sequence of control states. The state sequencer is a finite state machine. For each control state, microoperations define the actions which occur. Each microoperation is further subdivided into *control point activations*. The action part of the control unit is described when a boolean expression is obtained which defines when each control point is activated. The corresponding control signals resulting from control point *gathering* can be implemented by gates or a PLA.

Virtual memories were studied, first from the motivational standpoint of the application programmer and system programmer. Foremost among current techniques are segmentation and paging. Demand paging and cache memories have much in common, and depend on the locality phenomena for their performance. A double look-up dynamic addressing technique combines advantages of both segmentation and paging. The translation table lookaside array improves access times. Associative lookaside registers and cache directories can be used together in a three-level hierarchy having a cache, main memory, and paging device levels. Finally, techniques for extending a small address space include (1) the partitioning of memory into blocks or modules, and (2) the use of paging in a multitasking environment.

PROBLEMS

4.1. The project is to design a 5-MIP 32-bit processor.

    (a) Estimate the main memory capacity the processor would require in a nonpaged system in order to keep in balance.

    (b) Estimate the expected average IO traffic, using $E/B = 2$.

4.2. What is the bandwidth of an 8-track (byte wide) magnetic tape unit whose tape speed is 120 inches per second, and tape density is

    (a) 1600 linear bits per inch?

    (b) 6250 linear bits per inch?

4.3. What are the advantages of distinguishing between program space (program-generated addresses) and memory space (physical memory locations)?

4.4. Consider the bus of §4.6 which was described in the context of a single user. Suppose the design is to include two users, the CPU and a DMA channel, where the DMA channel has priority. Define two additional bus signals, DMAREQ controlled by the DMA channel, and CPUACK controlled by the CPU. Describe in words how two users could share the bus, mentioning only concepts.

4.5. Consider the refresh problem for an array of dynamic chips whose addressed row is refreshed whenever accessed whether the chip is selected or not. Design a refresh controller for a "selective cycle steal" technique, where the next row is refreshed by cycle steal only if it has not been accessed within its "time out" period. Let REFADR counter (see Fig. 4.12) hold the next address to be refreshed. If that address is accessed, let the timer be reset and advance the counter.

4.6.   Consider manufacturing the memory array of Fig. 4.20 as a printed circuit card, and specifying the card access time tAcard(adr). Use the following delay notation: tP(decd), tAchip(CE), tAchip(adr), tP(wire-OR), tP(I) (inverter delay), etc.

(a)   Write an access delay equation for the card access time tAcard(adr lo-ord) for the access time from address validity of ADR(2-11) to DATAOUT validity.

(b)   Write an access delay equation for the array access time time tAcard(adr hi-ord) for the access time from address validity ADR(0-1) to DATAOUT validity.   Assume the decoder is always enabled.

(c)   How do the delays in parts (a) and (b) relate to the card access time which would be specified by the manufacturer?

4.7.   Discuss the statement "Since monolithic memories are nondestructive read, there is no need to provide for a read-modify-write cycle in the memory bus definition."   What about semaphore instructions such as "Test-and-Set"? (See Chapter 2.)

4.8.   Consider the cache design of §4.16 and data paths of Fig. 4.43. Following the first MBUSCLK cycle, called FIRSTCY, assume the next cycles are called respectively CYCOUNT0, CYCOUNT1, ..., CYCOUNT9, etc. Consider the implementation part which only involves the MDATA data transfer portion (Fig. 4.43) of the cache controller. *Design the microoperations which govern each MBUSCLK cycle for the macrosequence RDNOWB* (Read miss, no write-back of Table 4.4). Assume main memory read data is available by the end of cycle CYCOUNT6. Signal LSBA defines the word required by the CPU, and cache directory bit RS defines the replaced slot. Timing signals SCYA and SCYB subdivide each MBUSCLK cycle into a first half and a second half. See Fig. 4.42. Registers are edge-triggered and are clocked at the end of each cycle. Let CWD(LSBA) and CWD(LSBA') denote CWD0 and CWD1 respectively if LSBA is 0, and CWD1 and CWD0 respectively if LSBA is 1.

4.9.   Why are cache systems not found in computer systems whose CPU has a low execution rate?

4.10. List some differences between virtual memory systems and the cache/main memory hierarchy.

4.11. Is there any advantage implementing a virtual memory in an architecture with a 16-bit virtual address?

4.12. Most paging schemes have 1K- to 4K-byte page sizes. What would be the advantages and disadvantages of a larger (8K-byte) page size?

4.13. What are the advantages and disadvantages of a double look-up address translation scheme over a single table scheme?

4.14. Let the S360/M67 translate table lookaside array (DLAT) have a hit ratio of 98%. With an access time of 750 ns for a hit and an access time of 2.85 μs for a DLAT miss but page table hit, estimate the mean access time for pages which have a main memory slot allocated.

4.15. Consider a scheme to determine the least recently used page in a three-page DLAT. Let a matrix be set up as follows:

	_P0_	_P1_	_P2_
P0:	0	0	0
P1:	0	0	0
P2:	0	0	0

When page "i" is referenced, let column "i" be set to all 1's and then row "i" be set to all 0's. Thus, a reference to page 1 followed by a reference to page 0 would affect the matrix as follows:

	_P0_	_P1_	_P2_		_P0_	_P1_	_P2_
P0:	0	1	0		0	0	0
P1:	0	0	0		1	0	0
P2:	0	1	0		1	1	0

Notice that the column pertaining to the least recently used page is all zeros. Let the next reference be to page 2:

	_P0_	_P1_	_P2_
P0:	0	0	1
P1:	1	0	1
P2:	0	0	0

Again the column pertaining to the least recently used page is all zeros. From symmetry arguments, show that only three bits, labeled x, y, and z, are needed to implement the algorithm. Devise the rule for setting or clearing these bits for each page (0, 1, or 2) which is referenced.

	_P0_	_P1_	_P2_
P0:			
P1:	x		
P2:	y	z	

REFERENCES

1. Richard Matick, *Computer Storage Systems and Technology*, Wiley-Interscience, New York, 1977. (See Chapter 1).
2. F. P. Brooks, Jr., "Mass Memory in Computer Systems", *IEEE Trans. on Magnetics,* vol. MAG-5, No. 3, 635-639.
3. G. Amdahl, "Storage and I/O Parameters and Systems Potential" *IEEE Computer Group Conf.,* June 1970, 371-372.
4. E. F. Codd, E. S. Lowry, E. McDonough, and C. A. Scalzi, "Multiprogramming Stretch: Feasibility Considerations", *Comm. ACM,* vol. 2, No. 11, November 1959, 13-17. See also W. Buchholz (Ed.), *Planning a Computer System* McGraw-Hill, New York, 1962.
5. M. O. Paley, "The Impact of LSI on Large Computing Systems", *IEEE J. Solid-state Circuits,* vol. SC-3, n. 3, September 1968, 258-261.

6. M. V. Wilkes, "Slave Memories and Dynamic Storage Allocation", *IEEE Trans. on Computers,* vol. C-14, April 1965, 270-271.

7. J. S. Liptay, "Structural Aspects of the System/360 Model 85: The Cache", *IBM Systems Jl.,* vol. 7, n. 1, 1968, 15-21.

8. R. J. Frankenberg and D. Cross, "Designer's Guide to Semiconductor Memories - Part 8", *EDN,* November 20, 1975, 127-137.

9. R. J. Frankenberg, "Designer's Guide to Semiconductor Memories", Parts 1 through 10, *EDN,* August 5, 1975 through January 20, 1976. (Available as single reprint from EDN magazine).

10. D. H. Gibson, "The Cache Concept for Large Scale Computers", *Rechnerstruckturen,* (H. Hasselmeier and W. Spruth, Eds.), R. Oldenbourg Verlag, Munich, 1974.

11. T. Kilburn, D. B. G. Edwards, M. J. Lanigan, and F. H. Sumner, "One-level Storage System", *IEEE Trans. Computers,* vol. C-11, April 1962, 223-235.

12. D. H. Gibson, "Considerations in Block-oriented Systems Design", *Proc. AFIPS,* vol. 30, SJCC 1967, 75-80.

13. C. J. Conti, "Concepts for Buffer Storage", *Computer Group News,* March 1969, 9-13.

14. R. J. Pankhurst, "Program Overlay Techniques", *Communications of the ACM,* vol. 11, n. 2, February 1968, 119-125.

15. R. M. Fano and F. J. Corbato, "Time-sharing on Computers", *Scientific American,* vol. 215 n. 3, September 1966, 129-140.

16. R. S. Barton, "Ideas for Computer System Organization", in *Software Engineering,* COINS III, vol. 1, (J. Tou, Ed.), Academic Press, New York, 1970.

17. J. B. Dennis, "Segmentation and the Design of Multiprogrammed Computer Systems", *JACM,* vol. 12, n. 4, October 1965, 589-602.

18. C. K. Tang, "Cache System Design in the Tightly Coupled Multiprocessor System", *Proc. AFIPS,* vol. 45, NCC 1976, 749-753.

19. D. W. Clark, B. W. Lampson, and K. A. Pier, "The Memory System of a High-Performance Personal Computer", *IEEE Trans. on Computers,* vol. C-30, n. 10, October 1981, 715-733.

20. Mary Poppendieck and E. J. Desautels, "Memory Extension Techniques for Minicomputers", *Computer,* vol. 10, May 1977, 68-75.

21. H. Raphael, "How to Expand a Microcomputer Memory", *Electronics,* December 23, 1976, 67-69.

22. J. D. Schoeffler, *IBM Series/1 - The Small Computer Concept,* IBM Corp., Atlanta, GA, 1978.

* CHAPTER 5 *

LOGIC DESIGN OF THE SC-16
ARCHITECTURE

5.1. INTRODUCTION

Engineers are proficient at using the building blocks or basic parts which the technology provides, and assembling them to perform useful functions. The engineer learns about three things: (1) the function of the machine to be built, (2) the parts, and (3) how to design. Chapter 3 focused on RTN statements for interpreting a very simple instruction set. In this chapter, the instruction set is more powerful, and we examine the data flow design, system timing, and logic design of the CPU in greater detail.

5.1.1. The End Result

First, the engineer must understand the function performed by the design result. We cannot properly design a computer program, for example, if we have no notion of its purpose or how it is to be used. In a sense, the engineer must mentally absorb the functional requirements of the end product. Here, the end product is an implementation of an architecture (instruction set, IO bus, and front panel controls) called the SC-16. Most computer designs implement an existing architecture, or some variation of an existing architecture. The SC-16 architecture is a variation of the

275

PDP-8 architecture, itself a variation of the PDP-5. The architecture incorporates a single-address instruction set which is nontrivial but not overly complex. The SC-16 is quite adequate for the purpose of teaching the fundamental principles of digital design as applied to the CPU.

5.1.2. Parts

The engineer must also acquire knowledge of each building block, learn the function of the part, how it is controlled, and how it is applied in the design environment. Similarly, the programmer must learn the instruction types and how to use them. The end result and the system parts share a common property: each comprises a single conceptual level. We do not require knowledge of the basic building blocks to describe what a computer does. We can describe the function of a "NAND" gate without specifying whether it is built from vacuum tubes or MOS or bipolar transistors. In this chapter our building blocks at various levels concern data flow components, the ALU, microoperations and system timing.

5.1.3. Digital Design Techniques

The most important skill an engineer should acquire is how to *design*. The design process bridges the conceptual gap between the constituent or primitive parts, and the end result. The greater the disparity in function between the parts and the end result, the greater the conceptual gap to be bridged. A one-level gap is bridged by a straightforward assembly of the primitive parts. Examples of well-understood single-level design problems include the design of an adder from NAND gates or the design of a counter from edge-triggered flip-flops. Similarly, the construction of a subroutine to perform floating point division bridges a single conceptual level. The construction of a CPU from NAND gates and flip-flops, in contrast, is a multiple-level design problem because the engineers must interpose intermediate conceptual levels between the basic parts and the end result. This same type of complexity is encountered in computer operating systems and database systems.

The *complex system* encountered in information processing creates a need for solving multiple-level design problems. The art has principles and techniques in common for both the computer engineering and the programming aspects of the field. The basic principle is to *divide and conquer*. We partition the problem into conceptual levels, and partition each conceptual level into semi-independent parts, each of which is a manageable single-level design problem.

Sometimes the task at hand can be approached *top-down* by successive subdivision in smaller subtasks. The subtasks represent a greater level of detail. At other times, the problem can be approached *bottom-up*, by building useful *superparts,* and solving a single-level problem by a straight-forward arrangement of the superparts.

Most often the designer must try to fill the intermediate conceptual levels of a complex problem by ingenuity: knowing where to define sub-tasks, and where to build superparts. Defining the intermediate levels is not a precise step-by-step procedure. We recall some engineering jargon: "How about this idea as a first cut?" "Let's see if it flies."

Computer design provides an excellent environment in which to address a useful multiple-level design problem with the desired property of complexity. The skills so acquired should be useful in attacking most complex problems in the information processing field. Unfortunately, courses on computer organization and courses describing the logic designer's SSI level building blocks deal in a single-level environment. Many computer design treatments are oversimplified. In the real world, iterative or "cut-and-try" techniques are used, so why make believe the solution follows a recipe? Simplistic treatments have a negative effect if a student loses confidence with real world problems.

5.1.4. SC-16 Design Overview and Objectives

We implement the SC-16 architecture in a version with a hardwired control unit called the SC-16H. ("H" is for "hardwired".) In chapter 6, the same architecture is implemented with two microprogrammed versions, the SC-16M and SC-16S. We make the point that there are many ways to implement the same digital function.

The TM-16 of Chapter 3, although a trivial architecture, introduced the notions of *data flow* versus *control unit,* of *microoperations* to describe data flow and control events, and of the *major state* to determine the current phase in the interpretation of the machine language instruction.

The SC-16 is a more sophisticated architecture. The TM-16 lacked a multiplicity of addressing modes, and had no register-reference instructions. In the SC-16H design, we cover *cost/performance* issues with very little extra effort.

In Chapter 3, the TM-16 data flow "happened" because we wished to emphasize the microoperation aspect of the control unit design. In this chapter, we treat the data flow as an independent design activity with attention paid to the cost-effective aspects. Also in the TM-16, the control state for a data flow cycle was a combination of a major state (I or E) and a timing signal from a counter (T0, T1, etc.). In the SC-16H, we assign a major state to each data flow cycle, eliminating the counter. The simpler approach was adequate for the TM-16 because there was only one operand addressing mode.

One of the weaknesses of RTN occurs with a complicated control state sequence. RTN offers no special advantages in describing what the next control state should be. The instruction event schematic shows the next control state, but representing the conditional information on such a diagram is difficult. We favor the *table of microoperations* as a solution. This table displays the *conditional information* which specifies the *data flow action* (microoperation), and also provides a column for declaring the *next control state*. This chapter also explores the system timing cycle in greater detail. The data flow is modified in some cases as a concession to performance.

The control unit design begins with instruction fetch, and proceeds with instruction event schematics for the "normal" instructions which can be handled as a group until the final execution cycle. The table of microoperations describes the control unit behavior. In the course of working out the instruction interpretations, we note the utility of certain *auxiliary circuits*. Auxiliary circuits assist in raising the conceptual level of the control unit design by handling certain troublesome control details at a lower level by providing useful control or conditional information signals. In some cases, the alternative to the auxiliary circuits is reduced performance. In other cases, it is increased complexity of the control unit.

After the sequences of microoperations for instruction interpretation have been designed, we implement the control unit behavior. The microoperations are *gathered* into the *control point activations* they imply, for which the corresponding control signals are implemented in a control PLA structure. The *implicants* for each next control state are readily obtained from the table of microoperations.

We implement the IO architecture of the SC-16. We also design programmed IO, interrupt scheme, DMA port, the Halt-Run controls and console operations of Load, Read and Write.

5.2. THE SC-16 ARCHITECTURE

The SC architecture possesses the basic attributes of a small computer: the data flow registers, the instruction set, and the IO bus. In many architectures, the bus to main memory interface, and the front panel or console, vary according to the implementation. Our design uses the memory bus (MBUS) of Chapter 4, and implements the console operations of the TM-16. We treat the interrupt architecture in a separate section.

5.2.1. Word Size

Data and instruction words have 16 bits. The opcode and address mode fields are three bits each, and the partial direct address (pda) field is ten bits. A *page 0/current page* technique defines how to obtain the full direct address (fda) of 16 bits. The program address space is 65536 (or 64K) 16-bit words; the addresses range from 0 through 65535.

5.2.2. Data Flow Registers Known to the Programmer

Program Counter (PC). The PC is a 16-bit register which points to the next instruction to be executed. Unless the current instruction being executed is a branch (skip, jump, etc.), the next instruction address is one greater (PC plus 1) than the current instruction address. For a skip instruction which is taken, the PC is incremented by 2.

Index Registers (IA and IB). Indexing is one of the addressing modes, and the data flow possesses two index registers: IA and IB.

Accumulator (AC). The SC-16 architecture is single-address. For binary data operations the implied first operand is the AC register, with the second operand being specified by the effective address of the instruction.

Accumulator Extension Bit (E). In some instructions which manipulate the accumulator, it is convenient to capture one bit of information in the extension bit E. For a shift left or shift right instruction, the "lost" (spill) bit may be saved in extension E. In adding an operand to the AC, the high-order carry-out value may be saved in the extension bit E. The E bit may be viewed as the left-most bit of a 17-bit AC register.

5.2.3. The Memory-Reference Instructions

The architecture of the SC-16 employs three basic instruction formats. The instruction format for the memory-reference class is shown in **Figure 5.1**.

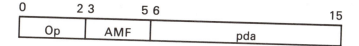

Figure 5.1. *Memory-reference instruction format.*

The majority of the instruction opcodes are memory-reference instructions, using instruction field (0-2) as the opcode. The address mode field (AMF) uses instruction field (3-5) as shown in **Table 5.1**.

Table 5.1. AMF Field		
Bit 3:	Page 0/Current Page to obtain the fda	
Bits 4-5:	**4** **5**	
	0 0	Direct addressing
	0 1	Indirect addressing
	1 0	Indexed, adding IA
	1 1	Indexed, adding IB

With a 10-bit partial direct address (pda) field (or offset), the page size is 1K words. Instruction bit 3 defines how to obtain the fda. If bit 3 is 0, the six high-order bits are forced to 0: the offset points into *page 0*. If bit 3 is 1, the high-order six bits are obtained from PC(0-5) for the current instruction. The offset points into the *current page*. Once the fda is obtained, bits 4 and 5 define how the effective address (ea) is obtained.

For the direct address mode, the fda is already the effective address:

$$\text{direct: } ea = fda \tag{5.1}$$

For the indirect address mode, the fda is the pointer to the effective address ea:

$$\text{indirect: } ea = M[fda]. \tag{5.2}$$

Note that only one level of indirection is employed; the full 64K words of the address space are indirectly addressable. For indexed addressing, bit 5 is 0 when IA is the index, and 1 when IB is the index. Let notation "I5A/B" denote the index register selected by instruction bit 5. The effective address is the sum of the fda and the index:

$$\text{indexed: } ea = fda \text{ plus } I5A/B. \tag{5.3}$$

The value in the index register is an unsigned number between 0 and 65535, as is the value of the fda. Because the sum can exceed 65535, the resulting address requires a 17-bit representation. In the SC-16, the address is "wrapped around" by ignoring the 17th (leftmost) bit. This is expressed by the following equation:

$$ea = fda \text{ plus } I5A/B \text{ modulo } 65536.$$

If the index is viewed as a *signed* two's complement number, the resulting address (with wrap-around) is as expected. (Some architectures test the effective address calculation and generate an interrupt (trap) if the result is not within the range of the physical memory capacity.)

We now describe the opcodes for the memory-reference instructions, using RTN statements. It is understood that:

- the ea is calculated according to Eqs. 5.1 through 5.3, and
- the PC has been incremented to point to the next instruction.

AND   - op 0:   AC←AC and M[ea]; E bit is left unchanged.
ADD   - op 1:   AC←AC plus M[ea]; E bit receives the carry-out.
LAC   - op 2:   AC←M[ea]; E bit unchanged.
SAC   - op 3:   M[ea]←AC; E bit unchanged.
JMP   - op 4:   PC←M[ea]; E bit unchanged.
SRJ   - op 5:   M[ea]←PC; PC←ea plus 1; E bit unchanged.
ISZ   - op 6:   M[ea]←M[ea] plus 1; E bit unchanged;
                0 = M[ea] (after the increment): PC←PC plus 1.

The remaining 3-bit opcode is "7", simply called "opcode 7" or OP7. Actually, this 3-bit code is "extended" by a fourth bit to make two extended opcodes, 1110 and 1111. These define the *register-reference* and the *input-output* operations respectively. The register-reference instruction is further refined by a "subop" field.

5.2.4. The Register-Reference Instructions

Figure 5.2 shows the format for the register-reference (RREF) instructions.

0	3 4	8 9	15
1110	Subop	Not used	

Figure 5.2. *Register-reference instruction format.*

The register-reference instructions either change (set, clear or complement) status or flag flip-flops, or skip on status, or manipulate values in data flow registers. A main memory operand is not needed. (Note that in architectures which use an explicit stack pointer, the register-reference class instruction could access main memory through the stack pointer.) Since register-reference instructions do not require a partial direct address field or an address mode field, the architect may *redefine* these fields for the register-reference instructions.

The first 3-bit field (0-2) of the instruction represent opcode 7, and bit 3 is a 0 to distinguish the register-reference instructions from the IO instructions. Field (4-8) is the subop field, and the decoded combinations can provide for up to 32 subops.

In the SC-16 architecture, we only define 18 of the possible subops. The 14 undefined (unimplemented) subops we say are *reserved* for future expansion. Subsequent models of the architecture may use the unused subops. Instruction field (9-15) is also unused. The provision for unused instruction combinations is quite common in computer architecture, and provides the flexibility for future "upward compatible" extensions of the basic architecture.

Table 5.2 describes the defined subops.

Table 5.2. Register–Reference Instructions

Name	_Subop_	_Description_
HLT	0	Halt the computer. Wait for console interrupt to restart the machine.
NOP	1	No operation. Continue with next instruction.
CLA	2	Clear the AC (AC←0).
STA	3	Set AC to all 1's (AC←1).
CMA	4	Complement the AC (AC←AC').
CLE	5	Clear the E bit (CLRE).
STE	6	Set E bit to 1 (SETE).
SPA	7	Skip next instruction if AC is positive (AC(0)=0: PC←PC plus 1).
SZA	8	Skip next instruction if AC is zero (AC=0: PC←PC plus 1).
SZE	9	Skip next instruction if E bit is 0 (E=0: PC←PC plus 1).
ROR	10	Rotate AC right, E bit provides the fill and accepts the spill (rotr (E,AC)).
ROL	11	Rotate AC left, E bit provides the fill and accepts the spill (rotl (E,AC)).
DTA	12	Deposit contents of AC into index register IA (IA←AC).
DTB	13	Deposit contents of AC into index register IB (IB←AC).
LFA	14	Load the AC from the IA register (AC←IA).
LFB	15	Load the AC from the IB register (AC←IB).
INA	16	Increment the IA register by 1 (IA←IA plus 1).
INB	17	Increment the IB register by 1 (IB←IB plus 1).

5.2.5. The Input–Output (DIO) Instructions

The DIO instruction performs the "programmed IO" capability of the SC-16 architecture. The format for the "Do IO" instruction is shown in Figure 5.3.

Figure 5.3. *Do IO instruction format.*

The opcode "1111" denotes the DIO instruction, which uses the IO interface. The IO interface consists of Data, Address, and Control parts, which interconnect the CPU with IO devices. The DIO instruction format uses bit 4 to distinguish an input operation (bit 4 is "0"), from an output operation (bit 4 is "1"). This is opposite from the TM-16 example. The "real world" also has such inconsistencies. Bit 5 is unused, and bits 6-15 are driven onto the IO bus. Thus, the partial direct address field of the memory-reference instruction corresponds to the "address/control" fields sent to the IO devices, offering some symmetry in the architecture. Bits 6-9 form the 4-bit device address (DEVADR) field, which provides for the attachment of up to 16 devices. Bits 10-15 form the device control (DEVCTL) field. This field is device-dependent, and must be agreed upon by the device interface designer and the programmer of the device driver routines. DEVADR and DEVCTL are activated for all DIO instructions. The addressed device must recognize its own address and respond either to the input or the output operation. For this, two mutually exclusive control signals feed all devices on the interface. On input, IO control signal "input strobe" (INSTR) is active, and the value placed on the IO data bus by the addressed device is loaded in the AC. On output, IO control signal "output strobe" (OUTSTR) is active and the value in AC is placed on the IO data bus for the addressed device. The detailed timing portion of the IO interface and DIO instruction are explained in §5.18.

5.3. CPU COST AND PERFORMANCE ISSUES

We have treated the computer at the architectural conceptual level. The memory bus and IO bus handle 16 bits each. The CPU fetches instructions and executes them out of main memory. The operands are also found in main memory.

Now consider the next lower level of detail, the *data flow component level*. System cost and performance issues imply that the data flow organization is the starting point for the design. The major factor affecting the performance of a *balanced* computer system is the rate at which instructions are executed. Each instruction execution requires one or more main memory references. A cost-effective CPU and main memory design has two properties:

1. the CPU keeps the memory relatively busy, and
2. the CPU is rarely waiting for memory.

If the CPU fails to keep the memory busy, the memory is poorly utilized. Perhaps cost could be saved on a lower-performance memory. When the memory is kept busy, the memory is neither "too fast" for the CPU, nor is the CPU "holding down" the memory utilization. When the

CPU rarely waits for memory, the memory is not "holding up" the CPU. For best system cost-effectiveness, the CPU designer should "target" the design to a particular memory, or at least to a targeted memory cycle time.

5.3.1. The Data Flow

The CPU of a computer system consists of two parts, the *data flow* or internal machine organization, and the *control unit*. Of these, *the data flow is more important.* Suppose the function and cycle time of the data flow have been worked out. A control unit can usually be found that can get maximum performance out of the data flow relative to the instruction set being interpreted. On the other hand, consider starting with the control unit (or the control sequence of microoperations for each instruction). How do we know we are not unrealistically assuming something happens in a data flow cycle which takes too much time? Or which may require an expensive data path which is rarely used? For this reason we prefer to begin with the data flow and then implement the control unit with *dependent* RTN microoperations. The data flow has the strongest impact on the cost and performance of the CPU. The performance of the data flow depends on *two items:*

item 1. the data flow cycle time, and
item 2. the concurrency (parallelism) of the data flow.

The performance of instruction set processors is usually measured in "millions of instructions per second" (MIPs), which relates to the number of instructions executed in a unit of time. For a given machine, any instruction execution can be subdivided into a sequence of data flow cycles. *CPU performance* depends on (1) how much time each data flow cycle takes, and (2) how many data flow cycles are required to execute each instruction. In contrast, *system throughput* concerns the instruction executions *and* IO operations required to perform a given programmed task. The throughput of many scientific "number-crunching" programs depends on the CPU. In contrast, the throughput of many commercial applications depends on the system printer.

Item 1 is important. If the data flow cycle time is increased or decreased, then the CPU performance decreases or increases respectively. (We assume the main memory is chosen to keep pace with the data flow.) The data flow cycle time can be reduced by using faster more expensive circuits or by reducing the number of levels of gate delay which govern the cycle time. Levels of delay are reduced by using more circuits, also increasing the cost. For example, the carry look-ahead technique reduces the levels of gate delay through an adder at the expense of more gates. (Any combinational logic circuit has a "two-level" realization, but some of the fan-in requirements may become quite high.)

Item 2 (concurrency) is also important; if the data flow cycle time remains the same and if each instruction takes less data flow cycles to execute, then performance increases. To reduce the number of data flow cycles per instruction executed, then more microoperations and/or more powerful microoperations must be performed each cycle. Increased data flow power is accomplished through more concurrency in the data flow. Wider data paths can transfer more bits per cycle. More data paths provide concurrency with simultaneous transfers. A more powerful microoperation in one data flow cycle can replace a sequence of two less powerful microoperations. Wider data paths, more data paths, and more functional unit capability in the data flow mean more components (buses, gates, circuits etc.). The increased functions translate into more components and higher cost (as expected). The designers often pause to tally the "component count" of the current version, and estimate what remains. The "component count" and cost per component of the design is a function of the desired performance.

5.3.2. Influence of the CPU Control Unit on Performance

The control unit has a secondary effect on CPU performance. Once the data flow is designed, the worst-case gate delay path determines the lower bound on the data flow cycle time. Also, the maximum concurrency is now determined. Therefore, *the control unit can only slow down the CPU.* If the control unit cannot provide for the concurrency desired, or if too many gate delays are in the paths which generate some control signals, the resulting CPU will be slower than its data flow potential. In some microprogrammed systems, the data flow may be capable of concurrent microoperations but lack a microinstruction to invoke the concurrency. In addition, certain control signals should activate (become stable) early in the cycle (such as ALU source selection control points). If they activate later, the data flow cycle will be longer. Cost and performance considerations may cause the designer to give up performance in some cases, in order to save components in the control unit.

5.3.3. The Data Flow Comes First

One of the hierarchical design principles is to *begin with the most important item* at each level. For CPU performance, the data flow dominates, and should be designed first to meet the performance goal. In low-cost designs, the data flow is a proper place to begin as well, because a low-cost data flow (within reason) is the target. We therefore concentrate on the data flow.

5.4. DATA FLOW COMPONENTS

The data flow consists of the data flow registers, functional units such as adders and shifters, and interconnection paths or buses. Data flow design is performed first at the block diagram level. The data flow control points are generally omitted from the diagram to avoid the clutter of lower-level details. The following building blocks are considered "basic" (primitive) to the conceptual level of data flow design.

5.4.1. Data Flow Registers

In early computer architectures, the data flow registers were generally known to the programmers. The AC, PC, and the index registers IA and IB, have been discussed in connection with the SC-16 architecture. We now define the following registers over which the programmer has no direct control.

Memory Address Register (MA). The MA register is as wide as the memory capacity implies, which is 16 bits. During the fetching of the instruction and the operand, MA holds the address steady while data is accessed from or written to main memory.

Memory Data Register (MD). The MD holds the data most recently read from main memory. In many systems it also holds data to be written into main memory. This register must be as wide as the word requested from memory, which is 16 bits.

Instruction Register (IR). The IR holds the opcode and other information from the instruction necessary for its execution. The SC-16H has a 6-bit IR: the 3-bit opcode field and the 3-bit address mode field AMF.

Other registers found in a data flow include *status,* which may be a collection of flags such as the arithmetic unit carry-out bit, a spill bit from a shift operation, a bit which is set if the arithmetic result is 0, etc. "Scratchpad" registers may exist for intermediate results in multiplication or division algorithms. If the architecture has a "stack", a stack pointer register may be incorporated in the data flow.

5.4.2. Arithmetic and Logical Unit (ALU)

An important component of the data flow is the ALU, where the arithmetic and logical operations are performed. The data flow design must ensure that the proper operands have paths to the proper input sides of the ALU. The ALU output must feed to the specified destination. To subtract, the ALU usually has at least one input which can be complemented. The logical (bit-wise) boolean operations (AND, OR, etc.), may also be performed in the ALU. Most adder designs internally generate the bit-wise AND, OR and exclusive-OR signals anyway.

5.4.3. Shifting, Incrementing, and Decrementing

For shifting, the data flow designer may choose to implement the AC as a shifting register. Alternatively, a *shifter*, consisting of one or more multiplexers per bit, may be used. (See Appendix C.) Shifting the AC left could be performed by doubling the value of the AC. The AC is fed to both ALU inputs and the sum is fed back to the AC register. We know of no simple technique such as this for halving or shifting right a value. A 2×1 MUX, of course, can selectively perform a shift right operation: let bit i of the MUX be fed bit $AC(i)$ and bit $AC(i+1)$. If the MUX control input selects $AC(i+1)$ for the ith bit, a shift right has been done.

The numeric value of 1 can be added to a data value in many ways. The operation is quite common in incrementing the PC or a stack pointer. The ALU can "one-up". Let one ALU source be the value to be incremented, the other source be forced to 0, and the carry-in input (CIN) be activated. The ALU output value is the incremented data input value.

A second way to increment is with a special "one-up" combinational circuit. The circuit which adds 1 to a value essentially handles the propagation of a carry signal, and is less expensive than an adder.

A third way to increment a value is to store it in a counting register. In the MSI technology, counter registers are available which may be parallel loaded, and counted up. In many architectures of the first generation, the PC was a counting register. (The counter was widely used in World War II radar circuits, and hence was a well-known vacuum tube circuit.)

The adder can decrement a number by 1 if the data value is fed to one adder input and the value consisting of all 1's is fed to the other. The carry-in must remain inactive. Some values can be counted down or decremented if stored in a counting register which has the decrement capability.

5.4.4. Busing

There are two ways of physically organizing multiple-source interconnection buses. A multiple-source bus is an electrical connection used to convey data signals which can originate from many sources, but the bus assumes the data values of only one source at a time. The logic circuit to perform this function is quite simple, consisting of an AND for each bit of each source, and an OR for each bit of the bus, as shown in **Figure 5.4**.

The MSI part known as the data selector, multiplexer (MUX), funnel, etc. performs the function of Fig. 5.4. When the MUX is used to implement the bus, it is a multiple-source MUX bus. The bus function is centralized, and the source outputs must be connected to the MUX inputs. Depending on the relative locations of the sources and the centralized MUX circuit, much wiring space can be consumed. In single wire-wrapped pc board and MSI component environments, the wiring space problem may be of little consequence.

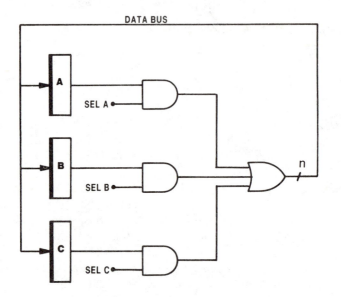

Figure 5.4. *The multiple-source bus function* where each source is also a destination.

In contrast, the *bidirectional bus* strategy is often employed in the VLSI and LSI chip design environment because only one pin per data bit is spent. Bidirectional data lines are also popular in interface buses. A bidirectional bus with the wire-OR is shown in **Figure 5.5.** Such a bus works well when the bus destination registers are the source registers. The OR of Fig. 5.4 can be implemented with any bus connective (wire-OR, transmission gate, or tri-state driver). The AND gate driver portion (open-collector NAND, or tri-state driver) is physically located near the source register. The proximity of the bus, at the AND gate driver output, makes the bus value closely available for feeding the source register. Functionally, a multiple-source MUX bus and a bidirectional bus are the same. The choice of one over the other is a matter of overall cost and performance.

5.5. SOME DATA FLOW DESIGN EXAMPLES

We have defined the architecture of the SC-16. The architecture is a behavioral specification of the design result. We presume familiarity with logic gates and flip-flops at the lowest level of detail of the design problem. The main intermediate level of design is the *data flow,* the single most important cost-performance determinant of the CPU; it is the focal point of

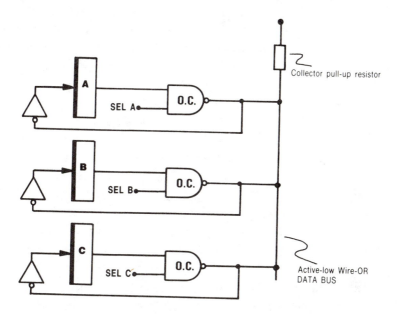

Figure 5.5. *A bidirectional bus.*

the design. In the TM-16 design, the data flow was treated as the consequence of an RTN-based behavioral description. In this chapter and the next, the data flow is designed first. This section exposes the reader to a variety of actual data flows.

5.5.1. The PDP-8

The PDP-8 [1], manufactured by Digital Equipment Corporation, is a simple 12-bit, single-address computer. Its data flow is shown in **Figure 5.6.** Data is written to or from main memory via MD. The IR only stores the 3-bit operation code; therefore it need not be a full memory word long. The ALU shows that the left adder input is complementable. To the left of the AC is the link bit (L). The link can receive the spill bit from a shift, or the carry-out of the MSB of the adder. The PC can be incremented by the ALU, since the left adder input can be blocked (made 0), and the CIN can be activated. The ALU may be used as a transfer mechanism. Programmed input data goes to AC via the left ALU input, then via the Z bus. For branch (jump) instructions, the branch address in MD goes through the ALU to the Z bus (with nothing added), and then to the PC and MA for the start of the next instruction cycle. The path from the MA to the ALU input is used in the execution of the subroutine jump instruction.

The basic *data flow operation* selects two source registers for the respective ALU data input points, processes the two operand values in the ALU/shifter, and deposits the result via the Z bus in the destination register. This action usually happens cyclically, under control of system timing, and its duration or period is called the *data flow cycle time*. For confidence in the timing scheme, the worst-case delays through the data flow loop must be determined to ensure that the system timing has allowed the Z bus to become valid before it is strobed into the destination register.

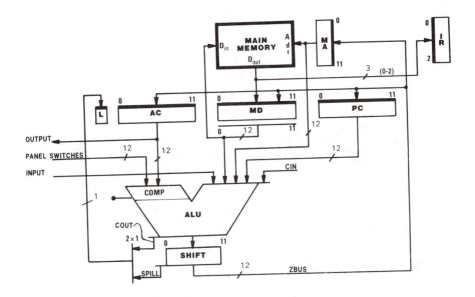

Figure 5.6. *PDP-8 data flow.*

5.5.2. The HP2100A

The Hewlett-Packard HP2100A [2] has a control unit which is implemented by microprogram, but the data flow is the "controlled part" of the CPU and need not differ greatly from a machine with a "hardwired" control unit. See **Figure 5.7.**

Like many computers, the HP2100A has three buses: the ALU left input, the ALU right input, and the ALU output. The names we have designated for the basic registers have been used in Fig. 5.7. The HP2100A is more powerful than the PDP-8, and has more registers. The F and Q registers are left-shifting, as indicated by the left arrow. There are two accumulator registers, AC0 and AC1. Registers SP1, 2, 3, and 4 are "scratchpad" registers used by the microprogrammer, and, like F and Q, are not visible to the programmer. As in the PDP-8, the MA register may

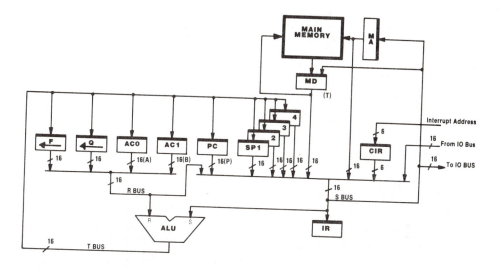

Figure 5.7. *HP2100A data flow.*

be fed to an adder input. The R bus may feed the S bus; in this way, AC0 and AC1 may be placed in MD for writing into memory.

The notion of one bus feeding another also appears between the S bus and the IO bus. A typical microinstruction execution selects an R bus source, an ALU function, and the T bus destination, thus defining the data flow cycle. The HP2100A uses unidirectional buses which improve concurrency but take more wiring space. The T bus is single-source multiple-destination, the R bus is multiple-source and has two destinations, and the S bus is multiple-source multiple-destination.

5.5.3.   PACE

PACE [3] is a simple cost-oriented CPU designed by National Semiconductor to fit on a small chip. In **Figure 5.8,** note the bidirectional data bus to MA and main memory. Due to pin limitations on the CPU chip, PACE must first transfer the memory address out through the IO Data Buffer, then reuse the IO Data Buffer as the MD. The architecture provides for a stack, which is implemented in hardware on the chip. Four accumulators, AC0 through AC3, are also provided. The IR is loaded from the IO Data Buffer following instruction fetch. Most of the control logic is placed in an on-chip ROM array, and IR helps determine the ROM address. The IR register, the IO Data Buffer, and the Status register appear to be implemented as flip-flops, whereas the stack, AC0-AC3, PC, TEMP1 and

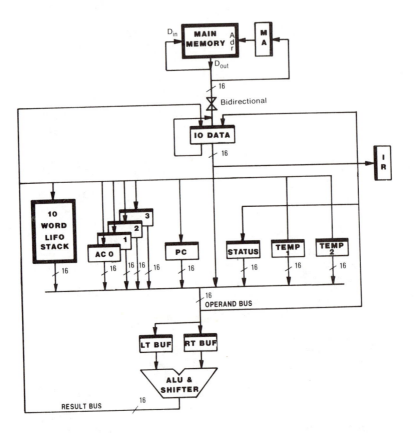

Figure 5.8. *Data flow of PACE microprocessor CPU.*

TEMP2 appear to be implemented in a local RAM array. The machine cycle consists of four clock timing points, probably distributed as follows: (1) one operand is read from the RAM array and placed in an ALU buffer register, (2) the second operand is read from the RAM array and placed in the other ALU buffer register, (3) the operands are combined in the ALU, and (4) the result is written back to the RAM register array or IO Data Buffer.

PACE is a two-bus system with an Operand bus and Result bus. Data buses consume chip area. Without a bus for each ALU input some concurrency is lost. Two timing points are required before the ALU is presented with both operands. PACE designers were willing to lose some concurrency in order to conserve chip area.

5.6. SC-16 LOGIC DESIGN: PRELIMINARIES

The logic design of a computer depends on the implementation technology. The designers already know whether the realization will be in dynamic MOS, CMOS, etc., in a custom VLSI chip design, in TTL, ECL, etc., with MSI parts, or chip slices on a pc board, etc. Thus the pin constraints, or chip area, or pc board area constraints, and other factors such as power limitations are already known, and the designers can make some preliminary trade-off decisions.

In the era of SSI (gate-level) technological domination (1963-1971), the SSI packages and main memory were relatively more expensive and pins and pc board area relatively less expensive. These factors influenced the architecture and logic design of computers. The PDP-8, for example, was designed in this time period, and is very miserly in its data flow registers, having only the major five. The word size is 12 bits, a reflection of the relatively high cost of memory of the time. These factors influence the trade-offs. We hasten to point out that the absolute costs of these components are not very relevant; it is the *relative* changes which are important. If pins, package, gates, memory and power all decrease (or increase) in cost by the same relative amounts, design trade-offs tend to remain the same. The most dramatic cost fluctuations in recent years have been the relative increase in cost of pins and higher-level package area versus decreased per-bit and per-gate costs at the VLSI chip level. These factors favor the use of on-chip register arrays instead of data flow registers, and favor the time-sharing of one or two interface buses among more functional units to conserve pins.

The SC-16 architecture has some of the flavor of the PDP-8, particularly in the register-reference instructions. We have been influenced by authors such as Hill and Peterson [4] and Mano [5] who have based textbook instruction sets on the PDP-8. For the logic design of the SC-16H in this chapter, we shall assume the following technological environment. Barring special considerations, the fewer gates of a data latch favor its use over the more expensive edge-triggered D flip-flop. Let us make believe that monolithic memory (local RAM) for a register array is not yet economical. This choice gives the reader some familiarity with the data latch, as the edge-triggered D was used in the TM-16. We use the MUX bus in the SC-16H. Two unidirectional MUX buses generally provide for greater concurrency than a bidirectional bus, and yield a higher-performance data flow. The local RAM approach to implementing the data flow registers is covered in the design of the SC-16S of Chapter 6.

Another factor considered early in the design is the type and timing of the interface to main memory. The main memory cycle time is a critical cost-performance factor in any computer. In well-balanced designs, the CPU and main memory both operate near full utilization. The TM-16 design was defective in this sense, because the main memory was capable of being cycled twice in a major cycle, and it wasn't. No computer designer likes to pay for expensive high-speed memory and receive the effective performance of slow memory.

Many CPU designs of the second generation (the core memory and discrete transistor era) used four data flow cycles to one main memory cycle. The transistor speeds were so much faster than the core memories that high memory utilization resulted. A crude but meaningful rule of thumb to system performance was the memory cycle time.

Today, a wide choice of logic and memory technologies allows the designer greater freedom to balance memory and data flow usage. We choose two data flow cycles per memory cycle, a compromise which balances memory and data flow utilization for our instruction set. (The reader, of course, is free to experiment with other strategies for designing a data flow in the context of a design project. See Appendix A.)

In another design consideration, we initially assume that the memory need not be refreshed. Realistically, the CPU designer ultimately must face the possibility that the memory data may not be available when needed, and build in a "wait" function.

In summary, the data flow is composed primarily of data latch registers, which implies a two-phase data flow clocking scheme. For convenience, we will implement the major control state flip-flops in edge-triggered JK flip-flops. After delivering the address to the memory system, the data flow will not expect memory read data to be valid until the second data flow cycle.

5.7. SC-16H DATA FLOW DESIGN

There are several ways to design a data flow. We suggest the following procedure. This procedure is valid if a local RAM is not used, or if the local RAM has been selected but the rest of the data flow has yet to be designed.

1. Learn the register transfer requirements.
2. Work out the ALU source and destination requirements.
3. Simplify the data paths, but within concurrency requirements.
4. Consider data flow clocking, delay locations, and possible need for holding registers.
5. Analyze data flow gate delays and estimate minimum reliable data flow cycle time Tmin(df).

5.7.1. An Iterative Procedure

We familiarize the reader with the SC-16 instruction set and the type of register transfers involved in I-fetch, effective address calculation, and execution. The reader will learn to determine the data paths required between data flow functional units, to apply techniques which reduce the number of MUX buses (data selectors) required, and to integrate the data flow cycle with the memory cycle and devise the timing signals.

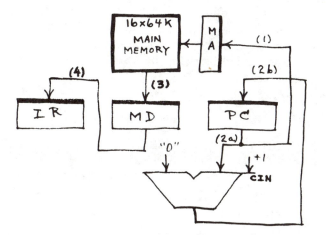

Figure 5.9. *Familiarization with I-fetch.* *(1) Load MA from PC; (2) increment PC by (a) letting adder receive PC with forced carry, and (b) loading result to PC; (3) load MD from memory; (4) load IR from MD.*

5.7.2. Preliminary Data Flow

We sketch some preliminary ideas, then iterate to a final solution. Consider the instruction fetch (I-fetch) portion of the interpretation of an instruction; see **Figure 5.9.** The labeled data paths show the following sequence.

(1) MA receives the instruction from the PC.
(2) While waiting for the main memory access time, the PC is incremented.
(3) The instruction is strobed into MD.
(4) The instruction is strobed into IR.

The technique for incrementing the PC uses the adder which already exists in the data flow for the ADD instruction and for indexing. With one adder input at zero, the other adder input receives the PC, and the adder carry-in bit is made active. This effectively adds 1 to the PC. The activation of the CIN input can be represented in RTN as CIN=1, or simply CIN.

Next consider an "unconstrained" or undisciplined data flow, with no restriction on data paths or multiplexers. **Figure 5.10** is constructed as follows. Assume the memory interface MBUS of Chapter 4. The data flow functional units (registers and ALU) are drawn. Then the addressing modes are considered, and the unconstrained register transfer paths for these are determined. To reduce the complexity of the problem at hand, we *postpone* the implementation of the full direct address (page 0 or current page). With the direct addressing mode, the direct address is in the IR, and a path is shown from the IR to the MA. As paths are added to the data flow, the new paths are labeled with the instruction or operation using the path. Actually, observe from Fig. 5.10 that after I-fetch the direct address is also in MD, and may be bused to MA from MD instead of from the IR.

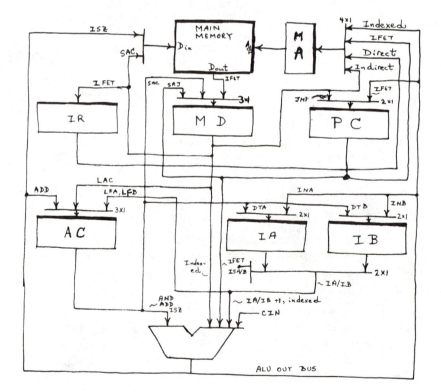

Figure 5.10. *A data flow for SC-16H with "unconstrained" data paths.*

Closer study reveals that the IR need not store the direct address bits at all; they are available in MD when required. This observation is reflected in subsequent data flow diagrams, where IR (6-15) is not needed.

A diagram such as Fig. 5.10 apprises the designer of the types of register transfers needed. Familiarization with these transfers enables the designer to eliminate data paths where concurrency is not possible or advantageous. In the diagram, control point I5A/B selects an index register; IR bit 5 selects IA if 0 and selects IB if 1. The selected register bus is called IA/IB. For instructions INA, INB, and ISZ, the values in registers IA, IB, and MD, respectively, must be incremented. (The result of MD plus 1, however, goes to memory input D_{in}.) The choices available are the same as for the PC: use the ALU with forced carry, a counting register, or a special one-up circuit. We choose the ALU with a forced carry, because in general, the required data paths already exist for other reasons.

We also note in Figs. 5.9 and 5.10 that the data path widths have been left out, as has the accumulator extension E. Our present concern is the existence versus nonexistence of a data path.

5.7.3. Minimize Multiplexers

The next step in the data flow design problem is to minimize the number of data paths, in other words, to *reduce the number and size of multiplexers in the data flow.* Using standard TTL MSI packages, the data flow of Fig. 5.10 consumes many more multiplexer packages than register packages. This expensive data flow is a lesson of what may result from the undisciplined use of a register transfer language, where any source register to destination register path is assumed to exist.

In our attack on reducing the number of multiplexers, we start by examining the ALU requirements. The ALU is the "heart" of the data flow. If a source register value is routed through the ALU, with zero added to it and no forced carry-in, then following a propagation delay, the same source register value appears on the ALU OUT BUS, which may then be used to deliver data to a destination register. This technique is called "using the ALU as a switch". Note from Fig. 5.10 that all registers except IR, which only has one source anyway, receive data from the ALU OUT BUS.

It is important that two registers to be added together not feed the same ALU input. We made this mistake in Fig. 5.10 by feeding both MD and the I5A/B multiplexer to the same ALU input. In order to add them during the effective address calculation phase for indexed mode, each summand must go to its own ALU input. Examination of the ALU input requirements show that MD and AC must feed separate inputs, as must MD and the I5A/B MUX. Our solution is to feed MD to one input, and to multiplex AC, PC, IA and IB to the other.

5.7.4. Holding Registers

Before completing the data flow design, the designer must know the type of register employed. We implement the registers as data latches. In MOS, ECL, and CMOS technologies, the data latch is an economical component. However, data latch registers are subject to the *race-through* problem, which means the data loop should have a "holding" register clocked at a different clock time from the "data flow" registers. A popular location for the holding register is the ALU OUT BUS, as shown in **Figure 5.11**. With the Z register implemented in data latches, the ALU output and Z register combination is called a *latched bus.* Notice also that memory is written from the Z register, saving a 2×1 MUX on the MD register input.

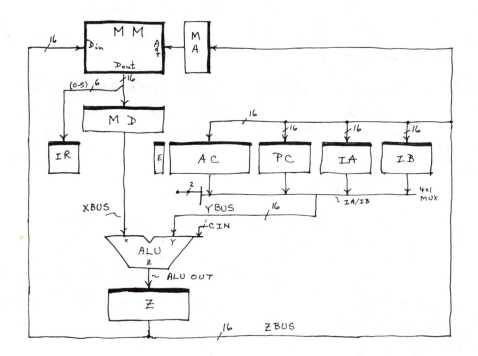

Figure 5.11. *Tentative SC-16H data flow with latched ALU OUT bus.*

Two deficiencies exist in having a holding register at the Z register. Consider the system timing. With the Z register holding the data for a memory write cycle, the data flow must remain idle until the Z register contents can be changed. A second problem with the holding register location at the ZBUS is the absence of any significant combinational circuit delays between the Z registers and the major data registers. To avoid the race-through problem, we wish to latch the ZBUS (fall of the Z register clock) before opening or passing data through the major destination register (rise of the destination register clock); therefore these clocking signals should not overlap. Unfortunately, there is no significant worst-case combinational circuit delay which could be accounted for during this non-overlap time. Perhaps with a large best-case delay through the ALU, and small relative skew between the clocks, a large nonoverlap time could be avoided. Depending upon guaranteed best-case delays is risky. The manufacturing process can improve and lower the best-case delays to the point where intermittent problems plague the assembled product at the test station. A reliance on guaranteed best-case delays also makes the process of reimplementing the same logic design in a faster technology more difficult, as the best-case to worst-case ratio may not be the same in the newer technology.

For these reasons, we seek a different location for the holding register. The next logical place in the data flow loop is at the ALU inputs. Operands on XBUS and YBUS are clocked to holding registers X and Y at clock "Y". The ALU operation is performed, and at clock "D", the result is clocked to the destination register. (This technique was employed in the IBM S360/40 data flow [6].) Note that no ALU operation is performed which has the MD as both a source and destination. We can eliminate register X.

We face the problem of a register to hold data to be written to memory. The MD register could be used, but this would require a 2×1 MUX on the MD register input, the second source being the ZBUS. Using the MD register would also require a holding register for the X ALU input for the MD ← MD plus 1 operation required in the execution of the ISZ instruction. Our solution to these problems is to provide a memory write data (MW) register, which holds all data to be written to main memory. Now the relevant ISZ microoperation becomes MW ← MD plus 1. We also eliminate the need for a 2×1 MUX on the input of MD. The new data flow is shown in **Figure 5.12.**

Avoiding the need to write from MD has an additional benefit for the execution of the SRJ instruction. When PC holds the address to be written to main memory, MD holds the new value to be stored in the PC. In the TM-16 design, a swap between MD and PC was accomplished on the same data flow cycle taking advantage of the edge-triggering property of the two registers. For the SC-16, the data latches and a single holding register make this swap difficult. However, with the MW register, PC can be sent to MW on one cycle, and MD can be sent to PC on the next cycle.

The data flow of Fig. 5.12 has some additional changes. First, the MA register has been given a 2×1 MUX, with the second source coming from the MBUS (memory data out bus). This change increases the performance

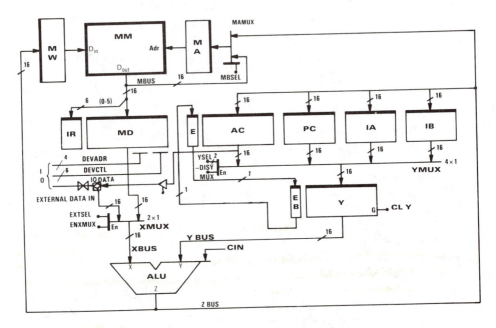

Figure 5.12. *The SC-16H data flow.*

considerably by getting the direct and indirect addresses into MA at the end of a READ cycle, in order to use the new address on the very next cycle. This change has required the MA to become edge-sensitive so that the leading edge of CLD does not perturb the address of the word currently being read. Edge triggering on MA avoids a race-through problem where the intervening circuit is the memory.

Another change in Fig. 5.12 is the addition of the EXTERNAL DATA IN bus to the XMUX. The designer must decide where to bring in external signals such as the IO bus and control panel switches before the design has progressed so far as to make the modification inconvenient.

5.7.5. Timing Considerations

With the Y Register located at the ALU input, the worst-case delays of the data flow loop are more equitably apportioned between the two clock phases. Let the major data flow registers be controlled (or enabled) by clocking signal CLD (D stands for destination), and let the Y Register be controlled (or enabled) by clocking signal CLY. The control signal activations for the YMUX delay happen before CLY. The ALU delays happen before CLD. This attempt to balance delays between two clock phases is a characteristic of dynamic MOS chip designs.

We define the falling edge of CLD, which latches data into the major data flow registers, to be "0-time", which denotes the start of a data flow cycle. Edge 0-time also causes the transition to the next major control state. In this first half cycle, there are propagation delays through major control state flip-flops, the activation of the new control points, and deactivation of the previous cycle's control signals. Also included in this first half cycle are the delays through the YMUX and the Y Register. CLY could possibly "open" (enable) the Y Register before valid data arrives at the input, and should go inactive (latch valid data) any time after its setup time has been paid; see Appendix D. Once valid data arrives through the Y ALU input, data should also be valid through the X ALU input, and the worst-case delays through the ALU must be accounted for. CLD may be active (enabled) after the deactivation of CLY. At the fall of CLD, the following chain of events takes place. After a delay through a clock-pulse AND gate or equivalent, the ZBUS is latched into the major data flow destination register(s) chosen for that cycle. Also, after an edge-triggered flip-flop propagation delay, new control signals are activated.

A delay analysis must be made to ensure that (1) no glitch appears during CLD on the enable input of a data latch register not selected as the destination register for the previous cycle, and (2) no new control signal can cause a change in the ZBUS value during CLD (while a destination register could see that change). The data latch setup time preceding the trailing edge of the enable signal is typically twice the propagation delay, but the hold time is typically zero. The ZBUS can change as soon as the deactivation of the data latch enable signal, when the hold time is zero.

We now consider a selective register clocking scheme with the aid of **Figure 5.13**. Consider the AC register as an example. In Fig. 5.13(a), a glitch on signal ENAC is possible if the skew in CLD is large. Assume that the AC does not receive the ZBUS on the present cycle, but that it does on the following cycle. Also suppose that due to clock skew, the trailing edge of CLD arrived at the major control state flip-flops first. If the best-case delays through the major state flip-flops and control logic for ENAC are less than the clock skew, then the AC clock signal CLAC will glitch, possibly causing an error. The designers of the IBM S360/50 faced this situation and solved it by making the following observation [6]. The destination control signals (such as ENAC) are required only at the end of the data flow cycle. By latching this fact into a Destination Controls register at CLY, the latched destination controls provide a "clean" level against which CLD can be gated. See Fig. 5.13(b).

The problem of maintaining the validity of ZBUS *through* CLD is similar except that the worst-case delay of the clock-pulse AND is added to the clock skew. To win the ENAC race condition, we wish the trailing edge of CLD to occur *before* ENAC changes. In the ZBUS validity situation, we require the deactivation of CLAC to occur before ZBUS changes.

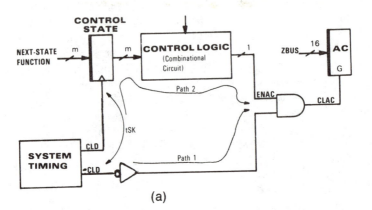

(a)

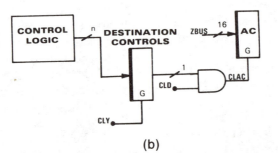

(b)

Figure 5.13. *Timing for register clocking.* (a) Illustration of a race condition upstream of CLAC. (b) Destination control register removes race condition.

The ZBUS could change at that point only with a change in the ALU or forced carry controls, or the XMUX controls. Again, the problem could be circumvented by latching these control signal values with CLY. A "messier" solution would be to insert delay into the CLD signal which changes the major state, relative to the CLD which strobes or clocks the destination register.

This completes the initial data flow design phase. The data flow meets the following requirements in an economical manner: the memory cycle has two data flow cycles, the data flow has a two-phase clock cycle, and the data paths are based on the SC-16 architecture. We learned the data path requirements via an "unconstrained" or undisciplined data flow, and began a more economical design by using the ALU as a switch. We consider the ALU to be one of the most important, and certainly the central, component of the data flow. We next studied the interface to main memory, and the two-phase buffer or holding register requirement, keeping in mind the requirements of the ISZ and SRJ instructions. Knowledge of the addressing modes and a desire to keep the main memory as busy as possible suggested the fast path from the memory read-data bus to MA. A "what if" approach was used to identify potential register clocking problems.

We have followed "first things first": isolate the most important items and attack them first, then modify the result as less important items are treated. Data flow design, like many other activities, requires not only knowledge of building blocks and techniques for putting them together, but a sense of the relative importance of each part used in the design.

5.8. SC-16H SYSTEM TIMING CYCLE

The system timing cycle is one of the most important considerations affecting system performance. The memory operations are integrated with the data flow cycle. Most computers use a central clock to measure out the fixed data flow cycle. The duration of the data flow cycle must exceed the worst-case delays of the operations performed in that cycle. One or more data flow cycles comprise the *system timing cycle*. In the SC-16H, the system cycle is one data flow cycle. The data flow cycle is a powerful construct comparable to what computer scientists call a "FORK-JOIN". The start of the data flow cycle is a FORK, in which each structure capable of independent operation may participate in a data flow action. The end of the data flow cycle is a JOIN. All concurrent actions of the cycle are presumed to have terminated. The designer does not worry that some of the actions could be terminated sooner. Often, at least one of the actions takes close to the allowed cycle time.

What should the data flow cycle time be? We shall assume that the SC-16H main memory uses the 2102A chip of Table 4.1, which has a minimum cycle time of 350 ns. We allow for a memory system cycle time of 500 ns and an implied data flow cycle time of 250 ns. (This estimate allows 150 ns for MA propagation delay, interconnection delays and MD setup delay.) These numbers have been generated in a rather loose fashion; normally, either the memory cycle or the data flow cycle tends to dictate the other.

In the second generation, the main memory technology dominated system timing in high-performance systems. The cache memory of the IBM S360/85 [7] was designed to break this dominance. In some high-performance systems, such as the Cray I, efforts are expended to meet a very fast data flow cycle, e.g. 12 ns; then all other timings are keyed to this. In the STRETCH [8] project, the critical timing parameter was the time to decode the instruction. This set the "pipeline" timing period and all functional units were designed to this period or a multiple of it. Instructions were prefetched (instruction look-ahead) and memory was subdivided into independent modules, which could be addressed concurrently, in an effort to keep the pipeline full. Generally, the memory system was not a determining factor for the timing of the early microprocessors: the system timing was the fastest permitted by the chip area and power constraints. In minicomputer families, the same architecture is implemented in models varying in performance from low to high. The medium- to high-performance models generally will have the memory and CPU timing designed in concert so as to offer a balanced system (neither component is a bottleneck to performance).

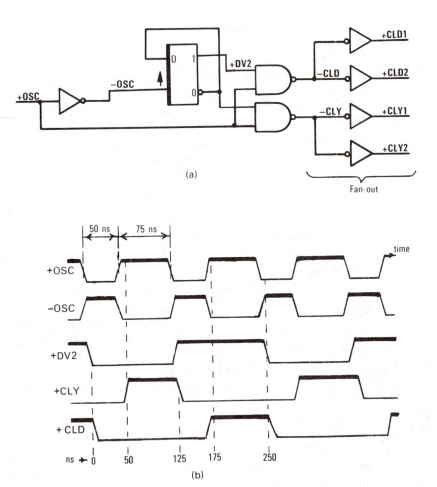

Figure 5.14. *SC-16H system clock circuit (with fan-out) and waveforms.* (a) Circuit. (b) Waveforms.

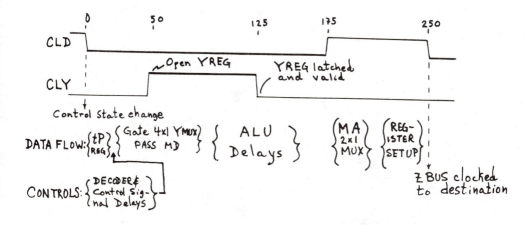

Figure 5.15. *Rough distribution of data flow delays.*

A 250-ns data flow cycle can be clocked by a scheme as shown in **Figure 5.14.** The oscillator does not generate a square wave, but nevertheless can be designed to perform as described. The edge-triggered D flip-flop is connected as a toggle. The basic system clock can be stopped very simply by inhibiting –CLD.

The distribution of the data flow delays are roughly laid out in **Figure 5.15.** The reader is referred to Appendix D for a discussion on two-phased timing. As the detailed design progresses, worst-case delay chains are checked to ensure the timing targets are met.

Consider next the memory operations. For read operations with a 2102A static memory, we need only ensure that delay specifications are met. At the trailing edge of CLD, a new address is presented so $tP(MA)$ is paid. The high-order bits are decoded for chip enable. The low-order MA bits must be powered up, causing additional delay $tP(driver)$. The MBUS signals must be similarly powered up, since the data bits fan out to MD and to IR or MA. There may also be line delays between the CPU and memory system. The powered memory bus MBUS must be valid for the worst-case setup times of IR, MD, and MA. With $tA(adr)max$ of 350 ns, a memory cycle of 500 ns is achievable if the sum of $tP(MA)$, $tP(da)$ for address and data, and $tSU(reg)$ is less than 150 ns worst-case.

For write operations, the write enable control signal (WRITE ENABLE) must be activated, and setup and pulse width specifications must be met. The setup time $tSU(WE\text{-}ad)$ means that WRITE ENABLE must activate no sooner than 100 ns following address validity. We can use the trailing edge of CLY at 125-ns time to activate WRITE ENABLE. This allows for a 25-ns difference between the worst-case $tP(MA) + tP(dr)$

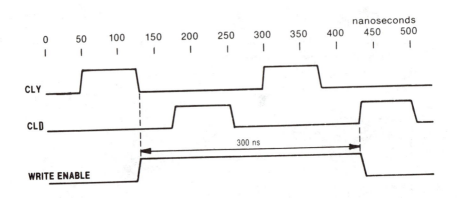

Figure 5.16. *Timing of signal WRITE ENABLE.*

+ skew for the address, and a best-case generation and powering delay of WRITE ENABLE. The minimum pulse width of WRITE ENABLE is 250 ns, suggesting that the leading edge of CLD at 175-ns time of the following cycle be used to deactivate WRITE ENABLE. **Figure 5.16** shows the timing of signal WRITE ENABLE. We defer the actual implementation of this signal, but assume that RTN statement WRITECY will cause WRITE ENABLE to be activated at 125-ns time of the same cycle.

5.9. SC-16 LOGIC DESIGN CONVENTIONS

Conventions implemented by auxiliary circuits are needed at the interface between the data flow and the microoperations controlling the data flow. In the previous section, we encountered such a case with the activation of the write enable signal. In the absence of an auxiliary control circuit we would proceed as follows. On the first data flow cycle of a write operation, the RTN statement could be:

condition•CLY: WRITE ENABLE ← 1

and on the second data flow cycle state

condition•CLD: WRITE ENABLE ← 0.

We feel this brings RTN to too low a level; it is preferable to generate a control signal WRITE on the first data flow cycle of a write cycle, and design an *auxiliary control circuit* to generate the write enable signal. Our conventions require that the address MA and data MW be set up by the end (trailing edge) of the CLD of the previous cycle. For the data flow cycle following the WRITE command, registers MA and MW must be stable.

Conventions provide context in which the data flow functions properly, and usually result in constraints on the microoperations. For example, a convention mentioned earlier requires that MD not be used as a source register on data flow cycles for which it is a destination register.   Constraints discipline the design, benefitting the designer by reducing the alternatives.

The opcode decoder is an auxiliary control circuit common to most "hardwired" control units. **Figure 5.17** shows the opcode and the address mode decoders. The opcode 7 instructions are decoded as shown in **Figure 5.18**. These circuits are at the interface to RTN statements and provide the conditional information. For example, instead of IR(0)•IR(1)•IR(2), we let JMP appear to the left of the colon of RTN statements. As the design progresses, the need to define additional auxiliary control circuits becomes evident.

5.10. SC-16H DATA FLOW FUNCTIONAL UNITS

5.10.1. MUX Control Points

Referring to Fig. 5.12, the 2×1 MAMUX has a single select line, which we call MBSEL (memory bus select). When active, MBSEL passes

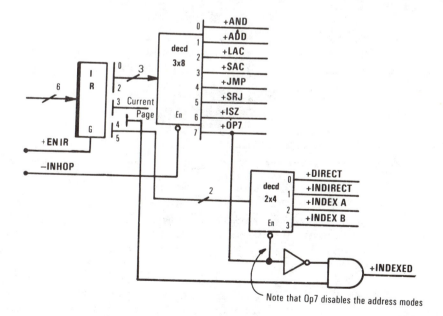

Figure 5.17. *Opcode and address mode decoding.*

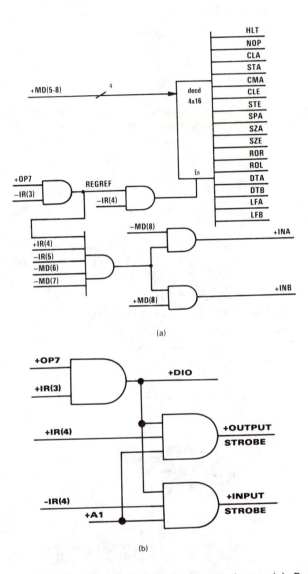

Figure 5.18. *Decoding the opcode 7 operations.* (a) Register-reference instructions. (b) DIO instruction (conceptual).

the value on MBUS to the MA.

The 2×1 XMUX has two control signals. When signal ENXMUX is inactive, it disables the XMUX, placing zeros on ALU input XBUS. When ENXMUX is active, the EXT DATA IN BUS data value passes to X when control point EXTSEL is active, and the MD data value passes when EXTSEL is inactive.

The 4×1 YMUX has three control points. When DISYMUX is active, the YMUX is disabled and places zeros on the Y ALU input. When DISY-MUX is inactive, the two select signals control which of four sources are fed to the Y ALU input: AC, PC, IA, or IB. We shall postpone the detail of encoding the YMUX select signals YSEL(0,1). The Y register is merely a holding register; its enable input is controlled directly by CLY.

5.10.2. The ALU

Table 5.3. ALU Functions Implied by the Opcodes

Opcode	Function
ADD	Binary addition
AND	Logical (bit-by-bit) AND
ISZ, SZA	One-up and/or Zero-detect
ROR	Rotate right
ROL	Rotate left
CLA	Place zeros on ALU out
CMA, STA	Complement Y input
SPA	Detect sign AC(0)
CLE, STE, SZE	Manipulate and test E bit

Table 5.3 shows the functions which might be required of the ALU. Binary addition is done with a binary adder. Because the adder is in the major delay chain of the data flow cycle, it is implemented with carry look-ahead. The AND function $G(i)$ may be obtained from 16 2-input AND gates. (Some MSI ALU chips have the AND function, as well as several others, available through functional select control inputs.) The one-up function is achieved by forcing the other ALU input to zero and activating the CIN input.

A large 16-input combinational circuit can detect a 16-bit zero value. One *zero-detection* method is to wire-OR the outputs of open-collector inverters. This technique takes advantage of the fact that the wire-OR function in TTL performs an AND function. A second method for zero detection requires a full data flow cycle. The number to be tested is inverted (bit-wise) and fed to one adder input, while the other adder input is 0 and input CIN is active. Thus the negative of the number tested is incremented. Only if the number is zero will the one-up of its bit-wise complement deliver a high-order carry-out (HOCOUT) signal. The HOC-OUT method can be used in the ISZ instruction because the result of all zeros occurs when one-upping an input consisting of all ones. The SC-16H employs this last technique for zero-detection.

For implementing the register-reference rotation instructions (ROL and ROR), a combinational shifter built from MUX elements is used, called ZMUX. See Appendix C. The same MUX can be used to select the AND function, which implies a 4×1 MUX at the binary adder outputs. For complementing YBUS, the Y adder input, we employ an exclusive-OR gate used as a selective inverter. A block diagram of the ALU may now be drawn, and is shown in **Figure 5.19.**

The ALU contrasts the way a logic designer views problems to the way a programmer views problems. In Fig. 5.19, the SUM, AND, and shifts are all simultaneously calculated via circuitry, and at the ZMUX the desired function is selected and gated to the ZBUS. In programming, the machine does nothing unless it is told. In digital logic, the combinational circuit continually performs the function.

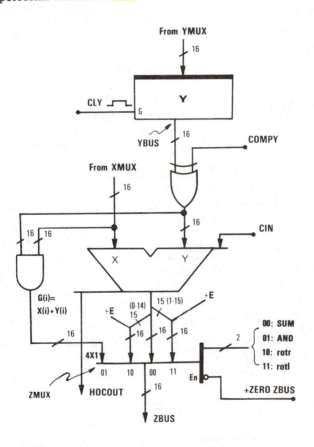

Figure 5.19. *Block diagram of SC-16H ALU.*

5.10.3. Page 0/Current Page and the MA Register

We now consider the detail of obtaining the full direct address from the instruction's address mode and partial address fields. Partial direct address bits 6-15 provide no problem; they are MBUS(6-15). However, the high-order bits MA(0-5) for the FDA Page (FDAP) must be obtained. The correct FDAP can be placed where needed by using auxiliary circuits as shown in **Figure 5.20.** The FDAP value is placed in the MA register by the proper design of the MA control signals. When the instruction appears on MBUS, bits (6-15) can be clocked into MA(6-15) by a control signal "ENMA615". If the instruction specifies the current page in forming FDAP (MBUS(3) is "on"), then no more actions are required because MA(0-5) already has the correct page. If the instruction specifies page 0, then MA(0-5) is cleared by loading zeros.   Zeros are fed through MAMUX(0-5) by disabling MAMUX(0-5) with ZEROMX05 active. The zeros are loaded to MA(0-5) by activating ENMA. This approach places the proper value of FDAP in MA for the indirect and direct addressing modes. See Fig. 5.20(a).

The FDAP value is also needed for *indexed addressing,* when either IA or IB is added to the full direct address to obtain the effective address. This sum is performed by the ALU, with IA or IB selected as the YBUS operand.   The XBUS(6-15) operand is from MD which is correct, but unfortunately XBUS(0-5) contains the opcode and address mode fields. We must design an auxiliary circuit which disallows MD(0-5) to pass to XBUS(0-5). The auxiliary circuit replaces MD(0-5) with the FDAP value via a 2×1 MUX called FDAPMUX as shown in Fig. 5.20(b). The FDAP value is obtained from MA(0-5), with the assistance of the circuit of Fig. 5.20(a). Note that these circuits have the *functional capability* of obtaining the proper FDAP at the proper place. The task of the microoperations designer is to ensure that the *control* signals are activated at the proper time.

5.11. CONTROL STATES

In a hardwired control unit, the action performed on each data flow cycle is determined by the total state: the *opcode, address mode, status flip-flops,* and the *control state* (used for sequencing purposes). In the TM-16, the control state was no more than a sequential counter which was advanced following each data flow cycle until it was reset to the initial I•T0 state. The number of control states was equal to the sequence of steps required to interpret the longest instruction.

Alternatively, we can visualize a control unit where for each combination of opcode, address mode, and step in the interpretation, there is (in general) a unique control state. Such a control state, for example, exists

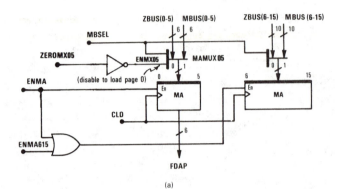

(a)

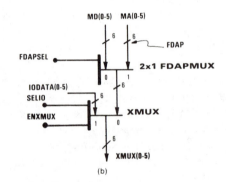

(b)

Figure 5.20. *Full direct address page calculation.* (a) FDAP circuit for direct or indirect addressing. (b) FDAP circuit for indexed addressing.

for microprogrammed control units in the form of the microprogram address register. Unfortunately, such an approach to hardwired control units, when applied to a minicomputer architecture such as the PDP-11, would involve hundreds of control states.

In the SC-16H implementation, we take a different approach. Here, we attempt to assign control states such that the same or similar microoperations occur on the same control state. The result should reduce the cost (number of p-terms) for the control signal activation logic. However, as a tradeoff, the cost of the next-state logic is increased over that of a counter.

There are three major activities in the execution of instructions:

1. instruction fetch,
2. operand address calculation and fetch, and
3. instruction execution.

We assign the control states as follows: I1 and I2 are instruction fetch cycles, corresponding to the two data flow cycles required for a memory system read.   Address calculation and operand fetch require at the most four data flow cycles for indirect addressing. It takes two data flow cycles to read out the pointer and another two data flow cycles to read out the operand. These four cycles are called A1, A2, A3, and A4. They are employed primarily for address calculation and operand fetch. All instructions except ISZ execute in at most one data flow cycle, E1. For ISZ, the operand must be incremented and rewritten to main memory, hence consuming cycles E2 and E3.

We require as a groundrule that the instruction address be in the MA for the start of the I1 cycle. This ensures that at the end of the I2 cycle, the next instruction may be strobed into IR, MD, and MA.

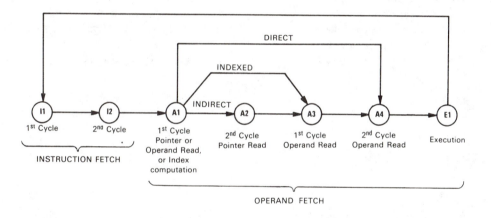

Figure 5.21.   *Next-state diagram of "general" instruction interpretation.*

We describe the basic control state sequence with the aid of **Figure 5.21.** The figure depicts a first iteration in a step-by-step decomposition of an instruction execution. This instruction control state sequence, in fact, works for the straightforward instructions of AND, ADD, and LAC. Our strategy is to handle these instructions first, and later incorporate less straightforward instructions into the design. We come back to the "first things first" aspect of the divide-and-conquer concept: first handle the most important, or most general, or "normal" case (or cases); then incorporate the less important cases (or exceptions). When faced with what to do next, solve the most important or most critical subproblem remaining.

5.12. INSTRUCTION EVENT SCHEMATICS

There are many ways of presenting the information resulting from laying out the interpretation sequence for an instruction. The *event schematic* is a sequence of *action blocks* and corresponds to a macrosequence of RTN statements, and helps the designer sort out the step-by-step interpretation of an instruction. We now develop the event schematics for the straightforward instructions. The sequence is instruction fetch, effective address calculation and operand fetch, and execution. This particular conceptual level of the design is very much like microprogramming, where the microprogrammer determines what to do on each data flow cycle.

The event schematics for instructions LAC, AND, and ADD are shown in **Figure 5.22.** Only cycle E1 is different. The longest execution time is for indirect addressing because two memory read cycles are required, the first for the pointer and the second for the operand itself. Consider Fig. 5.22(a). Cycles I1 and I2 are the same for all instructions as the opcode is not yet known. In I1 the PC is incremented. Recall the convention that the MA be set up prior to I1, so this is the first data flow cycle of a memory read cycle. I2 is the last data flow cycle of the memory read. Recall that the data latching defined by the RTN statements of I2

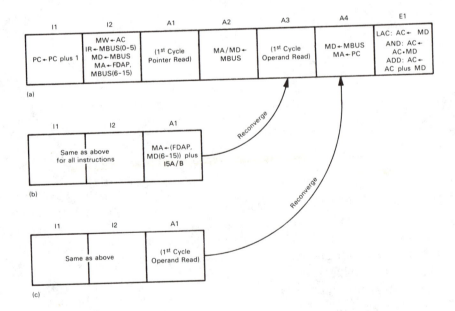

Figure 5.22. *Composite event schematics for instructions LAC, AND, and ADD.* (a) Indirect addressing. (b) Indexed addressing. (c) Direct addressing.

actually takes place at the *end* of cycle I2.   In I2 the instruction arrives from memory and is latched into registers IR, MD, and MA.

Also in I2, an apparently unrelated event is the transfer of the value of AC to MW! The technique involved is called *anticipation*. For the SAC or SRJ instructions, the MW must receive the value in AC or PC respectively. The SAC instruction occurs more frequently than SRJ; anticipating the SAC instruction has a more favorable influence on performance. In logic design, it costs no more to do something *all* the time than *some* of the time, in fact less. In I2, the data paths are free and would otherwise go unused. It does no harm to load the MW at this time. Note that this type of anticipation is a way of thinking not normally associated with programming.

Cycle A1 is the first data flow cycle for pointer read, and at the end of cycle A2, the pointer is conveyed over the "fast path" to MA. Cycle A3 is the first data flow cycle of operand read.   At the end of cycle A4 the operand is placed in MD, and the PC value is transferred to MA. A4 is a convenient time to load MA with the next instruction address. In E1, the unique operation required by the opcode is performed.

The instruction interpretation diverges at A1, depending on the address mode. However, each address mode is not unique thereafter. Being alert for common functions in each cycle, the address modes *reconverge*. The indexed mode of Fig. 5.22(b) diverges at cycle A1 but reconverges to the indirect mode at cycle A3 because interpretation is the same from then on.

In the RTN for cycle A1 Indexed, operand "I5A/B" to the right of the arrow means that IA or IB is selected through the YMUX as specified by instruction bit 5. This is handled by an auxiliary circuit at the YMUX select controls.

Fig. 5.22(c) shows that the direct addressing mode reconverges to cycle A4. The control unit can be greatly simplified by seeking to reconverge to control states where the desired microoperations are being performed. Although it is possible to design an instruction event schematic for each instruction and each address mode, we find the *table of microoperations* is a convenient descriptive technique for simple CPUs where many cycles are shared in common. The table of microoperations and a set of event schematics are descriptive techniques for the same conceptual level, and present the same information. Given a set of event schematics, we can generate the corresponding entries in a table of microoperations and vice-versa. The table of microoperations is more compact, and being organized on a data flow cycle basis, more readily displays commonality. Increased commonality reduces the size of the control unit.

5.13. TABLE OF MICROOPERATIONS

To continue the SC-16H design, we now use a table of microoperations to organize the RTN statements which interpret the instruction set. In normal RTN statements, data flow events take place conditioned upon the boolean expression to the left of the colon (:); one of the literals should always be a major control state. This *conditional* information is represented in the table of microoperations by the two leftmost columns, the first for the major control state and the second for the additional conditions (e.g. opcode) which invoke the microoperation.

Table 5.4 illustrates the table of microoperations technique for instructions LAC, AND and ADD. Table 5.4 is a reformulation of the event schematic descriptions of Fig. 5.22, and the reader should take the time to verify this fact.

For a given condition (e.g. state A1 *and* SAC *and* DIRECT) two items are of interest: (1) what *action* if any occurs on that cycle, and (2) what *control state* will govern the *next* cycle. Rather than use separate lines or two tables, the next control state is written in the rightmost column of the microoperation table.

<table>
<tr><td colspan="4" align="center">Table 5.4.
Table of Microoperations for LAC, AND, and ADD</td></tr>
<tr><td>*Control State*</td><td>*Additional Conditions*</td><td>*Microoperation*</td><td>*Next State*</td></tr>
<tr><td>I1</td><td></td><td>PC←PC plus 1</td><td>I2</td></tr>
<tr><td>I2</td><td></td><td>MW←AC; IR←MBUS(0-5); MD←MBUS; MA←FDAP, MBUS(6-15)</td><td>A1</td></tr>
<tr><td>A1</td><td>INDIRECT• (LAC+AND+ADD)</td><td></td><td>A2</td></tr>
<tr><td>A1</td><td>INDEXED• (LAC+AND+ADD)</td><td>MA←(FDAP, MD(6-15)) plus I5A/B</td><td>A3</td></tr>
<tr><td>A1</td><td>DIRECT• (LAC+AND+ADD)</td><td></td><td>A4</td></tr>
<tr><td>A2</td><td>INDIRECT• (LAC+AND+ADD)</td><td>MA/MD←MBUS</td><td>A3</td></tr>
<tr><td>A3</td><td>(LAC+AND+ADD)</td><td></td><td>A4</td></tr>
<tr><td>A4</td><td>LAC+AND+ADD</td><td>MD←MBUS; MA←PC</td><td>E1</td></tr>
<tr><td>E1</td><td>LAC</td><td>AC←MD</td><td>I1</td></tr>
<tr><td>E1</td><td>AND</td><td>AC←AC•MD</td><td>I1</td></tr>
<tr><td>E1</td><td>ADD</td><td>AC←AC plus MD</td><td>I1</td></tr>
</table>

We proceed to implement the remainder of the memory-reference instructions in tabular form. This is shown in **Figure 5.23**. We make a further simplification when individual control signals are made active. Instead of "WRITECY = 1", we put down "WRITECY" and it is understood that WRITECY is to be activated for the duration of the cycle.

We further state some *conventions* (e.g. auxiliary circuits) or defaults for generating the table of microoperations. The term FDAP (full direct address page) signifies the six high-order direct address bits for the page, either page 0 or the current page. Unless there is a statement to the contrary, by convention the XMUX is disabled. The AC is the default source for the YMUX, and the MD is the default source for the XMUX. The Next State column may contain an indirect reference to the lines which actually govern the next state. Independent statements invoked by the same condition are separated by semicolons. When a bus has multiple destination registers on a particular cycle, these registers are separated by a slash (/).

We can generate an output on the ZBUS, such as for zero detection purposes, but not have a destination. Here we use the phrase "No dest" as a reminder that none of the destination registers are enabled.

In composing Fig. 5.23, during the microoperation design phase, certain economies are possible in the "Conditions" column by the use of boolean algebra. Occasionally the ORing of conditions for microoperations may result in the "Next State" being unspecified on some lines of the table of microoperations. Moreover, some lines will have no microoperation specified but only the next state specified. For lines where no next state is specified, the line number(s) governing the next state are indicated in the next state column.

We can divide the microoperation phase of the design into three relatively independent subphases: (1) memory-reference instructions, (2) register-reference instructions, and (3) IO instructions. In the course of the dependent RTN, or table of microoperations activity, we become more familiar with our solution. As the "middle ground" between conceptual levels is filled, we discover ways in which the data flow can be modified to aid instruction interpretation, as well as the need for auxiliary circuits. When the microoperation phase is complete, the microoperations are decomposed into control signal activations. In this chapter, we use the *programmed logic array* (PLA) as a descriptive tool. All, some, or none of the control signals can be implemented in a PLA. The actual portion is a technological and worst-case delay trade-off. In order to relate the table of microoperations of Fig. 5.23 to the control signal PLA, the column to the left of "Next State" is reserved for the PLA p-term(s) used for the microoperations on that line.

See the control state diagram of Fig. 5.21 for the next states of the addressing phase. We have two exceptions to this basic pattern. First,

Line	Conditions (p-term)	Microoperations (RTN)	PLA p-term	Next State
1. I1		PC←PC plus 1	1	I2
2. I2		MW←AC; IR←MBUS(0-5); MA(6-15)←MBUS(6-15); MD←MBUS	2	A1
3. I2•MBUS(3)'		MA(0-5)←0	3	A1
4. A1•(INDIRECT+SRJ•INDEXED)		(p-term for Next State only)		A2
5. A1•INDEXED•SRJ'•JMP'		MA←FDAP,MD(6-15) plus I5A/B	4	A3
6. A1•DIRECT•SRJ'•JMP'		(p-term for Next State only)		A4
7. A1•DIRECT•SRJ		(p-term for Next State only)		A3
8. A1•DIRECT•SAC		WRITECY	5	A4
9. A1•DIRECT•JMP		PC←FDAP,MD(6-15)	6	I1
10. A1•SRJ		MW←PC	7	lines 4, 7
11. A1•INDEXED•JMP		PC/MA←FDAP,MD(6-15) plus I5A/B	8	I1
12. A2•INDEXED'		MA/MD←MBUS	9	A3
13. A2•INDEXED		PC/MA←FDAP,MD(6-15) plus I5A/B	10	A3
14. A3•JMP'		(p-term for Next State Only)		A4
15. A3•(SAC+SRJ)		WRITECY	11, 12	A4
16. A3•JMP		PC←MD	13	I1
17. A3•SRJ•DIRECT		PC←FDAP,MD(6-15) plus 1	14	A4
18. A3•SRJ•INDIRECT		PC←MD plus 1	15	A4
19. A3•SRJ•INDEXED		PC←PC plus 1	16	A4
20. A4•SRJ'•SAC'		MD←MBUS	17	E1
21. A4•ISZ'		MA←PC	18	lines 20, 22
22. A4•(SAC+SRJ)		(p-terms for Next State only)		I1
23. E1•LAC		AC←MD	19	I1
24. E1•AND		AC←AC•MD	20	I1
25. E1•ADD		AC←AC plus MD	21	I1
26. E1•ISZ		MW←MD plus 1	22	E2
27. E2•ISZ		WRITECY; No dest←MD plus 1; SKOZTEST	23	E3
28. E3•ISZ		PC/MA←PC (add SKIP FF via CIN)	24	I1

Figure 5.23. *Table of microoperations for memory-reference instructions.*

instructions SAC and SRJ cause data to be written to memory instead of read. Second, for instructions SRJ and JMP there is no operand to fetch; the effective address needs only to be loaded into the PC. These instructions therefore meander through the address control states in unique ways.

Instruction event or control state sequence timing schematics are useful in detailing how the instructions are interpreted. The event schematics for the entire instruction set can be organized into a single *control flow diagram* by placing *next-state* and *conditional information* between the action blocks which describe the microoperations. For more complex designs, the control flow diagram is a good starting point for the controls. Control states can be assigned to the action blocks at a later iteration, after the designer has become familiar with the general interpretation plan. **Figure 5.24** shows a part of a control flow diagram which describes the SRJ instruction. The

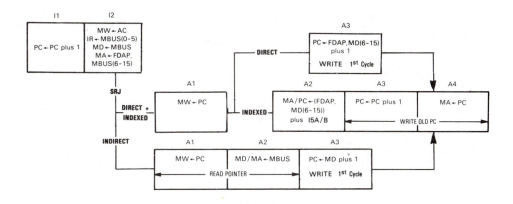

Figure 5.24. *Control flow diagram for the SRJ instruction.*

entire control flow diagram for the memory-reference instructions can be constructed from Fig. 5.23.

The register-reference instructions are all executed in one cycle, and A1 is the obvious control state for this. In cycle A4, the last cycle of the operand fetch, the PC is sent to MA in anticipation of the return to cycle I1. For the register-reference instructions, we lose the opportunity to anticipate transferring PC to MA during an unused data flow cycle. Therefore the next state following A1 for register-reference instructions is made E3, where MA is loaded prior to returning to state I1. **Figure 5.25** is a table of microoperations for the execution of the register-reference instructions. As a variation, instead of describing the *action* with RTN, we simply list the control points to be activated. The next state is always E3.

In summary, the approach comprises four steps, which are iterated:

1. Do the event schematics, possibly as a control flow diagram.
2. Assign control states to group common microoperations.
3. Estimate cost via table of microoperations or other means.
4. Implement control signal activation logic and next-state logic.

We began the control unit design at the data flow conceptual level with the instruction event schematics or control flow diagram. These may be translated to a table of microoperations which displays commonality and boolean minimizations in the "conditions" column, and is a convenient way to see what is happening in the same major state. The table of microoperations is close to a control PLA implementation. The microoperations themselves are decomposed into control signal activations. In Fig. 5.25 it is almost as convenient to list the activated control signals as to list the microoperations. Although we have presented this material as a series of steps com-

Condition	RTN Statement	Corresponding Control Signals	Next State
A1•HLT	Clear RUN flip-flop	HALT (Fig. 5.45)	E3
A1•NOP			E3
A1•CLA	AC←0	ENAC; DISYMUX	E3
A1•STA	AC←1...1	ENAC; DISYMUX; COMPY	E3
A1•CMA	AC←AC'	ENAC; COMPY	E3
A1•CLE	E←0	CLEAR E	E3
A1•STE	E←1	SET E	E3
A1•SPA	SKIP←AC(0)'	Auxiliary Circuit (Fig. 5.26)	E3
A1•SZA	No dest←AC' plus 1	SKOZTEST; FORCE CARRY; COMPY;	E3
A1•SZE	SKIP←E'	Auxiliary Circuit (Fig. 5.26)	E3
A1•ROR	AC←rotr AC	ENAC; ROTATER	E3
A1•ROL	AC←rotl AC	ENAC; ROTATEL	E3
A1•DTA	IA←AC	ENIA	E3
A1•DTB	IB←AC	ENIB	E3
A1•DFA	AC←IA	ENAC; IA2Y (Y mux select)	E3
A1•DFB	AC←IB	ENAC; IB2Y (Y mux select)	E3
A1•INA	IA←IA plus 1	ENIA; IA2Y; FORCE CARRY	E3
A1•INB	IB←IB plus 1	ENIB; IB2Y; FORCE CARRY	E3

Figure 5.25. *Microoperations and control signals for register-reference instructions.*

prising at least two conceptual levels, experienced designers may tend to "skip" some of the intermediate steps or levels. (In fact, perhaps too many designers jump prematurely into digital logic at the physical gate level.)

5.14. AUXILIARY CONTROL CIRCUITS

In generating the table of microoperations, we saw the need for several auxiliary circuits, which we now design.

5.14.1. The SKIP Functions

Several instructions perform a conditional skip of the next instruction. If the condition satisfying the skip is met, the PC must be incremented one more time before being placed in MA. The skip can be handled in several ways. Were PC a counting register, it could be clocked conditionally by the skip condition. In our data flow, however, the PC is one-upped by the ALU.

The instructions requiring the skip function are ISZ, SPA, SZA, and SZE. ISZ and SZA also require the ALU zero detection function. The zero test and one-upping cannot be done on the same cycle with only the

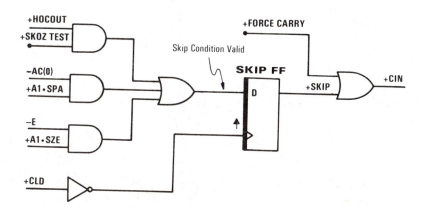

Figure 5.26. *The skip function auxiliary circuit.*

single ALU as designed. We can have a zero test on one cycle and one-up the PC on the next, based on the remembered result. We define an edge-triggered D *control flip-flop* called SKIP which remembers the result of the test; see **Figure 5.26.** A flip-flop is the only way to store a value for use on a following cycle. In our case, on the following cycle, we conditionally one-up PC depending on SKIP. The PC value is passed through the ALU to the ZBUS. The value of CIN is made equal to the value remembered in the SKIP flip-flop. Also on this conditional one-up cycle, the reasons for setting the SKIP flip-flop no longer exist, so it is cleared by the trailing edge of CLD. For the zero test, the ALU must be prepared with the operand which will cause a high-order carry-out if it is zero. This, with the skip-on-zero test (SKOZ TEST) control signal active, will set the SKIP flip-flop at the end of the cycle.

5.14.2. Multiplexer Controls

The 2×1 MUX elements have only one select control point, which has already been mentioned. If the 4×1 MUX elements are implemented with TTL MSI parts, the "one-out-of-four" source is selected by decoding two control signals. These control signals can be implemented by an auxiliary circuit.

Consider first the YMUX. A control signal named "ITOY" denotes selection of IA if IR(5) is 0, and IB otherwise. We also note from Fig. 5.25 that signals IA2Y and IB2Y select IA and IB respectively. We define a control signal PC2Y for selection of the PC. The assignment is made in the following table of combinations:

YSEL A	YSEL B	Source Selected
0	0	AC
0	1	IA
1	0	PC
1	1	IB

The table shows that YSELA is active when the PC or IB is selected, and YSELB is active when IA or IB is selected. We can write down the equations which implement the YMUX auxiliary circuit:

$$YSEL\ A = PC2Y + ITOY \cdot IR(5) + IB2Y$$
$$YSEL\ B = ITOY + IA2Y + IB2Y$$

We want these control signals to be valid early in the cycle, and they could be implemented in hardwired random logic instead of in a PLA. Consider next the ZMUX with assignment as follows:

ZSEL A	ZSEL B	Source Selected
0	0	SUM
0	1	ALUAND
1	0	rotr
1	1	rotl

Let control signals SUM, ALUAND, ROTATER, and ROTATEL, respectively, correspond to the MUX sources for the SUM, AND, rotr, and rotl operations. This yields equations for the ZMUX auxiliary circuit:

$$ZSEL\ A = ROTATER + ROTATEL$$
$$ZSEL\ B = ALUAND + ROTATEL$$

We have implemented the MUX controls by auxiliary circuits designed as for the TM-16. The control PLA generates control signals ITOY, IA2Y, IB2Y, PC2Y, ALUAND, ROTATEL, and ROTATER, and the YMUX and ZMUX auxiliary circuits generate MUX select signals YSELA, YSELB, ZSELA, and ZSELB.

When the SC-16H includes IR(5) as a control PLA input, signals YSELA, YSELB, ZSELA, and ZSELB can be generated directly by the PLA. Direct PLA generation for the MUX select signals is less expensive, and is done in practice. However, we use signals with more intuitively obvious meanings for teaching purposes. For example, activating signal "PC2Y" readily conjures the thought of conveying the PC contents to the Y adder input. The alternative, activating signal YSELB and deactivating signal YSELA, is an unlikely reminder that the Y adder input source is PC.

5.14.3. E Bit Implementation

Table 5.5. E Bit Requirements		
State	**Operation**	**Effect**
E1	ADD	Receives the higher-order carry-out
A1	CLE	Cleared
A1	STE	Set
A1	ROR	Receives SUM(15)
A1	ROL	Receives SUM(0)

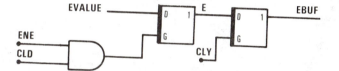

EVALUE = HOCOUT•E1•ADD + A1•STE + A1•ROR•SUM(15) + A1•ROL•SUM(0)
ENE = E1•ADD + A1•(CLE + STE + ROR + ROL)

Figure 5.27. *Implementation of the E bit.*

Table 5.5 lists the operations which affect the E bit, together with the major control state. **Figure 5.27** shows the implementation of the E bit. There is some subtlety here, as "don't care" conditions are employed in the generation of flip-flop output E. Note that data input EVALUE is low when clock enable ENE is activated by A1•CLE. The effect is to clear flip-flop E at the active transition.

5.15. CONTROL STATE IMPLEMENTATION

We have defined the machine implementation except for the console operations and DIO instruction. The console and cycle control signals RUNMODE and RUNCY perform a similar role as for the TM-16. A control state transition graph is shown in **Figure 5.28.** For the present table of microoperations, we assign one flip-flop per control state and determine the next-state equations for edge-triggered D flip-flops from the right-hand column of Fig. 5.23. The result is shown in **Table 5.6.** When OP7 is active, the address mode is inactive; see Fig. 5.17. The next-state signal name is "D" followed by the state name. The absence of RUNMODE

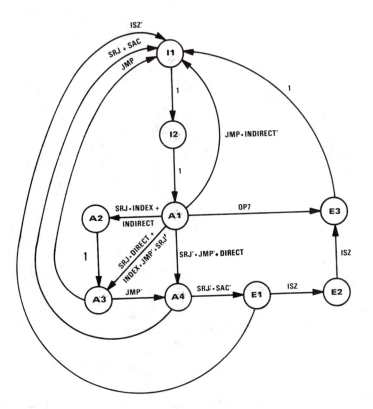

Figure 5.28. *State transition diagram for SC-16H in RUN mode.*

Table 5.6. Major Control State Equations

DI1 =   RUNMODE (A4(SRJ+SAC) + A1•JMP•INDIRECT′
        + A3•JMP + E1•ISZ′ + E3) +RUNCY

DI2 =   I1

DA1 =   I2

DA2 =   A1 (SRJ•INDEX + INDIRECT)

DA3 =   A1•DIRECT•SRJ + A1•INDEX•JMP′•SRJ′ + A2

DA4 =   A1•SRJ′•JMP′•DIRECT + A3•JMP′

DE1 =   A4•SRJ′•SAC′•DIRECT

DE2 =   E1•ISZ

DE3 =   A1•OP7 + E2•ISZ

deactivates the major control states at the end of the current instruction. To restart, signal RUNCY must be active for only one cycle.

5.16. CONTROL SIGNAL ACTIVATION LOGIC

As with the TM-16, the RTN statements for the SC-16H must be decomposed into the implied constituent control points which are active for the cycle. **Table 5.7** gives the decomposition of the more common RTN statements into the implied control points. Note the higher conceptual level of the RTN statement, as opposed to the greater detail and limited understandability of dealing directly with control point activations.

Table 5.7. Decomposing RTN Statements to Control Points

RTN Statement Level	*Control Point Activation Level*
PC ← PC plus 1	PC2Y; FORCE CARRY; ENPC
PC/MA ← MD plus I5A/B	ENXMUX; ITOY; ENMA; ENPC
AC ← AC•MD	ENXMUX; ALUAND; ENAC

All RTN statements in the table of microoperations of Fig. 5.23 are down-converted and the control signal logic conveniently gathered by the PLA. The PLA is shown in **Figure 5.29,** and the p-terms of this figure are cross-referenced to Fig. 5.23. We use the PLA structure to realize the behavioral description of this combinational circuit portion of the control unit. For single VLSI chip CPUs, a control PLA may be found on a portion of the chip. For MSI CPUs, discrete PLA chips themselves may be packaged on a pc card. PLA chips tend to be slow. In our case, for an MSI chip implementation, the control signals required at the end of the cycle (such as destination register clock enables) could be implemented in a PLA; signals needed promptly (such as YMUX controls) could be implemented in high-speed logic gates.

5.17. INTRODUCTION TO THE IO SCHEME

Programmed IO instructions can be very simple when the accumulator register is the medium for data exchange between the CPU and a peripheral device. We need a way to address (or select) the particular device, and coordinate the transfer. We also "tag" the data to provide an indication of whether the bus carries part of a block of data, as opposed to control or status information. We discuss and implement the programmed IO and the *interrupt architecture* for the SC-16.

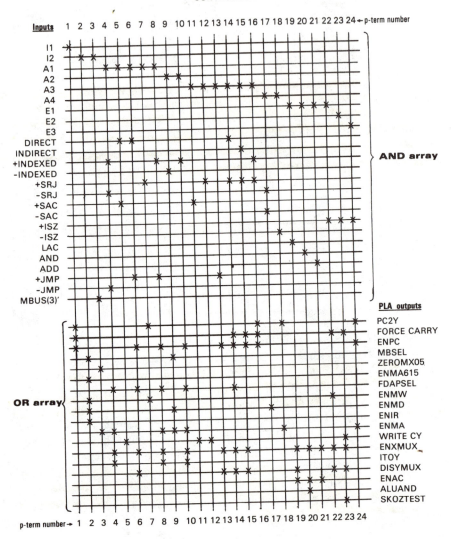

Figure 5.29. *A control PLA behavioral description of microoperations for the memory-reference instructions.*

The SC-16 architecture is more complex than the simple TM-16. We describe the relevant portion of the interrupt logic found on an interface card. Programmed IO and interrupts are part of the IO bus structure of the SC-16, but some high-speed devices may wish to seize the memory bus in order to transfer blocks of data between the device and main memory. The process of "stealing" a memory cycle from the CPU is an aspect of *Direct*

Memory Access (DMA) schemes.   The CPU clock is stopped, effectively
"idling" the CPU, and allowing the memory system to be used for DMA.

5.18. THE DIO INSTRUCTION FOR PROGRAMMED IO

As with the TM-16, the DIO instruction is executed in one data flow
cycle, control state A1.   For an output instruction, the AC contents are
placed on the IO data bus and the output strobe is generated.   Timing
signal CLD is made available so the selected devices may use it as a strobe
for copying data from the bus.   For an input instruction, the CPU generates
an input strobe INSTR.   INSTR tells the selected device to place the
appropriate data onto the bus.   The CPU strobes the data into AC at the
fall of CLD.

5.18.1. The IO Bus Structure

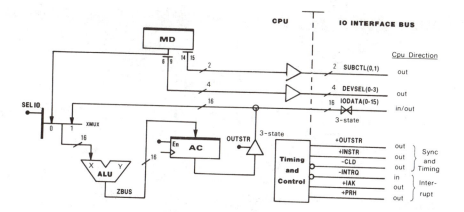

Figure 5.30. *General IO interface.*

We describe the SC-16H IO bus.   Instead of a data bus for input and
another for output, we use a single bidirectional, tri-state, 16-bit IODATA
bus.   Instead of a 6-bit control field as in the DIO instruction, we only use
the two low-order bits in a field we call SUBCTL.   These control bits select
one of four registers at the device.   The fields are shown in **Figure 5.30**,
along with the 4-bit device address field DEVSEL.   Since the correct
instruction bits are in MD at this time, they are driven to the IO bus from
MD.   Strobe signals INSTR and OUTSTR are the input and output strobes
respectively.   Clock CLD is provided on the bus for use by the IO device
adapter designer.

Three IO bus control signals, INTRQ (Interrupt Request), IAK (Interrupt Acknowledge), and PRH (Priority High) form part of the *interrupt architecture* to be explained.

5.18.2. CPU Logic Design for the DIO Instruction

Table 5.8. Execution of the DIO Instruction	
DIO•A1:	SUBCTL = MD(14-15);
	DEVSEL = MD(6-9)
DIO•A1•MD(4)•CLY:	OUTSTR ← 1
DIO•A1•MD(4)′•CLY:	INSTR ← 1
DIO•A1•MD(4)′:	AC ← IODATA

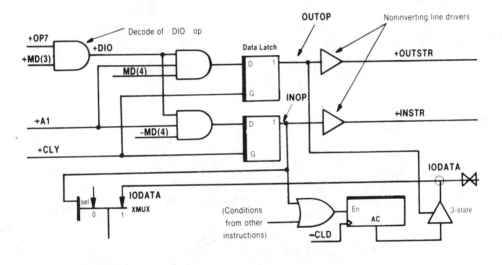

Figure 5.31. *Logic design for the DIO instruction.*

Table 5.8 describes the action in RTN statements for the execution of the DIO instruction. The data flow is as shown in Fig. 5.30. The DIO instruction is executed during state A1, and then in state E3, MA is loaded with the value of PC.

Figure 5.31 shows the generation of the control signals corresponding to these microoperations. The INSTR and OUTSTR strobes are generated by data latches during the A1 state, and remain valid through to the following activation of CLY for the next state (E3). The primary purpose for the latched strobes is to allow for skew in CLD at the device. The skew will be addressed in conjunction with the timing analysis for this operation.

5.18.3. Logic Design of IO Bus Interface at the Device

Now consider how logic at the device adapter to the SC-16 IO bus is expected to perform for the programmed IO instructions. The strobes tell the device the direction of transfer across the IODATA bus, whereas the SUBCTL field is intended to provide additional meaning. For the present, assume a *00* SUBCTL field means "data" and a *01* SUBCTL means "status" on input and "mode" on output. The device designer is allowed to define the other two combinations of the 2-bit SUBCTL field, *10* and *11*.

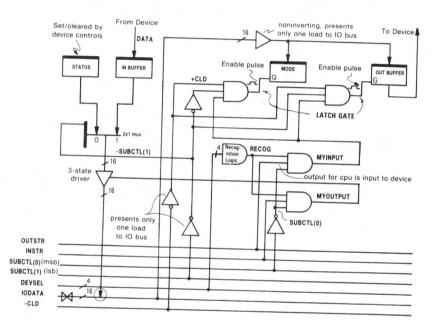

Figure 5.32. *Typical logic for device interface to IO bus.*

Figure 5.32 shows how a device adapter interfaces to the SC-16 IO bus. The interface as shown has two data registers, IN BUFFER for buffering data from the device to the CPU, and OUT BUFFER for buffering data from the CPU to the device. The AND gate denoted "Recognition Logic" decodes the device's unique selection code. For example, device 2 (0010) will have an AND gate as follows:

DEVSEL(0)′•DEVSEL(1)′•DEVSEL(2)•DEVSEL(3)′: Device 2.

In Fig. 5.32, the output of such an AND gate is called RECOG, and the contents of IODATA are neither delivered nor received without this signal being active. The signal MYINPUT is activated by device address recognition, *and* the output strobe from the CPU, *and* SUBCTL *00* or *01*.

For the SC-16 IO bus and DIO instruction architecture, all bus operations take one timing cycle. The device data flow requires a path from the STATUS and IN BUFFER registers to the IODATA bus, and a path from the IODATA bus to registers MODE and OUT BUFFER. The RTN statements are as follows:

RECOG•SUBCTL(0)'•SUBCTL(1)'•OUTSTR: OUTBUFFER ← IODATA
RECOG•SUBCTL(0)'•SUBCTL(1)•OUTSTR: MODE ← IODATA
RECOG•SUBCTL(0)'•SUBCTL(1)'•INSTR: IODATA = INBUFFER
RECOG•SUBCTL(0)'•SUBCTL(1)•INSTR: IODATA = STATUS

We next decompose the microoperations into the required control point activations so implied. The signal MYINPUT, together with CLD, provides the enable pulse for registers MODE and OUT BUFFER, which are built from data latches. SUBCTL(1) is the bit which chooses between the two possible destination registers at the adapter.

Similar control logic generates control signal MYOUTPUT: when MYOUTPUT is active, the device must place data on the IODATA lines. Thus, while bit SUBCTL(1) is selecting the source register for the 2×1 MUX, MYOUTPUT is turning on the tri-state drivers which place the data on the bus. Further, as a concession to detail, we show no bus signal being presented with more than one load by the device interface logic. In practice, many bus signals are of active-low polarity, so that the true polarity is obtained by an inverter which presents a single load; note signal −CLD of Fig. 5.32.

5.18.4. Timing Analysis of Programmed IO over the IO Bus

We can study the delay requirements of the SC-16 IO Bus. First, some assumptions are made. We want to place an upper bound on the bus interconnection delay tI(bus). Assume that the IO bus is confined to the backplane of a card cage. The device adapter interface is on a pc card which plugs to the backplane, with the adapter card edge-connector fitting into a backplane socket. If the device is a peripheral, the connection to the device from the adapter may be made by a hooded cable connector socket which plugs to an edge connector on the opposite side of the card; see **Figure 5.33.**

Consider the device interface of Fig. 5.32 and the output instruction. The timing chart of **Figure 5.34** shows a critical time duration from 250 to 290 ns, for the delayed or skewed trailing edge of OUT BUFFER enable pulse LATCHGATE. We do not wish IODATA to go invalid before

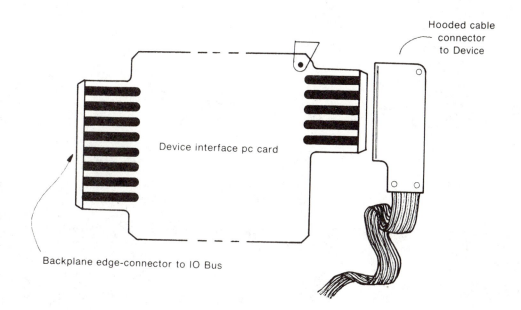

Figure 5.33. *IO bus connection to device interface.*

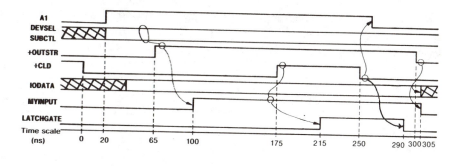

Figure 5.34. *Timing chart for output instruction.*

LATCHGATE has deactivated. This justifies the strategy of "holding over" the OUTSTR signal until CLD of the following cycle. A safer strategy for the interface design might be to implement OUT BUFFER as an edge-triggered register with the leading edge of CLD as the active transition. There is adequate setup time (from about 100-ns time to 215-ns time).

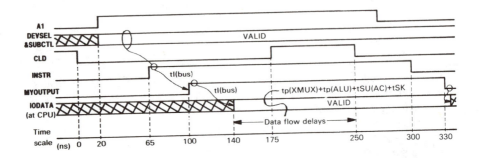

Figure 5.35. *Timing chart for input instruction.*

Figure 5.35 shows the timing chart for the DIO input instruction. Delays are longer here because the interconnection delay must be paid in two directions: once from the CPU to the device for address and control, and again from the device to the CPU for data. IO data passes through the ALU, and the resulting data flow delays leave little time to spare.

5.19. THE INTERRUPT ARCHITECTURE

Programmed IO is adequate to handle many IO transfer situations, particularly for small "dedicated" CPUs whose purpose is to control a single device (or at most a few devices). Under these circumstances, the CPU program can *poll* the device by causing the adapter to provide its status. If the status word of the device indicates a need for service, the polling program can execute a subroutine jump to the device service routine.

In some applications, there is enough additional work for the CPU program to make it advantageous not to spend time polling the device(s) continually. The TM-16 of Chapter 3 uses a simple interrupt scheme whereby the CPU program becomes aware of the need for service through an interrupt. The interrupt handler routine determines the identity of the interrupting device by reading the status of each device in turn, until it discovers a device whose status indicates a need for service. The TM-16 has only one PC save location; while the interrupt service routine is running, further interrupts are disabled. The IEN (interrupt enable) flip-flop is only set when in the "normal" or uninterrupted mode.

Determination of the interrupt requesting device by program is called "priority by software", because the program polls each device in the order determined by the programmer. The highest device in that order will be serviced first in case two devices interrupt at the same time. The SC-16 uses a *hardware priority scheme* and the highest-priority interrupting device receives attention from the CPU. Further, the SC-16 interrupt architecture permits a higher-priority device to interrupt a lower-priority device. To do this, the *save area* for the PC of the interrupted program must be kept distinct from the save area for the interrupting program. Each interrupt *level* has a distinct save area for the interrupted program.

The SC-16 has up to 16 device addresses, and we shall treat each as a distinct interrupt level with its own PC save location. As in the TM-16, device address 0 is reserved for the CPU. The hardware recognizes the lower addresses in the SC-16 memory address space as belonging to the interrupt system. Since the hardware is already identifying a save location with the device, it might also keep a pointer next to it for the device's interrupt service routine. This technique assigns the save area for device 0 to location 0 and its pointer to location 1. This leaves locations 2 and 3 for device 1, locations 4 and 5 for device 2, etc., as shown in **Figure 5.36**.

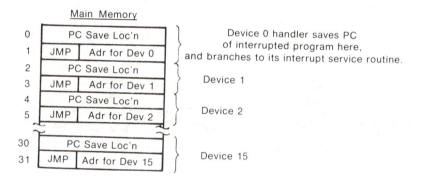

Figure 5.36. *Map of main memory "low core" showing PC SAVE areas, and jumps to interrupt service routines for the devices.*

The memory map of Fig. 5.36 leads naturally to the analogy between an interrupt and a subroutine jump. For example, when device 2 interrupts, the hardware "forces" a subroutine jump (SRJ instruction) to location 4 (obtained by doubling, or shifting left one bit, device address 2). The SRJ causes the PC of the interrupted program to be saved in location 4, and the instruction in location 5 to be executed next. For the scheme to work, the initialization part of the programming system must load the odd addresses 1, 3, ..., 31 with JMP instructions to the service routine of each active device.

We now describe the use of the three IO bus signals related to the interrupt system: –INTRQ, PRH, and IAK (interrupt request, priority high, and interrupt acknowledge, respectively). Interrupt request is activated by the highest-priority device requesting service. That device is determined by a priority *daisy-chain* as shown in **Figure 5.37.**

In Fig. 5.37, when the interrupt system is enabled, the CPU activates signal PRH(1). PRH (meaning "priority high") is a generic "cascade" type of signal such as the carry signal of a full adder. Signal PRH enters each device, and is employed in determining the PRH output value to be passed to the next device. Each device passes on the same PRH value, except when the device wishes to interrupt, and the incoming PRH value is high. When the device desires to interrupt, the outgoing PRH value is low, or inactive. If the incoming value of PRH is inactive, a higher-priority device is either interrupting the CPU or is requesting an interrupt.

The CPU interrupt request condition INTRQ is activated via an open-collector NAND which feeds a wire-OR connective. Therefore signal -INTRQ has the active-low polarity.

A new priority determination is made each cycle. If the interrupt request is accepted by the CPU, the CPU activates IAK. An active IAK signal causes the highest-priority device requesting an interrupt to place its device address on the IODATA bus. Thus, the "device determination" technique is automatic with IAK, and saves a considerable amount of time over "polling", i.e. identifying the interrupting device by software.

We can summarize the SC-16 interrupt architecture as follows. It is *multilevel* because a PC save area is provided for each unique level, and one level can interrupt a lower level. The scheme employs a *hardware priority:* the higher-priority source (or device) will interrupt the CPU when two or more devices wish to interrupt. *Source determination* is made by hardware; the CPU causes the interrupting device to place its device select code (address) on the IODATA bus. This device address, when doubled, indi-

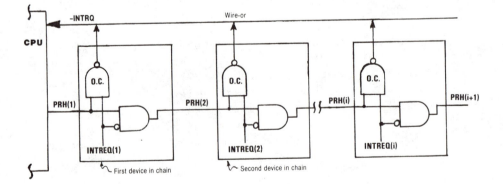

Figure 5.37. *A daisy-chain priority determination scheme.*

cates the PC save location in main memory. The address following the device's PC save location contains a pointer or *vector* to the device's interrupt service routine. This technique of branching directly to the interrupt source's service routine is called a *vectored interrupt* scheme.

5.20. IMPLEMENTATION OF INTERRUPTS FOR SC-16

In this section, we design the control logic for the CPU interrupt system. The logic at the CPU and the logic at the device adapter must cooperate to realize the architecture of the previous section. For the moment, at the CPU side, assume that the –INTRQ input signal is sampled during cycle I1. If active, the PC is not incremented and cycle I2 is used to "force" a subroutine jump (SRJ) to the address in low core reserved for the interrupting device. The SRJ causes the PC of the interrupted program to be saved, and the next instruction to be the JMP to the device's interrupt service routine. To return to (restore) the interrupted program, the interrupt service routine ends with an indirect JMP through its device's PC save location in main memory.

5.20.1. Device Interrupt Controls

We now design the interrupt control logic for a typical device interface card. The circuit is based on the Hewlett-Packard HP2116 interrupt scheme [9], which is simple enough to do by "trial and error".

When conditions within the device indicate the need for service, we set a device FLAG flip-flop; see **Figure 5.38**. The setting of this flip-flop occurs asynchronously with respect to the CPU clock, in particular with signal CLD, which is furnished over the IO bus to the devices. Let the FLAG flip-flop be an edge-triggered flip-flop, set on the leading edge of the signal SERVREQ (indicating a need for the device to be serviced). This permits the CPU to use a level-sensitive CLEAR input to clear the FLAG flip-flop. The "only once" strategy (see Appendix D) for the FLAG flip-flop means that the device must deactivate, then reactivate, signal SERVREQ before the CPU reacts a second time. The strategy also means that the device may deactivate the SERVREQ signal either before or after the device's interrupt request is serviced, giving the device interface designer greater flexibility.

Consider device i. Once FLAG(i) is set, the device must synchronize with the system clock, setting device flip-flop INTSYNC(i). With flip-flop INTSYNC(i) set, the device now contends for CPU service with other devices whose respective INTSYNC flip-flops are also set. The priority daisy-chain serves this purpose: only one device contending will see an active PRH signal. This device will be the only device to set its own flip-flop, called INTREQ(i), in turn activating the wire-OR INTRQ line into the CPU. This cascading of the three flip-flops FLAG(i), INTSYNC(i), and INTREQ(i) is shown in Fig. 5.38, along with a timing diagram.

Signals –CLD, +IAK, +PRH(i) and –INTREQ(i) are the IO bus interface signals. The logic circuit of Fig. 5.38(a) shows the interrupt control logic for typical device i. The relevant priority input is PRH(i), which it passes on as PRL(i) through AND gate 2. (The PRL(i) output point is connected to the PRH(i+1) input point of the "downstream" device.) The FLAG(i) flip-flop receives input +SERVREQ (from the device control logic) as a dynamic input. The data input to the FLAG(i) flip-flop is tied to 1; i.e. it is permanently high, so the positive edge of +SERVREQ always sets FLAG(i).

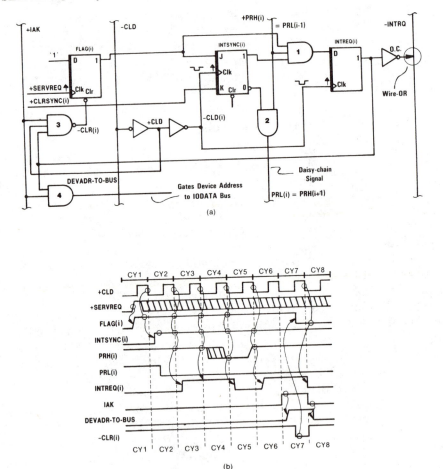

Figure 5.38. *Logic and timing of device interrupt logic.* (a) Logic schematic. (b) Timing chart.

The behavior of the circuit is described with the aid of the timing chart of Fig. 5.38(b). For convenience in explaining the operation, let signal +CLD divide time into CPU cycles, denoted here as CY1 through CY8. In CY1, the leading edge of +SERVREQ occurs, setting device i's FLAG. At the next trailing edge of CLD, the flip-flop INTSYNC for device i is set. INTSYNC(i) is a JK edge-triggered flip-flop, with the K input normally at 0. The INTSYNC(i) flip-flop is cleared by a CPU DIO instruction in the interrupt service routine for the device, which activates +CLRSYNC(i) before going to cycle I1, to restore control to the interrupted program. Signal +SERVREQ may be deactivated, once flip-flop FLAG(i) is set.

When INTSYNC(i) is set, all lower-priority devices are inhibited from interrupting, because PRL(i) is deactivated via AND gate 2. With INTSYNC(i) active in CY2, INTREQ(i) is set in CY3. INTREQ(i) is always changed with each trailing edge of CLD, so the daisy chain determines the highest-priority device whose INTSYNC(i) flip-flop is set once each CPU cycle. The one clock-time delay between setting INTSYNC(i) and setting INTREQ(i) allows for propagation delays in the daisy-chained priority signals. As shown in CY4, the CPU, or a higher-priority device, deactivates PRH(i). The inactive PRH(i) clears INTREQ(i) for CY5. Since FLAG(i) and INTSYNC(i) are still set, when PRH(i) is reactivated in CY5, INTSYNC(i) turns on again in CY6.

The CPU indicates acceptance of an interrupt by activating IO Bus signal +IAK as shown in CY7. Signal +IAK feeds all devices, but due to the daisy-chain, only one device will have activated CPU input INTRQ. This fact is used to clear FLAG(i) by signal –CLR(i). Signal –CLR(i) waits until CLD time before clearing FLAG(i) in case, on the previous cycle (CY6), a lower-priority device j was the device with active INTREQ(j). If the INTREQ(j) flip-flop of lower-priority device j is slow in being cleared, a glitch may erroneously clear the lower-priority FLAG(j) when IAK is activated. (Timing considerations such as this are common in multilevel priority interrupt schemes. The designer must learn to ask "What if...?".) Signal IAK also activates signal DEVADR-TO-BUS which causes device i to place its address on the IODATA bus.

We now explain why INTSYNC(i) is not cleared at the same time as FLAG(i), and why FLAG(i) is a condition for setting INTREQ(i). The interrupt acknowledge signal IAK means that the transfer of program control to device i's interrupt service routine has been effected, making it inappropriate to continue setting INTREQ(i). At the same time, it is undesirable to allow a lower-priority device to interrupt device i. Therefore, flip-flop INTSYNC(i) is not cleared with FLAG(i), but continues active to inhibit "downstream" devices from seeing an active value on their PRH input point. Clearing INTSYNC(i) is left to the interrupt service routine for device i. INTSYNC(i) should be cleared just prior to the indirect JMP which returns control to the interrupted program. If a lower-priority device wishes to interrupt, it sees its PRH input point active during I1, but is not able to activate CPU input –INTRQ until I2. Fortuitously, I2 is too late, and the device *i* service routine restores the interrupted program PC value from its PC save area. (This technique is covered in Chapter 3.) Once device *i*'s INTSYNC flip-flop has been cleared by the interrupt service routine, the device adapter control logic may correctly assume the system to be ready for another interrupt. Therefore, the PC save area for device *i* must be clear to accept a new value.

5.20.2.   CPU Interrupt Control Logic and Data Flow Change

The device address on IODATA enters the data flow at the XMUX and passes through the ALU. (See Fig. 5.30.) The incoming device address may be doubled by activating ALU control for rotate left (rotl) and forcing a "ZERO-FILL" into the low-order bit position: the desired main memory address will be on the ZBUS.

There are several ways to effect the interrupt at the CPU. We compare two alternative implementations. We first consider "simulating" a subroutine jump (SRJ) instruction. When the SC-16H data flow was designed, the details of the vectored interrupt scheme were postponed. The problem at hand is to place the SRJ opcode and the "direct" address control field code (101000) into IR, and the device address code (doubled) into MA and MD at the end of I2. This strategy on IR can be implemented many ways. With a MUX feeding IR, a constant (101000) can be a MUX source for getting the opcode into IR.

The left-shifted IODATA can be made to appear on the ZBUS. To simulate the SRJ instruction, this address must go to registers MA and MD. A path exists to MA; however, one has to be built for MD. A 2×1 MUX on the input to MD with MBUS and ZBUS as the two sources can provide a path for the device address from the ZBUS to the MD. Another problem is that the microoperation "PC←PC plus 1" takes place during I1. The incrementation of PC must be "undone" when an interrupt is accepted.

We now consider a second approach, which we actually implement. Instead of simulating an SRJ, we create an "interrupt" opcode. The circuit of **Figure 5.39** causes JK control flip-flop INTROP to be set at the same time I1 becomes valid if there is an interrupt request. Signal DI1, when active, means that I1 is to be the next control state. INTROP becomes the "opcode" for an "interrupt op", for which we can generate RTN statements, as shown in **Table 5.9**. **Figure 5.40** shows the instruction event schematic for interrupt acceptance.

The running CPU program may wish to disable the interrupt system temporarily. The first circuit design attempt is shown in **Figure 5.41**, where DEVADR0 denotes a device address of 0. The system may be disabled by inhibiting signal PRH(0) which emanates from the CPU. This can be done

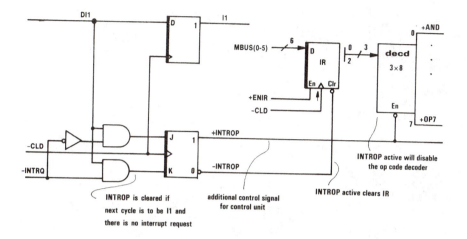

Figure 5.39. *Provision for an "interrupt" opcode.*

Table 5.9. Table of Microoperations for the Interrupt Op

State	Additional Conditions	Action	Next State
I1	−INTROP	PC ← PC plus 1 (unchanged)	I2
I1	+INTROP	MW ← PC	I2
I2	−INTROP	unchanged	A1
I2	+INTROP	PC/MA ← rotl IODATA, 0-FILL; IAK	A1
A1	+INTROP	WRITE CY; PC ← PC plus 1	A4
A4	+INTROP	MA ← PC	I1

by addressing the CPU as device 0, and using SUBCTL field combination *11* (otherwise unused) to disable the interrupt system. Similarly, SUBCTL field combination *10* enables it. The interrupt enable and disable circuit must be designed with the following "what if" problem in mind. No higher level should be allowed to interrupt before the current level executes the instruction which reloads the PC from its PC save area. Following A1 of a DIO instruction which clears the device INTSYNC flip-flop to disable the interrupt system, flip-flop INTROP should not be set. We wish to disallow an interrupt *following* the execution of the instruction which deactivates PRH(0). We do this by disallowing INTROP to be set while the interrupt state is being changed.

I1	I2	A1	A4
MW←PC	PC/MA←rotl IODATA, 0 IAK	PC←PC plus 1 **WRITE CY**	MA←PC

Figure 5.40. *Instruction event schematic for interrupt acceptance.*

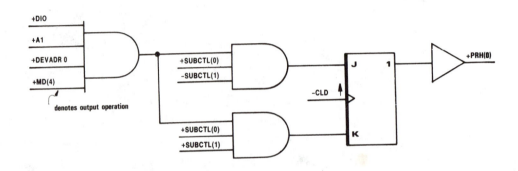

Figure 5.41. *Control of the PRH(0) signal.*

Fig. 5.41 shows the control of the PRH(0) signal. Since CPU input −INTRQ could be active during the A1 cycle which disables PRH, some way is needed to disallow accepting an interrupt following the DIO instruction. The reason is that the DIO instruction itself is capable of changing the state of the interrupt system. **Figure 5.42** describes the circuit modification (a "second-cut" to the INTROP flip-flop of Fig. 5.39) which prevents an interrupt following a DIO instruction.

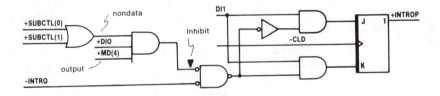

Figure 5.42. *Circuit to inhibit an interruption following certain DIO instructions.*

5.21. A DMA CAPABILITY FOR THE SC-16

In order to perform memory accesses independent of the CPU program, the memory system must be capable of accepting addresses from more than one source. If the memory system provides two distinct memory buses (each with its own address and data buses) it is said to be a *two-port* memory system. It is more common, however, for a CPU and one or more DMA channels to share a single port (data and address bus) to main memory. We implement the single-port approach in the SC-16H.

When a DMA channel requires a memory cycle, it cannot place the memory address on the memory bus until the CPU has relinquished that bus. Therefore, some coordination between the CPU and DMA channel is required to ensure that only one of them has the bus at any one time. Assume the buses are driven by *tri-state* drivers; the CPU must place its drivers in the high-impedance state before the DMA channel can use the bus. The CPU drivers are inhibited by signal HOLDACK, as shown in **Figure 5.43.** Now we need to determine when to activate HOLDACK.

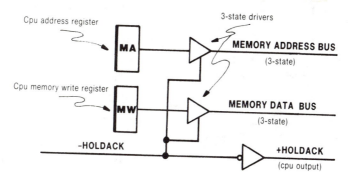

Figure 5.43. *CPU releasing the memory bus.*

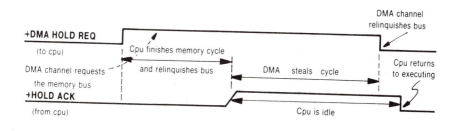

Figure   5.44.   *Timing   sequence   which   coordinates   a   DMA "cycle-steal".*

Figure 5.44 shows the "handshake" timing sequence which coordinates a DMA cycle-steal. The CPU-DMA synchronization occurs through two signals, DMA HOLDREQ and HOLDACK. Signal DMA HOLDREQ is a CPU input requesting a memory cycle. When the CPU has placed its bus drivers in the high-impedance state, it activates CPU output HOLDACK. After the DMA channel has received service from the main memory, it deactivates DMA HOLDREQ, and the CPU responds by deactivating HOLDACK.

When the DMA channel is accessing memory, the CPU is idle. This strategy requires the manipulation of the CPU system timing. However a DMA request is only one reason to manipulate the timing. Other reasons are considered next.

5.22. CAUSING THE CPU TO HALT OR IDLE

5.22.1. The Halt and Idle States

We list four reasons for causing the CPU to *halt* or *idle.*

Halt

1. In response to the execution of a "HALT" instruction.
2. In response to an operator stopping the CPU from the console.

Idle

3. To wait for a slow memory cycle.
4. To allow a memory cycle to be "stolen" by DMA.

The first two reasons were covered in Chapter 3 for the TM-16 design. In that design, the CPU halted by inhibiting the major control state I, while the clock-times T0, T1, T2, and T3 continued to occur.

In the SC-16H, we wait until the instruction has completed before idling the CPU in response to reasons 1 and 2. However, reasons 3 and 4 require the CPU to wait *even in the middle of an instruction.* This is clearly true for reason 3 (slow memory cycle) because the instruction interpretation should not continue if needed memory data is not ready. In the case of reason 4 (a DMA cycle steal), we increase the risk of data loss by failing to heed some DMA requests as soon as possible. Consider a disk write operation. When a long record is being written on the track, the disk controller must continually receive bits at no less than a specified rate. Data *overrun* occurs if the position on the magnetic media passes by the write head and the data to be written has not yet arrived from memory. In this section, we shall say reasons 1 and 2 *halt* the CPU by inhibiting cycle I1, and reasons 3 and 4 *idle* the CPU by inhibiting CLD. We first consider halting the CPU. At the same time, we provide for console controls.

5.22.2. Halting the CPU and Providing Console States

It is common practice for experienced logic designers to have some useful circuits in their repertoire of "parts". Whenever a situation requiring such a circuit arises, the designer modifies the circuit in the repertoire to suit the occasion. We do the same for the circuitry surrounding the front panel (console) controls.

Repeated here as **Figure 5.45** are control circuits from Chapter 3, which we appropriate and modify for the SC-16H. The console operation timing generator provides for three data flow cycles: CC1, CC2, and CC3, used to sequence the microoperations which interpret the console functions LOAD, READ, and WRITE. The console control knob is a 4-position switch which, when not in RUN position, clears the RUN flip-flop. This flip-flop must be set before major state I1 can be activated. When the knob is in the RUN position and the RUN flip-flop is clear, depressing the pushbutton initiates major state I1 through signal +RUNCY.

5.22.3. Idling the CPU

In the present implementation for idling the CPU, we allow the major control state to persist, but inhibit clock signal CLD. In the absence of CLD, no major register contents change, nor does the control state change. We point out that we inhibit only the CLD timing signal within the CPU (CLDG), and not that which is driven out on the IO bus as a synchronizing signal to the peripheral devices (CLDU). Consequently, DMA channels continue to receive this synchronizing signal even though the CPU may be idle. We also allow CLY pulses to occur; in fact, CLY could be used for synchronizing the logic which enables/disables CLD.

In **Figure 5.46**, we repeat the SC-16H system clock circuit, and show where signal CLDG is inhibited. (CLDG denotes "Clock D gated"; CLDU denotes "Clock D ungated".)

Two conditions idle the CPU: the "WAIT" condition indicates a slow memory access, and the "HOLD" condition indicates a DMA request. These conditions are handled by AND gates 4 and 5 respectively. Notice the presence of a signal called HOLD ENABLE. HOLD ENABLE ensures that the DMA channel does not steal a cycle immediately after the first data flow cycle of a CPU memory access. The complement of HOLD ENABLE ensures that the CPU waits only on the second data flow cycle of a memory access rather than the first. The meaning of HOLD ENABLE is now defined; it is active during the first data flow cycle of a memory access. HOLD ENABLE is generated by a combinational circuit as follows:

$$\text{HOLD ENABLE} = \text{I1} + \text{A1} + \text{A3} + \text{E1} + \text{E2}$$
$$+ \text{RUNMODE}' \cdot \text{CC1}' \cdot \text{CC2}' \cdot \text{CC3}'.$$

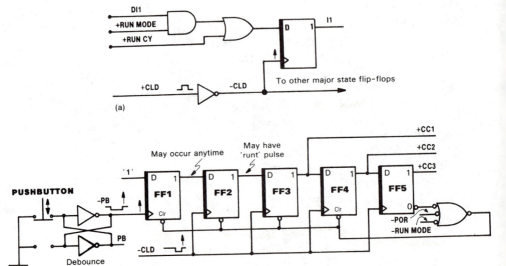

(a)

(b)

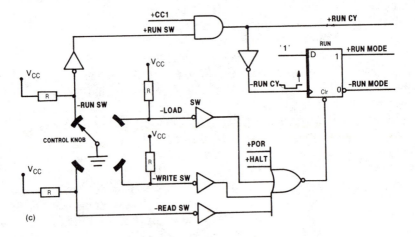

(c)

Figure 5.45. *Auxiliary control circuits involving console operations.* (a) Suspension of state I1, and restart. (b) Generation of console operation control states. (c) Control knob and RUN operation.

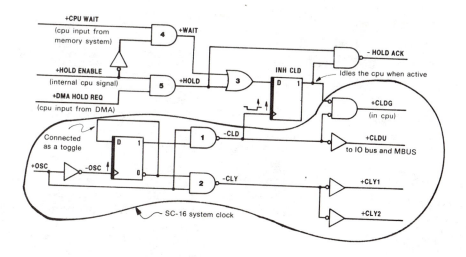

Figure 5.46. *CPU idling circuit.*

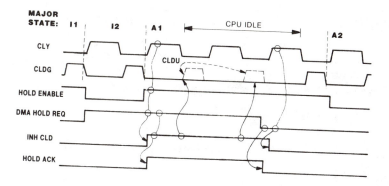

Figure 5.47. *Synchronization of a DMA memory cycle.*

The INH CLD data latch of Fig. 5.46 ensures that signal CLDG does not experience any "runt" pulses. It also delays acceptance of a request of a DMA channel until the second data flow cycle of a memory access has completed. See the timing diagram of **Figure 5.47.**

5.23. THE CONTROL PANEL OPERATIONS

Control panel architecture was covered in Chapter 3 for the TM-16. This section describes the control panel operations of LOAD, READ, and WRITE at the dependent RTN level for the SC-16H. For these operations, we assign the device address 0 and subcontrol field of 0.

LOAD Operation

```
LOAD•CC1 :   INOP; DEVADR=0; SUBCTL=0;
             AC/PC/MA←IODATA
```

We create signal INOP as a control point input to the "Timing and Control" logic of the IO interface; see Fig. 5.30. Activation of INOP sets flip-flop INSTR (whose output signal is +INSTR) for one cycle at CLY. Upon recognizing its address and subcontrol field, at the activation of signal +INSTR the value of the console switch is driven onto the IODATA bus. This value enters the data flow at the XMUX and appears on the ZBUS where it may be routed anywhere in the data flow. For LOAD, the switch data is sent to MA and PC. Typically, the LOAD operation specifies the memory address, and subsequent READ or WRITE operations cause memory operation on the address already in the MA. Loading the AC also provides visual feedback to the user.

READ Operation

```
READ•CC2:    MD←M[MA]; PC/MA←PC plus 1
READ•CC3:    AC←MD
```

The memory READ operation places the data in the AC. Assume the AC register outputs are wired to lights on the console. The PC is one-upped as a user convenience so the next block of consecutive data can be read out without reloading the address.

WRITE Operation

```
WRITE•CC1:   INOP; DEVADR=0; SUBCTL=0;
             MW/AC←IODATA
WRITE•CC2:   WRITE CY
WRITE•CC3:   MA/PC←PC plus 1
```

The switch value is also loaded into the AC to provide visual feedback to the user. The address is incremented as a user convenience.

Implementing the RTN statements takes place as before. Each RTN statement defines a condition of p-terms for which the control signals implied by the microoperation part are activated. To incorporate these console operations, the new p-terms are ORed (gathered) into the proper control signal generation circuits.

5.24. IMPLEMENTATION DETAILS

A *paper design* for the SC-16H has been done. All machines which have been built once passed through this paper design process on the way to realization. We have personally been through the prototype and debug phase enough times to conclude that there is really nothing mysterious or magical about taking the ideas expressed at the data flow block diagram, auxiliary circuit diagram, timing chart, and control signal activation level and converting them into hardware. Yet it never ceases to amaze us: it all works! There are no water wheels turning or valves opening and closing that one can watch; yet the simple low-level logic circuitry churns on, interpreting instruction after instruction.

The SC-16H as described herein has undergone the complex creative design phase. What remains is more or less a single-level *physical design* problem. In the MSI technology, with wire-wrap boards, the physical design may lack the challenge of bridging a large conceptual gap, but gives the reward of seeing the computer work. The data flow block diagram converts to the basic building blocks in a straightforward fashion. The major state control circuit behavior has been described, and the realization to the basic building block level can proceed as a sequential machine synthesis problem if desired. In our case, we derived boolean statements for the data inputs of edge-triggered D flip-flops. To implement the control unit, the p-terms are gathered. The control signal activation logic for the data flow control signals is realized by the OR of the p-terms which *imply* (activate) them. The output of each control signal combinational circuit is wired to the corresponding data flow control point.

At the completion of the paper design process, design automation (DA) programs have been most successful. The logic can be simulated and the design verified. Delay simulators can verify the signal timing. Either the designer or assignment programs convert the paper design descriptions into the building blocks or packages provided by the technology, and assign pin numbers. Placement programs assign locations on pc boards and draw up an interconnection list or net list. DA programs assign or assist in assigning pc boards to sockets and backplane nets to edge connector pins. Wiring programs can define the multilevel interconnection planes of the pc board. With components physically located and wired, more accurate worst-case delay calculations can be made on the critical delay chains. On the other hand, the physical design at the VLSI level presents many challenges in layout or placement, and interconnection.

The amount of power consumed by each component provides an estimate of the power supply rating required. Component power consumption, in conjunction with how far apart the components are placed, indicates the type of cooling required. The heat generated by those components must be carried away. The most popular cooling techniques are convection and forced air. Some high-performance machines use liquid cooling. On projects involving a large physical system, the "hardware" engineers specialize in the powering, packaging and cooling aspects.

A consideration at the packaging phase is how to test the pc board. Designers incorporate circuits on the board to aid maintenance and test. If the board has a manufacturing defect or defective on-board component, it is generally preferable to discover this before plugging the board into the machine. Once a machine has been operating well and suffers a failure, we desire convenient methods to locate the faulty pc board. We do not cover test and maintenance techniques here.

5.25. PERFORMANCE EVALUATION

CPU performance is difficult to evaluate. Many factors are involved, including the power of the instruction set and the type of program or application involved. The *instruction mix* is a simple technique for comparing computer models within a single architecture. The instruction mix assigns a percentage of time each instruction is executed by a typical member of a class of programs. For example, a "business mix" might be devised from programs generated from a compiler whose language was designed for business applications (e.g. COBOL).

To calculate performance under a "mix", the percentage of time assigned each instruction is multiplied by the time required to execute that instruction. These products are summed, and the result is the average instruction execution time corresponding to the given mix. A well-known example is the Gibson mix [10].

For the SC-16H, the state transition diagram in Fig. 5.28 is an excellent source for determining the *instruction timings*. The result is shown in **Table 5.10.**

Table 5.10.
SC-16H Instruction Timings (Data Flow Cycles)

Opcode	Direct	Indexed	Indirect
ADD	5	6	7
AND	5	6	7
LAC	5	6	7
SAC	4	5	6
JMP	3	3	5
SRJ	5	6	6
ISZ	7	8	9
Reg	4	–	–
DIO	4	–	–

The SC-16H instruction execution times vary from three to nine data flow cycles. At a cycle time of 500 ns, the execution time is from 1.5 μs to 4.5 μs.

5.26. LOGIC DESIGN VERSUS PROGRAMMING

The chapter has introduced some basic logic design techniques. The data flow employed data latch registers and the two-phase clocking scheme the data latch implies. Auxiliary circuits have been implemented as needed, but their design has been approached in more or less the same way a discovered bug would be fixed. A given circuit performs in a known way, and we wish to perform in another way. This type of activity is common at interfaces. The designer alters the circuit so it performs as desired. We know of no particular methodology for this single-level design modification problem other than the obvious. If a control signal is not active when it should be, "OR" in a signal which is active for the missing condition. If a control signal is active when it should not be, either use an "AND" to inhibit it, or remove from the circuit the unwanted p-term causing it to be active. If the occurrence of a combinational circuit output is to be remembered, then create a flip-flop which is set by that condition, and devise a proper reset. This is a type of skill which improves with practice, and is enhanced by visualizing circuits at the logic schematic level, together with timing diagrams.

We have also been sensitive to the logic designer's way of solving problems. In this vein, a technique introduced is that of anticipation. If the parallelism is available, it may be possible to perform a (free) microoperation blindly in *anticipation* of a later need.

Another concept inherent in hardware control units is that of *conditional execution*. In any data flow cycle and major control state, a control signal may be activated conditional on any valid data flow signal. The full direct address page (FDAP) value was obtained this way. The next chapter covers microprogramming, where the capability of conditional execution is not usually found.

We contrast programming and logic design in **Figure 5.48**. Fig. 5.48(a) is a flowchart of a decision process, typically found in programming. The problem is to invert input data Y if negative. Bit Y(0) is the sign bit. A programmer might solve it in RTN as shown in Fig. 5.48(b). Clock cycles T0, T1, and T2 are employed in that sequence, and working register X holds the input data. Time T1 is skipped over if X(0) is 0, indicating that X is already positive.

A logic designer does not view the problem as a "decision" at all, but as a "conditional execution". Also, no intermediate X register is needed. The solution is shown in Fig. 5.48(c).

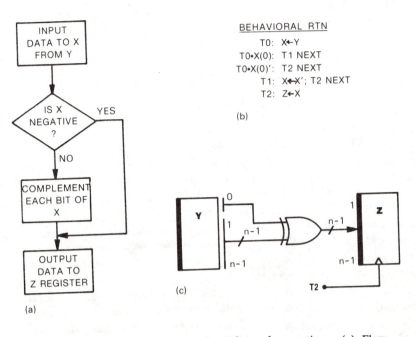

Figure 5.48. *Use of concept of conditional execution.* (a) Flow chart description. (b) RTN description. (c) A logic designer's approach.

Many CPU design problems benefit from a top-down, structured approach suitable to programming. But logic design is not like programming, because the basic building blocks are inherently different. Once a logic designer puts a gate into a circuit, that gate is always doing its job regardless of any other activity going on in the system. When a programmer inserts an instruction into a program, that instruction only functions when it is the active instruction being interpreted by the CPU. In a program there is a well-defined thread of control, creating a sequence of actions, "one thing at a time". In logic design all circuits behave concurrently, and the logic designer tries to pack as many concurrent microoperations into one data flow cycle as is economically feasible. Data flow and control unit design are more closely related to the *production system* model used in the artificial intelligence field [11].

5.27. SUMMARY

Chapter 5 is a central chapter of the book. The previous chapters provided the foundation for appreciating the many facets of the divide-and-conquer approach applied to a nontrivial multilevel design problem. The

CPU designed is more sophisticated than the PDP-8, and is on a par with many single-address machines. We believe the design is a competitive cost-performer. The reader has experienced the decomposition of a complex problem and the conceptual levels involved, and may wish to reread the portions of the Prologue and Chapter 1 dealing with design.

The CPU was decomposed into the *data flow* and *control unit.* The data flow consists of data paths and data transformation circuits, and the control unit controls *actions* on those objects. The data flow and control unit are interrelated with the *system timing,* probably one of the most important aspects of data flow level design. System timing includes data flow timing, delays of the data, delays in control signal activation, and integration with the memory cycle. The data flow, the control unit, and the system timing are each subjected to the designer's detailed analysis during the design. Each merit a language of their own, since the designer thinks of them in different ways. We use block diagrams, RTN, and timing charts respectively. At the instruction interpretation level, the RTN and the major state timing are combined. Event schematics and a table of microoperations are useful here. These two descriptive tools display essentially the same information. At this level, the need for auxiliary circuits is detected. Auxiliary circuits bridge the gap between the control points of the data flow, where the control signals generated by the control unit may not be exactly what is required by the data flow. Note the dichotomy between control and data signals. We think of control signals as being active or inactive. A data signal merely represents a binary digit, a data value of 0 or 1. Our interest in a data signal is whether it is valid or *stable.*

After each RTN statement is decomposed (down-converted) into control signal activations, the conditions for activating each control signal must be "gathered" or ORed together to generate (or implement) the control signal. The collection of control signal activations can be handled conveniently, conceptually as well as in practice, by a control PLA. Also at this level, the next-state controls may be designed. A state transition graph, such as Fig. 5.28, may be drawn from information inherent in the table of microoperations.

While the designer is handling the major or more frequent activities of the CPU, certain parts of the design may be postponed. In the SC-16H, we postponed the IO and console, continuing one of two long-standing traditions among CPU designers. (The other is for the console design to proceed concurrently with the CPU design, but under the responsibility of the most junior member of the design team.) We have introduced "ground-rules" as a means to simplify complexity by reducing choices through disciplining.

Although we have studied CPU design in the context of a relatively straightforward machine, a taste of complexity occurs in the address modes. Obtaining the full direct address, in conjunction with direct, indirect and indexed modes, has complicated the design enough to make it interesting. The memory interface, DMA port, IO interface, and console operations have been treated as realistically as is practical at this level. The design principles introduced do not change for large machine projects. Data flows have more concurrency; in fact some data flows may be viewed as a collection of intercommunicating functional units. But the cyclic nature, worst-case data flow delays, register clocking schemes, RTN-type microoperations, next control state determination, and decomposition of RTN statements into control point activations, remain the same. As more engineers work on the design, groundrules and proper subtask selection become more important.

The material covered in this chapter is sufficient background for the reader to undertake a CPU "paper design" project as described in Appendix A. The project is strongly recommended as the techniques we have described are best learned by doing. Many students state they have had several "Aha!" learning experiences from doing the project. We feel the arena of complex design problems is one where the teacher can lead the student to the problem area and provide guidelines, but to master the topic the student must do some independent work. After this, the student may correctly feel that computer design has been demystified!

PROBLEMS

5.1. The data flow of the TM-16 was designed using RTN first and determining register transfer path requirements. In the light of the SC-16 data flow design, redesign the TM-16 data flow such that performance remains approximately the same but the data flow is less expensive.

5.2. The SC-16 design depends upon a unit of time called a data flow cycle, which depends on worst-case delays. All data flow events are worked into this cycle. This approach uses a system clock, and a major control state. In another approach, data flow events may take an undetermined amount of time. They are sequenced by job completion signalling: the completion of one event signals the start of the next. Discuss performance and concurrency issues for each of these approaches.

5.3. The memory cycle consists of two data flow cycles. When performing a memory read or write operation, how does the CPU designer know the required time has expired before accepting data on a memory read or before cycling the memory again following a memory write?

5.4. Main memory holds three kinds of data: instructions, operands, and pointers. How do we know which kind of data the memory subsystem is delivering to the CPU at the completion of a memory read?

5.5. Consider the task of interpreting another single-address instruction set whose registers are compatible with the SC-16. Given the right to change or replace auxiliary circuits, but not the major data paths and functional units of the SC16-H data flow, discuss the probability that a control unit could be designed to interpret the new instruction set.

5.6. Consider the following three ways of selectively adding 1 to PC at the RTN level.

(a) E1·SKOP·SKIPCOND:PC←PC plus 1
(b) E1·SKOP:FORCED CARRY=SKIPCOND;
     PC←PC plus FORCED CARRY
(c) E1·SKOP:PC←PC plus SKIPCOND

Discuss how each would be implemented. Conceivably, could the implementation for each be the same at a lower level of detail?

5.7. Only the LOAD, READ, and WRITE console operations were implemented. Suppose the console knob also had a "Single Instruction Cycle" position, which would cause the interpretation of the next instruction, following the activation of pushbutton PB. Design the RTN for such an operation.

Table 5P.1. Instruction Mix (percent)			
Opcode	*Direct*	*Indexed*	*Indirect*
AND	1	1	1
ADD	6	5	4
LAC	5	5	10
SAC	5	5	8
JMP	5	3	3
SRJ	3	3	7
ISZ	2	2	5
DIO	1	1	1
Reg-Ref	8	N/A	N/A

5.8. State transition diagrams are useful in determining how many data flow cycles it takes for each instruction to execute. The average instruction execution time can be computed by knowing the percentage of time each opcode-address mode pair is interpreted. Given the percentages of **Table 5P.1,** what is the average instruction execution time, with a 500-ns data flow cycle, for this instruction mix?

5.9. We list several aspects of the design. Describe them as being a general design technique or an implementation opportunity. Indicate where you feel the relevant conceptual level lies.

(a) The control PLA as a behavioral description.
(b) Instruction event schematics.
(c) Converting RTN statements to control signal activations.
(d) Using the ALU as a switch in the data flow.
(e) Using a carry lookahead adder instead of ripple carry.
(f) Doing subtraction by inverting the subtrahend and forcing a carry.

(g) For current page addressing, using the fact the current page is in MA (0-5).

(h) Implementing MUX select signals directly as control PLA outputs.

(i) Choosing between a MUX bus and bidirectional bus strategy in the data flow.

(j) Routing AC to MW in I cycle.

5.10. Consider the problem solved by Fig. 5.42.   With the aid of a timing chart, describe how the modification prevents an interrupt following a DIO instruction.

5.11. Redesign console controls.   Replace the 4-position knob by four keys of a keyboard.

5.12. Consider the circuit of Fig. 5.38(a).   Can you design a simpler version which meets the same functional requirements?

A TEST MACHINE

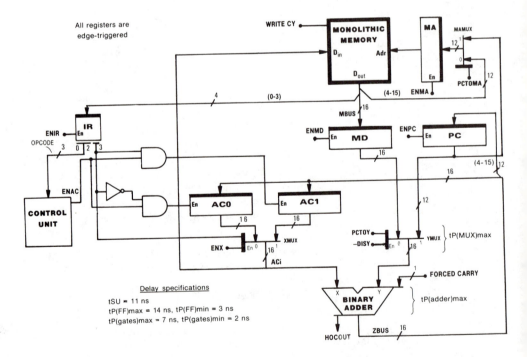

Figure 5P.1. *A test machine.*

A 16-bit "TEST" machine has been partially designed. The data flow is shown in **Figure 5P.1**. Also shown are some of the delay locations. This machine is a suitable vehicle for a final exam. Most of the questions are "uncoupled".

TEST is a simple machine with only one addressing mode, and the abbreviated address is already the full direct address (FDA). It has two accumulators: AC0 and AC1; the accumulator chosen for the instruction operand is indicated by instruction bit 3. The selected accumulator is denoted ACi where the variable i bit is 0 if IR(3)=0, and the variable i bit is 1 if IR(3)=1. The instruction format is as follows:

	Op	*i bit*	*Full Direct Address*
Bits:	0 1 2	3	4 ... 15

The instructions are as follows:

Op	*Name*	*Function (independent RTN)*
000	JUMP	PC←FDA (unconditional branch)
001	READ	ACi←M[FDA]
010	WRITE	M[FDA]←ACi
011	ADD	ACi←ACi plus M[FDA]
100	SKIPN	ACi(0): PC←PC plus 1
101	SKOP	General Skip. To be designed.
110	SUBJ	Subroutine Jump. To be designed.
111	Reg-Ref/DIO	Register-Reference/IO. To be designed.

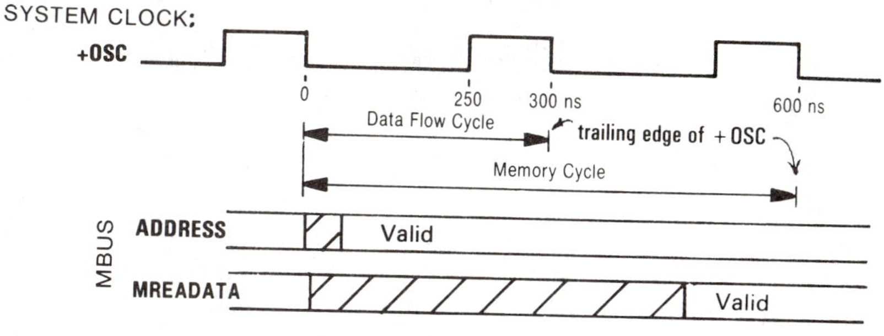

Figure 5P.2. *Timing.*

Figure 5P.3. *Register clocking for MA, PC, IR, and MD.*

Figure 5P.4. *Auxiliary circuit.*

The data flow cycle of the test machine is 300 ns and is shown in **Figure 5P.2.**
Registers are edge-triggered on the trailing edge of OSC, and the clocking is
single-phase. Registers are selectively loaded as shown in **Figure 5P.3.** The
memory cycle takes two data flow cycles, and is reading unless WRITECY is
activated at the start of a cycle. We shall not be concerned with the detail of a
properly timed write enable signal for the memory; a "black box" circuit which
handles this is shown in **Figure 5P.4.** If the memory is not writing, it is assumed to
be reading out the value at MA.

CONTROL STATE	ADDITIONAL SIGNALS	RTN Microoperations	NEXT STATE	PLA p-term(s)
I1		(read underway)	I2	1
I2		MD←MBUS; IR←MBUS(0-3); MA←MBUS(4-15); PC←PC plus 1	E1	2
E1	WRITE	WRITE CY; D_{in} = ACi	E2	3
E1	ADD+READ	(read underway)	E2	4
E1	SKIPN·ACi(0)	PC←PC plus 1	line 6	5
E1	SKIPN	(p-term for Next State only)	E2	6
E1	JUMP	PC←MD(4-15) (MA already has this)	I1	7
E2	ADD+READ	MA←PC; MD←MBUS	E3	8
E2	WRITE	MA←PC; D_{in} = ACi	I1	9
E2	SKIPN	MA←PC	I1	10
E3	READ	AC←MD	I1	11
E3	ADD	AC←AC plus MD	I1	12

Figure 5P.5. *Table of microoperations.*

The table of microoperations for the TEST machine as implemented so far is
found in **Figure 5P.5.** The microoperations in the table of microoperations have
been "keyed" via a circled number to the corresponding p-term of the control PLA
of **Figure 5P.6.** Note that this control PLA also implements the next-state equations for the major control state.

Beware: the function of the data flow is not exactly that of the SC-16. We
note here the important differences. The PC goes directly to MA. The ZBUS does
not go to MA. MD goes to the YMUX instead of the XMUX. The 12-bit instruction address field is the full direct address, so only 4K words can be addressed.

We also point out the following conventions or groundrules.

1. Like SC-16H, MA must be loaded with the PC before I1 occurs.
2. Like the SC-16H, the YMUX is normally enabled and XMUX is
   normally disabled. The YMUX normally selects MD.
3. The XMUX selects AC0 or AC1 in accord with bit IR(3).
4. The MAMUX is always enabled and normally passes MBUS.
5. The FORCED CARRY signal, the low-order adder carry-in, is
   normally inactive.
6. WRITECY will cause a 2 data flow cycle memory write operation beginning with the data flow cycle in which it is activated.

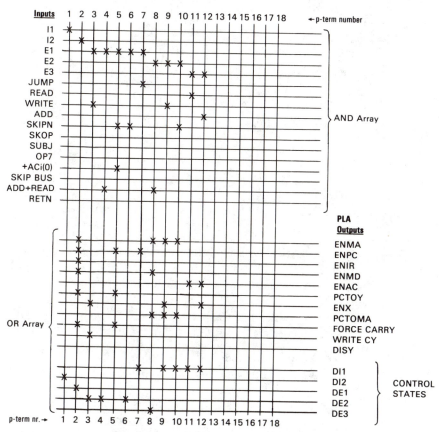

Figure 5P.6. *Control PLA*

The following test questions pertain to the TEST machine.

TEST QUESTIONS

5.13. A state transition diagram has been started for TEST in **Figure 5P.7**. Complete the diagram per Figure 5P.5.

5.14. Consider the elimination of E3: that is, going to I1 instead of E3. Now whatever would have happened in E3 should happen in I1. Can this be

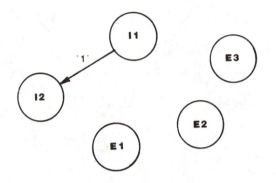

Figure 5P.7. *A state transition diagram.*

done? (Yes or No) Why or Why Not? (brief explanation).

5.15. We wish to obtain an expression for the worst-case data flow delays which govern Tmin (the best or fastest possible workable cycle time). Consider cycle E3 for ADD to be "worst", where the longest delay chain occurs for $ACi \leftarrow ACi$ plus MD. Assume the selected ACi value arrives at the X adder input before MD value arrives at the Y adder input. Denote the clock skew term tSK(AC)max. Write the delay equation for the delays determining Tmin, identifying them as tP(?), tSU(?), etc. *in the order of their occurrence*.

5.16. Consider whether any of the edge-triggered data flow registers could be replaced by the less expensive lower-power data latch. For data latches, the rise of OSC would "open" or pass the input to the output following tP(lat) and the fall of OSC would latch the value. The use of the data latch can be ruled out if, on a cycle for which it is a destination, it is also a source. (Recall the destination is latched on the fall of OSC.) Assume the best-case delay through each combinational circuit is 0 ns. Which of ACi, MA, MD, PC, or IR are implementable as data latches?

5.17. Do a control flow diagram which includes the ADD, JUMP, and READ instructions. (See Fig. 5.24.)

5.18. **Figure 5P.8** shows a timing chart which shows the activation of various control signals for cycles I1 and I2. The control PLA is useful in this exercise. **Figure 5P.9** shows a partially completed timing chart for the execution phase. Complete the timing chart of Fig. 5P.9 for the following instructions, for the signals given in the figure.

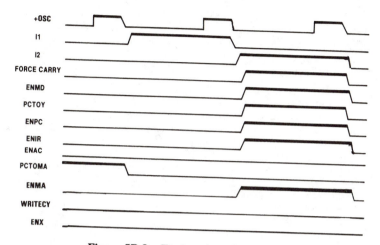

Figure 5P.8. *Timing chart for I1 and I2 cycle.*

(a) WRITE

(b) SKIPN, where ACi(0) has value 1

5.19. Implement opcode 5, SKOP, a skip-type instruction. During E1, if the skip condition is met, the *active-high* signal +SKIPBUS (a control PLA input) is active. Use this condition to add 1 conditionally to the PC in E1, depending on the value of SKIPBUS. Complete the execution in cycle E2. MA must have the proper address before I1 cycle.

(a) Give the RTN statements for the solution.

(b) On the Control PLA, "X" in the proper places, including "next state".

5.20. Opcode 6 is SUBJ, a subroutine jump. Design SUBJ using a "branch-and-link" approach where PC is stored in ACi (per IR(3)).

(a) Design the instruction event schematic.

(b) Suppose OP7 has a subop called "RETN" which is a subroutine return from SUBJ. Do the event schematic for RETN for cycles E1 and E2.

(c) Mark the control PLA for SUBJ and RETN.

5.21. Consider a register-reference instruction CMA which complements the selected ACi per IR(3). Describe how the data flow could be modified to do this (show a block diagram). What new data flow control point (points) is (are) required?

5.22. Consider a register-reference instruction DBA which doubles the selected ACi. Show a block diagram of the data flow changes needed to accommodate this instruction. Design the event schematic for the execution phase.

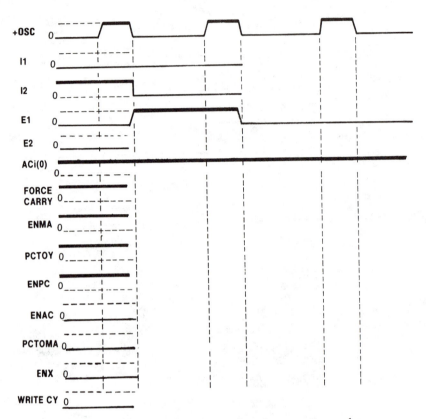

Figure 5P.9. *Timing chart for execution cycles.*

REFERENCES

1. Anon., *Small Computer Handbook,* Digital Equipment Corp., Maynard, MA, 1970 Edition.
2. Anon., *A Pocket Guide to the 2100 Computer,* Hewlett Packard Co., Palo Alto, CA, September 1972.
3. Anon., *PACE Technical Description,* Publication No. 4200078B, National Semiconductor, Santa Clara, CA, April 1976.
4. F.J. Hill and G.R. Peterson, *Digital Systems: Hardware Organization and Design,* Wiley, New York, 1973.
5. M.M. Mano, *Computer System Architecture,* Prentice-Hall, Englewood Cliffs, NJ, 1976.
6. S.S. Husson, *Microprogramming: Principles and Practices,* Prentice-Hall, Englewood Cliffs, NJ, 1970.
7. J.S. Liptay, "The Cache", *IBM Systems Journal,* Vol. 7, n. 1, 1968, 15-21.
8. W. Buchholtz, Ed., *Planning a Computer System, Project Stretch,* McGraw-Hill, New York, 1962.
9. Anon., *A Pocket Guide to Interfacing HP Computers,* Hewlett-Packard Co., Cupertino, CA, April 1970.

10. J.C. Gibson, "The Gibson Mix", *IBM Rep. TR00.2043,* IBM Corp., Poughkeepsie, NY, June 1970.

11. Nils J. Nilsson, *Principles of Artificial Intelligence,* Tioga Publishing Co., Palo Alto, CA, 1980.

✳ CHAPTER 6 ✳

MICROPROGRAMMED AND BIT-SLICE COMPUTER DESIGN

6.1. INTRODUCTION

Microprogramming was originally proposed by Wilkes [1] as an "orderly" way to implement the control unit section of a computer. Some improvements appeared shortly thereafter in [2]. In this chapter, we describe microprogramming in general, and then implement the SC-16 architecture. The hardwired design is called the SC-16H. This chapter covers two approaches to *microprogrammed* computers. We first implement the SC-16M with the same data flow as the SC-16H. Next, we implement the SC-16S with a microprogrammed bit-slice data flow; the "S" is a reminder that the data flow is *bit-slice*.

Figure 6.1 shows a general block diagram of a microprogrammed control unit. The data flow is a functional unit, with connection points for the control unit, main memory, and IO. Each word of the *control memory* is called a *microinstruction*. The microprogram memory is called the control memory because it "belongs" to the control unit. As with hardwired control units, two items are of interest for each cycle [1]:

1. the "action" part: activation of the control points, and
2. the "next state" part: sequence control via the next address determination logic circuits.

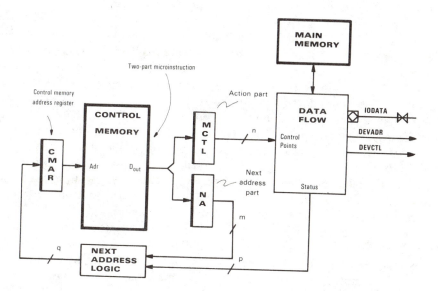

Figure 6.1. *Simplified version of microprogrammed control unit.*

Fig. 6.1 shows the microinstruction as composed of these two parts. The *action* field determines the concurrent microoperations or action performed in the data flow cycle. The *next address* field, together with status information from the data flow, determines the next microinstruction address. This address is loaded into the *control memory address register* (CMAR) to access the next instruction.

6.2. MICROPROGRAMMING CONSIDERATIONS

6.2.1. The Advantages of Microprogramming

If the microinstruction format is flexible, then bugs in the instruction interpretation logic can often be corrected by a change in the microprogram. It is usually easier to change a microprogram than to change hardwired logic. This is particularly true when the system reaches production. In general, the data flow and microinstruction format are designed to interpret a given or "native" instruction set. However, the system can often be microprogrammed to interpret another (foreign) instruction set. A microprogram application for a second instruction set is called *emulation*. Some microprogrammed machines use a control memory which is *writable*. A writable control store permits the selection of one microprogram to be loaded at power-on time, and other microprograms to be loaded at later times, as needed.

Many small computers are not microprogrammed. The control unit should have some minimum amount of "complexity" or functionality before microprogramming offers a cost advantage. We relate complexity and functionality (intuitive concepts) to the number of dependent RTN statements needed to describe the control unit behavior. We implement the SC-16M with a microprogrammed approach, but the control unit is really too simple to benefit from this. Some machines follow a mixed or hybrid approach; the instruction fetch phase is hardwired, and the operand fetch and execution phase is microprogrammed. Microprogramming seems to offer the most cost effectiveness for architectures with more than one execution cycle per instruction. Minicomputers with multiply or divide instructions are natural candidates for microprogramming.

Most of the implementations of the IBM S/360 architecture were microprogrammed. The instruction set's high functionality favors microprogramming, as explained in Tucker [3]. As the functionality of a data flow and control unit combination increases, so does the control unit cost. In the hardwired approach, more microoperations require more gates. This relationship is slightly more than linear; each p-term of conditional information represents an AND gate, but the fan-in of OR gates for each control point grows. With microprogramming, even for a simple machine, the control registers, branching logic and control memory cycle controls are designed once at a fixed cost. As functionality increases, however, we simply add more control memory. The resulting per-bit cost is less than the cost of the additional gates for the corresponding hardwired approach. The rate of increase is slightly greater than linear, as the addressing capability to the control store must increase one bit for each doubling of control memory size. The concept is illustrated in **Figure 6.2**. The microprogrammed approach was adopted for the design of the DEC PDP-11/60, and Mudge [4] explained similar motivations.

Microprogramming is also called "firmware" and conceptually falls between the instruction set level and the hardwired control unit (data flow) level. In conventional programming, typically only one action happens at a time. (Admittedly, the action may be at a higher level than an RTN statement.) In firmware, the capability for concurrency is improved over the single action aspect of software. In hardwired control the designer can take advantage of as much concurrency as the data flow permits.

6.2.2. Microprogram System Timing

Most microinstruction implementations have the microprogram cycle synchronized with the data flow cycle: each microinstruction controls the actions of one data flow cycle [3]. During the early portion (in time) of

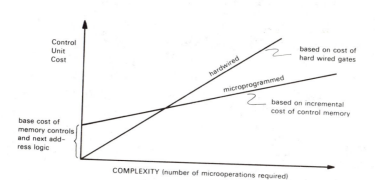

Figure 6.2. *Illustration of increased complexity favoring micropro-grammed control unit approach.*

the data flow cycle, the microprogram next address control logic must determine the value of the next microinstruction address. During the last portion of the data flow cycle the control or microinstruction memory must be accessed. This memory is often read-only (a ROM).

The action part and next address part of the microinstruction are both important, and are *overlapped* (executed in parallel). While the data flow is being influenced by the action part, the next address part determines the next address and accesses the next microinstruction. The propagation delays also occur in parallel. **Figure 6.3** shows a conceptual timing diagram which sketches the concurrency involved.

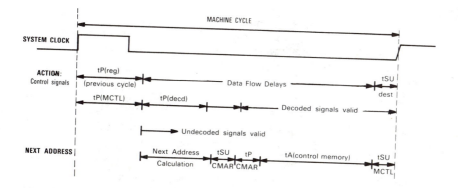

Figure 6.3. *Typical timing of microinstruction cycle.*

6.2.3. Microinstruction Word Format and the Action Part

Microinstruction format design is similar to instruction set design: place as much power and flexibility into as few instruction bits as possible. In this section we describe the relatively straightforward action control fields. The designer takes into account the data flow control points, the desired concurrency, and which actions are mutually exclusive.

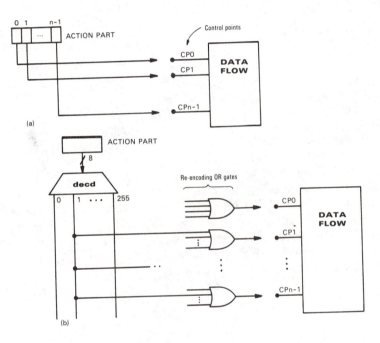

Figure 6.4. *"Pure" approaches to the microinstruction format.* (a) Pure horizontal approach. (b) Pure vertical approach.

There are two "pure" approaches to the design of the action part of a microinstruction. See **Figure 6.4.** When the *action field* contains one microinstruction bit for each data flow control point, then the microinstruction format is called *horizontal*. See Fig. 6.4(a). The action part of the pure horizontal microinstruction is said to consist of a set of independent 1-bit fields. For a control unit with n control points, the action part of a horizontal microinstruction has n bits. If a control signal is to be activated on that cycle, the microinstruction has a 1 in the bit position corresponding to that control signal. For example, on cycles that the PC is to be a destination register, then control signal ENPC is to be activated, and bit ENPC of the microinstruction is 1 (on). Horizontal microinstructions have complete freedom in that any combination of the control signals can be activated in any cycle, but usually have an unnecessarily large number of bits in the action part.

The second pure approach to microprogramming uses a *vertical* format. See Fig. 6.4(b). We can analyze the number of distinct yet concurrent microoperations performed in any given data flow cycle. Instances where more than one microoperation take place in the cycle are called a *multiple action*. Each multiple action can then be encoded in a few bits. For example, an 8-bit action field is sufficient if only one of 256 possible single or multiple actions is performed on each data flow cycle. The microinstruction action field is then decoded to cause the activation of the corresponding control points. Each vertical microinstruction is like a p-term which *implies* certain control point activations. The action part of the pure vertical microinstruction format is a single fully encoded field. Vertical microprogramming uses a small number of bits for the action field, but is inflexible in the concurrency of microoperations which can be performed on any cycle in future modifications.

Most microinstruction format designs use a *mixed* approach, as shown in **Figure 6.5.** The action part uses some combination of the horizontal and vertical approaches. The horizontal aspect is represented by defining a number of *independent fields,* usually formed by grouping control points which are not activated simultaneously. Thus, each field is encoded to control some set of control points. For example, two fields can select the respective information sources for the right and left ALU inputs and a third

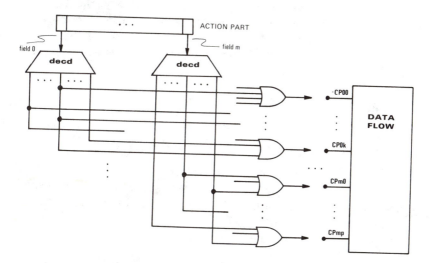

Figure 6.5. *Mixed approach to formatting the action part.*

field can select the destination of the ALU output. Each independent microinstruction field decode combination is called a *microorder* in Tucker [3]. The vertical format is represented by the encoding of the independent action fields. A microorder should *not* be confused with a microoperation. A microoperation may decompose into one or more microorders. Consider the microoperations of the following class:

$$R3 \leftarrow R1 \text{ "operation" } R2$$

A specific microoperation of this class could be implied by four microorders. In a practical microinstruction format, three microorders would specify the operands R1, R2, and R3; a fourth microorder would specify the operation.

As with instruction set design, we employ the concept of *field redefinition*. In this technique, the meaning (set of control points activated) of some fields depends on the microorder in another field. In the IBM S360/M50, for example, the first bit redefined the entire remaining microinstruction. If the bit was 0, the microinstruction was interpreted normally; if the bit was 1, the microinstruction was *reinterpreted* to do special input-output functions.

Note that the issue of *concurrency* is determined by the data flow, and not by the microinstruction format. Each independent bus or resource of the data flow gives rise to a class of microinstructions which use that resource and can be independently executed. A *concurrency class* is such a set of actions. The microinstruction can only constrain the available concurrency, and can never provide more concurrency classes than are inherent in the data flow. On the other hand, use of the horizontal microinstruction format cannot help if the "controlled part" of the implementation has a "bottleneck" which does not provide for more than one concurrency class.

6.2.4. Conditional Information and Next Address Determination

In this section we present a point. The three implementations of the SC-16 architecture, taken together, will make this point clear:

The control concept of *conditional execution* versus the notion of a "succession of microinstruction branches" is a key difference between the logic design of a hardwired control unit and a microprogrammed control unit.

The data flow of the SC-16H can be controlled by a microprogram. The control memory provides a microinstruction which on each cycle activates and deactivates the control points of the data flow. Such a scheme works if the actions performed by each microinstruction are correct, and the words from the control memory (microinstructions) appear in the proper sequence.

The *sequencing* aspects of the control memory are controlled by the next address placed in the CMAR, and are used to fetch the next microinstruction. The next address determination for CMAR corresponds roughly to the "next state" column in a table of microoperations. *The next address aspects of the microprogramming approach are perhaps the most difficult to grasp in microinstruction design.* The difficulty arises from the following problem.

In RTN statements, actions are invoked by the *conditional information* to the left of the colon in the statement. In the table of microoperations representation (see Chapter 5) this conditional information appears in the two columns denoted "control state" and "additional conditions". The conditional information represents a *status* of the data flow and control unit at the time of the execution of the microinstruction. This status is the current instruction opcode and address mode, the data flow carry latch value, and other flag, status, or condition code values in the control unit or data flow.

Actions ultimately are decomposed or down-converted to data flow control point activations, implemented in gate logic or a PLA. The gates or PLA implementation are determined by p-terms derived from the conditional information which implies the control point activations. Control point activations can be explained as boolean statements which are functions of conditional information such as the opcode decoder outputs, the address mode bits, the major control state, and status such as "HOCOUT".

Hardwired control units combine the major control state information with the status information early in the *current* cycle to determine the control signals to be activated in the same cycle.

Since the microinstruction action fields are generally not combined with the conditional information, the conditional values (status) must be reflected in the address used in reading out the *next* microinstruction. Microprogrammed control units determine the address of the next microinstruction from valid status information early in the current cycle: note that the action field retrieved from the address determined in Fig. 6.3 does not take effect until the next cycle. This one-cycle delay in the use of status information is a factor reducing the performance of microprogrammed control units relative to hardwired control units.

The action fields are not generally designed for *conditional execution* where the microorder is combined with current conditional information to determine the specific control point activation. If the microinstruction designer depends heavily on conditional information to assist the action fields, then a hardwired control unit might be as easily implemented.

The branching or next address fields of the microinstruction are very critical to performance due to the general unavailability of the conditional information once the microinstruction has been accessed. The design of the next address fields is difficult in the absence of any knowledge of the sequential nature of the instruction interpretation task. The microprogrammer must "know where the control flow is and where it is going" much more frequently for instruction interpretation than for general application programming. In fact, we suspect that if a microprogrammed machine does not need powerful branching, then either the control unit might better be hardwired, or the term microinstruction is being misapplied to the native instruction set. In some cases, the lack of good branching power can be compensated for by conditional execution. We employ conditional execution in the SC-16M for the register-reference instructions.

6.2.5. Techniques for Determining the Next Address

This subsection reviews the methods of determining the next address. Microinstruction designers have incorporated the techniques of instruction set architecture and have also developed some techniques of their own. The conventional methods are discussed in Chapter 2 and are listed in **Table 6.1.** We employ many of these techniques in the SC-16 architecture.

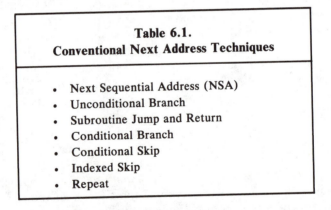

**Table 6.1.
Conventional Next Address Techniques**

- Next Sequential Address (NSA)
- Unconditional Branch
- Subroutine Jump and Return
- Conditional Branch
- Conditional Skip
- Indexed Skip
- Repeat

The NSA technique is quite popular, although not heavily used in many S/360 microprogrammed implementations. The NSA technique is employed together with a *microprogram counter* (μPC). Microprogrammed control units which do not have a μPC must use the unconditional branch. Subroutine stacks are popular in LSI parts which have been designed specially as general-purpose sequence controller chips. The conditional branch is used when a status bit selects between using the NSA or another target address. The conditional skip technique is used when a condition determines whether the last address (which is in μPC) should be incremented by the value 1 or 2. In microinstruction designs, the loop counter countdown in the control unit corresponds to the indexed skip. Similarly, the repeat function can be done as follows.   A counter is loaded   beforehand with a nonzero value. The repeated microinstruction decrements the counter and tests for 0. If 0, the value in the CMAR is replaced with the NSA value.

Of greater interest are techniques developed primarily for use in microinstructions. These are listed in **Table 6.2.**

Table 6.2.
Microinstruction Addressing Techniques
• Mapper
• CMAR Field Insertion (2^n-way branch)
• Bring-along (full or partial)
• Conditional Execution
• Late Branch

The first three techniques are illustrated in **Figure 6.6.** As an example, assume the CMAR is ten bits wide. In the *mapper* approach to the next address calculation, (Fig. 6.6(a)), we can retain a major control state sequencing mechanism similar to that used in the hardwired SC-16H. (See the state transition diagram of the SC-16H in Chapter 5.)   The designer can "map" (assign) the major control state, the opcode, and the address mode information to a unique microinstruction memory address, and a new major control state. Usually a ROM is used to translate the conditional information into an address. The ROM address mapper accepts signals from the major control state (e.g., I1, I2, A1, etc. in SC-16H) and the instruction register, and then determines a microinstruction address.   In practice the mapper approach is used in one place in the microprogram: after the instruction is fetched and before the individual routines are entered for executing the instruction.

The *field insertion* technique is called a "function branch" in [3]. See Fig. 6.6(b). The basic idea is suggested in [2]; the opcode is transferred to the high-order bits of the CMAR and the low-order bits are cleared to 0. This "breaks out" the opcode with a *multiway branch*. Located at each "target" is a microprogram routine which handles that particular opcode. Field insertion selects certain fields of the CMAR to receive the values of specific *branch bits* such as the condition code. See   path (1) of Fig. 6.6(b). The technique was used extensively in the IBM S360/M25 implementation where the CMAR field receiving the inserted branch bits was not always the low-order field. If the microinstruction following the target is also going to use field insertion, then bits other than the low-order bits need to be changed.

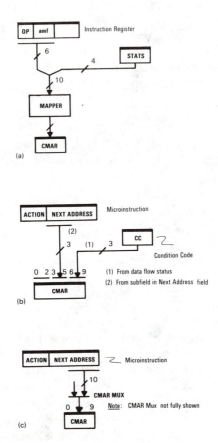

Figure 6.6. *Some techniques for microinstruction next address generation.* (a) Mapper approach. (b) Field insertion. (c) Full bring-along.

The branch bits correspond to the *conditional information* of hardwired control units. Branch bits can be:

- status latches which the microprogrammer can set or clear,
- condition code flags,
- part of the opcode or address mode fields of the instruction, or
- parts of a selected data word such as the MSB or LSB values.

For path (2) of Fig. 6.6(b), a field in the next address part of the microinstruction is inserted into CMAR(3-5). Since the address bits are partially brought along with the microinstruction, this form of branch is called partial *bring-along*.

In the *full* bring-along technique, the current microinstruction brings along the entire next address bits. See Fig. 6.6(c). Not too large a field is needed for many small-capacity microprogram memories. (For example, the Hewlett-Packard HP2100 has 256 microinstructions, expandable to 512 microinstructions.) The bring-along technique is slightly more powerful than the next sequential address incrementer. Bring-along easily simulates the next sequential address technique (the brought-along address is the NSA), but can also unconditionally branch to any target as for *reconverging*. A reconverging point in a program is an instruction location reached from (or following) more than one instruction. It is often the case that once the operand is fetched, microprogram segments which individually handle the ADD Indirect, ADD Indexed and ADD Direct reconverge to a microprogram segment for the execution of the ADD itself.

One way to bring along a full target address is to use field redefinition of the bits available for next address specification. In this technique, if the first bit of the next address part of the microinstruction is 1, then the remaining bits of the address part specify the full next microprogram address. In Fig. 6.6(c), the redefinition bit selects the CMARMUX data source to gate the relevant portion of the next address fields.

A combination of the bring-along and field insertion techniques is advantageous. One field of the CMAR may be unconditionally replaced by a short field of the next address part of the microinstruction. Another field of the next address part can specify how to insert bits into another CMAR field. This is the technique in Fig. 6.6(b).

The *conditional execution* technique actually *avoids* the need for a branch. The concept of *residual control* is a special case of conditional execution. The technique is called "data-dependent" microorders in Tucker [3]; a preloaded function register of the IBM S360/M50 controls certain logical storage-to-storage operations without branching to distinct microprogram routines. The location of the conditional execution information need not be a register specifically preloaded for the purpose as in residual control. Conditional execution can use any value available in the data flow or control unit. A microorder in an action field can be reserved to ask the hardware to "do the right thing". The register-reference instructions for the SC-16M are implemented in this fashion.

The S360/M50 had a *late branch* capability. Normally, the fetch of the next microinstruction is overlapped with the execution of the present microinstruction; see Fig. 6.3. The S360/M50 control memory was twice the width of the microinstruction; each cycle fetched two microinstructions. The low-order bit of the CMAR selected the microinstruction to be loaded into the microinstruction register. The low-order CMAR bit needed to be valid only at the end of the data flow cycle, and thus could be the carry-out bit of the ALU. The simultaneous read-out of two microinstructions coupled with the use of field insertion on the low-order CMAR bit provided a powerful late branch capability to the S360/M50.

6.2.6. Microinstruction Format Design

Most microprogrammed machines are designed with a combined top-down and bottom-up approach. The bottom-up approach interconnects parts into a system which performs a more powerful function. A general-purpose microprogrammed machine may be said to be designed bottom-up if it is not oriented to interpret a predetermined machine language instruction.

For a fairly complex machine language instruction, the bottom-up technique may not provide an efficient solution. A bottom-up design at best provides a "first cut" or "basis for complaints". Then the microprogrammers can improve the design by asking for this or that modification.

If the native machine language instruction is fairly simple, but has some features not amenable to a general-purpose approach, then the microoperations for each cycle may be laid out in an event schematic. The action fields and next address determination fields might then be designed based on what the event schematics need. This is close to a top-down approach, but should be done by a designer who knows the general data flow, the memory cycle, and bus concurrency available. In the top-down approach the microprogrammer-designer studies the instruction set to be interpreted and designs the best microinstruction format to do the job at hand.

In a combined approach, the microprogrammer will try to "lay out" a few key instruction event schematics or data flow cycles to see what is needed for interpreting the target instruction set. The microinstruction is designed from the intuition so obtained. Of course, there will be some iterations in each approach.

6.3. MICROPROGRAM CONTROL OF THE SC-16H

The SC-16M is the first microprogrammed version of the SC-16 architecture we consider in this chapter. We review the architecture of the instruction format. **Figure 6.7** depicts format 1, for the memory-reference instructions. **Figure 6.8** depicts format 2, for the register-reference instructions. **Figure 6.9** depicts format 3, for the IO instructions. This summarizes the architecture to be implemented by microprogram.

6.3.1. Differences between the SC-16H and SC-16M

A microprogrammed approach to the SC-16M requires a change in the way the designer views the implementation problem. The SC-16H has

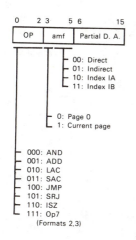

Figure 6.7. *SC-16 instruction format 1, memory-reference instructions.*

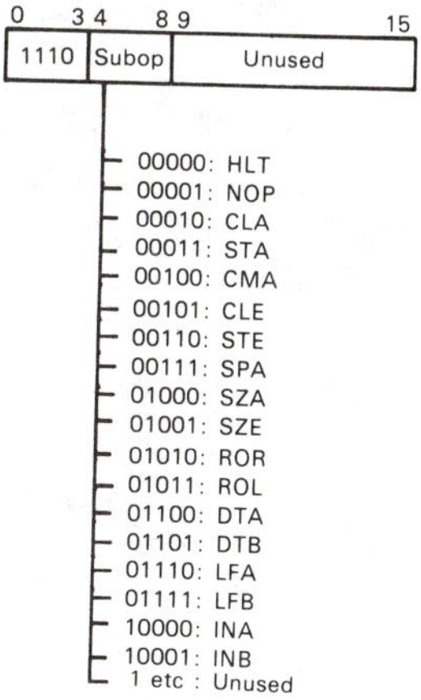

Figure 6.8. *SC-16 instruction format 2, register-reference instructions.*

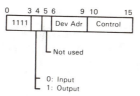

Figure 6.9. *SC-16 instruction format 3, input-output instructions.*

already been designed with a "hardwired" control unit, which we now review.

For example, in control state E1 for the hardwired control unit of the SC-16H, opcodes ISZ or LAC conditionally activate control point "DISYMUX". In a microprogrammed CPU, the current conditional information is used indirectly to affect the data flow control points through the action field of the *next* microinstruction.

It is also possible (but not common) for some action fields of the microinstruction to have decoded combinations which specify a conditional execution action. A trivial example is a microorder which adds the value in the carry latch to the AC. In a sense, the action to add 1 to the AC conditionally depends on the carry latch value.

A microprogrammed CPU does not give the microprogrammer the luxury of arriving at a control state, and then conditionally determining what is to be done. The designer must recognize that the only way to access any microinstruction action field is by satisfying a succession of microinstruction branches beginning at the start of I-fetch. This point of view becomes evident as the microprogrammed implementation of the SC-16M CPU unfolds.

6.3.2. The SC-16M Microinstruction: Action Part

Some microinstruction designs are "top-down"; a microinstruction format is designed first, and the data flow is designed to implement the microinstruction. The IBM S370/M145 was designed in this manner. Next, the microprogrammers perform the task of interpreting the "target machine" instruction set, while the logic designers implement the data flow and the control unit for the interpretation of the microinstructions. The microprogramming concept does not replace the hardwired control unit. However, the hardwired control unit is considerably simplified because it deals in the simpler conceptual level of microinstruction interpretation.

We designed the data flow of the SC-16H in the previous chapter. The present microprogrammed implementation is in one sense "bottom-up", since we accept the existing data flow. We reimplement the control unit with microinstructions. To simplify the microprogramming task, the register-reference and DIO instructions of opcode 7 (OP7) are implemented by conditional execution. The existing hardwired control logic for OP7 will be retained. (See Chapter 5.) A microorder in one of the control fields will cause the conditional execution of OP7.

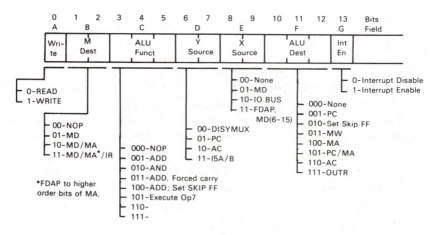

Figure 6.10. *The "action" part of the SC-16 control word.*

The action part of the SC-16M microinstruction is shown in **Figure 6.10.** It is general practice to decode individual fields into mutually exclusive microorders. The current microinstruction is assumed to reside in register MI. MI(0-13) comprises the action part of the microinstruction. A summary of the action fields follows:

Field A -   sets the WRITE flip-flop to initiate a write cycle. (For simplicity, assume the memory is static and is reading if it is not writing.) The WRITE flip-flop is set early in the current cycle, and is subsequently cleared by an auxiliary circuit at the end of the following cycle.

Field B -   denotes possible destinations for the memory word.

Field C -   controls the function performed by the ALU. Microorder ADD, Forced carry is used for 1-upping, microorder ADD, Set SKIP FF causes the SKIP flip-flop to be set. Microorder Execute OP7 causes the conditional execution of OP7.

Field D -   controls the Y source. Microorder I5A/B selects the proper index register per IR(5) (conditional execution).

Field E -   controls the X source. The IO bus or console switches are selectable, as well as MD.

Field F -   controls the destination of the ALU. Microorder Set Skip FF has no destination, but sets SKIP if the result is 0.

Field G -   enables the interrupt system at a time convenient to the microprogram. Interrupts are accepted by forcing a special microinstruction address where a PC save routine is located.

6.3.3. The SC-16M Microinstruction: Next Address Part

We employ a combination of techniques for determining the next address. The next address part of the microinstruction is subdivided into more than one field. One subfield brings along some of the next address bits, whereas others specify how the remaining address bits are obtained. Some microprogram address bits are the same as on the previous cycle. Field insertion is considered, for example, for the 2-bit address mode field IR(3,4). Inserting IR(3,4) into a 2-bit field of the next microinstruction address results in a 4-way branch mode: (1) direct, (2) indirect, (3) index IA and (4) index IB.

Consider the branching requirements of instruction interpretation, once I-fetch acquires the instruction. Generally, determining the addressing mode is most important; the effective address calculation (in the critical path for instruction execution) can proceed rapidly. Next, the operation itself is determined from the opcode, and the instruction is executed. Finally the microprogram reconverges to the beginning, which is I-fetch.

We do not wish to consume much time for the simple direct address mode. Therefore, in the SC-16M, we quickly determine the address mode. The state transition diagram for the SC-16H shows that different control states ensue from opcodes SRJ, JMP, SAC and OP7. The "break-out" of the other (more normal) opcodes does not take place until execution time. This suggests that SRJ, JMP, SAC and OP7 be broken out, together with the address modes (direct, indirect, or indexed). Furthermore, in the event of OP7, the address mode is not of immediate interest.

Field insertion is a compact way to create a multiway branch; we employ a 16-way branch, based on four bits R, S; T, and U. See **Figure 6.11,** which shows how these bits are devised. Conditions JMP, SRJ, SAC, and OP7, together with the instruction register bits IR(3-4), are encoded (mapped) into conditions described by the 16 combinations of R, S, T, and U. The truth tables in Fig. 6.11 show the encoding. Here a mapper approach obtains the branch bits for field insertion.

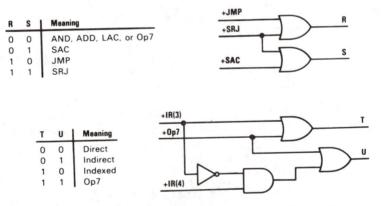

R	S	Meaning
0	0	AND, ADD, LAC, or Op7
0	1	SAC
1	0	JMP
1	1	SRJ

T	U	Meaning
0	0	Direct
0	1	Indirect
1	0	Indexed
1	1	Op7

Figure 6.11. *Determination of branch bits R, S, T, and U.*

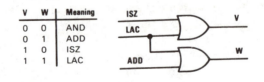

V	W	Meaning
0	0	AND
0	1	ADD
1	0	ISZ
1	1	LAC

Figure 6.12. *Determination of branch bits V and W.*

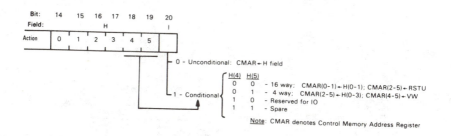

Figure 6.13. *The next address part of the control word.*

The same technique breaks out the four "normal" opcodes AND, ADD, LAC and ISZ. Branch bits V and W are encoded as shown in **Figure 6.12.** Again, a truth table is useful to describe the mapping or encoding of the branch conditions.

It appears that an addressing capacity of 64 microinstructions is adequate for the SC-16M; therefore an unconditional branch of six bits is sufficient. We use the bring-along technique. A seventh bit can cause the 6-bit field to be reinterpreted for conditional branches. The NSA technique is replaced by full bring-along. The result of this discussion is summarized in **Figure 6.13.**

6.3.4. The SC-16M Microprogram

The SC-16M microprogram is designed for all but the interrupt microinstruction routine. The noninterrupt portion of the microprogram can be located in the lowest 32 control memory addresses.

Since the microinstruction word boundaries for the 4- and 16-way branches need to be properly aligned, they dominate the address assignment. Address assignment is done by hand. The opcode group and address mode breakout from the 16-way branch occurs in I-fetch cycles and is shown in **Figure 6.14.** Note that Fig. 6.14 is a special flowchart, with each execution block (rectangle) representing the action part of one microinstruction. The assigned address is in the upper left of each block. Address 29 (instead of 0) is the "Start" of I-fetch. This is because the low-order 16 addresses are used for the 16-way target of the 16-way branch. A detail which decreases performance relative to the hardwired approach is that once the instruction is in MD, one cycle is lost in the 16-way branch.

For the "normal" instructions AND, ADD, ISZ, and LAC, the effective address of the operand can be calculated in common. See blocks 0, 1, and 2 of **Figure 6.15.** Also shown is a block for the register-reference and IO instructions of OP7. Once the operand is in the MD, the microprogram

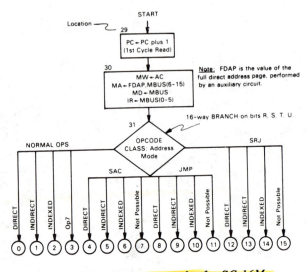

Figure 6.14. *Instruction cycles for SC-16M.*

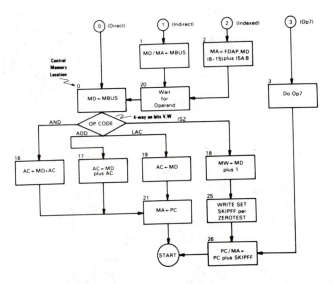

Figure 6.15. *Execution of normal ops and OP7 for SC-16M.*

(block 0) determines the required operation by means of a 4-way branch to break out the "normal" opcodes.

For "nonnormal" instructions SAC, JMP, and SRJ, the design approach breaks the opcode out first (block 31 of Fig. 6.14), because the microprogram must treat the address modes of direct, indirect or indexed

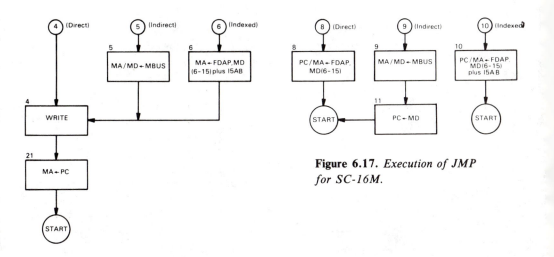

Figure **6.17.** *Execution of JMP for SC-16M.*

Figure **6.16.** *Execution of SAC for SC-16M.*

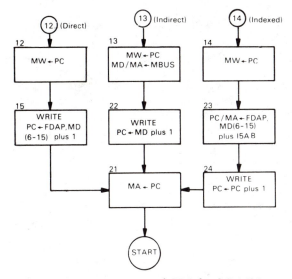

Figure **6.18.** *Execution of SRJ for SC-16M.*

separately. Instruction SAC is flowcharted in **Figure 6.16,** instruction JMP in **Figure 6.17,** and instruction SRJ in **Figure 6.18.**

Figure **6.19** shows the organization of the control memory with its microprogram. Columns A through I are a *bit map* of the fields of the same name. Due to the branching requirements implicit in the instruction interpretation, the microprogram does not look like a conventional program.

				FIELD									
Remark	Loc	ACTION	Next	A	B	C	D	E	F	G	H	I	Remark
Direct	0	MD←M (other ops)	4-way	01							010001	1	2nd cy read
Indirect	1	MD/MA←M (pointer)	20		10						010100	0	2nd cy read
Index	2	MA←MD plus I5A/B	20			001	11	11	100		010010	0	2nd cy read
Op7	3	Op7 (Reg ref, DIO)	26			101					011010	0	26
Direct	4	WRITE	21	1							010101	0	1st cy write
Indir	5	MA/MD←M	4		10						000100	0	
Index	6	MA←MD plus I5A/B	4			001	11	11	100		000100	0	
	7												unused
Direct	8	MA/PC←MD	29			001	00	11	101	1	011101	0	2nd cy read
Indir	9	MA/MD←M	11		10						001101	0	2nd cy read
Index	10	PC/MA←MD plus I5A/B	29			001	11	11	101	1	011101		
	11	PC←MD	29			001	00	01	001	1	011101		
Direct	12	MW←PC	15			001	01	00	011		001111	0	
Indir	13	MW←PC; MD/MA←M	22			001	01	00	011		001111	0	
Index	14	MW←PC	23			001	01	00	011		010111	0	
	15	WRITE; PC←FDAPMD plus 1	21	1		011	00	11	001		010101	0	
AND	16	AC←MD·AC	21			010	10	01	110		010101	0	
ADD	17	AC←AC plus MD	21			001	10	01	110		010101	0	
ISZ	18	MW←MD plus 1	25			011	00	01	011		011001	0	
LAC	19	AC←MD	21			001	00	01	110		010101	0	
	20	(wait for operand)	0								000000	0	1st cy read
	21	MA←PC	29			001	01	00	100	1	011101	0	possible cy 2
	22	WRITE; PC←MD plus 1	21	1		011	00	01	001		010101	0	1st cy write
SRJ	23	PC/MA←MD plus I5A/B	24			001	11	11	101		011000	0	
(con't)	24	WRITE; PC←PC plus 1	21	1		011	01	00	001		010101	0	1st cy write
	25	WRITE; ZTEST←MD plus 1	26	1		011		01	010		011010	0	1st cy write
	26	PC/MA←PC plus ZTEST	29			100	01	00	101	1	011101	0	2nd cy write
	27												unused
	28												
I1	29	PC←PC plus 1	30			011	01		001		011110	0	1st cy read
I2	30	MW←AC; IR/MD/MA←M	31		11	001	10		011		011111	0	2nd cy read
I3	31	(16-way branch)	0-15								000000	1	1st cy read op

(Marginal handwritten labels: SAC by rows 4–6; JMP by rows 8–10; SRS by rows 12–14)

Note: M denotes MBUS, FDAPMD denotes FDAP,MD(6-15), ZTEST denotes ZEROTEST

Figure 6.19. *The microprogram for the SC-16M.*

In location 3, OP7 is executed. In OP7 the control signals are activated as in the SC-16H. **Table 6.3** traces the execution of the SRJ Indexed instruction.

Table 6.3.
Trace of Execution of the SRJ Indexed Instruction

Cycle	Location	Action	Remarks
1	29	PC←PC plus 1	
2	30	MW←AC; IR/MD/MA←M	Concurrent actions
3	31	No action	16-way branch
4	14	MW←PC	
5	23	PC/MA←MD plus I5A/B	Conditional info
6	24	WRITECY; PC←PC plus 1	Minor concurrency
7	21	MA←PC	

6.4. SC-16M SUMMARY

The interpretation of the machine language instructions requires decisions. The three primary means of selectively performing actions are:

1. *conditional branches* to microinstructions which perform the action,
2. *conditional execution,* whereby in hardware, an existing data flow state is ANDed with an action field combination to generate the appropriate control point activations, and
3. *residual control,* a special case of conditional execution, whereby one or more flip-flops are preloaded with values which control an action on some subsequent cycle.

In the SC-16M, we use conditional branching for address mode and opcode break-out, and conditional execution for OP7. Residual control uses a control register loaded earlier in the microprogram, to be used later for conditional execution. Bit IR(5) is a residual control to select conditionally the proper index register when called upon to do so. The use of the SKIP flip-flop comes close to residual control; it is loaded in one cycle, and is used to add 1 selectively on the next cycle.

Figs. 6.14 and 6.19 indicate that the SC-16M microprogram reconverges to I-fetch at location 29. Many instructions reconverge before that. For the "normal" ops, once the operand is obtained, the execution reconverges to location 0 before diverging again four ways. For the SAC instruction (Fig. 6.16), the indirect and indexed cases reconverge to the direct case microinstruction segment at location 4. Many instruction execution segments complete execution without having loaded the MA with the updated value in PC. Such instruction segments reconverge to location 21 where MA is loaded before going to location 29.

Location 31 illustrates performance loss; no action is performed. In the case of the SRJ instruction, anticipation would be advantageous: move the value in PC to the MW register at this time.

6.5. MICROPROGRAM DOCUMENTATION PROBLEMS

The documentation for microprograms generally takes one of two forms: one- or two-dimensional. The first is an ordinary program listing; each line of the document describes a microinstruction, and governs a microinstruction cycle. The second is a flowchart or a flowchart-like document; each block describes a microinstruction.

A program listing is inherently one-dimensional. A listing is not convenient for describing microprograms with many concurrency classes (multiple actions) and with frequent multiway branching. However, some microprogrammed processors have very little concurrency. The IBM S360/M25 had a 16-bit "microinstruction", and used the NSA technique and the vertical format. The typical action consisted of combining one or two operands in the arithmetic unit. Branching was accomplished by special branch instructions which did nothing else. The microprograms were, in fact, described by program listings. The Hewlett-Packard HP21MX computer employed a similar approach: see [5].

Figure 6.20 shows a document called a *control flow diagram* or control flowchart. It is a simplified version of the microinstruction flowchart. This documentation technique was employed for the microprograms of most IBM S/360 series machines. These diagrams were generated by a system

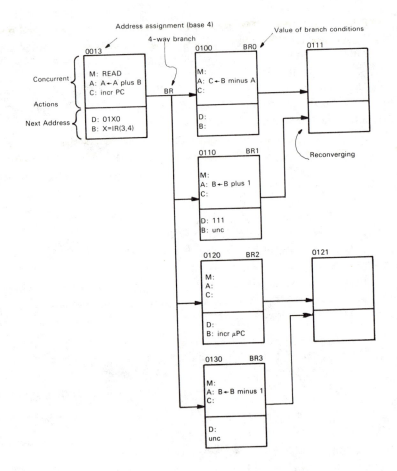

Figure 6.20. *The control flow diagram: a documentation technique which demonstrates concurrency and multiway branching.*

of computer programs called CAS (for Control Automation System) [6]. (See also descriptions in [3] and [7].) Each rectangle is a *control flow block* and describes one microinstruction (controls one data flow cycle). The top part presents the action microoperations. The bottom part describes how the next microinstruction address is obtained.

The control flow block action part has a line available for each concurrency class. As shown, there are three concurrency classes; the memory (M), the ALU (A), and a miscellaneous control signal field (C) which includes the incrementer for the PC.

The next address part of the control flow block has a line for a direct address (bring-along) field (D), and a line to describe how to obtain the next address (B). If blank, the "default" is the NSA (μPC plus 1). As shown in the next address part of the first microinstruction of Fig. 6.20, a 4-way branch is made by field insertion of the bits IR(3,4). Each of the four possible target addresses is called a *leg*. In general, microinstructions which can perform independent and concurrent actions are best represented in control flow diagrams.

<table>
<tr><td colspan="5" align="center">**Table 6.4.**
Example of a Multiway Branch Set</td></tr>
<tr><td>*Label*</td><td>*Leg*</td><td>*Next*
Label</td><td>*Leg*</td><td>*Statement*</td></tr>
<tr><td>NOSPEC</td><td></td><td>BR</td><td>N</td><td>N=IR BITS 3,4</td></tr>
<tr><td>BR</td><td>0</td><td>NOSUP</td><td></td><td>C=B minus A</td></tr>
<tr><td>BR</td><td>1</td><td>NOSUP</td><td></td><td>B=B plus 1</td></tr>
<tr><td>BR</td><td>2</td><td>SUPR</td><td></td><td>(no-op)</td></tr>
<tr><td>BR</td><td>3</td><td>SUPR</td><td></td><td>B=B minus 1</td></tr>
</table>

Microinstructions whose actions can be conveniently represented as a "line of code" tend to use an assembler language (one-dimensional) documentation technique. **Table 6.4** is an example of how multiway branching can be handled in assembler language: labels are given a field called leg, with a means to determine which leg of the branch is taken. The example coincides with that of Fig. 6.20, and is based loosely on documentation from the S/360 Model 25 microprogram listings.

6.6. MICROPROGRAMMED BIT–SLICE DATA FLOWS

In the previous section, the data flow we controlled by microprogram was specifically designed for the SC-16 architecture. In another approach, a functional unit which is a general-purpose *bit-slice* data flow is provided, and the designer's task is to interface and control that data flow [8]. Predecessors to this approach include ALU chips and multipliers, which are embedded in a system and provided with control signals.

The bit-slice data flow is usually implemented in the higher-performance bipolar technology. Where the gates per chip and the available chip pins are a limitation, the data flow is "sliced" vertically, e.g., into four bits per chip. The chip is provided with enough connection points for horizontal signals so the bit-slices can operate in parallel. The horizontal connection points include shift right and shift left bidirectional spill/fill pins, and pins for carry-in, carry-out, and carry lookahead.

The remainder of the chapter covers the microprogramming of a bit-slice data flow. The bit-slice is a local memory-based data flow. We introduce bit-slice technology as required for the system data flow and sequencer. Additional features and parts beyond this are not covered.

The implementation of the SC-16 architecture in a bit-slice data flow is called the SC-16S. Our initial approach to the problem is in general terms. The flowcharts of Figs. 6.14-6.18 describe the job to be done. Now we must learn the building blocks out of which the design is built. First consider the general concept of a 16-bit data flow organized around a local RAM. The 16-bit sliced data flow is a higher-level functional unit. This *data flow component* is assembled (built up) from the 4-bit wide parts.

In our general design approach using functional units, we learn (1) the behavior of the component, (2) the connection points and how they control the behavior, and (3) how to interconnect the unit into the system. To interface this data flow component into the CPU system, we consider the main memory and IO bus interfaces, and the control unit component. The resulting integration is called the *system data flow*.

Once the top-level system data flow is designed, the control unit component can be designed either with hardwired techniques or by microprogramming. To facilitate microprogramming, control chips have been defined to handle the problem of next address determination. Such functional units are called *microprogram controllers* or *sequencers*. Our final step at the general organization level is to learn the behavior and connection points of these sequencing components. Using conditional information (status and control) and a "current" microprogram counter (μPC) address value, the sequencers deliver the next microprogram address. This address may be the next sequential address (μPC plus 1) or some other bit configuration. Given the microprogram address, a control ROM or RAM is accessed to fetch the next microinstruction.

We summarize the steps in the design as follows. Normally, steps 4 and 5 are subject to iteration.

1. Design local memory data flow from bit-slice parts.
2. Design system data flow.
3. Study microprogram sequencers.
4. Design SC-16S control flow diagrams.
5. Design the microinstructions.

6.7. DATA FLOW DESIGN WITH A LOCAL MEMORY

This section discusses the composition and timing requirements of a local memory data flow organization at a high level. We postpone the detail of how it is vertically partitioned into bit-slices.

6.7.1. The AM2903 Basic Functions and Connection Points

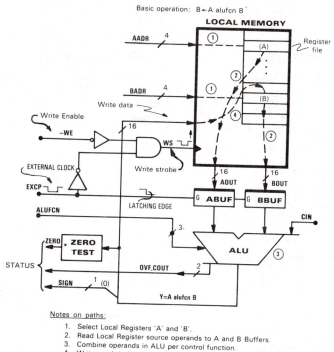

Figure 6.21. *Typical data flow cycle,* *16-bit local memory-oriented data flow.*

The general discussion describes the Am2903 bit-slice chip designed by American Micro Devices. **Figure 6.21** shows the basic elements. The data flow is organized around an ALU, and a *local memory* (LM), also called a local RAM or a local register file. The architecture's registers are implemented in local RAM. Consider a typical data flow cycle:

1. Two operands, A and B, are addressed in local memory LM.
2. Operands A and B are read out and loaded in buffer registers.
3. Operands A and B are functionally combined (add, subtract, add and shift, AND, etc.) by the ALU.
4. The result replaces the value of the B operand in LM.

The typical operation is represented by the RTN statement, where "alufcn" denotes any data transformation on the input data.

Typical op: B ← A alufcn B.

We note that the S370/M148 and S360/M25 CPU designs were early users of the local memory concept in conjunction with a microprogrammed control unit. In data flow implementations with local memory, parallel transfers are impossible because only one LM location can be written at a time. The basic system timing cycle of the S360/M25 local memory data flow used four timing points:

1. read the LM "A" source to register A,
2. read the LM "B" source to register B,
3. perform A alufcn B to register C, and
4. write the C register to the B source in LM.

In the S370/M148, the local memory was duplicated so both operands were read out at once, thus improving performance by combining points 1 and 2.

The Am2903 connection points are as follows; refer to Fig. 6.21. Input points to the local on-chip RAM include the two LM addresses, the A address (AADR) and the B address (BADR), and a local memory write enable WE control pin. The ALU receives the carry-in signal (CIN), and is controlled by the ALU function control field. The ALU data output is called Y. The ALU also delivers a status word, used by the control unit or sequencer as status information for the next address determination. Overflow signal OVF indicates two's complement arithmetic overflow. The adder carry-out signal (COUT), and the ALU output most significant bit (the sign bit SIGN) are also brought to pins. The ALU output also undergoes a "zero test", and the result appears on open-collector output signal +ZERO. The resulting ZERO signal is the wire-AND of the corresponding Y output for each data flow chip being zero. There are, of course, data input and output connection points. We discuss these items after learning what is required of them.

6.7.2. General Data Flow

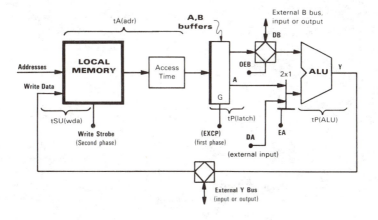

Figure 6.22. *Two-phase timing and external data buses.*

Figure 6.22 shows the data flow in block form with the location of external data input points (DA and DB), and data output points (DB and Y). The address is presented to LM, which has delay tSU(wd). Following the access time tA(adr), the word is loaded into the ABUF or BBUF register, whose output is valid following tP(lat). ALU input B enters through a bidirectional bus DB. A control point OEB determines the directionality. ALU input A permits an external data input DA. Register ABUF and input DA enter the ALU left side through a data selector governed by control point EA. The ALU delay is tP(ALU). The timing is two-phased; the first phase latches data into ABUF and/or BBUF, and the second phase writes Y bus to LM.

6.7.3. Local Memory Data Flow Timing Cycle

The data flow cycle timing delays are laid out in **Figure 6.23**. The cycle is much like that of a read-modify-write memory cycle. At time t0, the A and B addresses are valid. At t1, following memory access time tA, data is valid at the local RAM output. Valid data is delayed by tP through holding latch registers ABUF and BBUF before reaching the ALU inputs.

External clock pulse signal EXCP is the enable signal on ABUF and BBUF. Since data delays should not wait on a control signal, EXCP should "open" the holding latch register before local memory data is needed. This actually occurs at the end of the previous cycle. From t1 to t2, the latch propagation delay occurs. We can ask, why latch up operands A and B?

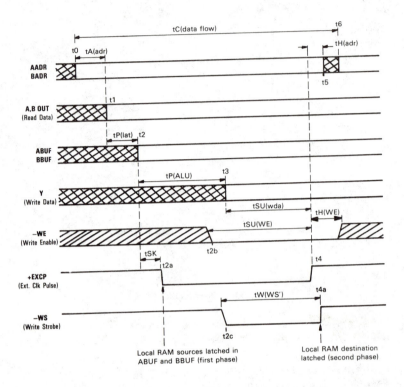

Figure 6.23. *Timing chart for local memory data flow cycle.*

The answer is that the read cycle is usually followed by the write cycle, and there is a danger that new write-data may *race through* LM back to the B operand, and corrupt the old write-data. Following t2, ABUF and BBUF can be latched. The latching of ABUF and BBUF is shown at t2a, which allows for clock skew. This completes the first phase of the two-phased timing scheme.

The delays of the second phase begin with the ALU propagation delay tP(ALU), which occurs from t2 to t3. Write enable WE must be activated (shown at t2b) by the amount of time tSU(WE) before clock EXCP has a positive transition and strobes local memory. The local memory internal write strobe WS is active when WE is active and EXCP is inactive. During the inactive period of EXCP, operands A and B remain latched, ensuring the stability of write-data before attempting the write cycle. The internal write strobe is shown activating at t2c. From t3 to t4 the local memory write-data setup time tSU(wd) (from Y to the clock) takes place. Therefore write enable WE must remain active for a specified amount of time tH(WE) following activation of EXCP. From t4 to t5, the hold times tH(adr) of the addresses and data take place. At t4a, the trailing edge of WS, data is written to the destination location in local memory. This ends the second phase of the timing cycle.

Following the hold time which defines t5, the ALU function controls can change, and new addresses AADR and BADR can be presented to local memory to begin paying the access time tA for the first phase of the next data flow cycle. The nonzero amount of delay required for new addresses (and control signals) to stabilize or become valid is shown from t5 to t6. The cycle time tC is from t0 to t6. This timing analysis demonstrates the delay sequence and indicates the race-through problem which requires the holding latches A and B. The holding latches and the two-phased timing scheme could be avoided if the local memory behaved as edge-triggered memory elements.

Table 6.5 shows some parameters from the AM2903 chip, as it appears in [8]. The ALU delay is a function of the number of bit-slice chips, and the delay of the carry look-ahead unit. The numbers are "typical" delays; we double the result as an estimate of the worst-case delay. A "typical" cycle time of 150 ns seems likely; therefore doubling this value suggests a cycle time of 300 ns.

Table 6.5.
Timing Parameters, 16–bit Am2903 Data Flow

Parameter	*"Typical" Value (ns)*	
tA(adr) − tP(lat)	35	(own estimate)
tSU(wd)	9	
tSU(WE)	15	
tW(WS')min	15	
tH(adr)	−3	
tH(WE)	0	

6.8. A DATA FLOW FROM THE AM2903 CHIP

The previous section covered the concept of a local memory data flow, and its basic timing cycle. This section covers the Am2903 chip in more detail, and builds up a 16-bit data flow from the basic 4-bit wide part.

6.8.1. The Personalization of the Am2903 Chip

Three applications of the Am2903 chip are distinguished, as determined by the significance of the four bits of the data word assigned to the chip. The leftmost four bits of the data word are assigned to the *most significant slice* (MSS). The rightmost four bits are assigned to the *least significant slice* (LSS). The 4-bit slices assigned to the middle of the data word are *intermediate slices* (IS).

The MSS chip delivers the high-order carry-out bit COUT, the overflow bit OVF and the sign bit SIGN. It also provides the leftmost fill/spill bits for shift operations. For arithmetic shifts (asl or asr) the sign bit is not involved in the shift. The LSS chip receives the low-order carry-in bit and the rightmost fill/spill bits for shifting operations. The LSS chip also receives the active "add one" input on an incrementation. The LSS chip plays a special role in multiplication and division algorithms. In the IS/LSS chips, the pins which correspond to the MSS chip connection points SIGN and OVF are redefined to the group generate (G) and group propagate (P) connection points needed for interconnection to the carry lookahead circuit.

The Am2903 chips are "personalized" through the use of two active low pins, called LSS and MSS. For the MSS chip, the MSS pin is tied low (to ground) and the LSS pin is tied high (to +5 volts). For the IS chip, both the LSS and MSS pins are tied high. For the LSS chip, the LSS pin is tied low, and the MSS pin is redefined to be a chip output useful for implementing an extended local memory external to the Am2903 chips. The Am2903 chip permits the external memory chips to extend the capacity of the local registers beyond the 16 which are on the chip. The DA and DB inputs are used when extended memory is the source. Our design does not use external memory.

6.8.2. The Am2903: More Detail

A block diagram of an Am2903 chip is shown in **Figure 6.24**. The ALU outputs labeled G and P indicate that the chip is employed in an IS or LSS position. We note two variations from the data flow of Fig. 6.21. First, a shifter is in the main data path following the ALU output F. The shifter is capable of passing value F straight, or shifted right one bit, or shifted left one bit. In the event of a *right shift,* bidirectional pin SIOR is an output and delivers the spill bit value, whereas bidirectional pin SIOL is an input and accepts the fill bit value. For a *left shift,* the roles of the bidirectional pins are reversed.

A second variation of the basic data flow is the existence of register Q, which is not part of local RAM. The Q register holds the least significant half of a double length floating point word which is to be normalized. For the multiplication algorithm, Q holds the multiplier. At the initialization for the divide algorithm, Q holds either a zero or the low-order half of a double length dividend. At the end of the division algorithm, Q contains the single length quotient word. The Q register can be shifted concurrently with ALU output F. The Am2903 can perform a multiply step, divide step,

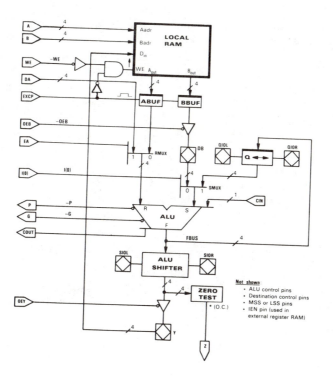

Figure 6.24. *Data flow of Am2903 as an intermediate bit-slice.*

or normalization step. These steps are "special functions" specified by a control field input combination to the chip. The SC-16 architecture is too simple to make use of the multiplication and division power the Q register provides to the Am2903 chip. We do not use the Q register, or describe it in further detail.

6.8.3. The Am2903 Major Activities

We now examine the main data loop, where four control activities are of interest:

1. selection of the ALU source data,
2. selection of the ALU function,
3. determination of the shifter function on ALU output F, and
4. Q register operations.

Left ALU data input R is selected through data selector RMUX by control point EA (the name means enable A). The two RMUX data sources are an off-chip input value from bus DA, and the ABUF latch value. Right ALU data input S is selected through SMUX by control point I(0), a bit of the primary input control bus I(0-8). The two SMUX data sources are the Q register and the bidirectional bus DB. Bidirectional bus DB is controlled by input connection OEB (the name means output enable B). If OEB is active (the connection point is active-low), the SMUX source DB comes from BBUF; otherwise the value on bus DB comes from outside the chip. When OEB is active, BBUF is driven off the chip through connection points DB.

The ALU function is determined by 4-bit control field I(1-4). The control of the ALU shifter and the Q register operation is combined into one control field I(5-8). Not all concurrency implicit in the data flow is available to the designer because of these control pin limitations. The designers of this chip have provided most of the common microoperations

---

Table 6.6.
ALU Function Control Field I(1–4)

Code (hex)	ALU Function
0	Special Function (Note 1)
1	S minus R (Note 2)
2	R minus S (Note 2)
3	R plus S plus CIN
4	S plus CIN
5	S′ plus CIN
6	R plus CIN
7	R′ plus CIN
8	0 (output forced low)
9	R′•S
A	R′ exclusive-OR S
B	R exclusive-OR S
C	R•S
D	(R+S)′
E	(R•S)′
F	R+S

Note 1: The *Special Function* decode redefines the decodes of the ALU Shifter control field to perform special operations used in multiplication, division and normalization.

Note 2: With an end-around-carry, this becomes 1's complement subtraction. With a forced CIN the operation is 2's complement subtraction.

through encodings of these two 4-bit control fields. The ALU functions are I(1-4) shown in **Table 6.6**.

In Table 6.6, code 0 is a special function which *redefines* field I(5-8). For Table 6.6 combinations other than the special function, control field I(5-8) is decoded as shown in **Table 6.7**. With only 16 control bit combinations, the ALU shifter and Q register functions are not independent. Table 6.7 is a compromise which attempts to include all useful function combinations.

Table 6.7.		
ALU Shifter and Q Register Control Field		

Code	ALU Shifter	Q Register
0	Y = ashr F	Hold
1	Y = shr F	Hold
2	Y = ashr F	Q ← shr Q
3	Y = shr F	Q ← shr Q
4	Y = F	Hold
5	Y = F	Q ← shr Q
6	Y = F	Q ← F
7	Y = F	Q ← F
8	Y = ashl F	Hold
9	Y = shl F	Hold
A	Y = ashl F	Q ← shl Q
B	Y = shl F	Q ← shl Q
C	Y = F	Hold
D	Y = F	Q ← shl Q
E	Y = SE(F)	Hold
F	Y = F	Hold

Control point OEY determines whether or not the value of the ALU shifter output F is driven off chip through connection points Y. If OEY is active, the Y bus assumes the value of the ALU shifter output. The Y bus value is available as write-data for the local memory. If OEY is inactive, external Y bus data may be written to local memory. The value on the active-low write enable control point WE determines whether or not local memory is written.

The pin-out names for the Am2903 chip are shown in **Figure 6.25**. The SIGN and OVF status outputs for the MSS chip are shown in parentheses, and are redefinitions of the G and P output pins.

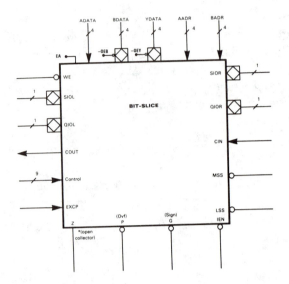

Figure 6.25. *Pin-outs of Am2903 bit-slice chip.*

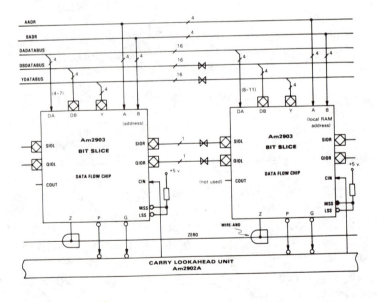

Figure 6.26. *Interchip connections for external data paths of Am2903.*

6.8.4. Interconnecting the Am2903 Chip

Consider the interconnection of four Am2903 chips to form a 16-bit local memory data flow. **Figure 6.26** shows IS positions (4-7) and (8-11) interconnected in parallel. The data connections are shown at the top of the block for each chip. 4-bit local memory address buses AADR and BADR fan out to each Am2903 chip, feeding the respective 4-bit A and B address input pins. Unidirectional bus DADATA is 16 bits wide, and is the name of the interconnection servicing four 4-bit data fields on the chip connection points called DA. Each of the 4-bit data fields of interconnection bus DADATA feeds the respective DA input points of an Am2903 chip. Similarly, 16-bit bidirectional buses DBDATA and YDATA are each assigned one 4-bit data field of each of the four chips, using respective connection points DB and Y.

The ALU shifter pins SIOL and SIOR are bidirectional, and are interconnected as shown in Fig. 6.26. The Q register bidirectional right and left spill/fill shifter pins are interconnected in the same way. The ALU carry signals can be handled in one of two ways. In the ripple carry method, the carry-out of a lower-position chip feeds the carry-in of the next higher-position chip. Ripple carry adders are extinct in all but least-cost systems, because the resulting large minimum cycle time based on a worst-case delay analysis is not an efficient trade-off. The carry lookahead technique considerably reduces cycle time at a very modest additional cost.

Carry lookahead chip Am2902 is designed for use with the Am2903 bit-slice chips. It accepts the active-low group generate (G) and propagate (P) signals, and delivers the chip active-high CIN signals for a 16-bit (4-chip) data flow.

For branching purposes, a useful test is the detection of a zero data value resulting from a data operation. The open-collector Z output pin of each chip is active (high) if the 4-bit output of the ALU shifter is zero. These outputs are wire-ANDed to provide a status signal called ZERO which is active only when the 16-bit data word is zero.

The result of our bottom-up design effort is the more powerful functional unit shown in **Figure 6.27**: a 16-bit data flow, composed of the properly interconnected four data flow slices and the lookahead chip. The like control signals of each chip are interconnected. Signals SIOL and COUT are respectively the SIOL and COUT pins of the MSS chip, and signals SIOR and CIN are respectively the SIOR and CIN pins of the LSS chip. Signals OVF and SIGN are the signals of the same name of the MSS chip. Signal ZERO is the wire-AND of the open collector Z pins of the individual chips. A pull-up resistor is required for this signal line.

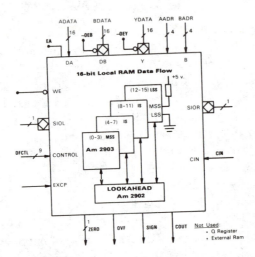

Figure 6.27. *Higher-level view of interconnected 16-bit sliced data flow.*

6.9. THE SYSTEM DATA FLOW

We now have the 16-bit Am2903-based data flow (Fig. 6.27) as a building block, and we must next determine the system data flow. We break this job down into three tasks which are iterated to find a solution:

1. assign the SC-16 architecture registers,
2. integrate the Am2903 data flow into the system, and
3. test system data paths against the microoperations.

To provide the scope of this problem, an architectural view of the SC-16 is shown in **Figure 6.28.** We show the CPU interfaces to main memory and to an IO bus.

6.9.1. Assignment of the Architecture Registers

For the first task, we deal with data registers AC, IA, and IB, and program counter register PC. These registers are shown in Fig. 6.28 as part of the data flow. Instruction register IR is shown with the control unit. The data flow registers are implemented in the local memory. The notation AC now denotes LM[AC]. Similarly the PC is assigned a 4-bit address in local memory, and is LM[PC]. In addition, a "work" register called MD (for memory data) is assigned a location in LM.

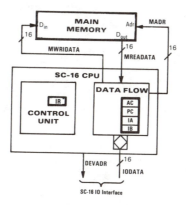

Figure 6.28. *Data and address paths for the SC-16 architecture.*

6.9.2. Integrating the Am2903 into the System

For the second task, the system busing functions must be assigned to the DA, DB, and Y connection points of Fig. 6.27. We propose an interconnection scheme, and then test the scheme against the microoperations which use the system interconnections. For the SC-16S design we employ a single bidirectional system bus. Data bus SDATA and address bus MADR serve both for main memory and IO. A single system bus is commonly found in cost-conscious systems. The architecture does not consume main memory capacity by using the memory-mapped IO technique. The RD and WR control strobes which activate main memory are distinct from the strobes OUTSTR and INSTR which control use of the system bus for IO purposes.

The result of the system interconnection exercise is shown in **Figure 6.29.** As in the SC-16H, the memory write-data MWRIDATA bus and the address MADR bus are buffered by registers MW and MA respectively. Two output buses, Y and DB, are available as pins of the Am2903 data flow.

6.9.3. System Buses for Microoperations

The system interconnections of Fig. 6.29 must support the data transfers required of the system architecture. The task is to test the data paths against the microoperations implied by the SC-16 architecture. This exercise helps us determine which Am2903 data flow output point should feed data bus SDATA, which output point should feed MW, and which output point should feed the address to MA.

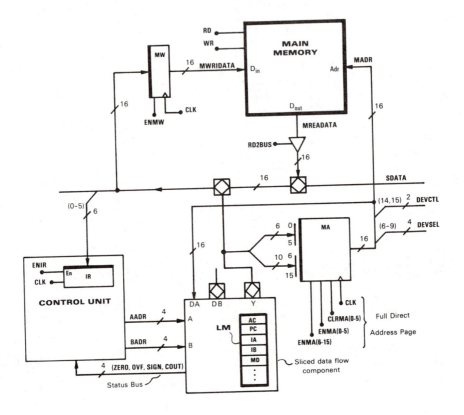

Figure 6.29. *System data paths for the SC-16S.*

We must meet the data flow specification on the one hand and the system requirements on the other. For example, output connection Y can produce the result of an arithmetic operation, whereas output connection DB can only receive its data from local RAM. On the system side, the microprograms of Figs. 6.14 through 6.18 show that MA most often receives data which has been operated on by the ALU in the same cycle. In other words, MA can receive data from ALU output Y, which suggests that the Y output connection feed MA. If the full direct address is to be placed in MA from the read-data bus as for the SC-16M and SC-16H, then memory MREADATA should also feed the MA. We let MREADATA and the Y output connection feed the same bus, called SDATA.

Let us stretch our imagination and think of ways of increasing concurrency. Since SDATA is connected to the ALU output, the ALU is idle when SDATA is being used for another purpose. We could improve system concurrency if the ALU were capable of operating independently of the

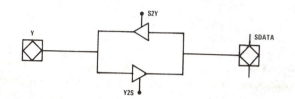

Figure 6.30. *Possible isolation of SDATA bus from Y pins of data flow component.*

SDATA bus (to which ALU output Y is connected). We can isolate the Y connection from the SDATA bus with additional tri-state drivers as shown in **Figure 6.30.** The tri-state drivers of Fig. 6.30 increase system cost and bus delays, so we do not pursue uncoupling the ALU output from the SDATA bus.

To improve concurrency, we might also be tempted to feed register MW from the DB connection point of the Am2903. However, the DB output does not provide an ALU result on the same cycle, which is disadvantageous for the ISZ instruction. Recall that the ISZ operand is incremented before it is written back to memory. Consequently, we let the SDATA bus feed MW, which allows MW to receive the incremented operand on the same data flow cycle.

Fig. 6.29 shows address register MA split into two parts, MA(0-5) (the page address) and MA(6-15) (the offset). This arrangement of the MA register implements the calculation of the full direct address page FDAP in MA(0-5). (The operation of the MA control signals to load FDAP is covered in Chapter 5, and we do not cover that again here.)

Note also that the MA output can feed back to otherwise "free" input connection point DA of the data flow. In this way, the index can be added to the full direct address to obtain the effective address for the indexed address mode. No use is planned for bidirectional pins DB of the data flow component. The DB connection is intended for expanding the capacity of on-chip local memory with off-chip RAM. The IO interface buses DEVSEL and DEVCTL receive the instruction device select field, and device control field from MA register fields (6-9) and (14-15) respectively.

On I-fetch, instruction register IR of the control unit receives the opcode and address mode portions of the instructions. Also, the Am2903 local memory A and B address connection points are fed by buses AADR and BADR from the control unit.

6.9.4. Summary of SC-16S Data Part

We summarize the SC-16S design at this intermediate stage, where the design of the data part has reached a point of relative stability. The dominant cost and performance factor in a computer is usually the data flow, so we dealt with this aspect first. We have designed the SC-16S to use the local RAM oriented data flow in the context of the Am2903 slice. The bit-slice timing is shown in Fig. 6.23. The detail of the Am2903 has been given (Fig. 6.24), and four Am2903s have been integrated into a 16-bit data flow component (Fig 6.24). This data flow component has been interfaced to main memory and the IO (Fig. 6.29). Registers MW and MA interface to memory and appear outside the sliced data flow. Except for the IR in the control unit, the other registers are assigned to local memory. The data part of Fig. 6.29 serves as a tentative result or "first-cut" against which the microoperations which interpret the SC-16 instruction set can be designed.

We assume that main memory can deliver read-data into the Y input connection point with the proper setup time tSU(wd) on the cycle following a read request. Each microinstruction controls one data flow cycle. The control points of the data flow are described in Tables 6.6 and 6.7. Two action fields of the microinstruction define the source operands AADR and BADR. The destination operand is BADR. The action part of the microinstruction appears straightforward, and its design is postponed.

Now we must consider the next address part of the control unit. Tables 6.1 and 6.2 summarize next address techniques. Recall that the next address design for the SC-16M made heavy use of the bring-along and the field insertion techniques. Chips called sequence controllers are available which perform the next address function.

6.10. SEQUENCE CONTROLLERS: AM2911

A dominant performance factor of a microprogrammed control unit is the next address determination and control memory access time. The next address calculation is thus in the critical path for a fast cycle time.

Before considering the SC-16S next address problem in detail, we first cover a typical *sequence controller* chip, the Am2911. A sequence controller accepts control information and delivers a next address. As with other functional units, the designer first learns the digital function, the meaning of the connection points, and the timing specifications. With this knowledge the designer either selects and properly applies the part or chooses an alternative solution for the application at hand.

In what follows, we construct the Am2911 bottom-up function by function. The Am2911 is capable of performing the following functions:

- NSA
- Branch to Immediate Target
- Subroutine Jump (Branch and save old μPC)
- Subroutine Return (Restore old μPC)
- Branch to Preloaded Target

The simplest sequence control function is the use of a microprogram counter μPC; see **Figure 6.31.** The Controller output (Address) feeds the control memory address register (CMAR). The μPC points to the next sequential instruction, and is used to load the CMAR. The μPC is incremented after its value has been used to fetch the microinstruction. The NSA technique implemented in Fig. 6.31(a) is used repeatedly for a sequence of microinstructions where no branching takes place.

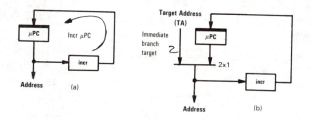

Figure 6.31. *Simple next address controllers.* (a) Next sequential address generation. (b) NSA generation with provision for immediate branching.

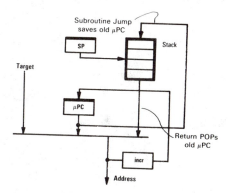

Figure 6.32. *NSA generation, provision for immediate branching, branching to subroutine with old μPC saved, and subroutine return with old μPC popped.*

When the control flow branches out of the NSA chain, a new *target address* (TA) is used to obtain the next microinstruction from control memory. Fig. 6.31(b) shows how the immediate target address of the branch function is switched to the CMAR. The new target address is also loaded to the μPC. Following instruction execution, the μPC is incremented, and the NSA technique is in force until the next branch.

A more sophisticated controller is shown in **Figure 6.32**. A subroutine jump can be performed by providing a stack to save the old μPC, as shown. The old μPC is saved on the same cycle the subroutine target address is transferred to the CMAR. At the proper subsequent time, the old μPC can be popped from the stack and transferred through the 3×1 MUX to the CMAR to effect the subroutine return.

One more technique is shown in **Figure 6.33**. The *preloaded target address* register (PTA) can be enabled on any cycle to receive an anticipated (future) target address. The PTA is loaded concurrently with the next address determination. The prestored branch (or loop-back) target address is available from PTA for use on a later cycle.

We put the above techniques together in **Figure 6.34,** which shows the basic data flow of the Am2911 sequence controller chip. Please *note* that the output labeled Y, which feeds CMAR, is the label used by the Am2911, and is not the same as pin Y of the Am2903. The chip is four bits wide and cascadable. A carry-in pin (CIN) and a carry-out pin (COUT) are provided for handling the incrementer function across chips. The ZERO input can be activated to return to address 0. This is useful in returning to the start of I-fetch if address 0 is assigned to the I-fetch "start".

The timing cycle of the Am2911 chip is shown in **Figure 6.35**. This cycle fits into the general scheme of Fig. 6.3. The μPC register and subroutine stack are edge-triggered on the positive edge of clock signal CLK.

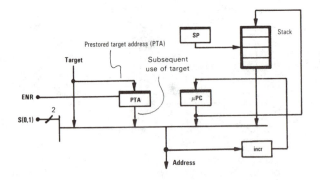

Figure 6.33. *NSA generation, provision for immediate branching, subroutine jump and return, and prestored target.*

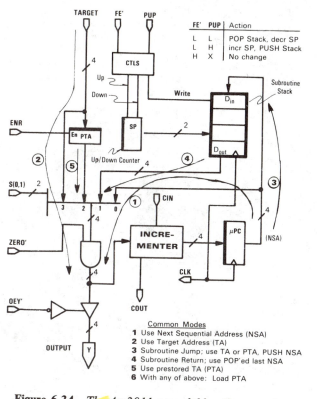

FE′	PUP	Action
L	L	POP Stack, decr SP
L	H	incr SP, PUSH Stack
H	X	No change

Common Modes
1 Use Next Sequential Address (NSA)
2 Use Target Address (TA)
3 Subroutine Jump; use TA or PTA, PUSH NSA
4 Subroutine Return; use POP′ed last NSA
5 Use prestored TA (PTA)
6 With any of above: Load PTA

Figure 6.34. *The Am2911 cascadable sequencer chip.*

At time t1, the inputs which govern the data input to the incrementer and determine the stack memory operation must be stable for time tSU(inp). The setup times for the inputs are specified on an individual basis.

At t1 we require the new microinstruction to be loaded into its holding register (see MCTL of Fig. 6.1). Following some propagation delay tP(inp), at t2 the control inputs to the Am2911 chip stabilize. Following delay tP(Y,inp), at t3 the selected next address is valid on output connection Y. There is also a propagation delay tP(Y,CLK) which must be paid from t1 before output Y is valid. Output Y becomes valid only when the longest delay (tP(inp) + tP(Y,inp) versus tP(Y,CLK)) has been paid. Once output Y has stabilized, the control memory access time begins. During this time the carry propagation delays in the incrementer can take place. At t4 the chip carry-in is shown stabilizing, and at t5 following time duration tP(C) the carry-out stabilizes. The carry-in must stabilize at some setup time tSU(CIN) before the incremented output Y value is clocked into the μPC at t6.

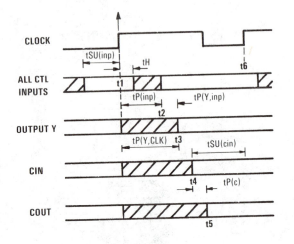

Figure 6.35. *Timing cycle of Am2911.*

Other sequence controllers perform similar functions. The Am2910 chip is similar to the Am2911; it is 12 bits wide but is not cascadable. The Am2910 can also employ the PTA register as a loop counter.

6.11. SC-16S CONTROL FLOW DIAGRAM

This section studies the interpretation of the SC-16 instruction set with the system data flow of Fig. 6.29 by creating the microprogram as a control flow diagram. The data flow capability and data flow cycle are almost fully determined at this point, so we can write *dependent* RTN statements for the actions. The RTN statements can be organized as control flow blocks in a form similar to an event schematic for each opcode and address mode; see Fig. 6.20.

In this exercise, we omit another constraint most microprogrammers have: we have not yet designed the microinstruction. In general, the microinstruction is designed by iteration. In our case, we design the control flow assuming we have the required microorders in the microinstruction. The functionality of the instruction set is simple enough to go ahead with the control flow and use the result as a basis for designing the microinstruction.

To integrate the event schematics into a control flow diagram, we face a very important problem: the next address or branching information must be added to the control flow blocks. We choose appropriate next address techniques from among the following: field insertion, subroutines, bring-along target addressing, and the NSA technique. We consider solutions such as conditional execution or delayed branching as these problems arise.

Finally, we determine the microinstruction word and ensure that action fields and next address fields have enough combinations to specify the required operations. The design is iterative: a desire to economize microinstruction bits may cause the designer to forego some concurrency.

6.11.1. SC-16S Control Flow Block

We now determine the format of the rectangular block for the control flow diagram. The action part has a line for each independent concurrency class of microoperations. Examine the system data flow of Fig. 6.29. The first concurrency class is called M for memory. Unlike the SC-16M, we assume two-way control for the memory, which needs explicit memory commands READ and WRITE. The control unit can independently cause the memory to initiate a read or a write operation. Also, unlike the SC-16M, we shall assume that the indicated memory operation is initiated early in the *next* cycle. Finally, the read or write command can be issued on the same cycle the MA or MW is loaded.

Next, consider concurrency class S, so named for the SDATA bus. We use bus SDATA only for one data source per cycle. Since SDATA is the interconnection for the Y connection point of the Am2903 data flow, the ALU output and data source for LM must also belong to this concurrency class.

The last concurrency class is called C for Control. This class involves the explicit activation of miscellaneous control signals, such as saving status values in "stat" flip-flops, or manipulating the stat values. Concurrency class C may also include actions of a conditional execution nature.

So far in this discussion, the next address part of the flowchart block merely includes a comment on how the next address should be formed. In creating the next address part of the control flow block, we must keep in mind that only values or status bits valid at the *beginning* of the cycle may be employed in generating the next address.

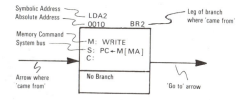

Figure 6.36. *Example of an SC-16S flowchart block* governing a data flow cycle.

Figure 6.36 shows an example of a control flow block for the SC-16S. Line M is a write command which is issued at the beginning of the next cycle. At the end of the current cycle, the MW is loaded with the write-data. Moreover, the current cycle also ends a read operation, because read-data (RD) is loaded to PC at the end of the cycle.

6.11.2. I-Fetch

We now begin the task of creating the control flow diagram for the SC-16S implementation. The challenge is to achieve a reasonable cost, but not to take too many needless cycles to execute the instructions. When in doubt, we *begin at the beginning,* which in this case is I-fetch. We require the MA to be already loaded with the value of the instruction address, and the read command to have been given. The control flow diagram for I-fetch is shown in **Figure 6.37**. The loading of the MA with the PC value is not incorporated into the execution of all instructions. Fig. 6.37 shows a "prestart" microinstruction which loads the MA and initiates the read operation.

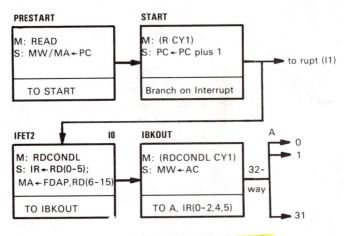

Figure 6.37. *I-fetch for SC-16S.*

In the I-fetch cycle START, the M field contains the comment (R CY1) as a reminder that the first data flow cycle of the read operation is underway. In this cycle, the PC is incremented. An interrupt test can also be made, as shown in the next address part for the START control flow block.

For microinstruction IFET2, consider first the SDATA bus. Main memory delivers read-data to the SDATA bus. The high-order six bits go to the IR register in the control unit. An auxiliary circuit determines the *full direct address page* (FDAP) and loads the direct address into MA.

Next, we explain the meaning of RDCONDL on line M of IFET2. The read-data bus which transfers the instruction becomes valid only toward the end of the current (IFET2) cycle. Consequently, only at the end of the *next* cycle can the opcode and address mode be "broken out" by the next address generation circuits of the control unit. Unless another approach is taken, we only know on the cycle *after* the opcode break-out whether a read or write command should be issued. To avoid memory idle time at this critical time, an alternate approach is to issue a read command *conditioned* on the instruction information (opcode and address mode) on the SDATA bus. The microorder is called RDCONDL, meaning "read conditional". An auxiliary circuit determines from the opcode and address mode on SDATA whether a read command can be issued. **Table 6.8** shows the conditions for issuing the read command.

	Table 6.8. RDCONDL Conditions for Issuing a Read Command	
Opcode	*Address Modes*	
AND	DIRECT, INDIRECT	
ADD	DIRECT, INDIRECT	
LAC	DIRECT, INDIRECT	
SAC	INDIRECT	
JMP	INDIRECT	
SRJ	INDIRECT	
ISZ	DIRECT, INDIRECT	

In the indexed address mode, it is pointless to issue a read command because the MA register has the wrong address. If the address mode is direct, then for instructions SAC and SRJ the proper command is write. For JMP Direct, it is premature to issue the read command, because this would be fetching the next instruction without testing for an interrupt. The fetch of the next instruction should either pass through the microinstruction located at START, or provide for testing the interrupt system.

The microinstruction controlling the third I-fetch cycle is the control flow block called IBKOUT. The major function of this cycle is to break out the opcode and address mode. The MW is loaded from AC, in anticipation of the opcode SAC.

6.11.3. Execution of AND, ADD, and LAC

The instructions AND, ADD, and LAC (opcodes 0, 1, and 2) all use the AC as the first operand and acquire the second operand from memory. These instructions are interpreted as shown in **Figure 6.38.** The control flow diagram for the instruction AND is in Fig. 6.38(a). Blocks ANDIND, ANDIA and ANDIB place the effective address of the operand into MA and set up the memory read operation. These three blocks reconverge to block ANDCY1 for the first cycle of the read operation. In cycle AND-DIR, the memory read-data RD is the operand value, which is delivered to the SDATA bus, from where it is written into the MD location of the data flow. On the following cycle (ANDEX), the operand is ANDed with the AC. Following the ANDEX cycle, the prestart cycle is the branch target.

The ADD instruction is similar to AND; the ALU operation of the final microinstruction is an ADD instead of an AND. See Fig. 6.38(b).

The operand fetch for the LAC instruction is the same as in Fig. 6.38(a). However since no ALU operation is needed, the instruction

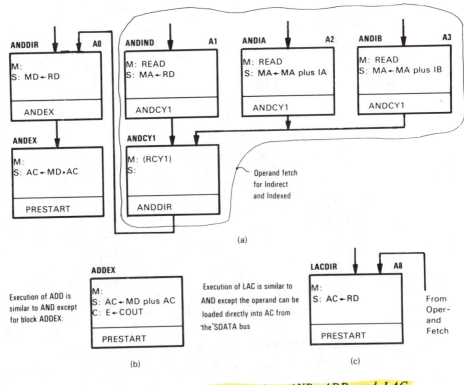

(a)

(b)

(c)

Figure 6.38. *Flowcharts for instructions AND, ADD, and LAC.*
(a) Execution of AND. (b) Execution of ADD. (c) Execution of LAC.

execution can be completed in cycle LACDIR, one cycle earlier than for AND and ADD. Cycle LACDIR is shown in Fig. 6.38(c).

6.11.4. The SAC, JMP, SRJ, and ISZ Instructions

Figure 6.39 illustrates the SAC instruction. In the SAC direct address case, the MA and MW registers are already loaded. Here, the SAC Direct instruction could benefit from a microorder which causes the write operation to be initiated early in the cycle.

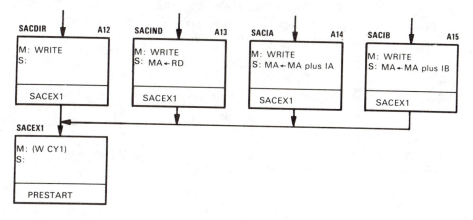

Figure 6.39. *Flowchart for SAC instruction execution.*

The control flow diagram for the JMP instruction is shown in **Figure 6.40.** For the JMP Direct instruction, the next instruction address is in MA. Then the address is routed to the PC and MW. For JMP Indirect, the next instruction address appears on the READATA bus from memory, and is routed to the PC, MW, and MA registers. These microinstructions are followed by START. For JMP Indexed, we cannot go directly to START, because the next instruction address is calculated in the ALU, and must go to PC as well as MA. The value of the BADR is the only address which can be written at the end of the cycle. BADR contains either IA or IB. The indexed JMP thus requires an extra cycle to write the new PC.

The SRJ instruction appears in **Figure 6.41.** For SRJ Direct, the MA contains the proper value but the old PC value must be transferred to MW for writing. The SRJ Indirect instruction could benefit from a concurrent path from PC to MW. As it is, the SDATA bus must be used to transfer read-data to the MA. Similarly, SRJ Indexed is executed by calculating the effective address and leaving it in MA. The indirect and indexed SRJ instructions reconverge to SRJ Direct once the effective address is in MA.

At SRJEX1, the effective address plus 1 is placed in the PC, and I-fetch is begun at the prestart microinstruction.

The ISZ instruction is shown in **Figure 6.42.** For the ISZ Indirect and ISZ Indexed instructions, the operand must be fetched after the effective address is obtained. These instructions reconverge to ISZCY1 where the first cycle of the read operation takes place. The microinstruction sequence then reconverges to ISZDIR for receiving the operand from memory. Next, at microinstruction ISZEX1, the operand is incremented and rewritten to MW, and a write command is issued. At this time, if the result of the increment is 0, line C indicates that a stat flip-flop named "C" is set. In the following microinstruction ISZEX2, this value (STATC) is added to the PC. If the memory operand was incremented to 0 on the previous cycle, then PC is incremented, causing a skip. Otherwise no skip occurs.

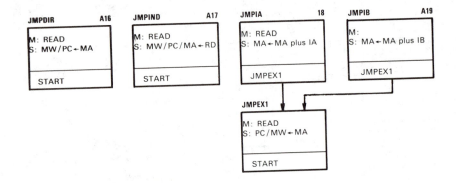

Figure 6.40. *Flowchart for JMP instruction execution.*

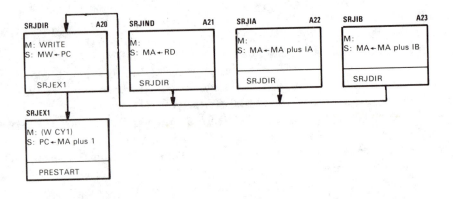

Figure 6.41. *Flowchart for SRJ instruction.*

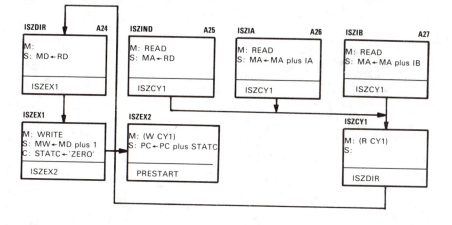

Figure 6.42. *Flowchart for ISZ instruction.*

6.11.5. The Input/Output Instructions

The OP7 instructions are broken out as shown on the top row of **Figure 6.43.** In I-fetch, we already broke out bits IR(4) and IR(5); see Fig. 6.37, block IBKOUT. The 2-way branch on IR bit 3 distinguishes between register-reference and IO instructions. The individual register-reference instructions are executed in control flowchart blocks F0 through F7, G0 through G7, and H0 and H1. These blocks are reached by multi-way branches from blocks B0, C0, and D0 on IR(6-8). For the DIO instructions, IR bit 4 distinguishes between input and output, so the microinstructions at the branch targets can execute the required DIO instruction, B1 and C1 for input, and D1 and E1 for output. The device address and control fields are already driven to the IO bus from register MA. On input, strobe INSTR is activated by line C, and data on SDATA is loaded into the AC. On output, strobe OUTSTR is activated. The contents of the AC are placed on the SDATA bus via pins of bus Y of the data flow component.

6.11.6. Register-Reference Instructions

The register-reference instructions are shown in **Figure 6.44.** To provide design variety, we do not employ conditional execution here as we did for the SC-16M. We break out the register-reference instructions for interpretation by microinstruction. Some special control microorders are required for the CLE and STE instructions. Instruction SPA, which skips on AC positive, causes the complement of SIGN (bit AC(0)) to be stored

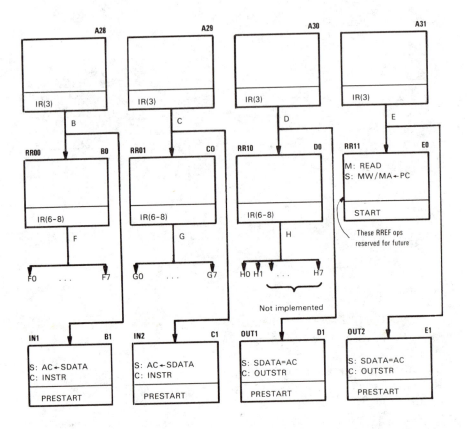

Figure 6.43. *DIO/RR opcode break-out and IO instructions.*

in the STATC flip-flop. (In microinstruction SPAEX, "nd" denotes "no destination".) Next, the microinstruction branches to ISZEX2 where the value in STATC is added to the PC as desired by the skip function. Register-reference instructions SZA and SZE are similarly executed by setting the skip condition into STATC.

On the microinstructions which rotate the AC (and the E bit), the right and left shift bidirectional input-output pins must be properly connected. The E flip-flop in the control unit provides the fill bit, and receives the spill bit value.

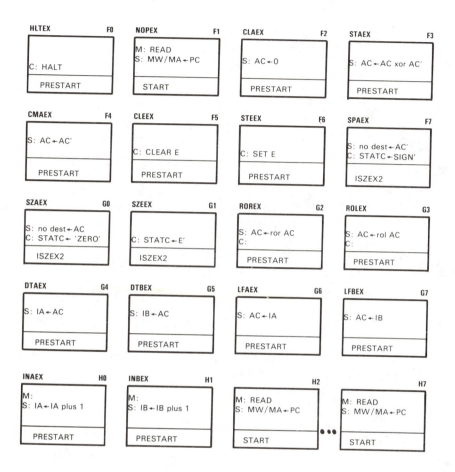

Figure 6.44. *Execution of register-reference instructions.*

6.12. SC-16S CONTROL UNIT

The *control unit* can now be specified from the control flow diagram of the SC-16S. This diagram comprises Figs. 6.37-6.44. The control unit is divided into two parts: the microinstruction action part and the next address part; see Fig. 6.1.

6.12.1. SC-16S Action Part

We first consider the SC-16S action part, shown in **Figure 6.45**. A 2-bit *memory control* action field (bits 0 and 1) controls the memory. The field would provide four microorders: no op, read, write, and conditional execution microorder RDCONDL.

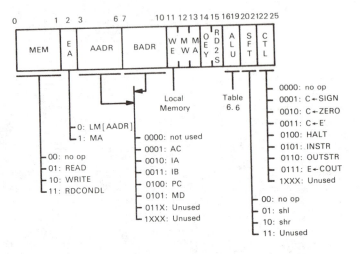

Figure 6.45. *Action fields of SC-16S microinstruction.*

The first ALU operand, *ALU input R,* is the RMUX output value (see Fig. 6.24), selected by Am2093 input point EA. The two data sources for RMUX are (1) the Am2903 connection point DA, for which MA is the off-chip source, and (2) the ABUF register. The ABUF register is loaded from LM from AADR. A 1-bit action field EA (bit 2), if active, selects the DA input. Otherwise, RMUX passes the value of the register indicated by the 4-bit address field (bits 3-6) called AADR.

The second ALU operand, *ALU input S,* is specified by the 4-bit field (bits 7-10) called BADR. This LM register also is the destination of the SDATA bus if SDATA is to be loaded to one of the data flow registers.

Three 1-bit fields (bits 11-13) define the *SDATA destinations:* none, one, or more destinations for SDATA. These are the data flow LM, the MW register, and the MA register. The action field bits are called WE, ENMW, and ENMA respectively.

Two 1-bit fields (bits 14-15) define the *SDATA bus source:* OEY and RD2SDATA. When "on", the first bit causes the data flow Y output to drive the SDATA bus. When "on", the second bit causes memory REA-DATA to drive the SDATA bus. When both bits are off, an IO device may place data on the bus. Both bits should not be "on" at the same time.

Corresponding to AM2903 control input field I(1-4), we connect the 4-bit *ALU function* field (bits 16-19) of the microinstruction. See Table 6.6 for the meaning of each combination.

The 2-bit microinstruction field (bits 20-21) defines four microorders for the ALU output *shift function:* "none", "shl", "shr", and an "unused" combination. The microorders are easily encoded to derive an acceptable combination of the data flow ALU shifter and Q register control inputs defined by Table 6.7.

The 4-bit microinstruction field (bits 22-25) controls the *miscellaneous control functions.* The control flow diagram shows seven such functions:

- STATC←SIGN
- STATC←ZERO
- STATC←E′
- Halt
- INSTR
- OUTSTR
- E←COUT

Of course, most of the time none of these microorders is being performed. This requires an eighth microorder: a "no op". To provide for expansion we defined a 4-bit control field, leaving eight unused microorders.

6.12.2. SC-16S Next Address Part

An important part of control unit design concerns how to obtain the address of the next microinstruction. Sequence control is achieved by the next address calculation. If the sequence does not have a conditional branch, then one of two techniques can be used to determine the next address: the next sequential address (NSA) technique or bring-along.

The control flow diagram shows many instances of reconvergence, which imply unconditional branches. Since we can always "bring along" the next sequential instruction, we choose the bring-along technique for all microinstruction sequences which do not contain a conditional branch.

We next search the control flow diagrams we have generated and list the branching conditions. The search uncovers the following branching conditions:

- Interrupt Request
- IR(0-2,4,5)
- IR(3)
- IR(6-8)

The SC-16 instructions are relatively simple and a subroutine stack for microinstruction addresses is not needed. Also, with a provision for an unconditional branch (bring-along), counter μPC is not needed. The primary advantages in using the Am2911 chip for next address generation are not present in the SC-16S application.

We choose an 8-bit address size, and use a 9-bit next address field. For an unconditional branch, one bit indicates the full bring-along mode.

When not in full bring-along mode, a 3-bit field indicates the conditional branch type. The conditional branches are handled by field insertion into the low-order CMAR address bits. The other five bits in the next address field are capable of being inserted into the CMAR higher-order bit positions.

6.13. PERFORMANCE COMPARISON

We have now implemented the SC-16 architecture three times, and it is interesting to discover what can be learned from three different approaches. A good first comparison is to find out how many data flow cycles it takes to execute each instruction. This exercise has already been done for the SC-16H, and we repeat the result in **Table 6.9.**

Table 6.9. SC-16H Instruction Timings (Data Flow Cycles)			
Op	*Direct*	*Indexed*	*Indirect*
ADD	5	6	7
AND	5	6	7
LAC	5	6	7
SAC	4	5	6
JMP	3	3	5
SRJ	5	6	6
ISZ	7	8	9
Reg	4	–	–
DIO	4	–	–

The flowcharts which define the SC-16 instruction execution for the microprogrammed versions can be studied in order to determine the data flow cycles required to execute each instruction; see **Table 6.10.**

The performance "winner" is the hardwired version of Table 6.9. The SC-16H is faster in terms of data flow cycles per execution. The performance advantage of the SC-16H over the SC-16M (which has the same data flow) illustrates that the microprogrammed approach can only lose to a hardwired approach. The primary performance advantage of the hardwired approach is the availability of the conditional information during the current data flow cycle. The hardwired version was able to receive the instruction on one cycle, and in the direct and indirect cases turn the effective address back to main memory. In both microprogrammed versions we

Table 6.10.
SC-16M and SC-16S Instruction Timings (Data Flow Cycles)

Op	SC-16M Direct	SC-16M Indexed	SC-16M Indirect	SC-16S Direct	SC-16S Indexed	SC-16S Indirect
ADD	6	8	8	6	8	8
AND	6	8	8	6	8	8
LAC	6	8	8	6	8	8
SAC	5	6	6	6	6	6
JMP	4	4	5	4	5	4
SRJ	6	6	6	6	7	7
ISZ	7	9	9	7	9	9
REG	5	–	–	7	–	–
DIO	5	–	–	6	–	–

were able to do the same, but only by means of the hardwired auxiliary circuits. Otherwise, the hardwired version would be probably even more dramatic in its performance advantage relative to the microprogrammed versions. Special-purpose hardware has boosted the performance of the microprogrammed versions by about one data flow cycle out of seven cycles.

Between the SC-16M which used the SC-16H data flow, and the SC-16S which used a bit-slice data flow, the performance comparison on a data flow cycle basis gives a very slight advantage to the SC-16M. Most of the instructions take the same number of data flow cycles to execute.

There is also a performance penalty in data flow cycle time between the hardwired and microprogrammed versions of an architecture. In the microprogrammed versions, there is typically a longer time delay from the start of the cycle to the point when the control signals which gate data to the ALU stabilize. As a result, in a given technology, the hardwired version probably is capable of being cycled at a faster rate.

6.14. SUMMARY

In this chapter we have covered the design of microprogrammed control units. When the instruction set is relatively complex, microprogramming offers a cost-effective approach to the design of the computer control unit.

Microprogrammed control is an alternative to hardwired control. For the purposes of instruction interpretation and cost-effective performance, the design of the *next address* calculation function of the microprogrammed control unit is a major consideration. Sequence controller chips are convenient when the control algorithm has many 2-way branches. The task of instruction interpretation invites the use of n-way branching, where n may be as large as 32. One can always use sequences of 2-way branches to achieve the effect of an 8-way to 32-way branch; however a performance penalty must be paid.

In this chapter we have treated microprogramming from the view of implementation. The action part of the microinstruction generally presents few problems. The next address part is critical to system performance. More cycles are required to interpret a specific instruction set if the microinstruction has less specialized branching capability. We studied a sequence controller for general-purpose use, but did not use it in the SC-16S design. Special hardware auxiliary circuits which "do the right thing" (i.e., conditional execution) can reduce considerably the number of data flow cycles required for instruction interpretation. In the SC-16, the three versions we have implemented have all benefited from an auxiliary circuit to calculate the full direct address page (FDAP).

Several advantages accrue to microprogrammed systems. The control unit organization is well structured, which increases the flexibility to handle changes during the debugging phase. Microprogramming is not a solution to *all* changes; some problems require hardwired solutions. In many cases, different microprograms can be loaded into control memory to perform emulation, i.e., to interpret various instruction sets. Also, the design team can be divided naturally into those who microprogram the application, and those who implement the data flow and the portion of the control unit which implements the microinstruction set. With the agreed-upon microinstruction interface, the design team is partitioned into two semi-autonomous parts. Another important benefit of microprogramming is the degree of internal testing and diagnosis afforded if the system is provided with the capability of accepting and executing such microprograms from a ROM or an external device. Diagnostic microprograms can be loaded into the system to determine the location of failed circuits.

The microinstruction set also offers documentation of the control flow at a higher conceptual level than is normally available in a hardwired system. Thus, system documentation for the control unit is simplified. The control flow diagram is certainly a superior behavioral description relative to a gate-level structural description of a hardwired control unit. Control unit design at this higher level reduces development costs for the implementation of sophisticated architectures. If the microinstruction is designed with generality in mind, then more than one instruction set may be conveniently interpreted with the microprogram language. Moreover, recent systems are improving the performance of the operating system by microprogramming certain heavily used procedures.

PROBLEMS

6.1. What are the two major parts of a microinstruction, and how do they relate to a finite state machine model?

6.2. Would the vertical or the horizontal microinstruction format facilitate a faster data flow cycle? Why?

6.3. Lay out a timing cycle similar to Fig. 6.3 for the nonoverlapped case, i.e., where the fetch of the microinstruction takes place in the first part of the cycle.

6.4. Discuss the advantages and disadvantages of the microinstruction control flow diagram as a documentation technique. What items of information does a control flow block show?

6.5. Compare (similarities and differences) the microinstruction control flow diagram with:

    (a) an event schematic
    (b) a flowchart
    (c) a table of microoperations

6.6. Suppose the AND instruction of the SC-16 were replaced by the BZE instruction which is a conditional branch on zero accumulator. Modify the current SC-16 designs to reflect the change by designing the sequence of microinstruction control diagram blocks which implements this instruction.

    (a) For the SC-16M, begin with block 16 of Fig. 6.15.
    (b) For the SC-16S, begin with block A1 of Fig. 6.38.

State any necessary hardware (auxiliary circuit) assumptions.

6.7. Consider the addition of an auxiliary circuit to do conditional execution on the third I-fetch cycle of the SC-16M (block 31, Fig. 6.14). Describe how the performance can be increased, using the ADD Indexed instruction as an example to illustrate the point. Design the microinstruction control flow diagram for this instruction, beginning with block 31 of Fig. 6.14.

6.8. Suppose a decision was made to increment a μPC counter for the SC-16M for all nonbranching nonreconverging next microinstruction addresses. Discuss how implementing a μPC could reduce cost elsewhere in the control unit. Indicate the items in the following list which apply to the new overall result, in comparison to the present SC-16M design.

    (a) increases cost   (d) increases performance
    (b) decreases cost   (e) decreases performance
    (c) cost stays about same   (f) performance stays same

6.9. Discuss the addressing modes found in a microinstruction, and relate the mode to the action and/or the next address part. For each part, explain where a microinstruction indirect address capability might make sense.

6.10. Consider the instruction mix of Table 5.P.1. Determine the mean instruction execution time, in data flow cycles, for the SC-16M and SC-16S. Identify the major source of the performance difference.

6.11. Your manager has decided to use the Am2911 sequence controller for implementing the next address function for the SC-16M. You have the design responsibility and can add a limited number of hardwired auxiliary circuits.

    (a)   Describe your new next address microinstruction format.

    (b)   Show the block diagram with the sequence controller.

    (c)   Give the microinstruction control diagram for the ADD Indexed instruction execution.

    (d)   Discuss the effect of the Am2911 on cost and performance.

6.12. Consider the use of a hardwired control unit with the system data flow of the SC-16S. Design the microinstruction control diagram sequence for the ADD Indexed instruction, and describe any auxiliary circuits you have assumed.

6.13. Draw a data flow cycle timing diagram for the SC-16S, to the level of Fig. 6.3, showing the SBUS delays, the Am 2903 delays, and the microprogram control unit delays. Show the main memory cycle and the control memory cycle.

6.14. Consider control flow block START for the SC-16S. Discuss the technique of anticipation relative to loading MW with the value of the PC, in case an interrupt occurs. Could unused Am2903 connection point DB (see Fig. 6.29) be utilized here?

6.15. Define the circuit which connects microinstruction field SFT (bits 20-21) to AM2903 input control bits I(5-8). See Table 6.7. Discuss your choice of combinations of I(5-8), keeping in mind the future possibility of emulating another architecture.

6.16. Provide a block diagram of the SC-16S control unit, showing the connection points to the system data flow, the control memory, the MCTL register for the action part, the NA register for the next address part, and the next address logic.

6.17. Make a hand assignment of control memory addresses for the control flow diagrams, and show the result in the form employed for Fig. 6.19.

REFERENCES

1. M. V. Wilkes, "The Best Way to Design an Automatic Calculating Machine", *Manchester University Computer Inaugural Conference,* July 1951, 16-18.
2. M. V. Wilkes and J. B. Stringer, "Microprogramming and the Design of the Control Circuits in an Electronic Digital Computer", *Proc. Cambridge Philosophical Soc.,* 49, Part 2, 1953, 230-238.
3. S. G. Tucker, "Microprogram Control for System/360", *IBM Systems Journal,* v. 6, n. 4, 1967, 222-241.
4. J. Craig Mudge, "Design Decisions Achieve Price/Performance Balance in Mid-range Minicomputers", *Computer Design,* v. 16, n. 8, August 1977, 87-96.
5. A. K. Agrawala and T. G. Rauscher, *Foundations of Microprogramming,* Academic Press, New York, 1976.

6. B. R. S. Buckingham, W. C. Carter, W. R. Crawford, and G. A. Nowell, "The Controls Automation System", *Sixth Annual Symposium on Switching Theory and Logical Design*, October 1965, 279.

7. Samir Husson, *Microprogramming Principles and Practices*, Prentice-Hall, Englewood Cliffs, NJ, 1970.

8. John Mick and James Brick, *Bit-slice Microprocessor Design*, McGraw-Hill, New York, 1980.

APPENDIX

A

A COURSE OUTLINE WITH A DESIGN PROJECT

A.1. INTRODUCTION

The author has given courses in computer design based on the material in this book. We provide an outline of a beginning graduate level two-credit one quarter course (20 lecture hours). Such a course is considered to be a minimum exposure to computer design. The course provides for midterm and final exams, and more importantly a **design project.** The course outline, project, and grading method presented here were developed over several years at the University of Santa Clara. The book itself contains more than enough material for a three-hour one-semester course.

The course can be taught by anyone with a good background in digital systems, and who has participated in at least a "paper design" project. A course which teaches *design* should have a design project to provide the proper focus. First, the project provides a stimulus to the student, because if properly graded and weighted, it is virtually impossible to achieve a course grade of **B** without completing the project. Second, the project serves as a challenge and stimulus to the instructor of a one quarter course, who must be well organized in order to present the material necessary to do the project. The instructor must bring the student to the point where the project is within reach. With the project requiring the instructor to present primarily useful and relevant information, the student is kept fairly active and busy during the course.

The project itself is a valuable teaching aid. Engineering design is much more than memorizing concepts and doing homework problems. We have organized the

424

project so that the student must solve subproblems at various conceptual levels. The student should see the divide-and-conquer nature of design, be sensitive to the control flow versus data flow aspects, and understand the advantage of bottom-up techniques as well as top-down techniques. These techniques are also useful in software design. Since system hardware operates on a different time scale from computer programs (nanoseconds versus milliseconds), some digital design techniques are expected to differ from software design. For example, the FORK/JOIN aspect of a system clock to coordinate data flow concurrency classes is generally missing in software.

The project requires some higher-level architectural decisions, and the student must implement the results of those decisions. We point out that more sophisticated architectures are not only more expensive to implement, they also consume more of the student's valuable design time. Thus more sophisticated architectures should not come at the expense of an incomplete design result.

People learn in plateaus. When introduced to a new course, a student may at first be confused and disoriented. Then, over a very short period of time, the jumble of information all comes together as the next plateau is reached. The project is a device which induces this plateau if the student has not yet reached it. Much of what is learned about design is learned while doing the project.

To achieve a passing grade on the project, the typical student may take over 40 hours' time. In that time, the student learns much more than mere concepts and definitions. The student undergoes a "baptism of fire", learning at the global level how all of the pieces of the design fit together in a nontrivial digital system. We feel anyone who can design a CPU can design any digital system, and this confidence should be transferred to the student.

A.2. COURSE PREREQUISITES

The course presumes an introductory knowledge of computer systems, binary number systems, and binary arithmetic. The primary prerequisite is a three-hour semester course (four-hour one quarter course) on combinational and sequential logic design. See, for example, the material in [1-3]. Combinational circuit topics include boolean algebra, popular TTL circuits, MSI components, programmed logic arrays, two-level realizations, bidirectional buses, multiplexers, adders and carry lookahead circuits. Sequential circuit topics include flip-flop types, data latch versus edge triggering, clocking and skew, minimum clock period calculations, setup and propagation delays, and the model of a sequential machine. Familiarity with assembler language programming, and operand specification techniques is useful.

A.3. SAM-16: A COMPUTER DESIGN PROJECT

In this project, the student does a *paper design* of a simple architecture called SAM-16. The project proceeds in three parts, each concentrating primarily on one conceptual level. Part 1 is at the architectural level, and is capable of being undertaken following the midterm exam (possibly after the TM-16 design of Chapter 3) and concurrent with coverage of the SC-16 design of Chapter 5. One architectural aspect concerns addressing main memory via a small partial address field in the instruction. This is a problem which has preoccupied computer architects for some time.   Part 2 is at the data flow and dependent microoperation (RTN) level, whereas Part 3 deals with a more detailed implementation level. These three parts teach the integration of the machine clock cycle, the data flow, the control unit, main memory, and the input-output bus. Since the student must communicate the design result, the importance of documentation is stressed.

The single-address architecture uses a single accumulator (AC).   Other registers include the program counter (PC), memory address register (MA), instruction register (IR), and memory data register (MD). Memory-reference instructions employ a 3-bit opcode, and must include the capability of direct and indirect addressing.   The formation of the effective address (ea) is to be described by the designer. Let M[ea] denote the memory location defined by the effective address.

The word size is 16 bits; both the data word and instruction word are this size, as are the CPU registers. Instruction addressable storage is 64K words, which needs a 16-bit address. The instruction itself requires the opcode field, an addressing mode field, and a partial direct address field. The partial direct address field of the instruction cannot itself address 64K words, because it is not 16 bits long.

Arithmetic is done in the 16-bit binary two's complement number system. The architecture as defined does not have an accumulator extension E or Link bit, nor a Carry or Overflow bit. The designer is free to define these bits as flags, if desired, and provide register-reference (RREF) instructions to manipulate them.

A.3.1. SAM-16 Instruction Set

Opcode	Name	Description
000	JMP	Unconditional Jump: PC←ea
001	SRJ	Subroutine Jump: to be defined (*Note 1*)
010	ADD	Add: AC←AC plus M[ea]
011	AND	And: AC←AC • M[ea]
100	LAC	Load AC: AC←M[ea]
101	SAC	Store AC: M[ea]←AC
110	BAP	Branch if AC Positive: AC ≥ 0: PC←ea
1110	RREF	To be defined. (*Note 2*)
1111	IOC	IO Command: to be defined. (*Note 3*)

Notes

1. Describe how subroutine jumps are performed for your SAM-16. If needed, define an RETN subop of RREF as a return.
2. Provide SAM-16 with a set of register-reference operations to do at least complement AC, AC shifts, a skip, and anything else which may be required.
3. Devise the bit configurations to control transfers to and from the AC over a common IO interface bus.

A.3.2. Project Description

This project is not a team effort, although the instructor may wish to organize it that way. As presented here, each student is to work alone, with the instructor as the *only* project consultant. (Through this consulting, the instructor gains greater insight into design, and learns a great deal about student stumbling blocks.)

The project is to be done in three parts, each having subparts. The project document should follow the subpart ordering *exactly*, properly titled. (This facilitates grading.) The subdivision of the project into parts aids the student in doing the project in a logical order. In our courses, the parts were submitted one week apart, spacing the work over the last three weeks and avoiding the last-minute rush. Each part concerns a conceptual level, which helps the student understand the multilevel nature of design. *Date all submissions.*

The structure of these three parts is independent of the particular architecture target (SAM-16). With appropriate modifications to the subparts, another architecture (or even digital system) could be substituted for the SAM-16. This particular project structure has evolved over several years of teaching the course and from providing many hours of telephone consulting to resolve student problems during the final weeks of the project. The consistent documentation, the required figures, the ordering and labeling of parts and subparts, is structured to help the student systematically attack the design.

There are many options open to the student. The architecture (and hence the design approach) can closely follow that of Chapter 5. Thus a "quick path" with very few design extras exists. On the other hand, the student will often wish to find out how a stack pointer functions, either for subroutines and/or for operand addressing. This is an "extra" and allows the student to be more creative. Thus, the project can be as simple or as complex as the student desires.

In the computer field, projects have a way of slipping schedules and missing deadlines. Some slippage is due to a failure to *freeze the design:* foolishly permitting changes in the behavioral specification up to the last minute. (Here, we do not mean debugging changes, which are changes to correct the structure to reflect the behavioral specification.) The instructor will receive requests to modify Part 1 after the student has turned it in. A suggested policy is to permit any changes which correct inconsistencies. Otherwise, only simplifying changes in the behavioral specification which advance the schedule should be permitted.

Part 1: CPU Architecture Design Level - Name, Date

1.0. Instruction Set Changes (permission of instructor required)

1.1. Effective Address
Discuss how the effective address **ea** is to be calculated, and how the address mode fields and partial direct address fields of the memory-reference instructions are used. In 1.1.1, describe, via independent RTN, how **fda** is obtained from pda. In 1.1.2, describe, via independent RTN, how **ea** is obtained from fda. Indicate the advantages of the approach. Provide an instruction format figure which shows the address mode and partial direct address fields. Provide an independent RTN statement describing each address mode. The project requires indirect addressing, but the student is free to employ other modes in the architecture.

1.2. Subroutine Jump
Explain how the subroutine jump instruction is designed and how a return from subroutine is invoked and accomplished. Include independent RTN.

1.3. Register-Reference Instructions
Describe the set of register-reference instructions implemented on your

SAM-16, subject to Note 2 of §§A.3.1. Explain anything unusual.

1.4. IO operations

Provide a figure for the IO instruction format, subject to Note 3 of §§A.3.1. Describe how programmed IO is done.

Part 2: Data Flow Design Level – Name, Date

2.1. Data Flow

Provide a block diagram of the data flow. Show all registers and functional units such as the adder, and fda formation. Show the *control points* with their names (as in Fig. 5P.1). Show bus widths, and the bits involved in any subword fields. Indicate by a triangle if the registers are edge-triggered.

2.2. Timing

A design constraint is that the memory cycle is two data flow cycles. Show timing diagrams keyed to "time 0" which describe the basic system timing and all clock signals. Indicate the timing of (1) the data flow cycle and memory cycles showing roughly where the delays (setup, propagation, access time, etc.) occur on a functional unit (ALU, MUX, etc.) basis. Show (2) the basic memory read and (3) write operation timing diagrams (see §§4.6.2), indicating on the diagram when memory address MA and data lines have valid information relative to time 0 of the data flow cycle.

2.3. I-Fetch

Provide an instruction event schematic for the I-fetch phase of instruction interpretation.

2.4. ADD Execution

Provide an event schematic of the operand fetch and execution phases of the interpretation of the ADD instruction for the *indirect* addressing mode. Indicate when and what memory is reading or writing.

2.5. SRJ Execution

Provide an event schematic of the operand fetch and execution phases of the interpretation of the SRJ instruction with *direct* addressing.

2.6. SAC Direct

If you have an address mode other than direct or indirect, show that event schematic for SAC. Otherwise, show event schematic for SAC direct.

Part 3: Detailed Logic Design Level – Name, Date

3.1. Control State Sequencing

Provide a state transition diagram for the major control states of SAM-16.

3.2. Table of Microoperations

Provide a table of microoperations or control flow diagram for:

    (a) memory-reference instructions
    (b) register-reference instructions (separate table)

3.3. Data Flow Control Signal Generation

Identify and generate the data flow control signals (do not include the IO or interrupt details). Mention any *auxiliary circuits* and *data flow conven-*

tions. We prefer a control PLA description to be used for control signal activation logic. Either a logic diagram (gate level) or list of boolean equations is also acceptable. Separate control signal descriptions can be done for memory-reference and register-reference instructions.

3.4. Interrupt

The IO and interrupt details are not to be implemented. However, in this subpart provide a *brief* high-level description of an interrupt structure you would propose for the SAM-16: describe (a) where the PC is saved, (b) the number of interrupt levels, (c) how the source is determined, and (d) how the interrupt address is delivered to PC and MA.

3.5. Extras

In this subpart, summarize any extras which your project contains. Extras can provide additional credit, and consist of:

- full direct addressing by other than the SC-16 technique,
- subroutine jump by other than the SC-16 technique,
- link bit handling,
- rich set of register-reference instructions,
- additional data flow registers,
- instruction format changes for greater function or additional address modes,
- input-output and interrupt scheme detail, and
- detailed ALU logic design.

A.3.3. Architectural Questions

Addressing Reminder

Architects have devised many ways to describe the operand locations or values. In single-address instructions, the accumulator is implied. Some instructions use immediate addressing where the partial direct address field holds a signed constant or literal.

Consider an 11-bit partial direct address field, and the need for a 16-bit address. The *page 0* or *current page* technique of the SC-16 can be employed. In *PC-relative* addressing, the partial direct address field is treated as a signed integer to be added to the PC. Another technique uses the 16-bit word following the instruction as an address. In effect, this constitutes a two-word instruction. Chapter 2 provides further details.

Subroutine Jump Reminder

Three popular methods are employed for handling subroutines: the LGP-30 method, the *branch-and-link* method of the IBM 704, and the *subroutine* stack used in the Burroughs B5000. Chapter 2 provides further details.

A.3.4. Additional Comments

A brief description of any architectural changes (replacing SUB, or including indexed addressing) is required. The description should include advantages and disadvantages of the change. The designer need not be concerned with details such as E-bit or Link bit implementation, generation of the memory control signals, stack overflow or underflow. The ALU can be shown as a block, with the functional capability evident from the diagram. For example, a capability to subtract is evident if one adder input value is selectively complementable.

Event schematics are a useful starting point for implementation, because each instruction must be interpreted in turn. The table of microoperations provides no new information over a properly devised set of event schematics, but presents the microoperations in a more convenient form for detecting common conditions which can reduce the implementation complexity (cost) of the control unit. For example, events common to a class of opcodes, or to a major state, can reduce the p-terms in the control PLA. In designing the control PLA, the table of microoperations is a more convenient starting point than a set of event schematics.

A.3.5. A Project Evaluation Procedure

The project is organized so that it should take no more than 20 to 30 minutes to grade. The evaluation procedure determines how well the student understands the architectural and design process. We assign six categories of understanding.

1. *Excellent:* The SAM-16 is efficient, complete, has no major or minor flaws (no loopholes), and possesses some extras.
2. *Very Good:* The SAM-16 is well designed, perhaps with a few minor inefficiencies and minor flaws, but no major flaws.
3. *Good:* The SAM-16 has some obvious improvements which could be made, no major flaw, but several inefficiencies and minor flaws.
4. *Fair:* The design has at least one major flaw or omission, but demonstrates an adequate understanding of the design process.
5. *Poor:* The design fails to demonstrate an adequate understanding of design methods, but shows some understanding of design techniques.
6. *Minimal:* The design demonstrates a lack of appreciation for design methods and techniques.

Major flaws include:

- an incorrect instruction interpretation step,
- a memory cycle which is not coordinated with the data flow cycle,
- a failure to reduce the set of conditions described by the RTN statements to control signal activations correctly,
- a state transition graph which does not correspond to the table of microoperations or control flow diagram, or
- an incomplete subpart.

Inefficiencies occur both in time and space. A time inefficiency occurs when some data flow cycles could be eliminated for one or more instruction executions at little or no extra cost. Space inefficiencies include more data paths than needed, or too large a number of major control states, or extra circuitry which could be significantly reduced in size. An architectural inefficiency is a feature which costs extra time and equipment, and the benefit to the user is minimal.

Minor flaws include poor organization, poor documentation, poor explanations, failure to organize and label the subparts as required, and weak subparts.

In assigning a numerical value to the project effort, it is convenient to indicate a major category which is scaled up according to the extras. Extras could promote a "good to very good" to "very good". The scale of **Table A.1** has been used.

Table A.1. Evaluation of Project		
Category	_Number Grade_	_Letter Grade_
Excellent	100	A+
Very Good to Excellent	94	A
Very Good	88	A–
Good to Very Good	83	B+
Good	76	B
Fair to Good	71	B–
Fair	65	C
Poor	50	D
Minimal	25	F

A.4. OUTLINE FOR 20-HOUR COURSE

A.4.1. Class Meetings

This section presents an outline for a ten-lecture course. Each lecture comprises two hours.

Lecture 1. Overview. _Text Ref.:_ Prologue, Chapter 1

Description of course and project. Review of prerequisites. Familiarization with standard use of instructor's nomenclature and "pencil and paper rule" used throughout the course. Design complexity and conceptual gaps. Description of a data processing system, CPU, main memory, IO. Instruction interpretation process. Descriptive tools: block diagrams, RTN statements, timing charts. Review of flip-flop timing characteristics.

Lecture 2. TM-16. _Text Ref.:_ Chapter 2 (skim), Chapter 3 (first half).

General instruction set information. Address modes (page 0, relative page, indirect, indexed) and program control (jumps, subroutine jump types, skips). TM-16 instruction set. Data word. Data flow cycle, system cycle, I and E major states. Data flow and data flow registers (MA, MD, IR, AC, PC). Sequence of microoperations for I state and LAC instruction, thus introducing RTN. Assign reading of remainder of TM-16 RTN statements.

Lecture 3. TM-16 (continued). _Text Ref.:_ Chapter 3.

Construction of data flow. Data flow cycle delays which govern minimum period Tmin. Simple description of IO and interrupt. Modification of I state to handle interrupts.

Lecture 4. TM-16 (continued). _Text Ref.:_ Chapter 3.

Control unit implementation from RTN statements to control signal activation logic. Gathering p-terms. MUX select control signals. Control signal timing chart example.

Lecture 5. Midterm Exam.

30 minutes: Description of SC-16 Architecture (Chapter 5).

75 minutes: Midterm exam based on Chapter 3.

Lecture 6.   SC-16H Data Flow and Memory Integration.   *Text Ref.:*   Chapter 4 (§4.1, 4.6, and 4.11), Chapter 5.

Review of static monolithic memory systems, introduction of memory bus interface MBUS. Importance of data flow design, and SC-16 data flow and timing. Use of ALU as a switch.

Lecture 7. SC-16H Control Algorithm.   *Text Ref.:*   Chapter 5.

Flowchart of SC-16H instruction interpretation, table of microoperations.

Lecture 8. SC-16H Logic Design.   *Text Ref.:*   Chapter 5.

Implementation of SC-16H control unit. SC-16 IO bus and interrupt scheme.

Lecture 9. Microprogramming and SC-16M.   *Text Ref.:*   Chapter 6.

Microprogramming, microprogrammed version of SC-16 data flow.
Due: Project part 1.

Lecture 10. Design and IO.   *Text Ref.:*   Chapters 5 and 6 (selected sections).

Review of implementation techniques for project. Concepts of IO interface design.
Due: Project part 2.

Final Exam

With the third part of the project due, the student may not have time or inclination to study for a final exam as well. Some instructors may wish to count the project as the final exam. Instead, we give a final exam for which doing the project is the best preparation. The design machine of the homework section of Chapter 5 is used as a basis for questions. For students who have done their own work on the project, the final exam grade correlates very well with the student's performance on the project.

The questions surrounding the problem machine of Chapter 5 have been "uncoupled" so that a wrong answer on one question does not affect the answer to another question. The questions seek to discover the student's understanding of the design process. The questions are designed for easily graded correct answers.
Due: Project part 3.

A.4.2. Course Grade

It is suggested that homework be assigned during the first five lectures. With a midterm and final, the weighting of the work handed in should be about 20% each for homework and midterm, and 30% each for the project and final. This weighting is used to compute a *number grade* representing the percentage achieved of the total possible points achievable. Where this falls depends on the instructor, and on the difficulty of the test questions and grading of the project. At the University of Santa Clara, the **A** was assigned to a number grade of 85% or better. Including students who dropped in lieu of a poor grade, this gave a well-deserved and hard-earned **A** to slightly less than half of the students. (The term "hard-earned" is applied because many students were employed by the semiconductor and microcomputer industry, and were "turned on" by the relevance of the course. As a result, the design project was attacked with considerable enthusiasm.)

A.4.3. Discussion

The 20-hour course is a bare minimum, but is better than *no* introduction to a realistic design problem. The text contains much more material than is needed for a course of 20 or even of 44 lecture hours. The course can be expanded to a three-hour one-semester course or a four-hour quarter course. There are four areas for expansion on the present core of 20 hours, for which the material appears in Chapters 4, 5, and 6:

- memory system design,
- design with bit-slice data flows,
- IO interfacing and peripheral control, and
- integration of IO, interrupts, and front panel.

An important reason for including more material than can be covered in a course is to give the instructor an advantage. We cannot expect all instructors to have relevant industrial experience. By studying the additional material the instructor acquires greater depth and breadth. The instructor can anticipate and be in a better position to answer student questions. The additional material also serves the student as a reference when the time comes to apply the course topic in a real design situation.

An area not specifically covered in this book, but important to a designer, is the *testability* of the design. The components and interconnections at various packaging levels should be designed to be more easily tested. Another area not treated in the book is the use of error detection circuits within the data flow and control unit. Treatments of testing, fault location, and other companion fields to digital engineering exist [4-7]. One characteristic shared by these companion fields is the presumption of knowledge of digital design. That is, one must be able to design a *structure* to meet the behavioral description of a *digital function* before one can test or protect that structure. In this book, then, we confine ourselves to providing the design prerequisites for more advanced topics such as testing and design automation.

REFERENCES

1. J. B. Peatman, *The Design of Digital Systems,* McGraw-Hill, New York, 1972.
2. J. D. Greenfield, *Practical Digital Design Using ICs,* Wiley, New York, 1977.
3. W. I. Fletcher, *An Engineering Approach to Digital Design,* Prentice-Hall, Englewood Cliffs, NJ, 1980.
4. F. F. Sellers, Jr., M. Y. Hsiao, and L. W. Bearnson, *Error Detecting Logic for Digital Computers,* McGraw-Hill, New York, 1968.
5. H. Y. Chang, E. G. Manning, and G. Metze, *Fault Diagnosis of Digital Systems,* Wiley, New York, 1970.
6. A. D. Friedman and P. R. Menon, *Fault Detection in Digital Circuits,* Prentice-Hall, Englewood Cliffs, NJ, 1971.
7. M. A. Breuer (Ed.), *Design Automation of Digital Systems,* vol. 1, Prentice-Hall, Englewood Cliffs, NJ, 1972.

APPENDIX

B

ELECTRONIC DEVICES
AND USEFUL INTERFACE CIRCUITS

B.1. INTRODUCTION

The digital systems designer deals in data flow component-level digital building blocks such as adders, multiplexers and decoders. These parts are themselves built from gate-level logic elements. In turn, the gate-level elements are built from electronic components and circuit devices such as diodes, resistors, capacitors and transistors. Thus electronics provides an important basis for digital systems.

There is general agreement among digital systems professionals that to do any digital systems work at the logic design or implementation level, sooner or later one must learn about capacitors, voltage, and the like. This appendix cannot do that. The treatment here is at the level of a "refresher" for someone who has some background. For those with no background, this appendix serves to narrow the gap to the electronic component level, but falls short of eliminating the gap. In other words, we provide the reader who has no electrical background with a "quick look" at electronics from a logic design viewpoint. For an in-depth treatment of many concepts covered in Appendices B, C, and D, see Malmstadt and Enke [1].

Boolean algebra and logic gates imply logic signals which appear on lines, wires, or interconnections. Wires are capable of conducting electrical *current*. Associated with any two points in an electrical circuit is a *voltage*. Voltage may also be measured with respect to ground, which serves as a reference value of 0 volts. Voltage is also called *potential*. Except during a power outage, voltage is always available between the two contacts of a wall socket, for example, whether or not a lamp or appliance is plugged in. Current is only drawn from the socket when the lamp is lit or the appliance is being used. Most logic systems use two voltage levels, high and low. The levels are the result of a quantization. For example, for many circuits in the TTL family, "high" is between +2.5 volts and +5.5 volts, whereas "low" is between 0 volts and +0.4 volts. Between 0.4 volts and +2.5 volts the signal is in transition. For control signals, the high and low values represent "true" and "false", or active and inactive. For data signals, values high and low represent the binary values 1 and 0. For most logic circuits, the signals are unidirectional. Unidirectional signal wires have a unique source, and the output from that source feeds one or more destinations.

The technology also provides circuits which permit bidirectional signals. Bidirectional signalling techniques are important because their effective employment can reduce system cost by reducing the number of interconnections. These circuits are called *bus connectives*. This appendix includes some electronics background in its description of these connectives.

At the digital system input and output interfaces, we often find members of a class of *special circuits*. Special circuits are those which provide timing reference sources (oscillators), time delays, or which convert the quantized low and high levels from one technology specification to another. The *transducer* is a special circuit which converts quantities to or from electrical signal levels used by digital logic. At the input interface, we find thumbwheel or rotary selection switches (knobs), pushbuttons, single or double throw switches, and keyboards.

B.2. ELEMENTARY DEVICE MODELS

For the most part, many of the important concepts of the computer and logic design profession can be expressed in terms of the logic element abstractions, independent of any particular technology. However, the professional designer always has a technology in mind, and is aware of the trade-offs particular to the technological environment.

B.2.1. Basic Electricity

Electrical engineering has been most closely linked to the computer design profession. For the benefit of those without this background, we briefly describe some very basic concepts.

Electricity is advantageous because it represents energy which is easily transported by means of *conductors* or wires. Metals provide the best conductors. Electric current exists when a quantity called *charge* is transported through the conductor. Electrons have a negative charge and ions have a positive charge. Charges of *like* polarity repel, and *unlike* charges attract. Thus, an electron is attracted to a positive ion. If we consider a molecule to be a "house", then the electrons are like "bachelors" which like to occupy a spare room in the house. A positive ion is a house with a spare room available. Bachelors repel each other and are attracted to spare rooms. Initially each bachelor occupies a spare room. In the absence of voltage, bachelors are randomly swapping rooms. In the presence of voltage, a current flows. This amounts to the bachelors moving in the same direction. The flow is relative, since the empty rooms flow in a direction opposite to the bachelors. Similarly, electron flow in one direction corresponds to a positive ion flow in the other. By convention, the direction of the current corresponds to the movement of the positive ions. (Bachelors are considered to move in the negative direction!) Materials which do not conduct charge are called insulators; materials which readily conduct charge, like metals, are called conductors. Material which is sometimes a conductor and sometimes an insulator is called a semiconductor. Many electronic components with interesting properties are made from semiconductors, including resistors, capacitors, diodes and transistors.

B.2.2. Electrical Quantities and Relationships

Table B.1. Primary Electrical Quantities		
Quantity	*Symbol*	*Unit*
Charge	Q	Coulomb
Voltage	V	Volt
Current	I	Ampere
Resistance	R	Ohm
Capacitance	C	Farad

Table B.1 describes the primary electrical quantities. Charge, voltage and current represent abstract quantities dealing with the flow of electricity. Current is related to charge as follows:

1 ampere = 1 coulomb/second

The ampere is a measure of the flow rate of charge. Voltage and current are interrelated. The existence of a source of voltage can cause current to flow. The existence of a source of current can cause voltage to appear across two points in a circuit. In digital systems, we view the current as a result of a voltage source or a potential in the circuit.

Resistance and capacitance are properties of two terminal devices. Unlike voltage, current, and charge, the devices retain their value of resistance and capacitance independent of current flow or the voltage appearing across the terminals.

A resistor presents resistance to current flow; other things being equal, a doubling of the resistance halves the current flow. Current can flow through a resistor in either direction.

A *short circuit* presents no resistance. In most circuits, the resistance of the wire is so small compared to the other elements that the wire is assumed to have zero resistance. Resistance adds in series, so for long wires we cannot ignore the resistance value of the wire. An *open circuit* presents an infinite resistance, which means that no current can flow between the two points in question, no matter how much voltage is across the points.

One important concept related to resistance is described by Ohm's Law:

$$V = I \times R \tag{B.1}$$

Ohm's law states that if 0.1 amps passes through a 2-ohm resistor, then a voltage of 0.2 volts (or 200 millivolts) is across the two terminals of the resistor. If we make an analogy between electrical current and water, then the speed of the flow of water corresponds to the speed of the flow of electric charge. Recall that one ampere means a flow of one coulomb per second. Voltage corresponds to the height of the storage tank or reservoir from which the water is flowing. A large resistance is analogous to a narrow pipe which slows the flow of water. When two resistors are connected in series, there is an intermediate voltage level between the two resistors. This is like creating an intermediate reservoir.

A capacitor is a two-terminal device consisting of two parallel plates (conducting surfaces) separated by an insulator. A capacitor can store a quantity of charge Q between the plates in the form of an excess of electrons on one plate and an excess of positive ions on the other plate. A charge on the capacitor creates a voltage between the terminals of the capacitor. Conversely, if a voltage is placed across the terminals of a capacitor, the capacitor will take in a charge. The relationship between the charge and the voltage is as follows:

$$Q = C \times V \qquad \textbf{(B.2)}$$

If V volts are placed across a capacitor of C farads, then the capacitor acquires a charge of Q coulombs. The capacitor does not acquire the charge instantaneously, but by means of a current flow. That is, the acquisition of positive ions on one plate and electrons on the other is accompanied by a flow of current. Once the capacitor is charged, the fact the terminals are separated by an insulator tells us that current ceases to flow until a new voltage appears across the capacitor terminals. When the terminals of the charged capacitor are connected through a resistance R to ground, then the capacitor *discharges* through the resistance. Again, this induces a current flow. When the terminals of the capacitor reach the same potential, no charge is on either capacitor plate, and there is no current flow. The duration of time that the current flows is proportional to, and within an order of magnitude of, the *RC time constant* of the circuit. This value is measured in seconds, and is the product of the resistance R in ohms and the capacitance C in farads:

$$RC \text{ time constant (sec)} = R \text{ (ohms)} \times C \text{ (farads)} \qquad \textbf{(B.3)}$$

Capacitance and the RC time constant can be important in digital systems because signal wires possess a capacitance. Here, one "plate" is the signal wire itself, and the other is the ground plane on a pc board, or the voltage plane of the power supply. When a logic signal changes value, the line capacitance is charged or discharged at the rate of its RC time constant. This interconnection or wiring delay must be included in the timing calculations used to estimate when signals become stable.

B.2.3. A "Voltage Divider" View of Logic Gates

Ohm's Law is useful for determining how voltage divides across resistors, as illustrated in **Figure B.1**. When the same current flows through two resistors, the voltage across both resistors is split between them. In Fig. B.1(a), five volts is across a 900-ohm resistor in series with a 100-ohm resistor, so the current flow is 5/1000 or five milliamps. Five milliamps through 900 ohms drops the voltage by 4.5 volts, and five milliamps through 100 ohms drops it the remaining 0.5 volts. Except when describing a voltage difference or voltage drop, voltage is measured

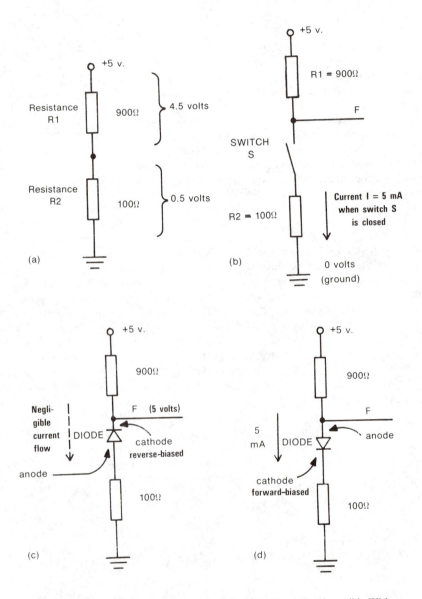

Figure B.1. *Voltage divider.* (a) A simple voltage divider. (b) With a switch. (c) With diode reverse-biased. (d) With diode forward-biased.

with respect to ground, defined to be 0 volts. An electrical ground is assumed to be an arbitrarily large source of electrons or positive ions, whichever is called for. The ground (earth) itself, when moist or when penetrated deeply enough with a metal rod, is such a source.

In Fig. B.1(b), a switch is opened, creating an open circuit. Point F is at +5 volts if no current is being drawn. If point F were connected to ground through a 900,000-ohm resistor, then point F, although at 4.999 volts, would still be considered to be at +5 volts ("slide rule accuracy"). For many practical situations, one million ohms is very close to an open circuit (infinite resistance).

B.2.4. Diodes

A *diode* is a device which presents an open circuit to current flow in a *reverse-biased* direction and a closed circuit to a *forward-biased* direction. It is like a horizontal pipe of rectangular cross-section which has a flap or door which the water can push or swing aside in one direction. In the other direction is a stop which prevents the door from swinging open.

The diode is a two-terminal device. The two terminals of the diode behave differently, so they each have been given a name. The anode accepts current as an input terminal but does not deliver current as an output terminal. The cathode delivers current, but does not accept it. When current flows inside the diode, it flows in the direction of the anode terminal to the cathode terminal.

Fig. B.1(c) shows the voltage divider circuit with the diode reverse-biased, preventing the flow of current. (The bias is with respect to the applied voltage.) To logic designers, a reverse-biased diode is approximated by an open circuit. In Fig. B.1(d), the diode is forward-biased with respect to the applied voltage, and offers very little resistance to current. It can be approximated by a short circuit.

B.2.5. Transistors

Often we need a device to act as a switch. Sometimes the switch is open and at other times it is closed. Rather than solder and unsolder diodes to control current flow, a three-terminal device called a *transistor* is used. A transistor has two terminals which behave similarly to the anode and cathode of the diode. The emitter only delivers current out of the transistor. The collector only accepts current into the transistor. Therefore, internal to the transistor, current flows from collector to emitter. The amount of flow, if any, is controlled by the third terminal called the base. The transistor is like the faucet of a garden hose. If closed, no current flows. If open, the amount of flow depends on the setting of the valve. When the valve is fully open, the flow is limited by the diameter of the fully opened valve. The analogy to a fully open valve occurs when the transistor is *saturated*. In digital systems, the transistor is either closed (switched off) or very close to saturation (switched on). (In radios, the transistor operates in between, called the linear range, where the current flow is most sensitive to the small variations on the base voltage.)

A transistor may be used as a switch, in digital technology, as shown in **Figure B.2**. A transistor behaves as two diodes in series, back to back, (facing away from each other), with one of the diodes controlled by the base terminal. See Fig. B.2(a). Resistor R1 is the collector load resistor, and is often called the *pull-up* resistor. When the base of the transistor is at a relatively high voltage, in this case perhaps +3 volts, the transistor is "turned on" by neutralizing reverse-biased diode D1. (*How* diode D1 is neutralized is beyond the scope of this book.) With D1 neutralized, the output voltage on signal line F approaches ground voltage. The

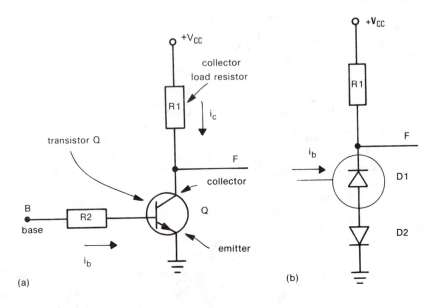

Figure B.2. *The transistor as a switch.* (a) Circuit. (b) Representation as two diodes, one controlled by the base current.

voltage on F does not quite reach ground due to an internal voltage drop between the collector and emitter of the transistor. (Nobody is perfect.)

On the other hand, if the voltage on base B is low, say 0.5 volts, then diode D1 is not neutralized. The transistor "cuts off", and behaves like an open circuit. This causes the voltage on point F to approach V_{CC} or the collector supply voltage. The circuits are designed to a collector supply V_{CC} of 5 volts (plus or minus ten percent) in the popular TTL logic family. When the output is high, it is used to feed current to, or *drive,* the inputs of other circuits. Point F *fans out* to other circuits; each of those circuits draws some current from F. This drive supplied from point F causes current to flow through the collector load resistor R1. From Ohm's Law, as this current increases, so does the voltage drop across R1, which serves to lower the output voltage at F. Therefore the number of inputs driven from point F is restricted to no more than some limit. The limit is calculated such that the output voltage drops no lower than some value, say 2.5 volts. Thus a "high" voltage level represents one of two states for output F.

When the transistor is saturated, output F is at the "low" voltage state. This voltage must not become too high, lest it be misinterpreted for the other state. The output voltage level is determined from the collector to emitter drop when in saturation. In TTL, the low level is between 0 and 0.4 volts.

Note that the transistor behaves like an inverter. With +4.5 volts on the input (the base B), the output (collector F) goes to 0.4 volts. With 0.5 volts on the input, the output goes to near +4.5 volts. We also note that the voltage levels on the output are compatible with the levels expected at the input.

B.2.6. Diode Logic

The use of diodes to perform logical functions on voltage levels is shown in **Figure B.3.** This figure illustrates *diode logic*. Fig. B.3(a) is a diode AND gate. The output voltage on point F is *pulled down* toward the low voltage if any input is low, because of the easy path (low resistance) through the forward-biased diode.

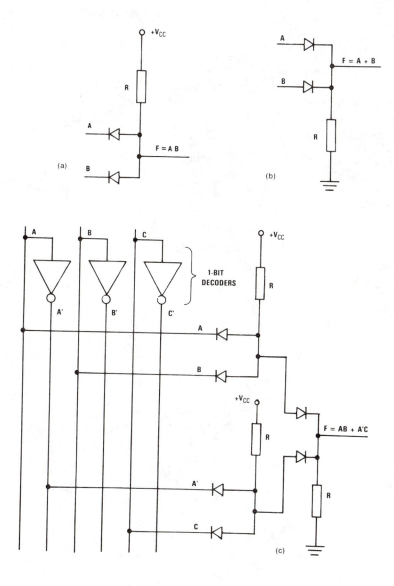

Figure B.3. *Diode logic.* (a) AND. (b) OR. (c) AND-OR.

For F to be at the high voltage level, points A and B must both be at the high voltage level.

Fig. B.3(b) shows a diode OR gate. Output F is held high if either point A or point B is at the high voltage. Either A or B (or both) can supply current through the forward-biased diode. For point F to be low, both A and B must be low.

Fig. B.3(c) shows diode AND gates feeding a diode OR gate, which is a realization of a boolean function in two levels of logic. The circuit is thus a *two-level* combinational circuit. First generation computers used diode logic of this type to a considerable extent.

We cannot indefinitely cascade the output of diode AND gates to diode OR gates, to diode AND gates, etc. At each level, the high voltage drops a bit and the low voltage rises a bit. Eventually it become impossible to distinguish high from low. Before the levels become indistinguishable, the levels are restored or readjusted by feeding the diode logic output to an inverter such as Fig. B.2.

Today, two-level diode logic circuits are organized into compact two-dimensional diode arrays on semiconductor chips. If the array designer provides the user with a convenient way to specify the locations of the diodes, the resulting chip is called a programmable logic array or PLA. A single fabrication process can provide a chip which can realize many functions. The logic array chip is a generalization of Fig. B.3(c), and the programmable part is the provision for a flexible and convenient way to locate the diodes.

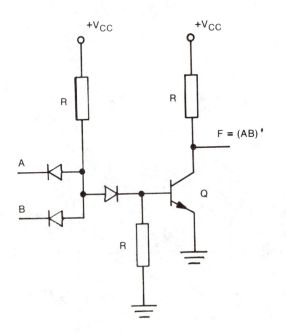

Figure B.4. *Diode-transistor logic (DTL) NAND.*

In the second generation, a popular circuit family was DTL (diode transistor logic), in which a diode AND gate fed a transistor inverter as shown in **Figure B.4.**

B.2.7. Gate Propagation Delays

When the transistor is turned on, a turn-on delay occurs. Similarly, when the transistor is turned off, a turn-off delay occurs. These are part of the overall gate

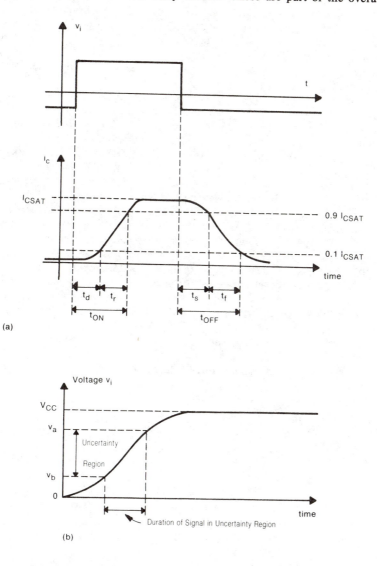

Figure B.5.   *Time response of transistor to input voltage* v_i.
(a) Response to square wave on input.   (b) Slower changing signal on input.

delay, called the *propagation delay*. The dynamic behavior of delays is studied in **Figure B.5.** A delay is only in evidence when the gate output is changing state. The response of the collector current of the circuit of Fig. B.2(a) to a negative square wave voltage pulse on input B is shown in Fig. B.5(a). The turn-on delay has two parts: the delay time t_d and the rise time t_r, as shown. Similarly, the turn-off delay has two parts: the storage time t_s and the fall time t_f.

In Fig. B.5(b), consider a slowly changing input to the circuit of Fig. B.2(a). The transistor must discriminate between a "low" (0) value on the input, and a "high" (1) value. In Fig. B.5(b), when $v_i < v_b$, the input is considered to be low, and when $v_i > v_a$, it is considered to be high. If the input voltage is between discrimination levels v_a and v_b, the input is in the threshold uncertainty region. The longer the rise or fall time, the greater the time spent in the threshold uncertainty region.

The gates whose inputs are fed by a particular gate's output signal are called that gate's *fan-out*. The delay experienced by a gate also depends upon its fan-out. In simple systems, each gate input represents a *unit load* to the gate driving the interconnection. Typically each gate can drive from seven to ten unit loads without violating a specification. Of course, fan-out considerations are not necessarily that simple in practice, because different circuit types draw different amounts of load current. It is also the case that when the logic gate output changes value, the capacitance represented by the interconnection must be charged or discharged. For drive from an inverter such as Fig. B.2(a), when the change is to the low level, the line capacitance is discharged rapidly through the low resistance of a turned-on transistor. Unfortunately, when the output changes to the high level, the line capacitance must be charged through the load resistor, so the delay is proportional to the RC time constant. In any case, adding more gate inputs to the interconnection always increases the signal transition delay. When some signals are heavily loaded, inverter fan-out trees are commonly used to increase the drive capability. This is shown in **Figure B.6.** For a more detailed discussion of fan-out drive, see Peatman [2], and Lancaster [3].

The electrical specifications and switching delay characteristics of the commercially available logic circuits are generally available in application notes or data books available from the manufacturer. Laws and Levy [4] cover many useful

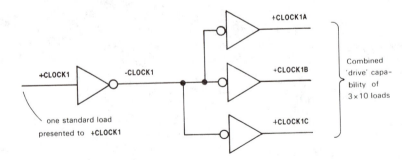

Figure B.6. *Example of fan-out tree (one level).*

topics, including input/output levels, fan-out capability, propagation delays, edge rates, setup, hold, and release times, effects of temperature and power supply variations, what to do with unused gate inputs, transmission line effects, line driving and receiving, and cross-talk and ringing.

B.3. THE BIDIRECTIONAL BUS CONNECTIVES

B.3.1. Bidirectional Buses

A *bus* is a general term reflecting the designer's grouping together a collection of signal wires to be treated as a unit. An interface bus connects a CPU to its peripheral devices. A data bus is a bus whose signals represent data bits, and which is used to transfer data from a *source* to one or more *destinations*.

Most logic signals encountered in a digital system are unidirectional, i.e. characterized by a single source which is always the same device. However, the relative cost of making interconnections is increasing. This is particularly true for pin-limited LSI and VLSI chips. To reduce interconnection costs, designers employ bidirectional busing. A bidirectional bus can have more than one source, but not more than one source can be active at the same time. Bidirectional busing thus implies coordination logic at each possible source, in order to avoid having more than one device driving each connection at the same time. For example, some microprocessor systems use a bidirectional memory DATA bus. If a control signal called memory write is active, then the memory user (say the central processor) is the source for the memory DATA bus. Otherwise, for a read operation, the memory itself is the source for the memory DATA bus.

Figure B.7 shows some busing examples. The data bus *width* is identified by a slash with the number of bits indicated nearby. An 8-bit data bus with a parity bit is indicated by "8,P". Unidirectional and bidirectional buses show an arrow at each possible destination. The bidirectional property is indicated by a square enclosing a diamond. A "bow-tie" symbol on a bus also indicates bidirectionality. In order to understand bidirectional busing, recall how a source signal is generated.

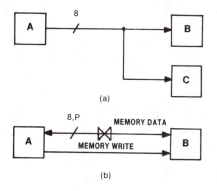

Figure B.7. *Examples of busing.* (a) An 8-bit unidirectional data bus. (b) An 8-bit plus parity bidirectional data bus.

See Fig. B.2(a). When transistor Q is turned on, output F is pulled low. When transistor Q is off, Q behaves like an open circuit. Point F is connected to V_{CC} through the collector load resistor. The collector load resistor is also called the pull-up resistor. When transistor Q is an open circuit, the pull-up resistor causes the voltage on F to be "pulled up" toward V_{CC}.

When the output of the circuit of Fig. B.2(a) is used as a source for a bus signal, transistor Q is designed to conduct more than usual current. Such a circuit is called a *driver* or *line driver*. See [4].

The low-level drive of the circuit of Fig. B.2(a) is *active* because when Q is on, there is only the resistance of Q when in the active state between output F and ground. Figure B.2(a) has a resistor between point F and V_{CC}. The circuit lacks an active high-level drive. This is an important distinction between two of the major bus connectives, the open-collector bus and the tri-state bus.

B.3.2. The Open–Collector Function

A logic function which was employed in the first generation, and again in the transistor technologies, has various names including collector-OR, OR-tie, DOT-OR, DOT-AND, wire-OR, wire-AND, virtual-AND, etc. The circuit is shown in

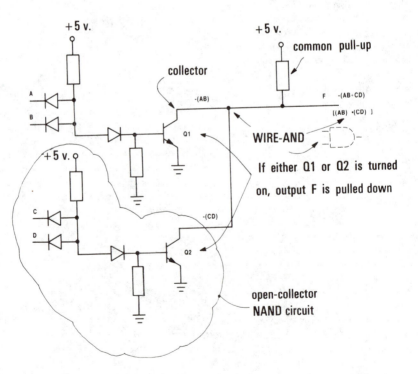

Figure B.8. *Collector-OR function by wiring two open-collector NAND gates.*

Figure B.8. The figure shows two two-input NAND gates. Output transistors Q1 and Q2 are typically packaged without a collector resistor, which make Q1 and Q2 *open-collector* (OC) circuit outputs. The NAND gates may be packaged on a chip. The open-collector outputs may be connected to a common collector load resistor external to the chip. Note that when so connected, the result is a realization of a two-level boolean statement. The second logic level, a *wire-AND,* or *collector-OR,* has little cost and almost no gate delay.

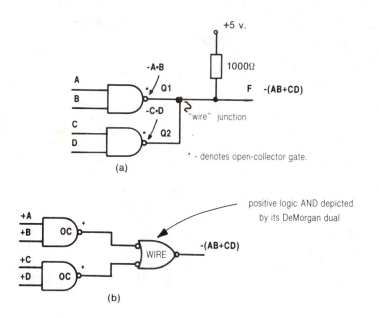

(a)

(b)

Figure B.9. *Collector-OR (DOT-OR) function by wiring two open-collector NAND gates.*   (a) Collector pull-up shown.   (b) As logic diagram symbol.

The role of the open-collector NAND gate is better shown in **Figure B.9.** The asterisk near the gate output indicates the gates have open-collector outputs. The circuits for Q1 and Q2 are conventional DTL NAND gates of Fig. B.4 with the exception that the collector pull-up resistor is missing. For "collector ORing", a common pull-up is required. Note from Fig. B.9(a) that the 1000-ohm load or pull-up resistor connection at the output is only pulled up to +5 volts when none of the gate outputs are low (pulling down). Otherwise the junction is held low. A way to show the wire-AND circuit on logic diagrams is shown in Fig. B.9(b). The NAND may be identified either by the asterisk or the "OC" notation. The wire-OR block as shown on the diagram is the DeMorgan dual of the wire-AND. In this case the DOT function is more easily understood as an OR. Since the function performed is AND-OR-INVERT, such circuits (when implemented as an SSI circuit) are called AOI circuits. In the TTL technology, open-collector NANDs, NORs, and inverters are available [5]. In the 7400 series TTL technology, open-collector outputs are convenient for *level conversion,* where the pull-up resistor can be tied to another voltage level.

In the first generation the vacuum tube DOT-AND was relatively "free". Since the third generation, the expense of packaging pull-up resistors reduces the cost advantage once enjoyed by using the "wire" function to do a level of logic. Today, the wire-OR is employed not so much in *random* or control logic, but for data *busing.* If several devices feed a common pull-up resistor, and only one device (source) is active at a time, then the value on the bus is known to be the value of the output of the unique source driver. The bus is used to transmit the value of that source driver to destination devices connected to the bus. Since the common bus driver is an open-collector NAND, the bus data is usually of the "active-low" polarity, as the NAND performs an inversion.

B.3.3. Tri–State Drivers

The normal circuit of the TTL technology does not readily permit a collector-OR function. See **Figure B.10.** Transistors Q3 and Q4 are called *totem pole* output transistors. When output F is low, Q3 is off and Q4 is on. If Q3 and Q4 are both on for any length of time, then in the absence of a current limiting device, Q3 or Q4 may burn out. (The same is true if two TTL outputs are tied together and the top transistor of one is on, and the bottom transistor of the other is on. In effect, they short circuit the power supply.)

A combination of the TTL totem pole transistors not yet mentioned is when Q3 and Q4 are both off. In this case, the output F has a high resistance to +5 volts, as well as a high resistance to ground. The output is said to be in a third state called the *high impedance* or HI-Z state. Noninverting amplifiers have been designed for TTL with a logic input which can place the output in the HI-Z state. Such a circuit is called a *tri-state* (or 3-state) *driver.* See **Figure B.11.** In Fig.

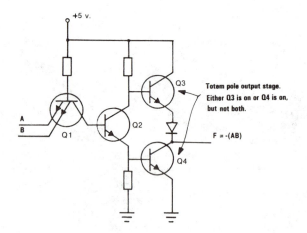

Figure B.10. *The TTL NAND gate.*

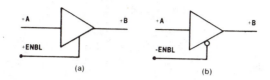

Figure B.11. *TTL Tri-state drivers.* (a) Active-high enable. (b) Active-low enable.

B.11(a), when the control signal ENBL is high, the input value A is passed to the output. It thus acts as an ordinary noninverting line driver. When ENBL is low, the driver is disabled, placing the output in the HI-Z state, where the output is an open circuit.

Figure B.12 shows the outputs for four tri-state drivers wired together. With the convention that at most one enabling signal is active, the popular data selector or data multiplexer function is performed. **Figure B.13** shows an n-bit bidirectional bus configuration. The tri-state bus has an *active pull-up* because the connection from the output line to V_{CC} is a transistor instead of a resistor. When the output goes high, the RC time constant is smaller for an active pull-up, so the tri-state bus is faster than an open-collector bus. The open-collector bus performs the active-high AND function. If the bus has more than one source, the resulting data is the bit-by-bit AND of the source data bits. The tri-state bus performs no logic function. If one tri-state driver is low and another high, the bus value may depend on the current limiting safety devices incorporated into the circuits. Fan-out drive calculations and groundrules are treated in Mick [6; p. 5.64].

B.3.4. The Transmission Gate

In the *complementary metal oxide semiconductor* (CMOS) technology, a bus connective exists called a *transmission gate*. The transmission gate also possesses a high impedance state when disabled. Enabled, the transmission gate passes current in either direction. In addition, the transmission gate is an analog switch which can also be employed as a multiplexer element and in a flip-flop circuit. The primary application of the transmission gate as a bus connective is within the confines of a large chip. In discussing bus connectives across chip boundaries, we restrict our attention to open-collector or tri-state devices. A connective with a similar function is called the *pass transistor*. For additional information, see Taub and Schilling [7; p. 479], and Mead and Conway [8].

B.3.5. Summary of Bus Connectives

The bus connectives are used to share signal wires between different portions of logic. The sharing reduces the overall number of interconnections or cables, at the expense of permitting only one use of the bus at one time. The buses are called bidirectional because more than one source is permitted. Data can go from a device to the CPU, or from the CPU to a device, over the same set of wires.

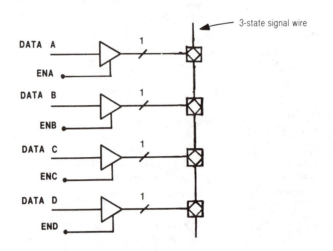

Figure B.12. *A tri-state signal wire, driven by four sources. (Destinations not shown.)*

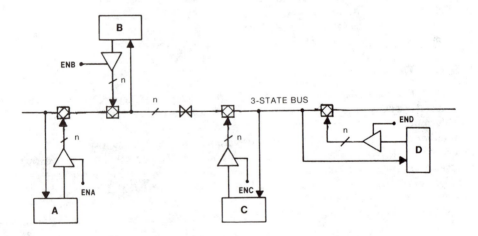

Figure B.13. *A bidirectional n-bit tri-state bus interconnecting four units.*

The open-collector bus is the oldest type in use. It is always used when the logical function is needed, such as for an interrupt line. Here, one or more devices wanting to receive attention can pull the interrupt line low.

The tri-state bus can be used over longer distances. The active high-level drive provides a lower series resistance to V_{CC} for the high output level. See Lenk [9; p. 366] for a more detailed discussion of multiple driver/receiver systems. Lenk also treats point-to-point delay versus line length calculations. The MOS transmission gate usage is generally confined to the MOS chip itself.

B.4. OSCILLATORS

This section covers circuits which provide the periodic signals upon which system timing is based. The term *system timing* (or system timing cycle) means a collection of periodic signals. A periodic signal is one which repeats the same voltage waveform each period. The number of periods which occur each second is the *frequency* or *rate*. If the period is 1 microsecond, the frequency is 1 megahertz (MHz), or one million cycles per second. The duration of the period is also called the *cycle-time;* which is occasionally (perhaps incorrectly) shortened to *cycle*. (Designers sometimes say "cycle" when "period" would be the correct word.)

Where a highly accurate or a high precision timing source is required, the timing reference is a *crystal* cut to the desired *fundamental* clock frequency. Where a less accurate, hence less expensive, reference is adequate, an RC (resistor-capacitor) network provides a basis for the fundamental frequency. In either case, the circuit which provides a signal which repeats at this fundamental frequency is called an *oscillator* circuit. The fundamental frequency of the oscillator signal is typically fed to a counter circuit (ring counter, etc.; see Appendix D) or otherwise is "counted down" (in frequency) to provide the system timing cycle [10]. The period of the system cycle is normally two to eight times the period of the fundamental clock signal generated by the oscillator. Any of the periodic signals generated in the system timing period may be generically called a *clocking* or *timing* signal.

B.4.1. Crystal Oscillators

Synchronous systems receive their timing signals from a central clock source. The heart of this source is a free-running oscillator circuit, or astable multivibrator. The frequency is controlled by a crystal if a precise frequency (within 0.1%) is required. Quartz crystals can be cut to resonate or vibrate (oscillate) at a specific frequency to great precision. They can be combined with electronic circuitry to provide precisely spaced signal transitions (pulses), which can be used as inputs to counters or frequency divider circuits [11]. A crystal-controlled oscillator using the crystal, one capacitor C, two transistors Q_i, and five resistors R_i, is shown in **Figure B.14.**

Instead of the discrete components of Fig. B.14, digital circuits are preferred. This is particularly true from the packaging standpoint since most printed circuit boards intended for use in digital systems more easily accommodate digital packages. Lancaster [3; p. 170] mentions the circuit of **Figure B.15,** which uses CMOS gates and can drive one TTL gate. Simpler oscillator circuits are shown in **Figure B.16.** Fig. B.16(a) was studied by Murata et. al. [12], and a variation is shown in Fig. B.16(b).

A further step toward integration is the availability of basic counter and clocking circuits on an IC chip, lacking only the crystal of the desired frequency to

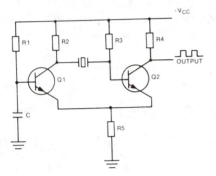

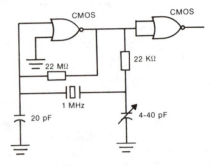

Figure B.14. *Electronic crystal-controlled oscillator.*

Figure B.15. *A crystal-controlled oscillator using digital parts.*

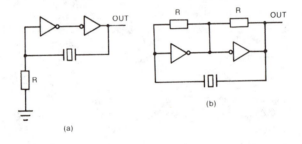

Figure B.16. *Simple crystal oscillator circuits.* (a) A simple circuit. (b) A variation of (a).

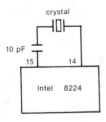

Figure B.17. *A system-timing IC using an external crystal reference.*

Figure B.18. *A popular quartz crystal package for microprocessors.*

be connected between the pins provided. Such a circuit is the Intel 8224 chip depicted as a block in **Figure B.17**. This IC provides the basic timing for some Intel computers of the SBC 80 line.

B.4.2. Piezoelectric Crystals

Crystals can be packaged in many ways. A popular microcomputer crystal package is shown in **Figure B.18**. In the electrical sense, the quartz crystal is quite complex. The electromechanical system which makes up the crystal is capable of more than one frequency (resonance) mode. The frequency reference application of the crystal is derived from the piezoelectric phenomena whereby a mechanical distortion is converted to an electrical surface charge, and vice-versa. See [13].

Some crystals can be operated in an "overtone mode" (at a multiple of the fundamental frequency) by use of a tank circuit (a parallel circuit of an inductance and a capacitor) tuned to the overtone frequency. See the Texas Instruments Data Book for a discussion of overtone frequencies and the clock generator circuits 74LS362 and 74LS424 [5; p. 7-507].

B.4.3. Resistor-Capacitor Network Oscillators

For waveform generators where 1% to 5% accuracy is adequate, then frequency determination by resistor-capacitor (RC) networks is common. A versatile semiconductor chip which performs many timing functions is called the 555 timer, or the MC1555 [14; p. 8-43]. The basic components of the 555 are two analog comparator devices and a set-clear flip-flop. By attaching two resistors and a capacitor external to the 555 chip, an oscillator function is performed [3; p. 170]. An oscillator for digital systems is also called an *astable multivibrator*. A multivibrator circuit generates a pulse, and "astable" means that after generating the pulse the circuit continues generating more pulses. (For a *monostable* multivibrator, the circuit output is stable in only one state. The monostable has an input, which when activated, causes a single pulse to appear on the output. A monostable is also called a *single-shot,* and is treated in Appendix D.)

The 555 circuit, when connected as an astable multivibrator, offers the designer the opportunity of specifying the pulse "on" time (duration) and "off" time. The ratio of the "on" time to the period is called the *duty cycle.* The duty cycle is changed by changing the ratio of the resistance of the two resistors. This facilitates the generation of an asymmetric clock signal.

B.4.4. Gated Oscillators

Occasionally it is useful to be able to turn on or off a string of oscillator pulses. For example, turning off the basic clock of a central processor is the designer's favorite way to cause the central processor to wait. When turning on or off a pulse string, it is desirable that no short or "runt" pulses occur at the transition from "wait" to "active" or vice-versa. The time delay calculations a designer uses to specify the clock period do not allow for any short pulse widths. The gated oscillator circuits of **Figure B.19** provide a means to start or stop a pulse train, in which no short pulses occur. Fig. B.19(a) appears in Marshall [15]. Fig. B.19(b) shows a gated oscillator which employs a simple edge-triggered flip-flop (see Appendix D), a NOR gate (see Appendix C), and an inverter. Signal +GATEIN

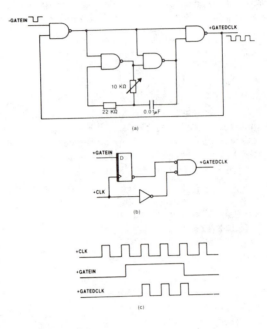

Figure B.19. *A gated oscillator circuit.* (a) Marshall's gated oscillator circuit. (b) A gated clock circuit where GATEIN is synchronized. (c) Waveform for gated clock.

must not change just prior to the leading edge of +CLK. The waveform is shown in Fig. B.19(c).

B.5. SWITCHES, JUMPERS, AND ADDRESS RECOGNITION

A digital system does not live in isolation of its surroundings. To control digital subsystems, manually-activated switches may dynamically initiate trains of events. To personalize a subsystem, switches may be statically set to certain positions. For example, the device address recognized by a device adapter may be set by jumper (or shorting plug) wires, or switch settings. Static switch settings generally "preprogram" a status or control state which may persist for a long duration. Dynamically controlled switches generally require the change in the switch setting to be synchronized to the system timing.

B.5.1. Electrical Terminology of Switches

Mechanical switches share terminology with relays. In fact, a relay may be viewed as an electrically actuated switch, whereas we normally view a mechanical switch as being manually actuated. **Figure B.20** illustrates some of the following definitions. Switches *make* (close) or *break* (open) an electrical connection between a *contact pair* (two contacts). A complementary contact pair exists if, when

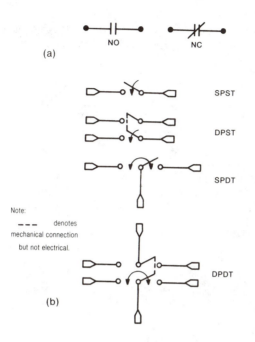

(a)

SPST

DPST

SPDT

Note:

− − −   denotes
mechanical connection
but not electrical.

DPDT

(b)

Figure B.20.   *Terminology for contacts and switches.*   (a) Contacts.
NO- normally open; NC- normally closed.   (b) Switches. SPST- single
pole, single throw; DPST- double pole, single throw; SPDT- single pole,
double throw; DPDT- double pole, double throw.

one pair of contacts is open, the other pair of contacts is closed, and vice-versa.
The complementary pairs have opposite polarity. A switch has a *normal* position,
and one pair is denoted *normally closed* (NC). The complementary pair is called
normally open (NO). Switches whose contact pairs do not possess a complementary
pair are called *single throw*. Switches whose contact pairs have a complementary
pair are called *double throw*. Some switches have a number of electrically independent contacts of the same polarity controlled by the same mechanical motion.
These are called *multipole* switches. In particular, a switch is *double pole* if two
electrically independent contact pairs belong to the same switch. The "pole" and
"throw" designations are mutually independent.

Switches can also be *maintained* or *momentary*. When a maintained switch is
moved off its normal position, it stays moved. When a momentary switch is moved
from its normal position, it remains there only so long as manual pressure is
applied. When released, the momentary switch returns to its normal position. This
distinction is most evident in pushbuttons, although some toggle switches are of the
momentary type.

B.5.2. Mechanical Aspects of Switches

A popular switch is the *DIP switch,* a collection of independent SPST switches packaged in a dual inline package and suitable for mounting on a pc board. See **Figure B.21.**

Figure B.21. *The DIP switch.* (a) Perspective view. (b) Electrical view.

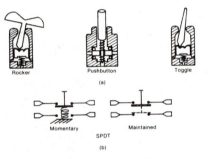

Figure B.22. *Rocker, pushbutton and toggle switches.* (a) Front view. (b) Electrical view.

The *toggle, rocker,* and *pushbutton* are generally found as SPDT switches (although some inexpensive toggles are SPDT), and can also be either momentary or maintained. These switches are shown in **Figure B.22.**

The *jumper* is a version of the SPDT switch of Fig. B.21. The jumper or shorting plug is illustrated in **Figure B.23,** and has an electrical connection between its two legs. It is typically plugged into plated-through holes on a pc board, as shown. The plug either makes contact between holes A and B, or between holes B and C.

A *rotary selector switch* is shown in **Figure B.24.** There is a mechanical detention (detent) mechanism which ensures that the center contact is connected to exactly one circumferential contact. A knob is attached to the shaft, so the switch is also called a knob. A 10-position knob is convenient for specifying a decimal number. The IBM S/360 used hexadecimal numbering, so 16-position knobs were found on S/360 front panels or consoles.

Keyboards are popular input devices and offer some advantage over thumbwheels, rotary switches and pushbuttons. A keyboard can replace several mechanical switches. Keyboards are available with mechanical or solid-state switches (hard

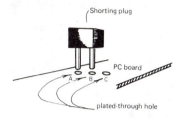

Figure B.23. *A printed-circuit board jumper connection.*

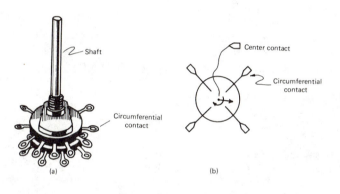

Figure B.24. *Rotary selector switch.* (a) Perspective view. (b) Electrical view.

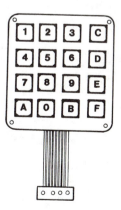

Figure B.25. *A 4×4 keyboard.*

contact, Hall-effect, capacitive, ferrite core, etc.) and in a large variety of size and key decoding configurations. A 4×4 keyboard, suitable for use on a front panel [16], is shown in **Figure B.25.**

B.5.3. Address Decoding with Switches

A common application for jumpers is to be able to recognize any designated address on an address bus. A nonpersonalized address recognition circuit is the simple AND gate, shown in **Figure B.26.** This AND gate recognizes the 8-bit hexadecimal '5D' (binary 0101 1101). This address recognizer is "hard-wired" because if the address to be recognized were changed, the circuit would need to be rewired. The employment of switches or jumpers resolves this problem; the designated address can be changed by switch changes or jumper changes.

From Fig. B.26, it is seen that the address personalization reduces to the choice of whether to feed the true or complement polarity of the address bit to the AND gate. The exclusive-OR gate is capable of selectively complementing a data-bit value on one input, per the value on a control variable on the other input. The technique is illustrated in **Figure B.27;** switch S(i) provides a selectable control variable value COMP(i). With the switch closed, the control signal COMP(i) is pulled low to ground, placing the true data-bit value on the EX-OR gate output. When the switch S(i) is open, pull-up resistor R(i) delivers a high or true value to control signal COMP(i), causing the data-bit value A(i) to be complemented on the output of the EX-OR gate.

The circuit of Fig. B.27 can be viewed in another way. The switch and resistor combination actually generates an 8-bit constant or value. This value happens to the complement of the designated address. The EX-OR gate and AND gate circuit is a *comparator* (see Appendix C), whose output is true only if the generated constant is the complement of the address on the bus. This higher conceptual level viewpoint is shown in the block diagram of **Figure B.28.**

Selectable constant generators appear on computer front panels to allow the operator to enter data or addresses. Rotary selector switches can also be used for this purpose; in fact it is easier to manipulate a 16-position knob than to move four SPDT switches manually. Keyboards are even more convenient.

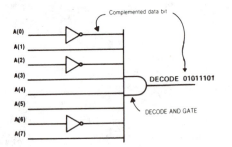

Figure B.26. *Nonpersonalized address decoder.*

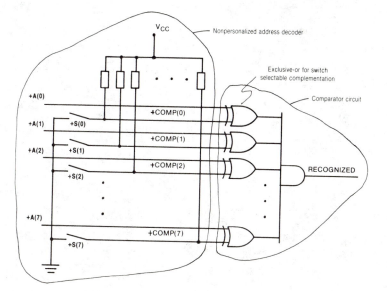

Figure B.27. *A switch-controlled personalizable address decoder.*

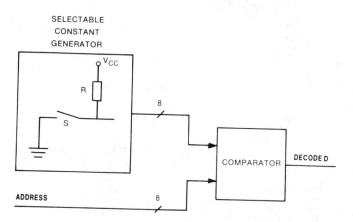

Figure B.28. *Block diagram of personalizable address decoder.*

B.5.4. Address Decoding with Jumpers

Jumpers are capable of convenient *4-to-1 jumper-selector* circuits as shown in **Figure B.29.** A single jumper can switch either of signals S0, S1, S2, or S3 to center position C. This capability can be used in conjunction with a 2×4 or 4×8

Figure B.29. *Jumpers can be used as a 4-to-1 selector. As shown, source S1 is selected.*

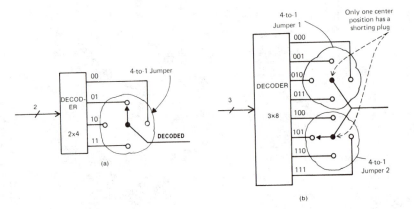

Figure B.30. *Use of 4-to-1 jumper selection for decode selection.*
(a) 2×4 decoder, "01" selected. (b) Use of two 4-to-1 jumper positions with a 3×8 decoder, "101" selected.

decoder (see Appendix C) to select and recognize the proper decoded address, as shown in **Figure B.30.** Fig. B.30(a) shows combination "01" selected by the jumper. In Fig. B.30(b), two 4-to-1 jumper-selectors are required, but only one shorting plug is used.

When a large address, such as an 8-bit address, is to be recognized, then the full decoder approach becomes expensive. An 8-bit decoder yields 256 individual decodes. This problem can be simply solved by using four of the 2×4 decoder/4-to-1 jumper-selector pairs found in Fig. B.30(a).

In **Figure B.31,** the four individual decodes are ANDed together so that only the designated combination will activate the recognizer output.

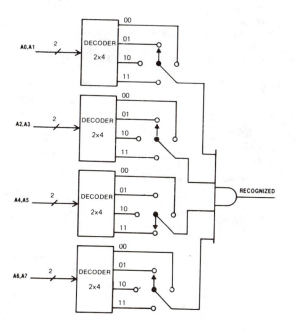

Figure B.31. *Combination of 2×4 decoder / 4-to-1 jumper pairs to recognize the 8-bit address "01011101".*

REFERENCES

1. H. V. Malmstadt and C. G. Enke, *Digital Electronics for Scientists,* W. A. Benjamin, Inc., New York, 1969.
2. John B. Peatman, *The Design of Digital Systems,* McGraw-Hill, New York, 1972.
3. Don Lancaster, *TTL Cookbook,* H. Sams Publications, Indianapolis, IN, 1974.
4. David A. Laws and Roy J. Levy, "Designer's Guide to High-performance Low-power Schottky Logic", *Schottky and Low-power Schottky Data Book,* Second Edition, Advanced Micro Devices, Inc., Sunnyvale, CA, 1977.
5. Anon., *The TTL Data Book,* Texas Instruments, Dallas, TX, 1976.
6. John R. Mick, "Using Schottky Tri-state Outputs in Bus-organized Systems", in *Schottky and Low-power Schottky Bipolar Memory, Logic and Interface Circuits,* Advanced Micro Devices, Sunnyvale, CA, 1975.
7. H. Taub and D. Schilling, *Digital Integrated Electronics,* McGraw-Hill, New York, 1977.
8. C. Mead and L. Conway, *Introduction to VLSI Systems,* Addison-Wesley, Reading, MA, 1980.
9. John D. Lenk, *Logic Designer's Manual,* Reston Publishing, Reston, VA, 1977.
10. G. G. Langdon, Jr., "A Survey of Counter Design Techniques", *Computer Design,* v. 9, n. 10, (October 1970), 85-93.
11. G. W. Harrison, "Crystal gives Precision to an Astable Multivibrator", *Electronics,* v. 41, November 1969, 121.
12. M. Murata et. al., "Analysis of Oscillator consisting of Digital Integrated Circuits", *IEEE J. of Solid-state Circuits,* vol. SC-5, n. 4, (August 1970), 165-168.

13. Jim McDermott, "Focus on Piezoelectric Crystals and Devices", *Electronic Design,* August 16, 1973, 44-54.

14. Anon., Linear Integrated Circuits, *Semiconductor Data Library,* vol. 6/Series B, Motorola, Phoenix, AZ, 1976.

15. Walter C. Marshall, "Fast-starting gated Oscillator yields clean Tone Burst", *Electronics,* Jan. 20, 1977, 98.

16. E. Dilatush, "Front-panel Controls", *EDN Magazine,* v. 23, n. 12 (June 20, 1978), 50-62.

DESCRIPTIVE TECHNIQUES
FOR COMBINATIONAL LOGIC

C.1. INTRODUCTION

Imagine what it would be like to build a house out of toothpicks. Suppose that the wooden toothpick is the only building block available. We would probably first glue the toothpicks together to build joists, framing members, flooring, etc., before proceeding. If we had to keep track of the location and function of each toothpick in the house, the job would be extremely tedious.

In many ways, the construction of a large digital system in the first or second generations was analogous to building a house out of toothpicks: the use of a low-level building block to construct a complex structure. The analogy also holds for the construction of a powerful computer program out of weak machine language instructions. Our primary weapon against complexity is the capability of abstraction. The low-level building blocks are organized into larger application-oriented units, and our thinking is now directed to the larger functional units. This provides some necessary structure. We are fortunate today in that the current technology provides basic parts which are functionally more powerful than the resistors, capacitors and vacuum tubes of the early computer engineers. We must raise our thinking to deal more directly with higher-level functional units. At higher levels (adders, shifters, etc.) we can comprehend a digital system design without becoming overwhelmed by the low-level SSI detail. The comment, "not seeing the woods (functional units) for the trees (SSI elements)", is applicable. The design first takes shape at the generalized MSI level. The SSI-level blocks (elementary gates) represent toothpicks.

It is not enough to think about a design at the functional unit level. We must be able to communicate our thoughts, which in turn requires a descriptive language. One purpose of this appendix is to correct the lack of emphasis on good descriptive techniques for the job at hand. In the familiar context of combinational logic building blocks we use block diagram shapes, block notation, a bus notation, and a register transfer notation (RTN). We introduce concepts and terminology for understanding and dealing with propagation delays attributable to these blocks, and present the timing chart notation. The function table is seen to be a compact form of the combinational truth table, which can be used to describe the behavior of a generalized MSI part. We use a representation of generalized MSI parts. For example, the multiplexer block has no constraints on the number of data inputs and data outputs. These details can be postponed until later in the design. One purpose of a block diagram is to present a higher-level design result without the clutter of excessive detail.

In this appendix, we use RTN to describe the behavior of MSI blocks. This is *not* the intended job for RTN; we do it for familiarization with the notation and its semantics. RTN is intended to describe actions which a yet-to-be implemented control unit is to perform.

One final introductory matter. This appendix helps refresh the reader's background in popular combinational switching circuits. Combinational circuit design techniques for MSI parts from SSI parts are trivial. What is important is that the reader assimilate the function and behavior of these parts, and know where and how to use them in a design.

C.2. AN OVERVIEW OF LOGIC DESIGN

C.2.1. Combinational Circuits

Some of the basic concepts of switching theory are briefly reviewed in this section. Switching theory comprises combinational and sequential circuits. A combinational circuit has no memory; its outputs are strictly a function of its inputs. A general combinational circuit of n inputs and m outputs is shown in **Figure C.1.** Fig. C.1(a) represents the circuit with a rectangular block. The behavior of the combinational circuit can be described in many ways. One of the more traditional methods is the truth table, as seen in Fig. C.1(b). When the number of input signal lines exceeds five, the number of lines in the truth table becomes unwieldy. Other descriptive methods include the use of a boolean statement for each of the m output signals.

The designer's viewpoint of most combinational circuits described here is that of an operation performed on an input vector of 0's and 1's. In many cases, a truth table which has a row for each possible combination obscures this operation by an overabundance of detail. A *function table* is a useful tabular descriptive tool which is based on the truth table but permits some "uncluttering" of detail. The function table is designed by example in §C.6.

A structural description of a combinational circuit consists of showing the actual arrangement of the gates which realize the desired behavior of the function. Once a combinational circuit has been designed, the structural description often

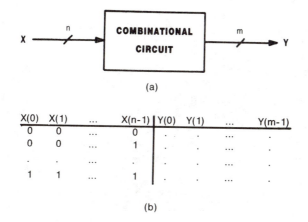

(a)

X(0)	X(1)	...	X(n-1)	Y(0)	Y(1)	...	Y(m-1)
0	0	...	0	.	.	...	.
0	0	...	1	.	.	...	.
.	.	...	.	.	.	...	.
1	1	...	1	.	.	...	.

(b)

Figure C.1. *A Generalized combinational circuit.* (a) Block diagram. (b) Truth table.

serves as the behavioral description. Many experienced logic designers are so adept at converting a structural description to a behavioral description in their mind, they are unaware a conversion is taking place.

C.2.2. Logic-to-Physical Mapping

The ancient Greeks studied deductive logic. Beginning with some true and false propositions, they deduced other true and false propositions. From the statement "Men are mortal" and "Socrates is a man", they deduced "Socrates is mortal". The British mathematician George Boole (1815-1864) studied logic, and authored a book titled *An Investigation into the Laws of Thought*. This study of truth functions takes place in the mind: the logic domain. A century later, deductive logic and its theorems were applied to switching circuit realizations in the physical domain.

One limitation of boolean algebra is the absence of the concept of time or change. The terms true and false have a connotation of permanence. Digital systems employ sequences of operations. Logical conditions are continually being activated and deactivated. Behavior is controlled through the technique of specifying that when certain *conditions* are active, then other *actions* take place. With this technique, in 1834 Babbage designed a machine without benefit of boolean algebra. A counter unit provides a sequencing mechanism, and certain count values can activate certain functional units.

Boolean algebra provides us with concepts and terms at a conceptual level independent of technological building blocks. Boolean functions deal with two-valued variables, and are the basis for combinational switching theory. It is possible to design systems as Babbage did: close to the physical level. The designer's thoughts originate in terms of circuit types, and signal levels. However, a hierarchical approach is needed to handle the ever more sophisticated and complex functional units of this era of improving VLSI technology. Consequently we need a technique to bridge conceptual levels.

For boolean algebra to be useful to the engineer, a correspondence from the logical world to the physical world must be defined. Sometimes in treatments of switching theory, these practical matters are not accorded adequate importance relative to the mathematical properties. The purpose of this section is to construct a bridge from switching theory to the logic drawings that represent physical circuits. This bridge is called the *logic-to-physical mapping*. The logic-to-physical mapping has two submappings. Relative to the digital function model introduced in the prologue, the first submapping concerns the meaning of the *operation* performed by the functional unit and the meaning of values on the connection points. The second submapping concerns the meaning of the *interconnections* and the values they take on.

Submapping 1: logic operations to logic circuits
Submapping 2: logic variables to signal lines

In the first submapping, the low-level digital functions of boolean AND and OR operations are implemented with physical logic gates. The physical circuit has input connection points and output connection points, which accept values denoted *high* or *low*. On the other hand, the truth tables describing the logic (boolean) operations use values *true* or *false*.

In the second submapping, Boolean or logic variables created in the designer's mind are *mapped* (assigned) to physical signal lines. The signal lines can possess two states corresponding to voltage levels which are also called *high* and *low*. Similarly, the logic variables in the designer's mind may have values *active* or *inactive*.

The interplay between the two submappings is nontrivial and concerns matching the values on the interconnections to the expected values on the connection points. The basic logical function (AND or OR) performed by the same physical logic circuit may be transformed from a basic AND operation to a basic OR operation and vice-versa. A complicating factor is that the transformation may be done by using one of two independent dualities. Only one duality is needed, so we have one duality too many! In the preferred duality, a theorem of DeMorgan is employed which does not affect the logic-to-physical mapping. In the second duality, the operation performed by the circuit may be transformed to its dual (AND to OR and vice-versa) by locally altering an instance of the first submapping (logic operation to physical circuit). We reduce the confusion by treating each submapping separately, and showing the *independence* of the dualities.

We do not claim that the logic-to-physical mapping is easy to grasp, but we present an approach which minimizes confusion if properly applied. This approach is (1) consistent, and (2) most nearly in conformance with current practices, specifications and documents. Many computer manufacturers have been using basically similar systems.

C.2.3. Submapping 1: Boolean Operations to Circuits

Boolean function inputs or outputs are either true or false. The voltage levels provided by computer technologies are called high and low. In assigning values true or false to the input and output connection points of a physical circuit, the *positive logic convention* identifies the high voltage with the true boolean value and the low voltage with the false boolean value. In the *negative logic convention,* the low level corresponds to true. The truth table for a 2-input AND element (gate) is shown in **Table C.1** for positive logic and negative logic. In the table, true is shown as a 1 and false as a 0. The output of an AND is 1 only if all inputs are 1. Variables (signals) A and B are inputs and variable S is the output. Similarly, **Table C.2** shows truth tables for a 2-input OR gate or element. The output of an OR is 1 if at least one input is 1. The boolean values are 0 and 1. In the physical domain, the signal values of the connection points are high (H) and low (L).

Table C.1.
Truth Tables for 2-input AND Element

AND Function			*Positive Logic AND*			*Negative Logic AND*		
A	*B*	*S*	*A*	*B*	*S*	*A*	*B*	*S*
0	0	0	L	L	L	H	H	H
0	1	0	L	H	L	H	L	H
1	0	0	H	L	L	L	H	H
1	1	1	H	H	H	L	L	L
a) 1 is true			b) H is true			c) L is true		

Table C.2.
Truth Tables for 2-input OR Element

OR Function			*Positive Logic OR*			*Negative Logic OR*		
A	*B*	*S*	*A*	*B*	*S*	*A*	*B*	*S*
0	0	0	L	L	L	H	H	H
0	1	1	L	H	H	H	L	L
1	0	1	H	L	H	L	H	L
1	1	1	H	H	H	L	L	L
a) 1 is true			b) H is true			c) L is true		

Now consider Table C.1(b) for AND and Table C.2(c) for OR, and note that they are identical: just reorder the rows. The output is high only when both inputs are high. This is the *negative logic duality:* a physical circuit which performs the positive logic AND function also performs the negative logic OR function. Similarly, note that Table C.1(c) and Table C.2(b), with reordered rows, represent the same physical circuit: positive logic OR or negative logic AND. Negative logic duality only depends on the second logic-to-physical submapping: the physical signal level used to represent "true" for the connection points. Note that between truth tables (b) and (c) of these tables, the names of the input and output signals were not changed, only the voltage level whose meaning is "true".

The circuit types of the most popular logic technologies are named according to the positive logic convention. In this book, we follow the positive logic convention and the *high voltage is always true.*

C.2.4. Some Switching Theory Terminology

The truth table is a descriptive tool which may be applied to any boolean function F. Truth tables have one row for each possible combination of values of the 2-valued boolean inputs. Each input combination (row) for which the value of F is 1 is called a *minterm* of function F. Function F can be represented as a boolean sum (OR operation) of its minterms. **Table C.3** defines a hypothetical function F with three input variables, A, B, and C. Each minterm, then, has three *literals:* A, B, and C. The output variable is F. Note that when variable A takes on value 0 in a row of the truth table, A is "not true", and is represented by A' as the minterm literal. Thus, A' is 1 when A is 0, and vice-versa.

Table C.3.				
Truth Table for a Boolean Function F				
_A_	_B_	_C_	_F_	_Minterm_
0	0	0	1	(A'B'C')
0	0	1	1	(A'B'C)
0	1	0	0	
0	1	1	1	(A'BC)
1	0	0	0	
1	0	1	0	
1	1	0	0	
1	1	1	0	

As a sum of minterms, Table C.3 is represented by the following equation.

$$F = A'B'C' + A'B'C + A'BC \qquad (C.1)$$

The AND operation is denoted by placing the variables side by side as in AB, or by the symbol "•" as in A • B. The OR operation is denoted by the plus sign as in A + B. Note that the complementation of a variable is indicated by the ' (prime). As a result, uncomplemented variables are said to be *unprimed.* Complementation of a variable can also be indicated by an overbar over the name. Complementation is a unary operation (operates on only one operand), and is also called the NOT operation. Eq. C.1 represents the minterms of the first, second, and fourth rows of the truth table. However, a more economical boolean equation for function F is:

$$F = A'B' + A'C \qquad (C.2)$$

In Eq. C.2, items A'B' and A'C are called *p-terms* (for product terms) of function F. In boolean algebra, the AND operation is called the boolean product. Items A', B' and C are the *literals.* A boolean *sum* corresponds to the OR operation. A p-term is a product (AND) of literals, and the equation represents a sum

(OR) of p-terms. A minterm is a p-term with a literal for each input variable. Eq. C.2 is a more economical description of function F in two respects: fewer p-terms and fewer literals. Eq C.2 is in "sum of products" (S-of-P) form.

We review a realization procedure in **Figure C.2.** Fig. C.2(a) shows the correspondence of the operations complementation, AND, and OR, with the logic diagram symbols for gates. Each *primed* (complemented) variable requires a complementary signal. An *inverter* performs the complementation function. The inverter, also called a NOT element, is a 1-input, 1-output gate.

Each p-term of an S-of-P expression corresponds to an AND gate with one input point corresponding to each literal. The output of each such AND gate feeds an OR gate. The OR gate output point corresponds to output variable F of Fig. C.2(a). In the physical domain, the OR gate *generates* signal F. Fig. C.2(b) shows a logic diagram representing Eq. C.2.

In Eq. C.2, literal A′ appears in both p-terms, and it can be factored out as follows:

$$F = A'(B' + C) \qquad\qquad\qquad (C.3)$$

However, Eq. C.3 is not in S-of-P form; it is realized with logic gates as shown in Fig. C.2(c).

More application detail appears in §C.19, where the minterm form is associated with a read-only memory (ROM). The S-of-P (or p-term) form of a logic equation is easily implemented in circuits with a programmable logic array (PLA).

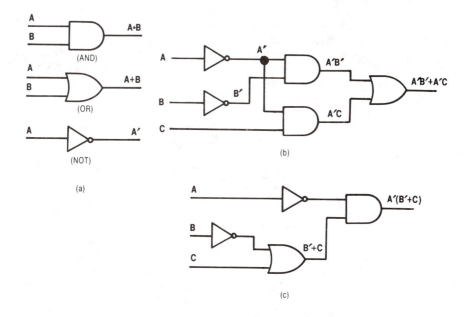

Figure C.2. *Logic gate functions.* (a) Basic functions. (b) S-of-P form. (c) Factoring A′.

C.2.5. Submapping 2: Signal Names with an Active Level

Logic variables originate in the designer's mind. Signal conditions are continually changing, so terms active and inactive are commonly employed to describe the two states of a logic variable. Also found in the system are binary *data variables,* whose values are 0 and 1.

Any logic variable which exists in a digital system has a complementary variable. For example, the property "ready" induces the complementary property of "not ready". When "ready" is true then "not ready" is false. Often a complementary variable may represent a useful condition in the system in its own right. A variable and its complement map to signal lines of opposite *polarity.*

Often the designers of a digital system are not those who must modify, update, or maintain the design. Some conventions in naming two-valued logic signals are needed to describe how the system works, and to avoid misleading those who attempt to understand the system from logic drawings.

Consider a signal named KEYON which represents a *condition* in the digital system. This signal is expected to assume the active value (high) when the key is depressed. In this case, signal KEYON is high, so KEYON is an *active-high* signal. Corresponding to signal KEYON may be a *complementary* signal named NOT KEYON whose value is inactive (low) when the key is depressed. This complementary signal is defined to be *active-low*. These terms do not mean the positive logic convention is changed. Notice that we are still mapping true into high and false into low relative to submapping 1 regarding logic operations. An active-low signal is a complementary signal, and can be generated from the active-high signal by an inverter. There is no avoiding the complementation operation on logic variables, and this fundamental boolean operation is *independent* of the mapping of logic variables to physical signal wires. We stress this point, as it is easy to confuse the unary complementation operation with a change in the convention for the logic-to-physical mapping. *An active-high signal is a signal which assumes the value "high" when the condition after which the signal is named is active.* Sometimes a required condition corresponds to a primed variable which identifies the inactive value of the given variable. For example, we may choose never to go on a picnic in the rain. "Not raining" is then one of the conditions for "picnic". Such signals are active-low because they are low when the condition from which they take their name is active.

If a given digital system behaves as desired, then we can randomly assign names to the signal lines and the system still works. Signals are given names to aid the recall of engineers who design, work on, interface to, or study the system. The assignment of a name to a signal is intended first as a reminder of what condition the signal represents. A second reminder is whether the signal represents the condition after which it is named in the low state or in the high state. This second item is called the *active level* of the signal. Active level naming has been practiced since the inception of computer design. In IBM, active-high signal names are preceded by a "+", and active-low signal names are preceded by a "−". In some Digital Equipment Corporation (DEC) documentation, active-high signal names are followed by an "H", and active-low signal names are followed by an "L".

In boolean algebra, wherever a sum or product operation requires the complement value, the single variable name is primed to denote the complementation operation. In the corresponding situation in the physical world, the signal is complemented once with an inverter. Often, as with many double-pole switches and flip-flops, a signal and its complement are both available. Now whenever a gate is implemented, it must be fed by input signals of the proper polarity. Thus active-high and active-low signals are respectively implementations of the unprimed and primed variables in boolean expressions. In the logical domain, we shall use primes (') to indicate complementation. In the physical domain, names corresponding to active-high signals are preceded by "+" (or blanks); names corresponding to active-low signals are preceded by "−".

When a signal line takes on its active level, it is *active*. Other terms which indicate this situation include asserted, on, up, or present. When a signal takes on the other level, it is *inactive*. Other terms for inactive are negated, disasserted, deactivated, turned off, down, absent, etc. We also use the verbs "activate" and "deactivate" to indicate the designer's thoughts about causing a transition from one signal value to the other.

Values in a digital system are continually changing, which places us in the time domain. An *edge* occurs when the signal acquires a new value. The transition to the active condition is a point in time called the *leading edge* of the signal change. The transition to the inactive condition is the *trailing edge* of the signal. The leading edge of an active-high signal is the low-to-high transition, and the leading edge of an active-low signal is the high-to-low transition. We mention here that some flip-flops or memory elements are edge- or transition-sensitive. Each signal has a leading and a trailing edge, but edge-sensitive elements only respond to one of the edges.

C.2.6. Gates, the Inversion Bubble, and the DeMorgan Duality

The elementary gates or logic blocks are shown in **Figure C.3**. These symbols are consistent with the "distinctive shape" version of standard ANSI Y 32.14 - 1973. The symbol for the NAND or NOR is the same as for the respective AND or OR, but the output line is shown leaving the symbol from an *inversion bubble*. The NAND operation is equivalent to an AND operation followed by a NOT operation, and a NOR operation is an OR operation followed by a NOT operation. The inversion bubble is logically equivalent to an inverter. See **Figure C.4**.

The primitive decision element of the second and early third generation technologies was the positive logic NAND gate. The NAND gate is universal, in the sense that any boolean expression can be implemented with a sufficient number of NAND gates. In this case, designers who think in terms of AND and OR operations, must convert their thoughts about these operations to the single NAND gate. Two problems are evident. What tool do we use to convert a boolean expression to NAND form? How can the designer reflect the basic AND and OR nature of the logic decision on the drawing? The basis for the answer to both these questions is *DeMorgan's theorem*, which states two boolean identities.

Logic designers can use the NOR gate to do an operation which the designer views as an AND, and the NAND gate to do an operation which is viewed as an OR. The notion may seem strange at first, but the basic idea is illustrated by DeMorgan's theorem:

$$(AB)' = A' + B' \qquad\qquad\text{(C.4)}$$
$$(C + D)' = C'D' \qquad\qquad\text{(C.5)}$$

Note that the left side of the first equation describes a NAND operation and the left side of the second equation describes a NOR operation. The DeMorgan "rule" shows that if one complements the literals one can replace the AND with an OR and vice-versa. The first equation states the NAND is equivalent to the OR of the complements of the inputs A and B. The second equation states the NOR is equivalent to the AND of the complements of inputs C and D. Thus, to obtain a signal representing the AND of signals +X and +Y, the designer can instead feed signals −X and −Y to a two-input NOR gate. By DeMorgan's theorem, the result is a signal representing XY. See **Figure C.5**. The manipulation of a boolean expres-

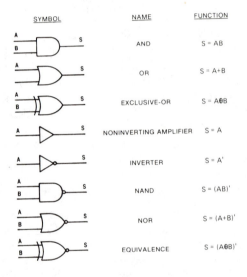

SYMBOL	NAME	FUNCTION
	AND	S = AB
	OR	S = A+B
	EXCLUSIVE-OR	S = A⊕B
	NONINVERTING AMPLIFIER	S = A
	INVERTER	S = A'
	NAND	S = (AB)'
	NOR	S = (A+B)'
	EQUIVALENCE	S = (A⊕B)'

Figure C.3. *Logic symbols for elementary logic gates and their function.*

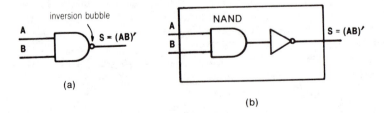

(a)

(b)

Figure C.4. *NAND element.* (a) NAND. (b) AND followed by inverter.

sion into a form suitable for NAND or NOR gates is a result of the boolean identities discovered by DeMorgan. A logician can use DeMorgan's theorem to convert *any* boolean equation into a form which uses only NAND operations and the complementation operation. Since a 1-input NAND is a NOT element, the NAND is sufficient to implement any boolean expression. Afterwards, the logician's result can be subjected to the logic-to-physical mapping. We note there are some who confuse this fundamental property of the logic domain with an interchange of the positive logic convention and the negative logic convention of submapping 2. Our explanation is *consistent* with the positive logic convention. NAND gates perform the AND operation of the left side of Eq. C.4 when the designer needs an AND function. Similarly, the NAND gate performs the OR operation of the right side of Eq. C.4 (A′ + B′), when the designer needs an OR function. When the designer views the NAND gate as performing an OR function, then the OR version of the gate should be used on the logic diagram. In a sense, the designer controls the logic operation performed by the physical circuit through the choice of the signal polarity to feed the gate input points.

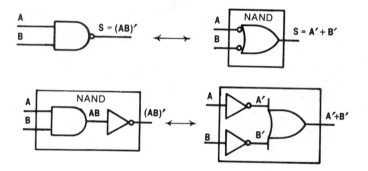

Figure C.5. *DeMorgan's theorem applied to the NAND gate.*

Figure C.6 shows the common gates and their *DeMorgan dual*. The DeMorgan dual is obtained by replacing OR with AND, and by replacing inversion bubbles with no bubble and no bubble with inversion bubbles.

Others [1] have used a mixed logic convention to describe what we call the DeMorgan dual. In mixed logic, the negative logic duality is applied locally to circuit types. The DeMorgan duality renders this confusing practice unnecessary: use positive logic and admit the existence of active-low signals. We generate active-low signals by inverters or NOT gates, or by the "bubble" on the output of a gate, but *not* by interchanging truth values. It is convenient, when logically combining the active-low signals, to feed them to gate inputs which have the inversion bubble. The bubble can be viewed as "cancelling" the active-low property, so the designer knows it is the "true" condition which is being ANDed or ORed by the gate.

Figure C.7 illustrates the DeMorgan dual. Suppose, for example, we desire to turn on a switch via a control signal T ON SW whenever a "key" is on (KEYON) or when another signal indicates a time delay has occurred (TIMEOUT). The

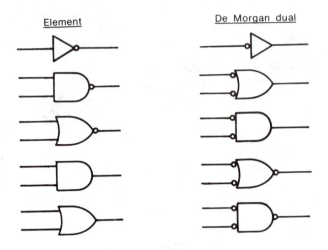

Figure C.6. *Logic elements and their DeMorgan dual.*

Figure C.7. *Two examples of the use of DeMorgan dual to combine complementary (active-low) signals and better convey meaning.*

design is to be done with a NAND gate. The designer is actually "ORing" two conditions, so the DeMorgan dual of the NAND is the proper logic drawing representation, as shown for the generation of +T ON SW in Fig. C.7. The second example in Fig. C.7 generates a signal whose meaning is poor weather, at least in the Santa Clara valley.

To pursue the use of the DeMorgan dual, consider a boolean function F in normal form:

$$F = AB + CD.$$

Figure C.8 shows a NAND realization. The equation

$$F = ((AB)'(CD)')'$$

is represented in logic diagram form with NAND gates as shown in Fig. C.8(a). However, Fig. C.8(b) is more understandable because it makes judicious use of the DeMorgan dual. We can make logic drawings more understandable with the proper use of the DeMorgan dual. See Wakerly [2].

Just as p-terms can have both primed and unprimed literals, it is not always possible to avoid feeding an active-low signal to an input which does not have a bubble. A case in point is when an active-low signal feeds an AND type gate to

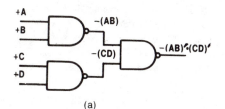

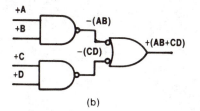

(a)

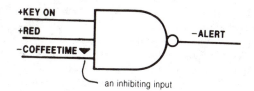

(b)

Figure C.8. *Use of DeMorgan dual on logic drawings.*   (a) Using only NAND gates. (b) Judicious use of DeMorgan dual on OR function.

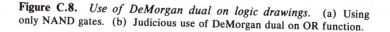

Figure C.9. *Example where active-low signal feeds nonbubble input.*

act as an inhibiting input. Suppose a condition "ALERT" is to be active when another condition is RED *and* a given key is on (KEYON), *except* during another condition known as COFFEETIME. If a NAND gate is used, the logic drawing is shown in **Figure C.9.** In this case, an active-low signal −COFFEETIME feeds an input point without an inversion bubble, which is called an "incompatibility". Incompatibilities occur normally, as in this case; COFFEETIME is an *inhibiting* input which is to disallow the activation of the NAND output. As a reminder, Fletcher [3] recommends the use of a solid triangle near the input.

So far, we have dealt primarily with logic signals of a control or conditional information nature. Another type of logic signal is not derived from a *condition* in the boolean algebraic sense, but from the *representation of numbers* in the binary number system. Such signals represent *data,* rather than conditions. If conditions in the system play an active role, then data plays a passive role. Bits have values 0 and 1, and in the positive logic convention, a 0 is a low value and a 1 is a high value. Data bits in numbers can also be complemented by inverters, so an active-low data signal is said to have the bit value 1 when the signal value is low. Thus for polarization, an active data signal has the binary value 1, and an inactive data signal has binary value 0.

C.2.7. Building Blocks: Naming of Pin-Outs

Two aspects of signal naming have been uncovered. The first is that the name given a signal line or connection concerns its purpose or what it does. Active-high or -low polarity indicators accompany a signal name. The second is the function or name of a logic drawing shape. We have seen NAND gates in the role of OR type functions, and have used the DeMorgan dual to move inversion bubbles and interchange the AND shape with the OR shape.

A simple rule to follow is noted here:

The active polarity *of an input or output pin is indicated by the presence or absence of a bubble. To perform the function, the inputs must have the active polarity. When the function is performed, the outputs take on their indicated active polarity.*

On a larger scale, the designer encounters functional units more complicated than the simple AND, OR, NAND or NOR functions. The simple rule easily extends to more complex functional units, such as data registers and memory chips. The chip manufacturer assigns pins, names, and meanings to the functional block inputs and outputs. This information generally appears on the *pin-out diagram* of a manufacturer's descriptive data sheet. A pin-out is a single input or output electrical connection or interface point for the chip or component, and corresponds to a signal source or destination. The pin-out is like a doorway and has a name. The pin-out is a connection point and should not be confused with a signal line or interconnection. We can use the term *label* when referring to the name of a pin-out. Some input connection points perform the function for which they are labeled when at the low level, and others at the high level. For example, the register CLEAR function for MSI parts almost always requires a low value. To indicate the need for an active-low signal on an input point, an inversion bubble is found on the pin-out diagram. The absence of an inversion bubble on the pin-out diagram means the function after which the input is labeled is performed when the input value is high.

Functional unit output points follow the same convention. If the output point originates from an inversion bubble, then when the condition corresponding to the pin-out label is active, that output value is low. On pin-outs without the inversion bubble, when the condition for which the label was assigned is active, the output value is high. Thus, the absence of an inversion bubble on an output indicates an active-high output signal. The abbreviation of the labels usually appear inside the block symbol with no polarity indication applied to the label. The bubbles convey the polarization information.

A functional block which performs a 4-bit counting function is shown in **Figure C.10**. The input point labeled L (abbreviation of "Load") controls the function performed. The inversion bubble indicates that the counter is loaded when this input point is low. When the L input point is fed by a signal in the high state, the counter is enabled to count up.

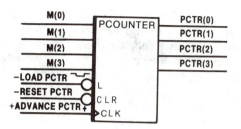

Figure C.10. *Example of active-low inputs on functional blocks.*

In Fig. C.10, the counter block is shown connected to signals which have names. Signal –LOAD PCTR controls the L input point. When condition LOAD PCTR is active, the –LOAD PCTR signal input is low, so the L input point is low, and the counter accepts parallel data (is parallel loaded) from its inputs, and presents the new value on its outputs. When the value of –LOAD PCTR returns to the high value, the last value on the data input lines is stored in the counter.

This method of loading data is *level-sensitive* to the low level, and a graphic appears near the input as a reminder of the low level. The counter outputs follow the input values being loaded while the LOAD input is low. An alternative loading method is called *edge-sensitive,* or *edge-triggered;* the data value is loaded and the output changes only upon the active transition of the controlling input. Edge-sensitive input points are indicated by a small triangle inside the block. If the change takes place on the positive (low-to-high) transition on the edge-sensitive input, no inversion bubble appears on the block diagram. An up arrow appears near the input as a reminder of the positive activating edge. An inversion bubble shows sensitivity to the negative-going edge.

Note that three concepts are involved here. Variable LOAD PCTR is a logical condition in the designer's mind. Signal –LOAD PCTR is a signal line corresponding to the logical condition. The line controls the value on input connection point (pin) labeled L of the building block or chip. To the logic designer using the building block, LOAD PCTR is an output signal to be generated. At a lower conceptual level, the chip designer views the connection point labeled L as a primary input to the chip.

Generally, the manufacturer assigns the label of the block diagram connection point. However, the designer is free to give any name to the signal line connected to that point. Often it is desirable to give the interconnection a different name. For example, the pin label UP/DOWN gives no indication of what polarity does what. If the high value on the pin input causes the counter to count down, then the signal line feeding the pin could be named +DOWN.

Many blocks of the same type may be used in a design, yet all will have the same label for the same pinout. Unless like pinouts are connected together, however, the pinouts will be connected to lines which have different names.

The key points of the naming approach in this section are as follows.

1. For any given condition in the system, there is a complementary condition which is inactive when the given condition is active.
2. Signal lines named after a condition must include a polarizing element (+ or −) to identify the level corresponding to the active condition.
3. The positive logic convention is always used for functional unit connection points. The inversion bubble on input always indicates that the pin expects a low value to perform the corresponding function; an inversion bubble on output indicates that the output condition appears as a low value. The bubble is viewed as a logic inverter.
4. The condition for which a signal is named is active when (a) the signal name indicates that the signal is active-high and the signal value is high, *or* (b) the signal name is active-low and the signal value is low. Thus a signal is active if its value corresponds to the polarizing element of its name.
5. An elementary OR type operation (OR or NOR) is converted to a DeMorgan dual AND type function by the application of DeMorgan's theorem. An AND type function is similarly convertible to an OR type function. The DeMorgan "rule" replaces AND with OR, active-high with active-low, and active-low with active-high.
6. Building blocks have pins or connection points which are given *labels* independent of the *name* of the signal wire connected to the connection point.

Table C.4 summarizes the important points in the mapping between the conceptual variables and boolean functions to the signal lines and logic gates.

Table C.4. Logic-to-Physical Mapping		
Item	*Conceptual Level*	*Implementation Level*
condition	variable (active, inactive)	signal (active-high, active-low)
name	variable name (DRY, DRY′)	signal name (+DRY, −DRY)
operation	function (AND, OR)	logic gate (NAND, NOR)

C.3. TIMING AND PROPAGATION DELAYS

In addition to the behavioral and structural properties of combinational circuits, we are interested in the property of time. On manufacturer's specification sheets (data sheets), timing is called "switching characteristics". Our interest in timing properties may seem inconsistent with the definition of a combinational circuit being independent of the past. The dependence only on the present, however, applies to when the inputs are stable. When one or more of the inputs change value, then a new line of the truth table governs the value of the circuit output. The outputs do not respond instantaneously: a *propagation delay* must be paid before the output stabilizes to the new value. This delay is denoted tP.

C.3.1. Delays and Timing Charts

The concepts of delays are illustrated in terms of the inverter element of **Figure C.11.** The element is shown in Fig. C.11(a) and the timing charts are shown in Figs. C.11(b) and (c). In timing charts, time is the horizontal axis, and increases from left to right. The timing charts in this figure also introduce the notion of the *cause-and-effect* arrow. In Fig. C.11(b), input signal +I reaches the low level, and *causes* the low-to-high change of signal –I. The change occurs following a delay tPLH(–I). Note here that the notation tP is expanded by appending "LH" to include the direction of signal change. The notation tPLH applies to an output level changing from low to high, and tPHL applies to an output changing from high to low. When dealing with 3-state devices, a third state (HI-Z) is brought into play. Notation tPZL denotes the delay when the output changes from the HI-Z state to the low level.

Fig. C.11 also shows that the name of the signal, or other identification of the delay, can appear in parentheses following the tP delay type. This reminder is useful when delays from more than one circuit are under discussion. In this light, the combinational delay of the generalized combinational circuit of Fig. C.1(a) is conveniently described by the notation tP(CC), where "CC" is an abbreviation for "combinational circuit". Unless otherwise stated, the value of tP(CC), if the HL or LH notation is not appended to the delay, is the larger of tPHL(CC) and

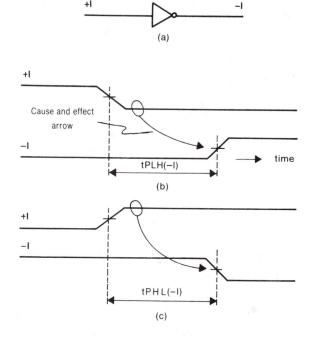

(a)

(b)

(c)

Figure C.11. *Combinational circuit propagation delays.*
(a) Inverter circuit. (b) Signal –I changing from low level to high level.
(c) Signal –I changing from high level to low level.

tPLH(CC). Also unless stated otherwise, tP(CC) includes the interconnection delay associated with the fan-out of the output line.

C.3.2. Worst-Case Delays

For any circuit, the propagation delays are only evident following an input transition. For each time +I goes from high to low, as in Fig. C.11(b), the delay value of tPLH(−I) can be different (within certain limits). In general we only know the maximum and the minimum values for a delay beforehand. Since combinational circuits are employed within digital systems which have a timing cycle, designers must be able to depend on the propagation delays being equal to or less than some specified maximum tPmax. This maximum is also called the *worst-case* delay. Most often, combinational gates are cascaded in a chain, one after another, and the designer must estimate the worst-case delay tP(CC)max for the combinational circuit itself. If the longest chain from input to output passes through ten gates, the circuit is said to have ten *levels of delay*. A very conservative approach is to add the worst-case delays for each gate or circuit in the slowest chain. However, this approach is unrealistic; some factors such as temperature may increase tPHL while decreasing tPLH. Therefore it is not uncommon (folk wisdom) to estimate tP(CC)max as a sum, with a few gates assigned less than the worst-case delay.

C.3.3. Ambiguity Duration and Skew

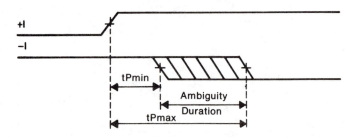

Figure C.12.   *Illustration of ambiguity region for propagation delays.*

Another timing specification of interest is the minimum possible propagation delay, tPmin, which corresponds to the *best-case* delay. The best-case delay is the soonest the output can change following an input change. Put another way, it is the duration of time for which the combinational circuit outputs are guaranteed to hold the former value following an input change. After tPmin, the output values are ambiguous; the output is not guaranteed to be either at the old value or the new value. Following tPmax, the output is guaranteed to be the new value. The *ambiguity duration* spans the time from the earliest an output value can change to the latest. **Figure C.12** shows a timing chart of an output signal transition where the ambiguity duration is shaded. Often the value of tPmin is assumed to be 0, which is certainly conservative. Since the combinational gates are cascaded in series, the ambiguity duration for "downstream" gates will widen. This phenomenon is shown for a fan-out tree in **Figure C.13.** The diagram of the circuit is shown in Fig. C.13(a), and the timing chart of delays appears in Fig. C.13(b). Such a tree is commonly used to "power" (provide the ability to drive a larger fan-out) the clocking signals of a digital system. It is not desirable to cascade clocking signals through too many gates because of the widening ambiguity duration for the downstream gates. Where the clock signals are involved, the duration of time between instants labeled t1 and t2 in Fig. C.13(b) is called the *clock skew.* Realistically, signals –CLOCK2A1 through –CLOCK2B2 are never activated and deactivated at the same instant of time. The edges of such timing signals can differ by as much as the value of the clock skew.

The ambiguity duration is represented differently for data signals, as is seen in **Figure C.14.** The critical aspect of a data signal is not whether it is high or low, but whether it has *stabilized* or not. Data signals are generally bused together; when the values on the bus are *valid* is important. The bus is valid when all data

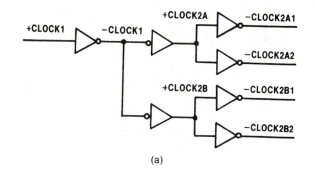

(a)

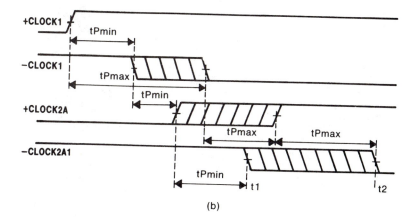

(b)

Figure C.13. *Effect of cascaded delays is to increase the ambiguity duration.* (a) Fan-out tree. (b) Timing chart.

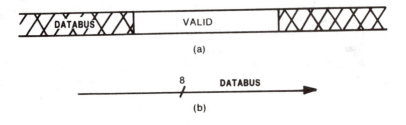

(a)

(b)

Figure C.14. *Data signal representations.* (a) Data bus timing information of interest. (b) 8-bit data bus block diagram notation.

signals have stabilized to their new values, whether the value is 0 or 1. The timing chart of Fig. C.14(a) shows the indifference to the actual values on the bus. Fig. C.14(b) shows the representation for a data bus eight bits wide without parity.

C.4.   BLOCK DIAGRAMS AND RTN STATEMENTS

Block diagrams allow the designer to describe digital operations on data signals concisely. The designer must not become unnecessarily bogged down with toothpicks at the gate level. The design should first proceed at the higher building block level. Therefore we present a block diagram notation. It is also convenient at this time to introduce a register transfer notation (RTN) to describe the function or behavior of the block.

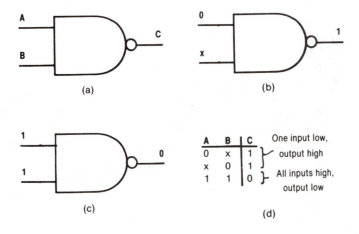

Figure C.15. *The NAND gate.* (a) Symbol. (b) If one input is low, the output is high. (c) The output is low only if all inputs are high. (d) Function table.

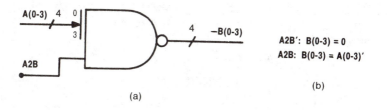

Figure C.16.   *Gated NAND bus.*   (a) Block diagram.   (b) RTN statements.

A two-input NAND is shown in **Figure C.15.**   The block is shown in Fig. C.15(a), with signal names on the inputs and output.   Fig. C.15(b) illustrates a logic designer's mental image of the gate: *if one input is low, the output is high.*   The dual view of the gate is shown in Fig. C.15(c) where *the output is low only if all inputs are high.*   These facts are summarized in Fig.   C.15(d), which is a function table.   The function table is like a truth table, but economically allows value "x" to mean either 0 or 1 as an input.   The truth table treats all input combinations equally, but the designer doesn't.   The function table is closer to the designer's thoughts.

The OR gate is similarly viewed.   If no inputs are active, the output is inactive.   If one (or more) input is active, the output is active.   The designer thinks: *an OR passes any active input value.*

Figure C.16 describes a NAND gate busing arrangement.   Fig. C.16(a) shows a block diagram which represents four NANDs.   The data line is slashed and tagged with a 4, so four gates are represented.   Signal A2B fans to all four gates; it is not slashed indicating a single control line.   The left endpoint of the line is a solid dot, a reminder that the line represents a control signal.   Fig. C.16(b) shows the register notation description for this function in the logical domain.   In RTN, we find a boolean statement to the left of the colon.   Here, control signal A2B is to the left of the colon.   When A2B is active, the action to the right of the colon takes place. The equal sign (=) indicates a combinational circuit function, where the signal or bus named to the left of the equal sign takes on the value to the right of the equal sign.   If a "primed" condition appears to the left of the colon, the action is performed when that condition is absent (inactive).

Information to the left of the colon is *conditional information,* which is either true or false.   The RTN statement does not indicate in this case whether the generalized MSI block *control point* is active-low or active-high.   The particular circuit shown performs an inversion of the data bits.   When the control signal is active, the bus is active-low.

In dealing with data which is bused, it is customary to give the collective data signals a name such as "AC" or "ZBUS".   The bits of the bus are assigned numbers ranging from 0 through $(n - 1)$ for an n-bit data word.   The first and last bit number may appear within parentheses separated by a dash: ZBUS(0-7) denotes an 8-bit bus.

The bits within the parentheses may be omitted if it is understood that the entire bus is described.   Individual bits such as bit 0 are denoted as ZBUS(0).   In many ways, the bus may be viewed as an n-component vector, with each bit being a component. The grouping of the bits together to form a bus may also be viewed as a concatenation. We represent concatenation by a comma (,). Thus the RTN statement:

$$DBUS = A(0-3), B(4-7)$$

indicates an 8-bit bus formed by the four high-order bits of A, and the fifth through eighth bits of B.

C.5. THE DATA SELECTOR OR MULTIPLEXER

One of the most important busing elements is called the data selector or multiplexer, or MUX. The function is basically one of *passing data* from one of the inputs to the output bus. See **Figure C.17.** (In England, the MUX function is called a "funnel".) A straightforward approach to the MUX is shown in Fig. C.17(a). The *select* control point(s) (indicated by a solid bubble) is encoded into two control points called X and Y as shown in Fig. C.17(b). Rather than increase combinational circuit delays by use of a decoder, the AND gates combine the select input decode function with the data "pass" function. Sometimes it may be desirable not to select any source to pass to the MUX output, but to "force" the MUX output to zero. On many MUX chips, there is an additional control point which most manufactures call an "enable" but can also be viewed as a "disable". The additional control point ENBL must be active in order to *pass* data. When ENBL is inactive, the MUX output is zero.

The block diagram symbol and RTN notation are shown in **Figure C.18.** The basic shape is a line perpendicular to the direction of data movement. This notation appears in data flow diagrams in many IBM maintenance documents, where clutter is avoided by not showing the control signals. To accommodate the control points, the symbol is a "T", with a cross on top of the stem. The cross on top of the "T" accepts the control points. On the source side of the cross, the "select" control points are placed, since they control the source data. Encoded select signals X and Y are shown as a 2-bit control bus. The "slash 2" indicates the bus width, and the solid bubble where the slash intersects the bus indicates a control bus (as opposed to data bus.)

The output side of the cross of the MUX block diagram symbol receives the enable or disable control point, because this control point controls the output. If the control point is active-low, a bubble appears.

The function is summarized as follows: the enabled MUX passes data from the selected source to the output. When the MUX is disabled, it forces the output to zero.

As an MSI part, a typical package contains two 4×1 MUX elements. The block diagram of Fig. C.18(a) concisely represents eight MSI packages. At the higher conceptual levels, more detail than this is undesirable. On some data flow diagrams, the MUX control points are removed, leaving only the stem of the "T". The designer should not become so overwhelmed by the detail that the global considerations are lost.

An RTN description of the behavior of the 4×1 MUX is shown in Fig. C.18(b). Referring to the top line, when the enable control point is inactive, then

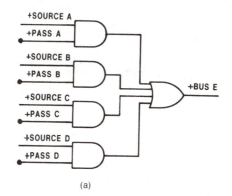

(a)

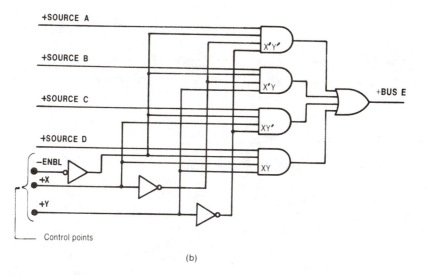

(b)

Figure C.17. *The 4×1 MUX circuit.* (a) Straightforward data selection. (b) Data selection via encoded select signals.

EN′ will be *true*. The output BUS E is zero. On the other hand, when EN is *true* (−EN of the block diagram is low), then the decoding of select signals X and Y determines which source data is passed to the output. For each of the four possible combinations of values for X and Y there is an RTN statement.

Recall that a *condition* either exists (is active or true) or does not exist (is inactive or false). A condition is mapped to a physical signal wire which represents the existence of the condition. The boolean algebra used to the left of the colon of an RTN statement deals with conditions which may be true or false (active or

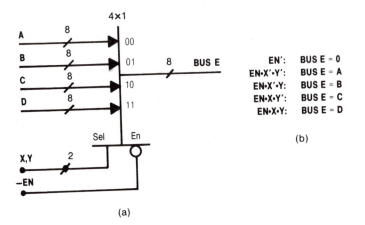

Figure C.18. *4×1 MUX descriptions.* (a) Block diagram. (b) RTN statements.

inactive). In RTN statements, all actions are performed for which the conditional information is true.

C.6. THE FUNCTION TABLE

The function table of **Figure C.19** is another method of describing the behavior of the 4×1 MUX of Fig. C.18(a). In this case, the function table is a physical description, so we use + and – signs before the signal names. In Fig. C.19, the function table describes the behavior for one data bit. This is the description required since the behavior is the same for all data bits. Notice that with four data sources, one *enable* control point, and two *select* control points, a boolean truth table for the 4×1 MUX has 2^7 or 128 rows! Fig. C.19 only has five rows. Yet under proper interpretation this 5-row table conveys information in a far more comprehensive manner. In truth tables, the rows must correspond to minterms, whereas in function tables the rows can be p-terms.

The top row of the function table indicates that when the signal –EN is high (Enable is false), the output is low (zero). When –EN is low, condition Enable is true and select inputs X and Y decode to pass values A, B, C, or D to the output BUS E.

We caution the reader in deciphering function tables on specification sheets. Although the L or H value on the designated pin of the package may produce the output value on the designated pin, unfortunately the signal names may not always correspond to the customary "active-low" or "active-high" naming convention.

SELECTS		ENABLE	OUTPUT
X	Y	-EN	BUS E
X	X	H	L
L	L	L	A
L	H	L	B
H	L	L	C
H	H	L	D

<u>Note</u>: L = low level, H = high level, x = either level

Figure C.19. *Function table for 4 × 1 MUX.*

C.7. MERGE, TAP, AND SPLIT NOTATION

Busing is an important function with data signals, and multiplexing is only one of the operations which may be performed. Another operation is *merging;* for example, an 8-bit bus and a 4-bit bus are merged into a 12-bit bus. The merge block is depicted in **Figure C.20,** where the concatenation operation is denoted by a comma. Also shown are data bus *tapping* (the main bus continues straight, the additional fan-out of the tap goes at an angle) and *splitting* (the opposite of a merge). Note that these operations do not involve any gates; they only concern the fan-out of the data lines. This notation is useful on data flow diagrams.

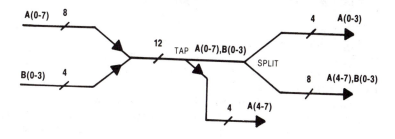

Figure C.20. *Merging, tapping, and splitting data buses on block diagrams.*

C.8. THE SHIFTER

Another common function which a MUX can perform is that of a *shifter.* A shifter is a combinational circuit used for shifting an input bus by an amount determined by values on control points. The shifter is distinguished from a shift register described in Appendix D.

A shifter is shown in **Figure C.21.** The input word is called A, and the output word is S. A right shift in RTN is denoted by *sr* or *shr.* In a right shift, each bit value moves right one position, toward the less significant end. A left shift is denoted *sl* or *shl* in RTN, and shifts each bit left, to a more significant position. The i-th bit value moves to the (i–1)-th position in a left shift. In RTN, shifting two bits left is denoted 2sl, which is two shift lefts.

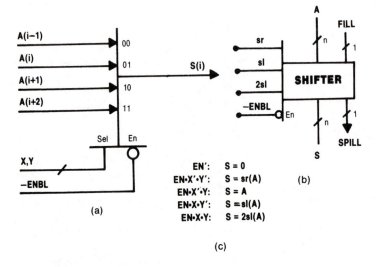

Figure C.21. *A shifter.* (a) Shifter using MUX. (b) Block diagram. (c) RTN statements.

In shift operations on n-bit numbers, the bit positions at the ends of the word, bit 0 (MSB) and bit n – 1 (LSB) are of special interest. For a right shift, we denote the MSB position as the *FILL*, and the LSB position as the *SPILL*. Similarly for a left shift, the MSB becomes the *SPILL* position and the LSB becomes the *FILL* position. The SPILL bit value is also called the end-off bit because there is no designated place for it to go. For an *end-off* shift, the bit value is lost. The FILL represents the opposite case, it is a position with no value specifically designated to occupy the position. Normally the FILL position receives a value 0, an operation known as *0-FILL*. Unless otherwise stated, shifts are end-off, *0-FILL*.

When the value in the spill position is received by the fill position, the shift is called a *rotate*, denoted in RTN as *rr* and *rl* for the right and left rotations respectively. The operation is also called an *end-around shift*.

Shifting a binary number to the right one position will halve the number, provided that the sign bit retains its value. When only the n – 1 magnitude bits of an n-bit binary number are shifted right, the operation is called an *arithmetic right shift*, and denoted *asr* or *ashr* in RTN statements. The spill bit is lost, and the fill bit is to the right of the sign bit. For one's and two's complement binary numbers, the fill position receives the value of the sign position, as it normally would.

For an *arithmetic left shift*, denoted *asl* or *ashl* in RTN, the sign bit retains its value. The fill bit value is 0. The bit to the right of the sign bit spills off and is lost. If this bit value differs from the value of the sign bit, an overflow occurs. The arithmetic left shift multiplies a binary number by 2.

An n-bit *barrel shifter* is a combinational circuit capable of shifting or rotating from 0 to n − 1 positions. In general, where n is a power of 2 and m = 2^n, m select-type control points determine the amount of the shift. The circuit can be systematically designed from m cascaded layers of 2×1 MUXes and some additional circuits, as described in Lim [4]. The design of a 4-bit barrel shifter, which shifts from 0 to 3 positions right or left, is described by Mick [5; p. 4-37]. This unit is also cascadable. A thorough discussion of combinational networks for shifting a variable number of bits appears in Davis [6].

Some shifters can shift one bit left or one bit right, and can be connected together. The shifters found in four bit-slice data flows such as the Am2903 (see Chapter 6), employ *bidirectional* chip pins at the right and left ends of the shifters. For a right shift, the right pin becomes the spill output and the left pin is the fill input. On the other hand, for a left shift, the left pin is the spill output and the right pin is the fill input. This arrangement permits the concatenation of the 4-bit wide shifters into 8-bit or 16-bit wide shifters.

The shifter function accepts a data input value, and either passes the bit value straight through to the output, or shifts it one (or more) position(s) to the right or left, as determined by the control point combination.

C.9. THE DECODER

The decoder is another popular MSI part, and is shown in **Figure C.22,** for a 2×4 decoder. The descriptions extend straightforwardly to decoders of size 3×8, 4×16, etc. The enable signal of the decoder is usually active-low, as are the outputs. The RTN decoder descriptor is *decd,* which implies a positive logic decoder function (active-high output lines). In the RTN of Fig. C.22(b) we only show the function as performed in the logic domain. The polarization of the signals is a detail left for the block diagram. The function table is shown in Fig. C.22(c). The enable signal and the outputs are active-low, as indicated by the minus sign accompanying those signal names. Decoders of a smaller dimension can be connected in a tree to implement higher dimension decoders. The technique is illustrated in Fig. C.22(d).

When the enable signal of the decoder is used to distribute a pulse (e.g. a trigger pulse) along a decoder output line, the decoder is renamed a *demultiplexer.* For example, an active-low clock pulse arriving at the enable input can be distributed, without inversion, to the output line selected by the value on the decoder inputs. See **Figure C.23.** The technique is useful for selecting a destination register to receive information from a common bus. The demultiplexer may also provide a control signal which selects among mutually exclusive 3-state drivers connected to a common bus.

C.10. THE PRIORITY ENCODER

Another common MSI block is the priority encoder of **Figure C.24.** The inputs are active-low, the output is active-high. The Enable is active-low, and an output is provided to indicate the validity of the encoder output. If *no* input is

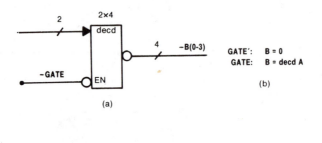

GATE': B = 0
GATE: B = decd A

(b)

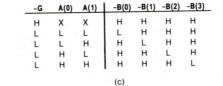

(c)

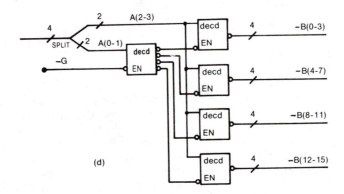

(d)

Figure C.22. *The 2×4 decoder.* (a) Block diagram. (b) RTN description. (c) Function table. (d) A 4×16 decoder with 2×4 decoder parts.

active, there is nothing to encode, which is indicated by the output labeled **GS** being inactive. In the priority encoder shown, only the most significant active input is encoded, where 0 is the most significant position and 3 is the least significant. Thus when the encoder delivers the value "3" on the output, no other input is active.

One application of the priority encoder is to convert the priority level of the highest-priority active input into a value which can be used as a portion of an address field. Another application of the priority encoder is to determine the bit position of the leading 1 in a number. The bit position may then be employed to control a shift amount for floating point number normalization.

In Fig. C.24(b), the semicolon is used to indicate *concurrent* RTN statements activated by the same condition to the left of the colon. The descriptor for the

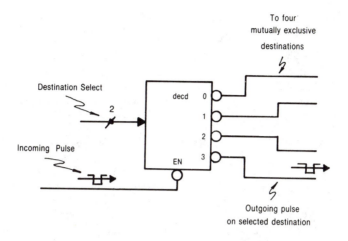

Figure C.23. *Use of decoder as demultiplexer.*

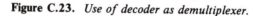

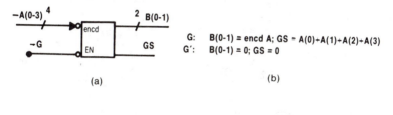

G: B(0-1) = encd A; GS = A(0)+A(1)+A(2)+A(3)
G': B(0-1) = 0; GS = 0

(a)

(b)

−G	−A(0)	−A(1)	−A(2)	−A(3)	B(0)	B(1)	GS
H	x	x	x	x	L	L	L
L	H	H	H	H	L	L	L
L	L	x	x	x	L	L	H
L	H	L	x	x	L	H	H
L	H	H	L	x	H	L	H
L	H	H	H	L	H	H	H

(c)

Figure C.24. *Priority encoder.* (a) Block diagram. (b) RTN statements. (c) Function table.

priority encoder is *encd*. Note that since the inputs are active-low, as opposed to the outputs, a minus sign does not appear in front of the output B. We also note in the function table that the names of active-low signals are preceded by a minus sign, reflecting the values found on the pins of the block.

C.11. THE 4-BIT MAGNITUDE COMPARATOR

The magnitude comparator accepts four bits from each of two data buses, A(0-3) and B(0-3), and compares them. See **Figure C.25.** We use the notation *gt, ge, eq, le,* and *lt* to indicate respectively the truth functions of "greater than", "greater than or equal", "equal", "less than or equal" and "less than". When values are operated on by these operators, the result is either true or false. If A(0-3) is greater than B(0-3) then the "AGTB" output is activated. If A(0-3) is less than B(0-3), then the "ALTB" output is activated. If A(0-3) equals B(0-3) then the output depends on the values of the cascading inputs.

The comparator is designed so that several can be placed in parallel, using the cascading inputs, to compare 8-bit, 16-bit, etc., values. The cascading inputs come from the next lower block in the chain. There are three inputs, which indicate the current comparison, considering only the low-order positions of the cascade. Inputs "G", "L" and "E" denote greater than, less than, or equal respectively. For the low-order comparator block, inputs "G" and "L" are made inactive, and "E" is made active. The blocks provide cascadable output points ">", "<" and "=" to be fed to the next higher G, L and E input points respectively. For the block diagram and the RTN statements, see Fig. C.25(a) and Fig. C.25(b). The function table is inefficient and is not shown. The cascading inputs are shown in Fig. C.25(c).

C.12. THE TRUE/COMPLEMENT/ZERO/ONE BLOCK

The exclusive-OR block is capable of passing either the true or complement value of a data bit line. This is a useful function to perform selectively on data

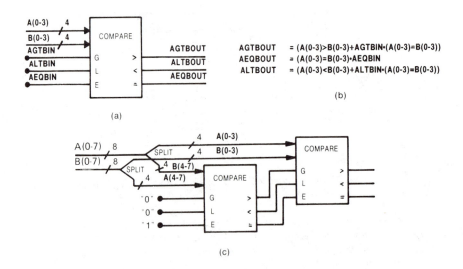

(a)

AGTBOUT = (A(0-3)>B(0-3)+AGTBIN•(A(0-3)=B(0-3)))
AEQBOUT = (A(0-3)=B(0-3)•AEQBIN
ALTBOUT = (A(0-3)<B(0-3)+ALTBIN•(A(0-3)=B(0-3)))

(b)

(c)

Figure C.25. *Cascadable 4-bit magnitude comparator.* (a) Block diagram. (b) RTN statements. (c) Cascading comparators.

before it enters an adder. In this way, addition and subtraction can be performed with just an adder circuit. Subtraction is performed by complementing the subtrahend and adding it to the minuend.

Figure C.26 shows operations on a single data bus. Fig. C.26(a) shows *selective complementation*. Sometimes it is convenient to force data values of all 0 or all 1 onto data lines. An MSI block which handles these applications is called the True/Complement/Zero/One block, shown in Fig. C.26(b). The RTN statements are in Fig. C.26(c) and the function table is in Fig. C.26(d).

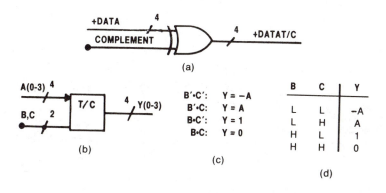

Figure C.26. *The True/Complement/Zero/One block.* (a) Gate to pass true or complement data. (b) Block diagram. (c) RTN statements. (d) Function table.

C.13. BINARY ADDER ELEMENT

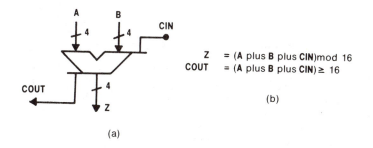

Figure C.27. *4-bit adder element.* (a) Adder block diagram. (b) RTN statements.

The binary adder is the key element of the computer. A 4-bit adder is shown in **Figure C.27.** The function of the 4-bit adder is identical to cascading together four 1-bit adders. See §§1.6.2 and the accompanying figures. The worst-case propagation delay in the adder is usually the ripple carry chain. This is the delay from the CIN input to the COUT output. Since the adder delay tends to be a limitation to the computer's performance, additional gates are employed to speed up the adder propagation delays. The *carry lookahead* is a popular technique to do this.

C.14. CARRY LOOKAHEAD CIRCUITS

Within a 4-bit adder group, the carry lookahead is implemented with the help of the *bit propagate*

$$P(i) = A(i) + B(i) \tag{C.6}$$

and *bit generate*

$$G(i) = A(i) \cdot B(i) \tag{C.7}$$

gates. Now the carry lookahead equations are:

$$COUT = G(0) + P(0) \cdot G(1) + P(0) \cdot P(1) \cdot G(2) + P(0) \cdot P(1) \cdot P(2) \cdot G(3) \\ + P(0) \cdot P(1) \cdot P(2) \cdot P(3) \cdot CIN \tag{C.8}$$

Similarly, the lookahead equations for the other carry-in signals (bits 0, 1, and 2) are similarly defined. They are combined within the adder with the respective half sum signals "A(i) *xor* B(i)" to form the respective sum signals.

$$CIN(0) = G(1) + P(1) \cdot G(2) + P(1) \cdot P(2) \cdot G(3) \\ + P(1) \cdot P(2) \cdot P(3) \cdot CIN \tag{C.9}$$

$$CIN(1) = G(2) + P(2) \cdot G(3) + P(2) \cdot P(3) \cdot CIN \tag{C.10}$$

$$CIN(2) = G(3) + P(3) \cdot CIN \tag{C.11}$$

Eqs. C.6-C.11 represent the application of the lookahead technique within a 4-bit adder group. The technique may also be applied across 4-bit groups. For each 4-bit group, the *group propagate* GP(0-3) and *group generate* GG(0-3) signals are defined as follows:

$$GP(0-3) = P(0) \cdot P(1) \cdot P(2) \cdot P(3) \tag{C.12}$$

$$GG(0-3) = G(0) + P(0) \cdot G(1) + P(0) \cdot P(1) \cdot G(2) \\ + P(0) \cdot P(1) \cdot P(2) \cdot G(3) \tag{C.13}$$

The group propagate and generate signals of Eq. C.12 and C.13 can be combined into higher-level lookahead equations, similar to what was done in Eqs. C.8 through C.11, to anticipate carry signals across 4-bit groups. Many MSI 4-bit arithmetic unit parts provide the group generate and propagate signals as outputs, whereas another MSI part implements Eqs. C.8 through C.11.

C.15. THE ARITHMETIC AND LOGICAL UNIT (ALU)

An ALU is typically a binary adder to which additional circuitry has been supplied to increase the functional power of the unit beyond the operation of binary addition. Notice from the previous section that the bit-by-bit logical functions of AND, OR, and XOR already exist in the form of the bit generate, bit propagate, and the half-sum functions respectively. If one or both inputs can be

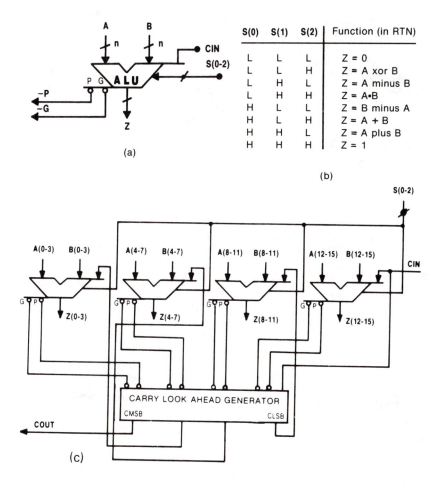

S(0)	S(1)	S(2)	Function (in RTN)
L	L	L	Z = 0
L	L	H	Z = A xor B
L	H	L	Z = A minus B
L	H	H	Z = A•B
H	L	L	Z = B minus A
H	L	H	Z = A + B
H	H	L	Z = A plus B
H	H	H	Z = 1

(a)

(b)

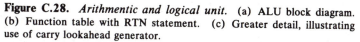

(c)

Figure C.28. *Arithmentic and logical unit.* (a) ALU block diagram. (b) Function table with RTN statement. (c) Greater detail, illustrating use of carry lookahead generator.

selectively inverted within the ALU, then addition, subtraction, and many logical functions are implemented.

The block diagram symbol of the ALU is the same as for the adder. However, the term "ALU" can be placed inside the symbol to indicate the expanded function. See **Figure C.28.** Control points are provided to indicate to the unit which operation to perform. The ALU is a nice example of a functional unit which performs a task. The unit performs an operation between two data inputs, and delivers the result on a data output. There are control inputs which define what the operation is to be. There are also status outputs. The carry-out signal is a status. Some ALUs are provided with an overflow (OVF) output. The functional unit is combinational because the unit does not have any memory. The operation is not invoked by a clock; the only timing consideration is that the output validity is subject to propagation delays. Figs. C.28(a) and (b) show the block symbol and functional descriptions respectively.

As an MSI part, this unit generally comes in 4-bit wide groups. Propagate and Generate output signals are meant to be used in conjunction with carry lookahead parts to generate the carry-in signals for each group. Fig. C.28(c) provides a more detailed diagram of how four 4-bit ALU groups connect to a carry lookahead generator.

C.16. SIGN EXTENSION

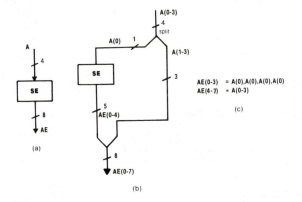

Figure C.29. *Sign extension.* (a) Block diagram. (b) More detail. (c) RTN statement.

It is often the case that a signed m-bit number must be combined arithmetically with a signed n-bit number, where m is less than n. The operation of sign extension (denoted *SE)* causes the m-bit number to be expanded to n bits by replicating the sign bit to the left by (n − m) bit positions. The 4-bit number +7 (0111) becomes the 8-bit number 0000 0111 by sign extension. See **Figure C.29.** A simple block diagram is in Fig. C.29(a). *SE* essentially signifies the fanning out of the MSB position to the (n − m) additional data lines required. Sign extension is thus accomplished by wiring. Unless greater fan power is called for, no gates are needed. Fig. C.29(b) is a more detailed block diagram of sign extension. Fig. C.29(c) shows the RTN statements.

C.17. PARITY GENERATION AND CHECKING

The parity check is a convenient way to check the validity of data on a bus. To do this, an 8-bit data bus will carry an additional signal line which carries information on whether the number of data bits at the high value is odd or even. An odd parity check is usual, so that the value of the parity line is such as to make the overall (the parity line is included) number of high (or 1-valued) bits odd. See **Figure C.30.**

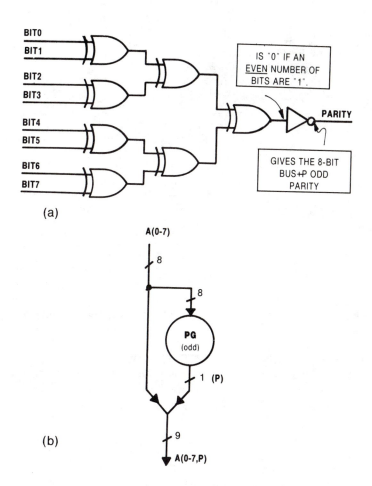

(a)

(b)

Figure C.30. *Odd priority generation.* (a) Circuit. (b) Block diagram.

Fig. C.30(a) shows an exclusive-OR tree used as an odd parity generator for an 8-bit data bus. We denote the circuit with a circle on block diagrams, as seen in Fig. C.30(b). The checking function is also performed by an exclusive-OR tree. See **Figure C.31.**

C.18. THE READ-ONLY MEMORY (ROM)

The read-only memory is a device which is presented with an n-bit address, and following an access delay, delivers a stable m-bit output value. See **Figure C.32.** The delay is called the *access time*. The memory contains 2^n words, one used for each possible combination of the address lines. The word size is m bits, and a distinct m-bit value is permanently stored for each of the 2^n distinct words in

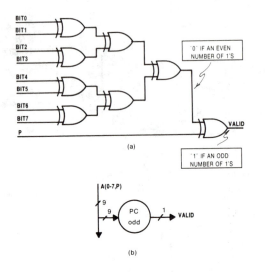

(a)

(b)

Figure C.31. *Parity check tree.* (a) Structure. (b) Block diagram symbol.

the ROM. The ROM *dimensions* are $(2^n) \times m$, and appear on the block diagram of Fig. C.32(a). We denote the address bus ADR, and the output bus READATA. The value stored at any location specified by the value on ADR is denoted M[ADR], as expressed in the RTN statement of Fig. C.32(b).

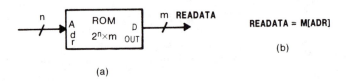

(a)

READATA = M[ADR]

(b)

Figure C.32. *Read-only memory.* (a) Block diagram. (b) RTN statement.

The value at each address is placed there during the fabrication process. For semiconductor ROMs, this "personalization" of the ROM usually constitutes the last of the several (perhaps four) masks used in the fabrication. Once the ROM has been personalized, it is nonvolatile: like the elephant, it "never forgets". The ROM is popular for storing data and programs or microprograms which never change. Many personal computers have the operating system stored in ROM.

Some ROMs (called PROMs) are reprogrammable; they can be removed from their socket and erased. They next undergo an electrical procedure which rewrites them before they are returned to the socket. Other varieties are *electrically altera-ble ROMs* (EAROMs) and *erasable programmable ROMs* (EPROMs).

Some ROMs are *field programmable,* and are called FPROMs. A *write-once* technique generally uses a fusible connection (link) which the user can "blow" by an overvoltage.

Another use for a ROM is as a replacement for an arbitrary combinational circuit. We note the analogy between Figs. C.1 and C.32. In the ROM, the address is decoded to what amounts to a minterm. A 1 is stored in the address if the corresponding minterm belongs to the boolean function; otherwise a 0 is stored.

As an example, consider a priority encoder of data inputs A(0) and A(1). A(0) has the highest priority. Subject to enabling signal G, the output B indicates the highest priority input which is active. If no inputs are active or if enabling signal G is inactive, then output signal GS is inactive. (See §C.10.)

A function table which describes the priority encoder is shown in **Table C.5.** The table is a simplified version of Fig. C.24(a).

Table C.5.
Function Table of Priority Encoder of Two Signals

	Inputs			*Outputs*	
G	*A(0)*	*A(1)*		*B(0)*	*GS*
0	x	x		0	0
1	0	0		0	0
1	0	1		1	1
1	1	x		0	1

The behavior of the priority encoder of Table C.5 can be realized by an 8-word by 2-bit (8×2) ROM. The ROM specification amounts to expanding the function table to a truth table, as shown in **Table C.6.**

Table C.6.
ROM Specification for Table C.5.

Minterm	*Address*			*M[ADR]*	
	G	*A(0)*	*A(1)*	*B(0)*	*GS*
0	0	0	0	0	0
1	0	0	1	0	0
2	0	1	0	0	0
3	0	1	1	0	0
4	1	0	0	0	0
5	1	0	1	1	1
6	1	1	0	0	1
7	1	1	1	0	1

In this table, the minterm number is the value of the address. Although minterms 0, 1, 2, and 3 are conveniently combined in Table C.6, they each have distinct addresses in ROM, and must each store the value "00". In general, if a combinational function can be easily realized, it is not economical to use a ROM implementation. Consider for example the MUX of Fig. C.17 in a dual 4×1 version. Such a part exists as a single MSI chip. A ROM realization would require a ROM of dimension 2048 by 2 (eight data inputs, three control inputs, and two outputs). However the dual 4×1 chip is probably less expensive and faster, due to a simpler geometry.

The use of a ROM implementation of a combinational circuit is most advantageous where the function to be realized is not subject to much combinational circuit minimization. Combinational circuits notorious for this problem are the translations from one code to another. In particular, ROMs are advantageously being used for translating from a keyboard code to an information interchange code such as ASCII.

C.19. PROGRAMMABLE LOGIC ARRAY (PLA)

C.19.1. Structurally a PLA is a Diode Matrix or Array

The term "programmable" as used here is a slight misnomer because the "programmability" is in the fabrication process. The analogy to a ROM is quite close; the personalization is usually a final masking step. Like the FPROM, an FPLA has a write-once capability via an overvoltage process which blows or melts a fusible link.

The PLA technique is not a new concept; it was employed in the first generation computers under the term *diode array*. The PLA is a clever way of organizing the diodes systematically to implement the AND-OR logic of Appendix B (see Fig. B.3(c)).

C.19.2. Behaviorally a PLA is a Combinational Circuit

Like a ROM, a PLA has n inputs and m outputs. However, a PLA has a constraint or a third specification we call P. Let P denote the maximum number of p-terms allowed in the PLA. Instead of decoding each of the 2^n input combinations, as in a ROM, the PLA follows a different approach. Each input and its complement are brought to each AND gate in the array. There are P such gates. These gates are called the *AND-array*. At each AND, the true, complement, or none of the signal lines corresponding to each input signal can be used as an input line. The output of each of the P AND gates in the AND-array can feed or not feed each of m OR gates. The OR gate section of the PLA is called the *OR-array*. Some PLA designs permit each OR gate output to be selectively inverted, as a part of the personalization process. The PLA, then, is a direct way to realize a two-level combinational circuit of the AND-OR type, or AND-OR-INVERT type. Not all n-input, m-output combinational circuits are realizable with PLAs because of the p-term limitation. For example, an 8-input, 96 p-term, 1-output PLA cannot realize the parity function. Any 8-input function has 2^8 input combinations, half of which ($2^7 = 128$) are 1 for the parity function. None of the minterms of the parity function can be combined.

C.19.3. Structural Description of a PLA

The circuit specification of Table C.6 is realized with a PLA in **Figure C.33**. On the left, the primary inputs are provided with drive and inversion. Each vertical line of the array is a p-term; in the actual diode matrix this line is tied to $+V_{CC}$ through an appropriate pull-up resistor. The presence of a diode is indicated by an "X" at the intersection. In the AND-array, the diode conducts current from the p-term pull-up resistor line toward the input line (of the p-term). Each output horizontal line of the OR-array is grounded through an appropriate resistor value. Before being driven off the PLA, each output signal is amplified or "powered up". Note in Fig. C.33 the direct analogy in the AND-array to each p-term in the sum-of-products expression for each output. Since each p-term can have as many literals as needed, minimization of literals is not critical. The limitation to realizability for multiple-output combinational functions is the maximum number of p-term lines built into the PLA. It is advantageous to minimize p-terms.

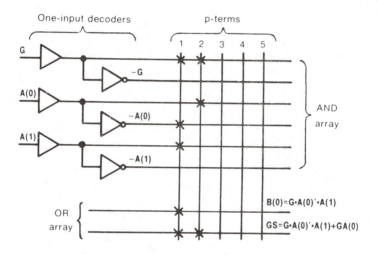

Figure C.33. *PLA implementation of Table C.6.*

As densities improve, the limit to realization of arbitrary combinational functions is the number of pins in the package. Consequently, the cost-effectiveness question of using ROM versus PLA parts disappears. The designer may be primarily interested in personalizing an n-input, m-output building block, and not care whether the part is a PLA or a ROM or some combination. Of course, cost and performance considerations will determine whether a PLA or a ROM is more economical in each application.

Other things being equal, the difference between ROMs, PLAs, or similar devices, is how the designer specifies the desired behavior. For the ROM a truth table is needed, and for a PLA the designer must specify the set of p-terms which imply each output. It is not difficult, of course, to devise a computer program to translate from one form to the other.

C.19.4. PLA Applications

PLA chips are commercially available and can be used as replacements for the "random logic" found in control units, provided the delays are not too long. The function assigned to the PLA in this case is to activate and deactivate control signals at the desired time under the right conditions. Other applications apply to data. These include the realization of systematic operations on data words such as barrel shifting, addition, multiplication, data formatting, or sign extension.

Both PLAs and ROMs have been used as substitutes for random logic. When employed in this application it is interesting to estimate how many bits of PLA or ROM replace how many elementary logic gates (such as NAND, etc.). Donath [7] has studied this problem and concludes that a logic gate is "equivalent" to 8.5 bits of memory.

C.19.5. Techniques for Arranging PLAs

Perhaps the most effective use of PLA techniques can be made by the VLSI chip designer. The chip designer works on a functional unit, and must meet area and power constraints. Only a portion of the active area is devoted to the PLA. In contrast, the MSI-level logic designer, once a PLA part is selected, cannot "juggle" the array. There is no advantage to rearranging the diodes by splitting, folding and reflecting submatrices to save chip area where there are no diodes. Such juggling results in packing the special-purpose array into a smaller area, at the expense of decreased flexibility. The VLSI chip designer thus employs several techniques to reduce the area needed for the diode array.

A description of many PLA chip area reduction techniques appear in Fleisher and Maissel [8], and in Weinberger [9]. Weinberger has designed a PLA for a high-speed 8-bit, 16-bit, or even 32-bit adder. One technique in Fleisher [8] replaces two 1-bit "decoders", by pairing two PLA inputs and feeding them to a 2×4 decoder. Since two input variables are handled in each case, four lines in the AND-array inputs are involved, and the AND-array size is about the same for each. However, the claim in [8] is that the two-input (2×4) decoder usage will probably reduce the number of diodes needed in the array. Another technique studied by Weinberger [9] is the pairwise exclusive-ORing of OR array outputs.

C.20. THE LOGIC DESIGN OF CONTROL SIGNALS

During the control signal design phase of a digital design project, all conditions which imply a given control signal are collected or *gathered* together. More specifically, each condition which activates a control point is viewed as a p-term (or ORing of p-terms), where the p-term inputs are either timing signals from the clock or status variables. The p-terms representing the conditions which activate the control signal are ORed together to implement (generate) the control signal. Each p-term can be implemented as an AND gate, and the control signal itself may be viewed as the output of an OR gate. The analogy with the PLA function is conceptually simple. Direct implementation of control signals with hardwired AND and OR gates in a two-level circuit may be difficult due to fan-in limitations. Fan-in can be increased at the cost of increased delays, as shown in **Figure C.34.** The wire-OR function also is useful for handling a high fan-in situation.

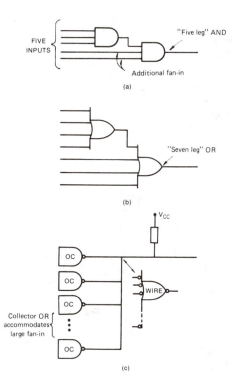

Figure C.34. *Fan-in expansion techniques.*   (a) AND function.
(b) OR function. (c) Wire-OR function.

Once the system and its control signals are initially implemented, the debugging phase is entered. This can be done either by simulation or by building a prototype. In any case, the designer who discovers and locates a bug other than a wiring error is usually confronted with a problem in a combinational circuit. The designer knows how the circuit actually works, and knows how it should work. The task is to modify the circuit such that its actual behavior corresponds to the desired behavior. Here, the intuition which all logic designers acquire comes into play.

Generally, the situation reduces to a control signal which is either (1) active when it should be inactive, or (2) inactive when it should be active. We shall call the erroneous control signal CTLSIG. The situations are illustrated in **Figure C.35.** In the first case, there may be an "upstream" p-term activating CTLSIG when it shouldn't, as shown in Fig. C.35(a). The entire "offending" gate can be eliminated if the offending p-term is always active at the wrong time. More likely, it may not have enough restricting conditions "ANDed" in. If an additional condition can be found to inhibit the activation of the offending p-term, except when it should, the bug can be fixed as shown in Fig. C.35(b). Otherwise, suppose we identify the conditions under which CTLSIG is erroneously activating. Now, a NAND gate can be used to generate a signal representing that condition, which in turn inhibits

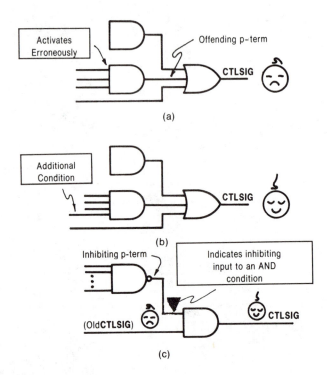

Figure C.35. *Correcting an erroneous control signal which activates when it should not.* (a) CTL goes active at wrong time. (b) Corrected CTLSIG. (c) Inhibiting CTLSIG by "brute force".

CTLSIG in a "brute force" approach; see Fig. C.35(c). More generally, a two-level circuit may be required to generate the inhibit condition.

For the second case mentioned, where CTLSIG is failing to activate when it should, see **Figure C.36.** Perhaps there is a p-term which should be activating but an offending input is inhibitive, as shown in Fig. C.36(a). More likely, the missing condition may have to be generated, hopefully by a single AND gate, and brute force ORed into OLDSIG. The brute force approach is shown in Fig. C.36(b).

The debugging phase develops a way of looking at a logic circuit which is not based upon truth tables or boolean algebra. This outlook depends upon knowing the behavior of the building blocks, and how the interconnections should be modified to obtain the desired behavior from the resulting logic circuit. The viewpoint induced by debugging a system is analogous to the way a craftsman knows what each tool can do. An AND gate input can be used to inhibit activation of the gate's output, and an OR gate input can be used to force the activation of its output. If a bug develops which is traced to a control signal, it may be possible to trace the problem upstream and correct the problem at the source. Otherwise a downstream fix may be possible. The approach to debugging is rather unsystematic. The technique is called designing by the "seat of the pants". We use this

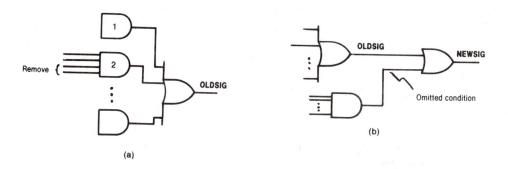

Figure C.36. *Correcting a control signal which fails to activate when it should.* (a) Removal of offending conditions. (b) "Brute force".

approach in the debug phase but do *not* recommend it for the design phase. Unfortunately, many engineers learn digital design by first debugging someone else's design. The danger is that "seat of the pants" techniques may then be carried to the initial design phase of the next project.

The concepts of inhibiting (disabling) and enabling (activating) control signals can also apply to data buses. An AND gate at each bit can be used to force 0's onto the bus, and an OR gate at each bit position can force 1's onto the data bus.

The techniques described here are part of the skills (stock in trade) acquired by digital systems designers. In forcing signals on or off, the designer is merely employing functional visualization at the gate level instead of at the functional unit level. On a larger scale, the designer as a craftsman can similarly manipulate and employ higher-level blocks such as registers, arithmetic units, and memories.

REFERENCES

1. F. Prosser and D. Winkel, "Mixed Logic Leads to Maximum Clarity with Minimum Hardware", *Computer Design,* v. 16, n. 5, May 1977, 111-117.
2. John F. Wakerly, *Logic Design Projects Using Standard Integrated Circuits,* Wiley, New York, 1976.
3. William I. Fletcher, *An Engineering Approach to Digital Design,* Prentice-Hall, Englewoood Cliffs, NJ, 1980.
4. R. S. Lim, "A Barrel Switch Design", *Computer Design,* v. 11, n. 8, August 1972, 76-79.
5. John R. Mick, "Am25S10 Four-bit Shifter", in *Schottky and Low-power Schottky Data Book,* 2nd Edition, Advanced Micro Devices, Sunnyvale, CA, 1977, 4-37 to 4-46.
6. R. L. Davis, "Uniform Shift Networks", *Computer,* v. 7, n. 9, September 1974, 60-71.
7. W. E. Donath, "Equivalence of Memory to 'Random Logic' ", *IBM Jl. Research and Develop.,* v. 18, September 1974, 401-407.
8. H. Fleisher and L. I. Maissel, "An Introduction to Array Logic", *IBM Jl. Research and Develop.,* v. 19, March 1975, 98-109.
9. A. Weinberger, "High-speed Programmable Logic Array Adders", *IBM Jl. Research and Develop.,* v. 23, March 1979, 163-178.

APPENDIX

D

A REVIEW OF SEQUENTIAL BUILDING BLOCKS

D.1. INTRODUCTION

Appendix D covers some basic sequential building blocks which have memory. Of special interest for each medium-scale (MSI) sequential circuit is its block diagram symbol, and its timing characteristics as described by a timing chart. The RTN statements are also a way to describe the behavior of medium-scale blocks. Although designers don't often use RTN statements for this purpose, such statements are of use to logic simulation programs.

By definition, a sequential circuit has memory. Sequential circuits remember something about the past history of the circuit's inputs. What is remembered is stored in a flip-flop, the simplest sequential circuit. Flip-flops are important. As in much of this work, a duality is discovered. The data type flip-flops are intended for use as data registers in data flows; the set-clear or JK flip-flops are more suited for control logic implementations or remembering status or conditions.

A data register is composed of flip-flops so it too is a sequential circuit. Most often, a data register does no more than store a word of 0's and 1's, to represent a binary number. Thus, a data register should not be viewed as a sequential circuit in all the generality so implied if a simpler functional view exists. Following a description of flip-flops, a sequential circuit is defined in a more formal fashion.

Of equal importance with the functional properties of the building blocks is the question of system timing. Timing requirements at the lowest conceptual level can be studied in terms of the requirements for individual flip-flops. There are basically two types of flip-flop timing requirements, based on the differences

506

between the latch-type flip-flop and the edge-triggered flip-flop. These individual requirements at the flip-flop level, together with clock skew considerations, influence the system timing requirements at the higher conceptual level of the system timing cycle. System timing considerations are studied in specific contexts in Chapters 3 through 6. The elements of timing covered in this appendix are very basic, and are considered to be an important part of the digital designer's stock-in-trade.

Signals provided by electromechanical switches must be properly *conditioned* or *debounced,* and *timed* (synchronized with a central clock) before being reliably employed in the digital system. Special sequential circuits also include single-shots, power-on reset circuits, and synchronizer circuits.

D.2. SOME PROPERTIES OF TIMING SIGNALS

A clocking signal whose period is symmetrically divided into identical durations of the high level and the low level is said to be a *square wave.* A square wave called CLK is shown in **Figure D.1.** The transition between levels is the *edge.* The signal repeats regularly, and the time duration of the clock signal between like edges (leading or trailing) is the *period.* One of the edges is distinguished by calling it the *initial transition* which starts a cycle. The start of one cycle is the end of the previous cycle. The clock period is also called the *cycle time.*

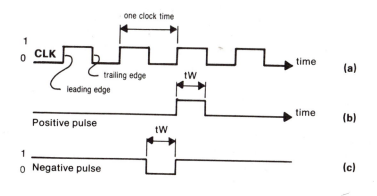

Figure D.1. *Examples of timing signals.* (a) Square wave. (b) Positive pulse. (c) Negative pulse.

Many timing signals have asymmetric waveforms. Such signals may aptly be called *pulses,* with the pulse being the level of shorter duration. In fact, pulse signals need not be periodic. In positive logic, a positive pulse is a signal whose duration in the high level is small, whereas a negative pulse signal spends less time in the low level. The concepts are illustrated graphically in Fig. D.1. For a positive pulse, the *leading edge* is the low-to-high transition; for a negative pulse the leading edge is the high-to-low transition. The opposite transition is called the *trailing edge.* A timing property of interest for some pulse signals (such as the write pulse to a monolithic memory) is the *pulse width* denoted tW.   For timing pulses which activate edge-triggered flip-flops, the instant of occurrence of the *active transition* is an important timing event.   The active transition is the transition which causes an output change.

D.3. FLIP-FLOPS

In this section we describe the properties and operation of common flip-flops. Of particular importance are the timing specifications of setup, hold, and output hold times. These specifications are also employed with monolithic memories.

There are two aspects of the flip-flop circuit which are of interest: how they are *clocked* and how they are *controlled*. These are shown in **Table D.1.**

Table D.1. Categories of Flip–Flops

1. How clocked
  a. Level-sensitive (latch)
  b. Edge-triggered
  c. Master-slave (pulse-width sensitive)
2. How controlled
  a. Data-type
  b. Set-clear
  c. JK (edge-triggered or master-slave only)

D.3.1. Level–Sensitive Flip–Flops

Level-sensitive flip-flops are also called *latches*. The simplest latch is the set-clear, which can be built from cross-coupled NOR or NAND gates; see **Figure D.2.**

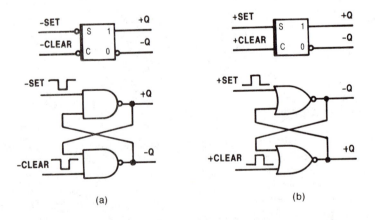

| (a) | (b) |

Figure   D.2.   *Cross-coupled   level-sensitive   flip-flops.*
(a) Cross-coupled NAND flip-flop. (b) Cross-coupled NOR flip-flop.

The symbol for a flip-flop is a rectangle with a heavy border on the input side. The set-clear flip-flop is a building block; its connection points receive *labels,* as distinguished from signal *names* assigned by the designer using the building block. The input connection points are labeled "S" and "C". The signal lines feeding these points are named by the designer. In Fig. D.2 the signals are named SET and CLEAR respectively. The flip-flop stores one bit, which is normally presented on an output connection point. Often, the flip-flop stores a data bit, whose value is 0 or 1. When a flip-flop is set, the value is 1, and when clear, the value is 0. The flip-flop may have two output connection points. The "true" or active-high output point is labeled "1" on the block diagram, and may be called the 1-output or "1-OUT". The complement or active-low output is labeled "0" inside the block, and may be called the 0-output or "0-OUT".

When the flip-flop stores a data value 1, the true output is high and the complement output is low. When the flip-flop stores the value of a condition or variable these same rules apply: the output labeled "1" is high when the condition after which the flip-flop is named is active or valid. On some manufacturer's specification sheets, the flip-flop outputs are also labeled "+Q" and "−Q" respectively, as in Fig. D.2.

The flip-flop activating signals cause the changes. For level-sensitive flip-flops as in Fig. D.2, changes are caused by nonoverlapping SET or CLEAR pulses. If both SET and CLEAR are active together, the normally complementary output signals take on the same value. The flip-flop's final state depends upon which pulse the flip-flop perceives as persisting longer. The delay specification for these flip-flops is simply the propagation delay tP from an input point to an output point. In fact, there are four such specifications, tP(S/1), tP(S/0), tP(C/1) and tP(C/0). Within the parentheses, the particular propagation delay is specified. The slash (/) separates the "from" label and the "to" label. Thus, tP(S/1) specifies the propagation delay from an activating change on the pin labeled S to a responding change on the 1-output pin. The timing unit of nanosecond (ns) is used for these specifications.

Another level-sensitive flip-flop is the *data latch,* also called a polarity hold (PH) flip-flop, or a D-latch. See **Figure D.3.** The activating control point is labeled G inside the block (for "Gate"). Recall that the signal or interconnection line feeding a connection point may have any name. For data latches, the activating signal is often named "ENABLE". When the G control point (i.e. the enable signal) is active, the latch is *open* and the value on the data input connection point (labeled D) passes to the data output connection point (labeled 1). When the G control point is inactive, the data latch *holds* or maintains its last output value.

Fig. D.3(a) shows how the data latch may be constructed from gates. Fig. D.3(b) shows the block diagram signal. The similarity of Fig. D.3(a) to a multiplexer circuit is illustrated by Fig. D.3(c). This similarity could be exploited, in fact, to employ a 4×1 MUX as a data latch combined with a 3×1 data selector on the input. However, we caution against this practice because of a possible timing problem.

The input value on the G control point is inverted twice, through inverters 1 and 2 of Fig. D.3(a). (On a 20-pin MSI chip, which may have eight data latches, inverters 1 and 2 fan out to all eight bits.) The input signal driving the enabling control point G sees only one *standard load,* (inverter 1 of Fig. D.3(a)). An active value on the G input allows the value on the D input point to pass through

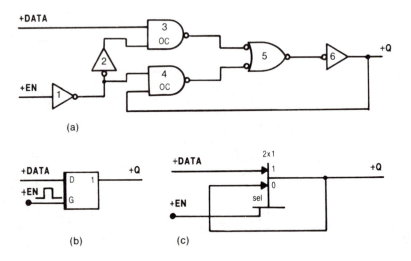

(a)

(b)   (c)

Figure D.3. *The data latch.* (a) Data latch built from open-collector NANDs and inverters. (b) Block diagram. (c) 2×1 MUX wired as data latch.

NAND 3 to the output point. In other words, NAND 3 is open, allowing input value D to pass. On the other hand, the complement (inactive) value on the enabling control point G closes NAND 3 and opens the feedback loop through NAND 4. The negative transition on input G (signal +EN) is critical. The opening of NAND 4 should occur before the output signal +Q reacts to the closing of NAND 3. The opening of NAND 4 occurs at the input to inverter 2, and the closing of NAND 3 at the output of inverter 2.

Inverter 2 is thus strategically placed to help assure that NAND 4 responds first to the change on enabling control point G. In Fig. D.3(c), a MUX output value is fed back to one of the data input points for data storage purposes (e.g. a latched bus). With this feedback, the delays following the deselection of the data signal must be considered.

A second potential data latch timing problem concerns the leading edge of +EN. When the data value is 1, and the output value is already 1, sometimes the output should not momentarily go to 0. A close inspection of Fig. D.3(a) reveals the problem. If the delay of inverter 2 is substantial relative to NAND 4, then for the case where +Q is 1, +DATA is 1 and a leading edge occurs on +G, output +Q may momentarily reach 0, even though +Q should remain at 1. Such spurious short pulses are called *glitches*. The glitch of Fig. D.3(a) may be removed by the addition of NAND 7 as shown in **Figure D.4.**

The timing diagram illustrating the behavior of the data latch is shown in **Figure D.5.** Inside the parentheses following the delay notation, "DL" is used as a reminder that the delay belongs to a data latch. The timing response of the data latch has two aspects. The first is a data propagation delay tP(DL-da) from the data input point labeled D to the output named Q. This delay is evident only if

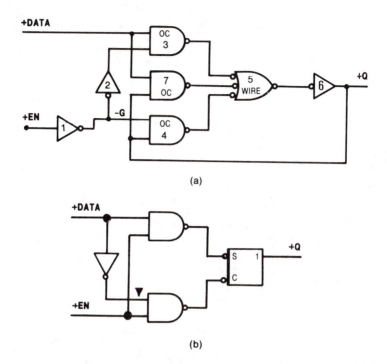

(a)

(b)

Figure D.4. *"Glitch-free" data latch circuits.* (a) Modification to circuit of *Figure D.3(a).* (b) Same using SC latch.

control point G is active when the data value changes. See times t1 and t2 of Fig. D.5. The second propagation delay tP(DL-en) is evident if data is stable when input point G activates. The enable propagation delay tP(DL-en) occurs from the leading edge of the value on G to the 1-output point (named Q) when the output is to change value. See times t3 and t4.

The concept of data latch *setup* time, tSU(DL), is illustrated by Fig. D.5 at times t5 and t6. If the value at the D input point changes at t5 just before the value on control point G deactivates at t6, it is not guaranteed that the data latch "sees" the input change: the value actually latched is not known. The value could be either the present or previous data value at connection point D. To guarantee that a known value is latched at the deactivation of control point G, that value must persist at point D for at least the setup time tSU(DL) prior to the deactivation at G. For most data latches, this setup time is equal to the propagation delay tP(DL-da). We make this assumption unless otherwise specified.

Some clocked data flip-flops have a *hold time* specification denoted tH. For a data latch, the value tH specifies that the data will be steady and valid for tH nanoseconds *after* control point G has been deactivated. Some latches in the TTL technology have a 0-ns setup time tSU and a 10-ns hold time tH. The hold time immediately follows the setup time, and the interval from setup time start to hold time end is very important. During this interval, the flip-flop is sensitive to (looks at) the data value, and no glitches should occur.

We summarize the data latch behavior as follows: *when the gate control point G is active, the data latch opens and passes data at point D. At the deactivation of control point G the latch closes and holds data.*

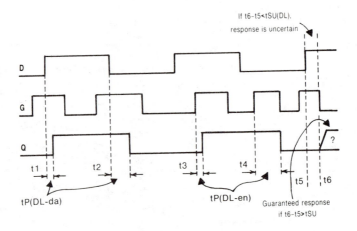

Figure D.5. *Timing diagram for data latch flip-flop.*

D.3.2. Edge-Triggered Flip-Flops

Edge-triggered flip-flops form the basis of many synchronous or clocked digital systems. One of the earliest treatments of clocked flip-flops appeared in 1958 by Phister [1]. He describes the R-S (Reset-Set), D (Delay), T (Trigger or Toggle), JK, and R-S-T (Reset, Set, Trigger) flip-flop types. In 1958, the flip-flops were activated by clock pulses on control points. Today, control points accept level input values and an additional (dynamic) control point receives the *active transition* which causes the flip-flop to change state. The setup time precedes this transition and the hold time follows it. On the block diagram, the control point receiving the active transition is a *dynamic* control point, and is indicated by the triangle. The flip-flops covered here are the D-type and the JK. The activating transition of the signal at the dynamic control point is also called the activating edge; hence edge-triggered flip-flops are also called *edge-sensitive*.

The type D edge-triggered flip-flop is controlled much like the data latch. See **Figure D.6.** The data input value feeds input connection point D, and a clocking signal named CLOCK feeds the control point labeled CLK. Control point CLK is activated or *triggered* by the leading edge of a positive pulse, at which time the value on point D is stored in the flip-flop. When the active transition is the trailing edge of a positive pulse (or leading edge of a negative pulse), the block diagram so indicates this condition by an *inversion bubble* at the dynamic control point. Fig. D.6(a) shows positive edge triggering and Fig. D.6(b) shows negative edge trigger-

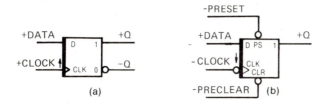

Figure D.6. *Edge-triggered D flip-flop.* (a) Positive edge triggering, double-rail output. (b) Negative edge triggering with active-low PRESET and CLEAR inputs, and single-rail output.

ing. As a reminder, an up arrow indicates positive edge triggering and a down arrow indicates negative edge triggering.

Fig. D.6(b) also shows two active-low level-sensitive control point inputs called PRESET and PRECLEAR, labeled inside the block as "PS" and "CLR" respectively. These control inputs are also called "dc" set and clear inputs, and behave like the SET and CLEAR inputs of the SC latch of Fig. D.2. When the PRESET and PRECLEAR inputs are inactive, the flip-flop is controlled by the dynamic control point. An active transition should not follow too closely the deactivation of a dc control input. The function table of the edge-triggered D flip-flop is shown in **Table D.2.**

	Table D.2.			
Function Table for Positive Edge-triggered D Flip-flops				
Input Values				*Output Value*
Preset*	*Clear**	*CLK*	*D*	*Q*
L	H	X	X	H
H	L	X	X	L
H	H	!	H	H
H	H	!	L	L
H	H	L	X	q (unchanged)
Note:				
* - Active low control point.				
! - active transition on signal.				

The name Q denotes the value of the *next* output. In the bottom row, we use the notation lowercase "q" to mean the *current* output value, before the active transition causes the flip-flop output to change to value Q.

The timing specifications for the preset and clear inputs are propagation delays like those of the SC latch. These input points are sometimes called direct preset or direct clear. In the era of vacuum tube and discrete transistor edge-triggered flip-flops, these signals were direct- (or dc-) coupled, as opposed to the dynamic control point (or trigger) which was ac-coupled through a capacitor.

There are two timing properties of interest with respect to the active transition. The first is the familiar propagation delay tP(CLK), the delay from the edge of the active transition until the instant the 1-output (or 0-output) point responds.

The second timing property concerns input data stability at the time of the active transition. For some *sampling interval* surrounding the edge of the active transition, the value on the D input point is sampled. The 1-output point value is guaranteed correct only if the signal value at the D input point remains stable throughout the sampling interval. The sampling interval is defined by the setup time tSU(FF) and hold time tH(FF). We use "FF" within parentheses to distinguish these delays from data latch (DL) delays. The value at data input point D must not change within the setup time tSU(FF) before the activating edge, and must remain stable until time period tH(FF) following the instant of the activating edge. Thus the minimum time of data sampling is tSU(FF) + tH(FF); see the timing chart of **Figure D.7**. The specifications tSU and tH do not affect the propagation delay tP, also shown in Fig. D.7. Prior to tSU and following tH, the value at input point D is shown as a cross-hatched rectangular area to indicate that point D need not be stable at that time. However during the sampling interval, the value of connection point D must not change. This stability requirement is represented on the timing chart by an open rectangle, inside of which may be a reminder indicating stability (or validity) of the data. The open rectangle means that regardless of the data value (0 or 1), it only matters that the data is stable. We say the edge-triggered flip-flop only "looks at" or "sees" the D input value during the sampling interval tSU+tH.

The value on output point 1-OUT (Q) is shown as being stable by means of an open area, and as being ambiguous (unknown, subject to change) with a cross-

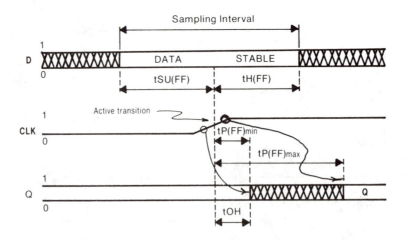

Figure D.7. *Timing chart of edge-triggered D flip-flop delay specifications.*

hatched area. Following an active transition, the output point holds or maintains the old value "q" for at least the best-case propagation delay time. This delay is called the flip-flop *output hold* time, denoted tOH. The output point 1-OUT assumes its final stable value by at most the worst-case flip-flop propagation delay tP(FF)max following the triggering edge.

In many flip-flops, the hold time tH(FF) is assumed to be 0 unless specified otherwise. The specification may be called a *release time,* denoted tR, in cases where the hold time is negative. Input data is allowed to change within the release time *before* the active transition.

In the first and second generation technologies, the edge-triggered flip-flop circuits employed capacitors. With the advent of the integrated circuit, it became uneconomical to use capacitors because of the large area of the chip consumed. It is advantageous to implement the flip-flop using NAND gates only. However the behavioral description of the flip-flop has the property of an *essential hazard transition*. The essential hazard transition may cause a malfunction, but need not if the delays are properly apportioned [2]. The term "essential hazard" means only that any circuit realization will have a race between changing signals on two or more paths. If the race is "won" by the undesirable signal, the flip-flop ends up in the wrong state. The undesirable path can always be defeated by inserting enough delay. It is also possible to favor the desirable path by confining it to an interconnection delay only, while forcing the undesirable path to pay at least one gate propagation delay.

We illustrate the hazard problem with the 6-NAND realization of the edge-triggered D flip-flop published by John Earle [3]. The circuit is shown in **Figure D.8** without the preset or preclear control points. With CLK inactive, the output values of NAND gates 2 and 3 are high. The output value of NAND 1 therefore is the inverse of the value of signal +D, and NAND 4 reinverts the value to that of +D, and feeds NAND 3. Similarly, the value D' is on the input to NAND 2. When CLK undergoes the active transition, NAND 2 inverts D' to D on its output, and NAND 3 similarly places D' on its output.

NANDs 2 and 3 feed a flip-flop formed by cross-coupled NANDs 5 and 6. Whichever output of NANDs 2 or 3 is low will set or clear this flip-flop. If the value on input point D is high, then the output of NAND 3 goes low, active-low setting the flip-flop whose output +Q becomes high. On the other hand, with input point D low, the output of NAND 2 goes low, active-low clearing the flip-flop so that output +Q becomes low.

The race implicit in the essential hazard is illustrated in **Figure D.9**. Let signal +D be low when +Q is high, and CLK experiences the negative edge. (This is not the active transition.) At the transition, the low input to NAND 3 forces line 8 high. If the CLK transition propagates too slowly on line 7, NAND 2 might see three high inputs and switch its output value low, creating a glitch. The glitch gives the undesirable result of changing the state of the flip-flop output. For an undesirable change to occur, however, NAND 3 would have to respond rapidly to the negative edge on CLK while NAND 2 still sees CLK as being high. Such behavior from NAND 2 has an extremely low probability for a rapid negative transition. If the negative transition is slow, NANDs 2 and 3 may spend too much time in the threshold uncertainty region (see Appendix B). The circuit will indeed malfunction when the threshold uncertainty region condition propagates through NAND 2 to NANDs 5 and 6.

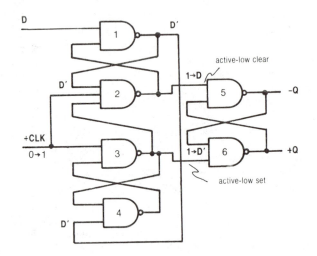

Figure D.8. *6-gate edge-triggered D flip-flop.*

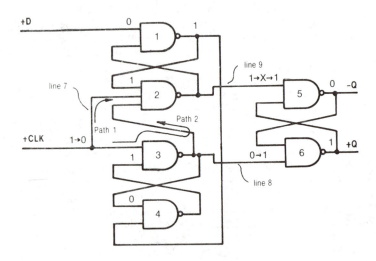

Figure D.9. *A race of line delay against gate delay.*

If the complement output of the edge-triggered D flip-flop is fed back to the D input point, then the flip-flop is connected as a binary toggle or counter element. The resulting toggle is designed from its behavioral description in Maley and Earle [4]. The capability of the edge-triggered flip-flop to perform as a shift register stage or binary counter stage makes it a powerful building block.

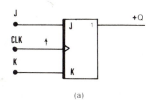

(a)

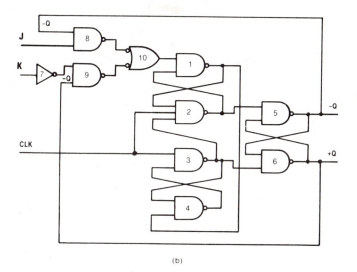

(b)

Figure D.10. *Edge-triggered JK flip-flop.* (a) Block diagram symbol of JK flip-flop. (b) Gate-level circuit.

The JK edge-triggered flip-flop provides a very versatile function. See **Figure D.10.** The block diagram is shown in Fig. D.10(a). The J and K input points may be thought of as calling for a set and a clear function respectively, at the active transition on CLK. If J and K are both inactive when the active transition on CLK occurs, the flip-flop state remains unchanged. When J and K are both active at the active transition, the JK flip-flop toggles as a binary counter element. The function table for the JK edge-triggered flip-flop appears in **Table D.3.** The notation "!" denotes the active transition.

Phister [1] showed that with a properly designed combinational circuit feeding the input points, one edge-triggered flip-flop could be made to look like (simulate) any other. The combinational circuit for simulating a JK flip-flop by a D flip-flop is shown in **Table D.4.** This circuit receives the values J, K, and flip-flop output signal Q as inputs. For each value of J, K, and Q, the appropriate value is fed to input D of the D flip-flop.

Table D.3.
Function Table for Edge-triggered JK Flip-flop

J	K	CLK	Q
L	L	X	q
L	H	!	L
H	L	!	H
H	H	!	q'

Table D.4.
Truth Table for Simulating JK Flip-flop

J	K	Q	D	
L	L	L	L	Maintain value
L	L	H	H	" "
L	H	L	L	Clear
L	H	H	L	"
H	L	L	H	Set
H	L	H	H	"
H	H	L	H	Toggle
H	H	H	L	"

The truth table of Table D.4 is realized by the boolean equation of Eq. D.1.

$$D = J \cdot Q' + K' \cdot Q \tag{D.1}$$

Eq. D.1 can be realized in NAND gates by adding three NANDs and an inverter to the circuit of Fig. D.8, as shown in Fig. D.10(b).

A shift register can be constructed from JK flip-flops, by connecting the 1-output (+Q) and 0-output (−Q) to the J and K input points respectively. The JK flip-flop can also be converted to a toggle by feeding the 1-output (+Q) to the K input point and the 0-output to the J input point of the same flip-flop. The JK flip-flop is well suited for implementing counters or sequencing mechanisms.

The JK flip-flop can also be used to implement a data register, by feeding the K input point the complement of the data value fed to the J input point. One JK flip-flop type which does not require the inverter for use as a D flip-flop is called the JK' flip-flop. The JK' behaves like the JK, except the K' input point is active-low. Feeding the same data value to the J input and the K' input produces the edge-triggered D flip-flop function.

For data register applications, the edge-triggered D flip-flop possesses a very important advantage over the JK flip-flop. The edge-triggered D flip-flop uses fewer pins, requiring only two input points, D and CLK. The JK flip-flop has three input points, J, K, and CLK. Also, the circuitry to implement the edge-triggered JK flip-flop is more complex.

D.3.3. The JK Master-Slave Flip-Flop

The use of master-slave flip-flops is not recommended. A 6-gate JK master-slave flip-flop implementation exists, but it lacks the edge-triggered property. The master-slave flip-flop is "pulse-width" sensitive, which gives rise to a timing problem called "glitch-catching". At one time (perhaps in the early 1960s) it may have offered a cost advantage, but that time has long since passed for MSI master-slave circuits. Under proper conditions, the circuit may offer some savings in area on a VLSI chip. The JK master-slave flip-flop can be found in many older SSI designs, and our treatment of the circuit consists of exposing its flaw.

The basic JK master-slave circuit is shown in **Figure D.11**. The block diagram is shown in Fig. D.11(a). Control point CLK controls the change in state. The input control point is not sensitive to the edge as in edge-triggered flip-flops, so instead of identifying the control input with a triangle, we use a small rectangle. The rectangle is a reminder that the circuit is pulse-width sensitive. Fig. D.11(b) shows a circuit for the master-slave. This is not the 6-NAND circuit mentioned earlier, but one which is more easily explained. The Slave flip-flop (NANDs 7 and 8) provide the 1- and 0-outputs +Q and −Q respectively. The Master flip-flop consists of NORs 3 and 4. At the activation of CLK, the Master flip-flop is capable of being changed. At the deactivation of CLK, the value of the Master is transferred to the Slave. When a flip-flop is *set,* the output is active (+Q high), and when *clear,* the output is inactive (+Q low).

The Master is set by AND 1, and cleared by AND 2. Only one of ANDs 1 or 2 is not inhibited by the output at any time. Slave output −Q is fed back to AND 1, so if the Slave is already set, AND 1 is inhibited from setting the Master. Similarly, +Q feeds AND 2, inhibiting the Master from being cleared when the Slave is cleared. When control point CLK is active, only one of NANDs 1 and 2 is enabled by the feedback of the 1- and 0-outputs. Note that only the AND which could cause a change in the output value is not inhibited. With CLK active, the Master responds to an active J or K value, whichever could cause an output change. This is the pulse-width time to which the flip-flop is sensitive.

We illustrate glitch-catching. Suppose AND 1 is sensitive because "−Q" is high. With CLK active and J inactive, a glitch on the J input is "caught" by the Master, and the Master is set. Even though J returns to the low level before CLK deactivates, and even if K is active indicating the flip-flop should be cleared, the Master flip-flop is set and cannot be cleared. In spite of any protests that J is low and K is high, at the fall of CLK, the Slave is set.

The same problem exists when the Slave is already set, and input point K momentarily activates while CLK is active. For proper operation, the values on input points J and K must remain stable for the entire duration of the pulse-width of the activating signal CLK. (If not, the glitch-catching problem will catch up to the designer.) Stated in another way, the setup time tSU for the master-slave flip-flop may be viewed as the entire duration of the pulse width of CLK. This is a factor encouraging narrow pulse widths in systems which use JK master-slave flip-flops. The problem is readily avoided by not using them in the first place. Since the outputs on most JK master-slave flip-flops change on the negative edge of the clock, the CLK input point is shown with an inversion bubble on the block diagram.

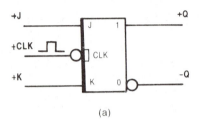

(a)

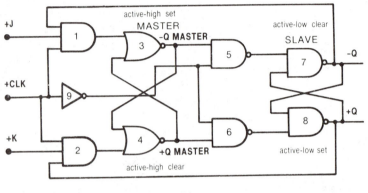

(b)

Figure D.11. *JK master-slave flip-flop.* (a) Block diagram symbol.
(b) Basic circuit.

D.3.4. A Sample Flip-Flop Application

In this section, an example is given which should assist in assimilating the
functional properties of flip-flops in control logic applications. Normally the
edge-triggered D remembers the value of a data bit sampled at the activating edge.
However the edge-triggered D can also be used to remember the occurrence of the
active transition itself. This requirement sometimes occurs in the input-output or
IO device interface. Referring to **Figure D.12,** consider the design of a digital
subsystem in which an input signal called CONDN requests or causes the subsystem
to perform a task. The task should be done exactly once for each activation of
signal CONDN. An initial approximation to the solution to the "exactly once"
requirement is shown in Fig. D.12(a) with accompanying timing chart Fig. D.12(b).

The cause-and-effect timing arrows use the following conventions. The small
circles on the arrow stem or shaft are placed either on a level or an edge. The
conjunction (AND) of the meanings of the circles represent the *cause*. The arrow-
head points to the *effect*, which is usually the activation or deactivation of signals.
If a circle is on an edge, that edge is the active transition for an edge-triggered
change. If an arrow has more than one edge circled, the designer is misapplying

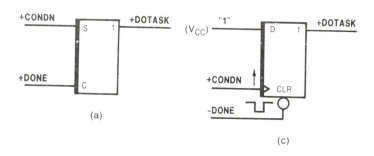

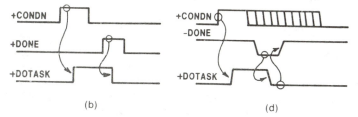

Figure D.12. *The "exactly once" problem.* (a) First solution. (b) First timing chart. (c) Second solution. (d) Second timing chart.

the convention, because edge-triggered flip-flops have only one activating input per output change.

Signal CONDN of Fig. D.12(a) sets flip-flop DOTASK. Signal DOTASK causes the task to be done. When the task is done, signal DONE clears the DOTASK flip-flop. Unfortunately, this simple solution has a problem (bug): *what if* signal CONDN has not deactivated by the time the task is done? (Many bugs can be found before implementation by asking "What if ... ?".) The deactivation of CONDN is outside the control of the subsystem designer. With this example, it is not immediately evident that the design requirement for performing the task is the *activation* (positive edge) of input signal CONDN, and not the fact that signal CONDN is active. The "exactly once" solution we seek is at hand if the flip-flop DOTASK is set by the leading *edge* of CONDN and cleared as before by the active *level* of condition DONE. Of course, if DONE is still active when the next positive edge of CONDN arrives, we may be in trouble again. Since DONE is under the subsystem designer's control, DONE can be deactivated when DOTASK deactivates, thus solving this second "What if?". The solution is shown in Fig. D.12(c), with the timing chart of Fig. D.12(d). The edge-triggered D flip-flop has its data (D) input permanently wired to the high level. The flip-flop is set for each activation of signal CONDN. The timing of signal CONDN in Fig. D.12(d) is shaded to indicate that it may deactivate at any time. Also note that the *edge* and not the *level* causes signal DOTASK to activate.

One remaining problem exists if signal CONDN deactivates and reactivates before the task is repeated. Hopefully the task requester will not request the task more frequently than the maximum rate of the cycle time of the task. Sometimes a signal called BUSY can be fed to the requester. When BUSY is active, the subsystem cannot accommodate a request. When BUSY is inactive, the task subsystem is assumed to be available. Note that in this circuit, signal DOTASK could be used as the BUSY signal.

This circuit belongs to the stock-in-trade of the logic designer, and is used in many situations similar to the one described. The design did not follow any particular algorithm, but proceeded from a first attempt followed by asking "What if?". The first attempt illuminated a problem, and was modified to correct that problem.

D.3.5. Flip–Flop Summary

We have not overwhelmed the reader with descriptions of all types of flip-flops, but have presented examples of the most popular and useful flip-flops encountered in bipolar and static MOS logic. For many applications, we favor the edge-triggered D flip-flop which represents a good balance between functional capability (ability to store, count, and shift) and the number of input pins required. For many control logic purposes, the JK flip-flop saves enough random logic combinational gates in control circuits to justify the extra input pin.

Level-sensitive flip-flops can be built from SSI gates, but require more wiring. SSI and MSI level-sensitive flip-flops generally need as many pins as the edge-triggered flip-flops. The data latch is less powerful than the edge-triggered D flip-flop. For the edge-triggered flip-flops, the designer need only be concerned about the time of occurrence of the active transition. For level-sensitive flip-flops, the pulse widths are of concern.

However, in the VLSI chip design application, the fewer gates and lower power consumption of the level-sensitive flip-flops are significant advantages. By sharing the enable (G control point) inverters of the data latch of Fig. D.3(a) across several data bits, registers can be built at a cost of slightly more than three easily connected gates per bit. In technologies which support the transmission gate, very economical data latches can be built. This is contrasted with a complex 6-gate edge-triggered D flip-flop (Fig. D.8) which consumes over twice the area.

D.4. SEQUENTIAL MACHINE MODEL

In the most general terms, a digital computer can be viewed as a *sequential machine* or *finite state machine*. The *state* is the totality of the values of all bits (flip-flops) in storage. Computers are certainly not designed as finite state machines from an abstract model. Rather, it is more convenient to view certain small portions of the computer as behaving like finite state machines. We introduce the notion here because conceptually it coincides with the *control unit* portion of a conventional computer design. The computer's *major state* or control phase corresponds to the present state of a sequential machine. The notion of state is a very powerful and general concept. Depending on its internal state, the machine can be made to react in different ways.

A sequential machine or finite state machine differs from a combinational circuit in that the sequential machine remembers information about its past inputs. This information, which is some function of the *past history,* is stored in memory elements (usually flip-flops). Two types of sequential machines have been studied in the scientific literature, the *synchronous* or clocked sequential machine, and the *asynchronous* or level mode sequential machine. The latter employs only level-sensitive flip-flops or direct feedback paths (Fig. D.2) and does not necessarily have a clock to synchronize operations. We shall not present the unclocked or asynchronous model here.

The clocked sequential machine is more suited to current computer design techniques. When all flip-flops change state at the same clock edge, the system timing is known as *single-phase*. The active transition of the clock CLK separates one clock-time from the next. The block diagram of the model is shown in **Figure D.13**. The circuit behaves as follows. With the *n* primary input signal values $X(0–(n–1))$ stable, and the *m* state variables $Y(0–(m–1))$ stable, the combinational circuit (CC) performs its calculation of the next-state values. The *present state* is the bit value combination in the Y Register during the present clock-time. The *next state* is what the Y Register will contain for the next clock-time. In many practical applications, a combinational circuit function of the present state also serves as the output value. In the more general case, the *k* circuit output signals $Z(0–(k–1))$ can be a combinational circuit function of the present state variable values and the primary input values. At the next active transition of the synchronizing signal (CLK), the next state is loaded into state register Y, and the new value becomes the present state value until the next active transition. Each bit in register Y is a state variable which can take on value 0 or 1.

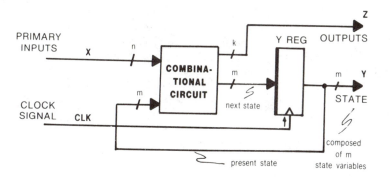

Figure D.13. *Finite state machine model;* n *inputs,* m *state variables, and* k *output variables.*

In Fig. D.13, we represent the collection of edge-triggered D flip-flops which comprise the present state as register Y with the block diagram symbol of a rectangle with a heavy border on the input side. In this way, the registers and their "directions" (input and output sides) are easily found on block diagrams.

Fig. D.13 shows how the *structure* of a sequential machine may be viewed. For some relatively simple sequential machines, a *state transition diagram* or graph, serves as a *behavioral* description. See **Figure D.14**. Each node of the graph represents a state, or a unique combination of values of state variables Y. When the machine is in a given state, that *active state* represents the *operating point* of the machine. Arrows connect a present state with a next state, and the label on each arrow is a boolean statement which if active causes the operating point to pass from the present state (tail of the arrow) to the next state (head of the arrow) at the next active transition. Now the next state of the previous clock-time becomes the present state for the next clock-time. The labels on the arrows are boolean functions of the sequential machine's primary input variables. (The state information is in the nodes of the graph.)

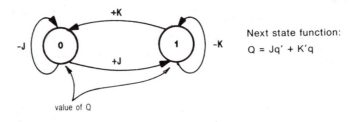

Next state function:

$Q = Jq' + K'q$

Figure D.14. *State transition diagram for J-K flip-flop.*

As an illustration, consider the JK flip-flop whose behavior is described by the state transition diagram of Fig. D.14. The CLK input point accepts the active transition, which is implicit in the clocked sequential machine model. The clocked sequential machine model has no provision for unclocked inputs such as "preset" or "clear". As in the level mode model, preset and clear input control points themselves directly cause the state change. The logic designer's notion of the building block as a functional unit, whose behavior is remembered as a timing diagram, or by RTN statements, is a versatile "model". The functional unit notion can handle many devices which do not conform to idealized theoretical models.

In Fig. D.14, the name of each state is shown inside the circle. In this case, the states 0 and 1 represent the value of the output variable Q. When in state 0 with a J input value of 0, the JK flip-flop doesn't change state. The occurrence results in a *self-loop*, where the next-state and present state have the same value.

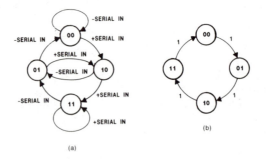

Figure D.15. *Further examples of state transition diagrams.*
(a) 2-bit shift register. (b) 2-bit binary counter.

As a further illustration of state transition diagrams, consider **Figure D.15.** Fig. D.15(a) is the state transition diagram for a 2-bit shift register, and Fig. D.15(b) describes a 2-bit binary counter. In each case, the nodes (states) are named after the value of the register contents. The shift register has a single input, SERIAL IN, which feeds the most significant bit (MSB) position. The state transition diagram of the counter is trivial; each state of the counter simply indicates a value of the number of active transitions modulo 4. Typically, shift and count registers have additional controlling inputs such as enabling signals. The shift and count functions are discussed in the next section.

D.5. DATA REGISTERS

The data register, or simply register, is the basic information storage building block. The register directly feeds a bus and so provides faster response than a semiconductor memory. Registers are useful to delay or to buffer (hold) information for one or two clock-times.

Registers are composed of individual flip-flops, usually edge-triggered D or the data latch, with common control and clocking signals. The register data input signal may come from a single source, from a bus, (possibly bidirectional) or from a data selector (MUX). Registers, like buses, are given names (e.g. AC, MAR, PC, BUFA) and the bit numbering is the same as for buses. The register output point may feed other registers, or a bus. Some registers provide 3-state output drivers, in which case an input control point called Output Enable is provided. When Output Enable is inactive, the register output values are in the high impedance (HI-Z) state.

When the active transition occurs on the dynamic input of an edge-triggered register, data is *strobed* or *clocked* into the register. These same terms are also applied to registers built from data latches when the enable (G) control point is active.

The block diagram and RTN statements for a data register are shown in **Figure D.16.** In Fig. D.16(a), the triangle on the clock input indicates the edge-triggered property, sensitive to a positive edge. The up arrow is optional and serves as a reminder that the positive transition is the active transition. The Enable and Clear control points are seen to be active-low. The register input is from the left, identified by the heavy line. At the output side, the notation shows that the bits are numbered 0 through 17, and that the full 18 bits feed a single place. In addition, the high-order three bits A(0-2) are "tapped" off to a second destination.

In Fig. D.16(b), the first RTN statement means that when signal CLEAR A is active (–CLEAR A is low), zeros are stored in register A. The left arrow implies that a storage function takes place; the equal sign is reserved for combinational (memoryless) circuits. The second RTN statement means that when CLEAR A is inactive (–CLEAR A is high) *and* when ENABLE A is active (–ENABLE A is low), then at the active transition of CLK, the *action* is to store the value of BUS B in register A. The positive transition on signal CLK is indicated by the up arrow. A negative transition on CLK can be indicated by a down arrow.

Sometimes a condition causes a data bus value to be loaded into more than one register. We denote multiple destinations by the use of a slash (/), where "A/B←BUS C" means the data on bus C is loaded into *both* registers A and B.

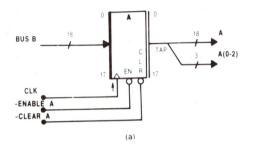

CLEAR A: A←0

(CLEAR A)'·ENABLE A·CLK↑: A←BUS B

(b)

Figure D.16. *Descriptions of a data register.* (a) Building block notation. (b) RTN statements.

D.5.1. Functional Registers

Figure D.17 describes a versatile binary counter with a parallel load capability, a count up capability, and a count down capability. It is cascadable; the building block can be connected with like building blocks to form a wider data path. The building block has a "min/max out" output point which can feed the dynamic (edge-triggered or master-slave) input point of a higher-order counter.

Counters which count from 0 through 9 are called *decade* counters or *divide-by-10* counters. Counters can be clocked with a high frequency clocking signal, and provide lower frequency clocking signals on the output points. This application

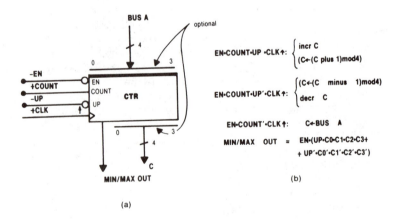

Figure D.17. *Binary up/down counter with parallel load.* (a) Physical building block. (b) RTN statements (behavior).

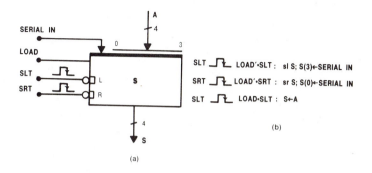

Figure D.18. *Universal shift register.* (a) Block diagram. (b) RTN statements.

is called *clock divider*. The horizontal lines of Fig. D.17(a) above and below the counter rectangle show the bit numbering, and are optional.

Figure D.18 shows a 4-bit universal shift register, so called because of the parallel load capability, and the capability of shifting either right or left. This building block is cascadable; bit 3 of a right-hand unit can connect to bit 0 of a left-hand unit to form an 8-bit shift register. The square dynamic control point indication shows that the master-slave type flip-flop is used.

A popular application of a shift register is the serialization and deserialization of data. Some communications lines and interfaces accept and deliver data which is serial-by-bit. However at each end of the serial interface, the data paths are parallel (for example eight bits wide). At the transmission end, an 8-bit data word is parallel-loaded into the shift register and shifted eight times. At the receiving end, each of the eight bits is shifted into the shift register and is then transferred in parallel to another 8-bit register. When functions such as serialization and deserialization are required, the designer should be able to visualize the motion of the data bits as they are assembled or disassembled through the shift register.

D.5.2. The Minimum Time for Register Transfers, Tmin

Within a data flow, an important timing constraint is the minimum time duration from the occurrence of one event (such as loading a first register), to the occurrence of a subsequent event (such as operating on and transferring the output of that register to a second register). The shorter the time duration, the faster the speed of the system, and the better the overall performance. Also relevant to performance is the ability to repeat the operation, with the first register receiving new data to be passed along. The notation *Tmin* is used to indicate the minimum period for cycling (repeating) a particular operation. Tmin includes propagation delays, setup delays, or any other delays which would prevent the operation from cycling at a faster rate. The calculation of Tmin is important for ensuring that a clocked sequential machine works as expected.

D.6. SYSTEM TIMING OF REGISTER TRANSFERS

The basic structural model for register transfers is shown in **Figure D.19.** At some point, CL A strobes data into Register A. Later, after paying the "appropriate" delay time, data can be strobed into destination Register B. What is the appropriate delay time? We must account for the stabilization of flip-flop output signals A OUT (tP(FFA)), the delays through the combinational circuit CC (tP(CC)), and whatever setup time is required by the flip-flops of Register B (tSU(FFB)). For the transfer, Register A is the source, the intervening combinational circuit is called CC, and Register B is the destination register. Many systems can be decomposed and analyzed in this way. The circuit CC may be no more than a direct connection, or may be as complex as a carry-save adder array which performs multiplication. The system timing takes into account the delays and the timing relationships between signals initiating changes and those responding to changes. (If no signal values were to change, the timing situation would be rather monotonous.)

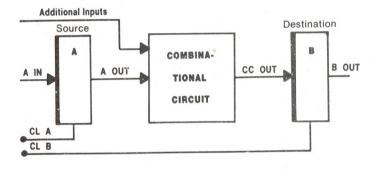

Figure D.19. *Structural model of register-to-register transfer.*

Clocking signals occur periodically, and are used to initiate changes in other signals. However, clocking signals must not be too closely spaced. The response to a last occurrence must have taken place before the next occurrence. The finite state machine model of Fig. D.13 can be used as a basis for calculating the *minimum cycle time* Tmin(CLK) for a single-phase clocked sequential circuit. In the single-phase case, Tmin specifies how often the active transitions of clock signal CLK can occur with circuit operation guaranteed to be correct according to the delay specifications. For simplicity, we postpone consideration of line or interconnection delays. (Once calculated, they are added to the value of Tmin.) In Fig. D.13, the source and destination registers are the same: the Y register. At first, we consider the active transitions to occur exactly when expected. Later, we show how to modify the calculation for clock skew.

D.6.1. Edge–Triggered Flip–Flop Timing

This subsection covers timing considerations for the use of edge-triggered D flip-flops in data registers. The circuit of Fig. D.13 (finite state machine) is used.

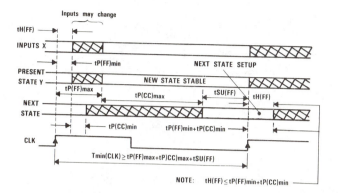

Figure D.20. *Timing diagram for finite state machine of* Figure D.13 *where source and destination registers are the same, and there is no clock skew.*

In the timing diagram of **Figure D.20,** the change is initiated by an active transition on signal CLK. Following hold time tH(FF), input X can change value. Following delay tP(FF)min, the Y register (present state) flip-flop outputs may become ambiguous. By time tP(FF)max, the new Y register outputs are guaranteed to be stable. Following an interconnection or line delay (assumed to be 0 on the timing chart), the combinational circuit CC is presented with valid present state information. By this time, the input values should be settled and stable. If not, then our timing analysis should include the additional time until input values X are stable. If the worst-case combinational circuit delay is tP(CC)max, then following this duration from when its inputs stabilize, the input values to the Y register should be stable. However, the Y register cannot be clocked or strobed until these values have been stable for the setup time tSU(FF). If the hold time tH(FF) of an edge-triggered flip-flop is less than or equal to the flip-flop's best-case propagation delay tP(FF)min (it usually is) plus any best-case combinational circuit delays, then the output of such flip-flop can be fed back to its input through that combinational circuit without a malfunction. What is more important is that the output of one flip-flop can be fed to its neighboring flip-flop whose change is initiated by the same active transition. Specifically this means that the edge-triggered flip-flop can be an element of a shift register. On the other hand, if tP(FF)min is less than tH(FF), the hold time may be violated for a single-phase system using a shift register function.

Figure D.21 shows the use of the edge-triggered D flip-flop as an element (a) in a *shift register* and (b) in a binary counter using the *ripple-carry* technique. To illustrate the ripple carry, the timing chart is shown in Fig. D.21(c). Cause-and-effect arrows show when the counter "rolls over" from a count of 7 back to a count of 0. The leading edge of signal CLK is seen to cause flip-flop C2 (least significant bit) to change state. The deactivation of flip-flop C2 corresponds to the leading edge of *ripple carry* signal −C2, which is the activating edge for changing flip-flop C1. Signal −C1 in turn provides the active transition for flip-flop C0.

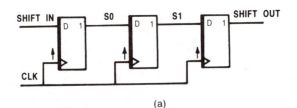

(a)

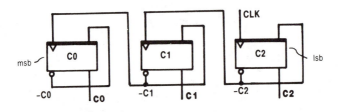

(b)

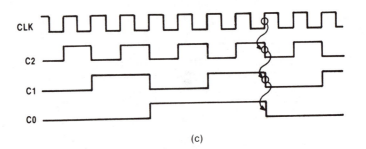

(c)

Figure D.21. *Shift registers and binary counters with edge-triggered D flip-flops.* (a) Shift register. (b) Binary ripple counter. (c) Timing diagram of 3-bit binary ripple counter.

D.6.2. Data Latch Timing

Figure D.22 illustrates the data latch register. The control points labeled G of each latch are connected together, and activated by the signal named ENABLE. The register propagation delays and setup times are the same as for each data latch. This subsection treats the timing problem associated with latch registers. In what follows, a problem called *race-through* is defined. Two-phase timing schemes are often a consequence of the race-through problem.

The data latch is level-sensitive; the edge of the ENABLE signal is not of interest. When the G input point is active (signal ENABLE is high), the data input (DATA IN) value is gated through to the output point (DATA OUT). The output value follows the input value so long as control point G is active. When the input value on point G goes inactive, the value which has been stable at the data input

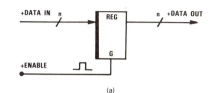

(a)

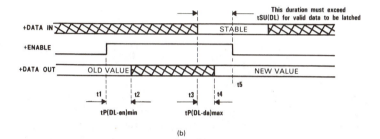

(b)

Figure D.22.   *The data latch register.*   (a) Block   diagram.
(b) Timing chart.

point for the setup time tSU(DL) is stored (latched).   If the output value is
inverted and fed back to the data input point, the data loop oscillates when input
point G is active.   If the value at the input data point changes during the setup
time, the latched value cannot be guaranteed.   The setup time tSU(DL) is usually
equal to the propagation delay tP(DL).

As seen from the timing diagram of Fig. D.22, the output of the data latch
goes ambiguous following tP(DL-en) when signal ENABLE (point G) is activated.
After ENABLE is deactivated, the value at the data input point no longer needs to
be stable.   Note that the delay through the data latch, when operated in this
fashion, is only the flip-flop propagation delay.   Further note from Fig. D.7 that in
the case of the edge-triggered D flip-flop, the best (shortest) possible guaranteed
delay through the flip-flop (from the instant of input data stability to the instant of
output data stability) is the sum of the setup time and the propagation time.   By
operating the data latch as shown in Fig. D.22(b) (the ENABLE signal is active
before input data is valid) the setup time tSU overlaps the propagation delay
tP(DL-da).   Observe that if tSU(DL) < tP(DL-da), then the output may change
(t4 of Fig. D.22) *after* the deactivation of the ENABLE signal (t5).

The level-sensitive property of the data latch prevents its use in a "one
flip-flop per bit" shift register, or a "one flip-flop per bit" binary counter element.
When signal ENABLE is active, the flip-flop loses its storage capability: the input
value is passed on as the output value.   Consider an attempt to construct a one-
flip-flop per bit shift register, as shown in **Figure D.23.**   For each ENABLE pulse,
the value of SERIAL IN should go to flip-flop A, and the value of A to flip-flop B.
What actually happens is that following two flip-flop propagation delays from the
activation of ENABLE, the value on SERIAL IN appears on both latch output

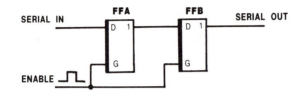

Figure D.23. *Attempt to use data latch as 1-FF-per-bit regis-*
ter: the "race-through" problem.

points.   Were a combinational circuit CC placed between flip-flop "FFA" and
"FFB", the signal value SERIAL IN could "race through" to point SERIAL OUT
after the additional delay tP(CC)min.

The Y register of the basic single-phase model of Fig. D.13 has the same
race-through problem.   The designer can avoid a malfunction only by a tight control
on clock width and circuit delays;   therefore, most systems with data latches do not
use a single-phase clock.   A malfunction will not occur if ENABLE is activated
long enough to effect the first change, and deactivated before the first change races
back to Y.   To accomplish this bit of magic, the pulse width of ENABLE (tW(EN))
must be less than tP(DL)min + tP(CC)min, but greater than tSU(DL) (usually
tP(DL)max).   Here, tP(CC)min should be large, which is not common.

Due to the race-through problem, when data latches are employed in counters
or shift registers, two data latches per bit are used.   An intermediate latch serves as
a temporary storage or holding place and is strobed at a different time.   In **Figure
D.24,** the deactivation of CLOCK1 latches the A and B data latches, whereas the
deactivation of CLOCK2 latches the intermediate data latches.   (In Fig.   D.24,
only one intermediate latch is shown.)   This is an example of a *two-phased clock.*

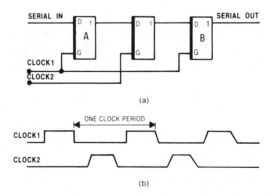

(a)

(b)

Figure D.24. *A 2-bit shift register built from data latches.*
(a) Circuit diagram. (b) Timing diagram.

Within one period of the system clock cycle, there are two timing points when data is latched or stored.

Note that in Fig. D.24(b), the clock signals are nonoverlapping. What if a single clock signal +CLK is used for CLOCK1, and its inverse −CLK is used for CLOCK2? The circuit and timing diagram is shown in **Figure D.25**. In each transition, signal −CLK is delayed from +CLK by the inverter propagation delay tP(I).

The cause-and-effect arrows of Fig. D.25(b) show the cause of changes to be levels (rather than edges as in Fig. D.21(c)). For the leftmost arrow, when +CLK reaches the high level, −CLK activates, going low. For the next arrow, when +CLK deactivates, going low, −CLK deactivates, going high. The use of an inverter on the clock does not provide a nonoverlapping two-phased clock. To show a possible malfunction, we consider the part of the timing diagram indicated tPHL(I) when both clock signals are high. At this point, flip-flop A is passing SERIAL IN to its output, which the Temporary Holding flip-flop is attempting to latch. If the propagation delay through flip-flop A can be less than the worst-case delay through the inverter plus the holding time of the holding flip-flop, the circuit malfunctions. The Temporary Holding flip-flop latches the "raced-through" value on SERIAL IN directly. For this reason, the inversion of a single clock signal to obtain a second phase involves a gamble, whereas the use of two nonoverlapping clock signals as in Fig. D.24(b) is a safe design practice.

In a system configuration, the race-through problem dictates that data latch registers clocked at one time never feed other registers clocked at the same time. This implies at least a two-phase system. The general model of such a system is

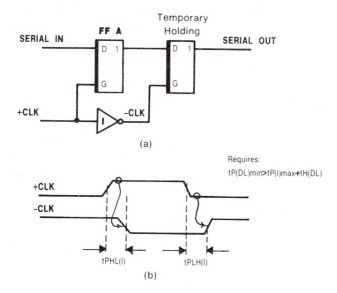

Figure D.25. *Use of single clock and inverse as two-phased clock.*
(a) Circuit diagram. (b) Timing of clock signals.

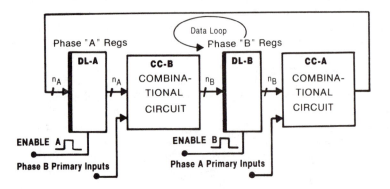

Figure D.26. *Model of two-phased system for data latch flip-flops.*

shown in **Figure D.26.** The data loop consists of combinational circuit A feeding the phase A registers (DL-A), followed by combinational circuit B feeding the phase B registers (DL-B).

We now work out the timing cycle for the two-phase scheme, and calculate the delays which control the minimum cycle time Tmin. The data loop contains at least the propagation delays of the A and B phase data latch registers (DL-A and DL-B) and combinational circuits A and B (CC-A and CC-B).

The basic timing diagram for a two-phased clocking scheme is shown in **Figure D.27.** For the data latches, we assume the propagation delay for data tP(DL-da) is also the setup time tSU(DL). These delays are concurrent, so we ignore tSU(DL). If tSU(DL) is actually larger than tP(DL-da), then we let tP(DL-da) be the larger delay, and our analysis for Tmin still holds.

From the discussion of Fig. D.5., recall that there are two propagation delays involving the data latch output, that from the data input tP(DL-da) and the other from the enable or gate input tP(DL-en). We can ignore tP(DL-en) if the enabling signal arrives sufficiently in advance of when the data input stabilizes. Thus, stable data occurs last, and controls the delay through the data latches. It is the designer's responsibility to ensure that the enabling control signal arrives first. Otherwise, the delay from data stability to the arrival of the enabling control signal must be added to Tmin.

The timing chart of Fig. D.27(a) illustrates the events which dominate the data latch timing cycle. Since the minimum cycle time Tmin is a function of the worst-case delays, in Fig. D.27(a) we assume maximum delay values. Begin with the phase A latches DL-A. At time t0, signal enable A (EN A) is activated. Later, at t1, the DL-A inputs are stable. Following delay tP(DL-da), at time t2, phase A register DL-A output values are guaranteed stable. At time t3, EN B activates before the combinational circuit B outputs stabilize. Later, following tP(CC-B) from t2, the CC-B outputs (or DL-B inputs) stabilize at time t4. Following delay tP(DL-da), the phase B register (DL-B) outputs are stable at t5. These outputs feed combinational circuit A; after tP(CC-A), at time t6, CC-A outputs stabilize. Observe that at point t6 in the cycle, we are back to t1, so we have encompassed the delays comprising the minimum cycle time Tmin. If there

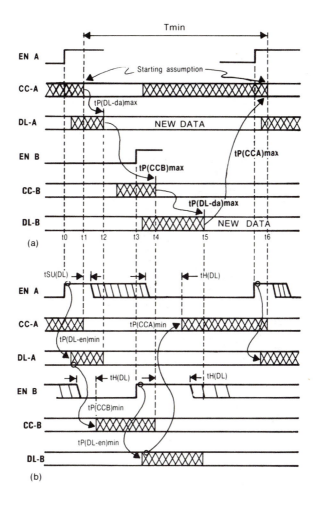

Figure D.27. *Two-phased clocking scheme with data latches*
(a) The dominant events for calculating Tmin. (b) Secondary events
determining deactivation time spans for ENABLE clocking signals.

are no problems in activating the enable signal before the data latch inputs, then
the Tmin calculation is as shown in Eq. D.2.

$$Tmin = tP(DLA\text{-}da)max + tP(CCB)max + tP(DLB\text{-}da)max$$
$$+ tP(CCA)max. \tag{D.2}$$

We achieved this Tmin value by assuming that enable signals EN A and
EN B were active before the respective data inputs to the latches was stable. If
this assumption is not the case, then Tmin must be increased by the time the data
must wait on Enable to activate.

In Fig. D.27(a), we accompany the activity of the worst-case delays which determine Tmin. In Fig. D.27(b), we observe the effect of best-case delays, and see when the enable signals must deactivate to avoid race-through problems. At t0, EN A activates, and at t1, DL-A inputs are stable. Following setup time tSU(DL) from t1, enable signal EN A can deactivate. This is the earliest EN A can deactivate.

Now consider what governs the latest time an enable signal can deactivate. We note that at t0, an active EN A opens DL-A allowing unstable data to flow to output DL-A following delay tP(DL-en)min. This unstable condition, following tP(CCB)min, appears on the inputs of data latches DL-B. By this time, preceded by hold time tH(DL), DL-B's enable signal should have deactivated. This time determines the latest time for EN B to deactivate. The analysis is similar for the earliest deactivation of EN B and the latest deactivation of EN A, and is shown in Fig. D.27(b).

It is interesting to note that whereas tP(DL-da)max governs the latches contribution to Tmin, the values of tSU(DL), tP(DL-en)min, and tH(DL) govern the range within which the enable signal must deactivate.

For the data latch, the two-phased clock is the most elementary. A generalization of the two-phased clock is the multiphased clock, but we doubt much can be gained within the data flow section of a central processor by having more than two "banks" of data registers in any data loop. In many multiphased systems, the additional clock times are used for control and interface purposes (to various memories or devices), rather than for data operations. In any case, within a multiphased clocked system, this basic rule is followed:

> *While the data latch destination register is accepting data, the source register output value must remain stable.*

Another variation within a data flow is to mix data latch registers with edge-triggered registers. In this case knowledge of both flip-flop types and the two basic timing schemes is fundamental to digital systems design. Knowing both timing schemes permits the reader to understand most other techniques as variations or combinations of the basic schemes.

D.6.3. Selective Register Clocking

Not all registers have their contents changed every cycle. For edge-triggered or data latch flip-flops, with one source of data, two selective clocking possibilities exist, as shown in **Figure D.28.** The "gating the clock" method of Fig. D.28(a) is more economical, and is in common use. The "loop-back" method of Fig. D.28(b) is employed in some technologies such as dynamic MOS, and corresponds to the classical synchronous sequential machine model. The loop-back technique applies to the use of data latch flip-flops as well.

The circuit of Fig. D.28(b) has the advantage that the control signal ENABLE A obeys the same setup and hold time specifications as the incoming data signals. The loop-back scheme of Fig. D.28(b) is commercially available in MSI TTL, and is endorsed here because there is considerably reduced clock skew variation in comparison to the arrangement of Fig. D.28(a). Furthermore, in Fig. D.28(a), if signal ENABLE A is either activated late or glitches when clock signal +CLK is

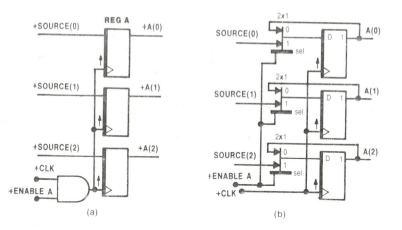

Figure D.28. *Selective register clocking.* (a) Gating the clock against a control signal, AND gate skew. (b) Clocking always, and "looping" old contents back to input using 2×1 MUX, minimal skew.

active, the register will receive a late active transition. Therefore the designer can use Fig. D.28(a) only by meeting tighter timing restrictions.

In many systems, the registers receive information either directly from a bus or through a data selector (MUX). In either case, source data must remain stable through the flip-flop setup and hold times. The control signal(s) selecting the data source must also remain stable. This stability may be difficult to guarantee in a data latch system. New control signal values themselves must be clocked at some point in the cycle. Here is an instance where a clock pulse other than the data register two-phased clock may be introduced for control purposes.

Consider next the select signals for multiplexing data to a latch register. In **Figure D.29,** signals SEL(X) and SEL(Y) must remain valid through the setup time for data latch FFA. Therefore the leading edge of CLOCK1 should certainly not make changes in these MUX select signals. Also, if the trailing edge of CLOCK1 is to cause SEL(X) and SEL(Y) to change values, the minimum time to effect that change must exceed the maximum delay through the AND gate which delivers the control signal ENABLE A. In other words, the MUX output value must be guaranteed stable through the setup time of FFA.

Fig. D.29 is also useful in explaining a related point. When registers are selectively clocked, there is only one time that data select signals such as SEL(X) and SEL(Y) are required to be valid: the duration of setup time prior to latching or strobing data into the register. At all other times, the values on these control signals can be ignored. The control signal specification for such data select signals can be characterized as having many "don't cares" (see Chapter 3). The control signals which control the active transitions on the registers, on the other hand, do not have such a liberty. The clocking signals must occur only when specified; at all other times control signals such as CHANGE A in Fig. D.29 are constrained to be inactive.

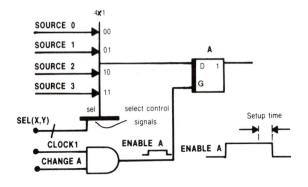

Figure D.29. *Multiplexing into a data latch.*

D.6.4. Clock Skew

Clock skew is important because of its effect on the Tmin system cycle time calculation. This section will show that the clock skew can be independently calculated, then added to the Tmin (without skew) to obtain the Tmin (with skew).

Consider the register transfer model of Fig. D.19, where registers A and B are edge-triggered. As shown by an analysis such as Fig. D.20, the minimum time between the active transition on CL A and the active transition on CL B is:

$$Tmin = tP(FFA)max + tP(CC)max + tSU(FFB). \qquad \text{(D.3)}$$

In an actual design situation, this equation may be used in several ways. First it can specify the system clock which prescribes the time period between the active transitions of CL A and CL B, T(A-to-B). Once T(A-to-B) has been specified, Eq. D.3 can be used to determine an upper-bound tP(CC)max for the delay through the intervening combinational circuit. Thus, if a first attempt at the design of that combinational circuit appears to be too slow, the designer can rearrange his circuits, doing more in parallel, to reduce the worst-case delay tP(CC)max.

The foregoing analysis is valid if relative delay variations do not displace CL A and CL B in time. Thus, if CL A occurs late, and CL B occurs early, the value T(A-to-B) becomes smaller than anticipated, and there is less time available for the data input values for register B to stabilize. Variations in the time of occurrence of the register clocking signals result in clock *skew,* denoted tSK(A-to-B). Although most system clock signals are generated from a common oscillator, which defines a common reference point, different clock signals may pass through different leaves of a fan-out tree, and be selectively gated through different combinational circuits.

First, some background. Clocking signals are *periodic:* the amount of time between successive activations of the clocking signal defines its *period.* The clocking signals also deactivate periodically. The point in time when a clocking signal changes state is called the *reference edge.* Corresponding to each unique clocking signal are two reference edges, one at the signal activation (turn on) and the other at the deactivation (turn off). Hopefully, clocking signals do not happen by accident; they are the result of the overall design of the central clocking scheme.

Within this scheme, the designer has defined a basic *machine cycle,* whose period T corresponds to the period of most of the important system clocking signals. The machine cycle period T can be subdivided into *timing points,* which in turn initiate or terminate actions described by RTN statements. The timing points are the reference edges of clocking signals. **Figure D.30** shows system clocking for a 100-nanosecond machine cycle with four timing points, called 0-time, 25-time, 50-time, and 75-time. One can use 100-time, which "wraps back" to 0-time, to describe the completion of a cycle. The timing cycle of Fig. D.30 describes the timing points, or occurrence of the reference edges, in "ideal nanoseconds".

The idealized wave forms reflect the designer's thoughts about the timing cycle, but not the realities of clock skew which necessarily result. The implementation involves logic blocks whose propagation delays are variable. Skew is not due to the existence of an absolute delay in logic gates or flip-flops, but to the *variation* between the worst-case and best-case delays. All types of clock skew result from an ambiguity in the exact moment a signal changes. Skew is the difference D between a worst-case and best-case delay:

$$\text{Skew} = D \ (\text{worst-case} - \text{best-case}) \tag{D.4}$$

Observe that the ideal timing scheme of Fig. D.30 could be implemented in logic blocks of known precise delay of, say, two ns. One need only generate each clocking signal with the same fixed number of gates and flip-flop delays in each path from the oscillator to the clocking signal. With ideal delay values there is no reason for skew. In practice, two types of skew are encountered, *relative skew* and *self-skew.* Relative skew is any *relative* variation (from the ideal) between *different* reference edges in the same period. Self-skew is any variation from the ideal between one reference edge and the *same* reference edge of the next period. In general, a low-to-high transition of a signal may have different worst- and best-case times from the high-to-low transition. Thus, the skew tSK(Ti) relative to the activation of a timing signal Ti may be different from skew tSK(Ti') of the deactivating edge of the same signal. To simplify the discussion, we assume the skew is the same for each edge: tSK(Ti)=tSK(Ti').

Another reality to contend with in clocking systems is the *powering* (achieving high fan-out) of clocking signals. Powering can be done with a fan-out tree. Clocking signals generated at different leaves of the same fan-out tree experience a *mutual* self-skew. **Figure D.31** shows the circuit block diagram and timing chart for the generation of clocking signals T1 and T2 of the clocking scheme idealized in

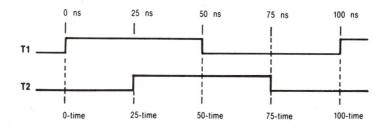

Figure D.30. *Ideal timing.*

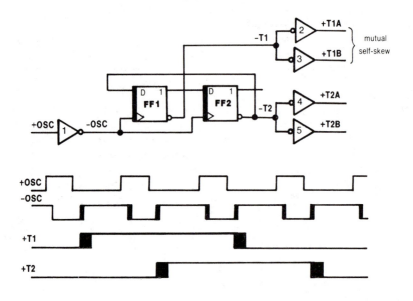

Figure D.31. *Illustration of clock skew.*

Fig. D.30. The mutual self-skew between signals T1A and T1B is the difference between the worst-case and best-case delays of inverters 2 and 3. Here, the *common fan-out point* is the complement output signal of flip-flop 1. Mutual skew is evident in the *same* period. The self-skew of T1A is the difference between the worst-case and best-case delays in the path through inverter 1, flip-flop 1, and inverter 2. The self-skew is only in evidence as a "jitter" from one clock period to the next. The common fan-out point for self-skew is the signal +OSC.

The relative skew between the clocking signals for T1 and T2 already takes into account the worst-case and best-case delays through the fan-out trees, and is evident in the same clock period. The relative skew delay calculations include a term $D(wc - bc)$ for inverter 1, because the jitter must be included from one edge to the next:

$$tSK(T1 - T2)rel = D(wc - bc)inv1 + D(wc - bc)FF1$$
$$+ D(wc - bc)FF2 + D(wc - bc)inverters \qquad \textbf{(D.5)}$$

Relative and mutual skews are more likely than self-skew to be real problems, because the former occur through different blocks. The self-skew calculation is very conservative since it presumes a variation from the worst-case to the best-case delays in the same block from one clock period to the next.

Consider the single-phased system of **Figure D.32.** The cause of the skew is seen to be combinational circuits 1 and 2. Were there not such intervening circuits, the only cause of skew would be variations in line or interconnection delays. (We include line delays with the propagation delay of the block furnishing the signal to simplify the exposition.)

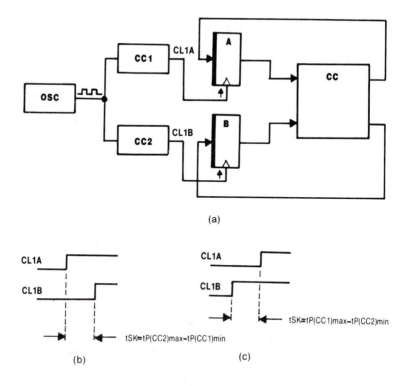

(a)

(b)

(c)

Figure D.32. *Illustration of clock skew tSK in a single-phased system.* (a) Block diagram. (b) CL1A preceeds CL1B. (c) CL1B preceeds CL1A.

In calculating the maximum skew, two situations must be considered, as in Fig. D.32(b) and (c). In each case the largest difference is calculated as shown, and for Tmin calculations, the maximum of the two values calculated is used. To correct a Tmin calculation for clock skew, use Eq. D.6 for edge-triggered flip-flops:

$$\text{Tmin (with skew)} = \text{Tmin (no skew)} + \text{tSKmax} \qquad \textbf{(D.6)}$$

Consider a symmetric situation in which the relevant tPmax − tPmin for CC1 and CC2 gives 15 ns for each case. Consequently CL1A could safely precede CL1B by 15 ns, or CL1B could safely precede CL1A by 15 ns. It is important to observe that the skew is not the sum, 30 ns, because both the cases of Fig. D.32(b) and (c) never occur at the same time.

In a multiphased system, such as in Fig. D.19 where CL A and CL B are different reference edges, variations in clock skew can always be compensated for by increasing the cycle time specification Tmin. However, due to the race-through problem, this does not hold for the single-phased system. Consider Fig. D.32(b), where CL1A precedes CL1B. Imagine CL1A causing register A to change after tP(A)min, causing the inputs to B to change after tP(CC)min. If, due to skew,

CL1B has not yet experienced the active transition, its setup time specification could be violated. A bad value could be strobed in. From the circuit delay parameters, the *maximum allowable clock skew* tMAS can be calculated as in Eq. D.7:

$$tMAS = tP(FF)min + tP(CC)min - tH(FF) \tag{D.7}$$

Note that tMAS applies only to single-phased systems, and is *not the actual skew tSK* which enters the Tmin calculation. Also, tMAS is independent of the setup time tSU, and tP(CC1) or tP(CC2). The single-phased scheme will not avoid the race-through problem unless:

$$tMAS > tSK. \tag{D.8}$$

Since a large tMAS is favorable, it is common in some high-performance systems to "pad" some of the faster combinational circuit paths with additional inverters in order to increase the value of tP(CC)min without increasing the value of tP(CC)max.

Consider now the two-phased timing scheme for the data latch approach. Refer back to the timing chart of Fig. D.27. Our philosophy in designing that scheme is that the data value not wait on the enabling of the latches. Rather, the latch should be enabled and open slightly before input data becomes valid. Once the data output value of the data latch is stable, the enable (EN A or EN B) can be deactivated. The enable must be deactivated before the data input value goes ambiguous. In an ideal case, a properly designed two-phased data latch scheme can be made insensitive to clock skew, and no correction for skew need be made to the Tmin equation. This ideal scheme, of course, does not tolerate large values of skew tSK. In practice, the synchronization of some primary input signals (from outside the system) with the system clock may affect the validity of some signals. Timing of these primary inputs may require a skew term to enter the Tmin calculation.

D.6.5. Timing Summary

We have studied some of the major system timing models. The use of data latches is cost-effective in VLSI chip technologies. Edge-triggered flip-flops prevail in many special-purpose designs using MSI building blocks where good functional power per pin is needed.

The system timing cycle must be designed in the light of the Tmin calculation, Eq. D.6. The delay specifications of the circuit family must be taken into account. We recommend the conservative approach for estimating delays. We have not covered all variations in synchronous clocking, but we have presented a sufficient basis for understanding most popular schemes.

D.7. SWITCH DEBOUNCE CIRCUITS

Synchronous systems must be prepared to accept inputs from unsynchronized outside sources, such as switches. In this section, we address the problem of dynamic switch position detection, where the activation of a switch can cause the digital system to respond. To prevent the system from responding more than once to a single activation, the *noise* caused by the closing and opening of mechanical contacts must be eliminated. The problem is that of *contact bounce;* the signal value contains noise and instabilities during a transition period. **Figure D.33** shows

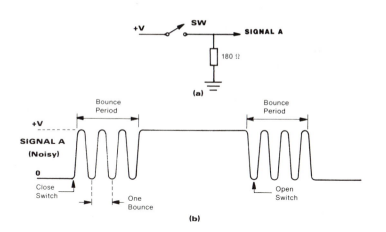

Figure D.33. *Contact bounce of single throw switch.* (a) Normally open switch. (b) Timing diagram.

a normally open (NO) switch, where we find (a) the circuit diagram, and (b) the timing diagram showing the noisy transition periods.

D.7.1. Double Throw Switches

The simplest mechanical contact to interface is the normally open, normally closed pair (SPDT arrangement), because only the leading edge of the contact signals is noisy. Use of a *debounce flip-flop* is shown in **Figure D.34.** A simple set-clear flip-flop of Fig. D.34(a) is used to clean the signal. A simple debounce flip-flop can be constructed by cross-coupling two inverters as in Fig. D.34(b). The activation or release of the switch causes an inverter output to be shorted for about the delay time for a signal to propagate through the feedback loop (equivalent of two inverter propagation delays), which is not harmful. This arrangement has the advantage of not requiring the pull-up resistors to V_{CC} of Fig. D.34(a). The timing chart for the debounced signal is shown in Fig. D.34(c).

The debounce circuit of Fig. D.34(b) generalizes nicely to handle rotary selectors for a small number of contacts [5]. The circuit is shown in **Figure D.35.** The alternate method to handle this switch is to provide a pull-up resistor to V_{CC} for each circumferential contact.

D.7.2. Single Throw Switches

Unfortunately not all switches have both normally open and normally closed contacts (or exactly one closed and several open contacts as in Fig. D.35). In the case of a single contact or single throw switch, the bounce period exists on both the leading and trailing edges of the signal. We know of no solution to the single throw debounce problem except to provide a delay time and patiently wait out the maximum bounce time. The delay time solution requires a knowledge of the

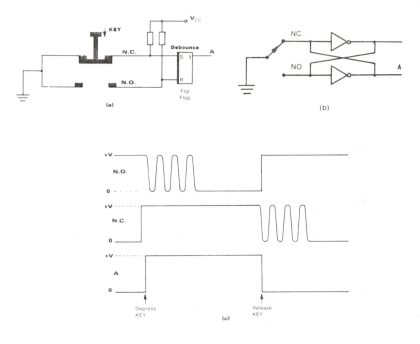

Figure D.34. *Debounce flip-flop to clean noisy SPDT* contacts.
(a) Conventional debounce flip-flop. (b) Simple debounce circuit.
(c) Timing chart.

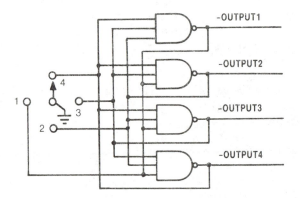

Figure D.35. *Rotary selector debouncing.*

maximum bounce period. Most mechanical switches have a bounce time of ten milliseconds or less, and almost all bounce times are less than 50 milliseconds.

Figure D.36 shows an arrangement for *cleaning* (removing noise from) both edges of a switch signal, where the delay period is five milliseconds (ms). The

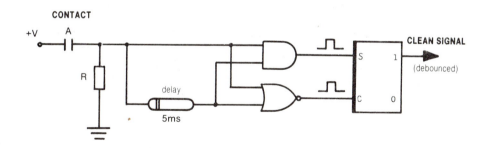

Figure D.36.   *Use of delay to clean or debounce contact noise.*

delays themselves are generally provided by an RC network: a capacitor C which is either charged or discharged through a resistor R.   The larger the value of the resistance R in the charging or discharging path, the longer the capacitor takes to charge or discharge.   The nominal delay of such an RC network is the *RC time constant*.   It is the product in seconds of the R value in ohms times the C value in farads (F).   For example, the charging (discharging) of a 1-nanofarad capacitor through a 1-megohm resistor has an RC time constant of 1 millisecond:

$$(1 \times 10^{-9}) \times (1 \times 10^{6}) = 1 \times 10^{-3}.$$

In Fig. D.36 the debounced signal is a level version of the contact state, delayed by the value of the delay element.

Some debounce circuits can provide a single pulse each time the contact is closed. This type of circuit is useful when the leading edge of the contact closure is designed to initiate a single operation within the digital system.   Although the contact may be closed longer than this time, it is not desirable to repeat the operation continually within the system.

A circuit described by Fontaine [6] which provides a fixed length pulse per contact closure is shown in **Figure D.37**. This single pulse must be shorter than the duration of one *bounce:* that is, one momentary contact closure within the bounce

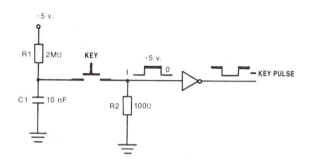

Figure D.37. *Pulse generator circuit.*

period (see Fig. D.33(b)). Initially capacitor C is charged to +5 volts. The switch is closed, the capacitor places five volts on the input to the inverter, and discharges current through resistor R2. The RC time constant with R2 is one microsecond (μs), so C discharges through 100 ohms during the first contact closure. The inverter sees its input at the high level for almost one microsecond, and so emits a negative pulse of that duration. When the contact opens, capacitor C is charged through R1, an RC network whose time constant of 20 milliseconds is 20,000 times larger.

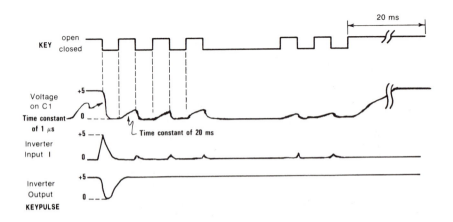

Figure D.38. *Timing diagram of pulse generator circuit.*

Since this time is long relative to the momentary contact bounce time, when C is discharged again through R2, it has not acquired enough charge to affect the inverter. The timing diagram is shown in **Figure D.38.** When the key switch bounces open, the capacitor only charges at the 20-ms rate, whereas when the key is closed, the capacitor discharges very rapidly at the 1-μs rate.

A debounce circuit is available as an MSI part (Motorola MC-14490) which consists of a 4-bit shift register with the parallel load capability. The shift register feeds an output flip-flop. The circuit must be provided with an outside clock signal such that four clock periods exceed the bounce time. If a "decision logic" circuit detects one or two 0 data bits in between two 1 data bits (or vice-versa), this is evidence of a bounce, and the shift register is parallel loaded with the value of the output flip-flop.

With a clock source available, a simple counter [7] can be used to provide a debounced signal, as shown in **Figure D.39.** When the contact is initially closed, the counter begins to count up. However, the bounce resets the counter. An appropriately large count (one of the more significant output signals) is used to set the debounce flip-flop. The flip-flop is cleared upon the first bounce of a switch opening.

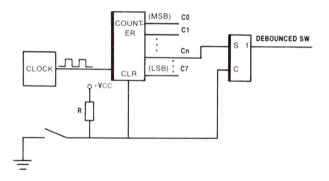

Figure D.39. *Use of a counter to debounce a switch.*

D.8. SINGLE-SHOT

The *single-shot,* also called a one-shot or monostable multivibrator, is a circuit which behaves in a fashion similar to the pulse generator circuit of Fig. D.37. The single-shot is a two-state device, only one state of which is stable. The circuit responds to the leading edge of the input with a pulse of fixed duration, before returning to its stable state.

Digital systems use single-shots to provide a signal of known time delay. When *triggered* or activated by a reference edge on the input, the circuit enters its unstable state for a predetermined time duration tD. Following time tD from the reference edge on the input, the single-shot returns to its stable state. The versatile 555 timer IC is capable of being employed as a single-shot by the proper attachment of a resistor and capacitor whose RC time constant provides an estimate of tD.

Single-shot circuits have the property of being retriggerable or not, as determined by how the circuit responds to a triggering edge while still in the unstable state. The retriggerable single-shot remains indefinitely in the unstable state if it is supplied with triggering edges at intervals less than tD. The retriggerable single-shot returns to the stable state following duration tD from receipt of the last triggering edge. The nonretriggerable single-shot ignores triggering edges while it is in the unstable state, and returns to the stable state following duration tD from when it first entered the unstable state.

A *timing chain* can be constructed from single-shots cascaded together, the return to the stable state of one triggering the next. Unless the delay values required are difficult to achieve by using one, or perhaps two, single-shots, in combination with counters to divide down the frequency, single-shot chains are not recommended. Packaging discrete resistors and capacitors is expensive in a production environment, and the time constant depends on the values of these components. If timing accuracy is needed, the RC time constants may require periodic checking and adjustment by service personnel. In the VLSI era, digital watches which lose or gain too much time are adjusted at service centers by placing a new watch in the old case.

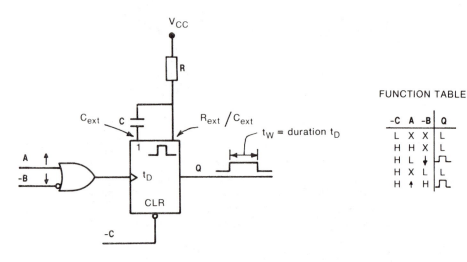

FUNCTION TABLE

-C	A	-B	Q
L	X	X	L
H	H	X	L
H	L	↓	⊓
H	X	L	L
H	↑	H	⊓

Figure D.40. *Single-shot.*

Figure D.40 shows a commercially available single-shot chip, the 74123, which can be cleared or reset by a level signal. The single-shot chip has a control point (an input pin) responsive to a positive triggering edge, and another control point responsive to a negative triggering edge. The time constant tD is determined by the values of an external capacitor and resistor.

D.9. SCHMITT TRIGGER CIRCUITS

Consider what happens when a smooth sine wave is used as the input to a logic inverter. The output will be slightly more "square" than the input because of the switching thresholds. Nevertheless, the inverter may be in its *uncertainty region* for too long a time, which may be detrimental if used as the active transition for an edge-triggered D flip-flop. To improve the rise and fall times of a slowly changing signal, we require an inverter with the *hysteresis* of a dual threshold. This means that a high threshold is used for recognizing a high input, and once a high input is recognized, a low threshold is applied for recognizing a low input. Such a circuit is called a Schmitt trigger.

Figure D.41 shows the block diagram and the corresponding waveforms for the device. The waveform shows the "snap action", where the device output makes its transitions rapidly. Logically, the device behaves like an inverter.

Input levels which lie between the two hysteresis thresholds do not cause the output to change. The device "squares" the edges of transitions which appear at its inputs. The inverter in Fig. D.37 is an application for a Schmitt trigger, because a high threshold for recognizing the high level on its input is desirable. The block diagram symbol for the Schmitt trigger is similar to an inverter. The snap action property is indicated by the symbol for a hysteresis loop.

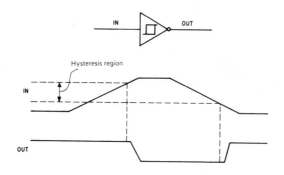

Figure D.41. *A Schmitt trigger with its waveforms.*

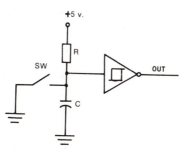

Figure D.42. *Simple debounce circuit with Schmitt trigger.*

A Schmitt trigger debounce circuit is shown in **Figure D.42.** With the switch S open, capacitor C charges up to +5 volts, and with its input high the Schmitt trigger output is low. When the switch is closed, the first bounce discharges C, as was explained for Fig. D.40, and the Schmitt trigger output OUT snaps high. Between subsequent bounces, due to the large RC time constant, capacitor C fails to charge up sufficiently to reach the Schmitt trigger threshold which now is quite high. When the switch remains closed, the Schmitt trigger input is held low. When the switch S opens, capacitor C begins to charge up to +5 volts, but is discharged each bounce. After the last bounce the capacitor will charge up, in accordance with its time constant, cross the high input threshold and snap the output OUT low within an order of magnitude of the RC time constant.

D.10. POWER-ON RESET CIRCUITS

D.10.1. Motivation

When power is first applied to a digital system, the flip-flops and volatile memories may turn on in any state. Unless some provision is made for initialization, the circuit may not behave as expected. This problem is analogous to running a computer program whose variables are not properly initialized. In the case of a digital computer, when power is applied, the contents of the program counter and instruction register, or major control state, should not be left to chance. For this reason, a signal called *power-on reset* (POR) or *power-clear,* is generated. The POR signal is activated only once, remains active for a short duration of time, and then remains in the inactive state for as long as the system power supply is on. To generate another POR signal, the system must be switched off and then on again. Conceptually, the POR signal could be ORed with a "Master Clear" button, so that either situation causes the system to be placed in the initial state.

D.10.2. A POR Circuit

A circuit to perform the power-on reset function is shown in **Figure D.43**. With power off, capacitor C is discharged to ground potential. When power is turned on, and reaches V_{CC} such that the logic gates are behaving normally, all the potential V_{CC} appears across the 1K-ohm resistor R. The inverter input is thus low initially, and the output is high. Now capacitor C is charged through R, with an RC time constant of 100 ms for the values shown. When the capacitor is sufficiently charged, the potential across C will appear to the inverter as the high state, which switches the output low. To enhance the speed of this change, use of a Schmitt trigger inverter is recommended. While power remains up, capacitor C remains charged, and signal +POR remains inactive.

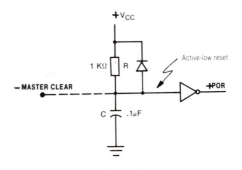

Figure D.43. *A power-on reset circuit.*

When power goes off, capacitor C is rapidly discharged through the diode. (This is the purpose of the diode.) The system can thus be rapidly turned on following power turn off, to clear the system and reinitialize it with the +POR pulse. The dotted line labeled –MASTER CLEAR shows where another signal causing a system reset could be ORed in to the same circuit.

D.11. NOISE SPIKE SHRINKING

Interface signals are sometimes noisy, and for control strobes, it is desirable to filter out short noise spikes (glitches). The type of noise called cross talk, for example, is caused by a signal change on a nearby conductor. The spike durations typically endure only for the signal rise or fall time, which may be on the order of ten nanoseconds (ns) or less.

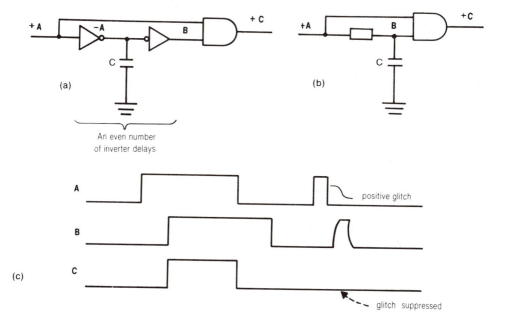

Figure D.44. *Positive pulse shrinker.* (a) Inverter delays. (b) RC delays. (c) Timing chart.

Figure D.44 shows circuits which eliminate these noise glitches. Assume input signal +A is normally low (an active-high signal pulse). We would like to filter out any incoming positive spikes on +A, preventing them from reaching output +C. The basic solution is to delay signal +A, making sure it does not revert back to the low value, before activating output +C. When +A is activated, Figure D.44(a) shows inverter pairs which serve to delay the signal at the B input to the NAND. Capacitors to ground (say at point −A) can further delay the signal. Output +C changes only when the original input +A *and* the delayed input +B have changed high. The circuit of Fig. D.44(b) shows an approach which achieves the same result with an RC network providing the delay. The effect of these circuits is to shorten the duration of the legitimate positive pulse, as seen in the waveform chart. When a glitch appears on +A which is shorter than the delay at signal +B, it is suppressed, as seen in the second half of the chart.

This circuit does not work at all on negative glitches; in fact, the circuit increases the negative pulse widths. The shortening of a positive pulse is achieved

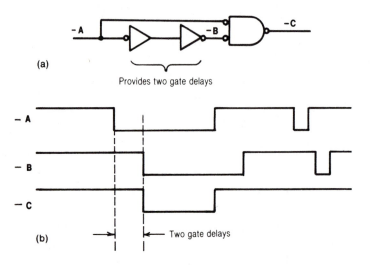

(a)

Provides two gate delays

(b)

Two gate delays

Figure D.45.   *Negative pulse shrinker.*   (a) Circuit.   (b) Timing chart.

at the expense of lengthening the negative pulse. Thus for active-low type signals, the circuit of Fig. D.44 must be changed by replacing the AND gate with an OR gate. See **Figure D.45,** where the DeMorgan dual (see Appendix C) of the OR gate is shown. This circuit is capable of suppressing short negative glitches but not positive ones. Therefore, in applying circuits such as these, care should be taken to determine the normal state of the signal. In this way, the proper polarity pulse undergoes the glitch suppression treatment.

D.12.   A USEFUL CONDITION-DETECTION CIRCUIT

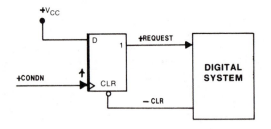

Figure D.46.   *A condition-detection circuit.*

In the circuit of **Figure D.46,** we recall the "exactly once" circuit of Fig. D.12, or a variation, which appears in many interfacing situations. The signal +CONDN may typically be a "cleaned" signal from a switch. The digital system employs flip-flop output +REQUEST to perform some function. However, the system should perform the function exactly one time for each activation of +CONDN and no more. If +CONDN is still active when the function has already been done, the active +CONDN should be ignored. This requirement calls for a circuit which only reacts to the leading edge of +CONDN, and is insensitive to when +CONDN deactivates. After the leading edge, +CONDN can deactivate whenever it wishes. The digital system remembers that it already performed the requested function by clearing flip-flop REQUEST. Now the digital system will not receive another request until the next leading edge of +CONDN.

D.13. SYNCHRONIZERS AND THE SYNCHRONIZER PROBLEM

The problem of interfacing contacts of pushbuttons to a digital system is often a two-part problem:

1) debounce the input signal, and
2) synchronize the debounced signal with the central clock of the synchronous system.

The *synchronizer* problem concerns deriving from an asynchronous input +A (which can activate at any time) a synchronous signal +S (of approximately the same duration) which is activated and deactivated in step with the clock. The signal is in step if its leading and trailing edges are within a propagation delay of the clock edges.

Two apparent solutions to this problem are shown in **Figure D.47,** one using NAND gates, and the other an edge-triggered flip-flop. The first activation of signal +A in Fig. D.47(c) shows how the circuits are intended to work. The

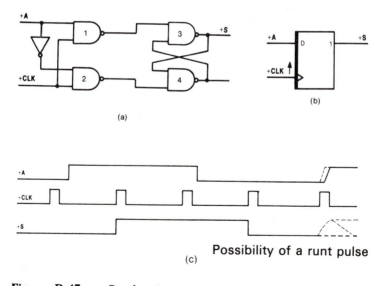

Possibility of a runt pulse

Figure D.47.   *Synchronizers.*   (a) NAND gate synchronizer.
(b) Edge-triggered D synchronizer. (c) Timing diagram.

second activation of +A is seen to occur in the proximity of the clock edge. Consider the response to this second activation by the circuit of Fig. D.47(a). One input to NAND 1 is falling while the other is rising. A negative "runt" pulse is emitted from NAND 1 to the input of NAND 3. If the pulse is weak enough, NAND 3 ignores it. If the pulse is strong enough, NAND 3 will go high long enough for NAND 4 to respond with a low level to latch the flip-flop with +S active. The synchronizer problem occurs when the strength of the runt pulse is not so short that it is ignored, nor so long that it causes NAND 4 to react. The problem which occurs is that the runt pulse can have enough strength to place the flip-flop of NANDs 3 and 4 of Fig. D.47(b) into a *metastable* state. When the metastable state manifests itself, the transistors internal to the synchronizer operate as linear amplifiers, the transistor "threshold uncertainty" region is entered, and oscillation or delayed response voltage occurs on signal +S. This metastable situation has been modeled, and experimentally verified.

The synchronizer problem has received some attention in the popular scientific literature [8], and has been brought to the attention of the technical community by Chaney and Molnar [9]. Mayne and Moore [10] study the problem and show it involves considerations of atomic physics. Chaney and Molnar observe that when the flip-flop propagation delays are longer than the rise times, then this metastable state is an oscillation between NAND 3 and NAND 4. When the propagation delays are small with respect to the rise and fall times, then the metastable state may cause NAND 3 and NAND 4 outputs to be somewhere in the uncertainty region. Mayne and Moore offer the comforting observation that thermal noise will cause the flip-flop to go eventually to one output state or the other.

The solution to the synchronizer problem is a probabilistic one: the longer one waits before actually using the flip-flop output signal, the less likely the chance of encountering the signal in a metastable state. Davies and Barber [11] calculate that with flip-flops of propagation delay ten ns and common values for the speed and amplification of the transistors involved, the output would be in a metastable state after ten ns with a probability of 10^{-4} and after 50 ns with a probability of 10^{-22}. Mayne and Moore [10] base a calculation on the Heisenberg uncertainty principle for a different circuit, and find that a wait of 50 ns produces a metastable state with probability of 4×10^{-6}. However an experimental setup showed a gross discrepancy, for which settling times of 50 ns to 100 ns had far less probability than Mayne and Moore expected.

In view of the existence of the metastable state, **Figure D.48** is the circuit of a more robust synchronizer. Here, the system waits a full clock cycle for the edge-triggered D flip-flop 1 to settle. If the active transitions are spaced on the order of

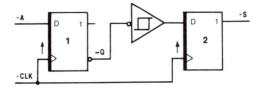

Figure D.48. *A more robust synchronizer.*

500 ns, this allows 500 ns of settling time, which should considerably reduce the likelihood of signal +S becoming metastable. The use of the Schmitt trigger provides additional discrimination to a signal which is in a metastable state.

D.14. READ-WRITE MONOLITHIC MEMORIES (RAMS)

Memories are covered in greater detail in Chapter 4. This section provides a brief introduction to the block diagram symbol of the RAM, and its RTN statement. A monolithic read-write memory is called a RAM, denoting *random access memory*. The term RAM is historical (and an anachronism), dating from the time when some main memories consisted of delay lines or drums.

Our treatment here is primarily at the functional level, as the system designer does not care about the circuit diagram of the on-chip flip-flops, or how the memory stores the bits. The important aspect is viewing the memory as a functional unit, and knowing what to do to get data into or out of the unit. In particular, the designer wants to read and write data with a minimum amount of "bureaucracy" imposed on the interface design. The static monolithic memory suits this requirement very well, and is the basis for the present description. The reader should keep in mind the operation of a data latch as a useful way to assimilate the function of a static RAM.

One type of monolithic memory has already been introduced in Appendix C, the ROM or read-only memory. The ROM building block does not remember any history from its past input values; it is merely a combinational circuit. A functional description of a ROM is: present a stable address to the ROM input points, allow a wait time tA (access time); then the output value is stable and valid.

The read operation of a RAM is similar. RAMs are presented with a stable address, and following access time tA the output data value is stable. RAMs are written into for a write operation, and for this purpose write-data input points are provided. A control point called write enable is also provided, and is used to write data into the addressed location. The past history remembered by the RAM (to make an analogy with a finite state machine) is the input data value which corresponds to each address value. The write enable control point is an active control point whose value initiates the change in the internal state of the RAM. We think of the write enable as the enable or G control point of a data latch. Write enable (WE) is also known as a write strobe or a R/W (read/write) control. The name and behavior vary according to the manufacturer.

Figure D.49 concerns the monolithic RAM. The block diagram is shown in Fig. D.49(a). To indicate a storage function, the rectangle has a dark or heavy border. Memory systems may be comprised of many chips. The memory block has the notation "4096 × 8", which means the RAM contains 4096 or 4K 8-bit words. The address input line is 12 bits wide, because $4096 = 2^{12}$. The input variable is usually named MA for "memory address". The data input bus is labeled MW for memory write-data, and is eight bits wide (the word size). The RAM data output is labeled RD for read-data bus.

In some lower-performance systems, the write-data and read-data buses can be implemented with the same bidirectional bus. Most memories cannot simultaneously undergo read and write operations, so there is no bus contention problem. A bidirectional bus conserves connection points or pins. Since the read and write

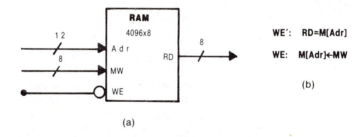

Figure D.49. *Monolithic RAM.* (a) Block diagram. (b) RTN statements.

operations are mutually exclusive, only one control point (WE) need be provided. When WE is inactive, the memory is reading the data at the address value; when WE is active, the memory is writing the data value at the data input. An inversion bubble is shown in Fig. D.49(a) as an indication of the active-low nature of the WE control point.

Fig. D.49(b) shows the RTN statements for the memory. "M[Adr]" denotes the memory word whose address is the value on the address bus labeled Adr. When not writing, WE is inactive, as expressed by condition WE′ being true. When WE′ is true, the data value at the addressed memory word, M[Adr], is placed on the data output RD bus. The read operation is a combinational function. The RTN statement reflects this by the equal sign.

For the write operation, control point WE is active. The value at input control point WE, being an activating input, has timing requirements which are covered in Chapter 4. For the present we simply treat the input like the G control point of the data latch. At the trailing edge of the signal feeding the WE input, a storage function is performed: the value on MW is stored in the word denoted M[Adr]. The storage function is indicated in the RTN statement by the left arrow.

Memory chips possess control inputs other than those discussed here. A *chip select* input point, when active, permits the chip to behave as described. When the chip is not selected, it neither writes nor reads. These details are covered in Chapter 4.

D.15. BUFFERING

"Buffer" is perhaps one of the most overworked words in the computer engineer's vocabulary. The general notion of a buffer is as a "go-between". The earliest computer use of the term buffer was probably to describe a storage device used to accommodate or compensate for the speed difference between two data rates. A block of words in main memory can be used for that purpose. The higher-speed main memory accepts or delivers data to a slower IO device as required, a word at a time. Typically an output buffer in main memory can be loaded by the computer program from a work area, at CPU instruction speeds.

To do *double buffering,* the CPU program loads a second output buffer area while the IO device is accepting words from the first output buffer area. When the transfer of the first buffer has been completed, the second output buffer is ready for transfer. In this way the slower output device can be kept busy. While the second buffer is being transferred, the first buffer can be reloaded. This technique is also called "ping-pong" or exchange buffering.

Another type of buffer is a register (built from flip-flops) at a device interface. The flip-flop buffer register holds data until a device at the other end of the interface is ready for it. Often at interfaces there is a change in data bus widths. Buffering techniques can convert two bytes of 8-bit data into one word of 16 bits.

Buffers can also do serialization and deserialization. For example, disk controllers or control units obtain data from a disk track in a serial-by-bit stream. The disk output is loaded to a deserializing shift register, which performs a parallel transfer to a buffer register in the controller while reloading the shift register from the disk output serial stream. Here, the controller buffer is a holding register. The controller must deliver the deserialized data to main memory before the next data word is transferred from the deserializer. When data is being read from (or written to) moving magnetic media, and cannot be taken from or delivered to the device in time, device *overrun* occurs. Overrun can result in the loss of data, and is to be avoided. Buffering techniques can prevent overrun problems. A first-in first-out (FIFO) buffer LSI storage chip is available; this chip can accept and deliver data at varying rates, and is useful in many applications.

Another use of the term buffer is as a synonym for a line driver circuit or a level converter. This buffer circuit "goes between" circuits whose input and output signal voltage (or current) levels do not match. A line driver may accept a logic signal at one voltage level, then amplify and convert the value to another voltage level. This type of circuit is *also* found at an IO interface, so the opportunity for confusion concerning "buffer" is evident. We prefer specific terms such as "level converter", "buffer register", "line driver", or "IO buffer area".

REFERENCES

1. Montgomery Phister, Jr., *Logical Design of Digital Computers,* Wiley, New York, 1958.
2. Glen G. Langdon, Jr., "Analysis of Asynchronous Circuits Under Different Delay Assumptions", *IEEE Trans. Computers,* vol. C-17, n. 12, December 1968, 1131-1143.
3. John Earle, "Logic and Timing in Digital System Design", *Electronic Design,* v. 8, n. 17, 1961, 30-42.
4. G. A. Maley and J. Earle, *The Logical Design of Transistor Computers,* Prentice-Hall, Englewood Cliffs, NJ, 1963.
5. Bob Cohn, "Debounce with Inverter or Logic Gates and out go the Pull-up Resistors", *Electronic Design,* September 13, 1978, 148.
6. G. Fontaine, "Gate suppresses Pulses from Switch Contact Bounces", *Electronics,* v. 44, n. 6, March 15, 1971, 76.
7. L. T. Hauck, "Solve Contact Bounce Problems without a One-shot", *EDN,* September 5, 1975, 80.
8. Anon., "Science and the Citizen", *Scientific American,* v. 228, n. 4, April 1973, 43-44.
9. T. J. Chaney and C. E. Molnar, "Anomolous Behavior of Synchronizer and Arbiter Circuits", *IEEE Trans. Computers,* v. C-22, 1973, 421-422.
10. D. Mayne and R. Moore, "Minimize Computer 'Crashes' ", *Electronic Design,* v. 22, n. 9, April 26, 1974, 168-172.
11. D. Davies and D. Barber, *Communication Networks for Computers,* Wiley, New York, 1973, 65-67.

SUBJECT INDEX

AUTHOR INDEX

A

Agrawala, A. K., 384(5), *422*
Alexander, C., 19, *21*
Allen, R., 27, *81*
Amdahl, G., 194, *273*

B

Barber, D., 554, *557*
Barton, R. S., 262, *274*
Bayless, J., 38(17), *81*
Belady, L. A., 13, *21*
Bell, C. G., 31, 44, 71, *81*
Bensky, L. S., 38(18), *81*
Blakeslee, T. R., 35, 40, *81*
Bottari, B., 38(20), *81*
Breuer, M. A., 36, *81*
Brick, J., 386(8), 391(8), *423*
Brooks, F. P., Jr., 5, 19, *21*, 49, *81*,
    86, 95, 98, 112, *139*, 194, *273*
Buchholz, W., 136(11), 137(11), *139*,
    303(8), *360*
Buckingham, B. R. S., 385(6), *423*
Burks, A., 62, *82*, 86, *139*

C

Carter, W. C., 385(6), *423*
Case, P. W., *81*
Chaney, T. J., 554, *557*
Clare, C. R., 14(20), *21*
Clark, D. W., 268, *274*
Codd, E. F., 194(4), *273*
Cohn, B., 543(5), *557*
Conti, C. J., 243(13), *274*
Conway, L., 449, *461*
Corbato, F. J., 257(15), *274*
Cragon, H. G., 86, *139*
Crawford, W. R., 385(6), *423*
Cross, D., 200, 213, *274*

D

Dahl, O.-J., 5(4), 7, 8(4), 18, 19, *21*
Davies, D., 554, *557*
Davis, R. L., 489, *505*
DeMarco, T., 13(18), 17(18), *21*
Dennis, J. B., 262, *274*
Desautels, E. J., 269, *274*
Dijkstra, E. W., 5, 7(4), 8(4), 18,
    19(4), *21*
Dilatush, E., 458(16), *462*
Dinneen, G. P., 62(35), *82*
Donath, W. E., 502, *505*

COLOPHON

Paper
> Body, 50 lb. Blue-white Finch
> Cover, Kivar 6

Composition
> Body, 10-pt. Press Roman, computer typeset by Marian Langdon using IBM software (YFL and Termtext), output on Autologic APS-5 photocomposer

Line Art
> Francisco Moreira and Glen Langdon

Cover Design
> John W. Jacobsen, White Oak Design, Inc., Marblehead MA

Printing
> R. R. Donnelley & Sons Company, Crawfordsville IN, narrow web offset press

Binding
> Hard cover - patent bound, .080 Binders board case